Doing Sociology

A BASIC TEXT

JAMES K. SEMONES

Kendall Hunt
publishing company
4050 Westmark Drive • P O Box 1840 • Dubuque IA 52004-1840

Kendall Hunt
publishing company

www.kendallhunt.com
Send all inquiries to:
4050 Westmark Drive
Dubuque, IA 52004-1840

*B*rief Contents

Contents

PART TWO   *Essential Elements of Social Life*   **121**

CHAPTER 5: Socialization: The Process of Becoming Human   123

Dedication

To my wife Lil, the love of my life,

and to our grandchildren, Maya and Jax,

our hope for the future.

About the Author

James K. Semones
Professor of Sociology, San Jacinto College
Adjunct Professor, Sociology, University of Houston—Downtown

James K. Semones holds both B.S. and M.A. degrees in Sociology from East Tennessee State University and a doctorate in Higher Education (College Teaching) and Sociology from the University of North Texas. In a career spanning more than 30 years, he has held both regular and adjunct faculty positions in sociology at several colleges and universities. They include East Tennessee State University, Jacksonville State University, University of Alabama—Birmingham, El Paso Community College, and Park College. Dr. Semones has been a full-time faculty member at San Jacinto College since 1984 and an adjunct professor in sociology at the University of Houston-Downtown since 2002. His teaching awards include Phi Theta Kappa Teacher of the Year, four-time campus nominee for the Minnie Stevens Piper Teaching Excellence Award, and three time recipient of the NISOD (National Institute of Staff and Organizational Development) Teaching Excellence Award.

Dr. Semones is a sociologist of education with primary research interests in the sociology of teaching and learning. His research and teaching interests also include the sociology of the family and deviant behavior. He has authored several books including *Sociology: A Core Text* (Holt, Rinehart and Winston), *Effective Study Skills: A Step-By-Step System for Student Success* (also with Holt), *The Experiential Guide to ESS* (Harcourt Brace Jovanovich), and *Survival Readings in Sociology: An Experiential Approach* (ESS Enterprises). In addition, Dr. Semones has co-authored several books, which include *Adult Education: Theory and Practice* and *Adult Learning and Program Development* (co-editor), *Key Issues in Higher Education and Society* (all from Burgess/Alpha Editions), and *Recruiting, Marketing, and Retention in Institutions of Higher Education* (University Press of America). He has also served as a consultant to many corporations, organizations, and schools including Xerox Corporation, Public Service Company of Oklahoma, Fidelity Investments, the American Heart Association, Phillips Petroleum, Bristol, Virginia Public Schools, Galena Park Independent School District (Texas), and the Learners Community at the University of Houston–Downtown.

Since 1991, usually accompanied by his wife (Prof. Lilian Romero), Dr. Semones has taken close to three hundred students on more than a dozen trips to eighteen countries on three continents. On these global adventures, students have been able to experience the sociological imagination firsthand. These two educators and their students have traversed up Mt. Regi in the snow in Switzerland, traveled in gondolas down the Grand Canal in Venice, explored the ruins at Pompeii in the shadow of Mt. Vesuvius, ridden camels in

Morocco, cruised to the sunny isle of Capri, seen and fed the Barbary apes in the caves on Gibraltar, and explored countless castles, cathedrals, palaces, and museums. Through these and numerous other experiences and adventures, both Dr. Semones and his students have come to better appreciate the application of sociological methods to the comparative study of societies around the world. This particular use of what might be called "global sociology" is an integral theme embedded into this text.

Preface

THE FOCUS OF THIS TEXT AND HOW TO USE IT

The challenge for any textbook author is to provide a learning resource that will meet the needs of both typical students and potential sociology majors, as well as provide the quality of coverage desired by their professors. This is not an easy task.

In any given year, there are perhaps two or three dozen nationally published and marketed textbooks in introductory sociology that enjoy some amount of success. Almost without exception, they are well researched, often well organized and elegantly written, and sometimes represent masterpieces of the bookbinder's art with slick covers and colorful illustrations. The obvious question then is "Why write and publish another sociology text?" The reasons should be obvious to those who critically examine current practices and trends in American higher education.

Critical Problems and Needs Addressed by This Text

This text was developed to respond directly to critical needs that are increasingly evident among faculty and students in many colleges and universities throughout the United States. Chief among these is the current disconnect between many academicians who author textbooks and their publishers and the end users—the students—they are supposed to serve.

The National Crisis in Reading   A review of the literature on the state of reading ability in America shows clearly that, in this regard, the United States is a country in serious decline. In 2004, the results of the Program for International Student Assessment (PISA) were released by the Canada-based Organisation for Economic Co-operation and Development (OECD). In its report based on data gathered during 2003, fifteen-year-olds from the United States ranked fifteen of thirty-one among adolescents of the same age in other countries that participated in the study. This mediocre performance by American teenagers placed them behind such countries as Australia, Canada, France, Ireland, Korea, and Japan. In a world characterized by the increasing number of highly educated and skilled workers, the fast-emerging global economy and occupational marketplace puts typical Americans at a serious competitive disadvantage (Organisation for Economic Co-operation and Development, 2004).

Recent U.S. research on reading shows similar alarming results. In late November of 2007, the National Endowment for the Arts (NEA) released the results of a comprehensive study on American reading habits and practices conducted in 2006 titled "To Read or Not To Read: A Question of National Consequence" (National Endowment for the Arts, 2007). This study was an expansion of a study conducted by the NEA in 2004 called

"Reading at Risk," which reported that literacy in the United States was in serious and steady decline. While the 2004 study focused on literary and academic reading of books, the most recent NEA research (2006) found a pattern of erosion in reading of all kinds, including reading conducted on-line over the internet. Although this newer study documented that children in elementary grades had improved modestly in reading scores and practices, reading and reading ability among teenagers, adults, and even college graduates has shown significant decline (Howard, 2007).

Why American Colleges Must Address This Crisis

Institutions of higher learning in the United States today face a daunting challenge that could significantly affect the role our country will play on the world stage in the coming century. The cover story of the May 12, 2008 issue of *Newsweek* entitled "The Rise of the Rest" represents a call to action for leaders of various American institutions with a clear message: (1) the world around us is developing—geopolitically, economically, and technologically—at an exponential rate and (2) the United States must face the prospects of a world characterized by "the end of Pax Americana" (Zakaria, 2008, p. 27). Put in plain language, while the twentieth century was clearly the American century, the twenty-first century portends a seismic shift in the bases of world power as other countries develop the capacity to compete with the United States head-to-head for various forms of capital—intellectual, political, social, and economic— that will shape the world of the future. To give one example, one hundred twenty-four "emerging market" countries increased their annual economic outputs by more than 4 percent per year in both 2006 and 2007. These and several other indicators show that, as the global economy continues to expand at an accelerating rate, the dominance of the United States in the world will be continually challenged on several fronts and American influence could significantly decline (Ibid). These realities are echoed in a growing sentiment among academics in several fields and educationists; that is, the way American colleges and universities currently function in designing and implementing their curricula and courses must also change in fundamental ways to meet the global challenges of today and those in the decades to come. One of those changes must be reflected in the text resources required of students and how they are used.

The Crisis in College Reading: Many Students Today Are Not Buying or Reading Assigned Texts

As a prerequisite to becoming an independent learner, it is widely accepted in academia that one must first develop an intimate relationship with the written word. This is a necessary precondition for becoming a scholar in any field of endeavor. Poor readers tend to perform poorly as students, and poorly prepared students do not fare well in the occupational marketplace later in life. Many professors would be dismayed to discover that twenty percent or more of their students in some introductory courses do not even purchase a textbook, much less read it. This problem is exacerbated by the fact that some professors test primarily from class notes and PowerPoint slides rather than from required texts. Other factors contributing to this sad state of affairs include a mediocre-to-poor public education (K–12) system with little academic rigor, the failed "No Child Left Behind" initiative implemented by the Bush Administration (2001–2009) with inadequate funding support, and a radical shift toward assessment of teachers in some states rather than a more balanced approach that places an equal emphasis on holding students accountable for their learning.

In summarizing the larger, societal implications of the ninety-nine page NEA report, Jennifer Howard in the *Chronicle of Higher Education* ("Americans Are Closing the Book on Reading, Study Finds," November 30, 2007), comments as follows:

> Twenty percent of American workers don't read at the level required by their jobs. In 2003, 58 percent of proficient readers earned at least $850 a week; only 13 percent of below-basic readers did.
>
> That reality hasn't been lost on employers, 38 percent of whom say that high school graduates don't measure up when it comes to reading comprehension. And those employers are shelling out large amounts—an estimated $3.1 billion on the part of corporations, for instance—for remedial training (p. A12).
>
> From *The Chronicle of Higher Education,* November 30, 2007 by Jennifer Howard. Copyright © 2007 by *The Chronicle for Higher Education.* Reprinted by permission.

Superficiality: A Critical Problem with Some Introductory Texts Today For anyone who undertakes a critical examination of comprehensive, full-color, hardbound textbooks today in sociology and several other fields, it is fair and accurate to say that, in general, they are excellent and, if anything, superior to their counterparts written several years ago. In terms of both content and pedagogy, *Psychology* by Don and Sandra Hockenbury (West) provides a notable benchmark. In my view, their text has set the gold standard against which traditional comprehensive texts in the behavioral sciences might be assessed.

Unfortunately, the same cannot be said of some so-called "core," "essentials," or "basic" texts, especially in the field of sociology. Rather than being designed from the ground up as a fundamental text with essential yet substantive chapters covering key content in some depth, they represent a cut-down derivative from a larger, comprehensive text written by the same author. Aimed primarily at students attending less-selective state colleges and universities and two-year, open-door community colleges, which serve large numbers of nontraditional, first generation college students, many of these texts "dumb down" course content by providing superficial, less-than-college-level coverage. In fact, some of these "texts" are so superficial as to be largely unintelligible to an uninformed reader who, as a beginning student, has no prior knowledge of the subject. Key qualitative indicators of superficiality include chapter lengths of only twenty to twenty-five pages, ten to twenty key terms at the end of most chapters instead of the number needed for a course of college rigor, no suggested readings, and numerous technological "bells-and-whistles" that often distract and confuse students rather than provide an integrated theme or direction. This rush to the bottom in pandering to the lowest common denominator by some authors and publishers is not what is needed for our students to meet the requirements of the future. We need to challenge our students to expand their knowledge and skills, not patronize and demean them. *Doing Sociology* has been written with this as a key focus in both content and design.

Key Features of This Text

It Is a Basic Text Yet a Substantive One
Rather than the "buffet" approach contained in the more traditional, larger texts that offer twenty to twenty-six different chapters, *Doing Sociology* focuses on the core essentials. As a basic text, fourteen essential topics have been chosen that reflect much of the core content of sociology as a discipline. With a "basics" emphasis, each topic can be treated more comprehensively with a greater depth of coverage than the approach used by many traditional texts. Because I identify just as strongly with the

role of teacher as I do with that of research scholar, this basic text has been designed to provide both the student and instructor with a teaching and learning delivery system designed to make the acquisition of sociology content efficient, effective, and enjoyable.

This approach offers many learning advantages to the student and teacher alike. First, it has been designed to communicate to students within their own frame of reference. Once a student's experiential background has been tapped into, he or she can then be stretched as a learner to develop new insights and formulate new questions. Second, it contains most of the basic topics in sociology explained in clear, concise language. In this regard, the text reads like a story or saga with each chapter building sequentially on the one that came before, yet standing alone as a separate body of reading. The professor who uses a basic text also benefits because he or she has greater flexibility to use a reader or to assign outside readings than would be the case with a bulkier and more expensive, traditional hardbound text. Therefore, both student and teacher are better able to benefit from the essential course content contained in a basic text.

The Design and Goal of This Text: The Achievement of Sociological Fluency

Reading experts in K–12 education speak of the development of basic reading fluency as children learn to master reading content through a process called metacognition. At the college level, textbook authors and college educators should focus significant efforts on designing text materials that incorporate teaching and learning strategies aimed at reading for content mastery by students at the academic, college level. In doing so, it is important that their efforts be focused on fostering the development of discipline fluency in their students. **Discipline fluency** is *the use of college reading assignments (depending on the subject) to recognize, comprehend, think with, and apply course content like a practitioner (e.g., computer analyst, economist, historian, biologist, sociologist, nurse, chemist, and so on.* By using reading assignments to master discipline-specific course content focused on specified and measurable learning outcomes, faculty can then make use of various strategies that should not only facilitate the development of discipline fluency at the college level, but enhance basic reading fluency as well.

In *Doing Sociology*, the fluency emphasis is on developing **sociological fluency**—that is, *the ability to accurately read about, comprehend, and apply the language, perspectives, and methods of sociology to analyze and better understand the social world around us and our place in it.* In its most advanced form, sociological fluency involves the ability to use the content and tools of sociology like a practitioner to better understand human social behavior at all levels of society. This key course focus is addressed in greater depth in Chapter 1.

An Emphasis on Active Reading Strategies   Reutzel (2006), in a chapter contained in *Fluency Instruction: Research-Based Best Practices,* provides key scaffolding that can be very useful in developing discipline fluency at the college level. His use of a three-category model—fluency concepts, fluency texts, and student fluency tasks—is useful for both college students and faculty in developing discipline fluency in their specific subject areas. By using such concepts, texts, and learning tasks, students are provided with a fluency path to follow. Though the use of such scaffolding, discipline fluency, and the approaches employed in *Doing Sociology,* sociological fluency can be facilitated. The result should be enhanced student performance and improved grades.

In order to achieve content mastery, the literature suggests that active learning strategies be employed. Bonwell and Eison (1991), for example, have proposed "that strategies promoting active learning be defined as instructional activities involving students in doing things and thinking about what they are doing (p. iii)." *Doing Sociology* has been written with this in mind. Specific strategies designed to actively engage students in reading and using their textbook as a learning tool include the following:

Strategy 1—BASF™: A Pretest/Posttest Fluency Assessment Tool The acronym BASF™ stands for Basic Assessment of Sociological Fluency. Developed by the author and included at the end of Chapter 1, the BASF™ is a useful tool for assessing where students are in basic sociological knowledge when they begin the introductory course. The fifty True–False items in the BASF™ instrument are representative examples of basic sociology content contained throughout the text. As such, this assessment can be taken by the student at the end of the first week of the semester to determine a student's level of sociological fluency going into the semester. By reading and studying the text, the student can discover the actual answers and supporting findings gleaned from sociological research. Then, the last week of the semester, either as preparation for the final exam or as a portion of the Final Exam itself, the student can take the BASF™ a second time as a posttest measure to see how much sociological fluency he or she has acquired.

Strategy 2—Interactive Chapter Study Guides: Benefits to Students and Their Teachers A companion volume, *Achieving Sociological Fluency: An Interactive Guide and Workbook*, is also provided with the text. The bulk of *Achieving Sociological Fluency* consists of fourteen interactive chapter study guides that mirror the chapters in the text. By engaging the text actively and using it as a resource to complete the chapter study guides, students benefit in the following ways:

BENEFITS TO STUDENTS:

1. *Task-Oriented Learning:* Students can become task-oriented in using the text as a resource to capture the essence of the text content in a concise, organized format by completing each Chapter Study Guide.

2. *Information Driven Class Discussions:* Students can use their completed Chapter Study Guides as a basis for discussions in class driven by course content, not uninformed opinion.

3. *More Effective Exam Preparation:* Students can prepare for exams much more effectively by having essential course content captured in concise, organized, and sophisticated outlines provided by the Chapter Study Guides. Note that the Chapter Study Guides make use of outline notation (to drill down into the material on several levels) rather than simply use "bullets" in simplistic, PowerPoint slides.

4. *Study Groups (and/or In-Class Group Work):* Students can use the templates provided in the Chapter Study Guides to interact with the text and perhaps with each other either in study groups for exam preparation or teacher-assigned group work in class.

BENEFITS TO PROFESSORS:

1. *Content-Driven Lectures/Discussions:* By either making transparencies from the study guides or projecting the pages in each Chapter Study Guide on a screen

using a document camera, the professor can use these as an instructional resource for lecture and/or guided discussion.

2. ***Use of the Socratic Method in Facilitating Student-Driven Discussions:*** Through the use of the format provided by the Chapter Study Guides, the professor and students can use the study guides as the basis for forming a dynamic partnership in which, literally, they will be focused in engaging text-driven course content. In class presentations and/or discussions, professors can use the study guides completed by students to ask key content-related questions and elicit student responses in the form of recitations, questions, examples, or insights.

3. ***Augmenting the Text Course Content with Outside Material:*** Professors can use the outline notation format furnished by the Chapter Study Guides as a frame to make additions by using their own material or deletions of certain portions as they see fit.

4. ***Holding Students Accountable for Their Own Learning:*** Students who do poorly on exams can be asked to submit their completed study guides to their professor and/or meet with the professor with the completed study guides for mentoring. Those with completed study guides can have them examined and then be counseled and guided by the professor on ways to improve them or more effectively use them for increased learning. Those with incomplete or uncompleted study guides can also be counseled and mentored.

Strategy 3: Use by Students of the SIVSI™ as a Visual Sociology Field Observation Tool The acronym SIVSI™ stands for *Semones Inventory of Visual Sociology Indicators.* It is included as an experiential learning resource in *Achieving Sociological Fluency.* Through the use of SIVSI,™ students make use of an inventory of one hundred visual sociology indicators divided into ten content topics contained in the *Doing Sociology* text. Driven by the text assignments, students are empowered to use the SIVSI™ as an active learning assessment tool to actually engage in "doing sociology" by completing field-based sociology projects in their own communities. In doing so, they are able to acquire the sociological imagination by first capturing and then evaluating the sociological information they gathered in the field.

As explained in greater detail in Chapter 1, **visual sociology** is the application of sociological concepts, perspectives, and techniques to better understand human behavior by using visual media such as photographs, movies, television, and so on. Although students may use existing photos or movies and the like for such a project, perhaps the most intriguing approach involves the application of sociological fluency to create information-rich visual documents (e.g., photographs or videos) that capture significant sociological information. For example, a student, either through photographs or a brief, edited video documentary, could first capture and then assess—through the use of SIVSI™—the stratification system (e.g., housing, occupations, recreational activities, modes of transportation, dress, demeanor, status symbols, dietary habits) of different class groups in their community. In addition, professors teaching from *Doing Sociology* and using their own expertise and creativity, can design additional field projects for students that best suit their instructional priorities and needs.

Acknowledgments

While responsibility for this book's content is mine alone, the efforts and talents of many people went into the development of the final manuscript. First, I am grateful for the comments and suggestions from dozens of colleagues nationally who have served as reviewers of my three previous texts and this latest effort, which was based on the previous three. Special thanks go to George Marchelos, my former Dean of Instruction and close friend for thirty years, and Greg Getz, Associate Professor of Sociology at the University of Houston—Downtown. The assistance of Acquisitions Editor Stephanie Ramirez, Project Coordinator Ryan Schrodt, and Permissions Editor Elizabeth Roberts of Kendall Hunt Publishing Company have also been invaluable.

Many colleagues from San Jacinto College provided me with encouragement and support in numerous ways. They include Richard Bailey, Vice President of Instruction, Sarah Janes, Academic Dean, Dennis Toombs, Professor of Government, and Charles Grant, my college President for over ten years and colleague and friend for over two decades. Other faculty and staff who helped me in numerous ways include Jan Crenshaw, Director of the Library and her staff including Richard Cuellar, instructional designers Patricia Petty, Sherry Nixon, and Huff Mann, and media specialist Lavena Wilder.

In addition, the legions of students who have matriculated through my introductory sociology courses at San Jacinto College since 1984 are deserving of special thanks. They have been the recipients of my text writing efforts through three separate volumes—*Sociology: A Core Text* (Holt, Rinehart and Winston), *Survival Readings in Sociology: An Experiential Approach (ESS Enterprises)*, and now *Doing Sociology* (Kendall/Hunt). My students have been very candid in telling me what works, what does not work, and what could be improved from their perspective. This text reflects what already has been thoroughly student tested for what has worked and worked well. Although I cannot mention them all by name, three students in particular were of special help during Fall 2008, as I developed the final manuscript: Tonya Granger and Edna Turner who served as student editors and Louly Contreras, an honors student, who used the SIVSI™ assessment tool for a visual sociology field project on social stratification in Houston, Texas.

Finally, I would like to thank Lil, my wife, life partner, and best friend. More than anything else, her love, patience, and understanding have helped sustain me in my many endeavors over the years.

El Yolo   James K. Semones
Dove Island on Lake Livingston, Texas
March 1, 2009

PART ONE

The Sociological Imagination

PART TWO

Essential Elements of Social Life

Socialization: The Process of Becoming Human

Terms to Know

anticipatory socialization	id	self-concept
apprenticeship in thinking	imitative (preparatory) stage	self-fulfilling prophesy
"bad blood" theory	inner directed	sensorimotor stage
bonding	instinct theory	significant others
cognitive development theory	looking-glass self	social Darwinism
concrete operations	mass media	social isolates
cultural mediation	other directed	socialization
didactic teaching	peer groups	sociobiology
dramaturgical analysis	personality	sociocultural theory
ego	play stage	superego
formal operations	preoperations	Thomas theorem
game stage	resocialization	youth subculture
generalized other	rites of passage	zone of proximal development (ZPD)
guided participation	role taking	

In Chapter 4, we began our survey of key topics in sociology by examining culture, the way of life we acquire as members of society. Through exposure to a culture, we are provided with a set of socially accepted patterns for thinking and acting that gives our lives order and predictability. In Chapter 5, we will focus on **socialization**, the process through which culture is transmitted to the individual and the personality and self-concept are developed. To begin, we will first examine the nature–nurture debate.

THE NATURE VERSUS NURTURE DEBATE

The crux of this debate is the question of how personality is determined and self-concept is formed. **Personality** refers to the sum total of a person's unique yet consistent patterns of thoughts, feelings, and actions. Are humans equipped at birth with a set of traits that largely direct and shape their personality development? Or are they instead shaped and influenced primarily by their experiences with the social environment that surrounds them? Proponents on both sides of this issue have argued vigorously for their respective viewpoints for well over a century. While each of us most likely possesses a genetic predisposition for being introverted or extraverted as demonstrated through neuroscience (Canli, 2004; Canli et al., 2002, 2004), much of what determines who we are and who we become depends on our cumulative experiences with others and society as we move through our life experience.

Socialization also provides the individual with a sense of identity in terms of "Who am I?," "What am I worth?," and "Where am I going?" This identity or self-image we each possess sociologists call the **self-concept**, the personal assessment people have of their own identity and self-worth and how they fit into the larger community and society. Our self-image forms much of the foundation for our personality. It is a complex area of study for the sociologist because (1) it has several dimensions and (2) it is constantly evolving due to a continuous, dynamic interplay that occurs between individuals and their social environment.

The Nature Argument

Those who subscribe to the nature position maintain that human beings possess a definite set of qualities determined largely by inborn traits. One's environment, therefore, represents only the background against which these inherited characteristics are played out (Adams, 1974). The notion of an "innate human nature" was proposed by social contract theorists of the seventeenth and eighteenth centuries. Some, like Jean-Jacques Rousseau, argued that humans are basically good but tend to become corrupted by modern civilized society. Others, such as Thomas Hobbes, argued that humans by nature are untrustworthy and selfish, characteristics that necessitated the formation of society with rules to keep people under control.

Social Darwinism   In 1859, Charles Darwin published his *On the Origin of Species*, which gave the nature argument a great deal of scientific legitimacy. He argued that human beings, like lower animals, are products not of divine creation but of evolution through natural selection. Those with the ability to adapt to changes in their environment survive, while those without such adaptability perish. Consequently, environment affects the genetic makeup present in all species and biological traits that are most adaptable emerge through natural selection.

The social Darwinists, led by Herbert Spencer, expanded this argument to include the nature of human societies. **Social Darwinism** was the argument that governments should not interfere in the lives of individuals or the operation of organizations so that the fittest can survive. Spencer and his followers asserted that European societies and the United States were more dominant in the world than other societies because they were more highly evolved. Other, less-advanced social systems were biologically and socially inferior because they occupied an earlier, and thus more primitive, stage of evolution (Spencer, 1860, 1874). The social Darwinists also used the natural selection argument to explain why certain individuals within modern societies were affluent, successful, and more "fit," while others, struggling in the throes of poverty were, therefore, "unfit." The glaring flaw in this argument soon became clear as the behavioral sciences developed substantively during the early part of the twentieth century: In the biological world, each member of a species—lions, for example—are born with essentially the same attributes and are exposed to the same environmental circumstances. However, humans are distributed throughout each society with diverse characteristics that are treated quite differently according to how each society is structured.

"Bad Blood" Theory   Other scientists during the late nineteenth and early twentieth centuries attributed human behavior to other inherited predispositions. Some subscribed to the "bad seed" or **"bad blood" theory**, the view that deviant behavior (such as crime and drug addiction) occurred because of a person's biological makeup and whether they possessed "bad blood" or was a "bad seed." In a 1994 motion picture titled *Natural Born Killers*, Woody Harrelson and Juliet Lewis played "bad seeds" who went on a random killing spree beginning with the massacre of the customers and staff at a diner. While this makes for an interesting movie plot, criminologists and other behavioral scientists have found little evidence to support the "bad blood" notion. The modern view by sociologists is that most criminal behavior, in large part, results from dysfunctional structural conditions impacting on individuals that lie within the fabric of the family, government, education, and other social institutions.

Instinct Theory   Another popular approach used by nature proponents during the late nineteenth and early twentieth centuries was that human behavior is determined mainly by "instincts." **Instinct theory** argued that human behavior was shaped largely by genetically inherited predispositions called instincts. Some proponents of this perspective held that such "instincts" caused specific types of behavior. Thus, people got married because of a "mating" instinct, fought wars due to a "killing" instinct, lived in homes and societies as a result of "nesting" and "herding" instincts, and birthed and raised children guided by "maternal" and "parenting" instincts. One researcher documented the increasing popularity of instinct theory during this period and, in reviewing academic and popular literature, found that over ten thousand alleged instincts had been claimed to exist (Bernard, 1924). However, by the 1930s researchers like anthropologist Margaret Mead and others were finding that, while some individuals and cultures had traits some called "instinctive," others did not. Therefore, *instinct* by this time had become a useless concept in science with which to explain human behavior in a meaningful way.

Sociobiology   Although most of the thinking of the twentieth century was dominated by "nurture" or environmental explanations of human behavior, a new discipline called sociobiology emerged during the late 1970s and 1980s that gave nature proponents renewed vigor. **Sociobiology** is the study of the biological aspects of social behavior in all species including humans (Wilson, 1978). The founder of this perspective is Edward O. Wilson, an entomologist (one who studies insects) who originated the term *sociobiology*. Wilson and his followers attempted to integrate or synthesize the research results of both the biological and social sciences. They argue that although culture rather than genetics is the prime cause of specific human behavior (Wilson, 1975), some forms of social behavior in general have a genetic foundation. They claim, for instance, that there are tendencies toward the exhibition of male dominance, territoriality, the incest taboo, the eating of meat, and religion that are genetically encoded in humans at birth.

This biological explanation has come under a barrage of criticism. In a debate with Wilson about three decades ago, Marvin Harris, an anthropologist, categorically rejected the idea that traits such as aggressiveness, territoriality, and male dominance were inherited by humans. He argued that there is tremendous variability in all these traits from culture to culture, and that even if there are certain biological tendencies for behavior, they are so weak and general as to be meaningless because they are so easily overridden by culture (Harris, 1980). Others argue that even some human behaviors long thought to be primarily biological—such as sexuality—are now being shown to be greatly influenced by cultural factors (Lauer and Handel, 1983). In short, there is little, if any, hard evidence to support the contention that most behaviors specific to humans as individuals are determined wholly or even significantly by genetic factors.

The Nurture Argument

While biology does play a role in affecting who we are as humans and our actions, available research indicates that we are impacted at least as much by environmental or "nurture" factors. We will begin a brief overview of this research with examples of findings on complex lower animals that are also capable of learning and that also need satisfying social contact with others of their kind.

Animal Studies: Examples by Pavlov and Harlow   A little over a century ago, researchers began to discover the impact of learning on behavior that previously was thought to be purely instinctive or otherwise inherited. At that time, the Russian physiologist Ivan Pavlov (1849–1935) demonstrated that, even among dogs, much behavior is subject to environmental conditions. Pavlov observed that dogs salivated any time food was present, a condition that appeared instinctive or reflexive. Through a process later referred to as _classical conditioning_, he conducted experiments with dogs in which, each time they were presented with food, a bell was rung. Gradually, he taught the dogs to salivate at the sound of the bell alone even when food was not present.

During the second half of the twentieth century, psychologist Harry Harlow and associates conducted experimental research to study the effects of social deprivation on rhesus monkeys (Harlow and Zimmerman, 1959; Harlow and Harlow, 1966; Novak, 1979). The researchers reared baby monkeys in total isolation from other monkeys, including their mothers. Instead, each monkey was given two artificial surrogate mothers made of wire. One "mother" was constructed of plain wire and was equipped with a bottle for feeding. The other "mother" was covered in terry cloth but contained no bottle. The monkeys became attached to the terry cloth mother and would cling to it most of the time, and went to the plain wire mother with the bottle only for food.

Invariably, these animals grew up extremely maladjusted. When approached, they would bite themselves repeatedly and cower in corners. They exhibited fear and hostility

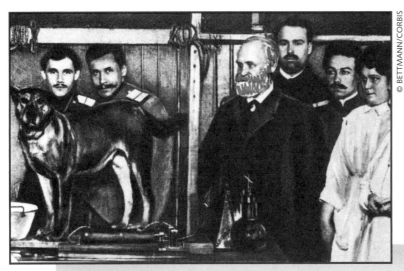

In his experiments with classical conditioning, Russian physiologist Ivan Pavlov demonstrated that, even among lower animals such as dogs, much of their behavior is learned.

when exposed to others of their kind. The females, after reaching maturity, would not mate and, when artificially inseminated, refused to care for or nurse their offspring. In a few cases, they even killed their babies before their caretakers could save them. Although one must be careful in generalizing from the behavior of lower primates to that of humans, it is clear that even with these animals, both sexual and maternal behavior are learned to a remarkable degree. Perhaps more important is the fact that monkeys, like humans, need love and nurturance in order to grow into functioning adults. Also, like humans, they may grow into neglectful and abusive parents if they themselves are neglected and abused while growing up (Kempe and Kempe, 1978; Polansky et al., 1981).

Even before the modern findings of Harlow and others, experimental animal studies cast such a serious shadow on biological explanations of human behavior that, by the 1920s and 1930s, the idea of human instincts ceased to be a meaningful concept in mainstream social science. The dominance of the nurture argument became fully established in the scientific community during the 1930s where it has remained to the present day.

Social Isolates   In 1924, psychologist James B. Watson (1878–1958) made his famous statement about the primacy of "nurture" over "nature" in human behavior:

> Give me a dozen healthy infants, well-formed, and my own specific world to bring them up in and I'll guarantee to take any one of them at random and train him to become any type of specialist I might select—a doctor, lawyer, artist, merchant, chief, yes even a beggarman and thief, regardless of his talents, penchants, tendencies, abilities, vocations, and the race of his ancestors (p. 104).

While Watson perhaps overstated the case, instances of children suffering extreme isolation from social contact with others provide a good illustration of the importance of socialization. Consider, for example, an experiment in which children were systematically isolated from certain socialization experiences and then observed to see how they developed. Such research, of course, would be condemned by present-day social scientists because of humane and ethical considerations. Nonetheless, this type of experiment was ordered by Emperor Frederick II during the thirteenth century. The emperor wanted to find out what types of speech patterns children would exhibit as adults if they had no interaction with others growing up.

> So he bade foster mothers and nurses to suckle the children, to bathe and wash them, but in no way to prattle with them or to speak to them, for he wanted to learn whether they would speak the the Hebrew language, the oldest, or Greek, or Latin, or Arabic, or perhaps the language of their parents, of whom they had been born. But he labored in vain because the children all died. For they could not live without the petting and joyful faces and loving words of their foster mothers (Ross and McLaughlin, 1949).

The twentieth-century cases of Anna, Isabelle, and Genie in the United States during the twentieth century all serve to illustrate clearly that children deprived of adequate social contact and stimulation in their early years do not develop into functional adults as a result. Sociologists refer to such deprived children as **social isolates**.

First, the cases of Anna and Isabelle reported by Kingsley Davis (1940, 1947, 1948) provide prominent early twentieth-century examples. Both were illegitimate children discovered and rescued by the authorities during the 1930s when they were about six years old. They both had been hidden from view in small attic rooms by their mothers because they were unwanted. Although the cases of these two little girls were unrelated and they were found nine months apart, their lack of socialization and states of physical condition were similar. Neither showed any human characteristics; they could only grunt and groan and were extremely ill from poor diet and lack of exercise. Anna could not walk, and Isabelle could only shuffle around because her legs were so bowed. Anna was placed in a county home and later in a school for the retarded where, by the time she was seven, she had advanced to the level of an average two year old. When she died at age ten from an extreme case of jaundice, she was toilet trained, could dress herself, and was able to show affection for a doll. The girl known as Isabelle was more fortunate. She had experienced greater social contact with her mother and, in contrast to Anna's limpness and total lack of expression when found, was often fearful and hostile around strangers. Her care and treatment were supervised by specialists who provided her with a much more intensive learning environment than Anna. Consequently, she made extremely fast progress so that by age eight and one-half years old, she was functioning almost at a normal level and eventually was able to enter school.

In a more recent case study involving a social isolate named Genie, the results were not so successful. Genie, a thirteen-year-old California girl, had been locked naked in a room and tied to an infant's toilet seat by her father since before her second birthday. When rescued in 1970 by the authorities, she could not utter a sound because her father had severely beaten her every time she tried to vocalize. In addition, she could not stand or straighten her arms and legs and could not chew because she had never been given solid food. When tested, she had the social development of a one year old. Placed in a special developmental program at UCLA, she made limited progress with speech over the course of four years, yet never learned to behave according to social norms. She learned to speak in short phrases but never learned to read. Her social behavior, however, was manifested by such acts as grabbing strangers she liked and refusing to let go, peering into people's faces from a distance of only a few inches, and near compulsive public masturbation (Curtiss, 1977).

Institutionalized Children   Research conducted on groups of *institutionalized children*—socially deprived children in institutional settings such as state-sponsored orphanages—have yielded similar results. One groundbreaking study was conducted in Europe during and after World War II. Rene Spitz (1945), in a two-year study, compared populations of infants in two different types of institutions, an orphanage and women's prison. Both groups of children had their physical needs attended to adequately, including food, clothing, cleanliness, and room temperature. In addition, each child in the orphanage saw a physician daily. In the prison, the children's mothers were with them regularly and were allowed to play with their babies for hours at a time. The children at the orphanage never saw their mothers and were rarely given any affection or emotional support from anyone, largely because the staff was small and overworked. They were also kept socially isolated from one another, whereas the children in the prison were in a collective nursery. Consequently, all the children in the orphanage were deficient both emotionally and socially by age two, and some were retarded. Most startling of all was that by the age of four, slightly over one-third of the children in the orphanage had died. When examined over the same period, the children in the prison had developed normally and none had died.

More contemporary examples of abandoned and isolated children continue to shock those who live in postmodern societies. India today has many orphanages where children, warehoused with no one to interact with them, lie in bed all day in darkened rooms. Behavioral scientists recently have conducted experimental research on these children. Their findings show that regular, structured 90-minute play sessions with groups of these children resulted in significant increases in motor skills and improved IQ scores (Taneja et al., 2002). Today, China furnishes some of the most glaring and pervasive examples of socially neglected children in the world. As a result of its one child per family policy, implemented during the 1980s to address dire overpopulation issues coupled with a largely village-focused agricultural economy, boys have been highly desired and prized. Girls, by contrast, were seen as worthless and have met an entirely different fate. Millions had been killed by their parents at birth, put out on the streets of large cities to beg from tourists, or abandoned outright and hidden in human warehouses away from the prying eyes of the world. Orphans who do survive to adulthood are often so developmentally deficient that they cannot live functional lives (Meese, 2005).

Feral Children   A final perspective that underscores the importance of nurture is the notion of *feral children,* alleged children of nature isolated from social contact with others and supposedly raised by wild animals. Largely devoid of evidence of actual cases, such "stories" have retained their romantic fascination to many people. In Roman mythology, Romulus and Remus, the founders of Rome, were suckled and raised by a wolf. During the twentieth and now the twenty-first century, several generations of Americans have been entertained by the fictional exploits of Tarzan the Ape Man, a boy from British nobility who, after his parents died in Africa when he was an infant, was reared by Kala, an ape. While these and other fictional accounts make interesting stories, it is unrealistic that a human being could actually survive with animals in early childhood, much less develop into a fully functional adult.

© SUNSET BOULEVARD/CORBIS

The fictional exploits of Tarzan the Ape Man have been enjoyed by generations of Americans. In reality, however, there is no evidence that a human child, virtually helpless as an infant, could be raised to maturity by animals.

Malson (1972), in reviewing the literature of fifty-three alleged cases of feral children between 1940s and early 1960s, found that almost all such persons who had spent significant periods in mid to late childhood living "in nature" had significant to severe problems of functioning and in adapting in a social environment. Most, for example, could not adequately work or communicate verbally with others. Therefore, real cases of so-called feral children are, in actuality, unfortunate children who are lost, abandoned, or cast out by their parents with very negative consequences to their emotional and social development (Ogburn, 1959).

Nature versus Nurture in Perspective   Each of us represents a unique combination of biological heritage and environmental experiences. From our biological backgrounds, we each are born with a genetic blueprint that includes a wide range of inborn traits and predispositions. Genes contained in this blueprint determine our complexion, our eye and hair colors, our body build and general size, our sex and blood type, and a variety of other characteristics. They also contain certain biological triggers that govern the aging process by signaling the onset of puberty, young adulthood, middle age, and old age. Biological factors also influence our level of intelligence, our personality, and our native talents.

However, unlike the lower animals, we humans are provided by nature with only the platform or the foundation necessary to reach our potential as the most advanced and sophisticated creatures on this planet. To actually reach this potential, to become a person and develop into a fully functioning human being with a fully developed personality and self-concept, each of us must rely on the environmental influences provided by socialization.

𝒥UNCTIONS (NEEDS) SERVED BY SOCIALIZATION

The human infant is virtually helpless at birth and is born *tabula rasa*, a social blank without any encoded experiences. Many lower animal species develop mainly in the womb and are fully capable of taking care of themselves within hours, weeks, or months after birth. The human infant, by contrast, cannot stand alone for the first year, is incapable of sexually reproducing for well over a decade beyond this, and may not be totally self-sufficient for still another ten or twelve years in many societies. Acquiring the skills and information necessary to get along with others and survive in society begins at birth and continues throughout the life cycle. How this process of acquiring culture and developing a personality takes place is one of the most fascinating topics within social science. To explore it, we begin with a brief examination of the basic needs served by socialization.

Bonding and Emotional Support

We humans are social creatures who require regular and satisfying contact with others. As we have already seen, the debilitating effects of social deprivation in small children can lead to dramatic maladjustment and, in some cases, even death. Although comprehensive studies to measure the effects of deprivation cannot be carried out on human subjects for obvious ethical reasons, research of this type has been conducted on some of the more sociable lower animals, most notably by Harry Harlow and others as previously discussed.

Bonding begins early in life and sets the stage for later emotional and social development.

In humans, emotional needs are met primarily through **bonding**, the process of forming close personal relationships with other people, such as the relationship between a parent and child. There are three major types of bonded relationships: (1) parent–child, (2) cross gender, such as a married couple, and (3) same gender, as typified by two close friends (Beach, 1973). Of these, the parent–child relationship is most crucial for the development of a well-adjusted child.

A growing body of research shows that the bonding that is important to the child's later social development may take place immediately after birth (Klaus et al., 1972; Kennell, Voos, and Klaus, 1979; Klaus and Kennell, 1982). Marshall Klaus and his associates, for instance, compared the bonding effects of two groups of women with their newborns. Those women in the control group had the typical level of contact with their newborns during the first few days after birth. Women in the experimental group had much more intensive contact with their newborns and, in addition to regular feeding times, spent at least one hour with their babies immediately after birth and an additional five hours each day with them during the first ten days. In longitudinal research conducted on these women over five years, it was found that children in the "extended contact" group developed more readily than the other children in several ways. As a result of more intensive bonding, these children were healthier physically; received more physical, emotional, and verbal contact from their mothers; and, at the age of five years, performed better on IQ and language exams than did the other children.

The Establishment of Behavioral Boundaries

In addition to meeting emotional needs, socialization also teaches the individual how to behave in a disciplined manner by placing behavior within certain boundaries. Undisciplined behavior is self-centered behavior that operates for the most part on impulse. Small children are self-centered or egocentric in orientation and, because they lack significant socialization, see the world as revolving around them. However, living in a society requires that each person learn to control impulses and act according to social rules. To do so, the child must learn to take the needs and wishes of others into consideration. Socialization, therefore, is a cultural process through which the developing child becomes equipped with guidelines for acceptable behavior. This in turn later will allow a mature person to survive and prosper as a member of society.

Goal Setting

Disciplined behavior simply for its own sake can be very unrewarding. Therefore, it is important for the individual to learn how to set and achieve meaningful goals so that disciplined behavior will have meaningful and beneficial results. Goals, therefore, act as rewards that reinforce disciplined behavior. To succeed as a society member, life essentially involves setting meaningful goals, achieving them, and then setting new ones. Some goals are short term, like getting out of bed in the morning, mowing the yard, or going out to dinner and a movie on Friday night. Others may be long-term goals, such as completing a college degree, reaching a certain career level, or raising a family. In any case, the nature of the socialization experiences one has significantly affects one's ability to set and achieve meaningful goals.

The Development of a Self-Concept

As discussed earlier, *self-concept* refers to the personal assessment people have of their own identity and self worth, and how they fit into their community and society. One way to describe self-concept is to say that it includes at least three key elements: *self-identity* ("Who am I?"), *self-worth* ("What am I worth?"), and *self-direction* ("Where am I going?") (Semones and Romero, 2007). Consequently, self-concept is much more multidimensional and complex than the overly simplistic "self-esteem," a term often used in the popular culture.

One way to assess self-concept is to make use of the concepts of *inner-directed* and *other-directed,* first developed by David Reisman (1961) and later refined by others such as Robert Merton (1964) and James Semones and Lilian Romero (2007). These two concepts represent a polar typology with inner-directed and other-directed representing *ideal types* placed on either end of a continuum. Most people, in regard to their own self-concepts and core personalities, would fall somewhere along this continuum as illustrated below:

$$\text{Inner-Directed} \quad\underline{\hspace{4cm}} \pm \underline{\hspace{4cm}}\quad \text{Other-Directed}$$

Inner-Directed People and Their Characteristics   Individuals whom sociologists today might call **inner-directed** are adults with a positive self-concept and an internal moral compass formed mainly during childhood that guides them during their life course (Reisman, 1961; Semones and Romero, 2007). Those who are inner-directed possess at least four distinct characteristics.

- **In Charge of Basic Life Decisions**   First, *they are in charge of their basic life decisions.* They do seek input and advice from others and often value such input.

But when key life decisions must be made, the inner-directed make such decisions based on their own appraisal of what they believe will be best for them. If others do not approve, the inner-directed have the ego strength to proceed regardless of "what others may think" because they understand that they alone will bear the consequences of such life decisions and be accountable for them. Therefore, such people operate out of their own "centers" and have the courage to be their own people. In doing so, they actively choose their own paths in life, which often lead to personal growth.

➤➤ *A Sense of Positive Self-Worth.* According to Semones and Romero (2007), what gives people the courage to "blaze their own trail" in life is this second characteristic: *They possess a sense of positive self-worth.* Inner-directed people feel comfortable in their own skin and see themselves as having dignity and value as human beings. This helps them avoid conformity for conformity's sake by simply "following the herd." When young people blindly succumb to peer pressure and follow the wrong crowd during the critical adolescent period of development, it can lead to very problematic consequences that include gang involvement, teenage pregnancy, criminal activity, incarceration, and sometimes even death from street crime.

➤➤ *Optimism.* Third, *they are optimists.* Inner-directed people look at their cups as half full rather than half empty, and consistently look on the positive side of most situations. When they experience failure, disappointment, or a life tragedy—loss of a loved one, financial failure, or serious accident or illness—they learn to put the best face they can on such things, play the cards they were dealt, turn the page, and move on. When they make mistakes, they take ownership by accepting responsibility for the mistakes. Only by doing so can they shape their destiny, set meaningful goals, and then take the corrective steps needed to achieve them.

➤➤ *Ability to Take Calculated Risks.* Finally, inner-directed people *take calculated risks to achieve personal growth.* From the world view of such people, living an authentic life requires that they *make* it happen by *doing* rather than by *wishing* for it. To use a recent popular expression, "They walk their talk." This action of getting out of their comfort zone to attempt new things and accept new challenges then reinforces their positive self-image when they are able to achieve new goals. When they sometimes fail, they muster the inner strength to engage in the introspection needed to determine why they failed, marshal their resources, and try again. By continually attempting new things, setting and achieving new goals, facing new challenges, making adjustments when they fail, and continually working to succeed, inner-directed people usually reach their goals.

The dynamic interplay of these four factors helps to foster and reinforce a positive self-concept in the process. This can then place inner-directed people on the path to what behavioral scientists call self-actualization.

Other-Directed People and Their Characteristics

Those who might be called **other-directed** are adults with a negative self-concept who allow others to guide their basic life decisions and shape their actions. The other-directed also have at least four characteristics that are observable from their actions.

➤ *Others Dominate Their Decisions.* First, *they allow others to dominate their basic life decisions.* By allowing others to, in effect, make decisions for them, "they dance to someone else's tune" and let themselves be "pulled by someone else's strings." Why would any adult human being play the role of marionette and allow others to control their basic life decisions? Why can't they be authentic people and live life largely on their own terms?

➤ *A Sense of Negative Self-Worth.* Much of the answer to the preceding questions lies in this second other-directed characteristic: *They possess a sense of negative self-worth.* Those nearer the extreme end of the inner-directed/other-directed continuum sometimes are so afraid they will be rejected and emotionally abandoned if they fail to abide by the wishes of others that they play the role of victim. When things do not go well for them, they then blame others rather than take personal responsibility for their inaction or failure. When this happens, they quite literally can become incapacitated by the third characteristic, their own pessimism.

➤ *Pessimism.* As a third characteristic, *other-directed people are pessimists.* They see their cup as half empty rather than half full and habitually look on the negative side of most life situations. When they meet with failure or disappointment, they then tend to assign blame to everyone around them except themselves. By projecting responsibility for what happens to them outward onto others rather than inward toward themselves, they quite literally become victims . . . of their own poor choices and refusal or inability to take personal responsibility.

➤ *Inability to Take Risks.* A fourth pattern exhibited by those who are other-directed is that *they take few if any risks.* They are not able to move out of their comfort zones and tend to "play it safe" by staying in their comfortable, womb-like environment. By sometimes wishing for a "24-carat" guarantee before they will try much of anything, they stagnate and "spin their wheels" while the world and their lives pass them by. Through their inability to act and, in some cases, their inability to make decisions when time-sensitive opportunities become available, they fail by default. If this dynamic becomes an on-going pattern, they may indeed become life-long victims of themselves. As the years and decades slip by, a person trapped in such a dynamic without any corrective steps being taken can become a very embittered, cynical, and tormented individual (Semones and Romero, 2007).

Social Survival Skills

To succeed in society, each individual needs to acquire a variety of coping skills. Some are general and needed by everyone, such as the skill to communicate effectively through mastery of both spoken and written language and the ability to get along well with others. Other skills are more specialized, such as occupational skills acquired primarily through formal education, training, and experience. Some socialization skills are gradually acquired as we learn the role demands placed on us by the social positions we occupy. For instance, during the course of a day, a person may carry out obligations that are the result of being a family member, an employee, a college student, a neighbor, and a consumer. Given the limitations of time and energy, it can be quite challenging to develop and implement the skills needed to balance all of these demands.

CLASSICAL SOCIALIZATION THEORISTS

How the personality and self-concept are formed and how we acquire culture have been investigated by socialization theorists throughout the twentieth century and continues today. In the next section of this chapter, we will examine the pioneering work of several theorists who have greatly enlarged our understanding of the socialization process. We will begin by discussing the work of two pioneering interactionists in sociology, Charles Horton Cooley and George Herbert Mead. Then we will briefly examine some of the work of psychoanalytic theorist Sigmund Freud, one of the founding fathers of modern psychology.

Cooley: Interactionism and the Looking Glass Self

One early American theorist who did much to popularize the interactionist perspective in sociology was Charles H. Cooley (1864–1929). This quiet, unassuming scholar, who spent his academic life teaching sociology at the University of Michigan and the University of Chicago, was greatly influenced by the work of William James, the nineteenth-century psychologist. James (1890) developed a concept of social self, rooted in the idea that the way people see themselves is greatly influenced by how others interact with and see them. Cooley built on this foundation to argue that, just as we see a physical reflection when we look at ourselves in a mirror, we also see a social reflection of how we look to others as we interact with them. This image we see of ourselves as a result of interacting with others is the **looking glass self**.

The Three Components of the Looking Glass Self   Cooley (1902, 1909) asserted that our self-image is shaped largely by three constantly interacting elements within the personality: (1) *presentation:* how we think we are seen by others, which affects how we present ourselves in each interaction situation; (2) *identification:* how we think others judge or evaluate us each time we interact with them; and (3) *subjective interpretation:* how we feel about and deal with their evaluations. This process, which is largely unconscious, occurs as a result of our varied and constantly evolving relationships with individuals and groups. Therefore, our self-concept is continually being influenced by these interactions as we "take readings" (*identification*) on how we appear to others by examining the image we see reflected in our social mirror.

Two Applications: The Thomas Theorem and the Self-Fulfilling Prophesy
Think back to Chapter 2 when the interactionist perspective was first discussed. The basic premise of interactionism is that *perception drives behavior;* i.e., we act on our perceptions of reality. Let's now break this down by examining two applications of Cooley's looking glass self.

The Thomas Theorem   Early in the twentieth century, American sociologist W. I. Thomas issued a simple yet profound statement known today as the **Thomas theorem**. When individuals "define situations as real, they are real in their consequences" (Thomas and Thomas, 1928, p. 572). In other words, we socially construct (invent) how we see ourselves, the world around us, and our place in it based on our socialization experiences. If a child is loved, encouraged, and consistently shown approval and affection while growing up, this will set the stage for how positively the child sees him- or herself and expects to be seen by others when he or she gazes into the social mirror. Abuse, neglect, and discouragement will tend to have an opposite impact. Therefore, if we then expect to be accepted or rejected, we often are. This theorem also has applications for specific areas of life and the roles we play including work, school, and relations with family and friends. What we invest in time and energy (behavior) in all these areas depends on how we see them (perception). In each instance, what we then receive (consequences) will depend on our priorities and what and how much, in terms of time and energy, we choose to invest or not invest in them.

 The Self-Fulfilling Prophecy   Second, adults can chose the types of social looking-glass they peer into, although children, because of the accidents of birth, are limited in their early years by the influences of family socialization. Those with positive self-concepts are conditioned to seek out positive people, and those with negative self-images often become caught up in the "misery loves company" syndrome. This often results in what sociologist Robert Merton has called the **self-fulfilling prophecy**, a prediction by a person that something will occur—their perception—which is then caused by that person to become true because of his or her actions (Merton, 1957). Therefore, if we believe in ourselves, we often make success happen, while if we expect to fail, we often do so and then blame our shortcomings on the situation or on others. Our inner realities—perceptions of reality based on what we think is true—become our outer realities—behaviors and actions—which then cause our perceptions to become true with very real positive or negative consequences.

Mead: Interactionism and Role Taking Theory

A contemporary of Cooley's who also viewed social behavior from an interactionist perspective was George Herbert Mead (1863–1931). Mead, a philosopher and early social psychologist, served on the faculty at the University of Chicago. Regarded as the Father of Social Psychology and a founder of symbolic interactionism, he disagreed strongly with the atomistic view of humans popularized by the social contract theorists and other "scientific" philosophers of the seventeenth and eighteenth centuries. These views assumed that humans could have a self-concept and reason in nature apart from the influences of society.

Mead noted that while we have many potentialities at birth, it is only through contact with society that we develop our humanity as manifested in the personality and self-concept. He felt that the important thing to be studied and understood is how society gets into the individual, shapes the personality or "self-hood," and determines to a great degree a person's social behavior. This takes place essentially during childhood as we acquire the norms of society and learn to engage in **role taking**, the ability to imagine ourselves in the social roles of others and act them out in order to learn the social standards that will be applied to our behavior.

The Three Stages of Role Taking   In Mead's view, we learn to take on the roles of others and become social beings in three general stages—the imitative (preparatory) stage, the play stage, and the game stage (Mead, 1934).

In the **imitative stage** (the first three years), children learn to imitate the behavior of others in their immediate environment such as parents and other close family members. Small children will indiscriminately imitate the behavior of parents, for instance, some attempting to read the paper, dress up, shave, or talk like Mom or Dad.

As children become older, they move into the **play stage** in which they begin seriously to act out the roles of adults. Children from three through seven or eight years of age typically go through periods of wanting to be a parent or a nurse, a doctor or astronaut, or any one of the myriad of fantasy figures like cowboys, Indians, Tarzan, Wonder Woman, Spiderman, and so forth. Although children at this stage do not understand the obligations that go with certain roles, the role taking itself facilitates social development.

Finally, in middle to late childhood and early adolescence, children enter the **game stage** in which they learn to play the game of society according to the rules or role obligations. As part of this process, children typically become significantly aware of the impersonal sanctions that increasingly will be applied to their behavior by the larger society as they grow to maturity.

The Emergence of Self: The "I and "Me"   As children progress through these three stages of role taking, two components of the self emerge, which Mead called the "I" and the "Me." The "*I*" is the acting self as represented by one's natural drives and impulses, talents, and creative energies. The "*me,*" by contrast, represents the socialized self that acts in response to the demands of society. The small child, undersocialized and dominated by the "I," acts on selfish whim and impulse. Older children and adolescents, because of the role-taking influences of socialization, become increasingly dominated by the "me."

For most of us as adults, Mead argued, the "me" normally keeps the "I" in check except in certain circumstances where it is acceptable, if not desirable, to allow the "I" to express itself. Although the "me" as the social component of the self is necessary for the purposes of conformity and social order, we must guard against the other extreme in which we become oversocialized automatons who have lost the spark and spontaneity of the "I" that we need in order to reach our creative potential as unique human beings.

Significant Others and the Generalized Other   As the self develops, it is most influenced by **significant others**, people with whom the individual has close personal ties. Parents and siblings are our first sources of intimate, personal relationships, followed by the friendship circles formed within our peer groups and important role models outside the family (e.g., a favorite teacher, a coach, or a public figure). Later, as adults, most of us typically form additional bonds with significant others such as best friends, lovers, and/or spouses. In addition to the specific demands placed on us by our loved ones, our social behavior is also subject to universally and applied norms in the form of community and societal standards for behavior. Thus, each of us is expected to conform to the requirements of the **generalized other**, standards of community behavior expected of anyone placed in a given social position. If a child is socialized by parents and other significant others to develop pro-social values and skills, the child will tend to "fit in" with the demands and expectations of the larger community and society (generalized other).

Freud: Elements of the Self in Conflict

Unlike interactionist theorists in sociology such as Cooley and Mead who saw socialization as largely a smooth, relatively uneventful process (in most cases) of merging the individual with society, Sigmund Freud (1856–1939) saw childhood socialization quite differently. Freud, an Austrian physician and the founder of the psychoanalytic school in psychology, viewed socialization as a process of coercion in which the child's freely expressed feelings and urges came under the force and control of parents and the norms of society.

Freud's Components of the Personality

According to Freud (1930), the personality (psyche) consists of three components—the id, the ego, and the superego—that develop in the child in stages and interact together in a dynamic mental process, which he termed the *psyche*. The first to develop is the **id**, a person's natural urges and "instincts" such as sex and aggression. Children under two years of age are thereby dominated by the "pleasure principle," are completely self-centered and obsessed with doing whatever feels good.

Sigmund Freud. The psychoanalytic approach.

COURTESY OF THE LIBRARY OF CONGRESS PRINTS AND PHOTOGRAPHS DIVISION

During the ages of two, three, or four years, the rational part of the self called the **ego**—the governor or manager of the personality—begins to emerge. The child's ego, governed by the "reality principle," consciously thinks through the consequences of acting before doing so. In a small child, the ego is aware of the power of parents to sanction behavior and, thus, learns to do what is rewarding and avoid what is punishing. The **superego**, an inner voice or conscience that makes us feel proud when we act properly and guilty when we do wrong, develops in middle childhood. Ruled by the "principle of ideals," it represents the ideal standards of behavior we live by in the form of internalized ethics or morality.

The Relationship between Components of the Psyche (Personality)

According to Freud, the ego comprises the most important component of our self-concept. It represents the governor or the main control mechanism in the psyche or personality. As mediator between the conflicting demands of the id and superego, it channels selfish id impulses into socially desired forms of behavior while, at the same time, reduces ideal expectations of the superego into realistic and manageable modes of behavior that conform to societal standards. If, however, the ego becomes weakened or destroyed, and either the id or superego becomes dominant in the personality, then maladjustment may set in, the result being deviant or antisocial behavior. Id-dominated individuals, in extreme cases, might commit a violent crime such as murder, assault, or rape. Likewise, people whose superegos have taken over could, in the extreme, become religious fanatics or political terrorists who become so obsessed with ideals that they lose their perspective. Freud might have interpreted the events of September 11, 2001, as having resulted from superego-dominated, personality maladjustment in the nineteen young Saudi men who—as functionaries for Osama Bin Laden—sacrificed themselves to kill over twenty-eight hundred innocent Americans. In this view, superego driven fanaticism drove this "mission from god."

Freud's Elements of the Psyche

Id	Ego	Superego
(Pleasure)	(Reality)	(Ideals)

*L*ATER SOCIALIZATION THEORISTS

While Cooley, Mead, and Freud were among the most prominent pioneers, others have greatly refined and extended our modern understanding of the socialization process. Among those who stand out in this respect are Erving Goffman, Jean Piaget, and Lev Vygotsky.

Goffman: Interactionism and Dramaturgical Analysis

One sociologist who sought to extend the work of interactionists such as Cooley and Mead was Erving Goffman (1922–1982), who used a somewhat novel and provocative approach. As discussed previously, Cooley sought to explain how the interacting self is created in a constant intermeshing of personality elements—*presentation, identification,* and *subjective interpretation.* His colleague and mentor, Mead, stressed how the self develops during three stages of role taking as we interact with others. Goffman's approach, however, perhaps could best be introduced with a brief quote from the great bard of English literature:

> All the world's a stage,
> and all the men and women merely players:
> They have their exits and entrances;
> And one man in his time plays many parts . . .
> —William Shakespeare, *As You Like It*, Act 2, Scene 7

Interaction as Dramaturgy: The Calculated Presentation of Self   In Goffman's view, our day-to-day, face-to-face interactions with others are the central ingredients or "stuff" that society is built from. This micro to macro perspective he called **dramaturgical analysis**, the study of how and why people intentionally interact with each other like actors in a play titled "society." Society, in this sense represents a continuous theatrical performance that, like the daily episodes of television daytime soap operas, go on for decades or a lifetime without end. In Goffman's view, each of us socially constructs how we will play each role that we take on according to socially agreed to scripts that we then often embellish with our own style and carry out according to our own purposes (Goffman, 1959, 1967).

Life as Theater: The Role of Impression Management and Face Work   As we carry out our roles or play our parts in this theatrical production called society, Goffman argues that it is not just what we do that matters but how we do it, and not just what we say but how we say it as well. And there is also the possibility, Goffman implies, that what we mean to do or what we mean to say may be misinterpreted by others or used against us in some way. Politicians, for example, must be very careful in what they say and do because those competing with them for political office may use their utterances and actions, often taken out of context, to discredit them.

Impression management refers to the conscious efforts we make to present ourselves to others in a way they will see as favorable. In doing so, we devote energy to studying for and practicing the role we will play so that we will give a good performance. Our role preparation includes the proper costuming or dress we should wear like the uniforms worn by nurses, police officers, and airline pilots or the "proper" attire for business professionals or exotic dancers. We also use what Goffman calls "expressions given," that is, our intentional use of language as a script we verbalize, and our "expressions given off," which are the nonverbal messages we convey with our facial expressions and eye movements, our mannerisms, and our body language usually aimed at creating a certain impression in our audience. In this regard, the verbal and nonverbal cues intentionally given off by politicians, professors, professional boxers, prostitutes, and bus drivers are all very distinct and different because they involve different scripted roles. In addition, each player needs the proper setting or *set* and the correct *props* in order to give a convincing performance. Examples would include soldiers in a battle formation with tanks, automatic weapons, and air support; professors with classrooms, lecterns, and media equipment for PowerPoint presentations; and physicians with examining rooms, white coats, thermometers, and stethoscopes (Goffman, 1959).

Face work is Goffman's term for efforts made by people to present themselves to others in a favorable light in order to avoid public embarrassment or "losing face" (Ibid.). In some places like Tokyo, Japan, for example, it is not uncommon for unemployed business executives to dress up in suits and ties, go downtown as if going to work, pass the day by frequenting movie theaters, museums, or libraries, and then go home. They do this because they want to "save face" in the eyes of their families and friends who are unaware they are unemployed (French, 2000). Other people use a variety of face work techniques as verbal rationalizations or "spin" when they feel ignored, embarrassed, marginalized, or rejected in social situations. For example, a student failing a particular course might say to his or her friends "That professor was such a lousy teacher that I dropped his course."

Piaget: Cognitive Development Theory

What is "cognitive development"? Swiss psychologist Jean Piaget (1896–1980) focused his socialization studies on how children develop intellectual abilities and moral judgments. He argued that children think and set priorities differently from adults, primarily because their intellectual capacities are limited and, therefore, must develop gradually in a series of observable stages. In a career encompassing more than forty years, Piaget developed and refined his **cognitive development theory**, which examined changes in thought processes and intellectual abilities that occur in four stages as children mature.

Piaget spent several decades observing thousands of children and talking to them about their thoughts, feelings, and actions. He concluded that children develop cognitively in four general stages—sensorimotor, preoperations, concrete operations, and formal operations. His work acted to reinforce and add a new dimension (namely cognition) to the socialization theories of Cooley and Mead (Piaget, 1929; Piaget and Inhelder, 1969) (Table 5-1).

The Sensorimotor Stage   During the **sensorimotor stage** (birth to two years), children develop motor intelligence and learn to distinguish different objects. *Motor intelligence*, Piaget argued, is the acquired ability by children to perceive their bodies as separate from the rest of their external environment. Small infants do not realize this or understand that they can use their bodies to make things happen in their environment. For instance, small babies do not realize that when they shake a rattle, they cause it to make a sound. Also during this period *object permanence* develops, in which children come to realize that people or objects, such as parents and toys, do not cease to exist when they leave one's

TABLE 5-1	Piaget's Stages of Cognitive Development
DEVELOPMENTAL STAGE	**CHARACTERISTICS (COGNITIVE ABILITIES)**
1. Sensorimotor (birth–2 years)	Motor skills development, perception of close surroundings, and object permanence (objects have their own reality apart from one's ability to see or experience them directly).
2. Preoperations (2–7 years)	Development of symbolic functions: Language ability emerges steadily along with ability to picture things in one's mind, the ability to take the role of another (although usually only one person at a time). Nonetheless, egocentrism remains.
3. Concrete Operations (7–12 years)	Logical thinking begins to develop: Child acquires ability to rank objects by size and class and understand their relations to one another by weight, mass, and volume. The ability to consider several points of view at once also develops.
4. Formal Operations (12 years–adulthood)	Abstract and hypothetical thinking is developed: individual learns to consider several options or hypothetical solutions to a problem before acting. The maturing person thus is free from the limitations of immediate and past experiences, can operate in the world of ideas, and consider future goals.

Source: Adapted from Ginsburg, H., and Opper, S. 1969. *Piaget's Theory of Intellectual Development.* Englewood Cliffs, NJ: Prentice-Hall.

sight. Perhaps you have played "peek-a-boo" with a two year old who has recently acquired the object permanence. The child knows you will reappear, but is still mystified at how it all works and greatly enjoys the game.

Preoperations   During the stage of **preoperations** (from two to about six or seven years), children develop the ability to think symbolically and use language to communicate with others. At this stage, children imitate the use of words with little understanding of what they mean. They also live to some extent in the world of "pretend" and "make believe" and usually perceive fantasy characters as real to some degree. Because they do not understand concepts like weight, size, category, and cause and effect during the early part of this period, they are not capable of many simple intellectual operations. If the same amount of water or milk is placed in two glasses, one short and the other tall, most children at this level of development will tend to choose the tall glass because they think it contains more. Likewise, "preoperational" children are likely to think large objects weigh more than small ones. By the time a child is six or seven, he or she has learned how to sort objects by size, weight, and class, and has developed to some extent the ability to see reality through the eyes of another person, although he or she typically can consider only one viewpoint at a time.

Concrete Operations   From seven to about twelve years of age, children move into and through the stage of **concrete operations** in which cause-and-effect relationships in the real world become understood and concrete reasoning ability is developed. As children move from preoperations to concrete operations, they learn to "factor in" several points of view simultaneously, and by age seven or eight, begin to largely abandon the world of intuition and fantasy (e.g., they learn the truth about Santa Claus, the tooth fairy, and the Easter bunny). At this stage, they can now test relationships between objects in a concrete way by weighing two objects in a literal manner or by measuring the quantity of liquid in two glasses. However, at this point in their intellectual development, they are still largely limited in their perceptions to their own life experiences and what they can and have experienced directly.

Formal Operations   According to Piaget, the stage of **formal operations** (from about twelve years to adulthood) represents the last and most advanced stage of cognitive development characterized by the development of higher order or abstract thinking abilities. During this period, adolescents develop the capability to hypothesize about possible cause-and-effect relationships and possible courses of action without the necessity of having experienced them directly. They can see the potential consequences of behavior in their "mind's eye." In terms of moral behavior, most individuals are no longer egocentric and selfish in their attitudes and behavior, but have internalized the concept of duty in regard to obeying social norms and the need to act for the greater good of the larger group or of society.

Piaget in Perspective   Piaget's central idea that children of different ages (corresponding roughly to his four stages) use different cognitive abilities and strategies to make sense of the world and operate successfully in it appears to be widely accepted by most researchers as a result of numerous studies (Kessen, 1996). His research seems particularly insightful regarding general cognitive development patterns among children in the United States and other Western societies.

However, his work has come under criticism for being too limiting in term of ages at which children develop certain abilities and somewhat culture bound by time and place. For example, Piaget and his colleagues, in their research on infants in Europe and the United States, found that *object permanence* (sensorimotor stage) did not occur until the baby was about nine months old. However, recent research has found that, given certain environments and learning opportunities, infants show mastery of object permanence as young as two and one-half months after birth (Aguilar and Baillargeon, 1999; Luo, et al., 2003). In addition, cross-cultural studies have shown that American children, particularly those from the middle class, follow Piaget's stages fairly closely in their development while children from lower classes and those from less-developed societies sometimes do not. Some American adolescents appear to reach the formal stage of development by age fourteen to sixteen years, while some adults never master this last stage.

Vygotsky: Sociocultural Theory

One important theorist whose ideas regarding socialization were largely unknown by Western scholars until recently was the Russian social-psychologist Lev Vygotsky (1896–1934). Largely because he lived in Russia during the totalitarian regime of Joseph Stalin and died prematurely at age 38 from tuberculosis, his writings have only become well-known since the 1960s and only in the past twenty years have they been recognized by behavioral scientists worldwide.

Sociocultural Context and Cognitive Development

Vygotsky's **sociocultural theory** represents a socialization perspective that focuses on the dynamic interplay between developing children and their guided participation in society by competent adults. In his view, cognitive development requires dynamic interaction between developing children and their guidance by competent adults within a particular sociocultural context. Vygotsky lived in Russia, a culturally diverse society, that covered a huge expanse of geographically varied territory. Its people were equally diverse with different ethnic backgrounds and occupations. They had economies that ranged from rural agricultural regions where farmers and herdsmen had to master the tools and techniques necessary to earn their livelihoods, to the very different life styles and occupations found among factory workers, trades people, and merchants in the large cities. Although *how* they learned to master their particular life situations remained the same, *what* they learned—as a farmer or factory worker, rancher or restauranteur, miller or merchant—depended on the particular requirements or contexts of their culture.

Premise 1: The Impact of Cultural Mediation

The key premise of Vygotsky's theory focuses on **cultural mediation**, the process by which children learn or internalize the ways of their culture and how to use them as tools to succeed both as a society member and as an individual. For example, milking a cow, using a computer, driving a car, and writing with a pen all represent cultural skills people learn to master to succeed as members of society. However, people, through the development of higher-order cognitive processes, can also learn to use these skills as tools for their own individual use that transcend the typical practical ways they are utilized within one's culture. So, while most people learn to drive cars as a means of transportation, the child who grows up to be a race car driver may use this skill at a higher level later in life to participate in a highly select and lucrative profession. Likewise, most people learn as children to use computers and pens for utilitarian purposes related to work, school, shopping, communicating with others, and recreation. However, for the child who grows up to be a professional writer and author—like J. K. Rowling who authored the Harry Potter series of books—he or she may learn to use them in ways that are unique to them (Vygotsky, 1978). In speaking to this, Vygotsky (1978) summarizes the powerful impact that socialization has on a person's development as follows:

> Every function in the child's cultural development appears twice: first on the social level, and later, on the individual level; first between people (interpsychological) and then inside the child (intrapsychological). This applies equally to voluntary attention, to logical memory, and to the formation of concepts. All the higher functions originate as actual relationships between individuals (p. 57).

Premise 2: Use of the Zone of Proximal Development (ZPD)

According to Vygotsky, the **zone of proximal development** (ZPD) is the potential for learning that a child possesses that can be developed with help from skilled mentors as compared to what the child already knows or can learn on his or her own. Reaching one's human potential depends largely on what happens developmentally in childhood. The relationships developed with competent, skilled adults—or lack thereof—determines, in large part, how children develop and what they will or will not be able to accomplish.

Apprenticeship in Thinking   In Vygotsky's view, a crucial element in how children develop cognitively is an **apprenticeship** in thinking, a process in which an unskilled person (novice learner) develops mastery of a cognitive competency through involvement with one or more engaged, skilled mentors. Children need these socialization apprenticeships with competent adults in order to reach their potential as human beings (Rogoff, 1990).

The Role of Guided Participation   Regardless of *what* we need to learn, Vkgotsky asserted, *how* we learn depends on **guided participation**. This, he defined as the process by which a skilled member of society serving as mentor—a parent or teacher, for example—actively assists an unskilled learner in mastering a particular cognitive competency. Consequently, learners, particularly children in their critical years of development, need and depend on the active assistance of dedicated, skilled mentors to help guide them to achieve mastery of a particular skill or activity (Karpov and HayWood, 1998). Without active intervention by competent and dedicated adults, a specific cognitive competency, whatever it might be, may not be achieved.

AGENTS OF SOCIALIZATION

Children are influenced in their individual and social development by a variety of factors. The family, peers, school, church, media, and the larger community and society all play an integral part in shaping our personalities and equipping us with skills for social survival and prosperity. In this portion of the chapter, we will focus on three of the most important agents of socialization—the family, the peer group, and the mass media—which, in the case of family and close friends, represent our primary sources of significant others and continue throughout our lives to play a significant role in shaping our attitudes and behaviors.

The Family

Of all sources of childhood socialization, the family is the most important. As mentioned earlier, the human infant is virtually helpless at birth and must rely on parents and other family members for physical care and protection during the many years required for maturation. More important for humans, however, is that our experiences with our families shape the way we see ourselves, the larger world, and our place in it. An American child grows up with a very different culture, language, and worldview than a child reared in Peru, India, or Japan. Likewise, family socialization patterns within pluralistic societies like the United States are quite diverse. For example, children reared in a rural farming community in the Midwest come to look at the world through a different filter than those brought up in a large industrial city in the Northeast. Likewise, children whose parents practice religious fundamentalism tend to grow up with different values and life priorities than those reared as Presbyterians, Catholics, or Jews.

Class as a Socialization Factor   One important factor involved in the transmission of culture to a child is social class. A family's socioeconomic level is important because different class levels represent distinct subcultures. Children's class backgrounds shape to a significant degree the values and beliefs they hold, their self-concepts, and how they come to relate to the rest of the world. These class subcultures are further reinforced by other factors, which include region, rural or urban residence, race and ethnicity, and religion. Children reared in lower socioeconomic circumstances, for instance, may tend to be fatalistic and see success as determined largely by luck. Those reared in more affluent circumstances, by contrast, tend to have an achievement orientation and see success in terms of individual effort and hard work.

Sociologist Melvin Kohn (1963, 1977) conducted studies that show distinct differences in how children are raised in working-class versus middle-class families. Working-class parents tend to stress strict conformity to traditional standards, punish the consequences of unacceptable behavior (what children do), and are more likely to use physical punishment. They stress to their children the importance of obeying the rules and keeping out of trouble. This parenting style, according to Kohn, is at least partially influenced by the fact that working-class parents typically have blue-collar jobs. In such occupations, they are given little, if any, discretion in how they do their own work and are expected to follow instructions precisely.

Middle-class parents, by contrast, tend to have white-collar jobs that, due to their complexity, require more independent thought and discretion. This is then reflected in how they socialize their children. Middle-class parents tend to stress and reward their children's initiative and creativity. When punishment is given, it is for the motives behind behavior instead of what the children did. Children in middle-class families are taught the importance of self-control rather than strict obedience and are less likely to be physically disciplined.

The impact of the family on the formation of self-concept is also important. As we saw with the cases of Anna, Isabelle, and Genie, and in Harry Harlow's deprivation research on monkeys, the lack of adequate emotional support during the formative developmental years can be devastating. Small children need consistent love, affection, support, and encouragement in order to develop positive self-images and the confidence required to deal effectively with life's adversities and challenges (Mortimer and Simmons, 1978). The family is the first social group to which they become members, and parents represent their first teachers, guides, and role models.

Birth Order   Even so, parents tend to treat their first-born and later-born children differently. Some research indicates that the first-born children tend to receive more attention, affection, and discipline than later-borns. These first-borns then tend to become higher achievers than their younger siblings, who tend to be more relaxed and sociable (Forer, 1976; Dunn and Kendrick, 1983). For instance, first-born children tend to earn better grades in school, score higher on IQ tests, and appear more likely to go to college. In addition, they are overrepresented among Rhodes scholars, those in *Who's Who in America,* and even presidents (52 percent) of the United States (Vander Zanden, 1985).

Methods of Family Socialization

There are three key methods of family socialization: reward and punishment, imitation and modeling, and didactic teaching. A combination of each of these methods occurs to some degree in almost all families as children progress through infancy into childhood, and then move into and through the years of adolescence. We will consider each briefly here.

Reward and Punishment: Three Parental Approaches   The dominant method of family socialization is **reward and punishment**, the primary tool used by parents to establish and enforce behavioral boundaries and standards for their children. There are three broad yet distinct parenting styles: the authoritarian approach, the permissive approach, and the authoritative approach (Baumrind, 1968, 1989). Each is practiced to a larger degree in some cultures or socioeconomic levels than others. In examining mothers cross-culturally, for example, German mothers are the most authoritarian, American mothers the most permissive, and Japanese mothers the most authoritative. In the discussion to follow, we will examine the viability of each approach as a parenting approach in America. In this brief narrative, each parenting strategy will be explained in terms of a definition, the primary parental tool used by such a parent, and their chief parental role. As you read the brief explanation to follow, keep in mind that each parent or set of parents tends to fall somewhere on the continuum that appears below in terms of parenting style.

The Continuum of Parenting
(Use of Reward and Punishment)

Authoritarian	Authoritative	Permissive
(Mainly punishments)	(Balance: Rewards and Punishment	(Mainly rewards)

Authoritarian Parenting   The **authoritarian approach** is one in which the parent uses mainly punishments and few if any rewards, and makes most if not all decisions concerning the child's behavior. With this strategy, *the parent's chief role is that of traffic cop or drill sergeant,* while *the primary parental tool used is coercion or intimidation.* While this strategy may be effective in village-focused, agricultural societies where children work shoulder to shoulder with their parents in the fields, participate directly in the economy as producers, and learn responsibility hands-on at a very young age, the authoritarian approach is very ineffective in modern and post-modern societies. Even with the best of intentions by such parents who love their children, this approach often spells disaster because it infantilizes children and shelter's them from the reality-testing experiences they will need to become full-functioning and responsible adults. While it is not difficult to intimidate small children, they do eventually mature into teenagers, physically as large or larger than their parents. Teenagers then often rebel against their parents and do wild and often destructive things to themselves and others because they have not been allowed to grow up.

Permissive Parenting   The second strategy, the **permissive approach**, is one in which the parent uses mainly rewards and few if any punishments and makes few if any decisions concerning the child's behavior. The *parent's chief role* with this approach *tends to be the parent as pal when children are young and the parent as martyr as they mature.* Like the authoritarian approach previously discussed, the permissive strategy represents an expedient, a parental shortcut, used by unprepared, ill-informed, and often overwhelmed adults. Usually they have not given parenting much thought or preparation beforehand and often are distracted by other demands placed on their time. As such, *this parent's primary parental tool is bribery,* which is every ineffective. Such parents often do not understand that small children are children, not miniature adults. As such, they are egocentric, extremely astute observers, and are and will continue to be very selfish and manipulative unless parents exert consistent and competent control and guidance very early on. In order for children to grow into competent adults, they must learn and appreciate that they are not the centers of the universe and that the world is not going to cater to them. Permissively raised children grow into immature, selfish, and incompetent adults who, even into their thirties and forties, sometimes are dependent on their parents to rescue them or "bail them out" when they prove incapable of being autonomous, self-reliant adults.

Authoritative Parenting   Finally, the **authoritative approach** is a parenting strategy in which the parent uses a balance of rewards and punishments, sets clear and consistent boundaries for the child's behavior, and gradually allows the child to participate in personal decision making. Behavioral research has clearly established that authoritative parenting is the most effective approach (Dorius et Al., 2004; Eisenburg et al., 2005). The *chief parental role* employed by such parents *tends to consist of five dimensions: teacher, counselor, coach, facilitator, and guide.*

Authoritative parents tailor which parental role dimension or combination is appropriate in a given circumstance with each child and parenting situation. How do they know which one or combination to use? They know their child. How do parents come to know their children? This can only be accomplished by investing large amounts of time and energy in them. By doing this and implementing the *primary parental tool of patience,* these parents tend to gradually guide their children, over an eighteen- to twenty-year period, into becoming competent, autonomous, and well-adjusted adults with the tools and strategies needed to survive and prosper in an increasingly complex and ever-changing world.

Imitation and Modeling   A second method of family socialization is **imitation and modeling**, a process in which, by imitating the behaviors and methods employed by parents, children use them as models for their own lives. Parents often may be unaware of the

The family is the primary agent of socialization.

power they as role models have over their children. For small children, parents usually are the first and most important adults in their lives and they usually want to be just like them. It is important to note that children will imitate their parent's bad habits and behaviors, as well as those seen as positive and adaptive. From a child's perspective "If mom and dad do it, it must be great. I want to do it too and be just like them." Consequently, parents should take care to model pro-social behaviors that, should the child employ them later as a life habit, will facilitate adjustment to the social demands of the larger community and society.

Didactic Teaching   The third and last method of family socialization to be discussed is **didactic teaching**, the actual hands-on instruction of a child by a parent in some skill or activity. Parents instruct their children in a variety of behavioral techniques they will need to acquire the skills to carry out a wide variety of behaviors and social habits necessary as adults. This instruction begins early in infancy as small children learn how to eat without being spoon fed, and dress themselves, tie their shoes, wash their hands, brush their teeth, and pick up their toys and clothes. Later they can be taught and required to make their beds, keep their rooms neat and tidy, and do a variety of household chores (e.g., washing, folding, and putting away their own clothes, mowing lawns, helping with cooking and washing dishes, etc.) as responsible members of a household. Recreational pursuits are also commonly taught by parents such as riding bicycles, playing ball, swimming, and playing a variety of games. Finally, beginning early in childhood, parents can teach their children how to talk properly, read, learn their numbers, and later, how to manage money, use their time wisely, etc.

The Peer Group

By the time children are five or six years old (and younger for the many children in daycare situations), their relationships with peers begin to play an important and integral role in their emotional and social development. **Peer groups** are groups of people of about the same age and social position whose members have significant influence on one another. Children are fascinated with one another because of the special standing of equality they share. This sets their relationships with each other apart from the inequality inherent in their dealings with adults. Because their states of physical, emotional, and intellectual development are about the same, they have experiences in common that are not applicable in their relationships with adults.

The Youth Subculture   In today's fast-changing modern society, children grow up in a very different world from the one their parents knew as children. This, among other things, has resulted in a gap between generations in several respects. Most notably, the twentieth century witnessed the emergence of a **youth subculture** consisting of life-style characteristics and preferences among children and adolescents very distinct from those of their parents. This is readily seen today in their use of "pop slang," distinct modes of dress, hair-styles, music, and other special consumer preferences.

The youth subculture acts to reinforce the impact of peer group socialization and can have both functional and dysfunctional consequences. On the positive side, it supports development of interpersonal communication skills and relationships outside the home, which become very important during adulthood in both career and recreational settings.

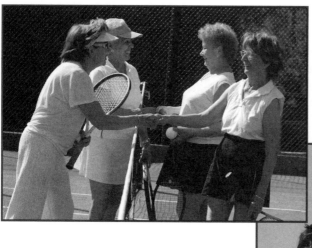

Peer groups influence our behavior throughout the life cycle.

Overidentification with the more superficial aspects of the youth subculture, however, can retard the development of an adult sense of responsibility. Involvement by children and adolescents with deviant elements such as the "drug scene" or delinquent groups can also have pronounced negative results.

Characteristics of Peer Groups
Peer groups function in several ways. First, *they introduce children to the impersonality of social rules.* In the home, rewards and punishments are administered by parents in a very personal manner, while in the peer group rules are impersonally set and sanctioned, and few if any people are given "special" consideration. Second, *they test the limits of adult tolerance.* Children will attempt things in peer settings that they would not dream of doing on their own in order to test adult authority and the strength of peer support and influence. In addition, *children's peer groups may or may not reinforce adult values.* For instance, one group of twelve year olds may have a lawn-mowing service to make money in the summertime, while another forms a burglary ring to rob the community (Broom and Selznick, 1968). Finally, *they teach children some of the more informal aspects of the larger culture that they often are not taught at home.* These may be adaptive or maladaptive in preparing a child for life success as an adult: Getting along with others, acquiring the etiquette of male–female social relations, learning about sex, the use of profanity, and the use of drugs are often reinforced or acquired in peer groups.

Mass Media: Its Impact on Child Development

Mass media consist of the various methods used to transmit information to large numbers of people in an organized manner. Through its many sources—including books, magazines, newspapers, television, movies, the internet—both children and adults are exposed to a vast array of images and topics.

Parents, in most cases, represent the most important source in guiding socialization for the developing child. There is an established and growing body of behavioral research on cognitive development—as related to the use and misuse of media—that parents can utilize to maximize the cognitive development of their children. Based on dozens of studies conducted over the past fifty years, cognitive research findings can perhaps best be summarized in the form of two key recommendations for parents who wish to foster intellectual development in their children.

Read to Your Child   A common characteristic of high school students who score in the top ten percent on college entrance exams is that they were consistently read to by their parents when they were small children. It is well established in the scientific literature that children who are read to each week from twelve months of age until they begin reading on their own typically are reading by age four and one-half years and, upon entering first grade, often read at the third to fourth grade level. Through such socialization, these children learn to love to reading and are intellectually curious and thirsty for knowledge. Parents who make an investment of their time and energy in fostering the development of their children's minds in this manner help to prepare their children for success rather than failure. The degree to which a child's mind is nourished by learning how to read as soon as possible provides a firm foundation for later development and self-actualization as an adult.

The following are key reasons why children benefit from being read to by their parents:

1. It activates listening skills.
2. It activates the imagination.
3. It provides interesting conversation topics.
4. It provides important language modeling.
5. It develops the ability to think critically.
6. It enhances the ability to think symbolically.
7. It stimulates writing abilities.
8. It's fun.
9. It's an affordable source of entertainment.
10. It increases a child's attention span.
11. It provides a peaceful family activity.
12. It develops a child's desire to read.
13. It models a rewarding lifelong habit.
14. It gives a child a sense of language rhythm.
15. It helps to pattern neural pathways.
16. It expands a child's vocabulary.
17. It increases a child ability to concentrate.
18. It gives a child needed practice in predicting information.
19. It expands a child's world view.
20. It's the single most important thing a parent can do to help a child succeed in school.

(Source: "Television, Computers, and Brain Development," Speechgoals.org 2004)

Set Quality Standards for a Child's Access to Television and Other Multimedia

Depending on which study is consulted, American school-age children spend an average of twenty-two to twenty-eight hours each week watching television. Do the math. There are twenty-four hours in a day. A minimum of eight hours are needed by children for nightly sleep. Two to four additional hours a day are required for getting dressed and undressed, bathing, eating meals, and taking care of physical hygiene and elimination needs. Subtract these hours from twenty-four and you get twelve to fourteen hours of functional living time each day. If a child watches twenty-two to twenty-eight hours of TV per week, this means that up to two-sevenths of a child's functional waking life may be spent sitting passively in front of a glowing screen. This is passive learning. By contrast, reading is active learning. Children being read to or reading on their own conjure up in their mind's eye what the characters in a story look like and how they relate to each other. In addition, they can determine the pace of their reading and stop to reflect on and think about what they just read. With television, everything is done for the viewer who is simply a passive receiver.

Too much television and other media with no quality controls can pose serious implications for cognitive development. If parents do not impose quality and quantity boundaries and limits on the television programming to which their children are exposed, the results, in extreme cases, can result in a variety of maladaptive consequences. These include impaired cognitive ability, deficiencies in reading skills, symptoms of attention deficit hyperactivity disorder (ADHD), poor social interaction and communication skills, social isolation, a negative self-concept, depression, a propensity toward aggressive and violent behavior, and poor performance in school. How much television should my child be exposed to? Of course, television is a wonderful medium for educational enrichment and entertainment. Used in moderation, it can enrich people's lives. Yet, like many things, including fat- and salt-laden fast foods, too much of it can have harmful effects particularly for young children. According to Jane M. Healy (1998) in "Understanding TV's Effects on the Developing Brain," too much television—particularly at ages critical for language development and manipulative play—can impact negatively on young minds in several different ways including the following:

Higher levels of television viewing correlate with lowered academic performance, especially reading scores. This may be because television substitutes for reading practice, partially because the compelling visual nature of the stimulus blocks development of left-hemisphere language circuitry. A young brain manipulated by jazzy visual effects cannot divide attention to listen carefully to language. Moreover, the "two-minute mind" easily becomes impatient with any material requiring depth of processing.

The nature of the stimulus may predispose some children to attention problems. Even aside from violent or overly stimulating sexual content, the fast-paced, attention grabbing "features" of children's programming (e.g., rapid zooms and pans, flashes of color, quick movement in the peripheral vision field, sudden loud noises) were modeled after advertising research, which determined that this technique is the best way to engage the brain involuntarily. Such experiences deprive the child of practice in using his or her own brain independently, as in games, hobbies, social interaction, or just "fussing around." I have talked to many parents of children diagnosed with attention-deficit disorder who found the difficulty markedly improved after they took away television viewing privileges.

The brain's executive control system, or pre-frontal cortex, is responsible for planning, organizing and sequencing behavior for self-control, moral judgment and attention. These centers develop throughout childhood and adolescence, but some research has suggested that "mindless" television video games may idle this particular part of the brain and impoverish its development. Until we know more about the interaction of environmental stimulation and the stages of pre-frontal development, it seems a grave error to expose children to a stimulus that may short-change this critical system.

A fair consensus among scientists who research learning would strongly suggest the following guidelines for parents: Infants and toddlers under two years should be discouraged from having little if any television exposure; for preschool children, one to five hours per week is recommended but no more than eight to ten; school-age children should have no more than ten to fifteen hours per week (American Academy of Pediatrics, 2001). Yet by age seventy, the average American will have spent seven to ten years of their waking life sitting passively in front of a television set (Strasburger, 1993). The foundation for such a lifestyle as a spectator rather than engaged participant is established early in childhood. One study found that one-third (32 percent) of children two to seven years old and nearly two-thirds of children and adolescents aged eight to eighteen years of age had a television set placed in their bedrooms (Gerbner, et al., 1994). In a policy statement issued by the American Academy of Pediatrics in February, 2001, it was recommended that parents "remove television sets from children's bedrooms" (American Academic of Pediatrics, p. 424.)

Effective childhood socialization requires that parents be engaged with their children by spending significant periods of time each week interacting with them one-on-one and in family activities. Too many uninformed and disengaged parents use television and other forms of information technology at potentially harmful levels as surrogate baby sitters to distract and entertain their children while they engage in things they consider more important. One price the child pays for too few restrictions on television and exposure to other media (e.g., movies, video games, internet) is impaired literacy development, which, according to recent research, is associated with poor performance in school (Sharif and Sargent, 2006; Moses, 2008). By contrast, children whose parents take the time and expend the energy to actively parent and guide them experience quite a different set of socialization experiences than "overstimulated children" whose minds are constantly bombarded and distracted by relatively unrestricted levels of "useless" information a mile wide and an inch deep. Children who are the recipients of competent parenting grow up learning how to concentrate for extended periods on key cognitive tasks, engage in introspection and critical thinking, and are able to stay task-oriented and focused in order to complete complex tasks and achieve meaningful life goals.

ADULT SOCIALIZATION

As behavioral theorists and researchers have known for quite some time, socialization does not end with adulthood but continues throughout the life cycle. Upon leaving childhood, we experience the transition to the world of adult responsibility and make various adaptations as we grow older and mature. These adaptations take several forms. Some have to do with the role transitions we make as we leave or continue school, obtain a job, and perhaps get married and start a family. Others involve how we adjust to our own aging process as we adapt first to being a young adult, then a middle-aged person, and finally a senior citizen.

Rites of Passage

Adult socialization is often reinforced by **rites of passage**, formal events that signal the end of one position or stage in life and the beginning of another. These key life events often take the form of ceremonies or rituals such as school graduation, marriage, completion of military training, and promotions or awards. These events, often involving the taking of photographs and attendance by close family and friends, are very special occasions that are remembered for years. But most important, they serve as benchmarks that mark our journey from one stage or period of life to another as we progress through our life cycle.

Anticipatory Socialization

The informal preparation for future life stages and life responsibilities is what Robert Merton and Alice Rossi (1968) have called **anticipatory socialization**. As George Herbert Mead found in his observations, this process of social preparation for the future actually begins in early childhood as children first imitate and then play out social roles they see enacted by parents and other adults. Children, for example, often look forward with eager anticipation to becoming a "teenager." Teenagers then prepare for entering the adult world. These mental rehearsals for the future, however, have their greatest impact during adulthood when we experience the greatest number of life transitions.

Anticipatory socialization is also evident in our personal relationships. Going steady prepares a couple to see if they are sufficiently compatible to carry it further. If the relationship endures and intensifies, a couple may become engaged. This, in turn, is a special period that allows two people to prepare for a married life together. If they do get married, the first year or two of marriage may be needed to decide about children and prepare for the responsibilities of parenthood. Life involves a series of these transitions that, if planned carefully, soften and make easier the changes and adjustments we all make as we grow older.

Resocialization

Role transitions made in adulthood often involve **resocialization**, an abrupt and often basic change in life style and life priorities. It involves, in most cases, the abandonment of one way of life for another. Being married, for example, involves a significant shift in priorities and a very different life style as compared to being single. A much more dramatic example is that of a person who experiences a religious conversion or joins the priesthood. The convert will sometimes claim a feeling of being cleansed or "born again," and essentially begins a new life as a believer. Resocialization is also in evidence when one joins the military. Other examples of resocialization would include becoming a parent, going to prison, getting divorced, losing one's job, winning the lottery, inheriting a fortune, or entering retirement from one's profession.

Resocialization tends to take two forms—voluntary and involuntary. *Voluntary resocialization* involves an independent and conscious choice by a person to undergo a fundamental change in his or her social identity and lifestyle. Sometimes, however, resocialization is imposed on people by virtue of the type of society in which they live or particular life circumstances. In this regard, *involuntary resocialization* is a basic life change imposed on a person by others or society. In rural areas of countries such as Indonesia, India, and China, for example, children are essentially forced by circumstances and parental pressure to become farmers or herds people. In several cultures, marriage is involuntary because it is arranged by parents who often give their children little or no choice in the matter.

The Middle Years and Becoming Elderly

As we become older, both anticipatory socialization and resocialization experiences play an important role in shaping our life course. During the middle years of the forties, fifties, and sixties, people look back introspectively at their previous accomplishments and examine their current life situations. "Have I used my life productively?" "Am I successful?" "Have I made a difference in the lives of others and in society?" The way such questions are answered affects how people see middle age and the future.

© KOH SZE KIAT, 2009. USED UNDER LICENSE FROM SHUTTERSTOCK, INC.

Resocialization carries with it a fundamental change in both life style and the norms one is expected to obey.

The middle years can be fulfilling and productive, or fraught with stress and crisis. Many mid-lifers experience some of the positives and the negatives both. This is a time in which income is highest, free time is often the greatest, and parental responsibilities are being phased out as children become adults and ultimately leave home. Although middle-aged people do not have the physical appearance of their youth, health and vitality are usually good and, combined with greater maturity and affluence, often provide them with very fulfilling lives. In fact, for many, the middle years are among the best.

Others in middle age, however, may experience crises in a variety of forms. Some feel they are caught in a "sandwich generation" between responsibilities to their adolescent and young adult children, and to elderly parents in poor economic circumstances or failing health. Others may have a mid-life crisis in which they feel trapped in a boring and unfulfilled life with no excitement or challenge. In any case, the middle years are a period of consolidation and reflection. For most, the majority of life decisions and accomplishments have been made, time is getting short, and the challenge is to make the most of what time they have left and to use it most productively to build the best future possible. Becoming elderly usually begins at about retirement. Because thirteen percent of Americans are now over sixty-five years of age or older (U.S. Census Bureau, 2000a), the elderly population is now much more visible than it once was.

Senior citizens face many challenges and problems. First, they live in a society that, during most of the twentieth century, had a "youth orientation," which viewed and treated many of the elderly as second-class citizens. The trend now, however, is shifting toward a much more positive view regarding the elderly and their capabilities, as evidenced by an increased use of elderly role models in the media and the abolition or extension of the mandatory retirement age formerly set at sixty-five. Second, the elderly often live on fixed retirement incomes that average only about one-half the earnings they had while working. Combined with increasing health problems and the difficulty in obtaining and paying for health insurance, senior citizens often face significant financial problems. Finally, retirement often brings reduced self-esteem, and the elderly must face grief crises when friends and spouses die.

Despite these problems, those over sixty-five often live healthy and productive lives for an additional fifteen years or so, and for some, much longer. As the ranks of the elderly continue to swell, with the numbers of those eighty-five and older increasing the fastest, positive role models are also becoming more common. At the age of seventy-eight, Ronald Reagan completed his second term as president of the United States in 1988; Senator John McCain was nominated for the presidency in 2008 at age seventy-one. Comedian and actor George Burns, who lived to be one hundred years old and made movies until he was 94, once said that people get old and feeble because of their attitudes. They "practice to get old. The minute they get to be sixty-five or seventy, they sit down slow, they get into a car with trouble. They start taking small steps." His approach was to attack life with "moxie" (Toufexis et al., 1988).

Evidently, an increasing number of senior citizens agree. Hulda Crooks, age ninety-one, climbed ninety-seven mountains between the ages of sixty and ninety, including Japan's Mt. Fuji . Other examples include seventy-four-year-old Dr. James Jay who, along with fifty-five others over the age of seventy, completed the New York City Marathon, and author Jane Stovall, one hundred three, who became a senior golf champion in her eighties and a student pilot at eighty-nine (Gibbs, et al., 1988).

▶ CHAPTER SUMMARY

1. The human personality is the product of two basic factors: nature (inherited characteristics) and nurture (social environment and experiences). Theories about the inherent nature of humans have varied from the social contract theories of the seventeenth and eighteenth centuries and social Darwinism during the nineteenth century, to the notion of human instincts in the early twentieth century. More recently, sociobiology has emerged as an attempt to study the biological origins of social behavior, although it has been widely criticized. The "environmental" or nurture explanation of behavior began to emerge in the late nineteenth century and early twentieth centuries with the work of researchers like Ivan Pavlov and James Watson. Recent case studies of children isolated from normal social contact and related research have demonstrated clearly that human development is significantly, if not largely, determined by socialization.

2. Because human infants are virtually helpless at birth and depend on others for a large portion of their lifespan, socialization serves several basic needs. Chief among these are bonding and emotional support, the establishment of behavioral boundaries, goal setting, social survival skills, and the formation and maintenance of the self-concept.

3. Three classical socialization theorists—Charles Horton Cooley, George Herbert Mead, and Sigmund Freud—laid much of the foundation for our modern understanding of human development. Cooley and Mead were interactionists who saw socialization as a gradual developmental process that resulted in the smooth merging of the needs and wants of the individual with those of society. Cooley stressed how our interactions with others influence our self-concept and behavior through his concept of the looking glass self. Mead stated that children learn the role-taking behavior necessary to conform to the demands of society in three stages: the preparatory (imitation) stage, the play stage, and the game stage. Freud disagreed with the interactionist view and maintained that socialization is an abrupt often coercive experience for small children in which the expression of their natural urges is severely restricted by parents and the larger society. Freud's theory of personality development stressed three interactive components of the psyche—the id, the ego, and the superego—that develop in stages.

4. Recent socialization theorists have concentrated on specific aspects of socialization as illustrated by the work of Erving Goffman (dramaturgy), Jean Piaget (cognitive development), and Lev Vygotsky (sociocultural theory). Goffman, in building on the work of Mead and other interactionists, focused his work on the social scripts that people learn and play out in their everyday lives, using such devices as impression management and face work. Piaget devoted his career to examining how children develop intellectually in four stages—sensorimotor, preoperations, concrete operations, and formal operations. Vygotsky, the Russian social psychologist whose work has only been fully discovered and appreciated recently by Western scholars, concentrated his analysis on how the sociocultural context shapes who children become as adults, which depends on consistent mentoring by competent adults.

5. Of the many agents of childhood socialization, three are stressed in this chapter—the family, peer groups, and mass media. The family is the most important agent of early socialization. Through exposure to parents and other family members, children acquire a set of basic values and learn the norms of acceptable behavior. In peer groups (groups of those about the same age and social position), children, among other things, learn about impersonal social rules and some of the more informal aspects of culture not acquired at home. Mass media and information technology provides another source for socialization in which the developing child may be exposed to images and content that reinforce dominant societal values. On the other hand, the child with unguided exposure, may become desensitized to the richness of face-to-face interaction and relationships that are possible and to the potentially harmful effects of violence as portrayed in the media and on the internet.

6. Socialization does not end with the onset of adulthood but, instead, continues throughout the life cycle. As adults, we mature and adapt in two basic ways. First, we engage in anticipatory socialization by mentally rehearsing for upcoming life events and stages. This acts to soften and make easier the changes and adjustments we all make as we get older. In addition, most of us have one or two to several resocialization experiences as we move through our life course in which abrupt and fundamental adjustments in life style and priorities occur. Common examples include marriage, parenthood, entering the military, and religious conversion. Through these processes of anticipatory socialization and resocialization, we also adapt not only to continuing changes in our society but also to our own chronological aging process as we first experience middle-age and then the retirement years later to come.

TERMS TO KNOW

anticipatory socialization: the informal preparation for future life stages and life responsibilities.

apprenticeship in thinking: a process in which an unskilled person (novice learner) develops mastery of a cognitive competency through active involvement with one or more skilled mentors.

"bad blood" theory: the early view that deviant behavior (such as crime and drug addiction) was caused by the biological makeup of a person who had "bad blood or who was a bad seed."

bonding: the process of forming close personal relationships with other people, such as the relationship between a parent and child.

cognitive development theory: Piaget's perspective that examined changes in thought processes and intellectual abilities that occur in four stages as children mature.

concrete operations: the third stage of cognitive development (Piaget) in which cause-and-effect relationships in the real world become understood and concrete reasoning ability is developed.

cultural mediation: the process by which children learn or internalize the ways of their culture and how to use them as tools to succeed both as a society member and as an individual

didactic teaching: the actual hands-on instruction of a child by a parent in some skill or activity.

dramaturgical analysis: Goffman's approach to socialization which studies how and why people intentionally interact with each others like actors in a play titled "society."

ego: Freud's term for the rational part of the self which acts as the governor or manager of the personality.

formal operations: the last and most advanced stage of cognitive development (Piaget) characterized by the development of higher order or abstract thinking abilities.

game stage: Mead's term for middle to late childhood and early adolescence, during which the individual learns to play the game of society according to the rules, in terms of role obligations.

generalized other: Mead's term for the standards of community behavior expected of anyone placed in a given social position.

guided participation: Mead's definition of the process by which a skilled member of society serving as mentor—a parent or teacher, for example—actively assists an unskilled learner in mastering a particular cognitive competency.

id: Freud's term for a person's natural urges and "instincts," such as sex and aggression.

imitative stage: Mead's term for infancy and early childhood (0–3 years), during which children learn to imitate the behavior of parents and others in their immediate environment.

inner-directed: adults with a positive self-concept and an internal moral compass formed mainly during childhood which guides them during their life course.

instinct theory: the argument that human behavior was shaped largely by genetically inherited predispositions that were called instincts.

looking-glass self: Cooley's term for how people see themselves based on their assessment of how others see them.

mass media: the various methods used to transmit information to large numbers of people in an organized manner.

other-directed: adults with a negative self-concept who, largely as a result, allow others to guide their basic life decisions and shape their actions.

peer groups: groups of people of about the same age and social position whose members have significant influence on one another.

personality: the sum total of a person's unique yet consistent patterns of thoughts, feelings, and actions.

play stage: Mead's term for middle childhood, during which the child begins to seriously act out the roles of adults.

preoperations: the second stage of cognitive development (Piaget) in which children develop the ability to think in symbolic terms and use language to communicate with others.

resocialization: an abrupt and often basic change in life-style and life priorities.

rites of passage: formal events that signal the end of one position or stage in life and the beginning of another.

role taking: the ability to imagine ourselves in the social roles of other people and act them out in order to learn the social standards that will be applied to our behavior.

self-concept: the personal assessment people have of their own identity and self-worth and how they fit into the larger community and society.

self-fulfilling prophesy: a prediction by a person that something will occur which is then caused to happen by his or her actions.

sensorimotor stage: the first stage of cognitive development (Piaget) in which children develop motor intelligence and learn to distinguish different objects.

significant others: Mead's term for people with whom the individual has close personal ties.

social Darwinism: Spencer's argument that governments should not interfere in the lives of individuals or the operation of organizations so that the fittest can survive.

social isolates: children deprived of adequate social contact and stimulation in their early years who do not develop into functional adults as a result.

socialization: the process through which culture is transmitted to the individual and the personality and self-concept are developed.

sociobiology: the study of the biological aspects of social behavior in all species including humans.

sociocultural theory: a socialization perspective that focuses on the dynamic interplay between developing children and their guided participation in society by competent adults (Vygotsky).

superego: Freud's term for the idealized part of the self or conscience that makes us feel proud when we act properly and guilty when we do wrong.

Thomas theorem: The assertion by W. I. Thomas that when individuals "define situations as real, they are real in their consequences."

youth subculture: life-style characteristics and preferences among children and adolescents very distinct from those of their parents.

zone of proximal development (ZPD): the potential for learning that a child possesses that can be developed with help from skilled mentors as compared to what the child already knows or can learn on his or her own.

SUGGESTED READINGS

Corsaro, W. A. 2004. *The Sociology of Childhood,* 2nd ed. Thousand Oaks, CA. An insightful survey of research into the social, interpersonal aspects of childhood that reveals information on the childhood experience of children in the United States as well as those of children in other cultures as well.

Croteau, D., and Hoynes, W. 2000. *Media/Society: Industries, Images, and Audiences.* Thousand Oaks, CA: Pine Forge Press. An interesting look at how mass media portray reality (contemporary events, social issues, and social problems) and how the public sees and reacts to them.

Hunt, S. J. 2006. *The Life Course: A Sociological Introduction.* New York: Palgrave Macmillan. Examines socialization as a lifelong experience requiring continuous adaptations to society and one's place in it throughout the life course.

Rymer, R. 1994. *Genie: A Scientific Tragedy.* New York: Harper Perennial Library. The tragic story of a 13-year-old social isolate named Genie, who, after being rescued by authorities from a life of neglect and abuse, was fought over by various academics and human services professional who claimed to want to "save" her.

Social Organization

READING PREVIEW

Terms to Know

accommodation	*group*	*role ambiguity*
achieved status	*horticultural societies*	*role conflict*
affinal kinship	*hunting-gathering societies*	*role set*
agrarian society	*industrial societies*	*role strain*
ascribed status	*institution*	*social control*
competition	*kinship*	*social interaction*
conflict	*macrolevel organization*	*social organization*
consanguineal kinship	*master status*	*social structure*
contract	*means of subsistence*	*society*
cooperation	*microlevel organization*	*status*
division of labor	*postindustrial societies*	*status inconsistency*
exchange	*role*	*status set*
fealty		

Concert tours for popular entertainers like Miley Cyrus (Hannah Montana) and the Jonas Brothers require a tremendous amount of planning and organization. Hundreds of details must be worked out starting with the necessary time set aside in the entertainer's schedule—decisions about the cities to be included; the concert locations to be used; negotiations concerning the "cut" of the proceeds to be received by promoters, ticket sellers, and concert halls. As the tour gets under way, "roadies" are hired to transport and set up the musical instruments and sound equipment, and advance people are sent ahead to ensure that arrangements for hotel accommodations, limousines, security, concession workers to sell programs, buttons, sweatshirts, and posters, and local publicity are all properly taken care of. Finally, a day or two before the concert series begins in each city, the performer and musicians, backup singers, choreographers, and technicians arrive to rehearse, to be interviewed by local media, and to ensure all details related to the performances are complete. In addition, some concerts today are technological spectaculars, often requiring computer-sequenced laser lights, smoke and fireworks explosions, wires and cranes to levitate the entertainer above the stage or over the audience, or other special effects. Only after all preparations are completed do the concert performances take place—often creating the illusion of spontaneous events that just unfold naturally.

In similar fashion, practically all aspects of social life involve **social organization**, the process by which society is structured as a system of social interaction to meet the needs of its members. Just as we may watch a live concert without thinking about the organization behind the scenes, we often carry out our day-to-day lives without consciously thinking about the organization or structure that surrounds us at all levels of our society.

Social organization actually is based on two concepts. First, there is **social interaction**, the process through which two or more individuals mutually influence each other's thoughts, feelings, and actions. We humans are social beings who need satisfying contact with others of our kind. We therefore engage them in conversation and make plans and decisions together that provide the rich texture and focus for social life. However, people do not interact with each other in random fashion. Instead, social interaction is shaped by **social structure**, a set of organized norms that govern how people are to interact with each other in various social situations. For example, there are norms that govern the structure of social interactions in the family, school, and the workplace. These two dimensions of *social interaction* and *social structure* then result in a comprehensive system of human interaction on various levels of society called social organization.

In this chapter, we will explore basically how social organization takes place. This structuring of society makes it possible for each generation to experience culture and socialization as the social system continues to evolve and change. To begin, we first will examine briefly how social organization is influenced by social needs.

MEETING SOCIAL NEEDS: THE BASIS FOR SOCIAL ORGANIZATION

The particular form a society takes depends in large part on how social needs are defined and addressed by its members. The basic categories of these needs are usually the same for most societies. However, specific aspects of each need may vary from society to society, as we will see. In addition, power and conflict often play a role in determining (1) how needs are defined and (2) which needs are given the greatest priority.

Population Maintenance and Control

Simply stated, *population maintenance* refers to the reproduction of society members. Every society, for its own survival, must guarantee the maintenance of its population base. This is accomplished mainly through the family institution—the structural unit in every society charged with, among other things, the reproduction of society members. The family is reinforced by a set of cultural norms that encourage people to have children and become parents. In addition, other institutional areas like religion, school, and government, through their norms, also act to reinforce the family and, in many societies, lend support and assistance toward the socialization of children.

Although population maintenance historically has been and still is an important social need, so is the need for *population control*, the limiting of fertility through family planning to prevent overpopulation. Today, we live on a grossly overpopulated planet in which one out of every six persons goes to bed hungry each night. Historically, however, when the average lifespan worldwide was under forty years and there were no modern medical resources, it was necessary for a couple to have five to seven children in order for two to live long enough to reproduce. Today the realities of the world are very different. This has necessitated a restructuring of social priorities worldwide aimed at limiting average family size.

Division of Labor

Every society must also address the need for a **division of labor**, a system in society through which essential tasks are assigned to and carried out by the necessary numbers of people. Traditionally, the division of labor was based largely on gender with needed functions allocated along the lines of "men's work" and "women's work." In modern technological societies, the trend has been toward the organizing of needed societal functions according to occupational specialization and technical competence. In this regard, the sex of the position holder is not nearly as important as it was once thought to be.

Today in modern postindustrial societies, technology and the need for specialized expertise have made characteristics such as size and brute strength totally obsolete as requirements for most social positions. In addition, women and their supporters throughout the twentieth century—particularly in the United States—organized politically and socially to effect changes in law and social policy, which has ensured their greater participation in society. Women today engage in practically all occupations, including such traditional male positions as police officer, construction worker, and airline pilot. For example, women pilots with combat training flew combat missions over Iraq in B-1B Lancet Bombers, F-16 Fighter Bombers, and other aircraft beginning in 2003. Pilots like Maj. Melissa Miles (call sign SHOCK for "Scarlet-Headed Ovulating Commie Killer"), recipient of the Distinguished Service Cross, have flown hundreds of combat missions and have amply demonstrated their ability to perform such functions very well, given appropriate socialization, training, and experience (Winn, 2008).

Likewise, men today can just be as effective as women in providing love, affection, and emotional support as primary caregivers to small children. Men also perform well in traditionally female occupations like elementary school teacher and nurse. Regardless of the occupations or functions carried out, people are motivated to fulfill these obligations by feelings of both accomplishment and personal satisfaction, which are reinforced by social rewards including money and social recognition.

The division of labor in American society today is based more on education, occupational training, and expertise than it is on gender.

Communication

Each society must make use of one or more learned systems of symbolic communication that permit and guarantee the effective functioning of socialization. In nonliterate cultures, this takes the form of conventional spoken language as well as oral histories of family and society which are memorized and handed down to each succeeding generation. Modern technological societies, by comparison, have additional means of communication, including books, other literary forms, and the electronic mass media including television, the internet, iPhones, and other venues.

The organizational apparatus needed to support and implement communication in modern societies is complex and is connected to the division of labor. The print media, for instance, require the coordination of organizations that include publishing companies, book stores and other vendors, schools, and libraries. People in occupations involved in this area include authors and writers, journalists, editors, photographers, layout and design artists, printers, bookbinders, marketing representatives, booksellers, educators, and librarians. The levels of organization needed to coordinate electronic mass media, such as television, is even more varied and complex.

In addition, those who own or have influence on the media determine in large part what is communicated, to whom, and for what purposes. In totalitarian countries, most forms of mass communication are closely controlled and monitored by their governments to ensure that the people receive the "correct" message. In the United States and other democratic societies, a free press furnishes people with varied viewpoints on most issues.

Shared Values and Goals: Consensus, Conflict, and Diversity

The need for shared values and goals is also important in every society. However, there is some debate among sociologists whether the societal values and goals needed for social organization are formed mainly through consensus, conflict, and/or a diversity of viewpoints.

The Functionalist View   From the functionalist perspective, the majority of members of any society must be in fundamental agreement with or at least give their consent to basic *shared values and goals*. Social agreement concerning key values forms the basis for both the formation of essential norms and the social order and cohesion that result from them. Shared values and norms, in turn, act as much of the foundation for establishing the dominant goals of a society. Often a society's future is influenced by the goals set by its people or their leaders. In 1961, President John F. Kennedy established as a national goal the landing of men on the moon by the end of that decade. This objective, supported by the American people, was met in July, 1969, and helped set the agenda for the continuing U.S. space program from the 1970s to the present. During the 1960s, public support for the space program was relatively easy to obtain because (1) landing men on the moon was a popular dream, (2) it did not interfere with the goals of most interest groups, and (3) the United States was in a perceived "space race" with the Russians to be the first on the moon, which appealed to the nationalistic pride of most Americans and the national security concerns of government leaders.

The Conflict Approach   From a conflict perspective, those in political, economic, and social leadership positions often use their power and influence to impose their values and goals on society as a whole. In the political arena, this is manifested in the ability to influence legislation and public policy regardless of public sentiment. The Prohibition Era of the 1920s, which banned alcohol under a constitutional amendment, and the 55-mile-per-hour speed limit of the 1970s and 1980s serve as notable examples of major policies foisted on the people by a small number of powerful interests. In both cases, political organization by certain groups in society were instrumental in having both prohibition and lower speed limits repealed. Individuals and groups with economic and political power may support certain candidates with "favorable attitudes" for political office, purchase the services of media to persuade the general public to their point of view, and affect the supply and demand for jobs and consumer products. Those with social power often have personal charisma or "contacts" with political and economic power holders to influence others concerning values and goals.

The Interactionist Perspective   Social consensus regarding shared values and goals is often difficult to obtain, however, particularly in fast-changing, pluralistic societies. The United States is, to a significant degree, a nation of diverse subcultures and interest groups. This has resulted to some extent in *anomie*, a state of confused norms (normlessness) brought about by rapid change and social complexity (Durkheim, 1966) (see Chapter 2). With so many value systems espoused by so many different groups in society, it becomes very difficult, at times, to establish what the dominant norms are or should be. For children growing up in a fast-changing, technological society, there is often confusion because the norms and values taught by parents, peers, teachers, certain subcultures, and the media often conflict with one another. As a result, individuals may become unsure of how they should act, because what is acceptable or unacceptable behavior is unclear. High crime rates, racial prejudice, and drug abuse serve as specific examples of conditions that derive from a complex social system where varying degrees of anomie are present.

The Maintenance of Social Order

To guarantee its survival and maintain social order, every society must have one or more forms of **social control**. This involves a process designed to maintain conformity to dominant norms. The most effective form of social control ideally occurs within the family institution as the child is socialized with a coherent set of values that correspond to the established norms of the larger society. This process is then reinforced by other institutions, including the church and the school. When socialization is successful, the developing individual internalizes societal norms as a personal code of conduct that governs his or her behavior to a large extent throughout life. For most people in most circumstances, these *internal social controls* are adequate to get them to conform.

When conventional internal controls are not sufficient to maintain conformity, much more punitive and formal sanctions must be applied. The society is then obliged to use *external social controls*, which may range from an official reprimand at a person's job or a traffic fine for double parking to the loss of liberty through imprisonment for the commission of a crime. Extreme violations of social order are handled in an organized manner through the legislative and criminal justice systems, which consist of law makers, police, the courts, and prisons. Each of these components, in turn, has its own form of organization. Police departments in large cities, for example, are complex organizations arranged in districts or precincts, each with its own captain who typically reports to a division chief. Officers with ranks under captain are specialists who carry out designated duties in specific areas: patrol, traffic control, narcotics and vice, and homicide (Taft and England, 1966). Although societies must rely primarily on successful socialization to maintain social control, it is sometimes necessary to apply external social controls to the behavior of individuals for whom socialization has been less than effective.

LEVELS OF SOCIAL ORGANIZATION

Almost every social act we perform—from the one-minute encounter with a department store clerk to the complex interworkings of large-scale organizations, basic institutions, and whole societies—involves structured forms of behavior. In this regard, sociologists generally distinguish between two basic levels of social organization: microlevel organization and macrolevel organization.

Microlevel Social Organization

Microlevel organization is concerned with the patterned ways people act at the local community level in social encounters, relationships, and groups. The emphasis here is on how we act, react, and interact in our everyday encounters with others and how the smallest elements of a society's social structure, such as social relationships, are structured. When we interact with others, even in the most brief and casual encounters with strangers, our behavior is usually somewhat patterned and predictable. In fact, much of what we do at the microlevel of society approaches social ritual. Many of us get up on the same side of the bed each morning, begin on the same side of the grocery store each time we do our shopping, and sit in the same seat at the kitchen table when we eat meals with our families. While it is

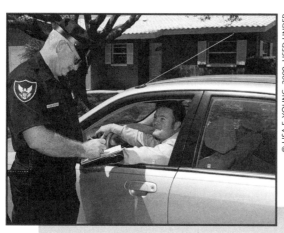

As societies have become larger, more diverse, and more complex, external social controls have become increasingly necessary.

true that the human experience is rich with individual diversity and opportunities for spontaneity, most of us operate within the structured boundaries set by our society and the habits we have acquired from our experiences with it. These habits take several forms.

Social Encounters
For instance, even the way we encounter people in our society is highly structured. Typically, many of us avoid making eye contact with a total stranger we pass on the sidewalk. A person we recognize as only a casual acquaintance is usually met with a "Hi," at which point he or she will respond back with a "Hi." This is a one-stroke greeting ritual. If we pass someone we know better, we will say "Hi," the other person will say, "Hi," we will then say, "How are you?" and he or she will usually respond with "Fine." This is a two-stroke greeting ritual. If the interaction goes beyond two strokes, the individuals normally will engage in a conversation that could last for several minutes or longer.

Using the family as an illustration, microlevel organization in the family begins with how we encounter our family members. Unlike an encounter with a stranger that may involve a nod or smile, or a business associate with whom we shake hands and begin by saying "How are you doing today?" followed by their response of "Fine, and you?," initial encounters with family members are different. Often, a family greeting includes a hug, a kiss, or both. Then when we part, the hug or kiss (or both) is often repeated. The way encounters (in the form of greetings) take place in family settings also vary by culture. In American families, males often shake hands. Among Filipino males, the younger male may take the hand of the older male relative and touch it to his forehead as a sign of respect.

Social Interaction
In numerous other ways, our social behavior at the microlevel is highly organized. Many of us say "Hello" when answering the phone, "Have a nice day" in a customer service role, and "Bless you" when someone sneezes. Likewise, many of us learn how to use certain cues to get people to respond to us in predictable ways. Depending on one's needs or purposes, a long and silent stare will cause most people to talk, standing up during a long meeting is a useful cue to end the meeting, and placing one's coat or sweater on a theater chair will usually reserve a seat in American society.

Social Relationships
Our relationships with family, friends, and co-workers are also structured in particular ways. Take a person's own individual family, for example. Most Americans come from a family background organized around a father, a mother, and one or more siblings. Others experience a childhood in which elderly grandparents or other relatives live in the home with them and the rest of their family members. Some, because of divorce, abandonment, poverty, or other disruptions, are reared partially or totally by grandparents or a single parent.

When a family is considered as a total group, individual family organization may depend to some degree on other factors including class, ethnicity, religion, and size. Some parents, because of these and other factors, may be more likely to be authoritarian, permissive, or authoritative in terms of how they rear their children. Size alone can affect the dynamics of the family as a group. Older children in large families, for instance, have often found themselves in the role of surrogate parent, responsible for the behavior of their little brothers and sisters. The eldest child with only one or two siblings rarely is expected to take on this responsibility. Other examples of microlevel organization include the structured patterns of interaction evident in a local high school, church, rock music band, grocery store, or garden club.

Macrolevel Organization

By contrast, **macrolevel organization** represents the manner in which large-scale organizations, basic institutions, and societies are organized and interact with one another. In other words, while microlevel organization focuses on how the small pieces of a society's social system are structured, macrolevel organization is concerned with how the large building blocks of a society are organized and interrelate together.

Large-Scale Organizations   What sociologists call *large scale organizations* include formal organizations like school systems or colleges, church denominations, and corporations, as well as whole industries devoted to the production and promotion of such things as cars, computers, rock music, education, defense, and health care. To illustrate, compare a community college with a major university as large-scale organizations. Both provide their students with a fine education but are organized very differently. The community college offers two-year academic degree programs along with vocational-technical certificate programs and continuing education courses. It stresses quality teaching with faculty members who teach in small classes and use a student-centered approach. A community college is often smaller than a university and is strictly a commuter institution that serves primarily a local population. A major university, by comparison, offers four-year academic degree programs and graduate programs leading to advanced degrees. Its faculty members are mainly research and publishing oriented, often teach large auditorium classes, and typically use a subject-centered approach. A major university also tends to be a large residential institution that attracts a regional and often a national or international student body.

Institutions   As mentioned earlier, an **institution** is a major structural part of a society that addresses a special area of human needs. Some simple societies are organized around one institution, the family group of kinship clan, in which all necessary social functions are carried out. Other more complex societies have *differentiated institutions*, each with its own specialized area of focus and concern. In modern social systems, there are five of these fundamental, yet specialized, institutions—the family, the economy, education, government, and religion—which together comprise the essential structural building blocks of society. Institutions in different societies vary in the ways they are organized. Government in the United States, for example, is structured as a representative democracy with a two-party political system and three relatively equal branches: the executive branch headed by a president, the legislative branch, and the judiciary. Cuba, by contrast, is governed by a military dictator as head of state; Western Samoa has a tribal chief; Oman, a sultan; Kuwait, an emir; and Jordan, a king (*World Almanac and Book of Facts,* 2005). The religious institution in some societies is predominantly Christian, while others may practice Buddhism, Islam, Confucianism, Hinduism, or any one or a combination of religious belief systems. In addition, the family institution is organized very differently in various societies, some allowing only monogamous marriage (one spouse), while others allow polygamous marriage (multiple spouses).

Societies (and Their Characteristics)   The largest and most complex system of social interaction is a **society**, the largest possible grouping of individuals with specific characteristics in a particular system of social interaction. Given this definition, there are two basic varieties of societies: animal societies and human societies. Many lower animal species including ants, bees, wolves, baboons, and whales have social interaction systems similar in many respects to those of humans (Table 6-1).

Animal Versus Human Societies   *Animal societies* have the following key characteristics: They (1) occupy a definite territory, (2) perpetuate their membership through sexual reproduction, (3) are completely autonomous and self-contained (like a hive of bees or a pride of lions), and (4) possess a way of life shaped in large part by instincts. Human societies have the first two characteristics in common with their animal counterparts: (1) territoriality and (2) perpetuation through sexual reproduction (although asexual means are possible now such as in vitro fertilization and possibly cloning in the future). However, human societies are (3) relatively independent (ties to other societies), and (4) possess a way of life shaped by culture rather than instinct (Biesanz and Biesanz, 1973).

Territoriality   One of the most interesting characteristics of both animal and human societies is territoriality. Like the lower animals, we humans also are territorial creatures who use various devices at both macro and microlevels to claim space. However, unlike lower animals who use, among other things, urine and claw scratches on trees to establish territorial boundaries, humans accomplish this politically at the macro level through treaty arrangements with other societies. Societal or national boundaries are taken very seriously and, if threatened, are defended under force of arms if necessary. In fact, disputes and wars between both tribal societies and nations are often caused by disputes over territory.

At the microlevel, most of us carry an invisible bubble of personal space with us everywhere we go. The size of this territorial bubble is influenced by one's culture and the social situation. In America, except for situations such as standing in line or riding in an elevator, it is normally about three to four feet in diameter. In American culture, this is usually the minimum distance we prefer to keep from other people, especially strangers. Americans will usually skip at least a seat or two, if possible, between themselves and other people in a movie theater. Suppose that two Americans are seated in a restaurant at a table that could seat four. Two strangers enter and sit down with them rather than occupy one of the available empty tables. The original occupants at the table would probably be very surprised and might feel threatened or offended. However, in Germany and other parts of Europe where other standards of territoriality apply, to sit at a separate table when two chairs are available at a table already partially occupied might be considered ill mannered. Physical

TABLE 6-1	Macrolevel Organization of Animal Versus Human Societies	
ANIMAL SOCIETIES (CHARACTERISTICS)		**HUMAN SOCIETIES (CHARACTERISTICS)**
1. Occupy a definite territory		1. Occupy a definite territory
2. Sexual reproduction		2. Sexual reproduction*
3. Completely independent		3. Relatively independent
4. Way of life shaped by instinct		4. Way of life shaped by culture

* This today is beginning to undergo some change. Various reproductive technologies that do not require sexual intercourse are now available or are in development.

objects are also used to "stake a claim" to personal space "as when sunglasses and lotion claim a beach chair, or a purse a seat in an airliner" (Goffman, 1972, p. 41). To further illustrate how territoriality differs from society to society, in some parts of both the Middle East and South America, it is not uncommon to get close to another person's face when interacting with them, close enough to feel the other's breath. Think of how most Americans and even Europeans might react to this.

Relative Independence   The third characteristic mentioned previously, relative independence, requires some further elaboration. Societies among the lower animals may require total group autonomy. In this sense, animal groupings—a hive of bees, a pride of lions, a band of hyenas—tend to be *independent,* wholly autonomous and self-contained. They typically do not interact with other animal groupings of their kind outside of their own territorially occupied group. Human societies, by contrast, tend to be much more *interdependent* and interconnect with one another through various alliances, treaties, and agreements. The United States, for example, is a voting member of the United Nations, has the NAFTA trade agreement with Mexico, and is a member of the North Atlantic Treaty Organization (NATO), the World Bank, and numerous other international bodies. In addition, most European countries are now members of the European Union (EU), an effort designed to combine Europe's separate national economies into one consolidated block of worldwide influence to compete favorably with the American dollar. With this move, the eurodollar has replaced French francs, German dueschmarks, and Italian lira, to name a few, which now are seen largely as artifacts of the past.

Levels of Organization in Perspective

Historically, sociologists have tended to see microlevel and macrolevel analysis as separate categories to be studied differently with distinct theoretical perspectives and research approaches. Microsociologists tended to be interactionists who examined the everyday behavior of people in relationships and groups. Macrosociologists usually were functionalists or conflict theorists, interested in investigating patterns of social behavior at the institutional or societal levels. Some sociologists today, however, see the division of social organization into the micro- and macrolevels to be a false dichotomy and favor a more integrated approach.

Functionalist, Conflict, and Interactionist Applications   As shown in Figure 6-1, perhaps it is more useful to see social organization as a continuum consisting of structured patterns at all levels of society, with overlapping characteristics and influences on one another. From this perspective, social organization is evident everywhere, from the most

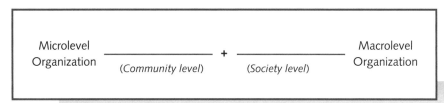

*F*igure 6-1

Primary and Secondary Group Relations: A Continuum

transitory and superficial encounters between two or three people, through relationships and groups, to the structured social patterns characteristic of the largest, most complex, and enduring organizations, institutions, and societies.

As we have seen, even the briefest, most superficial encounters at the microlevel can involve a tremendous degree of structure and predictability. Both the functionalist and conflict perspectives can be used here in addition to the interactionist approach to describe and analyze both functional and dysfunctional aspects of social relations and how power is acquired, organized, and used.

Likewise, the emphasis on meaning and perception by interactionists and the power perspective offered by conflict theorists are also helpful in studying the actions of large-scale organizations and institutions (Schelling, 1978). For instance, chief executive officers (CEOs) of corporations and presidents of universities can often influence the shaping of formal public policy concerning their respective institutions by having informal conversations with key legislators. In addition, corporations, governments, colleges, and other macrostructures often have organizational mindsets caused by the perceptions and actions of small groups of key decision-makers (micro-structures) who are in control.

TYPES OF SOCIETIES

There are several ways to categorize the organization of societies as macrostructures. Perhaps the most useful form of classification is **means of subsistence**, the specific process used by a society to provide food and other resources needed by its people for survival and prosperity (Table 6-2). Although there are numerous types of subsistence systems, they can be placed into five general categories for the purpose of identifying types of societies: hunting and gathering, horticultural, agrarian, industrial, and postindustrial.

Hunting-Gathering Societies   The first societies, which emerged with the dawn of humankind about three or four million years ago, consisted of small bands that hunted and foraged for a living. Lacking the means to either produce food or preserve it, members of **hunting-gathering societies** lived from day to day on what they could kill or find, and took life literally one meal at a time. Social organization revolved around one or a few nuclear families, the total band comprising only eight to ten or forty to fifty members. The division of labor was based largely on gender: Adult males were usually if not exclusively placed in the role of hunters, and women were usually assigned the role of gathers who searched for roots, berries, and other edibles. In hunting-gathering cultures, private property or personal possessions were of little value because of the necessity of a nomadic way of life.

Although this type of social system was largely replaced as more advanced forms evolved, a few hunting-gathering bands still exist today in some parts of the world. In the Kalahari desert region of southern Africa, the Kung Bushman still thrive in small wandering bands (Lee and Devore, 1976). In their society, food obtained by each family is shared communally with the rest of the band. Decision making among these peaceful and gentle people is quite egalitarian; there are no official leaders or laws. Disputes are settled by informal agreement between the parties involved, in consultation with other members of the band. The Arunta of Australia are also hunter-gatherers. These aboriginal people live in small one or two nuclear family bands and hunt animals for food, including the kangaroo

TABLE 6-2	Types of Societies	
SOCIETAL TYPE	**MEANS OF SUBSISTENCE**	**EXAMPLES**
Hunting-gathering (Nomadic bands)	Hunting for meat and foraging for edibles (bulb roots, berries, grubs, insects, bird eggs, honey, burrowing, rodents, etc.	Kung Bushmen of Africa; Arunta of Australia
Horticultural (Villages and tribes)	Simple slash-and-burn agriculture, and the use of domesticated cattle, goats, and fowl	Yanomamo of Brazil; Nuer of Africa
Agrarian (City or nation states with large peasant class)	Advanced agricultural methods (the plow, irrigation systems, crop rotation, etc.), some mercantilism, and centralized governmental authority	20th century: People's Republic of China; Today: much of Indochina
Industrial (Nation states)	High technology, mass production and specialized occupations	19th and 20th centuries: United States, Western European states; 21st century: emergent rise of China and India
Postindustrial (Nation states; confederations)	Emphasis on production of information rather than physical products, focus on computer/information literacy, "virtual" facilities	United States; Japan; European Union (EU)

and ostrich-like emu. Because they have no bows and arrows for hunting, they must rely on clubs, spears, and boomerangs (Elkin, 1954). To augment their diet, they also forage for edible roots and fungi, bird and reptile eggs, grub worms of moths and other insects, and snakes and burrowing rodents.

Horticultural Societies   Horticultural societies are village-focused societies that rely mainly on simple slash-and-burn agriculture and the use of domesticated animals for subsistence. They originated about 10,000 years ago with the *agricultural revolution*, which first made it possible to both produce food and store it for future use. With this new technology, wandering bands evolved into clans and tribes who lived in relatively permanent villages. Slash-and-burn agriculture involved cutting down all trees and foliage, burning it thoroughly, and then planting primitive grains in the ashes, which acted as fertilizer. Domestication of cattle, goats, and fowl resulted in a surplus of meat, which was readily available, as well as secondary protein in the form of milk, cheese, and eggs. As these types of societies emerged, they became characterized by charismatic headmen (who had significant unofficial authority over the group), emphasis on blood and marriage lineage within the clan, and the development of rites of passage to reinforce lineage and a sense of belonging.

Two notable examples of horticultural societies today include the Yanomamo of Brazil, a very warlike tribal people who live in small villages ruled informally by male elders. Although there are many villages that share the Yanomamo culture, each one is a separate social unit of about sixty to ninety people in which each person is considered to be related to all village members by blood or marriage. These different village groups often engage in war with one another, alternating raids and uneasy alliances which, more or less, become a continuous fact of life. In the Yanomamo villages, each family has its own garden, but the women are required to do most of the work. The culture is such that "marriage does not enhance the status of the girl, for her duties as wife require her to assume difficult and laborious tasks too menial to be executed by the men" (Chagnon, 1983, p. 111).

The Nuer of the Nile river area of Sudan in southeastern Africa consists of several large tribes of about 5,000 persons each, with each tribe divided into several clans. Although they cultivate crops including millet (sorghum) and corn, the Nuer are primarily pastoral people with a subsistence system centered on the raising of cattle for milk (their number one food) and meat. Cattle are privately owned, but land for cultivation belongs to the community. Although the family of the groom pays a price in cattle to the bride's family for her hand in marriage, women in the Nuer culture are treated in a much more egalitarian manner (Service, 1971) than those in Yanomamo society.

Agrarian Societies   About 5,500 years ago, **agrarian societies** began to develop. These were social systems organized around advanced agricultural methods for subsistence and centralized governmental authority. Specifically, they were marked by the invention of the plow, the development of sophisticated irrigation systems, the rise of technologies including the development of metallurgy and the use of the wheel, the emergence of first the city-state and, later, during and after the Middle Ages (400–1400 CE), the nation state. Therefore, the agricultural revolution that began earlier continued to gather momentum and was joined by the *urban revolution,* which was characterized chiefly by the rise of cities and the development of formalized government.

With centralized authority placed in the hands of a few, the resources and technology of the society could be rationally coordinated, as in the planning of irrigation systems, the rotation of crops, and the terracing of fields. Crop yields per acre of ground increased manifold over the yield of traditional slash-and-burn techniques, and food surpluses became common. The increased food supply caused populations to expand accordingly, a result of a higher standard of living that allowed more children to survive and become adults. Because intensive agriculture required that the division of labor be taken out of the family and placed under the jurisdiction of centralized authority, the organization of societies was made much more efficient. Consequently, societies grew in size from tribal chiefdoms to major civilizations in places like Egypt, China, Greece, Rome, and Central and South America.

As time passed, civilizations rose and fell. In Europe, the decline (beginning about 400 CE) and ultimate demise of Greco-Roman civilization (by 900 CE) was accomplished by a decline in traditional political, social, and economic institutions and a corresponding rise in the feudal system of the Middle Ages. However, the land and those with the desire to work it remained, and the agrarian system survived. Intensive agriculture came under control of an estate system administered mainly by lords who owned the land. These estates were in turn managed by supervisors appointed by the lords and were actually farmed by sharecropping peasants called serfs.

By the year 1400, the medieval period was giving way to the Renaissance, and the feudal system was being replaced by the nation-state and the reestablishment of large towns with fairly autonomous local governments. In addition, the economy was rapidly

The diverse ways in which societies are organized result in very different lifestyles among their inhabitants.

expanding from its agrarian base to include merchant and craft occupations. Other changes including growth in manufacturing, the development of modern banking and credit systems, the harnessing of water power for smelting iron and producing sheet metal, and, by the late 1400s, the printing of books (Easton, 1965). These and other developments set the stage for industrialization.

Industrial Societies   The industrial revolution began in England about 1750. Its tremendous impact has shaped the way many societies have been organized ever since. Industrialization involved the development of a means of subsistence based on a factory system of mass production. The British first developed machines for mass producing textiles. Later in the 1790s, the American Eli Whitney invented the cotton gin and also developed the principle of interchangeable parts to aid in mass production. These and other innovations made it possible for machines to do the work of thousands of workers and to do it much more quickly and efficiently (Bailey, 1966).

With mass production, an almost unlimited supply of goods could be produced at lower costs. This made it possible to increase the standard of living for the average citizen. The production process became divided into many specialized tasks and subtasks, and the concept of assembly line was ultimately developed for use in most industries. Workers were employed to carry out these specialized tasks for cash wages, which were in turn used to purchase the consumer goods—food, clothing, shelter, and other commodities—needed by the family unit. Thus, work shifted from the home and farm to the industrial factory, and the family became transformed from an independent unit of production (e.g., the family farm or business) to a more dependent unit of consumption.

Today **industrial societies** are among the most complex and technologically advanced social systems in the world due mainly to factors such as a cash economy, mass production, specialized occupations, and bureaucratic management. However, the very complexity and dynamism of industrial societies tend to make them more vulnerable to several types of social disorganization than many of the simpler hunting-gathering, horticultural, and agrarian societies. The contrast between the United States with its high crime and suicide rates and the Nootka Indians of British Columbia serves as one illustration. The Nootka live on the northwest coast of North America and make their living from fishing, hunting, and gathering.

> Murder, theft, and other crimes common to organized societies are very rare among the Nootka. There is no formal machinery of social control; most disputes are settled by private counsel or, if all else fails, public dressing-downs. Revenge by an individual seems to have been rare, and suicide, the ultimate protest against society, had not occurred within the memory of any informants (Service, 1971, p. 225).

Nonetheless, the industrial organization of modern societies has resulted in an average standard of living unprecedented in human history. Inhabitants of industrial societies that reached mature industrial development during the twentieth century—for example, Japan, the United States, and Western European countries—today have superior standards of food, housing, medical care, public health and sanitation, and transportation. Rising industrial countries today such as China and India hold promise in being able to achieve these goals for their inhabitants as well.

Postindustrial Societies According to sociologist Daniel Bell (1973) and several other social thinkers (Lipset, 1979; Toffler, 1980; Naisbitt, 1984; Linski and Nolan, 1999), the United States and other modern societies are now making the transition to **postindustrial societies**. These emerging social systems, in the view of some social scientists, increasingly are becoming dominated by service and information economies. This transition, now well under way, is being brought about primarily by an *information revolution* already in its first stages. With dramatic technologies being developed in computers, semiconductors, communication satellites, internet, and other areas, societies in the twenty-first century promise to be organized very differently from those of the twentieth century. For example, as a consequence of the internet, there are indications that we could see trends such as a decline in printed magazines and newspapers, fewer businesses housed in "brick-and mortar" facilities, and even fewer retail and grocery stores along with an increase in home-based businesses and jobs as many people shift toward shopping and doing business on-line (Edwards, 2000).

Author and consultant John Naisbitt (1984) reported more than twenty years ago that the shifting distribution of occupations is one sign that we are entering a new era.

> In 1950, only 17 percent of us worked in information-based jobs. Now more than 65 percent of us work with information in jobs such as programmers, teachers, clerks, secretaries, accountants, stock brokers, managers, insurance people, bureaucrats, lawyers, bankers, and technicians. And many more workers hold information-intensive jobs within manufacturing companies. Most Americans spend their time creating, processing, or distributing information. For example, workers in banking, the stock market, and insurance all hold information jobs (p. 4).

As we move fully into the twenty-first century, our lives and livelihoods and those of our children and grandchildren will be organized very differently from those of our parents and grandparents during the previous century. In this new world, computers will shape our lives perhaps more profoundly than the impact felt by the automobile on society during the 1900s.

Key Changes Occurring in Postindustrial Societies The information revolution driving emerging postindustrial societies is producing three key economic changes. These changes, briefly summarized here, likely will accelerate as we move fully into the flow of the twenty-first century:

1. ***Information Rather than Tangible Products.*** First, in contrast to producing tangible goods and products, which was a hallmark of industrialization, we will produce, store, organize, analyze, and disseminate information.
2. ***The Need for New Literacy Skills.*** Second, instead of developing and implementing physical and mechanical skills, we will be required—by necessity—to learn new literacy skills involving the use of new technologies and terms, expressions, and symbols both in our jobs and in our relations with others.
3. ***The Shift from Physical Facilities to "Virtual" Facilities.*** Third, we increasingly will shift from fixed, physical facilities—factories, schools, businesses, churches, governmental agencies—to "virtual facilities" that can be accessed practically anywhere by anybody (Macionis, 2007, p. 336.).

Such changes most likely will transform not only how we earn a living but how most aspects of our lives are organized—how we go to school and get credentialed, how we purchase needed and desired products, and even how our relationships with others including our loved ones are structured.

EY FORMS OF ORGANIZATION WITHIN SOCIETIES

Within the different types of societies [e.g., preindustrial (hunting-gathering, horticultural, agrarian), industrial, postindustrial] at both micro- and macrolevels are several forms of social organization. Among the most fundamental of these are those that are found in every society—kinship, fealty, groups, social statuses, and contract. Together, they comprise much of the foundation for the way human social interaction and social relationships take place.

Kinship

Kinship is a form of social organization involving the manner in which family relations are organized. In all societies, blood and marriage are universal bases for kinship organization, but it varies in which one or the other tends to be predominant. Most societies, particularly nonindustrial ones, have **consanguineal kinship**, a type of family organization based primarily on blood ties. These societies normally have an *extended family* of several generations of kin who depend on one another for mutual support and protection. Given the relatively simple division of labor in hunting-gathering and horticultural cultures, all societal functions are family-based and carried out mainly within this single institution. In these societies, male dominance is the usual pattern, women (wives and daughters) take a secondary role, and family name and property are passed from father to son. Some, however, such as the Navajo of the American Southwest, are female-focused or matrilineal, with property being passed between generations through the women's bloodlines (Witherspoon, 1975).

Industrial societies and emerging postindustrial societies are more likely to have **affinal kinship**, a type of family organization based primarily on marital ties. Here the *nuclear family,* consisting of only the married couple and their children, tends to be the dominant family form. This transition from consanguineal to affinal kinship began with the dawn of the Industrial Revolution as several functions that were once primarily family based—like education, religion, and economic production—gradually fell within the

With the emergence of the information revolution, and service-oriented economies, the United States and other technological societies are making the transition to postindustrial societies.

domain of separate, specialized institutions. With the shift away from an agrarian economy to one characterized by specialized occupations and cash wages, the consanguineal kinship system, with its emphasis on the extended family as a cooperative, self-supporting unit, became obsolete, at least from an economic standpoint.

Today in modern societies like the United States, extended family kin—including assorted grandparents, aunts, uncles, and cousins—tend to live in separate locations. In fact, given the demands for geographical mobility placed on many technical and professional workers in industrial and postindustrial societies, the nuclear family has become the only meaningful family unit in many instances, because extended kin often live several hundred miles away or farther. Consequently, affinal kinship became the primary family pattern in the United States and remains so today.

Fealty

A form of social organization involving the personal loyalty of a follower toward a leader is **fealty**. The leader in this regard may be an individual, a group, or a large organization or institution. Fealty involves a strong commitment to perform a service for or fulfill an obligation to the leader even, in many cases, at great risk and personal hardship. During the Middle Ages, from the ninth through the fifteenth centuries, fealty was an important ingredient in the organization of the feudal system. Not only did feudal lords band together in fealty to one another for mutual protection, each lord usually had in his service a group of soldiers or knights who would take oaths of fealty to lay down their lives if necessary, to protect the lord, his lady, and their family, property, and honor. Almost everyone is familiar with the legend of King Arthur and the Knights of the Round Table. As the story goes, the king went to fight in the Crusades and left Queen Guinevere in the care of Lancelot, his most trusted knight. While he was away, Lancelot violated his oath of fealty, he and the queen fell in love, and Arthur's trust was betrayed. While largely a fictional morality tale, it serves as a literary illustration of how fealty facilitates social cohesion and how its violation can cause social disorganization.

U.S. Secret Service Agents possess fealty to the point of using their bodies as human shields if necessary to protect the life of the president and others in their charge.

In modern society, fealty takes a variety of forms. Most large business organizations attempt to create a corporate climate that encourages loyalty to and identification with the organization by its employees. When this is successful, morale and productivity tend to be high, and affected employees become "company people." On the athletic field, it is called team pride and stems from a commitment to the coach, the team captain, and the team itself. The military term for fealty is *esprit de corps,* an identification with one's unit that extends from the squad and the platoon levels to one's branch of service. Regardless of the term used, fealty acts as a cohesive binding force to promote the effective functioning of several different types of groups and organizations in society.

Groups

One of the most fundamental forms of social organization is the group. A **group** consists of two or more people with one or more characteristics in common. Most groups are easily recognizable and have clear-cut boundaries that allow us to distinguish members from non-members. Group boundaries are established by the characteristics of members, the norms that govern their behavior, the behavior patterns that stem from such norms, and group goals. *Social groups* (informal social interaction) and *formal organizations* (formal social patterns) are types of groups largely governed by these factors. Therefore, family is easily differentiated from friends, members of a rock music group from members of a country-western band, and employees of General Motors from members of the U.S. Marines.

Other types of groups may be more difficult to precisely identify or understand because of their temporary nature and constantly changing characteristics. *Physical aggregates* that include *crowds* and *publics* (widely dispersed categories of people who share an interest in an issue or group of issues) are notable examples. Nonetheless, the groups we belong to and interact with play an important role in determining who we are and in shaping our social behavior. More detailed information about groups is provided in Chapter 7 to follow, which deals exclusively with specific types of groups and group behavior.

Statuses

The term **status**, as used by sociologists, refers to a socially defined place or position a person occupies in society, along with a set of expected behavior patterns that act to regulate that person's behavior. Most of us are involved in several statuses (social positions) simultaneously. In the most general sense, we are, first of all, members of a society. This status carries with it the responsibility to act in ways acceptable to the norms of our culture—speaking a certain language, obeying the laws, working at a job, paying taxes, and following a multiplicity of folkways. We also occupy several specialized statuses that may include family member, spouse, parent, employee, supervisor, student, citizen, or consumer. Take the position of family member as an example. As a member of this group, we may occupy a status as spouse, parent, child, sibling, in-law, etc. Therefore, every group or organization in which we participate involves a specific place or status that we occupy as participants within it. Each of these statuses, in turn, requires some of our energy and time and results in portions of our behavior being organized in particular ways.

Take your status as a college student for instance. Each week, you devote time and energy to attending class, taking notes, reading this textbook, and, it is hoped, organizing your work by completing the accompanying study guide in preparation for successful performance on exams. Your other statuses related to family and job can be demanding also. Thus, the statuses or social positions you and others occupy act to organize social behavior to a remarkable degree.

Basic Types: Ascribed, Achieved, and Master Statuses
The two most fundamental status types are ascribed and achieved statuses. An **ascribed status** is a social position assigned to a person at birth or otherwise imposed by society. The individual has little or no choice in determining an ascribed status he or she occupies. Examples include being born male or female, belonging to a particular racial or ethnic group, nationality, and being a child, teenager, or senior citizen. Although committing a felony and going to prison is a choice, how society labels and treats the felon upon release from prison is an ascribed status. By contrast, an **achieved status** is a social position earned through individual effort. Becoming a high school or college graduate, employee, spouse or parent, winner of the Nobel prize, and murderer are all examples of achieved statuses.

In addition, most adults typically choose to identify with or are defined in terms of one of their social positions above all others. This becomes the **master status**, the social position held by a person that becomes the primary source of his or her identity. In the United States, when two men meet for the first time at a social gathering, they usually will project a master status related to their employment or occupation. This is because men have been socialized traditionally to see themselves primarily in terms of being a family breadwinner. Women traditionally have identified primarily with the marital-homemaking position. Today, however, women typically choose from either their family status as wife-mother or their job or career. For college-educated, professional women in a dual-earner marriage, there is a pattern for some to see themselves primarily in terms of their jobs or careers, particularly after their marriages are established and their children are older with a firm foundation for their socialization having been firmly established.

Related Concepts: Status Set and Status Inconsistency
Two other concepts related to the status (or position) in society one holds are status set and status inconsistency. A

status set refers to the sum total of social statuses (social positions) a person occupies in his or her life situation. For example, one person may hold the statuses of family member, student, employee, church member, and club member (a hobby or personal interest organization) as his or her major social statuses. Another person may have a status set larger, smaller, or different in some regards. Because life in modern society is complex, it is relatively easy to take on more statuses (positions) than one can handle comfortably and overcommit time and energy resources that one might not have. For example, trying to work at a full-time job, take a full course load at college (another full-time commitment), and be an effective spouse and parent may be more than many people can handle comfortably. This, in turn, can lead to various problems such as *role strain* and *role conflict* that we will discuss shortly.

A second interesting concept related to statuses in modern society is **status inconsistency**. This refers to a contradiction or mismatch between statuses in which a person ranks high in one and low in another. For example, a person might rank low in their occupational position as an unskilled laborer but high in their social status as a deacon in their church. As another example, there is a wealthy "businessman and investor" who lives in a large mansion in a New Jersey village, has a chauffeur drive him into Manhattan each morning to work, and donates large amounts of money to his church and various charities. Then, he is arrested by the FBI, charged with racketeering, is convicted, and goes to prison. No one in his little village knew of his other status as head of a large criminal "family" that coerced millions in "protection money" over the years from dozens of businesses in New York.

Roles and Their Complications   In Chapter 5: Socialization, we saw how, according to George Herbert Mead and other interactionists, children mentally rehearse for the statuses they will carry out as adults by engaging in role taking, the imitation and playing out of adult roles. By adulthood, when statuses are actually occupied, each is characterized by a **role**, the expected forms of behavior, obligation, and privilege that go with a social status. Roles form the building blocks that make up the structure of the social positions we hold. They also determine in large part how we behave as participants. Largely through the influence of roles and how they are sanctioned by the larger society, the statuses we occupy not only shape our behavior but determine to a significant degree who we are. As Peter Berger (1963) says:

> One feels more ardent by kissing, more humble by kneeling and more angry by shaking one's fist. That is, the kiss not only expresses ardor but manufactures it. Roles carry with them both certain actions and emotions and attitudes that belong to these actions. The professor putting on an act that pretends to wisdom comes to feel wise. The preacher finds himself believing what he preaches. The soldier discovers martial stirrings in his breast as he puts on the uniform. In each case, while the emotion or attitude may have been present before the role was taken on, the latter inevitably strengthens what was there before. In many instances there is every reason to suppose that nothing at all anteceded the playing of the role in the actor's consciousness. In other words, one becomes wise by being appointed a professor, believing by engaging in activities that presuppose belief, and ready for battle by marching in formation (p. 96).

Statuses in modern societies often involve a **role set**, two or more distinct roles that relate to a single status or social position (Merton, 1968). The physician for example, carries out one role in regard to patients, another in relation to nurses, and others attached to interactions with colleagues, medical students, and pharmaceutical salespeople. In similar

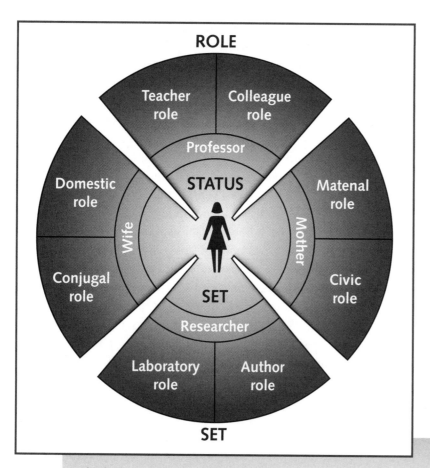

ROLE

Teacher role

Colleague role

Professor

STATUS

Domestic role

Matenal role

Wife

Mother

Conjugal role

Civic role

SET

Researcher

Laboratory role

Author role

SET

Figure 6-2

Each of us has a status set through which our life is organized according to the statuses we hold and the role that goes with each. Some of these statuses or social positions—such as family member or occupation—may also contain a role set.

fashion, a college baseball coach has different role obligations to players, the college as his or her employer, other college coaches, high school coaches while recruiting new players, and professional scouts.

Sometimes the obligations associated with our various social positions cause complications or problems for us in the form of role ambiguity, role strain, and role conflict. **Role ambiguity** occurs when the obligations attached to a social status are unclear. This often takes place in a new status or relationship. Most of us have felt a little unsure of ourselves on a first date, in the first few days at a new job, or in the first few weeks as a college student. Likewise, adolescence is often a confusing time for many young people with few, if any, clear-cut role demands. Role ambiguity can also occur when we are placed in an awkward situation in a social position that is normally well defined. A person might, for instance, feel very uncertain of how to proceed if a best friend asked for advice in how to handle his or her failing marriage.

Role Related Problems: Role Strain and Role Conflict   One problem commonly experienced in modern society is **role strain**. This is stress that occurs when conflicting

role demands are built into a single status, a person cannot fulfill the role demands of a given position, or both (Goode, 1960; Merton, 1976). Take the middle-management supervisor in a production plant, for example. Upper management wants lower labor costs and tries to freeze wages, while lower-level workers want wage increases and promotions. The clashing role demands placed on the middle manager by these two groups—whose needs, priorities, and demands are sometimes in opposition—can sometimes make it difficult to succeed in such a position.

The teenage marriage represents a good illustration of role strain that can occur when the role demands of a given social position simply cannot be met and the individual is overwhelmed by obligations. Young couples who marry while one or both are still in high school face role strain brought on by emotional and social immaturity, inadequate financial resources, the lack of credentials and experience needed to obtain adequate employment, family pressure, and a number of other problems. Taken as a whole, these elements of role stain contribute to a high teenage divorce rate. Regardless of type, unresolved role strain can lead to a negative self-concept, and, in some cases, even illness, heart attack, and premature death (Krantz, Grunberg, and Baum, 1985).

Role conflict is stress caused when conflicting role demands are built into separate statuses or positions, each of which an individual is expected to carry out successfully. Most of us experience role conflict from time to time when the obligations of the different positions we occupy interfere with each other. The role demands of one's job may conflict with those of one's marriage. If the requirement to spend extra hours at work becomes a long-term condition, a spouse may feel neglected and the marriage could suffer. You may have experienced role conflict as a college student, particularly if you have an outside job, are married, or both. If you do not put in sufficient study time, you may fail. But if you are not available to work when your employer needs you, you could lose your job. Obligations to a spouse or other family members may also require your attention. Consequently, many of us often feel like a juggler who must keep several balls in the air at the same time. It can be a difficult task and often requires careful planning and prioritizing. Even so, sometimes we must be wise enough to realize when we are overextending ourselves, and must establish firm priorities and reduce our obligations in certain areas when necessary.

Contract

Ever since the Middle Ages, *contract* has been an important basis for social organization, particularly in Western societies. A **contract** is a social bond between two or more parties that involves the exchange of one promise for another. As such, it has represented an important way to structure social relations for several hundred years. In feudal times, free peasants would often contract with a territorial lord to exchange their services for his protection. Unlike the general and implied nature of promises made and benefits received through kinship and fealty, contractual relations, as they evolved in Western societies, were very specific and explicit. As societies became larger and more complex, the need for specific and clearly defined contracts became more important. The rise of modern business economies after the Middle Ages, followed first by the Industrial Revolution and later by the high technology of the twentieth and twenty-first centuries, have made them even more necessary.

Today, the formal and specific nature of contracts has made them an indispensable form of organizing a wide variety of relationships in modern society. At the microlevel, we enter into contracts on a continuing basis each time we participate in the consumer economy by purchasing goods and services. All the activities of modern life, from charging a meal to a credit card, paying college tuition, to purchasing the clothes we wear, the cars we drive, or the houses we live in, usually involve contracts with one or more parties. Contracts at the macrolevel of society are more likely to have political and social, as well as economic, dimensions. They may include areas as diverse as labor contracts, corporate mergers, and nuclear test ban treaties.

Bureaucracy

With the development of early civilizations such as Mesopotamia and Egypt, decision making eventually came under the control of centralized authority. This was accompanied by the rise of *bureaucracy,* a form of social organization in which the work of participants (in large-scale organizations) is rationally coordinated by professionally trained managers. Without such leadership, the building of the pyramids in Ancient Egypt, the construction of the roads and aqueducts by the Roman Empire, and similar historical developments could not have occurred.

In modern times, the emergence of industrialization in the 1800s and the development of the factory system brought revolutionary changes to the production process. Of these changes, the most important involved the problems of managing extremely large numbers of factory workers engaged in a variety of specialized occupations.

Many traditional forms of leadership were ineffective in an industrial setting. Historically, those who rose to positions of authority did so as a result of personal power or charisma or were appointed on the basis of political favoritism by a king, lord, or other authority figure. The factory, however, represented a new phenomenon that had as its central purpose the mass production of economic consumer goods. In order to succeed, this type of enterprise required a rational, efficient form of management. In response to this need, professional managers were educated and trained especially for that purpose. This process of the professionalization of work roles has continued to evolve up to the present day. In speaking of this, Max Weber said that, in "place of the old-type ruler who is moved by sympathy, favor, grace, and gratitude, modern culture requires for its sustaining external apparatus, the emotionally detached and hence rigorously 'professional' expert" (Bendix, 1960, p. 422).

Today, most large-scale formal organizations involve the coordination of large numbers of people engaged in diverse and specialized functions. This applies not only to industrial and business organizations in modern societies, but also to institutions such as government. In France, for instance, government consists of a huge civil service apparatus. To qualify for a high-level civil service position, one must complete a special two-year school for government training after college graduation and score high on a battery of competitive examinations (Ridley, 1979). In the United States, many occupations are becoming increasingly professionalized, including law enforcement administration, nursing administration, and hotel and restaurant management. Given these trends, bureaucracy as a form of social organization appears destined to remain with us in the foreseeable future.

PATTERNS OF SOCIAL INTERACTION

Although many aspects of social organization vary from society to society—as in kinship structure and means of subsistence—social relations everywhere involve similar patterns of social interaction. *Social interaction*— previously defined as a process through which two or more individuals mutually influence each other's thoughts, feelings and actions— take five basic forms: cooperation, exchange, conflict, competition, and accommodation.

Cooperation

The most common form of social interaction is **cooperation**, the sharing of responsibility by people who work together to reach a shared goal. This joint effort and teamwork represents much of the foundation for maintaining social order and stability at all levels of society. By cooperating with each other through compliance with group and societal norms, our actions contribute to social survival, harmony, and, it is hoped, progress. More specifically, social cooperation makes it feasible to achieve goals that would be difficult if not impossible for a single individual to attain. Among the Eskimos of northern Canada, for instance, hunting and fishing are conducted in groups in order to acquire enough food for subsistence. The legislative bodies of modern governments operate under systems of parliamentary procedure in order to make laws and conduct related business. Throughout history, cooperation has made it possible to accomplish feats ranging from the construction of temples in ancient Athens to the development of space flight technology, computers, and particle accelerators today.

Forms of Cooperation According to sociologist Robert Nisbet (1970), there are four basic forms of cooperation. By far, the most common in both past and modern societies is

As members of a community and society, people learn the value of many forms of cooperation.

spontaneous cooperation, which takes place face-to-face at the microlevel in the form of mutual aid. Conditions that result in this type of cooperation tend to emerge from a set of situational circumstances. If a person's house catches fire, neighbors often work together to put out the fire and provide temporary support to the affected family. Likewise, college students sometimes form study groups to prepare for an upcoming exam. *Traditional cooperation,* by comparison, takes the form of social habit that is passed down from generation to generation as established custom. Americans, for example, cooperate with each other traditionally in hundreds of ways, ranging from standing in a line to get a check cashed at the bank to attending the weddings and funerals of close relatives and friends.

However, modern societies—characterized by ongoing change and increasing complexity—tend to depend less on spontaneous and traditional cooperation than on two other types. One of these, *directed cooperation,* involves cooperation that is enforced by an authority figure such as an employer, teacher, or police officer. The other, *contractual cooperation,* takes place when two or more parties mutually agree to specific conditions for cooperation. This can vary in form, from the teenager who agrees to baby sit a child for a married couple (microlevel), to several countries that form a formal trade agreement with each other (macrolevel).

Exchange

Cooperation is often reinforced by **exchange**, a form of social interaction in which all parties expect to benefit by receiving a reward. Sociologist George Homans (1961, 1974) has argued that we seek rewards in all our relations with others, and avoid negative consequences or punishments. We tend to continue relationships that offer more benefits than drawbacks and try to avoid those in which the negatives outweigh the positives.

Another exchange theorist, Peter Blau, has said that what is rewarding or punishing is not always clear cut or visible to the casual observer, but may be quite symbolic and subjective. In other words, what is meaningful as a reward may depend on the person, the situation, and the priorities or goals the individual seeks to have addressed or satisfied. For the student of behavior possessed by "the sociological imagination," Blau (1964) says that

> [s]ocial exchange can be observed everywhere once we are sensitized . . . to it, not only in market relations but also in friendship and even in love . . . as well as in many social relations between these extremes in intimacy. Neighbors exchange favors; children, toys; colleagues, assistance; acquaintances, courtesies; politicians, concessions; discussants, ideas; housewives, recipes (p. 88).

Exchange is based on the principle of *reciprocity,* the idea that people provide assistance to those who have helped them in order to maintain equality in social obligations (Gouldner, 1960). If someone comes along with jumper cables and helps you start your stalled car, you may reciprocate by offering to pay the person for his or her trouble. When you invite someone to your home for dinner or a party, that person may fulfill a felt obligation to you by returning the favor. If someone remembers your anniversary or birthday or sends you a Christmas card, you may respond in kind. In these and countless other ways, we exchange courtesies and resources with one another at all levels of society. This promotes alliances between individuals and groups and helps ensure cohesion and order throughout society.

Competition

Competition occurs when two or more parties attempt to reach a mutually prized goal that is limited in quantity. Unlike cooperation (shared goals) and exchange (mutual rewards), competition occurs when there can be only one winner of a ballgame, election, job promotion, or award for salesperson of the year. In these and numerous other situations, one must compete with others for scarce rewards. However, like the two previously mentioned forms of interaction, competition is governed by a particular type of norms (Friedsam, 1965). These norms act as rules of engagement to prevent competition from deteriorating into conflict which can be very destructive. The primary purpose of competition, therefore, is to achieve the goal, not to injure the other party or subvert the competitive process. If this process is threatened, it is sometimes necessary to impose punitive sanctions. These might include expulsion from the game for the abusive athlete, or job demotion or dismissal for the unethical sales representative.

Competition, like other forms of interaction, is found in all societies to some degree, whether it involves territorial hunting rights, soil resources for farming, cattle for breeding, or markets for industrial commodities. In the United States, the competitive spirit is an underlying element in dominant traditional norms that stress individualism, capitalism, and the upwardly mobile pursuit of the American dream. In this context, the primary advantage of competition is its usefulness as a mechanism to allocate scarce resources as rewards for hard work and high achievement. However, it can also result in discouragement and a sense of failure for those who, by virtue of poverty or emotional and social deprivation brought on by the accidents of birth and socialization, are not equipped with the necessary "cultural currency" to compete on an equal basis.

Conflict

When cooperation, exchange, and competition break down, there is often **conflict**, a pattern of interaction in which two or more parties seek to reach a goal by neutralizing,

© MORGAN DAVID DE LOSSY/CORBIS

Conflict is a pattern of interaction that may occur at any level of society and take a variety of forms.

dominating, or destroying all adversaries against their will (Williams, 1970). Conflict occurs in all types of groups, from the most intimate to the most impersonal, and at all levels of interaction, from the two people who bash their cars together on the freeway and pursue the matter in court to two or more countries that go to war. As the opposite of cooperation, conflict is characterized chiefly by hostility on the part of the concerned parties and often a lack of norms almost to the point that "practically anything goes." Although physical confrontation and violence sometimes occur, conflict more typically involves less dramatic approaches including verbal disagreements, written position papers, or exercises in social (e.g., petitions or demonstrations) and economic sanctions.

Forms of Conflict   The German sociologist Georg Simmel (1858–1918) argued that there were four basic types of conflict: wars, feuds, litigations, and ideological conflicts (Simmel, 1955).*Wars* represent the most extreme and destructive type of conflict from the standpoint of violence. During World War II (1939–1945), over 50 million people lost their lives. During the Vietnam conflict nearly a third of a century later, more than 58,000 Americans were killed and the civilian death toll for the Vietnamese exceeded 1,500,000. *Feuds* are disputes between or within groups, whereas *litigations* represent legal conflicts between parties that are fought in the courts. *Ideological conflicts,* the last of Simmel's categories, are conflicts over ideals or principles as illustrated by capitalism versus communism, conservatism versus liberalism, and Christianity versus agnosticism.

Accommodation

When conflict becomes disruptive, a process is needed to foster its reduction or resolution so that opposing parties can function together successfully. This process is called **accommodation**.

Forms of Accommodation   Although accommodation takes several forms, two of the most common are compromise and toleration. *Compromise* involves give-and-take negotiations between two parties in an attempt to find common ground sufficient to build a successful relationship. Examples might include the married couple with marital conflict (microlevel) that reaches an accommodation with or without the mediation of a professional counselor, or a labor–management dispute that is settled with or without third-party arbitration. Formal compromise often takes the form of written agreements, like labor contracts or treaties. In 1987, for example, twenty-four countries signed a treaty in Montreal, Canada, designed to help protect the ozone layer in the atmosphere. The ozone layer protects us from the harmful effects of the sun's ultraviolet rays. They agreed, among other things, to freeze world production of certain chlorofluorocarbons and fluorocarbons used in refrigerators and aerosol cans, which contribute to the destruction of the ozone layer.

Toleration is an agreement between two opposing parties to coexist since neither can easily defeat the other. In contrast to compromise, which involves active negotiations and sometimes formal agreements, toleration usually involves an implied arrangement between two relatively equal parties. In essence, they agree that although they do not like each other, it is in their best interests not to engage each other in direct conflict. The former Soviet Union (which dissolved in 1987) and the United States were bitter ideological enemies for over forty years. Yet, because each had sufficient nuclear armament to destroy the world several times over, they found it advantageous—through a condition called *détente*—to avoid direct confrontation and overt war. Although they did engage in compromise with each other in some areas and signed treaties together, the primary relationship between these two super powers was toleration.

CHAPTER SUMMARY

1. Social organization is the process by which society is structured as a system of social interaction to meet the needs of its members. To accomplish this, particular social needs must be addressed, which include population maintenance and control (reproduction of society members), division of labor (how work is allocated), communication, shared values and goals, and social control (to ensure social order).

2. There are two basic levels of social organization: microlevel organization and macrolevel organization. The patterned ways people act at the local community level in social encounters, relationships, and groups constitutes microlevel organization. By comparison, macrolevel organization is concerned with the manner in which large-scale organizations like school systems and corporations are organized, as well as how basic institutions such as the society's family, government, and economic systems are structured.

3. Although there are several ways to distinguish between different types of societies, perhaps the most useful is by means of subsistence, the process used by a society to provide food and other basic resources needed by its people for survival and prosperity. Hunting-gathering societies are the simplest. They consist of small bands of nomads who, because they have no means of producing or preserving food, live from day to day by hunting and foraging for food. Horticultural societies depend mainly on slash-and-burn agriculture and raising domesticated animals for food. Their members live in village-based clans and villages. Agrarian societies, which came later, developed intensive and sophisticated forms of agriculture and evolved into large, urban-based civilizations which included city-states with centralized authority. By the 1700s and 1800s, industrial societies emerged with the onset of the industrial revolution which were characterized by a cash economy, mass production and specialized occupations. Today, the United States and some other countries are fast moving toward an information-based economy as emerging post-industrial societies.

4. Within the various types of societies at both micro- and macrolevels are several key forms of social organization that include kinship, fealty, and groups. Kinship has to do with the way in which family relations are organized in given societies. As such, it occurs in two basic forms throughout the world: consanguineal kinship (based on blood ties) and affinal kinship (based on marital ties). Fealty is a form of social organization based on the personal loyalty of a follower toward a leader. Common forms include loyalty of an employee to an employer, team pride in athletics, and *esprit de corps* in the military. Social behavior is also organized according to the groups to which a person belongs, along with the norms and group goals that govern behavior within such groups.

5. Other basic forms of social organization include social positions (statuses), contract, and bureaucracy. A status is a socially defined location or position a person occupies in society. Some of the statuses we occupy are ascribed (imposed), like sex, race, and ethnicity at birth; others are achieved, including education, occupation, and marriage in modern countries. Each position or status in society also carries with it a role that consists of certain expected behaviors along with obligations and privileges.

6. Contract, which involves the exchange of one promise for another, has been an important form of social organization since the Middle Ages in Europe and is a common form in modern societies with cash economies today. Another form of social organization that has become equally important to modern societies is bureaucracy, the rational organization of work in large-scale organizations coordinated by professional managers.

7. Social interaction, the process through which two or more parties mutually influence one another's thoughts, feelings, and actions, takes several basic forms. Cooperation involves the sharing of responsibility by people who work together to reach a shared goal. This is reinforced by exchange, a form of interaction in which all parties expect to benefit by receiving a reward. When a relationship is rewarding, we are motivated to maintain it. Competition, an additional form of social interaction, takes place when two or more parties attempt to reach the same goal that is limited in quantity. Unlike cooperation (shared goals) and exchange (mutual rewards), there can be only one winner of a competition. However, order is maintained through a set of commonly agreed-upon rules that act to govern competition (as in the rules of play in professional sports).

8. When cooperation, exchange, and competition break down, there is often conflict, a type of social interaction marked by two or more parties attempting to neutralize, dominate, or destroy all adversaries against their will. There are essentially no norms (rules) that govern conflict, as there are in competition. Consequently, its results can be very destructive. When conflict occurs, another type of social interaction is often helpful—accommodation, which involves the use of various approaches to reduce or resolve conflict.

TERMS TO KNOW

accommodation: a pattern of social interaction that fosters the reduction or resolution of conflict so that opposing parties can function together successfully.

achieved status: a social position earned through individual effort.

affinal kinship: a type of family organization based primarily on marital ties.

agrarian societies: social systems organized around advanced agricultural methods for subsistence and centralized governmental authority.

ascribed status: a social position assigned to a person at birth or otherwise imposed by society.

competition: a pattern of social interaction that occurs when two or more parties attempt to reach a mutually prized goal that is limited in quantity.

conflict: a pattern of social interaction in which two or more parties seek to reach a goal by neutralizing, dominating, or destroying all adversaries against their will.

consanguineal kinship: a type of family organization based primarily on blood ties.

contract: a social bond between two or more parties that involves the exchange of one promise for another.

cooperation: a pattern of social interaction that involves the sharing of responsibility by people who work together to reach a shared goal.

division of labor: a system in society through which essential tasks are assigned to and carried out by the necessary numbers of people.

exchange: a pattern of social interaction in which all parties expect to benefit by receiving a reward.

fealty: a form of social organization involving the personal loyalty of a follower toward a leader.

group: two or more people with one or more characteristics in common.

horticultural societies: village focused social systems that rely on simple slash-and-burn agriculture and the use of domesticated animals for subsistence.

hunting-gathering societies: small bands of nomadic hunters and food gatherers who, because they lack the technology to produce or preserve food, literally take life a meal at a time.

industrial societies: complex and technologically advanced social systems with a cash economy, mass production, specialized occupations, and bureaucratic management.

institution: a major structural part of a society that addresses a special area of human needs.

kinship: a form of social organization involving the manner in which family relations are organized.

macrolevel organization: the manner in which large-scale organizations, basic institutions, and societies are organized and interact with one another.

master status: the social position held by a person that becomes the primary source of his or her identity.

means of subsistence: the specific process used by a society to provide food and other resources needed by its people for survival and prosperity.

microlevel organization: the patterned ways people act at the local community level in social encounters, relationships, and groups.

postindustrial societies: emerging social systems which increasingly are becoming dominated by service and information economies.

role: the expected forms of behavior, obligation, and privilege that go with a social status.

role ambiguity: a situation that occurs when the obligations attached to a social status are unclear.

role conflict: stress caused when conflicting role demands are built into separate statuses or positions, each of which an individual is expected to carry out successfully.

role set: two or more distinct roles that relate to a single status or social position.

role strain: stress that occurs when conflicting role demands are built into a single status, a person cannot fulfill the role demands of a given position, or both.

social control: a process designed to maintain conformity to dominant norms.

social interaction: the process through which two or more individuals mutually influence each other's thoughts, feelings, and actions.

social organization: the process by which society is structured as a system of social interaction to meet the needs of its members.

social structure: a set of organized norms that govern how people are to interact with each other in various social situations.

society: the largest possible grouping of individuals with specific characteristics in a particular system of social interaction.

status: a socially defined place or position a person occupies in society, along with a set of expected behavior patterns that act to regulate their behavior.

status inconsistency: a contradiction or mismatch between statuses in which a person ranks high in one and low in another.

status set: the sum total of statuses (social positions) a person occupies in his or her life situation.

SUGGESTED READINGS

Diamond, J. 2005. *Collapse: How Societies Choose to Fail or Succeed.* New York: Viking. A timely book aimed at examining the relationship between how a society is organized and adjusts its basic institutions and social processes to changing world and societal conditions. In the final analysis, the author contends, this adaptability or lack thereof largely determines whether societies succeed and prosper or decline and perhaps die.

Etzioni, A. 2001. *Next: The Road to the Good Society.* New York: Basic Books. One of the key modern theorists in organization discusses the importance of community—people being concerned with and focused on each other—as the only viable way to build a strong resilient society rather than just being focused on ourselves.

Putnam, R. D. 2000. *Bowling Alone: The Collapse and Revival of American Community.* New York: Simon & Schuster. A detailed and well-research examination as to why microlevel society—interpersonal and community forms of interaction—has declined and what steps are necessary to revive it.

Wilson, J. Q. 2000. *Bureaucracy: What Government Agencies Do and Why They Do It.* New York: Basic Books. An insightful look into how governmental agencies function with an emphasis on specific goals established by such publicly financed organizations and how they are organized to achieve them.

Groups in Society

► READING PREVIEW

Terms to Know

calculated formation	in-group	secondary group
coalition	instrumental group purpose	social category
collective conscience	mechanical solidarity	social distance
common attributes	networking	social group
consciousness of kind	organic solidarity	social networks
dyad	out-group	social solidarity
expressive group purpose	patterned social relations	socioemotional leaders
formal organization	physical aggregate	statistical category
gemeinschaft	polar typology	task leaders
gesellschaft	primary group	triad
group dynamics	reference group	

It was almost midnight in San Diego on a cold night in February and young Christopher Valva was arriving home from his second shift job at a printing company. The nineteen-year-old noticed three juveniles "hanging out" near his house, told them to go away, and then, after an angry exchange of words, was attacked and stabbed in the heart with a long hunting knife. As his assailants fled, Chris stumbled into his house, and his shocked mother, seeing her blood-soaked son, dialed 9-1-1. Within minutes, police and paramedics were on the scene and Chris was rushed by ambulance to the trauma center at Mercy Hospital and Emergency Center. En route, while the driver communicated with Mercy and a surgical team was hastily assembled, paramedics continued to apply CPR to Chris although he had almost no blood, collapsed veins, no pulse, and dilated pupils.

Upon his arrival at the hospital, Dr. Eugene Rumsey, Jr. and a team of other trauma surgeons, nurses, and technicians went to work on a patient that by most traditional indications was already dead. Knowing that the young man had only a one percent chance for survival, the team opened his chest and, while a breathing bag forced oxygen into his lungs and intravenous lines sent blood and solution coursing through his veins, Rumsey held Chris's heart in his hand and massaged it until it showed signs of life and finally began beating on its own. As it beat, the heart spurted blood through a one and one-half inch wound, which was carefully sewn shut and repaired by a thoracic surgeon. Over the next several hours after the surgery, the crises of restoring liver and kidney functions, treating heart arrhythmias, and combating the sudden drop in body temperature with blankets and blood transfusions were dealt with and successfully overcome. In March, thirty-five days after entering the Mercy Trauma Center, Chris Valva was released from the hospital. By Christmas, he was able to return to work and resume a normal routine after having been given a second chance at life (Michelmore, 1986).

This rather dramatic incident serves to illustrate how fundamentally important groups are and how critical they can be to each of us. In Chris Valva's case, one group of delinquents almost caused his death, while the intercession of his mother and two other groups—paramedics and the medical trauma team—saved his life. While nothing this extreme may happen to most of us, our group contacts and relations with others nonetheless have a profound impact on our behavior, emotional and social well-being, and happiness.

As we have already seen, both culture (Chapter 4), and socialization (Chapter 5) are the products of group processes. Likewise, the way we affiliate with and interact in groups play a crucial role in shaping the social organization of a society (Chapter 6). In the discussion to follow, we will build upon this foundation and focus our attention specifically on groups and how they operate in society.

GROUP CHARACTERISTICS AND TYPES

Although group processes form the foundation for the human experience, groups themselves represent a difficult phenomenon to classify and study. A *group,* as first defined in Chapter 6, consists of two or more people with one or more characteristics in common. As such, groups represent a key form of social organization. Each of us refers to groups several times each day to identify and distinguish among a wide assortment of different collections of people. Depending on who we are and the particular circumstances involved, we may talk or hear about Italian Americans, Fortune 500 companies, people infected with HIV-AIDS, farmers in Kansas, prostitutes and their customers, smokers, Democrats, country-western singers, bald-headed men, *Dancing with the Stars* contestants, people with hemorrhoids, Baptists, widows, students, and so forth. The list becomes practically endless.

In addition, many of these groups may be divided into subgroups. Students, for example, may be classified into elementary, secondary, college, and graduate or professional students. If we then concentrate attention on one of these subcategories, such as college students, it likewise may be divided even further by class rank (first year, sophomores, juniors, seniors), college major, grade point average (GPA), and membership in school organizations.

Many groups tend to be temporary and dynamic in nature. Some, like new social relationships or business organizations, are just beginning, while others are changing in focus and composition or, in some cases, may be in the process of dissolving altogether.

Characteristics of Groups

Given the diverse, temporary, and ever-changing nature of groups, sociologists use a variety of characteristics to distinguish among their different types. Of these, four in particular—common attributes, consciousness of kind, patterned social relations, and calculated formation—appear most useful. Some types of groups may possess only one or two of these characteristics, while others typically may have three or all four.

Common Attributes   The term **common attributes** refers to the characteristics members of a group have in common with one another. In all groups there are one or more shared characteristics among members that act as boundaries to distinguish members from

nonmembers. For instance, age, gender, and special dress and activities represent common attributes (characteristics) that distinguish members of a Girl Scout troop from those in other groups. In similar fashion, professional basketball players may be identified by such commonly held characteristics as physical height and uniforms, professors by education and academic rank, convicted felons by their criminal records, and corporations by method of organization.

Consciousness of Kind   In 1906, sociologist William Graham Sumner originated the concept of **consciousness of kind**, the tendency of people to recognize others like themselves and, in many cases, to feel a common sense of identification or connection as a result (Sumner, 1906, 1960). This is often evident when people find themselves in an unfamiliar social setting comprised mainly of strangers with whom they have little if anything in common. Noncommissioned military personnel, for instance, tend to congregate while waiting at large airports during layovers between flights. In an unfamiliar place full of strangers, they are immediately drawn to the uniforms of those with whom they share a common bond. Those who ride motorcycles, particularly Harley-Davidson owners, share a special affinity with one another that they acknowledge when passing other bikers like themselves on the road. In numerous other instances, consciousness of kind acts as a pervasive characteristic of many groups in society. We are continually drawn to people with whom we have things in common.

Patterned Social Relations   In many groups, members influence the feelings, attitudes, and behavior of one another through personal social interaction or **patterned social relations**. In today's world, these relations may also include some indirect system of social contact (e.g., emails, chat rooms, and distance learning courses on the internet). These form the foundation for human interaction at the microlevel of society. They include rules of conduct called norms (Chapter 4) and patterns of social interaction including cooperation, exchange, competition, conflict, and accommodation (Chapter 6). Together these elements shape to a significant degree how we interact meaningfully with family, friends, neighbors, co-workers, and acquaintances. In addition, patterned social relations are also characteristic of large-scale organizations and institutions at the middle range and macrolevels of society. Both General Motors and the United States Government, for instance, make use of patterned social interaction both internally and in relating to other large-scale organizations and institutions. This often involves more indirect and impersonal forms of social contact such as conventions and other large meetings, along with newsletters, blogs on the internet, emails at one's job, text messaging, and other means of correspondence.

Calculated Formation   Finally, some groups also possess **calculated formation**, the action taken by group members to organize together in pursuit of one or more specific, practical goals. Often, these shared goals are fairly complex in nature as well as the plans that must be implemented to achieve them. Take, for example, a group of workers in an industrial production plant who are disenchanted with their pay, fringe benefits, and working conditions. If they then form a local chapter of a labor union to address these concerns, they will be organizing themselves formally as a means of achieving one or more complex goals. Groups with calculated formation tend to be larger than many social groups (like families and friendship circles). In fact, size alone can make calculated formation a necessity.

Consequently, large charitable organizations are formed and organized deliberately to raise money for the disadvantaged, corporations organized to make profits, college's to educate society's future leaders, and governmental agencies to meet specific needs of the public at large.

Types of Groups

As mentioned earlier, some groups may have only one or two of the characteristics just discussed, while others may have three or all four (Figure 7-1). In this regard, sociologists generally classify groups into five general categories: physical aggregates, statistical categories, social categories, social groups, and formal organizations.

Physical Aggregates   Sometimes we find ourselves in the midst of a collectivity of people by simply being in the same place at the same time. This form of social experience involves a **physical aggregate**, a group distinguished primarily by the physical proximity of its members. We briefly participate in physical aggregates each time we stand in a line, get on an elevator with others, attend a concert, go to a movie, and otherwise find ourselves in crowds. We normally tend to feel neutral toward such groups and give them little if any thought at all. Although we share one or more common attributes with these people (like concert attendees each holding a ticket), there is little else to make a lasting impression. If there is any social interaction in a crowd—such as our asking someone in front of us in a movie line what time the show starts—it tends to be momentary, superficial, and unstructured. Therefore, we usually forget our encounters with fellow members of physical aggregates the moment they are concluded.

Statistical Categories   Another type of group to which we are largely oblivious is the **statistical category**, an artificial group formed by researchers for the purposes of social analysis. Because it is not formed by the members themselves, it is a contrived group that

Physical aggregates (or crowds) are a common occurrence in modern urban societies.

holds the greatest meaning for those who conduct various forms of social research. In this regard, each of us belongs to dozens, if not hundreds of these groups although we are not consciously aware of inclusion.

We show up in census data, consumer surveys, popularity ratings for television polls, and political polls to name a few. Even the "junk mail" we receive tends to be based in significant part on our membership in statistical categories by age, marital status, income, occupation, and so forth, in which we are placed for marketing purposes. Like physical aggregates, statistical categories lack consciousness of kind, patterned social relations, and calculated formation.

Social Categories   The **social category**, unlike the two previously mentioned group types, is characterized by both common attributes and consciousness of kind. This is a group distinguished by its members having one or more visible or otherwise identifiable special features or characteristics in common. The chief factor here is consciousness of kind. We tend to identify with fellow members of the social categories in which we hold membership. Men, therefore, feel a special bond with other men, women an identification with other women, and Mexican Americans a connection with others of Mexican descent. Likewise college students, U.S. Marines, Cherokee Indians, senior citizens, rodeo riders, Methodists, and sociologists feel a special affinity for others of their kind. However, social categories as total groupings of people typically lack both patterned social relations and formal organization. These additional characteristics may appear, however, in social groups and formal organizations that are often formed within social categories.

Social Groups   The most important and fundamental of all group types is the **social group**, a group of people bound together by common interests and values in a definite pattern of social relations. A person's family, a circle of close friends, a sociology class, two couples on a picnic, and several neighborhood children at play with one another all serve as representative examples. They each possess common attributes, consciousness of kind, and patterned social relations.

Social groups and the relations members share with each other are at the core of the human experience. Culture (Chapter 4), socialization (Chapter 5), and social organization (Chapter 6) all take place within group settings. In addition, both a person's self-concept and social identity are shaped primarily through patterned social relations with others. For these reasons, this chapter is devoted primarily to an exploration of the different types of social groups, the factors that shape the way they are organized, and the forms of behavior that take place within them.

Formal Organizations   The last of the five types of groups is the **formal organization**, a group deliberately formed to pursue one or more specific practical goals. Like social groups, formal organizations also are very important to human survival and prosperity, particularly in large technological societies with differentiated institutions and a specialized division of labor. They too are characterized by common attributes, consciousness of kind, and patterned social relations. However, unlike most social groups, formal organizations have the additional characteristic of calculated formation, which allows the most complex of human endeavors, from performing open heart surgery to landing men on the moon, to first be planned and then carried out in a highly organized and efficient manner. Through

TABLE 7-1	Types of Groups and Their Characteristics			
		TYPICAL CHARACTERISTICS		
TYPE OF GROUP	COMMON ATTRIBUTES	CONSCIOUSNESS OF KIND	PATTERNED SOCIAL RELATIONS	CALCULATED FORMATION
Physical Aggregate	Yes	No	No	No
Statistical Category	Yes	No	No	No
Social Category	Yes	Yes	No	No
Social Group	Yes	Yes	Yes	No
Formal Organization	Yes	Yes	Yes	Yes

calculated formation (the intent, plan, or means), the formal organization is then able to achieve its primary goal, whatever it might be, such as earning a yearly profit, curing a disease, or winning a military battle (Table 7-1).

OCIAL GROUPS

Because culture, socialization, and social organization take place largely within the framework of social relations, the bulk of this chapter is devoted to a discussion of how sociologists distinguish between two fundamental types of social groups, primary groups and secondary groups.

Primary Groups

Charles Horton Cooley (1909, 1956) originated the concept of **primary group**, a small group characterized by personalized, ongoing relationships. In his formulation of the "looking glass self" theory of personality (Chapter 5), Cooley was particularly interested in examining group relationships that have the greatest impact on the developing child. He felt that the family and children's play groups are among the most important influences on a child's socialization because they are the first groups a person is exposed to and they represent the primary source of social and emotional support. In elaborating on primary groups, he had this to say:

> By primary groups I mean those characterized by intimate face-to-face associations and cooperation. They are primary in several senses, but chiefly in that they are fundamental in forming the social nature and ideals of the individualities in a common whole, so that one's very self, for many purposes at least, is the common life and purpose of the group . . . Primary groups are [also] primary in the sense that they do not change in the same degree as more elaborate relations, but form a comparatively permanent source out of which the latter are ever springing. Of course they are not independent of the larger society, but to some extent reflect its spirit. . . . These groups, then, are the springs of life, not only for the individual, but for social institutions (1956, pp. 23–29).

Primary group relations are very personalized, with levels of emotional intimacy and social sharing that make them special for each of us.

Characteristics of Primary Groups   Based on Cooley's initial formulation and subsequent observations and refinements by other sociologists (King and Koller, 1975), it is clear that primary groups have several distinct characteristics. The eight key characteristics are listed below.

1. *Relative Smallness.* Given the fast-paced and relatively specialized nature of social relations in technological societies today, it is relatively rare for primary groups—such as one's family or circle of best friends—to exceed more than eight to ten individuals. Most contain only two to five people. Indeed, given the geographically mobile nature of life for many Americans, it is difficult to sustain long-term and personalized relationships with relatives and friends that one no longer lives near or sees more than a few times a year or less.

2. *Strong Affectional Ties.* The relationships among primary group members are personal and emotion laden. We tend to build an emotional investment with our significant others, and they with us. Given this degree of intimacy, our primary group relations serve as our basic source for emotional and social support.

3. *Strong Personal Identification.* As a result, in large part, of our very personal relations with our primary group members, we also identify strongly with them and desire their approval. Therefore, primary groups play an instrumental role in socialization, and influence to a remarkable degree the formation of a person's self-concept.

4. *Multidimensional Relationships.* Interaction among primary group members tends to be relatively open, free, and extensive. Because our fellow members care about us and accept us as we are, it is possible to interact with them as a whole person and to "be ourselves." In many social encounters, however, we share only a single facet of our personality with others because of the special role demands—such

as those of an employee, student, or customer—placed on us as well as on those with whom we interact.

5. ***Continuous Face-to-Face Contact.*** Members of primary groups interact with one another on a one-to-one basis frequently and over a continuous period of time. We usually see and interact directly with our immediate family and best friends daily or weekly on an ongoing basis over many months, years, and in some cases, several decades during our lives.

6. ***Durability.*** Primary group relations are very durable and often border on permanence. This is partially due to the fact that personal relationships, especially in modern technological societies, are difficult to form and maintain and, once established, are not easily transferable to other people. It is quite difficult, if not impossible, to replace the strong ties felt with a close relative or best friend.

7. ***Trust.*** As a result of the close personal nature of primary group relations and their durability, we tend to trust our fellow members; likewise, they feel they can trust us. Most of us, for instance, would not hesitate to take the word of a close family member or close friend but might be skeptical about many things told to us by acquaintances or strangers.

8. ***Informal Social Controls.*** Because of many of the preceding factors, formal or official social controls are usually unnecessary in primary groups. Informal sanctions such as praise (positive) or criticism (negative) are usually sufficient in maintaining conformity to group rules or standards.

The Scope of Primary Relations

Our interactions with others in our primary groups represent "the ties that bind." By connecting to others in a personal and ongoing manner, we not only obtain satisfaction of our basic needs for emotional intimacy and social sharing, but we also contribute to the cohesiveness of the larger community and society. Primary group relations thus furnish us with a sense of belonging, a feeling of being connected to the larger human experience. This need to belong is important to us and manifests itself throughout life not only in family and typical friendship groups, but in a number of other diverse primary group circumstances as well. Two interesting examples involve primary group bonding in the military and among social deviants.

Primary Group Bonding in the Military

People are capable of making some rather unusual informal adaptations in order to form and maintain primary group relations. Take military life during wartime, for instance. During World War II, both German and Allied soldiers possessed a sense of fealty toward their fellow soldiers at the combat unit level that rivaled the intimacy of families (Shils and Janowitz, 1948; Shils, 1950). German infantry units were effective not so much because of their loyalty to the Nazi cause, but because of the primary group affiliations with their units on a company level. Unlike the American military, the *Wehrmacht* sent men into battle who had already formed strong bonds by having trained together (Van Creveld, 1982). Whenever a German fighting unit became depleted through heavy casualties, the entire unit would be pulled back from the front, reconstituted, and then returned to action.

The Americans, by contrast, constantly added new recruits to depleted units and formed primary group bonds on the battlefront. In addition to eating, sleeping, and fighting together, they shared the most intimate details of their past lives, read each other's mail, shared their belongings and gifts from home, and generally considered each other brothers. The formation of these primary groups, above all else, contributed to their cohesiveness and fighting effectiveness during the war.

In the Korean conflict, although there was similar loyalty to one's fighting unit, the most pervasive and effective primary groups consisted of pairs of soldiers who would stick together as "buddies" and look out for each other. The buddy system in Korea became necessary, in part, as a result of a personnel rotation system that constantly changed the makeup of fighting units. Roger W. Little (1970), a sociologist who lived with an American infantry rifle company as an observer from November 1952 through February 1953, chronicled this situation. In an excerpt from one of the many interviews that Little conducted, a soldier had this to say about the buddy system:

> A buddy understands you and is interested in your story. Some big mouths talk as if everyone is interested in their story but they're not. You've got to find a guy you like and he likes you, then you're buddies and you know he will listen to you when you want to talk. A buddy shares everything; if you don't get mail, he lets you read his (p. 364).

More recent observations concerning the value of primary groups in the military have also been illuminating. Close personal relations were much less prevalent among American soldiers during the Vietnamese conflict (Moskos, 1975). This military action was officially termed a "conflict" rather than a war, had no battlefront, unclear objectives, and a rotation period of twelve to thirteen months that kept most soldiers dealing with it in their own particular fashion. Each man had his own designated departure date that marked the end of the war for him. He spent his time "in country" counting down the days until he could return to "the world." Consequently, morale in many units was low, dissension was high, and whenever a man was "short" (with less than sixty days to go), he was much less likely to be "gung ho" about anything that involved potential contact with the enemy.

The experiences from the 1980s to the present observed by both Israeli and American military leaders are somewhat related. They have found that unless combat units are formed and trained carefully over a designated period of time, the development of *esprit de corps* will be significantly impaired. Soldiers in quickly formed units, when placed in a combat situation, do not perform well and are more likely to suffer mental breakdowns compared to units characterized by primary group affiliation (Solomon, Mikulincer, and Hobfoll, 1986).

In the recent American military involvement in Iraq, American military personnel not only bonded strongly with each other but often with their Iraqi counterparts in the newly reconstituted Iraqi army as well. This sense of brotherhood and mutual support between American and Iraqi soldiers, facilitated by the U.S. strategy of a "surge" of 20,000 thousand additional troops deployed to critical areas in Iraq during 2007–2008 (along with 110,000 newly trained Iraqi soldiers and police on the ground), helped the Iraqi military become more autonomous and capable. Consequently, by early 2008, the Iraqis were conducting most major military operations against enemy insurgents with U.S. troops used as backup support. This, in turn, set the stage for a planned drawdown in U.S. troop strength in Iraq, along with plans for a phased withdrawal of a significant U.S. military presence (Mills, 2008).

Primary Group Bonding among Social Deviants   Primary group relations also develop within the context of deviant behavior. Partially because of the pressure and felt desperation of an "us" versus "them" mentality, as well as family disorganization and other factors, juvenile gangs and subgroups within them sometimes take on many of the characteristics of a primary group. The same can be said of adult criminal gangs. You probably are already familiar, for instance, with the story of Bonnie Parker and Clyde Barrow—commonly known as Bonnie and Clyde. These two lovers headed a gang that robbed banks in several states during the 1930s until they were finally killed in an ambush by law enforcement officials. In like manner, the relationship between pimp and prostitute sometimes involves professed love and romance, although in reality it is usually one-sided, the pimp "conning" the woman in order to exploit her for money (Bryan, 1965; Harmatz and Novak, 1983).

Among the most interesting of primary group relationships among those regarded as deviant is the homosexual "marriage" that takes place in coercive institutions like women's prisons. Sociologist Rose Giallombardo (1970) has researched this phenomenon and gives the following description:

> (T)he *femme* or *mommy* is the inmate who plays the female role in a homosexual relationship. . . . The complementary role to the femme is the *stud broad* or *daddy* who assumes the male role. . . . Cast in the context of a "marital" relationship, the homosexual dyad is viewed by the inmates as a meaningful personal and social relationship. From the mass of interview data it is clear, however, that this mode of behavior would be repugnant to most prisoners, but the uniqueness of the prison situation compels the inmate to redefine and attach new meanings to this behavior within the prison structure. . . . For the vast majority of the inmates, adjustment to the prison world is made by establishing a homosexual alliance with a compatible partner as a marriage unit. Although we cannot discuss the dynamics of mate selection, courtship, and marriage in this paper, it should be pointed out that when a stud and femme have established a homosexual alliance, they are said to be "making it" or to be "tight"; that is to say, they are socially recognized as constituting a legitimate married pair. Since one of the important goals in establishing a homosexual marriage alliance is to strive for what is referred to as a "sincere" relationship, which is one based upon romantic love, the *trick* is held in low esteem by the inmates because she allows herself to be exploited rather than to develop a relationship that is sincere (p. 404).

Secondary Groups

In contrast to the primary group is the **secondary group**, a relatively large collection of people with whom one has superficial and somewhat impersonal relations. Our interactions with secondary groups tend to be more task oriented and specialized compared to our primary relations, which are focused on friendship and personal intimacy. Although our experiences with them may be pleasant (such as discussing career possibilities with a school counselor) or unpleasant (like complaining about poor service in a restaurant), we tend to feel neutral and somewhat aloof concerning most of our secondary group encounters and interactions.

Characteristics of Secondary Groups   Secondary groups have these characteristics:

1. ***Relatively Large Size.*** Secondary groups generally are larger than primary groups and may include thirty, forty, or fifty people or more (e.g., students in a college

Secondary group relations are the most common. They involve superficial and somewhat impersonal relations with others.

sociology class, employees who work in a particular department or division of a company, etc.).

2. ***Weak Affectional Ties.*** Relationships among members of secondary groups tend to be relatively impersonal with little, if any, emotional investment. As a result, secondary relations are easily transferable to other people and social situations. Take the "face-to-face classes" in which most students enroll each semester for example. At the end of each college term, few, if any, people feel pangs of loss at the prospect of never seeing their classmates again. Most people enroll for the next semester or term, form new secondary relations with teachers and students, and have at most only fleeting thoughts concerning the "relationships" they left behind. Courses taught over the internet tend to be even more impersonal. Distance learning classes are becoming increasingly popular for some students and provide some advantages, particularly for highly disciplined and autonomous learners for which they often provides a good fit. However, under the best of circumstances, such courses tend to be less personal than on-campus classes because of a lack of face-to-face contact and interaction with professors and fellow students.

3. ***Little or No Personal Identification.*** Because our secondary group relations are generally interchangeable, they tend to have much less influence on our self-concept than our relations with family and close friends.

4. ***One-Dimensional Relationships.*** Interaction in these groups tends to be specialized and somewhat inhibited. Secondary group relations are structured primarily in terms of specialized social statuses (positions) and the role demands that go with them. Therefore, especially in modern societies, people in most social situations tend to reveal to others only the single facet of themselves required by positions such as employer or employee, teacher or student, store clerk or customer, IRS

representative or taxpayer. Some of us—particularly sociologists—realize that, because of the highly specialized and complex nature of modern society, we remain unaware of the multi-dimensional nature of most people with whom we come into contact. However, most of us probably are so preoccupied with our own lives and priorities that we do not even think about it.

5. *Limited Face-to-Face Contact.* Members of secondary groups tend to interact with each other rather infrequently on a one-to-one basis over a relatively short period of time. Take most college students, for example. Think for a moment about your status as a member of a sociology class and perhaps other classes that meet on campus two or three times per week. How many of your classmates have you verbally interacted with directly in a one-on-one, face-to-face manner during the course of the semester? How often? What does this say to us about the quality of our relationships at school or, for that matter, in most of the social encounters we have with others in modern society? What does it say about the way your society is organized in terms of social relations as compared with a much smaller, village-focused, non-industrial society?

6. *Nonpermanence.* These group interactions tend to last for only a relatively short period of time, in part as a result of their specialized nature and easy transferability to other people and to other situations. A secondary group transaction between a customer and a counter person at a fast-food restaurant may last only a minute or two. A college class will meet for a school term or semester and then disband forever.

7. *Distrust.* Because of the somewhat reserved, impersonal, and temporary nature of secondary groups, distrust often tends to replace trust as an assumption on which relationships between members are based.

8. *Formal Social Controls.* Conformity to group standards, in most cases, is ensured through a system of formal rules that apply equally to all members. Company employees must conform to rules related to working hours, workloads, lunch hours, and vacations. Students must contend with rules concerning attendance, curriculum requirements, grading standards, and registration procedures.

The Scope of Secondary Group Relations   In mass urban societies today, most social contacts with others involve secondary rather than primary relations. Most Americans, for example, spend the bulk of each weekday either at school or at work. Both schoolchildren and college students typically come in contact with several teachers and dozens, if not hundreds, of other students each day. Likewise, physicians, teachers, department store cashiers, and those in numerous other occupations come in contact with many people in a variety of different specialized circumstances. In a given day, a college professor, for instance, may teach several classes, have individual conferences with students, interact with colleagues, administrators, and textbook salespeople, and sit on one or more committees. In fact, many occupations involve working with people in a variety of capacities including project groups, task forces, and committees, which are all typical secondary groups. Members usually know little about one another so that liking or disliking one another personally tends to be irrelevant as long as they can interact together successfully in the context of their jobs or the task at hand (Olmsted and Hare, 1978).

Regarding the scope of secondary relations, Luis Wirth commented (1938) that

the city is characterized by secondary rather than primary contacts. The contacts of the city may indeed be face to face, but they are nevertheless impersonal, superficial, transitory, and segmental. The reserve, the indifference, and the blasé outlook that urbanites manifest in their relationships may thus be regarded as devices for immunizing themselves against the personal claims and expectations of others (pp. 1–2).

The Psychological and Interpersonal Impact of Secondary Relations   The German sociologist Georg Simmel (1918, 1950 A), a contemporary of Wirth's, spoke of the psychological and interpersonal impact that resulted from the indifference and reserve characteristic of social relations in the modern metropolis:

As a result of this reserve, we frequently do not even know by sight those who have been our neighbors for years. And it is this reserve which, in the eyes of small town people, makes us appear to be cold and heartless. Indeed, if I do not deceive myself, the inner aspect of this outer reserve is not only indifference but, more often than we are aware, it is a mutual strangeness and revulsion, which will break into hatred and fight at the moment of a closer contact, however caused (1950 A, p. 415).

Social Group Relations in Perspective

Although the concepts of primary and secondary groups are useful for discussion purposes, few social groups are strictly one type or the other. Instead, most are composites that, though they may be predominantly primary or secondary in nature, still contain elements of the other type. Consequently, primary groups and secondary groups are perhaps best understood as ideal types at either end of a continuum as shown in Figure 7-1.

Secondary group elements may develop within primary group relationships and vice versa. In the family group, for example, a young person may move back home with parents for a while after graduation from college and pay rent just like any other boarder. Likewise, a person who works for a large corporation will interact socially with most fellow employees on a secondary group basis. However, within a given department or office, people may see each other socially outside work and sometimes form fairly strong friendships. Behavioral scientists find that one important factor leading to the formation of primary groups among relative strangers and acquaintances is continued proximity. The longer we are near people on a regular basis, the more likely it is that we will develop an ongoing pattern of interaction, get to know them, and form meaningful friendships (Gergen and Gergen, 1981).

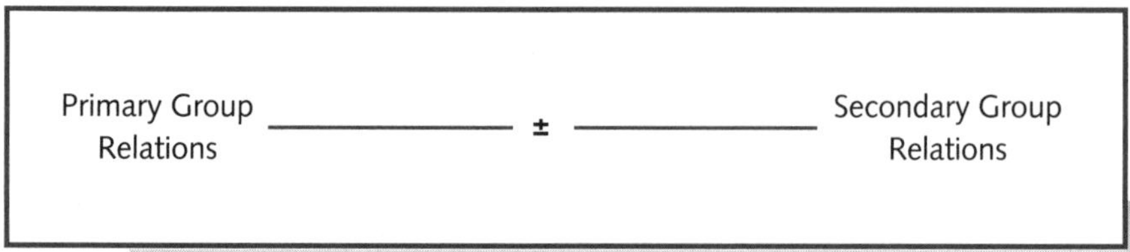

Primary Group Relations ———————— ± ———————— Secondary Group Relations

Figure 7-1

Primary and Secondary Group Relations: A Continuum

SOCIAL STRUCTURE AND THE QUALITY OF GROUP RELATIONS

The manner in which a society is structured or organized affects to a significant degree the overall quality of social relations that occur within it. This is perhaps best illustrated in the work of two late nineteenth century and early twentieth century European sociologists, Ferdinand Tönnies and Emile Durkheim.

Tönnies: *Gemeinschaft* and *Gesellschaft*

Ferdinand Tönnies (1855–1936) was a German sociologist who spent his entire academic life at the University of Keil in northern Germany. His most important contribution to sociological theory, *Gemeinschaft und Gesellschaft* (community and society), was published in 1887. In this ground-breaking work, which was subsequently published in six other editions, Tönnies developed a typology in which he distinguished between the social organization of village-focused societies and that of mass societies characterized by large cities and an urban way of life. His pioneering use of the **polar typology**—the placing of two dissimilar concepts as ideal types at either end of a continuum—is a tool of analysis still used by sociologists today (Timasheff, 1967). There are illustrations of polar typologies throughout this book , including Figure 7-2.

The *Gemeinschaft* Society: Basic Characteristics
The *gemeinschaft* is a community-oriented society in which most social relations are personal, informal, and tend to be based on tradition. Both horticultural and agrarian societies (Chapter 6), for example, tend to be largely *gemeinschaft* in terms of how social relations are organized. In speaking of this, Tönnies (1887, 1957, 2003) said:

> Family life is the general basis of life in the *Gemeinschaft*. It subsists in village and town life. The village community and the town themselves can be considered as large families, the various clans and houses representing the elementary organisms of its body. . . . Here, original kinship and inherited status remain an essential, or at least the most important condition of participating fully in property and other rights (1957, pp. 228–229).

In the *gemeinschaft* environment, primary group relations abound because of a variety of structural factors. These nonindustrial, village-focused societies typically have *low levels of material technology* and *slow rates of change*. These attributes, coupled with *common ancestry*, combine to produce a system of *commonly held norms and values*. In a farm-based

Gemeinschaft Society ————— ± ————— *Gesellschaft* Society
(Primary Group Relations)   (Secondary Group Relations)

Figure 7-2

Tönnies's Polar Typology of Societies. Based on the discussion in this chapter, where would you plot the United States along this continuum? What about Thailand or Bolivia?

economy, life tends to be organized around *tradition-based social positions* into which people are socialized from birth. Men, women, and children all have their own prescribed roles that govern not only how they interact within the family but also how they identify with and contribute to the community as a whole. Because most occupations and functions revolve around farming and animal husbandry, people have a great deal in common with one another and form *close-knit and long-term ties* with family and community members. In these societies, there is also *geographical stability* as many of their members grow up, get married, raise their families, and grow old and die within a few miles of their birthplace. These factors tend to create a societal climate conducive to primary group relations.

The *Gesellschaft* Society: Basic Characteristics

By contrast, Tönnies argued, the *gesellschaft* is an urban, industrial society with impersonal and somewhat informal relations that tend to be based on contract. Tönnies was concerned about the decline of primary relations and offered at least a partial explanation by identifying several key characteristics of emerging urban societies. In his view, the intimacy and sense of community characteristic of *gemeinschaft* societies were being replaced by

> the rational will of the *gesellschaft*. In the course of history, folk culture has given rise to the civilization of the state. The main features of this process can be described in the following way: Economic control is achieved in many forms, the highest of which is planned capitalist production or large-scale industry. It is through the merchants that the technical conditions for the national union of independent individuals and for capitalist production are created. This merchant class is by nature, mostly also by origin, international as well as national and urban, i.e., it belongs to *gesellschaft* not *gemeinschaft*. Later all social groups and dignitaries and, at least in tendency, the whole people acquire the characteristics of the *gesellschaft*. . . . Simultaneously, along with this revolution in the social order, there takes place a gradual change in the law, in meaning as well as in form. The contract as such becomes the basis of the entire system, and rational will of the *gesellschaft* formed by its interests combines with the authoritative will of the state to create, maintain, and change the legal system (1957, pp. 225–226).

Largely because of its size and complexity, the way a *gesellschaft* society is organized acts to create barriers to primary group relations. Given such factors as *high technology, rapid change,* and *diverse ancestry* among society members, *diverse and specialized norms and values* emerge. People develop very different perceptions of appropriate and inappropriate behavior, given their particular cultural heritage, varied occupations, and other quite diversified life situations.

An industrial economy results in *contract-based social positions* in which long-standing traditions may be of little relevance in light of changing social conditions. Personal relationships give way to business and professional relationships that are highly specialized in nature. Relationships based on friendship, trust, and good will are replaced by those that stress profit, productivity, and the achievement of other rational goals. Long-term close ties are replaced by *temporary and specialized friendships,* which are spread over several groups and tend to change in membership as time passes and conditions change. Finally, a *gesellschaft* society is characterized by *geographical and social mobility* among members. In a modern cash economy, people often must go where the jobs are, even if it means leaving extended relatives and friends behind and moving to another city or state.

Durkheim: Mechanical and Organic Solidarity

The French sociologist Emile Durkheim, a contemporary of Tönnies, also was interested in exploring the relationship between the way a society is structured and the overall manner in which social group relations take place. Like other analytical sociologists of his day, including such notables as Tönnies, Georg Simmel, and Gabriel Tarde, he favored the comparative approach, particularly that of comparing simple versus complex societies.

Durkheim's main research interest throughout his academic career was focused on the issue of **social solidarity** (social order) and its fundamental causes. In his first book, *The Division of Labor in Society* (1893, 1933), he sought to explain from a historical perspective the types of social solidarity characteristic of both simple rural societies and modern industrial social systems. Although he concentrated mainly on social solidarity, much of what he said had significant relevance toward explaining the quality of social relations in different types of societies.

Durkheim distinguished between simple nonindustrial societies characterized by *mechanical solidarity,* and complex industrial societies characterized by *organic solidarity.* He felt that social solidarity (order and cohesion) was the result of a **collective conscience**, a state of mental and moral agreement among members of a society concerning basic norms and values. Thus the collective conscience of a society, as expressed in a particular form of social solidarity, was the moral and social cement that held society together.

Mechanical Solidarity   Among the results of Durkheim's analysis was his finding that the primary group relations prevalent in simple nonindustrial societies was related to **mechanical solidarity**, the solidarity (cohesion) of resemblance characteristic of traditional nonindustrial societies. Most people in simple societies of the past, such as feudal societies of preindustrial Europe, were almost identical in their occupations, interests, and values. The low level of material technology in these societies resulted in a very simple division of labor. Therefore, the actions of most people tended to take the form of automatic or mechanical responses to rather predictable life situations. With everyone engaging in the same activities and thinking similar thoughts about most things, it then followed that social relations in these small societies tended to be personal and open for the most part. Because almost everyone knew almost everyone else in the hamlet or village, there were few obstacles to interfere with primary group relations. Durkheim found that in these societies the collective conscience was very strong and social solidarity was, therefore, relatively easy to maintain. This friendly, open sort of orientation toward others in the community can still be observed even today in rural pockets of largely industrial societies and postindustrial societies like the United States.

However, something developed in recent history to undermine mechanical solidarity, weaken the collective conscience, and alter the nature of social relations. That something was the Industrial Revolution, which began about 1750 but did not have a significant impact until after 1800. The factory system of production, Durkheim asserted, resulted in the emergence of a specialized division of labor and with it a different type of social cohesion, which he termed organic solidarity.

Organic Solidarity   Durkheim used the term **organic solidarity** to mean the solidarity of differences. In modern societies, individuals are differentiated by their occupations, values, and life styles. The result of this societal condition brought on largely by industrialization is a society composed of different types of people. These different individuals function much like the various organs of the body. They carry out different functions, but ones that complement or blend with each other for the smooth working of the society as a whole. Just as the heart, lungs, stomach, and other organs perform different yet complementary functions to maintain equilibrium in the physical organism, the same could be said for the way differentiated occupations interrelate smoothly to maintain order in the industrial society.

To carry the organic analogy further, a breakdown in one functional area can cause dislocation all across the system in either a physical organism or a human society. If, for example, a person experiences a heart attack or a serious back injury, his or her entire body is rendered incapable of functioning properly until the injured part recovers. Durkheim asserted that the same is true in a society. In the United States, for instance, coal miners produce coal and coal runs the steel mills; steelworkers produce steel and steel is used in the production of automobiles; car manufacturers distribute the cars to car dealers and the dealers then sell the cars to consumers. Hypothetically speaking, a long and unresolved coal miners' strike could create somewhat of a domino effect, which in turn could possibly impair a large part of the economy.

Durkheim was concerned because organic solidarity was more precarious than the earlier type and, given the differentiated nature of modern societies, the collective conscience was weakened. He felt that the sheer complexity of these societies often resulted in a condition of *anomie* (Chapter 2) the absence or breakdown of norms.

In terms of social relations, modern societies—composed of huge numbers of people who are different from one another in occupation, values, and life styles—are structured in a manner that discourages primary group relationships. One may come into contact with so many different types of people in so many different situations that it becomes difficult to maintain anything other than secondary group relationships with most of them.

Social Group Relations Today

Some sociologists such as Harold L. Wilensky and Charles N. Lebeaux have argued that "the breakdown of primary group life and informal controls has been greatly exaggerated" (1958, p. 125). They cite studies that show that the need to form primary relations is fairly universal and manifests itself in urban as well as rural settings. Even in a geographically mobile, industrial society, people who are isolated from one source of primary relations seek out and find others.

While it is true that people everywhere desire and need primary group relations, an impressive body of research shows that the nature of urban industrial society makes it difficult for people to form and sustain primary relations. Stanley S. Guterman (1969), for instance, concluded from his research that urban dwellers are less likely to have primary group bonds with close friends than those who live in small towns. In 1985, a national study asked those in the sample to identify the person with whom they could discuss important matters. Through the use of this measure, the study found that the average person had strong personal ties with only three other people as close confidants (Marsden, 1987).

Since that time, Americans have increasingly become a nation of observers rather than participants in meaningful social connections with others, their community, and society. In 2000, Robert Putnam's thoroughly researched book *Bowling Alone* chronicled the fact that

Americans have become increasingly disconnected from one another in civic engagement; by the mid 1990s participation in church, community organizations, clubs, volunteerism, and philanthropy was only one-tenth of what it was during the 1970s. Civic and organizational participation had declined significantly in every measurable area "from the most common—petition signing—to the least common—running for office" (p. 41). In addition, based on national sampling data, the average number of close confidant relationships for typical Americans had been reduced from three people in 1985 to only two confidants in 2004. Nearly twenty-five percent reported that they had no one with whom to discuss personal matters important to them (*Science Daily,* 2006).

GROUP DYNAMICS

To gain a basic understanding of the richness and diversity of the human experience requires an examination of groups and group processes. Because we are social creatures, our lives are shaped significantly by not only by our exposure to a multiplicity of groups, but by our impact on these groups as well. So far, we have devoted most of this chapter to a discussion of the architecture of groups and how the characteristics of certain types of societies shape the way group relationships are structured. However, groups are not static things, merely to be classified and cataloged in the abstract for analytical purposes. Instead, they represent dynamic processes that impact directly on each of us. Therefore, let us now focus our attention on **group dynamics**, the systematic study of small group processes.

Basic Principles of Group Dynamics

The study of group dynamics is a relatively new development in sociology, which originated during the late 1940s and early 1950s. Although several scholars have conducted research in this area of microsociology, three names stand out from the rest: Robert F. Bales, George C. Homans, and Alex Bavelas. Together, through their research, they have formulated many of the basic principles of group dynamics. Five of these are discussed below.

Task-Oriented Groups Use a Three-Stage Process
Robert F. Bales (1950) pioneered a method for investigating small-group interaction that became known as *interaction process analysis.* Over many years, Bales and his associates studied small groups of research subjects behind one-way glass. Each group was given a task to perform, and the verbal responses of each member were recorded and a record kept as to which person each comment was addressed.

The entire interaction process for each individual and group was charted according to twelve categories of response. Examples of these categorized responses include defends or asserts oneself, agrees, demonstrates antagonism, understands, gives help, asks for opinion, and so on. One of several findings derived from this research was that groups went through three distinct behavioral phases in addressing tasks. First, there was the *orientation phase* in which participants sought and gave information. This was followed by the *evaluation phase* in which all input was evaluated and opinions given. Finally, the group entered the *control phase* in which information was prioritized, solutions offered, and conclusions made (Bales, 1950; Bales and Strodtbeck, 1951; Bales 1970).

Group Behavior Is Norm-Based

A founding father of group dynamics, George Homans, in his seminal book *The Human Group* (1950, 2001), set forth several basic principles of small-group processes. Among these, the most important are the principles that group behavior is norm-based, interaction encourages friendship, and initiative promotes status.

First of all, Homans found that all groups operate according to a set of norms that are established and maintained by each group. These norms provide the group with structure, order, and focus. In established groups, the new member in most cases must find out what the norms are and adapt to them in order to be accepted. Groups that are newly formed invariably go through a process of establishing what the norms will be. As this occurs, a group structure emerges that includes leadership and interaction patterns and a certain style of decision making. Think back for a moment to your first few days at college. What norms did you discover and adjust to that were different from those in high school? Which norms in your sociology class (usually set by the professor) are similar to or different from those in some of your other classes?

Interaction Encourages Friendship

Homans also asserted the principle that interaction encourages friendship. Not only are primary group relations characterized by greater interaction among members than are secondary groups, but taking the initiative in talking to others can cause friendships to develop. Stated in simple terms, there are many lonely people just waiting to be "discovered," those who are in need of a friend or friends. Sociologists like Homans have found that the most effective way to establish friendships is to muster the courage to make the first move. By thrusting ourselves into the world of social action by being the first to smile, put out a hand, introduce ourselves, and initiate conversation, we can usually satisfy our desire for friendship. Research has shown that most people will respond to us in like manner.

© PETRENKO ANDRIY, 2009. USED UNDER LICENSE FROM SHUTTERSTOCK, INC.

Those who initiate contact with others are more likely to make friends.

Initiative Promotes Status   Homans (1950, 2001) and others have also found that initiative promotes status. By taking the initiative in interacting with others, a person is able to promote him- or herself to a position of high status within the group. Those who interact least in groups tend to be low-status members. In addition, some researchers have found that the person who initiates the most interactions often is perceived as the leader by other group members. This individual, by virtue of the force of personality in both keeping the group task-oriented and supporting the ideas of other members, gains their loyalty and support (Bales and Slater, 1955).

Group Communication Is Affected by the Positioning of Members   During the 1960s, sociologist Alex Bavelas (1962) conducted a series of communication experiments on task-oriented groups each consisting of five persons. He arranged these groups into different configurations including a circle, a wheel, a Y and a chain (Figure 7-3). Of these arrangements, the wheel—in which the leader tended to be the person in the center—was found to accomplish tasks most efficiently, although group morale suffered. By being located in the hub of the wheel, the leader could both effectively communicate his or her wishes to the group and control all communication that went to individual members who were cut off from one another. By contrast, the circle was found to be less effective from a task-completion standpoint because there was no definite leader. However, it had the highest morale among members because of the high level of communication that was possible. Bavelas found that both the quantity and style of communication resulted from the way members were positioned in the group, which in turn affected both leadership and morale.

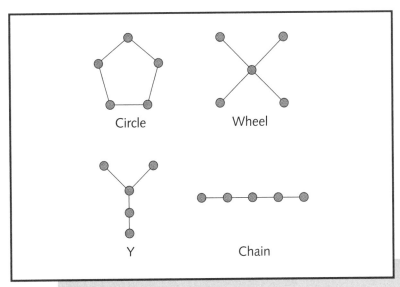

Figure 7-3

Group Position and Communication. The manner in which people are positioned in groups affects their ability to communicate with other group members. If you were the leader of a five-person group, which group communication structure would you prefer, and where would you locate yourself in it? Each dot portrayed above represents a person, and each line between dots represents a line of communication.

Source: Adapted from Bavelas, A. (1962). Communication patterns in task-oriented groups. In D. Cartright and A. F. Zander, eds. *Group Dynamics.* New York: Harper & Row.

Relating to Groups as an Individual

In-Groups and Out-Groups Probably the most fundamental way each of us relates to groups as an individual is in terms of "us" versus "them." Early in the twentieth century, William Graham Sumner (1906) addressed this issue by distinguishing between in-groups and out-groups. An **in-group** is a group that a person belongs to or identifies with. It is a "we" group as compared to a "they" group. In-groups have a sense of "we-ness" or *consciousness of kind* that usually is based on commonly shared values or experiences among group members. Nongroup members are typically viewed as outsiders or "they." Our in-groups may range in size from the smallest of social groups, such as a marriage or friendship circle, to the largest of social categories, such as "we" women, "we" Methodists, "we" New Yorkers, or "we" Americans. These types of group identifications reinforce both our need to belong and social cohesion as manifested in *ethnocentrism* (Chapter 4).

An **out-group**, by contrast, is a group that a person does not belong to or identify with. It is a "they" group as compared to a "we" group. Groups distinguished according to in-groups and out-groups differ in membership and orientation, and are often characterized by rivalry and tension. If one is Catholic, an out-group would be Protestants. In similar fashion, the old would represent an out-group for the young, those who like mainly classical music would be an out-group for country-western fans, and Palestinians would be an out-group for Israelis.

Social Distance The manner in which an individual relates to groups can also be examined by measuring **social distance**. This refers to the degree of acceptance an individual feels toward those who belong to various groups to which he or she does not belong. Sociologist Emory S. Bogardus (1959) devised a seven-point system to measure social distance. When it is administered to research subjects in the form of a scale, they are asked to answer yes or no to whether they would be willing to include a certain category of person—a member of a different ethnic group for instance—as (1) a family member by marriage, (2) a personal friend, (3) a close neighbor, (4) a co-worker, (5) a citizen in their country, (6) a visitor to their country, or (7) would ban the person from their country.

Through the use of the Bogardus Social Distance Scale and other measures, sociologists are able to ascertain how close or distant people feel toward certain groups according to certain characteristics, such as age, ethnicity, race, class, religion, sexual orientation, and nationality. This allows us to predict with some accuracy the extent to which some groups will either be cooperative or antagonistic towards one another.

Reference Groups In 1942, Herbert Hyman used the term *reference group* to describe another way people relate to the groups that surround them. A **reference group** is a group to which a person may or may not belong, which is used as a standard of comparison to evaluate his or her values, behavior, and goals. A person's primary groups, including family and close peer relations (see Chapters 5 and 6), may be reference groups in the sense that they usually are seen as models for value formation and behavior.

Many reference groups, however, are social categories that we use strictly as a basis for comparing our own attitudes and performance. Using them as benchmarks can be a valuable device for assessing or own social identities, performance, and decisions regarding what we wish to achieve in life. For example, it is important for a person serious about obtaining a college degree to identify strongly with college graduates, just as high school and college athletes often identify with professional ball players, aspiring writers with published authors, and beginning employees wishing to get ahead with those in the upper ranks of management.

Both success and failure tend to be defined in terms of the groups in which we choose to participate and those with which we identify. To identify with the success of a particular reference group only as a dream, with little or no commitment or effort devoted to it, will not be sufficient to attain a wished-for standard of performance or objective. However, without beginning with a vision, as measured by the behavior and accomplishments of others, the achievement of success, regardless of how it is socially defined and measured, will most likely not occur.

Social Networks and Networking

Each of us possesses one or more **social networks**, linkages maintained with specific types of people for the satisfaction of personal and practical needs. By way of elaboration, some people may have developed a variety of large, established social networks while others may have only a few that tend to be very small. Some reclusive and socially disconnected people may have no social networks to speak of at all. Most of us, however, tend to have a family network, a friendship network, a network of work associates, a network of classmates if we attend college, a network of fellow church members if we are affiliated closely with a church organization, etc.

A very important life skill is learning how to engage in **networking**, the conscious and planned cultivation of social networks to achieve personal or practical goals. Politicians and those successful in business and careers are masters of networking. Similarly, people with large circles of fairly close friends usually have expended significant time and energy to cultivate them.

Size and Group Behavior: Dyads and Triads

Almost everyone is familiar with the expression "Too many cooks spoil the broth." Although many clichés have little basis in truth, this one, as it relates to group complexity, appears to have some validity. For instance, sociologist John James (1951), in a classic study involving nine thousand people in both work and recreational situations, found that seventy-one percent of all interactions engaged in by the research subjects involved only two people, and twenty-one percent included only three people. Of the rest, only two percent of the interactions involved more than four people. Subsequent research carried out over past six decades has yielded similar results.

Principle: As the Size of a Group Increases, the Number of Potential Relationships Increase Geometrically
Much of the basis for the fact that we often prefer interactions that are one-on-one with others has to do with the factor of complexity. The smaller the group, the less complicated it is to establish and maintain the qualities of rapport, effective communication, and successful decision making. Thus, the size of a group plays a very important role in affecting the patterns of interaction that take place within it. For instance, sociologist Paul Hare (1962) mentions that in a two-person group, there is only a single relationship between the two members. But with a three-person group, the number of

potential relationships increases geometrically to six. By the time we arrive at a seven-person group, there are 966 potential relationships (Table 7-2).

This exponential rise in group complexity can be readily observed when the interaction dynamics of a **dyad** (a two-person group) are compared with those of a **triad** (a three-person group). Among the first to study these two different types of groups was the German sociologist Georg Simmel (1858–1918), who in 1905, published an analysis of dyads and triads in a seminal article titled "Quantitative Aspects of the Group." He found the dyad, or two-person group, to be very fragile because it "depends on each of its two elements alone—in its death though not in its life; for its life it needs *both*, but for its death, only one" (1905, 1950 B, p. 124).

A dyad is both the most intimate and the most vulnerable of groups. Because there are no others with which to divide time and energy, there can be a degree of rapport and mutual sharing between the two participants not possible with larger groups. Dyads, however, tend to be difficult to maintain because, unlike larger groups, individual responsibility is an "all or nothing" situation that cannot be shifted onto the group or delegated to others. In addition, conflict that may arise between the two parties is not subject to either mediation or interference by other group members. Consequently, it is normally the complete responsibility of the two members to resolve a dispute, accommodate it, or dissolve the group by parting company (Gupta, 1983).

When a dyad becomes a triad through the addition of a third party, the dynamics of the group become much more complex. A triad is a more durable group in that the leaving of any one member is not essential to group survival; the two remaining members can continue their relationship. Intimacy is not as profound as with the dyad, because each member must now divide time and energy between two persons. In addition, when conflict breaks out between two of the members, the third party can act as a mediator to help resolve the conflict.

An Example: Married Couple Versus Married Couple with Child   Perhaps the most complicating aspect of all, however, is that in the triad (six potential relationships as portrayed in Figure 7-4), power coalitions of two against one are possible, whereas they are

TABLE 7-2 Group Size and Number of Potential Relationships

GROUP SIZE	NUMBER OF POTENTIAL RELATIONSHIPS
2 persons (dyad)	1
3 persons (triad)	6
4 persons	25
5 persons	90
6 persons	301
7 persons	966

As the number of people in a group increases, the number of potential relationships increase geometrically. Even in a group of only three or four people, the communication and power combinations are not only complex but are constantly subject to adjustment.

Source: Hare. A. P. 1962. *Handbook of Small Group Research*. Glencoe, Illinois: Free Press, p. 229.

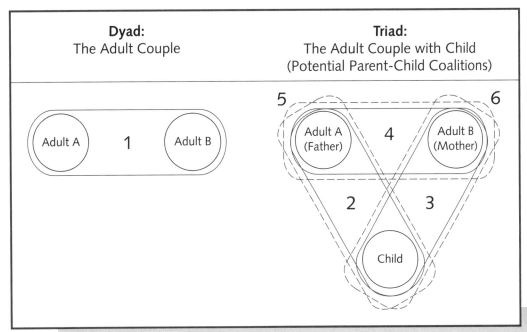

Group Size and the Rise of Complexity: The Adult Couple Versus the Adult Couple with Child. The six potential relationships created with the formation of the couple plus child triad above include the following: 1. adult A plus adult B bond (e.g., marriage bond); 2. father–child bond; 3. mother–child bond; 4. adult couple–parenting coalition; 5. father–child coalition; 6. mother–child coalition. NOTE: Coalitions 5 and 6 interfere with an adaptive family dynamic and should not be allowed by the couple to occur.

not feasible in the dyad. A **coalition**, in the context of group dynamics, is a relationship formed when some group members align themselves against others. Thus, any member can play the role of opportunist in joining forces with another member to overwhelm the third party or act as a strategist in seizing power through the use of "divide and conquer" tactics. With the opportunity for shifts in power ever present, alignments between members can and often do change from time to time and from issue to issue (Caplow, 1969).

Nowhere is the distinction between a dyad and triad more apparent and important than in the interaction dynamics of a married couple versus a married couple with a child. Given the previous discussion, a newly married couple typically would do well to postpone having a child for at least a year or two in order to adjust to the role obligations that go with being married. With this foundation firmly established, the couple would then be in a better position to handle the increasing complexities that accrue to adding a third family member. For example, having a child means that ideally both partners are able to successfully carry out and balance the role obligations of both spouse and parent without overidentifying with or neglecting either. In addition, parenting represents an extension of the partnership established at the onset of marriage, in which both spouses work together as a team to establish consistent standards for child rearing.

A common trap permissive parents fall into is not setting clear and consistent behavioral boundaries (see Chapter 5 for a discussion of parenting strategies) for their developing child or children. When parents do not form a united partnership in mutually agreeing to and putting into practice a uniform set of "ground rules" for a child's behavior, their child intuitively but effectively will fill this ill-defined area of required behavior by pitting one parent against another. By forming an implied coalition with one parent (e.g., "But Daddy said I could do it") through the use of "divide and conquer" tactics, the egocentric child "wins" and gets his or her way and the disorganized and "clueless" parents often never see this coming. The result often is that the child becomes the boss of the parents, at least for a time, until and unless the parents learn to intervene together as partners with clearly defined behavioral boundaries, ongoing monitoring, and consistent reinforcement. In extreme cases, inattention to this one factor alone can create so much stress and disorganization in the marriage that the couple may divorce and/or the child may grow into an insecure, incompetent, and manipulative yet overly dependent adult.

THE FOCUS OF GROUP BEHAVIOR

In the last section of this chapter, we will briefly examine some of the basic factors that shape the focus of group behavior. The direction and momentum that groups exhibit are determined to a significant degree by their purposes, as well as by their types and styles of leadership.

Group Purposes

Most groups tend to be characterized by a predominance of one or the other of two basic purposes, expressive or instrumental. *Primary groups* have, for the most part, an **expressive group purpose** in which the main goal is the emotional benefit derived from participation. Here, group interaction in the family and one's circle of close friends represents an end in itself; namely, the sense of intimacy, community, and belonging one receives from interacting with others on a personal level. *Secondary groups,* by comparison, typically have an **instrumental group purpose** in which interaction with others is used as a means to a practical end. In this regard, we interact with servers in restaurants mainly to receive a meal, teachers to obtain an education, employers to earn a living, and salespeople and clerks of various types to acquire needed consumer items. *Formal organizations* also make use of instrumental purposes of a much more specific and complex nature through the formal ways in which they are organized, for example, to sell products and services, make a profit, and/or serve the public.

Group purposes act to organize and structure social interaction in specific ways which, although not expressly stated, are understood by practically everyone. In this regard, our primary group members (family, close friends) are likely to feel manipulated and "used" if they discover we have ulterior motives aimed at personal gain in interacting with them. Likewise, those with whom we interact in secondary group situations (e.g., work, school, commerce, and government) may feel uncomfortable or exploited if we take up too much of their time or try to get too personal with them.

Types and Styles of Leadership

Two Basic Types of Leadership
The focus of group interaction is also affected by the type of leadership found in a group. A *leader* is a person who is able to wield more authority or power than other members in influencing the way the group functions. Some leaders influence the group by virtue of their official position of authority, while others are informal

leaders who influence members through the force of their personalities. Nevertheless, there are two basic types of leaders generally recognized by sociologists, task leaders and socioemotional leaders (Bales, 1953; Fiedler, 1981).

Task leaders focus their attention on instrumental group purposes aimed at reaching practical goals. They tend to concentrate on "getting the job done" as their first consideration. Some researchers hold that task leadership competence is the most important leadership element (Hollander, 1964). They cite findings that small groups tend to look for task competence in their leaders and appear somewhat adept in being able to identify such individuals (Firestone, Lichtman, and Calamosca, 1975). Yet, as other research indicates, members of some groups can develop, over a period of time, a significant amount of hostility and resentment toward the task leader and "taking orders," as well as toward each other, particularly when their interest in the task at hand is not high (Burke, 1967, 1968). When this occurs, another type of leadership, socioemotional leadership, is often more effective.

Socioemotional leaders concentrate their energies on expressive group purposes aimed at promoting morale and harmony among members. They focus attention on meeting people's emotional needs for acceptance and appreciation and in reducing conflict. Socioemotional leaders tend to be better liked than task leaders, especially when groups function over a long period of time and initial enthusiasm for a task has diminished (Slater, 1955). Whether the task leader or socioemotional leader is the more effective depends on several factors relating to the group situation. In most groups, both large and small, both types of leadership are needed.

Three Basic Leadership Styles Another important consideration is leadership style, which takes three basic forms: authoritarian, laissez-faire, and democratic (Lewin, 1954; White and Lippitt, 1960). The leader who uses the *authoritarian* style basically give orders and makes most if not all decisions pertaining to the group. This approach normally is effective and efficient when the leader is present but often breaks down when the leader is absent. Members of authoritarian groups often have low morale and may exhibit frustration and

© SONYA ETCHISON, 2009. USED UNDER LICENSE FROM SHUTTERSTOCK, INC.

Different types of social situations often call for certain types of leadership. What type of leadership style would be most appropriate here?

hostility toward the leader. Many if not most people, however, prefer an authoritarian "take charge" leader in a crisis, and some people, perhaps those with low self-esteem or those who lack competence in the area of behavior required by the group, prefer to have the leader tell them what to do.

Leaders who use the *laissez-faire* style occupy the other polar extreme, in that they remain passive and uninvolved and allow the group to proceed on its own. Consequently, there is little group productivity, and conflicts between group members are usually quite apparent. However, sometimes the laissez-faire approach may be effective such as with the corporate leader who, at times, gives project teams almost complete freedom to experiment and innovate, or the caring parent or teacher who allows their offspring or students the freedom to fail in teaching them the lessons of accountability.

Those leaders who embrace the *democratic* style occupy the middle ground between the two extremes. Typically, they are effective regardless of whether the group is a family, a local organization or club, a major corporation, or any one of several other types. Participation in decision making is spread across the group, which heightens morale as a result of an increased sense among members that their ideas are appreciated. However, democratically run groups are much slower in responding to changing social conditions and are thus less efficient than authoritarian groups because of the time required to seek input from members. In addition, some groups, like military organizations in wartime, would probably be totally ineffective if they functioned democratically.

Leadership in Perspective   The most effective leaders, including the most effective teachers and parents, exhibit a rare blend of leadership types and styles that is part art and part science, but mainly craft developed and refined over many years of dutiful application. Such leaders are rarely found. They are those who possess the rare ability to integrate both types of leadership—task and socioemotional—and, given the situation, project any or a combination of the three leadership styles—authoritarian, laissez-faire, or democratic—in operating effectively with subordinates. This integrated model of leadership is portrayed in Figure 7-5.

You have learned throughout this chapter that the groups to which we belong play a crucial role in shaping our self-concept and in affecting our thoughts, feelings, world view, and actions both as individuals and as members of society. In our discussion, you were introduced to several different types of groups—physical aggregates, statistical categories, social categories, social groups, and formal organizations—along with their distinguishing characteristics. Of these, the largest emphasis was placed on social groups, the source of our most important group affiliations. In Chapter 8, we will next focus attention on other groups and structures that significantly impact our lives, formal organizations, and bureaucracy.

(Instrumental Group Purpose)		(Expressive Group Purpose)
Task Leaders ———————————	± ————————	**Socioemotional Leaders**
(Authoritarian style)	*(Democratic style)*	*(Laissez-faire style)*

Figure 7-5

The Leadership Continuum: An Integrated Model.
Leader Types, Group Purposes, and Leadership Styles

CHAPTER SUMMARY

1. There are four basic characteristics that are useful in distinguishing among different types of groups in society. One characteristic all groups possess is that of common attributes, which are used as group boundaries to distinguish members from nonmembers. Whether or not a given group has one or more of the other three characteristics—consciousness of kind, patterned social relations, and calculated formation—depends on what type it represents.

2. There are five basic types of groups, the most fundamental of which is the social group. The other four types consist of physical aggregates (crowds), statistical categories (groups designated for research and comparative purposes), social categories (those with visible or special characteristics like women over six feet tall or retired persons), and formal organizations (groups with planned practical goals). Given the importance of the social group, it remains the focus for most of the remaining chapter.

3. Social groups occur in two basic forms: primary groups and secondary groups. The primary group is a small group distinguished by personal, ongoing relationships between members. Our primary group relationships (e.g., our family or circle of best friends) are very important in that they serve as our basic source of emotional and social support. The qualities of primary group relationships include multidimensional relationships, continuous face-to-face contact, durability, trust, and informal social controls. Secondary groups, by comparison, involve relatively superficial and impersonal relations with various groupings of people. Relationships of this kind, which tend to be the most common form in modern societies, are one dimensional, nonpermanent, usually based on distrust, and make use of formal social controls.

4. The predominance of either primary or secondary group relationships is affected in large part by the way a given society is structured or organized. This is perhaps best explained and illustrated in the work of two late nineteenth-century European sociologists, Ferdinand Tönnies and Emile Durkheim. Tönnies, a German sociologist, is best known for his *gemeinschaft–gesellschaft* typology, in which he distinguished between the social organization of small village-focused societies (*gemeinschaft*) and large, urban industrial societies (*gesellschaft*). Because the *gemeinschaft* social system has a low level of material technology, common ancestry among inhabitants, tradition-based social positions, close-knit and long-term ties between members, and geographical stability, it fosters a social climate conducive to primary group relations. The *gesellschaft* society, with largely opposite characteristics, has a social structure more amenable to secondary group relations.

5. French sociologist Emile Durkheim was also interested in studying the relationship between social structure and the nature of social relations. He sought to discover and compare the nature of social order (solidarity) in simple, nonindustrial societies with that of modern industrial systems. He found that traditional nonindustrial societies had mechanical solidarity—the solidarity of resemblance—which was more conducive to primary group relations, while modern societies possessed organic solidarity—the solidarity of differences—which was better suited for secondary group relations.

6. Group dynamics is the systematic study of small-group processes. Basic principles of group interaction include the following: groups approach tasks in a three-step process, group behavior is norm based, interaction encourages friendship, initiative promotes status within the group, and group communication is affected by the positioning of people within the group, the ways in which we relate to groups as individuals, as well as the size of groups and the manner in which they function.

7. In terms of relating to groups, each of us perceives in-groups ("we" groups) with whom we feel a bond or a sense of connection. This personal identification promotes group solidarity and ethnocentrism. We also perceive out-groups ("they" groups) with whom we may feel a sense of rivalry or tension.

8. In addition, the size of a group plays an important role in group dynamics, a dyad (two person group) being much simpler in several respects than a triad (a three-person group). An illustration is provided (adult couple versus adult couple with child).

9. The focus or thrust of group behavior is affected by a variety of factors, including group purposes and leadership types and styles. Primary group relations usually involve an expressive group purpose (emotional benefit), while secondary group relations typically have an instrumental purpose (practical benefit). With regard to leadership, there are two basic types of leaders: those who are socioemotional in orientation (concerned with group morale) and those who are task-oriented (focused on getting the job done). Additionally, leaders tend to have a leadership style that may be authoritarian (high efficiency–low morale), democratic (low efficiency–high morale), or laissez-faire (low productivity–high conflict).

TERMS TO KNOW

calculated formation: the action taken by group members to organize together in pursuit of one or more specific, practical goals.

coalition: in the context of group dynamics, it is a a relationship formed when some group members align themselves against others.

collective conscience: in Durkheim's view, a state of mental and moral agreement among members of a society concerning basic norms and values.

common attributes: the characteristics members of a group share in common with one another.

consciousness of kind: the tendency of people to recognize others like themselves and, in many cases, to feel a common sense of identification or connection as a result.

dyad: a two person group.

expressive group purpose: the focus of relations in primary groups in which the main goal is the emotional benefit derived from participation as an end in itself.

formal organization: a group deliberately formed to pursue one or more specific practical goals.

gemeinschaft: Tönnies's term for a community-oriented society in which most social relations are personal, informal, and tend to be based on tradition.

gesellschaft: Tönnies' term for an urban, industrial society with impersonal and somewhat informal relations that tend to be based on contract.

group dynamics: the systematic study of small group processes.

in-group: a group a person belongs to or identifies with.

instrumental group purpose: the focus of relations in secondary groups in which the group is used as a means to an end to achieve a practical goal.

mechanical solidarity: Durkheim's term for the solidarity (cohesion) of resemblance characteristic of traditional nonindustrial societies.

networking: the conscious and planned cultivation of social networks to achieve personal or practical goals.

organic solidarity: Durkheim's term for the solidarity (cohesion) of differences found in modern complex societies.

out-group: a group a person does not belong to or identify with.

patterned social relations: a process by which group members influence the feelings, attitudes, and behavior of one another through personal social interaction.

physical aggregate: a type of group distinguished primarily by the physical proximity of its members (e.g., a crowd).

polar typology: a tool of analysis in which two dissimilar ideal types are placed at either end of a continuum for the purposes of comparison.

primary group: a small group characterized by personalized, ongoing relationships.

reference group: a group to which a person may or may not belong, which is used as a standard of comparison to evaluate his or her values, behavior, and goals.

secondary group: a relatively large collection of people with whom one has superficial and somewhat impersonal relations.

social category: a type of group distinguished by its members having one or more visible or otherwise identifiable special features or characteristics in common.

social distance: the degree of acceptance an individual feels toward those who belong to various groups to which he or she does not belong.

social group: a type of group consisting of people bound together by common interests and values in a definite pattern of social relations.

social networks: linkages maintained with specific types of people for the satisfaction of personal and practical needs.

social solidarity: Durkheim's term for social order and its fundamental causes.

socioemotional leaders: those who concentrate their energies on expressive group purposes aimed at promoting morale and harmony among members.

statistical category: a type of group not formed by the members themselves but by researchers for the purposes of social analysis.

task leaders: those focus their attention on instrumental group purposes aimed at reaching practical goals.

triad: a three-person group.

SUGGESTED READINGS

Cooley, C. H. 1956. *Social Organization: Human Nature and the Social Order.* New York: Free Press. Originally published in 1909). A classic discussion in this early text by Cooley on the primary group and its basic characteristics.

Goffman, E. 1963. *Behavior in Public Places.* New York: Free Press. A series of classic observations concerning the ways in which casual social encounters (secondary group relations) take place in contemporary urban society.

Janis, I. L., and L. Mann. 1977. *Decision Making.* New York: Free Press. A valuable resource that presents a thorough explanation of both sociological theory and research on the group decision making process.

Nye, J. L., and A. M. Brower (Eds.). 1996. *What's Social about Social Cognition?* Thousand Oaks, CA: Sage Publications. Readings and essays on social interaction patterns that occur at the microlevel of society, with emphasis on how boundaries of groups are established and maintained and how decision making in groups takes place.

Putnam, R. 2003. *Better Together: Restoring the American Community.* New York: Simon & Schuster. An analysis of the impact of new social linkages being created via the internet and other media sources that promise to bring back a sense of community (e.g., Craig'sList) and create new ways for people to meaningfully connect with each other.

Tönnies, F. 2003. *Community and Society.* New York: Dover Publications. Originally published in 1887 in German as *Gemeinschaft und Gellschaft.* Tönnies classic comparative societies and how their structural characteristics respectively affect the quality of social relations occurring within them.

PART THREE

Organizations, Rank, and Diversity

Formal Organizations and Bureaucracy

Terms to Know

authority	*goal displacement*	*protection of incompetence*
bottom-up decision making	*groupthink*	*rational-legal authority*
brainwashing	*hierarchical authority*	*ritualism*
bureaucracy	*informal structure*	*specialized division of labor*
careers	*iron law of oligarchy*	*technical competence*
charismatic authority	*mortification*	*total institution*
coercive organization	*Parkinson's law*	*traditional authority*
collectives	*Peter Principle*	*utilitarian organization*
conformity	*power*	*voluntary organization*
formal structure		

"In general, service in America stinks." The view reflected in this quote by Thomas J. Peters, prominent management consultant and coauthor of *In Search of Excellence*, was written in 1982. Yet according to many recent indicators and the observations of rank-and-file citizens who see the evidence all around them, conditions of service since then have deteriorated on many fronts. As an example, airlines today routinely overbook flights, charge customers a fee for each checked bag, and have dropped meal service on many routes. However, today, service in the broader sense has to do with the actions of many leaders of large-scale organizations and institutions, their core values, and their abandonment of the social contract and a service ideal in favor of furthering their individual careers and fortunes.

From a sociological, macro perspective, we currently are seeing the results of failed leadership based on flawed assumptions in several sectors of society. These visible and measurable results range from broken public school and health care systems to a failing social security system for the elderly, all of which are in dire need of reform.

To illustrate the scope of these systemic problems, we might examine some basic infrastructure issues. According to a 2009 report released by the American Society of Civil engineers, the United States gets a grade of "D" for the state of its infrastructure. One-third of America's major roads and highways are substandard and in need of repair. This contributes to Americans sitting more than four billion hours in traffic each year, which costs drivers sixty-seven billion dollars annually in added operating and repair costs. In addition, one-fourth of all bridges are structurally unsound or obsolete, aging water mains and pipes lose seven billion gallons per day due to leaks, and America's levees are operated with a "patch and pray" mindset. Other

© RENE JANSA, 2009. USE UNDER LICENSE FROM SHUTTERSTOCK, INC.

Many of us have regular contact with large-scale organizations and bureaucracies in our jobs, community activities, and at school.

critical elements of infrastructure—aviation, dams, hazardous waste, schools, and transit—also received "D" ratings. In summarizing the society's report, executive director Patrick Natale said of America's infrastructure crisis: "We haven't had the leadership or will to take action on it. The bottom line is that a failing infrastructure cannot support a thriving economy" (CNN, Wed. January 28, 2009).

Despite these pressing problems, Americans appreciate the many aspects of "service" and the life-style that the service economy has made possible. Although many may look back with fondness at "the good old days" when life was less complicated and relationships were more personal, few would actually elect to go back to a society devoid of air conditioning, television, cell phones, the internet, and the other benefits of modern society. Our occupational progress and ability to provide for our families are greatly influenced by how well we understand and perform in large-scale organizations. In fact, those with little understanding of how their society and the large-scale organizations within it operate are in a poor position to be very successful.

Given the tremendous impact that formal organizations have on modern societies today, it is important to understand (1) the nature of organizations and their different types, (2) the historical development of social authority and how it is manifested in large organizations today, (3) the development and nature of bureaucracy, (4) the manner in which large-scale organizations operate as formal social systems, and (5) some basic problems related to organizations and bureaucracy. This chapter, therefore, will build of the material presented in Chapter 7 and discuss these basic issues in some detail.

TYPES OF FORMAL ORGANIZATIONS

As you will recall from Chapter 7, a *formal organization* is a group deliberately formed to pursue one or more specific, practical goals. Formed from secondary social groups, formal organizations typically possess all four of the basic group characteristics discussed preciously: common attributes, consciousness of kind, patterned social relations, and calculated formation. Thus constituted, such organizations form much of the foundation for modern society today.

Sociologists have offered several classifications of formal organizations (Parsons, 1956; Blau and Scott, 1962; Perrow, 1967; Hass and Drabek, 1973; Etzioni, 1975). Of these, the typology devised by Amitai Etzioni (1975) is one of the most useful. It clearly shows (1) the diverse manner in which complex organizations are structured and how they function, (2) the reasons that people participate in various types of organizations, and (3) the types and degrees of control that organizations assert over members. Etzioni lists three types of organizations—voluntary, utilitarian, and coercive—that act as a general umbrella under which most formal organizations can be placed. In addition, Erving Goffman's analysis of the total institution as an extreme form of coercive organization provides additional depth and insight.

Voluntary Organizations

An organization people join freely as a part-time activity because they agree with its values, norms, and goals is a **voluntary organization**. Common examples include civic and fraternal organizations like Moose, Kiwanis, and Rotary clubs; professional associations

© ROBERT KYLLO, 2009. USE UNDER LICENSE FROM SHUTTERSTOCK, INC.

Many Americans belong to one or more voluntary organizations that they join out of interest and sometimes for fun.

such the American Bar Association and American Sociological Association; and personal interest organizations such as those related to hobbies, political orientation, religion, age, background, and even gender (for example, the Boy Scouts and Daughters of the American Revolution).

In America historically, people have tended to be joiners, with about two out of every three holding membership in at least one voluntary organization. This orientation for joining sometimes is socialized into children early in life as they participate in Little League ball, Girl Scouts, and a number of other organizational activities. We learn to participate in voluntary organizations in our spare time perhaps because they address interests and fulfill needs not met through our day-to-day encounters with family and friends. Consequently, they represent very specialized affiliations that tend to meet specialized needs. According to Etzioni, this type of organization involves the least amount of control (*low control*) over the lives of participants. The influence that is exerted is due to *normative power* (peer pressure), effective only because members' values are in agreement with the norms and goals of the organization.

Voluntary organizations are distinguished in other ways as well. First, because they consist of like-minded people, they tend to be organized along class lines. Both Pentecostals and Presbyterians worship as Christians, but their churches are organized very differently, and their memberships tend to reflect different socioeconomic strata of society, particularly in regard to types of occupations and levels and types of education. Income can also be a consideration. Relatively few members of the upper class participate in bowling or belong to camping clubs. Likewise, few working-class people join golf and polo clubs because sports such as bowling are much less expensive. Second, large and well-organized voluntary organizations often affect public policy. Some notable examples include the National Rifle Association (NRA), Mothers Against Drunk Driving (MADD), and the National Association for the Advancement of Colored People (NAACP) (Table 8-1).

TABLE 8-1	Etzioni's Three Types of Organizations and Selected Characteristics	
TYPE OF ORGANIZATION	**LEVEL OF CONTROL ASSERTED OVER MEMBERS**	**FORM OF POWER USED**
Voluntary Organization	Low	Normative Power
Utilitarian Organization	Medium	Remunerative Power
Coercive Organization	High	Coercive Power

Source: Etzioni, A. (1975). *A Comparative Analysis of Complex Organizations.* New York: Free Press.

Utilitarian Organizations

A **utilitarian organization** is an organization in which people participate for practical gain or profit. Examples include businesses, corporations, and professional organizations such as brokerage, law, and consulting firms. While people are not coerced into affiliating with them, participation is not strictly voluntary either. Most adult members of modern society today feel some pressure to work with or for one or more utilitarian organizations in order to provide a living for themselves and their families. As a result, these organizations fall somewhere in the middle of the continuum, between the extremes of voluntarism on one end and coercion on the other. Etzioni found that these organizations can exert a fair amount of control (*medium control*) over a person's life through the use of *remunerative power,* the ability to reward a person in a significant, practical way. Particularly in difficult economic times when jobs are not easy to obtain, the "tyranny of the paycheck," whether real or imagined, can significantly influence a person's behavior and life as a whole.

Coercive Organizations

An organization in which people participate due to force or the threat of force is a **coercive organization**. Conscriptive military systems, prisoner-of-war camps, prisons, custodial mental institutions, some monastic religious communities and sects, and even elementary schools serve as representative examples. Those placed or retained in this type of organizational environment as a requirement, against their will, or as a result of brainwashing have few if any options and little if any freedom of action. In Etzioni's analysis, these organizations exert *high to complete control* over their members through the use of *coercive power.* This can range from notes of disapproval sent home to parents of elementary school children, to psychological and physical torture, starvation, and even death in some prisoner-of-war camps.

Total Institutions: Mortification and Brainwashing

Erving Goffman's (1961) term for an extreme form of coercive organization that exerts control 24-hours per day over participants is a **total institution**. In his research, he found that, although these organizations exist for different purposes, they tend to have one characteristic in common. They encapsulate their "recruits" or "inmates" by cutting them off from the outside world. Then they resocialize their new members through **mortification**, a process in which a person's old identity is stripped away through a systematic program of degradation and humiliation, and replaced with a new self more suitable to the organization (Table 8-2).

Techniques Used in the Mortification Process   Mortification is often made possible by *degradation rituals*, procedures and activities intentionally designed to emotionally disorient, program, and/or shock new members into submitting to the demands of the new environment. Army recruits may be cursed at by their sergeant's, made to do demeaning and self-effacing tasks, and may be called only "recruit" in most instances. Prison inmates are stripped, deloused, subject to strip searches and periodic shakedowns, and often are referred to only by number. And members of some religious sects are placed in a very isolated, insular environment, often at a rural ranch or compound where they are wrapped in a psychological cocoon of "love."

Mortification is also facilitated through a variety of environmental devices aimed at destroying the individuality of people; they can then be easily "programmed" and thus controlled (Table 8-2). First, the organization maintains *twenty-four hours a day control* over inmates (or recruits) and participants are monitored on a constant, ongoing basis. Second, *members are kept in isolation* from the outside world. In prisons and mental hospitals, this is accomplished by walls and other physical barriers, whereas in POW camps this may also include the monitoring and censoring of mail. During the Korean conflict in the early 1950s, North Korean captors, as part of their mortification program, did not allow warm, reassuring letters from loved ones back home to "get through" to American prisoners of war. However, all the bad news—the "Dear John" letters, divorce notices, and news of family illnesses and death—were delivered.

Mortification is aided in other ways as well. Some coercive organizations use the *confiscation of personal effects* such as clothing and jewelry to discourage individuality and maximize efficient control over participants. In some religious orders all priests or nuns or believers must wear identical habits or uniform clothing with the same or similar colors and styles. In the military all recruits wear identical uniforms, and in most prisons and county jails all inmates must wear the same type of clothing. Life in a coercive organization also involves *comprehensive scheduling*. Members are told when to do almost everything—eat, sleep, work, recreate, bathe—so that all important decisions concerning how their time is spent are taken out of their hands. Violations of any kind are met with *swift and*

TABLE 8-2	**Techniques Used in the Mortification Process**
	Degradation rituals
	Twenty-four hours a day control over participants
	Isolation of members
	Confiscation of personal effects
	Comprehensive scheduling
	Swift and negative sanctions

effective negative sanctions such as solitary confinement, rigorous exercise, missing meals, or doing penance.

One Result of Mortification: Brainwashing

In some extreme cases, the use of these devices can result in **brainwashing**, a process of almost complete thought control in which the victim's existing values and beliefs are made useless and replaced with those desired by the agent of influence. This most extreme form of mortification renders the individual psychologically helpless and dependent on captors or "leaders" for satisfaction of basic emotional and psychological needs. Peers who have already been brainwashed are often enlisted to apply pressure and make the individual feel even more worthless and guilty. Then, when the victim begins to exhibit the "right" attitudes, rewards including praise, encouragement, and affection are given (Muller, 1974). Although brainwashing can occur in most any type of total institution—such as with American prisoners of war (POWs) who were culturally "reprogrammed" by their North Korean captors during the Korean conflict—most recent examples tend to be from extremist religious sects, two of which are to be briefly discussed.

The "People's Temple" Sect: Mass Suicide

A prominent example of brainwashing is evident in the story of the "People's Temple" sect that ended tragically in 1978. This group, affiliated with the Disciples of Christ, was headed by a mentally disturbed but charismatic "bishop" named Jim Jones who appealed mainly to the poor and undereducated. Alienated from society and fearing that secular authorities were plotting against his group, he ultimately moved his flock of followers to the Central American jungles of Guyana where they founded a settlement called Jonestown.

Once there, Jones and his close disciples confiscated all passports and kept his followers isolated from contact with their relatives and friends in the United States, who became increasingly worried. During the last several months, he kept these people preoccupied with religious activities and rituals and had them write him letters of self-deprecation

Brainwashing can result in tragedy, as illustrated by the 900 followers of charismatic religious leader Jim Jones, all of whom participated in mass suicide in 1978.

addressed to "Father" or "Daddy." After an investigative visit by outsiders from America, some of whom were murdered as they were trying to depart, Jones had his followers prepare large quantities of Kool-Aid to which was added cyanide. Believing that Jones either talked with God or was the messiah himself, his nine hundred followers, on orders from Jones, drank the lethal Kool-Aid, lay down in the grass in fairly neat groups and rows, and died, many with their arms wrapped around one another. Jones himself died from a gunshot wound to the head, apparently administered by a loyal follower under his direction, who subsequently committed suicide as well (Reiterman, 1982).

The "Yearning for Zion" (YFZ) Polygamist Sect   During April, 2008, in one of the largest child custody cases in American history, Texas Child Protective Services officials, assisted by law enforcement agencies including the Texas Rangers, conducted a massive raid of a seventeen-hundred acre ranch in isolated El Dorado, Texas. There, they took over four hundred children into protective custody arguing that a spin-off sect from the Church of Jesus Christ of Latter Day Saints called "Yearning for Zion" were sanctioning the assigning and reassigning of wives by "revelation." This alleged practice included underage girls who were being "married," raped (according to Texas law), and impregnated by assigned "husbands," some as old as their fifties. At an unprecedented court hearing that took two days and involved over three hundred fifty defense attorneys, a state District Judge ordered DNA testing on all members—children and adults—of the sect until family identities and parental rights could be sorted out and children's rights, including under-aged girls (some of whom were pregnant) could be ensured (Langford, 2008). Upon appeal, two months later in June the Supreme Court of Texas affirmed the ruling by the Third Court of Appeals which vacated the actions of the judge, and ordered the children returned to their families. In the appellate rulings, Child Protective Services was mandated to investigate each case of alleged abuse on a case-by-case basis (Holusha and Johnson, 2008)

FORMS OF SOCIAL AUTHORITY

The power and authority of their leaders significantly affect the functioning of both small groups and formal organizations. Power and authority, as we will see, come in different forms. The juvenile gang leader, for instance, has little in common with the high school teacher, although they may affect the behavior of the same people. In similar fashion, a European monarch, an American president, and a terrorist such as Osama Bin Laden lead the people of their countries or their followers in very different ways.

The Nature and Types of Power

Power is the ability to influence or control the behavior of others with or without their consent. Leaders everywhere exert power by actively influencing if not actually determining how group and organizational decisions are made and the particular forms they take. Some are very direct and blunt about how they exercise their prerogatives, while others are quite indirect and subtle. Leaders can also use power to guide gently or to dominate totally; they may be kind or cruel, noble or dishonorable, lawful or unlawful, competent or incompetent.

Types of Power   There are five basic sources of power which, in turn, result in five corresponding power types: reward, coercion, referent power, expert power, and legitimate power (French and Raven, 1968). These power types may be used singly or in combination with one another. The first mentioned, *reward power,* results from the ability of a person to provide others with something of value that they desire. The employer, for instance, rewards the employee with a paycheck and the incentive for a bonus or promotion if the individual performs accordingly.

The opposite of reward power is *coercive power,* which derives from the ability of an individual to punish those whose behavior does not meet expected standards. Employers have this type of power as well and can freeze wages, demote, or fire an employee who performs below acceptable levels. The arrest powers of police, the prosecution powers of governmental agencies and officials such as district attorneys, and the legislative power of elected officials provide additional illustrations.

Referent power stems from the ability of a person to personally attract or appeal to others. The source of attraction may be that of parent figure, sex object, mentor or other form of personal influence or inspiration. The leader of the "People's Temple" sect, Jim Jones, for instance, had a magnetic personality that drew hundreds of followers and gave him ultimate control over their lives. In addition, athletes, television and movie stars, and other well known personalities are sometimes paid millions of dollars to make advertisements for the selling of commercial products or to provide endorsements for products ranging from beauty aids to automobiles to golf clubs and other sports equipment. In addition, such personalities also may, at times, promote causes or political candidates running for office.

Expert power results from people's belief that a particular type of individual possesses more knowledge than they do in a certain area of expertise. Doctors, lawyers, teachers, accountants, and other professionals have this type of power because of the respect accorded them by those they serve, usually based on formal credentials they hold and/or expertise they possess.

The final type of power, *legitimate power,* is usually referred to as *authority.* It is derived from people's belief that it is right and proper to do what a certain individual or organization directs them to do. As such, legitimate power forms the basis for formal authority and often contains elements of one or a combination of the other power types just mentioned.

Authority and Its Basic Types

Authority is legitimated power generally recognized and supported by those over whom it is exercised. It is formal or official power held by certain individuals, organizations, and their representatives. A tribal chief, a dictator, and a king all have authority, as do governmental agencies and their representatives, corporations and their managers, and schools and their administrators and teachers.

Max Weber (1922, 1968), one of the early masters of sociological thought, died unexpectedly of pneumonia in 1920 before he could finish his most ambitious book, *Economy and Society* (Coser, 1971, p. 242). The manuscript, which was published posthumously in 1922, included his classic analysis of authority and bureaucratic organization. In this work, Weber developed a typology of three forms of legitimate authority: charismatic, traditional, and rational–legal authority.

© GEORGIJEVIC MIROSLAV, 2009. USE UNDER LICENSE FROM SHUTTERSTOCK, INC.

Power comes in several forms. What type of power is being exhibited by this performer?

Charismatic Authority Historically, some of the simplest societies have been characterized by **charismatic authority.** This authority form is based on the commonly accepted belief by followers that the leader possesses special qualities or unique characteristics. Cultures and organizations that subscribe to this authority system have participants who "believe" the charismatic leader to have a special destiny, unusual vision, divine grace, or special heroic qualities that, in most cases, are "self-evident." Weber elaborates as follows:

> The charismatic leader gains and maintains authority solely by proving his strength in life. If he wants to be a prophet, he must perform miracles; if he wants to be a war lord, he must perform heroic deeds; Above all, however, his divine mission must "prove" itself in that those who faithfully surrender to him must fare well. If they do not fare well, he is obviously not the master sent by the gods (1946, p. 249).

The term *"charisma"* originates from the Greek language, meaning "gifts of grace," and sometimes is used in reference to divinity. Both historically and in recent times, some charismatic leaders have been regarded as divine or representatives of God or the gods. Examples include Buddha, Jesus, the Pope in Rome, and even destructive "prophets" such as Osama Bin Laden and certain Muslim Mullahs, who are radical Islamic extremists. In other instances, followers have believed in the heroic qualities of their leaders, as illustrated by Alexander the Great, George Washington, Napoleon, and, more recently, Theodore Roosevelt and Franklin Roosevelt. Those who have derived their large following due to a magnetic, forceful personality or special vision included, during the twentieth century, individuals such as Adolf Hitler, Winston Churchill, Martin Luther King, Jr., and John F. Kennedy. Most recently, President Barack Obama has exemplified magnetic, charismatic qualities by his oratorical skill and youthful, energetic appeal.

In simple societies of the past especially, the greatest disadvantage associated with charismatic authority was instability and the problem of succession. Who was to take over the responsibilities of leadership when the charismatic leader became too old and feeble to lead, or died? How was the new leader to be chosen? Beyond the charismatic leader himself—who alone made decisions, ruled on disputes, and provided order solely by virtue of his presence—there were no traditions, laws, or rules for guidance. Although many societies tried to work out a succession system, societal decline, chaos, and even civil war between competing factions often marked the period between effective charismatic regimes. This dilemma was finally resolved historically when the alleged divine grace of a leader became institutionalized into a family bloodline and stable traditions. This *routinization of charisma*, as Weber termed it, marked the transition from charismatic authority to other forms. This process set the stage for the emergence of a second authority type, traditional authority.

Traditional Authority   Although societies marked by charismatic authority may be routinized into either traditionalism or bureaucratization (Gerth and Mills, 1946), historically, in most cases they evolved into traditional authority, a premodern form of leadership. **Traditional authority** is a type of authority based on followers' acceptance of the legitimacy contained in long-standing traditions and customs. With this type of leadership, the concept of monarchy developed, and many kings and queens, by virtue of accepted custom and tradition, ruled by "divine right." Because of the accepted belief that the monarch possessed charismatic grace and was thus the intermediary between God or the gods and the people, his or her authority was solidified and rarely if ever questioned.

Succession under traditional authority was established through accepted custom. Most societies historically were characterized by patriarchy, or rule by males. At the macrolevel, a royal line of succession was established by custom so that, in many societies, the firstborn son inherited the throne and was given total authority to rule for life. At the microlevel, the authority structure of the family mirrored that of the government. The father was the "ruler" of the family and, on his death, his sons inherited his lands or business, with the firstborn son, in some societies, entitled to most or all of the estate. Women were usually accorded "second-class citizen" status and played only a minor role in decision making.

Few people living under a traditional system of authority questioned such laws and customs, which were rarely if ever written down. The people simply accepted them because that was what they were accustomed to doing. Little has changed in today's traditional societies, and people still revere old customs, which are seen as "normal" because "things have always been done this way." While in a sense this represents an irrational system of authority based largely on an accident of birth, it nonetheless has provided societies with a means of stability and continuity not possible under the charismatic system.

Rational–Legal Authority   Under traditional authority, there were no guarantees that a newly crowned monarch or a son with a newly inherited farm or business would be competent or capable of learning the responsibilities that lay ahead. While this did not appear to be an insurmountable problem before the nineteenth century, the industrial revolution brought with it a different economic system that required a rational system of authority based on expertise.

Weber named this **rational–legal authority**, a type of authority based on the legitimacy of a formal set of laws and rules that define the scope of a leader's rights and responsibilities. With the substitution of a system of laws for one based on rulers, loyalty and obedience, authority shifted away from personalities to a system of rationally determined procedures. This became necessary during the 1800s because of the tremendous

complexities involved with the emerging factory system, an increasingly specialized division of labor, and a cash economy.

Rational–legal authority is the cornerstone of modern bureaucracy and social organization today. As a system, it is rational in the sense that specialized positions occupied by workers, professionals, and management officials are carefully planned and specified in terms of the types of education and training called for and the levels of performance required. It is also legal in the sense that the state and political bodies within it often set, monitor, and enforce the standards of performance required of those who occupy particular positions. Corporations and other organizations that employ various workers and specialists also have their own "legal" requirements in terms of company policies and procedures, position requirements, and job descriptions.

Women in modern rational–legal systems often find themselves relatively free from the tyranny of patriarchy so characteristic of earlier charismatic and traditional systems. Particularly in societies like the United States, they are increasingly able to compete with men for high status positions on a relatively equal basis because they too can acquire recognized and approved credentials.

During the last hundred years, the United States has steadily become more rational–legal in terms of the way authority is structured and work is preformed. Physicians, lawyers, teachers, beauticians, electricians, police officers, and many other individuals must meet both educational standards and legal licensing or certification requirements in order to function in their respective occupations. As we move into and through the twenty-first century, this trend continues to become increasingly pronounced. Therefore, those without specialized skills and a positive orientation toward continued education, which are both needed in today's ever-changing economic and social environment, may find themselves joining the ranks of dislocated workers.

Types of Authority in Perspective   As we reflect on these three types of authority—charismatic, traditional, and rational–legal—it is important to note that Weber saw these concepts as *ideal types* (see Chapters 2 and 7). They represent conceptual models that are useful in assessing and comparing phenomena as they actually exist. In most societies, a single type of authority tends to be dominant. However, many social systems and institutions represent composites of two or even all three forms of authority. The United Kingdom, for instance, is officially a monarchy with established and revered customs and traditions that specify, among other things, how succession will take place. Nonetheless, its authority today is grounded in basically rational–legal institutions related to government and the economy. As another illustration, the Catholic Church is presided over by a Pope, a charismatic leader who "sits in the chair of Peter," a disciple of Jesus, another charismatic leader. Yet this religion contains traditional elements that have been passed down for close to two thousand years. However, the Catholic Church also contains rational–legal elements—it controls billions of dollars in assets that necessitate management and coordination by a small army of accountants, business and investment professionals, lawyers, and even architects, construction engineers, and art and conservation experts.

THE NATURE OF BUREAUCRACY

In Chapter 6 (Social Organization), the concept of bureaucracy was first introduced. **Bureaucracy** is a form of social organization in which the work of participants in large-scale organizations is rationally coordinated by professionally trained managers. In this regard, bureaucracy

> . . . is not a new phenomenon. It existed in simple forms thousands of years ago in Egypt and Rome. But the trend toward bureaucratization has greatly accelerated during the last century. In contemporary society bureaucracy has become a dominant institution, indeed the institution that epitomizes the modern era. Unless we understand this institutional form, we cannot understand the social life of today (Blau and Meyer, 1971, p. 10).

Michels' Iron Law of Oligarchy

Robert Michels (1876–1936), a friend and colleague of Max Weber, argued that bureaucracy is incompatible with democracy and, therefore, is oligarchic in nature. In his classic book *Political Parties* published in 1911, he set forth his **iron law of oligarchy**, which states that the power in organizations invariably becomes concentrated in the hands of a few people who use it to further their self-interests. Michels studied emerging socialist political parties and labor unions in Europe. He found that though they stressed broad-based, democratic participation by rank-and-file members, the result was a monopoly of power by a few, who it appeared, paid little attention to the opinions of the masses.

Michels sought to explain this apparent contradiction by examining the innerworkings of large formal organizations. He found that as a practical matter, the extremely complex and diversified nature of such organizations required a hierarchical structure of authority with day-to-day decision making and control placed in the hands of a group of managerial elites. Even when ultimate authority was held by the rank-and-file membership who were able to attend periodic meetings and vote on designated issues, those in the upper levels of management held certain advantages that allowed them to consolidate their power and ultimately control the organization.

Concentrated Energy by Leaders: Information Control and the Illusion of Inclusion

First of all, in the political parties and labor unions that Michels examined, leaders were full-time paid employees and elected officials. Therefore, they could devote their full energies to running the organization, unlike the general membership who participated only on a part-time voluntary basis in monitoring the ways in which the organization operated and was managed.

Leaders also had complete access and control over all information concerning the organization. This allowed them to manipulate the rank-and-file members by deciding what and how much information to provide to and what to withhold from them in order to further their own interests. Control over information gave upper management the ability to craft propaganda with which to control the perception of the organization and important issues by the general membership. This, combined with other political devices—such as speech making, disseminating information through newsletters, setting times and agendas for general meetings, and designing committees and other activities for "active" members who tended to curry favor by mirroring the wishes of those in power—gave management almost full if not total control.

Needed Actions by the Rank-and-File to Gain Inclusion and Power

Add to this the fact that democracy can be a cumbersome process in large-scale organizations, Michels found that active participation by general members requires an independent assessment and commitment to what is best for the organization. These requirements, coupled with the members' willingness to attend meetings, gain some control over setting agendas, research important issues, and demonstrate the courage and initiative to have their voices heard, are some of the essential ingredients necessary for genuine democracy and resulting inclusion.

The Nature of the Rank-and-File

Instead, Michels (1966) found among the organizations he examined that members tended to be apathetic regarding active participation. They were more than willing to delegate all responsibilities to elected officials. This apathy, combined with their general lack of education and sophistication, part-time involvement because of other life priorities, and their tendency to blindly trust and respect those in authority, resulted in what Michels called "the incompetency of the masses." As a result, his most succinct assessment of bureaucracy was this brief statement: "Who says organization says oligarchy" (p. 365).

Weber's Ideal Model of Bureaucracy

Max Weber (1922, 1968) disagreed with the position of his friend and colleague Robert Michels that bureaucracies were, by nature, oligarchic. He took the position that many could be, and in some instances were, democratic in nature. Weber asserted that if an organization is structured properly, advancement within it is indeed democratic in that promotion to top-level positions is based on competence and merit. He was concerned, however, by the way some large formal organizations he observed were being managed. As a result, he developed a model based on his assessment of what constituted the ideal bureaucracy (Table 8-3). Bureaucracy as a pervasive form of social organization emerged with the industrial revolution and the corresponding necessity for rational–legal authority. *Rationalization,* therefore, in Weber's thinking, represented the dominant force in modern society, not only in the present but in the foreseeable future as well.

In Weber's view, the ideal bureaucracy contains the following characteristics.

1. ***Specialized Division of Labor.*** For maximum efficiency, Weber argued, there must be a **specialized division of labor**, a process in which participants in large-scale organizations are assigned positions that center on specific, specialized tasks. By dividing work into small, specialized tasks, the greatest output can be generated. For instance, if the only automobiles available for purchase were hand-crafted like the Rolls Royce or Ferrari, most of us would be riding bicycles. However, given the efficiency of mass production, most of us can enjoy a higher standard of living by purchasing vehicles—new or used—that were produced on a factory assembly line.

2. ***Hierarchical Authority.*** It is not enough that tasks be specialized. They must be managed or coordinated as well. In this regard, Weber stressed three key characteristics of what others would come to call "the managerial pyramid" or "organizational chart." He saw the ideal organization as one involving **hierarchical authority**, a process in which "offices" or positions in an organization are arranged vertically in terms of authority and responsibility.

   Such a vertical "chain of command," Weber argued, must possess at three organizational elements if the organization is to operate effectively. First, *the higher the position in the organization, the greater should be the area of jurisdiction.* By "jurisdiction," Weber meant both authority and responsibility. In a properly functioning organization, he asserted, bureaucratic officials are accountable to the person directly above them in authority and are responsible for the performance of others

TABLE 8-3 Weber's Ideal Model of Bureaucracy

1. A specialized division of labor
2. Hierarchical authority
3. Written rules
4. Impartial performance of duties
5. Reward based on technical competence
6. Careers

"I almost fell off the treadmill."

below them in the organization. To carry out such responsibility effectively, each official must have the necessary amount and type of authority to get the job done. Second, *the authority of each official must be clearly defined and limited in scope* so that duplication of effort and avoidance of responsibility will not occur. In essence, what he was discussing here was the need for each official to have a written and clearly defined job description. In addition, *authority must be positional*, not personal. It is rational–legal in that requirements and duties accrue to the position and not the person placed in it. The individual who occupies it may come and go, but the position will remain and be perpetuated.

3. **Written Rules.** Management of the bureaucracy is based on a system of written policies and procedures. These rules of operation are permanently recorded and remain fairly stable. They provide the formal structure within which the very complex and diversified activities conducted by the organization can be managed and coordinated smoothly. This way, operation of the organization can be focused with everyone "pulling in the same direction." The alternative, which Weber observed personally in some organizations he examined, is a situation in which one part of the organization is operating at cross purposes from the organization as a whole, primarily by being out of touch or "operating in the dark." Consequently, Weber noted, such organizations may operate in a climate in which "one hand doesn't know what the other hand is doing."

4. *Impartial Performance of Duties.* In contrast to the conduct of authority in non-industrial societies, in which relationships in groups and organizations are based largely on inheritance and personal favor, the bureaucratic official is ideally neutral and attempts to treat everyone impartially and fairly. Personal feelings are not allowed to prejudice the manner in which the official administers his or her position. Subordinates are to be treated solely on the basis of how well they perform their jobs. In Weber's words, the official operates in "a spirit of formalistic impersonality . . . without hatred or passion and hence without affection or enthusiasm" (Gerth and Mills, 1946, p. 340).

5. *Rewards Based on Technical Competence.* Weber was adamant in stressing the importance of rewarding only technical qualifications and performance. To accomplish this, *objective measures* are to be used both in hiring people and in judging their performance. In the bureaucracy, it is assumed that trained individuals are more likely to perform their jobs well than are those whose positions, like those in nonindustrial societies, are based largely on personality, political favors, family ties, or personal friendship. In Weber's view, people should be allocated to positions purely on the basis of **technical competence**, and rewards (placement and promotion) should be based on formal education, training, experience, and job performance. These four elements together comprise the essential ingredients of technical competence in Weber's model of bureaucracy.

6. *Careers.* In Weber's assessment, those in the middle to upper levels of an organization have careers, not jobs. **Careers** are positions held by managerial and professional officials through which, in exchange for loyal and adequate performance, extended employment and opportunities for advancement are provided. In a career position, the official is paid *a salary instead of wages.* Under a salary arrangement, an organization purchases competence rather than a certain amount of work as measured by an hourly wage. The career official is also provided with *a distinct degree of social esteem* by the bureaucracy. As a person moves up through the ranks, esteem is increased as measured by several indicators, many of them concrete and visible. They include, in addition to salary and fringe benefits, such "perks" as titles, expense accounts, company cars, corner offices, etc. Finally, the career path of the bureaucrat is made possible through *promotion by superior officials.* An individual's record of performance is periodically examined, and, if it is found to be acceptable according to predetermined performance benchmarks, he or she may qualify for advancement within the organization. Normally, promotion for career officials would require two or more superior officials in the organization to jointly provide their approval.

Weber's Model in Perspective Weber sought to explain how bureaucracy could best be used to "rationalize" human societies. He asserted that widespread bureaucracy was an inevitable outgrowth of the industrial revolution. However, he also expressed serious concern about its potential for misuse and harm. Nonetheless, he also felt that it possessed "technical superiority over any other form of organization" (1946, p. 214). His model represented an attempt to show how bureaucracy could be most efficiently and effectively harnessed to serve humankind and, in the process, improve the quality of life for all.

Weber has not been without his critics. Some have argued that while he gave a classic and penetrating analysis to the formal side of bureaucracy, he overlooked the importance of the informal or human side of large formal organizations. Others note that Weber's bureaucratic model is not the only rational way to organize large-scale organizations (Parsons, 1947; Gouldner, 1954; Blau and Scott, 1962). Alternatives, including the Japanese system, may function just as well, given different cultural contexts, goals, and technologies.

Criticisms aside, Weber's contributions represent a pioneering benchmark in the analysis of large-scale organizations. His bureaucratic model is still taught to those majoring in business and management in colleges and universities around the world. Indeed, most large formal organizations in the United States still reflect several of Weber's characteristics, and the trend is toward more bureaucracy rather than less. If recent growth in government and trends in the corporate sector toward increased consolidations are any indication, the twenty-first century promises to be even more "bureaucratic" than previous ones.

Conformity

Conformity is behavior that is in agreement with the norms of society or one of its smaller structural elements. As with other types of groups, bureaucratic organizations can place a great deal of pressure on participants to conform through the use of both formal and informal mechanisms for social control called "sanctions" (Chapters 4 and 6). In formal organizations, this pressure to conform can occur at all levels, from the most superficial interactions of people in their formal work settings to the behavior of those at the highest levels of decision making.

Conformity in Formal Work Settings
The extent to which individuals may succumb to group pressure is well documented. Work-related conformity in organizational settings can occur, first of all, as a result of pressure from peers.

The Asch Experiments
In a series of classic experiments, Soloman Asch (1955) tested college students to see how susceptible they were to group pressure. The research subjects were told that they would participate in groups of seven to nine people in which a series of fifteen trials would be conducted to measure visible perception. Each trial involved the members of a group being shown two cards placed next to each other. Then each group participant was asked by the researchers to compare the visual image or images on Card A with those on Card B and announce verbally to the group the correct answer. What the actual research subject was not told was that the other members of the research group were paid stooges who were in on the experiment (Figure 8-1).

As the experiment got underway, the research confederates gave the correct answers as they had been told to do. The research subject, of course, gave the right answer as well, and the votes were unanimous. Then, midway through the trials, the other group members all started giving the wrong answers and did so for several trials. For instance, in one trial, Card A had a single vertical line, Card B had three vertical lines, and the task was to choose the line on Card B that was the same length as the one on the other card (Figure 8-1). The paid students all gave the same wrong answer (as they had been instructed to do). Asch found that in the trials involving the wrong answers given by the rest of the group, the naive students (research subjects) agreed with the wrong answer thirty-seven percent of the time. This experiment demonstrated to a significant degree the power of peer pressure.

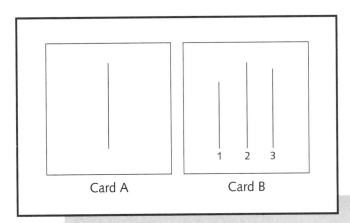

Figure 8-1

Comparison Cards in the Asch Experiments. How would you react if everyone in your group agreed that line 1 or line 3 on Card B matched the length of the line on Card A? Would you go along with the group, or express disagreement even under peer pressure?

Source: Adapted from Asch, S. 1965. Effects of group pressure upon the modification and distortion of judgments. In H. Proshansky and B. Seidenberg, eds. *Basic Studies in Psychology*, 393–401. New York: Holt, Rinehart and Winston.

When Asch interviewed the actual research subjects a few days later, most reported that they felt anxious and uncomfortable but went along with the group in order not to cause trouble or stand out. However, some claimed that they gave honest answers based on what they actually saw. For these people, it seemed that the group pressure they experienced was so strong that it caused them to not see what was plainly evident. But the larger issue is this: If such a large proportion of people can be pressured by total strangers into compliance, or be beguiled into doubting the evidence seen with their own eyes in simple matching tests, think of the influence on behavior that might be generated if they had ongoing contact with fellow participants in large-scale organizations at work, at school, or on the job.

Milgram's Organization-Placed Experiments   Some insight into the implications of the previous statement is provided by the controversial yet revealing experiments conducted by social psychologist Stanley Milgram during the 1960s. The research question he sought to answer was this: How far can people be pressured to go in their behavior when instructed to perform certain tasks by an authority figure within a certain group or organizational environment?

Specifically, Milgram structured experiments to find out how much pain, as measured by electric shock, people would be willing to inflict on others if ordered to do so by an authority figure. The research subjects, who were paid for their participation, were led to believe that the experiments had to do with the effect of punishment on memory. Milgram (1965) gives the following description of the procedures he used:

> A rigged drawing is held so that the naive subject is always the teacher, and the accomplice becomes the learner. The learner is taken into an adjacent room and strapped into an "electric chair."
>
> The naive subject is told that it is his task to teach the learner a list of paired . . . [terms], to test him on the list, and to administer punishments whenever the learner errs in the test. Punishment takes the form of electric shock, delivered to the learner by means of a shock

generator controlled by the naive subject. The teacher is instructed to increase the intensity of the electric shock one step on the generator on each error. The learner, according to the plan, provides many wrong answers, so that, before long the naive subject must give him the strongest shock on the generator. Increases in shock level are met by increasingly insistent demands from the learner that the experiment be stopped because of the growing discomfort to him. However, in clear terms the experimenter orders the teacher to continue with the procedure in disregard of the learner's protests. Thus the naive subject must resolve a conflict between two mutually incompatible demands. . . . He may continue to follow the orders of the experimenter and continue to shock the learner with increasing severity, or he may refuse to follow the orders of the experimenter and heed the learner's pleas (pp. 59–60).

No actual shocks were given by the research subjects, and the screams of pain and agony by the "learner" in the next room were, in reality, tape recordings made especially for the experiments by paid actors. Nonetheless, the "teachers" in the experiments thought everything was real, and, in one series of experiments, sixty-five percent of the research subjects administered what they thought were four hundred fifty volts of punishment.

Conformity at the Highest Levels of Decision Making   Many of the factors that influence conformity at the lower levels of organizations can also be observed at policy-making levels. Compliance with group norms is, of course, a desirable outcome of social interaction at all levels of society. Without it, social order and group cohesion would be impossible to maintain.

Groupthink: A Form of Overconformity   In large-scale organizations, however, conformity for conformity's sake sometimes becomes over-conformity, which can be very dysfunctional, especially when it occurs among high-level decision makers. When conformity reaches this extreme, it becomes what Irving Janis (1982A) calls **groupthink**, a form of over-conformity in which, for the sake of cohesion and "good relations," group decisions are made uncritically with little if any conflict.

This "all for one and one for all" mentality, according to Janis, emerges out of several conditions resulting from high cohesion that members of the group come to exhibit as characteristics. These include the members' unanimous belief that they as a group are superior, morally right, and invulnerable. Add to this their collective ability to rationalize the group position and apply simplistic negative stereotypes to those perceived as the enemy. Finally, there is strong pressure both from the group and the individual's sense of duty to keep reservations and possible criticisms to a minimum. To do otherwise would be interpreted by the group as disloyalty. Consequently, ideas, information, and suggestions that do not conform with the group's predetermined mindset are largely ignored and people become "team players" and "go along to get along."

The "Bay of Pigs" Incident   One example is the John F. Kennedy administration that covertly sponsored an ill-fated invasion of Cuba in 1961 at the Bay of Pigs. The invasion by Cuban rebels, trained and equipped by the CIA, was a total failure, and most of the rebels were either killed or captured. President Kennedy's advisors totally overlooked the strength of Fidel Castro' forces and failed to seek out other relevant intelligence sources. In the meetings between Kennedy and his advisors on this subject, the atmosphere was one of "assumed consensus" and the vote to support the project was unanimous. This fiasco further alienated the Castro regime from the United States, reinforced and encouraged the already growing relationship between Cuba and the Soviet Union, and ultimately influenced attempts by the Soviets to place nuclear missiles in Cuba. The confrontation between the two super powers that followed in October, 1962, called the Cuban Missile Crisis, brought the United States and the Soviet Union to the brink of nuclear war.

Research on Groupthink: 1945 to Present   Janis (1982 B) examined numerous foreign policy decisions made by the United States after World War II. He found that of nineteen international crises identified from 1945 up through the 1970s, American government used groupthink decision making to a significant degree in eighty-seven percent of them. Included in these were the Bay of Pigs fiasco by the Kennedy administration and the behavior of the Johnson administration that led to the escalation of military involvement in Vietnam by the United States during the 1960s and 1970s.

U.S. Automakers during the 1970s   In the business and corporate sector, automakers in the United States—the same country that landed men on the moon—exhibited groupthink by claiming during the early 1970s that it was "technologically impossible" to produce small, high-quality, fuel-efficient cars that met the Environmental Protection Agency's (EPA) emission standards for pollution control. Japanese automakers like Honda did so with ease over the next few years, setting the stage for their capture of a large portion of the U.S. auto market in the 1980s, which largely has been sustained up until the present.

The Nixon, Reagan, and Bush Administrations   Groupthink among high-level governmental officials in the executive branch of government continued through the remainder of the century and into the 2000s. For example, it contributed to both the cover-up of "Watergate," which led to the downfall of President Richard M. Nixon in the 1970s and the Iran–Contra scandal that plagued the Ronald Reagan administration during the 1980s. More recently, over-conformity to the flawed mantra of "weapons of mass destruction" in Iraq exhibited by President George W. Bush and his inner circle after the September 11, 2001 terrorist attacks on the United States led to a military invasion of Iraq in 2003. Weapons of mass destruction—stockpiles of chemical and biological weapons—and clear-cut evidence of a nuclear weapons program were not found. Soon thereafter, the Senate Intelligence Committee appointed a bipartisan subcommittee to investigate this matter chaired by Pat Roberts (R-Kan.). In a scathing four-hundred-page report released in July, 2004, panel chair Roberts, in a press conference summarizing the findings, was recorded by journalists in attendance as saying the following:

> This groupthink caused the [intelligence] community to interpret ambiguous evidence such as the procurement of dual use technology" . . . [to mean Iraq had an active weapons program, Roberts said] . . . "It is clear that this group think also extended to our allies . . . all of whom did believe that Saddam Hussein did have an active WMD program (Porteus, Fox News, 2004).

Resources Needed to Combat Groupthink   Several steps can be taken by groups at all levels of an organization to combat groupthink. According to Janis (1982B), they include, first of all, educating members to both the nature and dangers of groupthink. Members should also be encouraged to "speak their minds" critically on all issues and express their true feelings without fear of personal condemnation or reprisal. The responsibility for creating this type of group position rests with the leader or leaders who must attempt to remain impartial. At least one group member should be assigned the responsibility of taking an alternative viewpoint that challenges the most popular position.

Another valuable tool is the use of "independent" outside experts who attend meetings and feel free to challenge any and all opinions. Although this may appear on the surface to encourage chaos and disruption, critical analysis of key issues and give-and-take between conscientious professionals lead to more effective decisions. Research has demonstrated that superior decisions usually are made when minority views are strongly and consistently voiced, causing the majority to rethink and reevaluate its position (Nemeth, 1985).

Alternative Forms of Organization

The Collective   For America, the decades of the 1960s and 1970s represented a tumultuous time in which many traditions were challenged and many ideas were shared. It was also a time in which many young people experienced alienation from modern society and searched for viable alternatives through social experimentation and the formation of *countercultures* (Chapter 4). Some of these alternative groups espoused an "anti-establishment" and "anti-bureaucratic" view of the world. To them, bigger was not better and the bureaucracy was impersonal, exploitative, and dehumanizing. Although most of these groups faded with the times, some of their ideas remain and have been incorporated by others.

One of the visible results of that generation and era has been an increase in the popularity of **collectives**. These are alternative organizations consisting mainly of small businesses and nonprofit volunteer groups that function on nonbureaucratic principles. Examples include community service organizations such as free schools, legal aid groups, and food and library cooperatives along with small businesses such as alternative newspapers, health food stores, and bookstores. These organizations operate for the most part as collective partnerships. They are intentionally antibureaucratic in organization and make use of consensus instead of authority, few rules, personal as opposed to "bureaucratic" relations, few status distinctions, and little or no specialization (Rothschild-Whitt, 1979). When things need to be done, members just "pitch in."

The collective appears to work well on a small scale when the number of participants is small, time and energy commitments among members are high, and profits are small. However, as the number of people increases to more than ten or twelve, primary group relations tend to break down and the group may dissolve or be taken over by a small coalition of "elites" (Rothschild, 1986). For these reasons, the collective, by its very nature, does not seem to offer a viable alternative to bureaucracy as a means of organizing large-scale formal organizations.

The Japanese Model of Organizations   Unlike collectives, Japanese corporations compete very well with Western bureaucracies in the world marketplace although they are structured differently. In the wake of World War II during the late 1940s and throughout the 1950s, the words "Made in Japan" conjured up images of poor quality goods and shoddy workmanship in the minds of American consumers. Those same words today, in association with brand names like Nikon for cameras, Mitsubishi for television sets, and Toyota for automobiles, result in very different perceptions.

As shown in Table 8-4, the Japanese approach to organizations contains elements that contrast significantly from the characteristics stressed in Weber's model. In addition, its emphasis on active participation and input into decision making by participants—in effect a form of democracy—offers a viable and successful alternative to Michels' *iron law of oligarchy*.

1. ***Participants as Cross-Trained Generalists.*** In contrast to Weber's model in which each participant is trained as a specialist who has mastered a specific task or step in the production process, the emphasis in the Japanese model is to develop a generalist who has mastered all aspects of a particular category of work or occupation. So a nurse, over the course of a career spanning several decades, might spend one to a few years in mastering each of several nursing concentrations—pediatrics, critical care, surgery, geriatrics—before becoming a director of nursing at a major hospital during the last years of his or her career. In similar fashion, a college graduate pursuing a career in banking might spend the first year in management training, then gain some experience as a teller followed by multiple years each in commercial banking, human resources, loans, and other areas until, after more than ten years or so, reaching the ranks of banking management. Americans in similar careers usually are trained and gain experience as specialists in one area of professional practice (Ouchi, 1982).

2. ***Team Organized Labor.*** Although Japanese organizations appear similar to American corporations, the underlying foundation of the Japanese corporation is the cultural emphasis on loyalty to the group. By contrast, American society stresses individuality and individual choice (Zandu, 1983). The Japanese orientation toward the group is based on several important customs including the centuries-old tradition of bringing honor to one's family through one's deeds.

   In contrast to the American system, which stresses and rewards individual achievement, the Japanese emphasize group performance. Employees are typically divided into performance groups or work teams and are evaluated on the performance of the entire group. Such a system requires both cooperation and collective decision making even at the lowest levels of the organization.

3. ***Bottom-Up Decision Making.*** Though a process called **bottom-up decision making**, information and decisions travel from bottom to top based on consensus rather than from top to bottom in the organization. Because the Japanese stress consensus at all levels—which they feel promotes group loyalty and productivity—

TABLE 8-4	**The Japanese Model of Organizations**

1. Participants as cross-trained generalists

2. Team organized labor

3. Bottom-up decision making

4. Employee as "total person" or family member

5. Lifelong employment

top-level executives provide general goals and guidance but leave much of the practical how-to aspects of operation to the lower-level employees. In the Japanese view, this arrangement promotes a sense of personal pride and responsibility in the employees, which reinforces both loyalty and productivity (Vogel, 1979).

As lower-level individuals and teams develop ideas, arrive at consensus, and then make recommendations to those higher up in the organization, a process is used called the *ringi-sei* (bottom-up) system based on "implicit understanding." Intentionally somewhat ambiguous, a *ringi-sho* (proposal) captures the essence of an idea without specifying too many details, which are left for those higher up in the organization to sort out. This allows each level of the organization to share ownership of an idea without it being driven by the egos of an individual or small group. While seemingly slow and inefficient by American standards, particularly in the early stages, implementation can be accomplished with surprising speed and efficiency once higher level executives realize the value of a proposed idea. (Tomlinson, 1996/1999). Once they do, they must convince lower-level personnel of the same regarding the specifics of implementation through an elaborate informal process of persuasion, negotiation, and bargaining. One advantage of this approach is that everyone affected by ideas gets input in determining if and how they will be implemented. In addition, formal leaders, instead of imposing changes from above—as in the Western model—work with lower-level participants every step of the way in building consensus (Jacoby, 2004).

4. ***The Employee as "Total Person" or Family Member.*** In American corporations, the participant is an employee whose work status (and employee role) is separate from his or her private life. Although there are many excellent organizations to work for in the United States where employees are treated very well—Google, Genetech, Starbucks, and Methodist Hospital System (CNNMoney.com, 2008), to name a few—the American system stresses a "strictly business" relationship between company and employee (Ouchi, 1982). When carried to the extreme, employees in some organizations are regarded mainly as "labor costs" and treated as "expendable commodities." The debacle surrounding the fall of Enron in 2001, one of America's largest corporations, is a case in point. When Enron collapsed as a result of an elaborate pyramid scheme that included phony bookkeeping that artificially inflated company assets and stock values and huge claimed losses for income tax purposes, Ken Lay (CEO) and other complicit corporate leaders quietly divested themselves of their stock holdings while, in the case of Lay, telling employees to buy more company stock. Then, when Enron fell, thousands of employees, who had placed their entire retirement portfolios in Enron stock, found themselves on the street with no jobs with their retirement accounts wiped out. Former Enron CEOs Kenneth Lay and Jeffery Skilling were both convicted of conspiracy, fraud, and other charges in 2006 (Richardson, 2006).

In Japanese companies, the leadership reinforces the family ethic by exhibiting *treatment of the employee as a "total person" or family member.* Recruited immediately after graduation from school, workers are employed by companies that provide them with housing and food, medical benefits, continuing education, and various types of recreational facilities in addition to their wages. When an employee goes through important rites of passage—graduations, weddings, and other important events—company representatives also attend for support. After retirement, which usually takes place at age fifty-five, the company continues to help take care of former employees until they die (Noda, 1975).

5. ***Lifelong Employment.*** In Japan, the company often becomes the "second family" for workers through the practice by corporations of furnishing employees with *lifetime employment.* For the Japanese worker, this results in an ethic of lifelong commitment to the company. The employee, therefore, wishes to bring as much honor to the second family as to the first. Life in the second family (the company) begins, as described by one Japanese steel company executive, with a "company birth" which, as an event, "has the same importance as our crying birth" (Abegglen, 1958, pp. 569–570).

The Japanese Organization in Perspective   Despite these characteristics, Japanese organizations can seem somewhat regimented from an American perspective. Japanese employees in many companies wear company uniforms and perform physical exercises and sing company songs in groups before starting each workday. In addition, they are expected to attend several company sponsored functions. While Americans, with their individualistic orientation, would find these activities paternalistic and restrictive, they work well for the Japanese whose particular brand of bureaucracy produces impressive results in the international marketplace.

Although during the 1990s and 2000s, there have been voices of dissent from among both *avant-garde* Japanese executives and some workers to adopt the Western model of organizations or move toward a hybrid or convergence model, the established "Japanese way" of structuring organizations, particularly corporations, has largely prevailed due to its success (Tanikawa, 1995; Jacoby, 2004). For example, during 2008, the Toyota Tundra was poised to eclipse both Ford and Chevrolet/GMC as the best selling pickup in both the United States and other parts of the world.

© TAN KIAN KHOON, 2009. USE UNDER LICENSE FROM SHUTTERSTOCK, INC.

The Japanese corporation is often characterized by lifelong employment, concern for the employee as "total person" or family member, emphasis on group performance, and bottom-up decision making.

THE ORGANIZATION AS A SOCIAL SYSTEM

Large formal organizations may be divided into two major structural components, the *formal structure* and the *informal structure*. Together, they make up the social interaction system of the organization.

The Formal Structure

One of the remarkable results of modern society is that in some respects "the more things change the more they stay the same." If you travel cross-country by car today or travel to Europe, Asia, or South America, you will experience regional differences in topography and culture and, in the case of foreign travel, will be exposed to cultures quite different from your own. Yet, in some respects, you can have a cultural experience remarkably similar to what you experience back home. Holiday Inn, Walmart, Coca Cola, Starbucks, and American fast food chains such as McDonalds and Pizza Hut have corporate footprints today that are worldwide. You can find a Starbucks along the harbor in Hong Kong and order a special coffee as easily as if you were in Houston. Although they serve beer at McDonalds in Germany, Germans put mayonnaise on their "pomme fritz"(French fries), and in Beijing a fried egg is placed on top of the bun, the hamburger is prepared according to a standardized formula and is basically the same everywhere in the world. What makes this paradox of uniformity in an ever-changing world possible is the formal structure of large-scale organizations.

Formal structure refers to the official set of goals, policies, and procedures of an organization that specify the behavior of its members. An organization's formal structure, therefore, is the result of the process called *calculated formation* (Chapter 7). Since many of the products, stores, and other service facilities we as consumers come into contact with represent small parts of larger national or international corporations, the "sameness" we experience with them is due largely to their being a part of a larger formal structure.

Weber's bureaucratic model is the most widely accepted standard against which the formal structure of most organizations is measured. The Japanese approach, in some respects, represents an interesting alternative. Regardless of whether the Japanese or the American model is preferred—or the Indian or Chinese models which are now in their formative stages—each offers an approach to formal structure that may be quite effective within specific cultural contexts. The fact remains, however, that the formal structure is a rational, effective, and indispensable element in efficiently organizing the specialized work of large numbers of people in highly complex organizations. Without it, it does not appear possible that most inhabitants in modern societies could enjoy the affluent life style of convenience that is an ongoing characteristic of modern life. As essential as the formal structure is, however, it alone is not sufficient for the effective operation of a large-scale organization. Although overlooked in Weber's analysis—a common criticism—it is also necessary to examine and understand the importance of another key component in all bureaucracies, the informal structure.

The Informal Structure

Organizations consist of people, not merely company policies, organizational charts, job descriptions, operating budgets, and other formal aspects. This human side of the organi-

The informal structure of a large-scale organization can contribute to higher morale and greater productivity by creating a personalized work setting.

zation, which can be observed in any bureaucracy, is the **informal structure**. It consists of the nonofficial norms and interaction patterns of an organization that emerge from the interaction patterns of its participants.

The informal structure serves several functions. First of all, it acts to create *a personalized work setting*. The rules and positions in large-scale organizations are, by necessity, impersonal. Everyone must abide by them and be held equally accountable for their actions under them. However, morale and the motivation to do a good job are also important. They both can best be kept at a high level through an informal means of interaction that allows for personal contact and friendship within the organization. This human side of the organization also contributes to *flexible decision making*. Formal policies and procedures cannot anticipate every possible contingency. Therefore, some reliance must be placed on the informal structure to make spontaneous adjustments and changes when needed. There is also a system of informal interaction, often called "the grapevine," which creates *streamlined communications*. The "rumor mill" as it is sometimes called, can be very effective in disseminating information much more quickly than would be possible through official channels.

In addition, the informal structure is useful in *the promotion of special interests*. This can help or hurt an organization, depending on the situation and the ability by top management to create an organizational climate conducive to high morale and productivity. Highly motivated participants, in an informal manner, can reinforce each other's morale because they feel positive about the organization. Likewise, poorly motivated and alienated workers can informally agree to perform at a minimum level, withhold creativity, and even sabotage the organization in extreme cases. Consequently, it is in the best interests of large-scale organizations to create an organizational climate conducive to the successful management of human resources.

According to Thomas J. Peters and Robert Waterman, Jr. (1982) in their groundbreaking book *In Search of Excellence,* a "people orientation" by management is one of the key principles that creates organizational effectiveness. Their message to top-level managers on this topic is excerpted as follows:

Treat people as adults. Treat them as partners; treat them with dignity; treat them with respect. Treat *them*—not capital spending and automation—as the primary source of productivity gains. These are the fundamental lessons from the excellent companies research. In other words, if you want productivity and the financial reward that goes with it, you must treat your workers as your most valuable asset. . . .

The orientation toward people in these companies often started decades ago—full employment policies in times of recession, extraordinary amounts of training when no training was the norm, everybody on a first name basis in times much more formal than ours, and so on. Caring runs in the veins of the managers of these institutions. People are why those managers are there, and they know it and live it. . . .

Perhaps surprisingly, the people orientation also has a *tough* side. The excellent companies are measurement happy and performance oriented, but this toughness is borne of mutually high expectations and peer review rather than emanating from table pounding managers and complicated control systems. The tough side is, in fact, probably tougher than that found in the less excellent and typically more formal systems-driven companies, for nothing is more enticing than the feeling of being needed, which is the magic that produces high expectations. What's more, if it's your peers that have those high expectations of you, then there's all the more incentive to perform well (pp. 238–240).

The Organization in Perspective

The formal structure and the informal structure represent two halves of the same whole, namely, the organization or formal organization, some of which are bureaucracies as well. In most cases, neither component can function well without the other, and the organization as a total interaction system requires both in order to function with maximum effectiveness. In this sense, these two parts of an organization are closely related to the two basic types of leadership discussed in Chapter 7. Effective management of the formal structure in an organization requires *task leadership*, while successful coordination of the informal structure necessitates *socioemotional leadership*. While most organizations have leaders of both types, they, like the organizational components they represent, should not be seen as mutually exclusive. Rather, the challenge for organizations in the future, as indicated by Peters and Waterman, is to integrate these elements successfully. Ideally, organizations should represent an ever-changing and flexible blend of both formal and informal structures and leaders who incorporate both task and socioemotional skills to maintain a dynamic equilibrium. To be successful in creating such a balance—which varies depending on the organization, its goals, and its circumstances—is not easy. Yet, particularly for private sector corporations that must compete in a constantly evolving world marketplace, this balance is increasingly necessary and will become even more important in the future.

In the wake of increasing information technology and pressures placed on corporate leaders by shareholders to maximize profits per dollar invested, recent trends also include outsourcing facilities and employees in foreign countries where regulations are less encumbering and labor costs are lower. The use of fewer levels of management (leveling the organization), temporary employees, foreign recruitment for American jobs, the use of part-time workers to minimize the costs of benefits, and other practices are resulting in leaner organizations. These new and changing variables will make the balancing of the elements we have discussed even more challenging. In addition, such processes resulting in the "reinvention of the organization" could pose some very real problems in the future, some of which are now known and some that are yet to be revealed.

PROBLEMS IN LARGE-SCALE ORGANIZATIONS

Too great an emphasis on rules, rituals, and costs (formal structure/task leadership) or on member's feelings and interpersonal relations (informal structure/socioemotional leadership) can be a contributing factor leading to organizational problems. In this regard, we will briefly examine several common problems that plague some organizations today: ritualism, goal displacement, and the protection of incompetence along with the dilemmas that have been described as the Peter principle and Parkinson's law.

Ritualism

One of the most pervasive problems found within bureaucracies is **ritualism** (sometimes called trained incapacity), an overconformity to the rules of the organization by an individual participant. Such a person often is described as having "tunnel vision" or "not being able to see the forest for the trees," or "think out of the box." Most of us have had experience with ritualists. Examples are the clerk who cannot help you because of "company policy" even though the slightest demonstration of flexibility would solve your problem; the police officer who tickets you for going four miles per hour over the speed limit; or the teacher who appears more interested in grades than in whether learning takes place. Participants in bureaucracies are socialized to see the rules and regulations of the organization as the important elements that should be taken seriously. Because many organizations reward their workers and officials more for following rules that for providing effective service or actually achieving stated goals, overconformity often occurs.

Goal Displacement

When ritualism is carried to the organizational level, it becomes **goal displacement**, a problem in which the means (rules) of an organization become substituted for the goals and many to most participants lose sight of their original objectives. Although ritualism usually occurs with lower-level workers who have responsibility but little or no authority or with the occasional high-level bureaucrat in a similar situation, goal displacement can permeate an entire organization or one if its key elements. Usually, for goal displacement to occur, at least tacit agreement must flow from the highest echelons of decision making at the departmental, divisional, or higher-level managerial levels. A charitable organization that spends much if not most of its income on "administrative costs" rather than on its stated purposes represents one example. Governmental agencies that offer contrived excuses to justify their existence long after their stated purposes have been achieved or otherwise made obsolete serves as an added illustration, one that robs tax payers of millions of wasted dollars annually.

The Protection of Incompetence

The **protection of incompetence** is a problem that occurs when an organization fails to first identify and then to promptly develop, reassign, or remove inadequate performers.

While loyalty to hand-picked subordinates along with group morale are important and high turnover is to be avoided in most cases, these considerations should not take precedence over the ability of the organization to successfully accomplish its goals. Incompetence often becomes prevalent in an organization in which formal goals have become sacrificed to the extremes of socioemotional leadership. In other cases, policies that were designed to provide rewards and job security to those who have given faithful service also act to insulate and protect the mediocre and incompetent. Aspects of the U.S. civil service system of employment and the seniority system in some companies provide examples. It is also apparent that the informal structure of organizations can create a condition of poor performance when workers decide informally on a relatively low rate of production. Under this arrangement, any worker who exceeds this level of production is considered a "rate buster" and is severely ostracized by fellow workers (Semones, 1977).

The Peter Principle

Lawrence J. Peter and Raymond Hull (1969) identified another bureaucratic problem that they described as the **Peter principle**. The Peter principle is the assertion that officials within an organization tend to keep rising until they eventually reach their level of incompetence. An excellent classroom teacher, for instance, may become an assistant principal because of the incentives of higher pay and increases status. However, if this person is a poor administrator, advancement to a principalship over a school will probably not occur. Because this individual normally would not return to teaching, he or she becomes "locked in" at their level of incompetence.

Parkinson's Law

As organizations expand and grow more complex, it becomes more difficult to manage and coordinate the diverse activities of all participants. This creates a condition ripe for problems related to waste and inefficiency, described by *Parkinson's law* (named after its originator, British historian C. Northcote Parkinson). In its simplest form, **Parkinson's law** is the argument that "Work expands to fill the time available for its completion" (Parkinson, 1957). When people in organizations have very little to do, they may try to keep this from being detected by appearing busy and engaging in "make-work." They shuffle papers, duplicate their efforts, and develop a whole array of empty rituals in order to seem productive. In some cases, this can go on for years if the perpetrators are good at it and their supervisors are preoccupied with other matters.

In closing, this discussion has attempted to build on the material in Chapter 7 to present you with an overview of formal organizations and bureaucracy. While it is not an exhaustive treatment of the subject by any means, it is hoped that some of your questions about large-scale organizations have been answered and that your curiosity has been sparked concerning many others. Because most of us will spend the majority of our adult lives working in and dealing with large-scale organizations, many of which are bureaucracies, it is in our best interests to understand "from whence they came," how they operate, and where they are likely to be going as we move into the future. This brief treatment has been aimed at helping you gain some insight in these regards.

▶ CHAPTER SUMMARY

1. As originally defined in Chapter 7, a *formal organization* is a group deliberately formed to achieve one or more specific practical goals. Some organizations also involve *bureaucracy*, a form of social organization in which the work of participants is rationally coordinated by professionally trained managers.

2. Sociologist Amitai Etzioni has developed one of the most useful means of classifying organizations based on the reasons that people participate in them and, in turn, the degree of control certain organizations can exert on their lives. In this respect, the voluntary organization is one people join freely as a part-time activity because they agree with its norms and goals. It has low control over the individual and may take the form of civic, professional, or personal interest organization. The utilitarian organization is one that an individual participates in for practical gain or profit. It can be a business, a corporation, or a professional firm and tends to exercise a significant (medium) degree of control over the life of a participant as in the case of one's job. Finally, the coercive organization makes use of force or the threat of force. It exercises high to total control over the individual, as illustrated by structures ranging from elementary schools on one end of the continuum through religious orders to mental hospitals, prisons, and POW camps on the other. Extreme forms of coercive organizations called total institutions, such as some religious sects, POW camps, and so on, often make use of mortification and brainwashing techniques to control and manipulate participants.

3. Power is the ability to influence or control the behavior of others with or without their consent whereas authority is legitimated power generally recognized and supported by those over whom it is exercised. Max Weber identified three basic forms of authority that exist in society: charismatic authority, traditional authority, and rational–legal authority. Charismatic authority (the force of personality) is based on followers' belief that the leader possesses divine grace, heroism, or other special qualities. Traditional authority (monarchy) involves followers' acceptance of the legitimacy contained in long-standing traditions and customs. Rational–legal authority (objective qualifications representing technical expertise), the most prevalent form found in modern societies, is based on the legitimacy of a formal system of laws and policies that define the nature and scope of a leader's authority and responsibility.

4. Regarding the nature of bureaucracy, sociologist Robert Michels argued that bureaucracy is incompatible with democracy. His iron law of oligarchy, for which he is most noted, states that power in organizations invariably becomes concentrated in the hands of a few people who use it to further their own self-interests.

5. Max Weber disagreed with Michels' oligarchic perspective and felt that large-scale organizations could be democratic. He developed an ideal model of bureaucracy that consists of six key elements: a specialized division of labor, hierarchical authority, written rules, impartial performance of duties, reward based on technical competence, and careers. He argued that if these characteristics were emulated by actual organizations, the "rationalization" of modern societies could be realized.

6. Conformity is an essential ingredient of any large-scale organization. In this regard, it occurs at all levels, from the smallest of formal work settings involving people at the lowest levels of authority in the organization to the highest echelons of decision making. When conformity is carried to an extreme, it can result in groupthink, a situation in which group decisions are made uncritically, with little or no conflict, for the sake of cohesion and "good relations." This can result in very negative consequences.

7. There are alternatives to bureaucracy as Michels and Weber envisioned it. The collective and the Japanese corporation serve as notable examples. A collective is a small business or nonprofit volunteer group that functions on nonbureaucratic principles, including consensus decision making and little or no specialization. While it sometimes works well with small numbers of participants, the collective does not appear to represent a viable alternative to bureaucracy as a means of organizing large-scale organizations. The Japanese corporation, however, with a system based on lifetime employment, concern for the "total person," group performance, and bottom-up decision making, functions very successfully in the international marketplace.

8. Complex organizations often experience a wide variety of problems. Some of the most common include ritualism, goal displacement, protection of incompetence, and organizational consequences described in the Peter principle and Parkinson's law. An organizational imbalance created by too great of an emphasis on either the formal structure or the informal structure can contribute to most if not all of these problems.

TERMS TO KNOW

authority: legitimated power generally recognized and supported by those over whom it is exercised.

bottom-up decision making: a characteristic of Japanese corporations in which information and decisions based on group consensus travel from bottom to top, rather than from top to bottom in the organization.

brainwashing: a process of almost complete thought control in which the victim's existing values and beliefs are made useless and replaced with those desired by the agent of influence.

bureaucracy: a form of social organization in which the work of participants in large-scale organizations is rationally coordinated by professionally trained managers.

careers: positions held by managerial and professional officials through which, in exchange for loyal and adequate performance, extended employment and opportunities for advancement are provided.

charismatic authority: Weber's term for authority based on the commonly accepted belief by followers that a leader possesses special qualities or unique characteristics (e.g., military heroism or divine grace).

coercive organization: Etzioni's term for an organization in which people participate due to force or the threat of force.

collectives: alternative organizations consisting mainly of small businesses and nonprofit volunteer groups that function on nonbureaucratic principles.

conformity: behavior that is in agreement with the norms of society or one of its smaller structural elements.

formal structure: the official set of goals, policies, and procedures of an organization that specify the behavior of its members.

goal displacement: a problem in which the means (rules) of an organization become substituted for the goals and many to most participants lose sight of their original objectives.

groupthink: a form of over-conformity in which, for the sake of cohesion and "good relations," group decisions are make uncritically with little if any conflict.

hierarchical authority: a process in which "offices" or positions in an organization are arranged vertically in terms of authority and responsibility.

informal structure: the nonofficial norms and interaction patterns of an organization that emerge from the interaction patterns of its participants.

iron law of oligarchy: Michels' principle that power in organizations invariably becomes concentrated in the hands of a few people who use it to further their self-interests.

mortification: a process in which a person's old identity is stripped away through a systematic program of degradation and humiliation, and replaced with a new self more suitable to the organization.

Parkinson's law: a problem in organizations in which "Work expands to fill the time available for its completion."

Peter principle: the assertion that officials within an organization tend to keep rising until they eventually reach their level of incompetence.

power: the ability to influence or control the behavior of others with or without their consent.

protection of incompetence: a problem that occurs when an organization fails to first identify and then to promptly develop, reassign, or remove inadequate performers.

Rational–legal authority: Weber's term for a type of authority based on the legitimacy of a formal set of laws or rules that define the scope of a leader's rights and responsibilities.

ritualism: a problem involving over-conformity to the rules of the organization by an individual participant.

specialized division of labor: a process in which participants in large-scale organizations are assigned positions that center on specific, specialized tasks.

technical competence: in Weber's model, the basis for rewards (placement and promotion) in a bureaucracy as measured by formal education, training, experience, and job performance.

total institution: an extreme form of coercive organization that exerts twenty-four-hours-a-day control over participants

traditional authority: a type of authority based on followers' acceptance of the legitimacy contained in long-standing traditions and customs (e.g., authority possessed by a king or queen).

utilitarian organization: Etzioni's term for an organization in which people participate for practical gain or profit.

voluntary organization: Etzioni's term for an organization people join freely as a part-time activity because they agree with its values, norms, and goals.

SUGGESTED READINGS

Jacoby, S. M. 2004. *The Embedded Corporation: Corporate Governance and Employee Relations in Japan and the United States.* Princeton, NJ: Princeton University Press. A well-written and thorough comparative examination of the corporate systems used in Japan and the United States, the advantages and disadvantages of both, and a consideration of convergence or a hybrid approach which could evolve into prominence in the ever-changing global economy of the twenty-first century.

Peters, T. J., and R. H. Waterman, Jr. 1982. *In Search of Excellence: Lessons of America's Best Run Companies.* New York: Warner Books. A well-written, entertaining, and disturbing look at the American corporation, along with eight principles for organizational success and detailed examples from successful corporations including Frito-Lay, Hewlett-Packard, IBM, and others. This classic in organizational leadership is as fresh and relevant today as it was when first published three decades ago.

Whitman, M. N. 1999. *New World, New Rules: The Changing Role of the American Corporation.* Boston: Harvard University Press. A look at the realities of competing in the global economy in retaining market share of existing markets and penetrating new ones.

Social Stratification

READING PREVIEW

Terms to Know

absolute poverty	intragenerational mobility	relative poverty
caste system	life chances	reputational approach
class system	life style	slavery
conflict perspective	objective approach	social class
culture of poverty hypothesis	objective poverty	social mobility
evolutionary perspective	pluralistic theory	social stratification
felt poverty	poverty	structural unemployment
functionalist perspective	power	subjective approach
horizontal mobility	power elite theory	vertical mobility
intergenerational mobility	prestige	wealth

For some Americans, the first part of the twenty-first century has resulted in great prosperity. Today, nearly nine percent of Americans are millionaires; there are four hundred billionaires in the United States with over 1.1 million millionaire households concentrated in just ten U.S. counties (Sahadi, 2006; *Forbes 400*, October 29, 2006) (Table 9-1). While running for president in 2008, Democratic candidate Hillary Clinton and her husband, former president Bill Clinton, released their U.S. federal tax returns to the American public. Despite leaving the White House in 2000 and being millions of dollars in debt for legal fees incurred by the president's involvement in the Monica Lewinsky matter and other scandals, the Clinton's quickly recovered and reported earnings for 2000–2007 of $109 million. Most of this money came from speaking fees that garnered Bill Clinton up to $250,000 per event and a $15 million dollar publisher's advance for his 2004 autobiography *My Life*. During this time, they also paid $33.8 million in taxes and gave $10.2 million in charitable contributions. Nonetheless, these earnings placed the Clintons in the top one-hundredth of one percent of all U.S. wage earners (Dilanian, 2008).

Yet the earnings of ex-presidents pale in comparison to the incomes of the really super-rich. As an illustration, hedge fund manager John Paulson earned $3.7 billion ($3,200 million) during 2007 and the top twenty-five mutual fund managers averaged $872 million each for the same year (Fletcher, 2008). The top fifty hedge fund managers earned a combined total of $29 billion for 2007 while the median household income for all American families was $60,500 (Anderson, 2008). How is it that celebrities such as Jennifer Lopez and Marc Anthony could spend $2 million on their wedding in 2004 and Oprah Winfrey, a billionaire, could give away a $1 million wedding on her syndicated television show (July, 2004). By contrast, a poor family in the United States may subsist on less than $1,800 per month and the per capita income for an agricultural laborer in India and other parts of the Third World is no more than a dollar a day or $350 to $400 per year?

Some form of structured inequality exists in most places throughout the world. Sociologists refer to this as **social stratification**, a system in each society that defines how

TABLE 9-1	The Millionaires Next Door: Top Ten Counties in 2005 with Millionaire Households	

U.S. RANK	COUNTY	NO. OF MILLIONAIRE HOUSEHOLDS
1	Los Angeles County, CA	262,800
2	Cook County, IL	167,800
3	Orange County, CA	113,299
4	Maricopa County, AZ	106,210
5	San Diego, County, CA	100,030
6	Harris County, TX	95,593
7	Nassau County, NY	78,816
8	Santa Clara County, CA	75,371
9	Palm Beach County, FL	69,871
10	Middlesex County, MA	67,552

SOURCE: TNS Financial Services; Sahadi, J. 2006; Top 10 millionaire counties. CNNMoney.com March 29. http://money.cnn.com/2006/03/28/news/economy/millionaires/

social rank is determined and social rewards are distributed. Within a society, people are ranked in a hierarchy of social respectability and worth. This vertical arrangement of rank involves two or more layers or strata, which sociologists call "classes" in some societies and "castes" in others. In the United States, for example, there is a class system of stratification with three general levels: upper, middle, and lower class. The occupants of each class tend to think, feel, and act somewhat differently from those in other classes regarding religion, politics, recreation, and many other areas of preference and behavior. Likewise, each stratum represents an unequal distribution of social rewards in the form of power, prestige, and wealth. For instance, a physician in America tends to enjoy a great deal more of all these benefits compared with a postal worker or plumber.

In this chapter, we will address a variety of key questions about stratification. They include the following: How is social inequality organized in different societies? How do sociologists explain why there seems to be a need for different levels of social position in all societies? What are the major components of social rank? What forces and factors make it possible for many Americans to own two or more homes while others live on the streets with no homes at all? These are some of the basic issues to be examined in the pages to follow.

TYPES OF STRATIFICATION SYSTEMS

To begin, let us examine how social inequality is organized in different societies. In this regard, social systems worldwide tend to have one or a combination of three different types of stratification systems: slavery, caste, or class. A variety of factors, including characteristics of the economic system, forms of political organization, levels of technology, and even the nature of religions, may influence the particular form of ranking that becomes dominant in a given society.

Slavery

Slavery refers to an involuntary system of bondage in which human beings are bought, sold, or exchanged for money or other resources. Although many Americans tend to think of slavery as an artifact of the past, it is a flourishing practice today, particularly in developing countries. For example, human beings captured as the spoils of war in intertribal conflicts in parts of Sudan and other African countries are still placed into bondage—men, women, and children. However, the trafficking in humans in most parts of the world involves mainly women and children. Bought, sold, and traded as commodities, they serve two main functions for their captors, as a cheap source of labor and for use as prostitutes and sex slaves in the flesh trade.

Examples are numerous and evidence is ample, often because those responsible are so callous and brazen about their exploitation of fellow human beings. In many developing countries, very little value is put on human life and the ethic for many is quite literally "eat or be eaten, steal or be stolen from, and take or be taken." Living at a bare subsistence level, this is seen as the natural order of things.

In the golden triangle of India—Delhi, Agra, and Jaipur—thousands of children as young as eight years old are sold into bondage by their parents to "apprentice" in rug and stone finishing factories. Here, they tie the fine knots in hand crafted rugs that only small nimble hands can tie; their hands are often bleeding by the end of the day until hard calluses form. By age fourteen, the work done by these children and those who work in stone finishing factories insetting small, mosaic tiles in polished stone for the tourist trade takes a toll on their eyes, and they must "retire," often nearly blind from their work. This is but one example of many that can be observed in different parts of the world—from children leased out to companies by their parents for as little as two dollars a month in China to work at hard labor on farms and construction projects, to Indonesia and Thailand where girls by the thousands are sold into prostitution by age eight. Likewise, in the Ukraine and Romania, boys and girls are sold into prostitution and then taken to Western European capitals by their "owners" to turn tricks on the street. Estimates as to the numbers of people worldwide caught in the trap of slavery range from 12.3 million to over 30 million (BBC News, May 11, 2005).

The Caste System

A **caste system** is a rigid and closed system of social ranking in which most statuses are ascribed and tend to remain so. While several societies, including portions of Africa, Ceylon, and traditional Japan, have experienced caste stratification of one form or another, the traditional caste system of India perhaps serves as the best illustration. This system, practiced for more than three thousand years, was legally abolished by the Indian government in 1950. Nonetheless, while it has significantly declined in urban areas, caste ranking has continued in the rural parts of the country where laws are difficult to enforce (Robertson, 1974).

Although it was made illegal in 1950, the traditional Hindu caste system still remains and "untouchables" occupy the lowest levels of society in some parts of India. Often members of such subcastes have been forced to live in "other" sections of a village and be required to drink water from a separate well.

The Traditional Indian Caste System

The Indian caste system is closely intertwined with the ancient Hindu religion from which it evolved. The Hindus believe that the only life after death is through *samsara,* or reincarnation, in which the soul is reborn in the body of another. If one does not adhere strictly to the *dharma,* or behavior specified for the caste one is born into, then one may be downgraded in caste during the next reincarnation. Hindus believe that the only way to improve one's caste level is by strictly adhering to the dharma of one's present caste, which may bring a rebirth to a higher station as a reward in the next life.

Traditionally, this system of ranking included four main *varnas,* or castes: the *Brahmans* (priests and teachers), the *Kahatriyas* (princes and warriors), the *Vaisyas* (merchants and craftsmen), and the *Sundras* (laborers). Below these were many subcastes of untouchables, or "outcasts," that constituted about twenty percent of the population. These lower caste members were to be avoided at all costs and were therefore shunned by those of higher castes. Rituals related to one's caste governed practically every aspect of life: which occupations were allowed, whom one could have as a friend or could marry, the proper way to enter a town; one's diet; and so forth (Rossides, 1976). In recent years, however, Indian leaders have been pushing for industrialization, scientific farming, and a more diversified economy, and India has increasingly become a class society (Weisman, 1986) in the urbanized areas. However, despite assertions by Indian governmental officials that caste no longer exists, it is still very visible in rural parts of the country where the majority of Indians still live (BBC, "Religion and Ethics-Hinduism," 2005).

The Apartheid System in South Africa

The apartheid system practiced until the early 1990s in South Africa represented a caste system that in some ways were as rigid as those practiced in traditional India. *Apartheid* refers to a strict system of racial segregation.

South Africans historically were divided into four caste-like categories: white, African, Asian, and colored (mixed racial background). Each group was strictly segregated into separate districts of each town, and anyone who visited different racial districts had to possess a pass that was periodically inspected by officials. South African whites displayed (and some still do) an attitude of overt, up-front racism not unlike that exhibited by Southern whites in the United States during the nineteenth century and first six decades of the twentieth century.

Caste in the United States   It should be noted that even in the United States, historical conditions of caste have existed as applied to certain categories of people. Originally, the freedoms espoused by the founding fathers in the Constitution and Bill of Rights applied, for the most part, to white, Anglo-Saxon, Protestant, property-holding males. It has taken well over two hundred years for the caste limitations placed on blacks, Native Americans, women, Jews, and other minorities to finally be openly addressed and, to a significant degree, put aside. Consequently, class and caste are not mutually exclusive; elements of both usually exist to some degree in all societies.

The Class System

A **class system** is a relatively open and flexible system of social ranking in which most statuses are achieved. Where a person is positioned in such a system depends upon what they achieve in terms of occupation, education, and wealth. Class systems are the products of industrialization, for the most part, and, although they take several different forms, can be found in all industrial and postindustrial societies to a large degree.

The number and characteristics of classes in a given society are determined in part by the productivity of its economic system. Because of the capacity of nations like the United States and Japan to generate surpluses, they tend to have more class levels and more complex stratification systems than, for instance, Cuba, the former Soviet Union before it collapsed in 1987, and other "classless societies" with very sluggish economies. Class in the United States remains a somewhat elusive concept to define precisely. This is due in part to the diverse and ever-changing nature of American society. Nonetheless, one could accurately define **social class** as a grouping of people on the socioeconomic continuum who share similar levels and types of power, prestige, and wealth.

How Many Classes Exist in America?   Sociologists today generally agree that within the three major subdivisions of upper, middle, and lower classes, there are at least five distinct American classes. One of the most useful typologies of class has been the one developed by Daniel Rossides (1998): (1) the *upper class* (high achievement and/or inherited wealth), (2) the *upper-middle class* (degreed professionals with substantial incomes), (3) the *lower-middle class* (lower-level white-collar workers), (4) the *working class* (skilled and semiskilled blue-collar workers paid hourly wages), and (5) the *underclass* (unskilled workers, the underemployed, and the unemployed poor).

Regardless of how we define these general categories, there are problems and contradictions. How, for instance, should the three key variables of occupation, education, and wealth be weighted? While sociologists today tend to place occupation and education higher than mere income in assessing social rank, it is indeed ironic that many blue-collar *only the strong survive.*

workers, including coal miners and plumbers, have higher incomes than some in professional occupations, such as social workers and public school teachers. Therefore, rating social class is much more complex than merely considering income.

Social Mobility: The Key to How Class Systems Work   In the United States and elsewhere, the chief characteristic of a class system is **social mobility**, the ability to move from one social location or level in society to another. A caste system, by contrast, offers little if any opportunity to change one's socioeconomic position. Although there are several ways to discuss social mobility, perhaps the most useful is to distinguish between its two basic types: vertical mobility and horizontal mobility.

Vertical Mobility   **Vertical mobility** refers to any upward or downward change that occurs in a person's social class level. American society encourages upward mobility. Some working-class parents, for example, encourage their children to go to college, which for most people, is the surest and most direct route to middle-class and upper middle-class status. Such parents wish options and choices for their children that they never had because of a variety of circumstances. However, vertical mobility can also go the other way. The son or daughter of a research chemist who fails to finish college and elects instead to become a car salesperson, employee of a department store, or pursue the dream of becoming a first-tier fashion model, will most probably experience downward mobility.

There are two basic forms of vertical social mobility in modern class societies, *intergenerational mobility* and *intragenerational mobility.* **Intergenerational mobility** is change in social class level that occurs across generations between parents and their children. Most college students twenty-five years old and younger fall at or below their parents' social class level. However, particularly for those with working-class parents, completion of a four-year degree usually will result in significant upward mobility. By studying the over-all trends of both upward and downward intergenerational mobility among various segments of the population, sociologists can more accurately access such factors as inequality and opportunity.

Social scientists also are interested in tracking **intragenerational mobility**, changes people experience in social rank within their own lifetimes or careers. Research show that while many Americans change jobs and occupations, most experience only slight to medium gains or losses in relative status during the course of their careers (Sorensen, 1975). However, in a class system that places such an emphasis on degrees and credentials like that in the United States, a hospital technician can become a physician and then later a surgeon, an accounting clerk can become a certified public accountant (CPA), a college student can eventually earn a Ph.D. and become a professor, and a B movie actor like Ronald Reagan, a peanut farmer like Jimmy Carter, or a community organizer like Barack Obama can become president.

Horizontal Mobility   Class systems of stratification also provide opportunities for horizontal mobility if citizens decide to choose such an option. **Horizontal mobility** involves change in social position, usually occupation, without any significant impact on social class level. The factory worker who becomes a store clerk or the carpenter who becomes a firefighter would change their jobs but experience little or no change in social class.

Chief Determinants of Social Mobility

In the United States, the chief factors that determine social mobility are changes in social norms, technology, and, most importantly, occupational supply and demand.

Changes in Social Norms

When structural changes occur in one institution driven by changes in social norms (mores and folkways), they impact other areas of society as well. During the 1960s and 1970s, in the wake of the women's movement and changes occurring in the economy, women began entering the workforce in unprecedented numbers. As one consequence, there was a restructuring that took place not only in many American families but the workplace itself, as some occupations became obsolete and new types of jobs became necessary. The demise of the home-delivery milkman provides one example. By the middle to late 1970s, with the steady decline of stay-at-home wives and mothers, home-delivery milkmen had become obsolete because there was no longer a person at home during the day—particularly during peak summer and winter months— to collect the milk from the front porch. Consequently, the jobs of milkmen were replaced by those who worked in convenience stores.

Changes in Technology

Today, the internet revolution brought about by ever-expanding computer technology in the new century is changing the way we shop, acquire an education, pay our bills, and conduct our jobs. As a result, some functions and occupations are becoming obsolete while others are being newly created. This results in significant shifts in both occupations and upward and downward social mobility.

The Key to Social Mobility: Changes in Occupational Supply and Demand

As changes continue to occur in both social norms and technology, and social institutions then adjust by altering their structures and organization, changes also take place in both occupational supply and demand. This is mainly what drives social mobility.

© DEAN MITCHELL, 2009. USE UNDER LICENSE FROM SHUTTERSTOCK, INC.

The key to social mobility in modern societies today is due to changes in occupational supply and demand. More and more jobs in the future will require technical expertise and "computer literacy" obtained largely from formal education and training.

As we move forward beyond the first decade or two of the twenty-first century and prepare for the future, we must learn to anticipate social change and make the appropriate adjustments in order to maintain our class position and perhaps be able to achieve some upper mobility. The idea of holding one occupation that changes very little for one's entire working life is now largely an artifact of the past. College teaching and learning represents one example of such seedbed changes that are now occurring throughout modern society. "Chalk and talk" forms of instruction and "brick and mortar" colleges will continue into the foreseeable future. However, distance education via the internet and "colleges without walls" are also emerging as viable alternatives for students who can benefit from alternative forms of course delivery. As students get accustomed to distance learning as a way of "going to school," they are being socialized into becoming more comfortable with using various sorts of informational technology to streamline many aspects of their lives. Those who do not learn how to use informational technology and do not keep up with the changes that will continue to occur in the delivery of such technology, most likely will experience downward social mobility that could threaten their socioeconomic position.

SOCIOLOGICAL EXPLANATIONS OF STRATIFICATION

Why is there such a disparity in practically all societies between those with power, prestige, and wealth and the very poor? Sociologists address this question from several major perspectives. In the following discussion, we will examine three major approaches—the functionalist, conflict, and evolutionary perspectives.

The Functionalist Perspective

As we discussed is Chapter 2, the *functionalist approach* studies basic social structures in society in terms of the ways they function to promote social order and harmony. This paradigm may be applied to the study of most aspects of social behavior, including social stratification.

The Work of Davis and Moore Kingsley Davis and Wilbert Moore (1945) made the classical application of functionalism to stratification. According to their view, the **functionalist perspective** sees stratification as necessary and beneficial to society because it uses a system of rewards to motivate people to acquire the skills needed to obtain the most valued positions. They stated that society, in effect, "dangles social carrots" in front of people in the form of social rewards such as power, prestige, and monetary gain to provide them with the incentive needed to seek and obtain positions that call for scarce skills and lengthy training.

Davis and Moore argued that because not all people have the same levels of ability and motivation, and some societal positions require more or less skill, training, and discipline, social inequality is inevitable. If physicians were rewarded at the same level as laborers, it would make little sense to expect them to undergo the expensive, arduous, and time-consuming process of acquiring a medical education. Because society needs physicians and others with rare talents in order to function properly, social inequality is needed to ensure that a sufficient number of people will have the motivation to gain qualification for all the necessary positions.

The Concept of Meritocracy   The functionalist explanation of stratification is based primarily on economic incentives and other forms of extrinsic rewards. Davis and Moore and others of the functionalist school subscribe to the concept of **meritocracy**, the idea that society is dominated by the most talented who, therefore, deserve most of the social rewards. The poor, in contrast, tend to have the least talent and skill, but, nonetheless, their experience benefits certain segments of society in a "functional" way (Gans, 1972, 1973). For example, the existence of poverty creates a need for certain service occupations that include social work, public health and housing administration, and law enforcement. The poor also create markets for a variety of goods and services including pawn broking, secondhand clothing and furniture, and a variety of other used and inferior consumer goods. Finally, poverty functions to ensure that the jobs the affluent do not want to do— the menial, undignified, uncomfortable, dirty, and dangerous jobs—will be filled.

Criticisms of the Functionalist View   While some sociologists adhere to this approach (Cullen and Novick, 1979), others have criticized it on a variety of grounds. One apparent shortcoming of functionalism is that *it ignores preexisting inequities and differential opportunities that many inherit at birth* (Bottomore, 1966). The poor, women, and many minorities, because of their "place" in the existing social system, face obstacles rarely encountered by white middle-class males. Women, for example, were not allowed to vote until the 1920s, and blacks were segregated from any significant participation in mainstream society until the late 1960s. Such barriers built into the structure of society tend to render the talents and abilities of certain groups invisible and of no consequence. The concept of a true meritocracy, therefore, is a myth. Functionalism, as Melvin Tumin (1953) argues, serves mainly to justify the status quo, which would keep those with most of the power and prestige in their positions of privilege and encourage resentment among those with the least number of opportunities.

Another criticism of functionalism is that *the social rewards "earned" by individuals often do not match the value of their contributions to society* (Wrong, 1959). Which position is more important to society as a whole—that of a professional baseball player or a U.S. Supreme Court judge? The answer, of course, is obvious. Yet, some athletes are paid fifty times the annual income of all federal officials, including the president of the United States. Likewise, movie actors, rock music stars, and other media personalities are sometimes paid enormous sums of money and enjoy a significant amount of social visibility and prestige, although the actual value of their objective contribution to society is questionable. As of 2009, actor Tom Cruise, for example, was being paid $25 million dollars for each motion picture in which he acted. Yet public school teachers, who, though highly educated and entrusted with the minds of society's next generation of leaders, remain among the lowest paid of all professionals.

The Conflict Perspective

While functionalists argue that stratification is beneficial to society because it matches individuals with the greatest skills to positions requiring the greatest expertise, conflict theorists take an opposite view. The **conflict perspective** sees stratification as harmful to society because it allows those with the most power, prestige, and wealth to dominate and exploit the less advantaged and maintain a condition of inequity.

Marx: Origins of the Conflict Approach   The conflict perspective on stratification originated with the work of Karl Marx during the nineteenth century. As you will recall from our discussion in Chapter 2, Marx argued that human history is largely a chronicle of class struggles that have existed in every age between two basic groups, the *"haves"* and the *"have nots."* The "haves," whether they are represented by the feudal lords of the Middle Ages or capitalists of modern times, comprise the ruling class, whose members possess most of the power and wealth. The "have nots," as represented by feudal serfs and modern factory workers, are the economically dispossessed with little or no hope for the future. In Marx's view, human history has consisted of a continuous cyclical process in which the tyranny and exploitation practiced by each ruling class ultimately led to its overthrow by the "have nots," who then became the new ruling class.

Marx viewed social class strictly in economic terms as related to the means of production. Those who owned the means of production were the ruling class, and those who worked for the owners were the "have nots." In the modern industrial era, he predicted the "have nots," whom he named the *proletariat,* would realize that they were being exploited, develop *class consciousness,* and overthrow the ruling class or *bourgeoisie* in a revolution that might be peaceful in some societies and violent in others. Then, he asserted, the sheer efficiency of industrial production would create such an abundance, that further class conflict over scarce resources would be unnecessary, the public would own the means of production and a truly classless society would emerge. Although Marx's notion of a proletarian revolt did not materialize in most societies and his ideas were far too simplistic by modern standards, his perspective was a powerful one and his ideas regarding the importance of power established an important foundation for further sociological exploration.

Modern Conflict Theory   Since the 1950s, American sociologists have greatly expanded Marx's narrow economic perspective on conflict. One characteristic that distinguishes conflict theory from functionalism is its emphasis on the impact of social structure on stratification rather than on individual factors such as training and talent. Some conflict theorists, for instance, might argue that no woman or black person, regardless of ability, could have been nominated for—much less elected to—the presidency of the United States before 2008 because of the social and political inequities built into the structure of American society. Others, like Ralf Dahrendorf (1959), have examined how various groups such as unions, companies, and a multitude of interest groups compete with one another for political as well as economic power. Organizations like Mothers Against Drunk Driving (MADD) and the National Education Association (NEA), for instance, have no ownership in the means of production (as in Marx's view), but nonetheless wield a significant amount of political power.

The Evolutionary Perspective: An Integrated View

Both the functionalist and the conflict approaches provide us with valuable insights but should not be seen as mutually exclusive. Instead, a synthesis of the two is perhaps the most useful perspective, as societies in general exhibit a basic stability yet contain elements of conflict and discord. Sociologist Gerhard Lenski (1966) has developed an **evolutionary perspective**, an approach that attempts to integrate both functionalist and conflict explanations of stratification. He argues that societies initially try to match rewards to the skills required for particular positions, but as technology evolves and surpluses develop, those in power attempt to retain control over this wealth. Lenski's basic thesis is summarized as follows: The functionalist perspective holds true initially as societies attempt to provide the most substantial rewards to those willing to undergo training and develop skills needed for important positions. However, as social systems evolve over time and develop additional technology, they may produce surpluses in highly valued goods and services. When this occurs, conflicts may develop over who should control or own this additional wealth. Those already in positions of political and economic power develop a vested interest in using whatever leverage they can to ensure that they retain control over these resources. Lenski maintains that, in general, as societies become more technological and complex, the level of control appears to rise as well.

*L*IFE CHANCES AND STRATIFICATION

Social rank profoundly influences both our general attitudes and our behavior. This process begins with early childhood socialization in which, because of the accident of birth, the social stratum that our family occupies significantly affects how we come to view the world and our place in it. In American society, children from different social classes develop distinctive value orientations. Working class adolescents, for example, must decide whether or not to go to college after high school graduation. Among upper middle-class teenagers in general and certain ethnic groups including several Asian American subcultures, not going to college is rarely considered an option because of the way they are socialized by their parents. Instead, their key decision has to do with which college to attend. Upper middle-class and upper-class teens, for example, often are focused on choosing a college during their junior year of high school and often apply to several colleges during the fall and early spring of their senior year through a process called early admission. For adolescents occupying the lower social classes, such patterns of behavior are much less prevalent.

Differential Life Chances and Their Indicators

The Concept of Life Chances   Stratification also affects what Max Weber termed **life chances**, the opportunities for survival and prosperity in society. These life chances which, together, determine in large part the way a person will live and what social mobility, if any, he or she will experience are identified and studied carefully by sociologists.

Life Chance Indicators   In the United States and elsewhere, life chances significantly impact on both the length and quality of life. Take *life expectancy* as one example. The higher one's social class, the longer one's life expectancy tends to be, according to numerous studies. Infant mortality, for instance, is much higher among the poor (Gortmaker, 1979; Mare, 1982), and overall mortality rates as well as rates of specific diseases like cancer are also higher among the poor (Shai, 1986). Americans in the middle and upper classes are better fed, housed, and educated, and this contributes to longer life expectancy. They also have much better access to adequate *health care* than their less affluent counterparts. Although public assistance programs, such as Medicaid, have helped narrow the health care gap significantly, these programs tend to serve only those living in the most dire circumstances, such as the elderly, the disabled, and those living in single-parent households.

The underemployed "working poor," who constitute the majority of people living in poverty, tend to have little or no health insurance and, consequently, receive only sporadic medical attention at best.

Another indicator of differential life chances is *nutrition.* Families with middle-class incomes spend about 15 percent of their income on food as compared with 35 percent spent by families with incomes below the poverty line (Gallo, Zellner, and Smallwood, 1980). The more affluent also pay less than the poor for food items because they can shop around for bargains in suburban chain grocery stores that buy foodstuffs in bulk. By contrast, the urban poor often have no personal transportation and, especially the disabled and elderly, are limited to small neighborhood markets where prices are higher and perishable goods like bread, produce, and diary products are often stale, overripe, or semi-spoiled. Consequently, the diets of those in the lower strata of society are substandard, and this contributes to high infant mortality, low birth weight in babies, and millions of malnourished children.

In terms of social policy, the 1980s under the Reagan administration was a period of declining support for several forms of public assistance, including maternal and child health care programs. These cutbacks were made in order to reduce federal bureaucracy and governmental costs (Aldous, 1986). Yet a growing body of research shows that public programs designed as preventive measures to enhance life chances actually save money in the long run, not to mention the social costs involved. In a study conducted at Harvard University, for example, it was found that the incidence of low birth weight in babies of mothers who did not receive supplemental nutrition benefits during their pregnancies was three times higher than babies of mothers who did receive such assistance. As a result, it was estimated that each dollar spent on such preventive prenatal care for poor mothers would net a savings of three dollars in long-term costs of health care for the children of these women (Amidei, 1981). Although some marginal improvements occurred during the Clinton administration (1993–2001), life chances among the poor did not improve on President George W. Bush's watch (2001–2009) except for reductions in poverty among the elderly.

Poverty

Poverty is a condition experienced by those who possess the lowest levels of life chances in a given society. These not only include life expectancy, health care, and nutrition, but are also reflected in other indicators such as inadequate housing, low levels of education, high fertility rates, and low income. Sometimes referred to as the *underclass* (Myrdal, 1962), those experiencing poverty in America and elsewhere typically are people who lack the basic resources necessary for long-term survival and prosperity.

Absolute Versus Relative Poverty   Sociologists define poverty in several different ways (Light and Keller, 1982). First, there is a distinction made between absolute poverty and relative poverty. **Absolute poverty** exists when people lack essential resources for survival, such as food and shelter. Compared to some societies, relatively few people in the United States starve to death each year. When these things do happen, they occur mainly among abandoned infants, the elderly poor, and "street people." In the world's poorest countries, however, absolute poverty is a reality for a large proportion of their populations. During the 1984–1985 drought in Africa, for example, two million people died of malnutrition and disease.

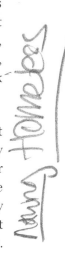

many homeless

These photographs were taken by Louly Contreras, an honors student in sociology at San Jacinto College. She analyzed them using the SIVSI™, a visual sociology assessment tool developed by the author. They portray life style elements of those who live on the streets of Houston and were part of a visual sociology project on stratification. How many SIVSI™ indicators can you find in each of these images? See *Achieving Sociological Fluency: An Interactive Guide and Workbook* that accompanies your text. Would you be able to write a brief essay on the sociological content contained in these photos and the messages they convey? If so, what do these photos tell you?

Relative poverty, by contrast, refers to a standard of living that is substandard in relation to that of the majority of society members. Using this definition, millions of Americans, including the underemployed and those in steady, but unskilled occupations, may have the essentials such as food, shelter, and basic health care but lack the purchasing power to acquire many of the nonessential "luxury" items many to most people in the middle class often take for granted.

Objective Versus Felt Poverty   There is also a distinction made between objective and felt poverty. **Objective poverty** is a state of official deprivation as determined by an agreed-upon standard of measurement. Since 1964, the U.S. government has used a poverty index developed by Mollie Orshansky (1965) of the Social Security Administration. This index, now known as the "poverty line," is set yearly, based on the amount of money needed each year per person to maintain minimum but adequate nutrition under temporary circumstances. Researchers use an elaborate formula to establish this cutoff point; it is based on the type of family, the number of adults and children under eighteen years of age living in the household, the type of residence (farm or nonfarm), and other factors. They then calculate these factors in terms of the consumer price index. In 2008, the poverty line for a nonfarm family of four was $22,200 (U.S. Department of Health and Human Services, 2008) Consequently, about fourteen percent of all Americans were officially poor in 2008 (Table 9-2).

Felt poverty refers to hardships experienced by those who fall slightly above the poverty line and/or those who experience psychological and emotional deprivation. Many

TABLE 9-2	United States Poverty Lines 2008 by Yearly Family Income (48 Contigious States and District of Columbia*)	
SIZE OF FAMILY	POVERTY UNIT LINE**	125 PERCENT***
1	$10,400	$13,000
2	$14,000	$17,500
3	$17,600	$22,000
4	$22,200	$26,500
5	$24,800	$31,000
6	$28,400	$35,500
7	$32,000	$40,000
8	$35,600	$44,500

SOURCE: U.S. Department of Health and Human Services; Annual Update, Poverty Guidelines: Posted January 23, 2008.
 *Guidelines for Alaska and Hawaii calculated separately due to costs of living.
 **To qualify for federal public assistance programs.
 ***To qualify for Affidavit of Support (125% of poverty line) for petitioning immigrants.

such families may be worse off in standard of living because they cannot qualify for federal assistance programs that are open to those who are "officially" poor. Others may be distinguished from the "officially" poor primarily because of felt emotional deprivation because their standard of living has been reduced. Felt poverty, therefore, should not be confused with relative poverty because it often has more to do with the psychological and emotional dimensions of poverty than with actual standard of living. Say, for example, a very affluent upper-class family lost their family business due to bankruptcy and were forced to live a middle-class lifestyle with only one home instead of several and with fewer amenities. While many people would feel little if any sympathy for them, members of this family, nonetheless, might perceive themselves as poor and experience a great deal of psychological and emotional distress.

The Poor in America

Those at the bottom of America's socioeconomic ladder vary widely in circumstances. Some are dislocated workers temporarily out of work who are "down on their luck." Although they and their families often suffer significantly and lose homes, cars, and other possessions, many if not most are able to return to work and/or retrain for other jobs. Others are marginal workers engaged in seasonal or unskilled jobs that offer low pay and often little job security such as farm workers, and manual laborers, domestics, dishwashers, car washers, and shoe shiners.

There are about thirty-seven million people living in poverty within the United States, which include almost eight million families (U.S. Census Bureau, 2005b). As many as thirteen million (approximately one-third), however, form the "hard-core" poor who appear destined for permanent poverty. Of these, an estimated one to three million are the homeless of various types, including those with mental disorders, who help make up the ranks of the "street people." An additional several million are undocumented aliens who live on the fringes of society and continually face deportation. A few million more are single women with dependent children caught up in a long-term cycle of poverty (Harrington, 1984; U.S. department of Health and Human Services, 2008).

Regardless whether the experience of deprivation is temporary or long term, poverty appears to be a growing problem for the most vulnerable people in society. Most of America's poor occupy one or more of the following overlapping categories: women, children, minorities, the elderly, and the disabled (U.S. Bureau of the Census, 1986a).

Of these groups, the large majority of the poor are women, children, and minorities. A trend toward the feminization of poverty is obvious since most adults living in poverty today are women. In 2005, the poverty rate for all women eighteen years of age or older was nearly thirteen percent (14.6 million women) as compared with nearly nine percent of all American men. In addition, of the twelve and one-half million adults who participated in the Federal Food Stamp Program, about eight and one-half million (68 percent) were women, with forty-five percent of these being young women in the eighteen to thirty-five year age group (U.S. Department of Health and Human Services, 2007). As a result of such factors as teenage pregnancy, divorce, desertion, and widowhood, more than forty-eight percent of households headed by single women suffer from poverty. In large part due to this factor, more than half of all poor children in the United States live in these households. Consequently, about thirteen million children—almost one out of every five Americans under eighteen years of age (eighteen percent)—live in households with incomes below the poverty line. When racial and ethnic backgrounds are factored in, ten percent of white children, twenty-eight percent of Hispanic children, and thirty-five percent of black children live in poverty (Fass and Cauthen, 2006).

The rates of poverty among the elderly are not as dismal. A couple of generations ago during the 1960s, about thirty percent of those over sixty-five were living in poverty. However, due to better retirement programs offered by both private and public employers and the fact that many Americans today who are sixty-five or older continue to participate in the labor force, the poverty rate for the elderly had fallen to only ten percent by 2005. Consequently, only about ten percent (more than three and one-half million) of all poor in the United States today are elderly.

The Culture of Poverty Hypothesis

A Culture of Poverty as a Cause?
Perhaps the most popular explanation of poverty among social scientists historically has been the culture of poverty hypothesis developed by anthropologist Oscar Lewis (1961, 1966, 1968). Using data gathered from field observations made primarily among the impoverished in Mexico and the United States, he argued that poverty involves a subculture that socializes its children with attitudes of despair and acceptance of being poor as natural and normal for them. The poor, Lewis asserts, tend to have little sense of what is going on in the larger society and remain socially isolated from it in their own neighborhoods and communities. They appear relatively unaware of opportunities for improving their life chances and fail to see how collective organization on their part could help to diminish their problems as well as influence public policy in the larger community

Poverty takes several forms. Although the urban poor are highly visible in the media today, there are many like this rural family who also suffer impaired life chances.

and society. Poverty, then, can become a self-perpetuating cycle. On an individual level, the child reared in this environment tends to develop a set of values and personality characteristics very different from those of the middle-class child in the suburbs. As Lewis explains,

> The individual who grows up in this culture has a strong feeling of fatalism, helplessness, dependence, and inferiority; a strong present-time orientation with relatively little disposition to defer gratification and plan for the future, and a high tolerance for psychological pathology of all kinds (1966, p. 23).

A Critique: Poverty for Most Is Temporary   While Lewis's hypothesis may help to explain poverty at least in part among segments of the chronically poor (Kerbo, 1981), it has come under criticism by some social scientists. Perhaps most important is the fact that for most who experience poverty in the United States, being poor is a temporary situation from which they recover in a few months or years (Duncan, 1984). Consequently, many to most sociologists do not accept Lewis' hypothesis as having much validity today.

The majority of today's poor are represented by an ever-changing pool of unfortunates caught up in the throes of temporary deprivation. Some are single mothers with young children who, because of teenage pregnancy, separation, or divorce and other factors, experience poverty and must seek public assistance for a time until they can obtain jobs. Others are displaced workers victimized by structural unemployment, the loss of employment as a result of changes in the economy that render certain occupations obsolete. In recent years, for example, changes in demand and technology have affected the gas, oil, steel, auto, and farm industries, which in turn have resulted in millions of "new poor."

A Culture of Poverty as a Consequence?   Some sociologists, such as Garth Massey (1982) and others, have argued that the culture of poverty—when it does exist—is not so much the cause of poverty as it is the consequence or adaptation to the condition of being poor. Ian Robertson (1980), in summarizing much of the literature on this point, reports that from the perspective of some writers,

> any distinctive culture of the poor is the result, not the cause, of their continuing poverty, and their characteristics and attitudes are a realistic and understandable response to their situation. The poor have to abandon the attitudes, values, and expectations of the predominantly middle-class society around them because middle-class culture is irrelevant to their circumstances. For example, middle-class culture emphasizes "deferred gratification"—saving income and postponing pleasures today in order to reap greater benefits tomorrow. The culture of the poor, however, tends to emphasize "instant gratification"—spending one's money and enjoying what one has while it lasts. Clearly, the value of deferred gratification makes no sense to someone who does not have money to save and is pessimistic about the future. Instant gratification is a rational response to this situation, but it is the result not the cause of poverty. Indeed, empirical studies of impoverished ghetto residences show that if they do manage to get jobs that offer stable income, they become "mainstreamers," concerned with such middle-class values as deferred gratification and respectability (p. 189).

The Poor and Welfare: Myth and Reality

There are several commonly held myths about the poor and the amount of public assistance they receive in the United States. Perhaps two of the most prevalent and interconnected misconceptions are as follows: *The myth of able-bodied recipients* and *the myth that most of America's poor are on welfare.* In fact, so-called welfare chiselers, while they do exist, are the exception rather than the rule. Most public assistance dollars go to help children, the ill, the elderly, and the disabled. Of these, single mothers and their offspring represent the one category that comprises the large majority of welfare recipients. Factors that contribute to this include emotional immaturity and ignorance about birth control, rape, divorce, and abandonment or desertion by live-in partners or husbands. In addition, contrary to popular belief, only about one-third of America's poor today receive welfare assistance. Contributing factors include the increased stigma attached to receiving welfare, increased requirements including paperwork to receive benefits, and federal requirements imposed since 1996 that limit benefits to five years of lifetime eligibility (Shirk, Bennett, and Abner, 1999; Deparle, 2004; Etter, 2006).

A third misconception is *the myth that women on welfare keep having babies to increase their benefits.* In fact, adults in a "welfare family" (1) have a life-time limit of four years in which to receive federal Temporary Assistance for Needy Families (TANF) benefits, (2) must participate in a work plan designed to reach economic self-sufficiency to receive any benefits, and (3) ultimately receive benefits for an average of only eighteen months. Of those adults who are single parents receiving benefits, eighty-two percent have only one or two children and fewer than seven percent have more than four offspring (U.S. Department of Human Services, 2006).

As a final illustration, there is *the myth that benefits discourage working.* In fact, welfare payments alone in all fifty states are not sufficient to raise a recipient family's above the poverty line. And people have to eat to survive. Just for the sake of illustration, suppose a family of four living at the allotted poverty line of $22,200 (2008) spend one-third of its income on food and choose to purchase it at McDonalds. According to sociologist Leonard Beeghley, that would give each family member just one Big Mac sandwich and a one medium soft drink per day on which to live (Beeghley, 2008).

CLASS IN AMERICA: ELEMENTS OF RANK

Weber's Multidimensional Approach: The Elements of Class   Although Marx saw class in economic terms as consisting of two groups, the propertied ("the haves") and the nonpropertied ("the have nots"), another early theorist, German sociologist Max Weber, was the first to take a multidimensional approach and divide class into its essential elements. Weber viewed social class as consisting of a dynamic interplay among three major elements: "political status" or power, "social status" or prestige, and "economic status" or wealth (Weber, 1946; Parsons, 1947). His assessment of class generally has been the most widely accepted in contemporary sociology. Consequently, his three key dimensions of class—power, prestige, and wealth—will provide the general framework from which we will next examine the specific aspects of class in America. In addition, life style, a factor Weber saw as related to prestige, deserves to be treated as separate class characteristic in its own right.

Power

As introduced in Chapter 8, **power** is the ability to influence or control the behavior of others with or without their consent. For the purposes of social stratification, the most important types of power tend to be "referent power" or influence and "legitimate power" or authority. These factors determine how decisions are made and who makes them. In a given instance, does more power reside in a factory supervisor or a shop steward, a classroom teacher or a PTA president, a city mayor or a chief campaign contributor? Such issues are decided each day based on a constantly shifting balance of power in all sectors and at all levels of society.

Two Forms of Power Related to Stratification   First, there is *influence*, the ability to affect the actions of others through the power of persuasion. This is informal power, which results from the possession of knowledge and the force of personality, rather than official prerogatives that go with a formal position or rank. Even if a person had the official title "fund-raiser," for instance, he or she would be an abysmal failure without certain interpersonal skills and personal characteristics. Many influential people, therefore, tend to operate without need of formal position, and some prefer to operate behind the scenes.

Although those with the power to persuade may not have a legitimate right to make decisions, they can influence those who do. Three notable examples during the twentieth century were Mahatma Gandhi, Martin Luther King, Jr., and Eleanor Roosevelt who, each in his or her own way, were able to influence policy makers and social policy as well. During the last decade of the previous century, Hillary Clinton as first lady wielded tremendous influence during the eight-year administration (1993–2001) of her husband, President Bill Clinton although she possessed no formal authority.

Authority, as previously defined (Chapter 8), is legitimated power generally recognized and supported by those over whom it is exercised. In other words, it is legitimate power that results from an officially held position in society. As such, it is formal in nature. Like influence, authority is found at all levels and classes of society. Parents have authority over their children (microlevel), and the state has some authority over parents (macrolevel), particularly in cases of neglect or abuse. We can also consider as examples of authority the police officer who has the authority to arrest and detain, the public school teacher to pass and fail, and the physician to diagnose and prescribe. Those with the greatest authority (and in some cases, influence as well) include heads of institutions like Pope Benedict XVI, corporate CEOs such as Bill Gates of Microsoft, and heads of state like Gloria Aroyo of the Philippines. Shortly after the end of her husband's administration, Hillary Clinton transformed her influence and popularity as first lady into formal authority as an elected U.S. senator from New York who was subsequently reelected. She then ran for President in 2008, was narrowly defeated by Barack Obama for the Democratic presidential nomination and then, upon his election as president, parleyed her influence and that of her husband into becoming nominated and confirmed as Secretary of State, a position which carries a great deal of authority.

Two Sociological Explanations of Power

One of the most intriguing issues relating to power has to do with who wields it and how it is concentrated. Is power in America limited to a small "ruling class" of elites, or is it instead more widely dispersed among a variety of specialized factions? The majority of social scientists have not reached agreement on this question. Perhaps this is partially due to the complexities of analysis brought on by the ever-changing economic and social conditions of American society. Then, too, the use of power, particularly influence, is not readily visible to the investigator. Those with power often keep it secret and exercise it as a guarded rite behind closed doors.

Power Elite Theory

Some sociologists subscribe to the **power elite theory** developed by C. Wright Mills in his book *The Power Elite* (1959). Here, Mills asserted that American society is shaped largely by an informal unified group of elites from the highest levels of government, the military, and the corporate sector. According to Mills, these individuals—who have both high authority and substantial influence—operate through interlocking networks to make decisions that serve their own vested interests. However, by working together, they can also largely determine the nature and direction of social policy. Large defense contractors, like General Dynamics, Haliburton, and Honeywell, for example, must work with Pentagon officials who, in turn, must cooperate with legislators to get defense appropriation bills passed through Congress. The results serve the needs of all concerned. The defense contractors make money, the military obtains the latest combat hardware, and the legislators ensure that the needed level of national defense is maintained. The majority of these elites, although they occupy top positions in different sectors of society, are white males, graduates of the same twelve private universities, members of the same clubs, and have similar worldviews (Domhoff, 1967; Dye, 1986).

Pluralistic Theory

Other sociologists (Dahl, 1961; Reisman, 1961; Martin, 1977) subscribe to **pluralistic theory**, the assertion that power in America is distributed among a wide variety of interest groups that tend to cancel each other out, thus preventing any one group from dominating public policy. Some sociologists argue that no single group has a decisive advantage in being able to rule America. Instead, a wide variety of groups, each with its own vested interests, compete with one another for their own slices of the public policy pie. There are the various manufacturing and business lobbies centering on products like cigarettes, automobiles, oil and gas, and agricultural products. There are interest groups focused on furthering positions on issues that range from abortion, gun control, conservation, and religion, to civil rights for women, blacks, and other minorities, the elderly, and children. Sociologist David Reisman and others have argued that because of the large numbers of these interest groups and their many agendas, they ultimately cancel each other out, resulting in no single group being able to gain decisive advantage.

Prestige

Prestige is the relative degree of honor and respect a person receives from others. The basis for such esteem and deference depends on the personal qualities seen as important by the members of any given society. In the feudal system practiced in medieval Europe, family membership, amount of property, and demonstrated loyalty were all considered important criteria. The caste system in India traditionally stressed birth as the basis for esteem. In other societies, prestige may be based on a combination of these and other possible factors including power (heads of governments and corporations), wealth (billionaires), physical beauty (top fashion models), credibility (network anchor people), intellect (Nobel Prize recipients), dramatic ability (movie stars), athletic prowess (professional ball players), and life style. Elements of all these variables may be seen in the American class system. Old, established families like the Rockefellers, DuPonts, and Mellons, for example, are noted for their family background, power, wealth, and life style.

However, some of these factors—particularly newly acquired wealth and media exposure—have little or no bearing on the relative level of prestige experienced by most Americans. Few people will have an opportunity to co-star with Cameron Diaz and Drew Barrymore in the next installment of the *Charlie's Angels* chronicles, to anchor an evening news show like *CNN: 360 with Anderson Cooper*, or to appear on the cover of *Vogue* magazine. Therefore, we will focus our discussion briefly on a common misperception about class prestige held by many Americans, and the factors that tend to be the most important common denominators of prestige in America: occupation and education.

Wealth and Prestige: A Common Misperception   The idea that wealth is the most important source of prestige is a common misconception. Who has the greatest amount of prestige (and power): the president of the United States, a CEO of any top U.S. corporation, or a manager of a major mutual fund? The answer is obvious. Yet the president's annual salary of $400,000 is paltry compared to that of corporate leaders and mutual fund managers. In 2007, for example, the top fifty hedge fund managers averaged $580 million each for the year or just over $1.1 million per week and $27,500 per hour (based on a forty-hour week) (Anderson, 2008). Yet how many Americans have never even heard the names of finance and investment leaders such as John Paulson (annual salary $3.7 billion), George Soros (annual salary $2.9 billion), or James Simons (annual salary $2.8 billion), whose earnings for 2007 led the list (Anderson, 2008). These top three fund manager alone, in terms of extrapolated wealth accumulation, each had an average salary of $3.3 billion for the year or a mind-boggling $6,346 million per week and more than $1.56 million per hour.

The different elements that constitute class do not necessarily go together. Billionaire Sheldon Adelson, for example, has great wealth but limited prestige and power. The Dalai Lama has great international prestige as a world spiritual leader but little if any wealth.

Occupation and Prestige   Occupation generally is regarded by sociologists as the most important indicator of prestige in America because, in most cases, it represents the primary means to both power and wealth. As such, it represents the closest fit—as compared to other class indicators—to power and influence over other people's lives. According to the National Opinion Research Center (2001), Americans hold professionals such as physicians, college professors, lawyers, and scientists, who have undergone many years of intensive education and earn relatively high incomes in greatest esteem. Those ranked at the bottom of the prestige hierarchy are unskilled workers including farm laborers, maids, garbage collectors, etc. (Table 9-3).

Education and Prestige   Education is the second most important indicator of prestige because it represents the primary means of gaining entry into the most valued occupations and achieving overall upward social mobility. There is an increasing need for a high school diploma or equivalent by anyone wanting to gain any type of regular, full-time employment, and a four-year college degree is almost a universal minimum requirement for entry into the upper-middle class. As far as income alone is concerned, education in a "credential-oriented" society is a key ingredient to maintaining or increasing one's standard of living. According to the U.S. Bureau of the Census, the median annual income for American workers eighteen years of age and older in 2005, by level of education, was $26,933 for those who completed four years of high school as compared with $52,671 for those with four years of college. Individuals with doctoral degrees averaged $91,370 in average annual earnings (U.S. Census Bureau, 2006b) (Table 9-4).

Some research has shown that family background including, for example, the occupations of parents, plays a crucial role in affecting the amount of education an individual acquires (Jencks, 1972). Middle- and upper-class parents socialize their children to see a four-year college degree as an essential ingredient in the transition to adulthood and self-sufficiency, and often plan carefully for their children's college years. Most parents from the lower classes, in socializing their children, do not place as much emphasis on education.

TABLE 9-3 Prestige Rankings of Selected American Occupations

OCCUPATION	SCORE	OCCUPATION	SCORE
Physician	86	Secretary	46
Lawyer	75	Insurance agent	45
College professor	74	Bank teller	43
Dentist	74	Nurse's aid	42
Architect	73	Farmer	40
Clergy (degreed)	69	Correctional officer	40
Pharmacist	68	Receptionist	39
Registered nurse	66	Carpenter	39
High school teacher	66	Barber	36
Accountant	65	Child care worker	35
Elementary school teacher	64	Hotel clerk	32
Airline pilot	60	Bus driver	32
Police officer	60	Auto body repair person	31
Prekindergarten teacher	55	Truck driver	30
Librarian	54	Salesperson (shoes)	28
Firefighter	53	Garbage collector	28
Social worker	52	Restaurant server	28
Dental hygienist	52	Bartender	25
Electrician	51	Farm worker	23
Funeral director	49	Janitor	22
Mail carrier	47	Newspaper vendor	19

NOTE: Prestige ratings could be from 100 (highest) to 0 (lowest).
SOURCE: National Opinion Research Center, 2001.

Wealth

The primary indicator of strictly economic stratification is **wealth**, the net worth of an individual or group in terms of property and income. For most Americans, however, the degree of wealth they possess is more a reflection of their overall social class level than its cause. Wealth accrues essentially as a consequence of achieving higher levels of power, occupation, and education. Of the four hundred richest people in the United States, for example, only about one-third inherited their wealth. Instead, the majority are self-made billionaires (Forbes, 2004). Nonetheless, those in the upper classes can and do use wealth to solidify their class position and provide opportunities for their children that most Americans could not hope to offer. The yearly cost in 2009, for instance, of sending a son

TABLE 9-4	Mean Annual Income in 2005: U.S. Workers 18 Years and Over by Educational Attainment	
LEVEL OF EDUCATIONAL ATTAINMENT		**MEAN YEARLY INCOME**
Did Not Complete High School		$17,299
High School Graduate (including GED)		$26,933
Some College (no degree)		$30,627
Associates Degree (A.A., A.S.)		$36,665
Bachelor's Degree (B.A., B.S.)		$52,671
Master's Degree (M.A., M.S.)		$66,754
Professional Degree (M.D., J.D., D.D.S, etc.)		$112,902
Doctoral Degree (Ph.D., Ed.D.)		$91,370

SOURCE: U.S. Census Bureau, Current Population Survey, 2006b Annual Social and Economic Supplement.

or daughter to an elite private college or university such as the MIT or Harvard was over $40,000 per year.

How Rich Are the Rich?   There are also striking indicators that wealth is becoming increasingly concentrated in the hands of a few. When *Forbes Magazine* released its list of the four hundred wealthiest Americans in October, 2006, "the collective net worth of the nation's wealthiest climbed $120 billion, to $1.25 trillion" (Special Issue: "Forbes 400: The Richest People in America," *Forbes*, October 9, 2006). For the first time, beginning in 2006, the four hundred richest Americans were all billionaires. See a list of the ten wealthiest in Table 9-5.

Property   *Property* refers to all material assets owned by a person, such as real estate, stocks and bonds, pension funds, antiques and art, and cash on hand. It is difficult to arrive at a precise breakdown on how property in America is distributed because assets are so easily hidden, for instance, funds are held in foreign banks and art collections in private homes. However, it is clear from available estimates that property is distributed throughout the population quite equally. Using the broad definition above, we can say that the top ten percent of property holders own about sixty-four percent of all wealth in the United States. The bottom half own only three percent of the nation's total wealth (Rose, 1986).

Income   *Income* refers to all money earned through all sources including wages or salaries, interest on savings, and investment dividends. For most Americans, income derives almost exclusively from their occupations in the form of wages and salaries. By contrast, the wealthy obtain most of their income from a variety of investments, including rental property, stocks and bonds, and interest on funds held in financial institutions. Income in the United States is also unequally distributed, although not so greatly as is property. In terms of annual income, the wealthiest twenty percent of the population in

TABLE 9-5	The Ten Wealthiest Americans: 2006

NAME	WEALTH	SOURCE OF WEALTH	AGE
William H. Gates	$53.0 Billion	Microsoft	50
Warren Buffet	$46.0 Billion	Berkshire Hathaway	76
Sheldon Adelson	$20.5 Billion	Casinos, Las Vegas	73
Lawrence Ellison	$19.5 Billion	Oracle	62
Paul Allen	$16.0 Billion	Microsoft	53
Jim C. Walton	$15.7 Billion	Wal-Mart	58
S. Robson Walton	$15.6 Billion	Wal-Mart	62
Christy Walton	$15.6 Billion	Wal-Mart	50
Alice L. Walton	$15.5 Billion	Wal-Mart	57
Michael Dell	$15.5 Billion	Dell	41

SOURCE: Special Issue: *Forbes.* 2006. *Forbes 400: The Richest People in America,* Oct. 9.

TABLE 9-6	Distribution of Median U.S. Family: Income by Quintile 2004

QUINTILE	LOWEST INCOME THRESHOLD
Highest Fifth	$88,030*
Second-Highest Fifth	$55,331
Middle Fifth	$34,738
Second-Lowest Fifth	$18,500
Lowest-Fifth	Poverty

SOURCE: U.S. Bureau of the Census, 2005b.
*In 2004, 15.73 percent of households had incomes exceeding $100,000 annually.

2005 earned more than forty-three percent of all available income, compared to the poorest twenty percent, who earned only about four and one-half percent of all available income.

Life Style

Power, aspects of prestige including occupation and education, and wealth are all important indicators of social class. However, an individual's membership in a given society is usually not fully recognized and accepted by others of similar status unless that person also exhibits the "appropriate" life style that goes with it. To be fully accepted as belonging to a given class level by its other members, a person is expected to demonstrate to some degree that he or she identifies with and practices its culture.

There are a multitude of ways a person may exhibit class identification, ranging from certain forms of language, carriage, and dress, to diet, consumer and recreational preferences, and preferred forms of social etiquette. Taken as a whole, these and other related characteristics affect to a significant degree how we see ourselves, our place in the community and society, whom we choose for our friends and companions, and how we relate to other people in general.

Sociologically speaking, **life style** refers to the general value orientation, tastes and preferences, and pattern of living characteristic of those belonging to a particular group or social class. Some people prefer country-western music, cold beer in a can, jeans and baseball caps, and *TV Guide*. Others have a preference for classical music, gin and tonic, clothing from Ralph Lauren or Neiman Marcus, and the *Wall Street Journal*. Therefore, life style represents a class subculture in which the way people feel, act, and live in general reflects their class status, along with other factors including power, prestige, and wealth. In terms of child socialization, for example, working-class parents rear their children to conform to and respect authority and to be neat and orderly. Middle-class parents, in contrast, teach their children to develop attitudes of initiative and autonomy, and tend to give them more freedom of action aimed at developing their creativity (Bell, 1979).

Nonetheless, writer Paul Fussel (1983) argues that the lower the social class, the less likely it is that its people will recognize the importance of life style in shaping the level of social esteem given them by others:

> At the bottom, people tend to believe that class is defined by the amount of money you have. In the middle, people grant that money has something to do with it, but think education and the kind of work you do almost equally important. Nearer the top, people perceive that taste, values, ideas, style, and behavior are indispensable criteria of class, regardless of money or occupation or education (p. 5).

Social Class in Perspective

Social scientists find that social class is difficult to measure precisely for a variety of reasons. First, there is the dimension of power and its complexity. While authority is related to the duties of an occupation or office and is thereby official and usually somewhat open to inspection and measurement, influence is not. Influence is more emotional and subjective in nature, and those who exert influence often do so quietly and discreetly.

Social class also has to do with prestige. Both the elements of occupation and education can be correlated with relative degrees of power and wealth and with the esteem (reputation) accorded them by most Americans. However, level of education alone does not guarantee a person a certain social position or the lack of it. There are people with college degrees in working-class occupations, and there are those who have never been to college who have been able to start and build successful businesses and have a significant impact on their communities.

Wealth too can be a complicated variable in placing people in specified social classes. An organized crime boss may live in a mansion on a large estate, drive a Rolls Royce, and have huge sums of ready cash. Likewise, high-priced call girls and even small-time drug dealers often generate six-figure incomes. How do they rank on the social class ladder compared with social workers, librarians, and nurses or, for that matter, with dentists, lawyers, and college professors?

Finally, there is class life style that is subcultural and also difficult to measure. Dramatic differences in life style are evident between those in the upper class versus those in the working class. However, the life styles of adjacent social classes, like the lower-middle and working classes, for example, may be distinctive in some ways but overlap in others.

These are but a few examples of status inconsistency (see Chapter 6) by class, a contradiction that exists when a person appears to rank higher in one aspect of stratification than another. In the United States, occupation (and to a lesser degree, education) usually take precedence over wealth. A person with a deviant occupation, such as a criminal, would be ranked very low, regardless of their wealth. Similarly, many in the working class, including truck drivers and union laborers, are paid higher wages than those in some middle-class occupations, including public school teachers, but are ranked significantly lower in overall social class.

THE ANALYSIS OF STRATIFICATION

In an attempt to lend precision to the concept of social class and to analyze its impact on social behavior in general, sociologists use a variety of research approaches. Of these, the most important are the subjective approach, the reputational approach, and the objective approach.

The Subjective Approach

A method of stratification analysis in which people are asked to identify their own social class category is the **subjective method**. One useful benefit of this method is that it furnishes sociologists with a means of comparing perceived social class by individuals and groups with their actual approximate positions on the stratification scale as determined by objective measures. Most Americans, regardless of their actual class ranking, identify themselves as belonging somewhere in the middle class, while only about eight percent perceive themselves as lower class and one or two percent see themselves as upper class (Hodge and Treiman, 1968; Jackman and Jackman, 1983).

These findings tend to indicate, among other things, that people perceive their own social class level based on their reference groups (whom they would like to be like). Sometimes people's perceptions tend to be at odds with the way their community and society would actually rank them. In a society like the United States that is dominated by middle-class values, however, those who are objectively working class who wish to obtain a college education need to identify with much of the mindset of the middle class, such as seeing a need for a college education, practicing deferred gratification, and being time conscious, which are requirements for upward mobility and actual middle-class status. Class then, for individuals engaged in self-ranking, often represents a social category they identify with as a goal, rather than one they occupy in actuality.

The Reputational Approach

While the use of subjective techniques involves getting individuals to rank themselves, the **reputational method** is a method of stratification analysis that asks people to identify the social class of others in their community. As such, it represents an approach that focuses on the dimension of class prestige. The best known early stratification studies that used this approach were conducted during the 1930s and 1940s by W. Lloyd Warner and his associates in communities such as Newburyport, Massachusetts ("Yankee City") and Morris, Illinois ("Jonesville") (Warner and Lunt, 1941; Warner, 1949; Warner et al., 1949). In his "Yankee City" study of a New England community, Warner found six distinct class levels which, as shown by later research, he felt were fairly typical of communities throughout the United States. These class levels are briefly described as follows:

1. ***Upper-upper class.*** In Warner's research, the *upper-upper class* was found to be an old aristocracy of upper-class families. These families could trace their prominence in the community and nation back at least three generations. Meeting the lineage test of birth and family name was therefore seen as more important than "mere wealth," which tended to be substantial. Nationally prominent upper-upper-class families today include the Vanderbilts, the Hearsts, the Carnegies, and the Fords. The Kennedys and Bushes would also probably qualify at this time.

2. ***Lower-upper class.*** Those with newly acquired wealth and social standing comprised the *lower-upper class.* These people, Warner found, had acquired wealth through developing industries including shoes, textiles, and finance. They were separated from the upper-upper class only by the lack of long-term family status. Members of the lower-upper class today are referred to as "new money" by members of the general public. Bill Gates, Michael Dell, Arnold Schwarzenegger, and Oprah Winfrey would represent prominent examples today.

3. ***Upper-middle class.*** The next group, the *upper-middle class,* consisted of college-educated professionals and successful business people. Members of this class tended to be property owners and were often quite active in civic affairs. They lived in better neighborhoods and had substantial incomes, but not enough to constitute wealth. Today, the upper-middle class are degreed professionals for the most part.

4. ***Lower-middle class.*** The highest of what Warner called the "common classes" was the *lower-middle class,* which consisted of small business people, lower-level white-collar workers, and skilled blue-collar workers. People of this class lived in small houses in neat neighborhoods, tended to be politically conservative, and were careful with their money. Their reputation was that of good common, hard-working people.

5. ***Upper-lower class.*** Warner identified semiskilled and unskilled blue collar workers as *upper-lower class.* These people lived in less desirable neighborhoods and had a reputation of being "poor but honest." The term "working class" is used by some sociologists today to identify essentially the same group (*Encyclopedia of Sociology,* 2002).

6. ***Lower-lower class.*** The underemployed and unemployed represented the *lower-lower class.* Its members had a reputation of being lazy, shiftless, and dependent and, therefore, were seen as not respectable. Based on what we know today about poverty from sociological research, many if not most of the poor in America are undeserving of such a reputation, although it is still prevalent.

The reputational approach has been very useful in studying stratification in small communities. However, it is difficult to use in large cities where people do not know others in their community and cannot, therefore, accurately judge their reputations.

The Objective Approach

The method most often used today in sociological research is the objective approach. Although both the subjective and reputational approaches have their place in stratification research, many to most sociologists prefer the **objective approach**, a method of stratification analysis that makes use of standardized criteria—such as occupation, education, and income—for objectively measuring social rank. In this manner, feelings and perceptions of evaluators are exchanged for more precise scales that weigh several stratification factors. The objective approach is also more amenable to being used with large populations and in evaluating the stratification characteristics of whole societies.

The most common applications of the objective approach involve measures of socioeconomic status (SES), which sociologists use to rank individuals depending on a combination of occupation, education, and income. Occupation is ranked according to established prestige scales, which, in turn, is determined through research on large samples of Americans who are asked to rank most of the standard occupations from highest to lowest. Of chief concern here is the relative importance of certain occupational skills for society. Some occupations require greater responsibility and involve higher degrees of influence and control over people's lives than others.

Evaluators are also interested in the likelihood that certain occupations will attract highly educated people. Education, as determined by years and levels obtained, is used because it reflects the difficulty and length of preparation required to qualify persons for given positions. It is generally assumed that the longer and more extensive the training, the more highly valued will be the skills that are developed.

Finally, income is considered, as measured in yearly earnings. Here we see the unequal reward system which, generally speaking, pays more money to those in the most prestigious occupations who have the most education.

In closing, it is hoped that this topic has helped you to further appreciate how fascinating, varied, and complex social stratification is and can be. Sociologists are interested primarily in assessing the impact of social rank at the macro level on the structure of society and vice versa. They are also interested in its impact at the micro level on people's attitudes, opportunities, and behavior, as well as in identifying apparent trends for the future.

The United States, with its class system, has become—especially in light of the reforms of the twentieth century, which include the civil rights and women's movements—one of the most open societies in the world. Nonetheless, structured inequalities exist in all social systems, and America is no exception. In addition to its class system, America retains a few caste-like aspects, as mentioned earlier. These are applied to a few notable categories of people—racial and ethnic minorities and, to some degree, women. The ways in which these elements of a caste-like system arose and have changed, in regard to racial and ethnic minorities in particular, represents much of the focus for the chapter to follow.

▶ CHAPTER SUMMARY

1. Societies today tend to have one or any combination of three different types of stratification systems. Slavery, which still exists in several forms throughout the world, is a system of involuntary bondage in which human beings are bought, sold, or exchanged. The two dominant forms of stratification systems found today are caste and class, with a caste system being basically closed with few if any opportunities for social mobility (e.g., traditional India) while a class system (e.g., the United States) is open with many opportunities to change or improve one's social rank.

2. Each society has some form of stratification that defines how social rank is determined and social rewards are distributed. One consequence of rank is what Max Weber called "life chances," the opportunities for survival and prosperity in society. In terms of such life chance indicators as life expectancy, availability of health care, and good nutrition, the upper classes in America fare much better than the poor.

3. Those with the lowest levels of life chances live in poverty, which sociologists categorize in various ways. Absolute poverty describes the plight of people who lack the essentials for survival while relative poverty indicates a standard of living below average for some when compared with the standard for most people in a given community or society. A distinction is also made between objective poverty (official poverty as determined by agreed-upon criteria) and felt poverty (the physical, psychological, and emotional experience of deprivation).

4. Most of America's poor tend to belong to one or more of the following categories: women, children, minorities, the elderly, and the disabled. One popular explanation of deprivation, historically, has been the culture of poverty hypothesis, which holds that attitudes of despair and hopelessness are socialized into children and passed from generation to generation. While this may hold true for some, poverty in America generally tends to be a temporary situation for most who experience it.

5. There are three dominant sociological approaches in examining and explaining the causes of stratification—the functionalist, conflict, and evolutionary perspectives. The functionalist approach holds that unequal rewards are necessary to motivate enough people to seek and fill the jobs requiring the most education and skill. The conflict approach, in comparison, sees ranking as harmful, because those with superior positions of power and wealth can keep the system structured to benefit themselves and thus dominate and exploit the disadvantaged. A third approach, the evolutionary perspective, essentially combines the other two perspectives.

6. The primary dimensions of social class in America are power, prestige, wealth, and life style. Power is the ability to influence or control the behavior of others and is divided into two basic types—authority (one's official position) and influence (the ability to persuade). Prestige is the honor and respect a person receives from others, as measured by occupation, education, and wealth. Wealth, a third class indicator, tends to be a reflection of overall class, rather than its prime determinant, and is divided into the categories of property (what one owns) and income (what one earns). Finally, life style refers to the general value orientation, tastes and preferences, and patterns of living characteristic of those belonging to a particular group or social class.

7. Precise measurement of social class is complex, in part the result of status inconsistency, a contradiction that exists when a person appears to rank higher in one aspect of stratification than another. To deal effectively with this and other related issues and difficulties, sociologists employ a variety of research strategies: the subjective approach (self-placement), the reputational approach (community studies), and the objective approach (socioeconomic status).

TERMS TO KNOW

absolute poverty: a condition that exists when people lack essential resources, such as food and shelter, for survival.

caste system: a rigid and closed system of social ranking in which most statuses are ascribed and tend to remain so.

class system: a relatively open and flexible system of social ranking in which most statuses are achieved.

conflict perspective: an approach that sees stratification as harmful to society because it allows those with the most power, prestige, and wealth to dominate and exploit the less advantaged and maintain a condition of inequity.

culture of poverty hypothesis: Oscar Lewis' argument that poverty involves a subculture that socializes its children with attitudes of despair and acceptance of being poor as natural and normal for them.

evolutionary perspective: an approach that attempts to integrate both functionalist and conflict explanations of stratification.

felt poverty: a condition of hardship experienced by families that fall slightly above the poverty line and/or those whose members experience emotional deprivation because their standard of living has been reduced.

functionalist perspective: an approach that sees stratification as necessary and beneficial to society because it uses a system of rewards to motivate people to acquire the skills needed to obtain the most valued positions.

horizontal mobility: change in social position, usually occupation, without any significant impact on social class level.

intergenerational mobility: change in social class level that occurs across generations between parents and their children.

intragenerational mobility: changes people experience in social rank within their own lifetimes or careers.

life chances: opportunities for survival and prosperity in society (Max Weber).

life style: the general value orientation, tastes and preferences, and pattern of living characteristic of those belonging to a particular group or social class.

objective approach: a method of stratification analysis that makes use of standardized criteria—such as occupation, education, and income—for objectively measuring social rank.

objective poverty: a state of official deprivation as determined by an agreed-upon standard of measurement (e.g., the poverty line for a family of four).

pluralistic theory: the assertion that power in America is distributed among a wide variety of interest groups which tend to cancel each other out, thus preventing any one group from dominating public policy.

poverty: a condition experienced by those who possess the lowest levels of life chances in a given society.

power: the ability to influence or control the behavior of others with or without their consent.

power elite theory: the assertion by Mills that American society is shaped largely by an informal unified group of elites from the highest levels of government, the military, and the corporate sector.

prestige: the relative degree of honor and respect a person receives from others.

relative poverty: a standard of living that is substandard in relation to that of the majority of society members.

reputational approach: a method of stratification analysis that asks people to identify the social class of others in their community.

slavery: an involuntary system of bondage in which human beings are bought, sold, or exchanged for money or other resources.

social class: a grouping of people on the socioeconomic continuum who share similar levels and types of power, prestige, and wealth.

social mobility: the ability to move from one social location or level in society to another.

social stratification: a system in each society that defines how social rank is determined and social rewards are distributed.

structural unemployment: the loss of employment as a result of changes in the economy that render certain occupations obsolete.

subjective approach: a method of stratification analysis in which people are asked to identify their own social class category.

vertical mobility: any upward or downward change that occurs in a person's social class level.

wealth: the net worth of an individual or group in terms of property and income.

SUGGESTED READINGS

Ehrenreich, B. 2001. *Nickel and Dimed. On (Not) Getting By in America.* New York: Metropolitan. An insightful account of the use of participant observation by an investigative writer who lived a year attempting to survive in America by holding a variety of menial jobs that paid the minimum wage. She worked at various jobs including Wal-Mart, restaurants, and served as a maid while recording the struggles and stresses—both emotional and physical—experienced by those who just "barely get by."

Keister, L. A. 2005. *Getting Rich: America's New Rich and How They Got That Way.* New York: Cambridge University Press. An examination of the sources of wealth and the occupations and strategies used by those becoming wealthy in America today.

Schor, J. 1999. *The Overspent American: Why We Want What We Don't Need.* New York: Harper-Collins. An overview of the spending patterns of Americans as consumers—almost comical at times—whose self-images and emotional well-being appear to be based on the perceived quality of the "things" we own, use, and wear.

Shipler, D. K. 2005. *The Working Poor: Invisible in America.* New York: Vintage. A "pull-no-punches" exposé of the conditions faced by the working poor today who tend to get caught in a vicious cycle of structural unemployment, discrimination, and powerlessness.

Racial and Ethnic Relations

Terms to Know

accommodation	hate crimes	prejudice
amalgamation	individual discrimination	race
anti-Semitism	individual racism	racial minority
authoritarian personality	institutional discrimination	racism
discrimination	institutional racism	reverse discrimination
dominant group	Jim Crow	reverse racism
ethnic minority	minority group	segregation
ethnicity	normative prejudice	stereotypes
exploitative prejudice	pan-indianism	
genocide	pluralism	

On November 4, 2008, U.S. Senator Barack Obama of Illinois was elected as forty-fourth President of the United States. Obama, the first African American elected to the nation's highest office, beat his Republican opponent, John McCain, decisively and in doing so, garnered most votes numerically from white Americans. In choosing him, voters saw not a black man but the candidate they thought best suited to lead the country. Consequently, this election served—among other things—as a referendum on race in this country. It marked an important turning point in the history of racial and ethnic relations, and, as such, offered a resounding repudiation of past values and practices by American society that will be explored briefly in the pages to follow.

DOMINANT GROUPS AND MINORITY GROUPS

What Is a Dominant Group?

A **dominant group** is a social category comprised of those in society who are dominant in power, prestige, wealth, and culture. Its members use this advantage to have their values and cultural orientation legitimized as society's dominant norms and the social policies that result from them.

The Historically Dominant Group in America: White Anglos

America was first settled predominantly by those of English, Scotch–Irish, and German descent. The United States originated largely from thirteen British colonies during the 1600s and 1700s. In the wake of a successful eighteenth-century revolt against British rule (1776–1789), the next two centuries saw rapid industrialization and, with it, massive immigration by diverse racial and ethnic groups drawn by the prospects of a better life. Some, however, did not come as

TABLE 10-1	Ethnic Backgrounds of the U.S. Population, 1790*
ETHNIC BACKGROUND	**PERCENT**
English	60.1
Scottish, Scotch–Irish	14.0
German	8.6
Irish	3.6
Dutch	3.1
French, Swedish	3.0
Other	7.0

* Total may not equal 100 percent due to rounding. Estimates based on the first U.S. Census, 1790. They do not include the 20 percent who were slaves.

Source: Parrillo, V. N. (1985) *Strangers to These Shores,* 2nd ed., 119. New York: Wiley.

willing or paying passengers, but as commodities from Africa to be sold in commercial auctions, packed tightly in the bowels of slave ships. Others—white ethnics, Asians, and Hispanics—came voluntarily, but often found themselves, upon arrival, the victims of prejudice and discrimination which, in many cases, limited their life chances significantly (Table 10-1).

Regardless of whether immigration was voluntary are forced, however, it created a rich diversity of racial and ethnic groups in America. Given the values of freedom and individual rights and choice that formed the bedrock upon which the United States was founded, it was perhaps inevitable that the monopoly on power and policy established by the white Anglo establishment would eventually change. By working within the system of government set forth by the founding fathers, twentieth-first century Americans of all colors and creeds found themselves by the year 2008 at a tipping point in American history as the seeds of significant change planted during the 1950s and 1960s began to ripen and bear substantial fruit.

Societal Dominance Today: The Gathering Momentum of Change   The laws and policies of the United States, even today, continue to be shaped largely by the Anglo-Saxon orientation of the original colonies. Such obvious examples as English language and legal traditions still dominate the norms of American culture. In addition, the upper classes who make up the affluent and powerful establishment and those wishing to emulate them exhibit an almost compulsive attraction to anything related to traditional English or European life from the architectural styles of their homes and their furnishings to the community developments they live in with names like Wimbleton Estates, Georgetown Colony, and Hampton Court.

Nonetheless, the United States today, in terms of both opportunities and racial and ethnic relations, is a far different place than it was just one-half century ago and is continuing to undergo significant if not dramatic change. Today, those from minority backgrounds increasingly are better represented in leadership positions. In the arts, Oprah Winfrey has dominated daytime talk TV for over well over two decades beginning in the mid 1980s and, in doing so, became the first African-American woman billionaire and one of the five hundred wealthiest Americans. In 2001, Halle Berry and Denzel Washington each won the Oscar for best actress and actor, respectively, for a dramatic performance in a motion picture. Other minority actors garnering top acting and artistic awards in recent years have included Benicio Del Toro (Best Supporting Actor, 2001), Jamie Fox (Best Actor, 2004), Morgan Freeman (Best Supporting Actor, 2004), Ang Lee (Best Director, 2005), Forrest Whitaker (Best Actor, 2006), and Jennifer Hudson (Best Supporting Actress, 2006) (*The World Almanac and Book of Facts*, 2008, p. 262). Increasing diversity also is reflected today in the backgrounds of chief executive officers (CEOs) who lead America's five hundred largest corporations, which include seven African Americans and twelve women (RP News Wires, May–June, 2008).

However, perhaps the most profound changes in leadership positions have occurred within the institution of government. When Barack Obama won the Democratic nomination for president on August 13, 2008, exactly forty-five years to the day after Martin Luther King, Jr. gave his "I have a dream" speech at the base of the Lincoln Memorial, it became clear that American minorities had turned an important corner in terms of inclusion that would set the stage for the future.

What Is a Minority Group?

A **minority group** is a social category of people distinguished by their physical or cultural characteristics whose members have experienced a historical pattern of prejudice and discrimination (Wirth, 1945). Minorities usually are smaller in number than the dominant or majority group, but not always. In South Africa, for example, nonwhites outnumber whites four to one. Historically, this country has been dominated by the white Afrikaner establishment, descendents of British colonists that from the nineteenth century until the 2000s, have dominated law and public policy. Although minorities in the United states have made tremendous strides in recent decades, it is important to examine sociologically their key characteristics, outline the history of racial and ethnic relations in America, and discuss some key racial and ethnic groups of today.

Key Characteristics of Minorities

Sociologists generally agree on the following five characteristics that distinguish a minority group from a dominant group (Wagley and Harris, 1964; Vander Zanden, 1983).

1. *Impaired Life Chances. Those belonging to a minority group have suffered disadvantages at the hands of those comprising the majority group.* Historically, minorities have not been accorded the same life chances as those in the Anglo-American majority, the "good things" in life. Even today, their members generally rank lower in terms of power, prestige, and wealth. Members of most minorities are more likely to live in poverty than those in the dominant group, are often more poorly educated, and remain underrepresented in positions of authority and influence in major institutions. In addition, they often represent the source of the advantages enjoyed by the majority. For one group to have tremendous privilege, another must be

oppressed. Although such differential treatment has been reduced dramatically from one-half century ago, a certain amount of bigotry and discrimination still exists today, sometimes in new forms from different sources. For example, in the wake of the September 11, 2001 attacks on the United States by Islamic extremists, some Americans were subjected to prejudice and discrimination simply for being Middle Eastern or Muslim in ethnic origin or religion.

2. ***Visible Characteristics Used as a Basis for Differential Treatment.*** *Members of minorities are identifiable on the basis of visible physical and/or cultural characteristics and, as a result, are treated differently by the majority group.* Some minorities are identified primarily on the basis of physical attributes such as race, gender, or age. Others are defined by the dominant group primarily in terms of cultural characteristics including language, religion, family structure, dress, mannerisms, or even sexual orientation. Members of the dominant group historically saw minorities as deviant, condemned their norms and practices based on their cultural characteristics, and often made them the subject of jokes. And differences based on physical characteristics were often the basis for doctrines of supremacy leading to such attitudes as racism and sexism. Although times and norms have changed and most dominant group members today have left such attitudes and practices in the "dustbin of history," it would be inaccurate to say that bigotry and discrimination have been eradicated. They still exist, although they largely have gone underground and their practitioners and their actions—to the extent to which they still exist—are not socially accepted today in the American cultural mainstream.

3. ***Strong Group Identification.*** *Members of minority groups possess a strong sense of group identity.* This feeling of identification is due partly to distinctive subcultural characteristics that give minority members characteristics in common with each other, such as similar language patterns, modes of dress, music, and value orientations. Historical patterns of oppression and persecution experienced by previous generations also acted to drive them together and caused sharpened distinctions between their group and others. This heightened self-consciousness resulted in a "stick together" attitude and intense loyalty to the group that remains with some minorities today, particularly among older generations.

4. ***Membership Based on Ascribed Status.*** *Minority group membership is an ascribed status.* Membership in most minorities is imposed by society on the basis of birth, not achievement. In Nazi Germany, for instance, Jews were persecuted mercilessly. It mattered not that some Jews looked just like non-Jew Germans or had adopted the Christian religion. They were still regarded as Jews because of their ancestry. In the United States, a person who appears white but who has even a single black grandparent is often viewed as black (Vander Zanden, 1983). For example, in the United States historically, particularly in the South, there was the "one drop rule." A person with any African ancestry—even though light skinned or sometimes Caucasian in appearance—was labeled as black and usually self-identified themselves in like manner. This traditional pattern of ascribed identity still exists to a significant degree today.

5. ***Ingroup Marriage.*** *Minority group members, by social pressure or choice, typically marry within their own group.* Societies in general tend to put pressure on people for "like to marry like." Such pressure, termed *endogamy* by sociologists, is felt by members of dominant and minority groups alike. This theme was explored in depth and with great sensitivity in the now-classic 1967 motion picture *Guess Who's Coming to Dinner?*, starring Spencer Tracy, Katharine Hepburn, and Sidney Poitier. In the story, a white liberal newspaper publisher (Tracy) comes face-to-face with his own supposedly progressive values when his daughter brings home her fiancée (Poitier) to meet her parents, who are surprised to discover that he is black.

Types of Minorities

Minority groups are difficult to classify precisely because many people fall into two or more historically disadvantaged groups. A black Jewish woman, for example, may find herself treated differently due to her race, ethnicity, gender, religion, or some or all of these factors. Of chief consideration, according to sociologist Louis Wirth, is that membership in a minority "carries with it the exclusion from full participation in the life of the society" (1945, p. 347).

Although minority membership can be based on a variety of discrete criteria including gender, age, religion, and sexual orientation, sociologists generally distinguish between two major overlapping types of minorities: racial minorities and ethnic minorities. A **racial minority** is a social category whose members have suffered social disadvantages because of visible physical characteristics (such as skin color). Racial minorities in the United States include Native Americans, African Americans, Asians (such as Japanese, Chinese, Filipino, Korean, and Vietnamese Americans), Hawaiians, and those of East Indian descent. An **ethnic minority** is a social category whose members have experienced social disadvantages mainly due to cultural characteristics such as language or national origin. There are many diverse ethnic minorities in the United States today. They include Hispanic Americans, such as those of Mexican, Puerto Rican, and Cuban descent, and white ethnics, such as Irish, Polish, and Jewish Americans.

*P*REJUDICE AND DISCRIMINATION

One useful way to begin a discussion of minority relations is to concentrate on the sources of minority group members' unequal life chances in society. Historically, racial and ethnic minorities have been denied full and active participation due to three primary factors: prejudice, discrimination, and racism. We will focus first on prejudice and discrimination. Then later in the chapter, we will discuss racism in some depth as a separate topic.

The Nature of Prejudice

What Is Prejudice?: General and Sociological Applications
Prejudice in general refers to judgment based on preconceived ideas. It is a biased attitude that usually stems from faulty inductive reasoning. To overgeneralize about dozens of things based on an

inadequate and unrepresentative group of specific observations is quite easy (see Chapter 2). All of us do this from time to time. People often have prejudices about the best and worst of everything ranging from brands of cars, fast-food hamburgers, and styles of dress, to more substantive topics such as the "only" acceptable political affiliation or religion. Some individuals, particularly those with untrained and undisciplined minds, may feel that they not only have cornered the market on truth but have both a right and obligation to impose their preferences and prejudices on others so that they also will become "enlightened." A few such people become fanatics, who, in their emotional zeal to convert the world to their particular political ideology or religious viewpoint, engage in behavior seen as obnoxious or oppressive to most others.

Sociologists, however, are interested primarily in a particular form of **prejudice**, the negative judgment of individuals and groups because of preconceived ideas held about them. The prejudiced individual, as social psychologist Gordon Allport states it, exhibits "an aversive or hostile attitude toward a person who belongs to a group, simply because he belongs to that group, and is therefore presumed to have the objectionable qualities ascribed to that group (1954, p. 7)."

Three Types of Prejudice   When prejudice becomes focused on people, it generally takes one or a combination of three basic forms—normative prejudice, exploitative prejudice, or the authoritarian personality. Each of these three major prejudice types is best explained from one of the three major sociological perspectives first introduced in Chapter 2—functionalism, conflict theory, and interactionism. Together, they provide us with an integrated and very useful typology of prejudice (Table 10-2).

Normative Prejudice: A Functionalist Perspective   **Normative prejudice** consists of negative attitudes toward members of a particular group that are accepted as "normal" through the process of socialization. Sociologists from the functionalist school maintain that children in practically all cultures are socialized with prejudices about those who comprise their out-groups. These attitudes ultimately become elements of the ethnocentrism most people exhibit. Because people in general tend to lack the sociological imagination, it

TABLE 10-2 A Typology of Prejudice		
TYPES, CHARACTERISTICS, AND SOURCES OF SOCIOLOGICAL EXPLANATION		
TYPE OF PREJUDICE	**CHARACTERISTICS (AND EXAMPLE GIVEN)**	**SOCIOLOGICAL EXPLANATION**
Normative Prejudice	Bigotry resulting from socialization. (e.g. "Jews are stingy with money.")	Functionalism
Exploitative Prejudice	Bigotry used to justify discrimination. ("It's a lot of money to a Mexican.")	Conflict theory
Authoritarian Personality	Deep-seated, hate-filled bigotry ("We should deport all Muslims and imprison or kill all that resist.")	Interactionism

is tempting for them to blindly accept the orientations toward people and everything else taught to them by their families, peer groups, and other agents of socialization in their communities. For example, many to most white children reared in America prior to the 1960s were taught as a matter of course that blacks were inferior to whites, Jews were "tightwads" who were stingy with money, and Japanese—because of the 1941 attack at Pearl Harbor—were sneaky and not to be trusted. Internationally, some children raised in North Korea and portions of the Middle East today are taught that Americans should be distrusted and hated. Consequently, prejudices of this type are built into the structures of institutions and societies and are used by those in power to justify their agendas and maintain the status quo. They are culture specific and vary from place to place. They are also subject to change with the passage of time.

Exploitative Prejudice: An Explanation from the Conflict Perspective

One mechanism used by the dominant group ("the haves") to sustain their advantaged position is **exploitative prejudice**, negative attitudes toward minority group members held by members of the dominant group that are used as justification for keeping them in a subordinate position. Conflict theorists argue that those in the dominant group often seek to sustain an atmosphere of hostility and/or paternalism toward a minority group as a means of maintaining their position of dominance over them. Many signers of the Declaration of Independence, for instance, were slaveholders and property owners who used slave labor to sustain their economic position. Consequently, it was not in their financial interests to condemn slavery. The forced migration of Native Americans (American Indians) westward during the 1830s (the Trail of Tears) furnishes an additional illustration. The notion that Indians were "heathen savages" *accustomed* to hardships who could survive as readily on the desolate plains and deserts of the West as they could in the forests of the Southeast

© BETTMANN/CORBIS

The 1970s show, *All in the Family,* is still popular in syndication on Cable TV. In its many episodes, the main character, Archie Bunker, exhibited normative prejudice toward several categories of people. His attitudes and actions placed him in one humorous and embarrassing misadventure after another. It portrayed bigotry as increasingly inappropriate in a changing society in which the rights of all groups are to be respected.

served to justify actions by the U.S. government in stripping them of their traditional lands and relocating them to what is now Oklahoma. Some conflict sociologists (Davis, Gardner, and Gardner, 1965) have argued that these attitudes of superiority by those in power helped to create and reinforce a *caste system* historically for Native Americans, blacks, Asians, and other minorities. Even today, exploitative prejudice is used as a justification for paying undocumented aliens substandard wages. Excuses given include "what we pay them is a lot of money to Mexicans" to "Americans won't work for minimum wages or less for day labor jobs." These attitudes are self-serving to many American businesses and consumers who benefit economically from the exploitation of illegal workers. Consequently, many governmental agencies, especially those in places designated as "sanctuary cities," basically "look the other way" by choosing not to enforce immigration laws.

The Authoritarian Personality: An Application Of Interactionism   Some behavioral scientists have found that deep-seated prejudice in some people is linked to personality traits developed in people at the micro level of society during childhood. T. W. Adorno and his colleagues (1950) at the University of California at Berkley concluded from their research that highly prejudiced people may possess what they termed the *authoritarian personality*. Using the F-scale, a personality scale designed to measure fascism, they found the **authoritarian personality** to be a highly rigid and intolerant person who tends to exhibit a group of identifiable personality characteristics. These include *an overly simplistic view of reality* in which almost everything is neatly compartmentalized into dichotomies of good or bad, black or white, us or them. Such views are taught to them as children by their caregivers. Authoritarian personalities also tend to have had *an extremely authoritarian upbringing* with punitive parents who handed out very harsh punishment, often at the slightest deviation from the "proper way" to act. Because of such ongoing intimidation, the child grows up with a submissive attitude toward authority figures, which carries over into adulthood. Such a person also may develop unresolved anger against parents and other authority figures, which then becomes focused on those who are different and less fortunate and who have little or no power (Pettigrew, 1980). Authoritarian personalities, therefore, *tend to be very submissive to those above them in authority and very punitive toward those over whom they have authority*. They often focus their deep-seated anger on minorities, who, because of small numbers and a lack of power, have been vulnerable historically. Expressions of hate-filled bigotry makes authoritarian personalities feel important and, for the moment, adequate. Members of hate groups are often products of such a socialization process.

Prejudice in Perspective   These three types of prejudice often overlap and, therefore, are not mutually exclusive. The development of an authoritarian personality, for instance, is facilitated by a cultural climate in which the structural characteristics of society encourage certain forms of normative prejudice. As an illustration, the Ku Klux Klan (KKK), an extremist organization that contains an abundance of authoritarian personalities, originated in the deep South immediately after the Civil War (1861–1865) where the cultural climate encouraged prejudice toward blacks in particular. During its period of greatest popularity and visibility during the 1920s, thousands of Klansman clad in white, sheet-like costumes marched in parades and some colleges in the deep South had campus student chapters. Although the Klan and its derivatives have all but disappeared from the public eye, groups derived from the KKK and other groups still exist in small cells led by those who are fueled by deep-seated hate and intolerance.

Stereotypes   Regardless of type, however, those with prejudices usually make use of **stereotypes**, fixed mental images about the characteristics of entire categories of people that are not tested against reality. These images form much of the content of prejudice. Some common examples of stereotypical thinking are: Mexicans are lazy, blacks have rhythm, Southerners are slow, athletes are dumb, male homosexuals are effeminate, old people are senile, and Jews are stingy. While certainly some individuals in these categories have the characteristics described, so does a percentage of the general population. Therefore, to label everyone in terms of exaggerated negative characteristics is to distort reality. Nonetheless, stereotypical perceptions are often used as a rationale for unequal treatment (Table 10-3).

The Nature of Discrimination

What Is Discrimination?   Whereas prejudice is a judgmental attitude, **discrimination** refers to differential treatment of people based on their membership in a particular social category. Applied to minorities, such treatment at the hands of a dominant group is a negative and destructive force in society and often is based on prejudice. When established as a pattern, discrimination acts to reduce life chances for the group affected. The resulting deprivation, once visible, reinforces the prejudice that the minority group is inferior. This, in turn, breeds further discrimination and the circle is complete. According to Robert

TABLE 10-3	Common Stereotypes		
BLACKS	**CHINESE**	**HISPANICS**	**ITALIANS**
Great athletes	Sly, sinister, deceitful	Big on machismo	Stupid, ignorant
Sexual prowess	Learned, wise	Lazy	Distrust education
Stupid	Love to gamble	Refuse to learn English	Great singers
Musically gifted	Cruel	Don't value education	Talk with hands
Great rhythm	Strong family ties	Warm, emotional	Belong to the Mafia
Lazy, shiftless	Quiet, polite	Violent, hot tempered	Cowards in battle
Violent criminals	Deferential	Don't mind using welfare	Great shoemakers
IRISH	**JAPANESE**	**JEWS**	**POLES**
Heavy drinkers	Chauvinistic	Cheap	Dumb
Good at politics	Hardworking	Shrewd businessman	Dirty
Sexually repressed	The "sneaky Jap"	Control the banks	Racists, bigots
Very religious	Great imitators	Pushy, aggressive	Boorish, uncultured
Highly nationalistic	Law abiding	Rich, ostentatious	Low class
Witty, gregarious	Educated, intelligent	Have big noses	
The "fighting Irish"			

Source: W. B. 1982. *The Things They Say Behind Your Back.* New York: Doubleday.

MacIver (1948), discrimination thus feeds on itself in a vicious cycle that he has illustrated as follows:

discrimination → lower income level → lower standards of living → lower education → lower earning capacity → discrimination (p. 64).

Types of Discrimination   There are several forms of discrimination that will be discussed briefly.

Individual Versus Institutional Discrimination   First, sociologists recognize discrimination that occurs on both micro- and macrolevels of society. **Individual discrimination** is unequal treatment that occurs when individuals belonging to one group treat individuals of another group differently because of their group membership. During the era of legal segregation in the United States (1896–1954), African Americans, other minorities, and women at the interpersonal and community (micro) levels endured an incalculable number of small acts of ongoing discrimination in social relations on a daily basis, maintained and reinforced by those in the dominant group. Present-day examples would include a landlord who intentionally finds a way to refuse to rent apartments to people of Mexican or Middle Eastern Muslim descent, although they may be U.S. citizens. **Institutional discrimination**, by contrast, involves unequal treatment of certain categories of people as a result of inequities built into basic institutions. In this regard, the norms and values of the majority group take precedence over those of minorities in areas such as law, politics, education, business, and general customs. Black males, for example, were not allowed to vote in the United States until the 1860s, and American Indians and women did not gain suffrage until 1919 or later. While discrimination like this is direct and intentional, it sometimes takes indirect and often unintentional forms. The results, however, are the same.

A case in point was the minimum height requirement for police officers used by the Chicago Police Department during the 1960s. This had the effect of discriminating against otherwise qualified Puerto Ricans who, as a group, are shorter than white and black Americans. This height requirement was later changed in the wake of riots in the Puerto Rican community in 1966, which included charges of police brutality. Consequently, Puerto Ricans could then enter law enforcement and community relations were improved (Schaefer, 1985).

Reverse Discrimination   **Reverse discrimination** is unequal treatment of individuals based on their membership in the dominant group. In 1978, for example, the U.S. Supreme Court ruled in *Regents of the University of California v. Bakke* that reverse discrimination did occur in the case of Allan Bakke, an older white male with an engineering background who was denied admission to medical school mainly due to a racial quota system established for minorities. The court ruled that the university abridged Bakkes's constitutional rights based on his charge of racial discrimination. However, the court also ruled that racial background could be use as one factor in establishing admission requirements (Schaefer, 2008).

Affirmative action programs mandated by the U.S. government have provoked much of the controversy involving charges of reverse discrimination, and several lawsuits have been filed and decided on by the courts in recent years. The original aim of affirmative action, as first put into effect through an executive order issued by President John F. Kennedy in 1961,was for organizations and institutions receiving federal funds to actively seek minority applicants for employment and use their minority status as one factor in selection. However, in recent years, the original intent of affirmative action was modified and expanded, which resulted in controversial practices by organizations and several recent court rulings.

One example was the Gruttner case ruled on by the Supreme Court in 2003. This lawsuit was filed against the University of Michigan Law School by Betty Gruttner, a white woman who was not accepted into law school. Her attorneys argued that only about nine percent of white applicants with her LSAT admission test scores and grade point average records were admitted when she applied as compared with 100 percent of those with similar credentials who were African American. In a two-part decision, the court rejected Ms. Gruttner's claim regarding her own admission and ruled that the racial backgrounds of applicants could be used as a factor in admissions due to the need to encourage a diverse student body. However, the court—in the second part of its decision—set aside the school's policy for undergraduate admissions, which gave applicants points solely based on race or minority background. In the ruling of the court, race can be used as one factor in admission as long as several factors are considered that view each applicant mainly on their merits as an individual rather than their membership in a particular social category (Stout, 2003).

The Relationship between Prejudice and Discrimination

Prejudicial attitudes and discriminatory behavior are closely associated with each other because prejudice often serves as the basis for discrimination and vice versa. However, in some cases, the relationship between the two is not so easily explained. Some people are prejudiced but do not discriminate, while others discriminate but often are not prejudiced. In an attempt at clarification, Robert Merton (1976) identified four ways the two concepts relate to each other:

1. *Unprejudiced nondiscrimination* involves "all-weather liberals" opposed to both prejudice and discrimination who consistently act on their principles in various social situations. Most civil rights advocates and activists would be unprejudiced nondiscriminators.

2. *Unprejudiced discrimination* is carried out by "fair-weather liberals" who, although not prejudiced themselves, will discriminate and support discrimination by others for their own gain. Although they sometimes talk about being progressive in certain social circles, they will not jeopardize business profits, reputation, or votes if pressure to discriminate is strong. At the end of the segregation era in the late 1960s, for example, some white business owners who harbored no ill will toward African Americans still refused to serve blacks because they feared losing most of their customers who were white.

3. *Prejudiced nondiscrimination* involves "fair-weather bigots," who reluctantly engage in equal treatment of groups they dislike because of social pressure to do so. Both federal laws and recent Supreme Court decisions reaffirming such laws have made most forms of discrimination illegal in the United States. Therefore, some people in power positions who otherwise would not hire minorities do employ minority applicants because they fear legal sanctions if they do not comply with the law.

4. *Prejudiced discrimination* is carried out by "all-weather bigots" who consistently discriminate against groups they dislike because of principles they subscribe to based on prejudice. Although they represent an anachronism today, numerous "hate groups" who maintain an extremist "lunatic fringe" position in society and exhibit blatant bigotry still exist although their numbers tend to be low. Examples of hate groups, as identified and monitored by federal law enforcement agencies and other organizations, include a variety of Ku Klux Klan groups, neo-Confederates, anti-Semitic groups, neo-Nazis, and black separatist groups (Southern Law Poverty Center, 2008).

WHAT IS RACE?

Race can be a confusing concept that often means different things to different people. Even scientists use this term differently. In this regard, race can be seen from either a biological or sociological perspective.

The Nature of Race: Two Approaches at Definition

Race as a Biological Concept   From a biological perspective, *race* refers to a social category of people with certain visible physical features in common that are genetically inherited and passed on to future generations. There are numerous racial groups (called stocks or strains) throughout the world, with varying physical characteristics. Yet scientists have been unable to reach a consensus on how many such groups exist in the world or how they might be classified. No matter what "identifiable physical characteristics" are used as criteria—skin pigmentation, hair texture, facial features, blood types, etc.—different numbers and types of "races" appear.

Three commonly used racial categories used traditionally are Caucasian (fair skin; straight or wavy hair), Mongoloid (yellow to brown skin; epicanthic eye folds), and Negroid (dark skin; wooly hair) (Kroeber, 1948). Yet, many East Indian Hindus have Caucasian facial features and straight hair but dark skin like Negroids. Bushman are classified as Negroid but have some Mongoloid features, including epicanthic folds under the eyes and light yellow-brown skin. The Polynesians of the South Pacific and the Aborigines of Australia have so many contradictory characteristics that they cannot be placed into any of the three general categories.

Added to this is the complication raised by intermarriage between so-called races. In the United States, for instance, eighty percent or more of black Americans have white ancestry, at least fifty percent of Mexican Americans have both Indian (Native American) and white ancestry, and approximately twenty percent of white Americans have either African or Indian ancestry (Stuckert, 1976). Consequently, "race" as a clearly definable biological concept in science is a useless means of classification (Ferris and Stein, 2008) (Figure 10-1).

Race as a Sociological Concept   What is important about "race," however, is how various individuals, groups, and cultures perceive it. This social meaning is of particular interest to sociologists. From a sociological perspective, **race** refers to a social category of

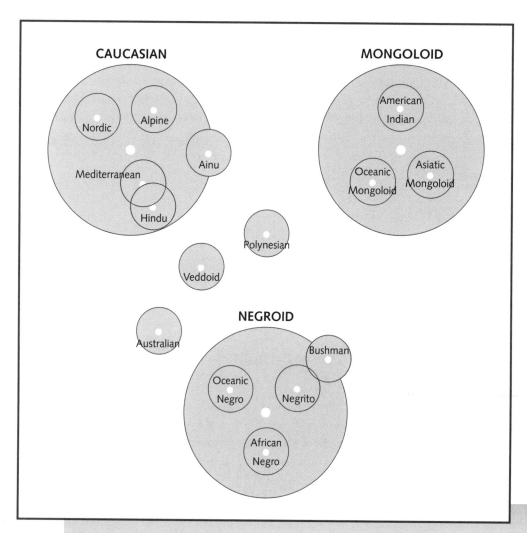

Three Major Racial Categories

SOURCE: Kroeber, A. L. 1948. *Anthropology,* 10. New York: Harcourt Brace and World.

Figure 10-1

people perceived and treated in a distinct manner on the basis of certain visible physical characteristics. As such, race as a concept represents a social invention used to assign meaning and value to people on the basis of so-called "racial" differences (Van den Berghe, 1978). Consequently, members of one "race" often see themselves as distinct from others. They assume that their physical traits are related to their intellectual ability and social fortunes, whether they be high or low, positive or negative. They expect to be treated a certain way by virtue of their "race" and are treated as expected in many cases.

In some societies, the racial background of the dominant group is often seen as superior to others, along with the life style or ethnicity that goes with it. Other racial groups and their life styles are similarly defined as inferior in the minds of some people in varying degrees. To some extent, the culture of the "majority race" is socialized into all offspring, including those of racial minorities. Because "race" and minority membership traditionally were ascribed, children of minorities historically were often left with a negative image of themselves because they could not become members of the dominant racial group.

When the concept of race is equated with expectations of success or failure, privilege or hardship, and self-worth versus self-deprecation, it can have a very negative impact on the self-image of minority children. In his autobiography *Nigger,* comedian and author Dick Gregory (1967) relates what it was like growing up in the inner city of St. Louis during the 1940s. Being poor, black, and fatherless, his experiences were not unlike those experienced by many poor and minority children of his time and even more recently.

> I never learned hate or shame at home. I had to go to school for that. I was about seven years old when I got my first big lesson . . . [and] learned to be ashamed of myself. It was on a Thursday. I was sitting in the back of the room, in a seat with a chalk circle drawn around it. The idiot's seat, the troublemaker's seat.
>
> The teacher though I was stupid. Couldn't spell, couldn't read, couldn't do arithmetic. Just stupid. Teachers were never interested in finding out that you couldn't concentrate because you were so hungry, because you hadn't had any breakfast. All you could think about was noontime, would it ever come? Maybe you could sneak into the cloakroom and steal a bite of some kid's lunch out of a coat pocket. A bite of something. Paste. You can't really make a meal of paste . . . but sometimes I'd scoop a few spoonfuls out of the paste jar in the back of the room. Pregnant people get strange tastes. I was pregnant with poverty; Pregnant with dirt and pregnant with smells that made people turn away; Pregnant with cold and pregnant with shoes that were never bought for me, pregnant with five other people in my bed and no Daddy in the next room, and pregnant with hunger. Paste doesn't taste too bad when you're hungry.
>
> The teacher thought I was a troublemaker. All she saw . . . was a little black boy who squirmed in his idiot's seat and made little noises and poked the kids around him. I guess she couldn't see a kid who made noises because he wanted someone to know he was there (pp. 29–30).

Race: Myth Versus Reality

Because of the long and divisive history attached to "race" and the ways in which it has been used and misused against various racial minorities, it remains a sensitive and contentious subject even well into the twenty-first century. Just when many Americans—both dominant-group and minority-group members—begin to feel that their culture is about to transcend the typing and treating of people by so-called "racial" characteristics, there sometimes occurs a "racial incident" which brings old sentiments and resentments bubbling back to the surface in full focus and gives them renewed life. Charges of racism fly about with unbridled abandon, often from more than one side. And old wounds, once thought healed or nearly healed, are at least temporarily reinfected with bigotry, hate speech, and calls for justice and retribution as a reaction. To partially address such factors bearing on race and racial issues, we will discuss a few of the dominant myths that surround this subject.

Myth 1: The Notion of Racial Superiority
Throughout history, conquering societies have used the physical characteristics of the people they conquered as a justification for subjugating or enslaving them as part of the spoils of war. When the Mongol hordes descended on the Roman Empire in the fifth century BCE, the physical features of the Caucasian Romans were used as an excuse by the invading Asiatics for enslaving them. In similar fashion, white colonists in America over one thousand years later during the 1600s and 1700s used the dark features of the Africans sold into bondage to them as a rationale

for slavery. Even as recently as the late twentieth century, similar attempts have been made to justify a doctrine of racial supremacy.

However, scientists operating independently from one another in several disciplines have found no convincing evidence that any so-called "racial" group is superior or inferior to any other "racial" group regarding talents or characteristics of significance. Therefore, racial superiority argued for some groups over others in areas ranging from musicality and "natural" athletic ability to sexual prowess and intellectual capacity represent little more than cultural mythology.

Myth 2: The Concept of Pure Race

Most of us represent an amalgam of different "racial" influences. African women brought to America as slaves were often impregnated by white planters and other white males because, as slaves, they had no power to resist or protest. The children born of such unions were legally considered slaves based on "the status of the mother." During the 1960s, the U.S. Supreme Court overturned state laws banning miscegenation (interracial marriage). Based partly on this but mainly the legacy created in the wake of the civil rights movement, which was a cultural attitude of tolerance about race relations, bi-racial and/or ethnically mixed children have become normative in society's mainstream. Consequently, children today produced from racially mixed marriages do not grow up with the social stigma that was pervasive prior to the 1970s.

Myth 3: "Race" as a Meaningful Biological Concept in Science

Biologists, geneticists, and biomedical researchers generally have joined with behavioral scientists in finding that "race" generally is not a meaningful biological concept in science. Beyond the problem of an agreed-upon and consistent classification system for "so-called races" and the complication of few if any people coming from a single "racial" background, there are

© TONY ROBERTS/CORBIS

Tiger Woods claims a rich racial heritage that includes Caucasian (one-eighth), black (one-fourth), American Indian (one-eighth), Thai (one-fourth), and Chinese (one-fourth). He embraces all these ethnic influences and calls himself Cablinasian.

Source: White, Jack E. 1997. "I'm Just Who I Am." *Time*. May 5, 32–36.

few if any significant biological differences between alleged "racial groups." The distinctions that do exist—skin pigmentation, hair texture, facial structure, eye folds, and so on— are cosmetic and superficial, not determinative. We are all *Homo sapiens sapiens* under the skin, with the same chromosomal characteristics, blood types, brain structures, and body architectures. Because of these considerations, the biological concept of race as a "pure type" is regarded as a social myth and is of little or no value to science (Montagu, 1972). Although physical "racial" differences do exist among humans, they are largely superficial and, by themselves, play no significant role in shaping intellectual capacity, biological potential, or social behavior. One finding from genetics is particularly interesting.

There actually is more genetic similarity between so-called racial groups than within them (Witherspoon et al., 2007). One consequence of this is that a person in need of an organ transplant who goes on the national organ recipient list is more likely to receive an organ from a person from a different so-called "racial group" than from his or her own. Consequently, there is a significant number of white Anglos walking around with African American hearts beating inside their bodies, African Americans with "white" kidneys or Asian livers, and Asian Americans with "white" or "black" corneas that better allow them to see. Other possible combinations are too numerous to mention. Such consequences stem from the fact that about eighty-five percent of genetic variations occur within populations or so-called racial groups (Barbujani, et al., 1997).

The Nature of Racism

When an awareness of racial differences includes a higher value placed on membership in one racial group as compared to another, then racism occurs. **Racism** is a doctrine—and acts stemming from it—that holds that one racial category is superior and all others, in varying degrees, are inferior. Therefore, racism includes both prejudice and discrimination in that it combines racial prejudice with the use of power to negatively affect how people are treated. The dominant or majority group benefits in several ways from such an ideology (Nash, 1962). First, racism serves as a convenient moral justification for unequal treatment of a minority. Second, a racist doctrine, once institutionalized, is often viewed as normal by everyone, including oppressed minorities. This, in turn, acts to discourage them for questioning the "system." Finally, racial mythology tries to justify itself on the grounds that members of the "inferior race," being untalented and helpless people, would be much worse off if major social changes occurred and freedoms were allocated to them that they could not handle responsibly.

The historical treatment of blacks in America serves as a classic example of racism put into practice. During the summers of 1966 and 1967, racial unrest spread across America in a wave of riots and civil disturbances involving blacks and whites in dozens of cities. In places like Tampa, Atlanta, Newark, and Chicago many black communities erupted in violence that resulted in looting, arson, assault, and several deaths. By the end of July, 1967, President Lyndon Johnson had appointed a Commission on Civil Disorders to find the causes of these upheavals that were splitting the country into two polarized camps, one black and the other white. This is a brief excerpt summarizing the commission's findings:

> [T]he single overriding cause of rioting in the cities was not any one thing commonly
> adduced—unemployment, lack of education, poverty, exploitation—but . . . was all of these
> things and more, expressed in the insidious and pervasive white sense of the inferiority of

black men. Here is the essence of the charge: "What white Americans have never fully understood—but what the Negro can never forget—is that white society is deeply implicated in the ghetto. White institutions created it, white institutions maintain it, and white society condones it" (*Report of the National Advisory Commission on Civil Disorders*, 1968, p. vii).

The Origins of Racism in America

To trace the origins of racism leading to the unrest of the 1960s and beyond, one must examine the early American experience. The first blacks in servitude were brought to the Jamestown settlement in Virginia in 1619 as indentured servants. By the 1660s, however, black slavery was becoming sanctioned by law and by 1700 had replaced indentured servitude as the primary source of cheap agricultural labor in the colonies (Quarles, 1969).

Slavery was justified by a doctrine of racial supremacy that consisted of several arguments. One was a biblical justification quoting various passages from the scriptures, including the Genesis account of Noah's curse on Canaan, which allegedly gave slavery God's sanction (Lincoln, 1968). A second defined the Negro as a subhuman, depraved beast. A third and somewhat more benign approach portrayed blacks as half-pathetic, half-comical creatures—simple-minded children that required constant supervision.

This last attitude toward the Negro became the basis for a stereotypical view of black people that continued well into the twentieth century. The following is fairly representative of the view of blacks offered by Thomas Dixon's racist novel *Leopard Spots* (1902) and other literary material of the early twentieth century:

> The Negro is an amoral creature . . . unable to discriminate between right and wrong. The power to make a free and intelligent moral choice has been denied to him by his Creator, leaving him a permanent cripple in the evolutionary struggle for existence. At his best he is a good child, for whom one may feel a genuine affection . . . akin to the love of a master for a loyal dog. But just as a dog must be told what to do if he is to be of any use in a human society, so the Negro must be guided and controlled by his Anglo-Saxon superiors, on whose shoulders rests the burden of civilizing him, so far as his limited capacities will permit (quoted in Bloomfield, 1970, p. 118).

Even as late as the 1940s, popular American literature and motion pictures used images like Stepin Fetchit, a black movie character, to depict blacks as having rolling eyes, a shuffling gait, a whiny voice, and experiencing a never-ending series of predicaments brought on by simple-mindedness.

Racism and the Use of IQ Tests

By the 1930s and 1940s, some forms of racism were much more subtle and indirect. One example is the manner in which IQ tests were used and interpreted. Although IQ tests were not designed with racist intentions, their use and abuse has had a discriminatory and stigmatizing effect on minority children and white children from lower socioeconomic backgrounds. In addition, supporters of white supremacy have used IQ test scores of minority children as "evidence" for racially biased arguments.

Psychological tests to measure intelligence or IQ (intelligence quotient) have been used in various applications—the military, education, industry, law—since the early part of the twentieth century. Traditionally, IQ tests have been structured according to the pattern as established by L. L. Thurston (1938) to measure ability in three broad areas: verbal skills, spatial skills, and logical skills. IQ tests, such as the Standford-Binet and Wechsler,

Movie and TV characters like Amos and Andy in the 1940s and 1950s portrayed blacks as simple-minded and in constant need of supervision by their white "superiors."

have been administered to several generations of American school children and have been shown to be good predictors of academic success (McCall, 1975).

The extensive use of IQ tests, however, has been highly controversial in recent years and has been criticized as invalid in assessing the abilities of minority children and those from lower socioeconomic backgrounds. Such children, including blacks and Hispanics, who historically have scored 10 to 15 points lower than white middle-class children, also have not done as well in school.

The term "IQ" or "intelligence test" is misleading because it implies that what is being measured in innate learning capacity. In truth, behavioral scientists are not in agreement as to precisely what intelligence is. Some see is as "adaptability," others "specific skills," and still others "scholastic aptitude" (Haber and Runyon, 1974). At best, IQ tests are imprecise measures of certain narrowly defined skills or abilities. Even these have not been measured directly but have been inferred from the behavior (scores) of children taking the tests. In partial recognition of this lack of clarity, a panel of experts appointed in 1975 by the American Psychological Association's Board of Scientific Affairs stated that IQ and other psychological tests "do not prove or disapprove anyone's capacity to learn" (Roediger, et al., 1984, p. 361).

In particular, the verbal and analogy sections of standardized IQ tests have been criticized for being culturally biased and representing little more than socialization keyed to a white middle-class cultural model. Many minority children and poor whites cannot be expected to "know" that cup goes with saucer, symphony with composer," or that silence is the "appropriate behavior" in church (Havighust and Neugarten, 1967; Vander Zanden, 1972). These things are not part of their cultural experience.

As a result of such test scores, an untold number of minority and poor children have been perceived as slow learners and tracked accordingly. Consequently, some teachers have exhibited a tendency to expend less time and energy on them than on "normal IQ" and "high IQ" children with more "potential." These children also have been more likely than their white middle-class counterparts to wear the label "mentally retarded" and to be placed in special education programs (Beeghley and Butler, 1974). At the same time, ironically, children of interracial and black parentage adopted by white middle-class couples with above average education, income, and IQs consistently score ten points above the national IQ average and twenty points above that of black children raised in poverty (Scarr and Weinburg, 1976). In summarizing the research on whether or not so-called "IQ" translates into life success, psychologist Don Hockenbury and science writer Sandra Hockenbury have stated that "[a]lthough intelligence is necessary for success in any field, the kind of intelligence that is reflected by high scores on traditional IQ tests is no guarantee of vocational success or professional eminence" (2006, p. 308).

Two Historically Dominant Forms of Racism Sociologists generally recognize two major categories of racism, individual and institutional. **Individual racism** is unequal treatment that occurs when ideas and actions based on a doctrine of racial supremacy are applied to members of one racial category by members of another. The individual racist may do little more than talk, gossip, or joke about members of the "inferior race" with friends of like mind. However, sometimes such a person may put these attitudes into action, as in the case of the manager who tries earnestly to hire as few members of certain racial groups as possible. **Institutional racism**, by comparison, is unequal treatment of members of a racial category that results when ideas and actions based on a doctrine of racial supremacy are embedded into the structure of basic institutions (e.g., government, education, and the economic system). This particular type of racism, and the discrimination that results from it, historically took several specific forms. The era of legal segregation in America (1896–1954), for example, divided practically every aspect of life—neighborhoods, schools, businesses, transportation, churches, and even restrooms and drinking fountains—by racial category. The traditional practice of "ability grouping" and the tracking of minority children in school, based in large part on IQ test scores, could be considered as an additional illustration. Internationally, the apartheid policy practiced by the South African government until 1994, separating neighborhoods into "white," "black," and "colored," serves as an additional example of institutional racism from another part of the world.

The State of Racism Today: New Forms Due to such factors as the Civil Rights Act of 1964, affirmative action, the formation of the Equal Employment Opportunity Commission (EEOC), numerous supreme court decisions, and other reforms and mechanisms, racism, as manifested in racial discrimination, is illegal at federal, state, and local levels, and has retreated to the backwaters of American society. In addition, racism in America, once worn as a badge of pride by many and used to justify the enslavement of an entire people for two hundred years, is now socially unacceptable in almost all sectors of society. However, despite such beneficial changes, racism still remains today, although in anachronistic forms for the most part. Three of the more important of these will be briefly discussed here—hate groups, hate crimes, and reverse racism.

Hate Groups White racists still exist, the most extreme of which belong to small, but organized hate groups such as the Ku Klux Khan and the Aryan Brotherhood that have cells in all but four states. (Southern Poverty Law Center, 2008). Neo-Nazi groups tend to be prevalent in states such as New Hampshire, Michigan, and Minnesota. In addition, neo-Confederates have many cells in South Carolina and Georgia while the Ku Klux Klan has numerous active chapters in several states including Florida, Texas, Louisiana, and Arkansas. There are also anti-Semitic groups who focus hate on the Jews. As a final example, numerous Black Separatist cells are active in states including North Carolina, Texas, and California; they focus their hate on what they stereotypically label as "white America." Many hate groups, such as white supremacist groups, have web sites from which they promote their pamphlets and other forms of propaganda aimed at blaming various contemporary problems facing America today on minorities and recent immigrants (Rivlin, 2005).

Hate Crimes   In 1990, the Hate Crimes Statistics Act was enacted into law that called for the U.S. Department of Justice to develop an ongoing database on hate crimes. **Hate crimes** are ordinary crimes in which victims are chosen because of some characteristic they possess such as racial background, religion, ethnicity, or sexual orientation. As of 2005, national data compiled by the Justice Department as reported through local and state law enforcement agencies throughout the United States indicated that, out of eighty-eight hundred hate crimes and incidents reported, fifty-one percent were motivated by race, eighteen percent by religion, sixteen and one-half percent by sexual orientation, and nearly fourteen percent by ethnicity (Harlow, 2005). By 2006, the total number of reported hate crimes had increased to nearly 9100. See Table 10-4 for a breakdown of offenses by type and known offender's race.

Reverse Racism   Members of the dominant group do not hold a monopoly on racism, particularly now in the twenty-first century. There is also *reverse racism* as exhibited by some African Americans, Asian Americans, and some members of other minorities. **Reverse racism** is a resentment and acts stemming from it focused on the group in power by some minority members driven by deep-seated bitterness at the wrongs done to their ancestors by the ancestors of the dominant group. Empowered by recently acquired rights and life chances, such racists try to invoke *white guilt* in members of the dominant group by using a technique that African American scholar Shelby Steel (1990) has called *raceholding*. By intentionally invoking the "race card" in charging racism when most anything negative happens to

TABLE 10-4	U.S. Hate Crimes: 2006 (by Offense Type and known Offender's Race)					
				KNOWN OFFENDER'S RACE*		
OFFENSE TYPE	TOTAL OFFENSES	WHITE	BLACK	AMERICAN INDIAN	ASIAN/PACIFIC ISLANDER	MULTIPLE RACES
Total	9,080	3,710	1,026	66	75	
Crimes against persons	5,449	3,122	832	53	66	
Crimes against property	3,593	573	173	13	8	
Crimes against society	38	15	14	0	1	

SOURCE: *Hate Crime Statistics,* 2006. U.S. Department of Justice, Federal Bureau of Investigation, Table 3.

* In many instances, the offender's race was (were) unidentified by the victim or victims.

themselves or to others in their social category, such individuals often try to avoid taking personal responsibility for their actions by scapegoating members of the dominant group whom they perceive as vulnerable. In doing so, they engage in a form of racism themselves.

In other cases, some such racists attempt to inflame emotions and exaggerate or even invent so-called racially motivated "incidents" or controversies out of thin air. The actions of Reverend Jeramiah Wright, President Barack Obama's pastor for twenty years, during the 2008 presidential campaign, provides a prominent example. The inflammatory rhetoric, comments, and hate speech emanating from Reverend Wright both from the pulpit and in speeches made in the network media and most notably at a National Press Club luncheon on April 28, 2008 where he was a keynote speaker, were astounding in their apparent display of hatred toward the United States, its leaders, and the majority of its people. Among other things, he suggested that the United States was a terrorist nation that brought the September 11th attacks on itself and that the HIV virus was concocted by the U.S. Government as a form of genocide aimed at eradicating people of African descent (Halloran, 2008).

In commenting directly the next day after Wright's Press Club speech, then presidential candidate Barack Obama soundly denounced his former pastor of twenty years and characterized the reverend's rhetoric as "divisive," "destructive," and comforting to those in society who feed off of hate. In doing so, the man who six months later would be elected as the first African American president informed the American people that Wright's world view was a contradiction of who he was and what he represented as a person (The Associated Press, "Obama Denounces Former Pastor," April 29, 2008, pp. 1–2.)

Racism in Perspective   Racism—like sexism, ageism, anti-Semitism, homophobia, and other forms of bigotry—is a form of dehumanization. Its purpose, used by those who practice it, is to objectify those seen as powerless by labeling, ridiculing, or reviling them in various ways that reduce them as individual human beings and negatively impact on their life chances. In this sense, racism is used as a psychological weapon by those seeing themselves as having power against those whom they resent and wish to exploit or harm—for whatever reason or reasons—and perceive as powerless. Up until the later decades of the twentieth century, which were marked by the end of legal segregation and enabling civil rights reforms, racism and other forms of bigotry in America appeared in blatant, overt forms used by many members of the group in power—the white Anglo establishment—to dominate and belittle minorities and women and keep them "in their place."

However, the last half century has witnessed seedbed changes in the fabric of American culture, and racial bigotry has declined to relatively insignificant levels when compared to the benchmarks of the past. Particularly among the college educated and those Americans who grew up in the postsegregation world, racism and racist expressions have all but disappeared in social discourse in most sectors of society. White racists still exist but in much smaller numbers than in the past. There are also racists that have emerged from other racial and ethnic groups, who harbor deep-seated resentment toward members of today's dominant group for past social policies and acts that harmed their parents, grandparents, and certainly ancestors. Many sociologists would agree that in a progressive, enlightened society, there is no place for racism in any guise or for any other form of bigotry, regardless of who espouses it or the group on which it is focused.

RACIAL MINORITIES

Native Americans

American Indians, or Native Americans, were the first to settle in North America and also the first to be dominated and placed in a minority position by European immigrants. It is estimated that in the year 1500 there were approximately ten million indigenous people north of the Rio Grande River. They were divided into so many different tribal groups that approximately seven hundred languages were spoken. However, by 1850, they numbered only about 250,000, decimated by a loss of food supply and exposure to such "white man's diseases" as influenza, measles, and smallpox (Schaefer, 2008, pp. 167–168). In 2008, it was estimated that there were about 2.4 million American Indians living in the United States (including Alaska) based on updated 2000 census data (*The World Almanac and Book of Facts*, 2008, p. 604). According to the Bureau of Indian Affairs, the number of Native Americans in 2006 within states with federal reservations ranged from 2,420 people in Vermont (one reservation) to 333,346 in California (twenty reservations).

Native Americans under Colonial Rule At first, these original Americans were seen by many European colonists as "noble savages," well meaning but ignorant in the ways of civilization. Early missionaries, after some contact with Indian groups, declared that these native inhabitants were the "Ten Lost Tribes of Israel" (Deloria, 1970, p. 13). Even today, children in elementary schools are taught stories—partly mythical and highly romanticized—of Squanto and the Pilgrims and how the Indians and the early white settlers shared in the feast of the first so-called "Thanksgiving" in a spirit of goodwill. However, by the eighteenth century, Native Americans—who had their own strongly held cultures and ethnocentric pride and who wanted nothing to do with the white man's civilization, including his religion—had been redefined by many in the dominant group as heathens or beasts.

As European settlers demanded more and more territory for permanent settlement that had been used by Native Americans for centuries, confrontations between the two groups escalated and became increasingly hostile. The English authorities responded in the 1750s by declaring members of some Indian tribes vermin by official proclamation and calling for their extermination.

It was the English and not the Indians—as commonly portrayed in nineteenth-century American literature and twentieth-century motion pictures—who introduced scalping to America. In 1755, for example, a proclamation was issued at Boston sanctioned by King George II that called for all Penobscot Indians to be destroyed and a bounty of forty pounds sterling each was to be paid for the entire scalps of all adult males and twenty pounds for the scalps of all females and children under twelve years (Deloria, 1970).

Yet at the same time, some Indian groups were highly respected by the colonists. The Iroquois, for instance, consisted of a league of six tribes—the Cayuga, Mohawk, Oneida, Onondaga, Senaca, and Tuscarora—which collectively were regarded as very civilized. Portions of their system of government served as a model for some provisions incorporated into the U.S. Constitution. For example, the method used by a joint Senate–House conference committee to arrive at a compromise bill from separate bills passed in each legislative body is based on an Iroquois concept (Parrillo, 1985).

Native Americans after the Formation of the United States With the formation of the United States and the end of English rule, Native Americans as a group did not fare well during the nineteenth and early twentieth centuries. Under the onslaught of Western expansion and the continuing demand for Indian territory, the U.S. Government entered into numerous treaties with various tribes for the settlement of their lands However, many of these treaties were broken by the government, and the pressure to move from one reservation to another, sometimes with the threat of force, destroyed much of the traditional culture and food sources of many tribes.

In 1871, the government ceased to make treaties with the Indians and, instead, made them wards of the U.S government under the administration of the Bureau of Indian Affairs (BIA). The BIA did little on the Indians' behalf, and most Native American groups were left to their own resources. The destruction of the American buffalo (bison) by American sportsmen and hide hunters, for example, pushed the Plains Indian tribes to the brink of starvation. Some tribes reacted with violence and fought back in numerous encounters with settlers and the U.S. military forces, but to no avail.

Native Americans in Recent Times and Today Today, Native Americans represent the poorest of all American minorities. Not granted full citizenship until 1924, they have suffered under many confusing and often contradictory shifts in government policy throughout the twentieth and into the present twenty-first century. Most of these policies have not helped them to better their social and economic position. Indicators of poor life chances abound. Overall, thirty-eight percent live below the poverty line and, on reservations, the figure is forty-eight percent. Fifty-five percent of those on reservations live in substandard housing, seventy percent must haul drinking water at least a mile to their homes, and fifty-eight percent of their children receive less than an eighth grade education (Vander Zanden, 1983).

Nonetheless, some improvements are being made, most notably what sociologist Richard T. Schaefer (2008, p. 178) calls *pan-Indianism*. Similar in many respects to the political organization of blacks during the civil rights movement of the 1960s, **pan-Indianism** involves attempts by Indian groups to develop coalitions between several tribes to deal effectively with common problems. One perceived common problem is the insensitivity of the federal government, which many Native Americans feel treats them and their tribes as captive colonies. The most successful of the pan-Indian groups in recent years has been the Council of Energy Resource Tribes (CERT). By 1986, CERT had membership and representation from forty-two tribes. This coalition was able to negotiate a deal for the Navajos with Atlantic Richfield Company (ARCO) which brought in an estimated $78 million in revenues by 2006. If pan-Indianism is to grow into a consistent social force, fragmented and isolated Indian tribes must overcome their differences and learn to work together as a force for social change.

African Americans

The largest racial minority in the United States consists of African Americans who, as of 2006, numbered thirty-eight million and accounted for nearly thirteen percent of the population (*The World Almanac and Book of Facts*, 2008, p. 601).

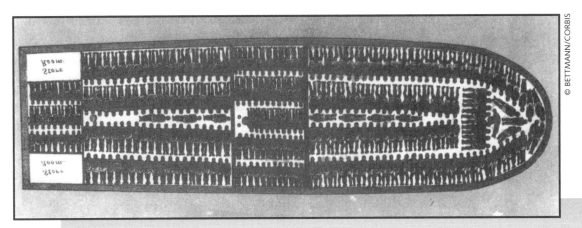

For Portuguese, English, and Dutch merchants and ship owners during the 1600s and 1700s, the African slave trade was a lucrative business. As shown in the print above, most slavers were "tight packers" who tried to cram as many slaves as possible into the holds of their ships to maximize profits. Forced to lie side by aside in their own excrement with only two feet or so of crawl space, one out of every eight slaves died during the fifty days it took to make the Atlantic passage (The Bettman Archive).

A Cultural Experience Rooted in Slavery   The black experience in this country is rooted in slavery, which lasted for more than two hundred years. The period of what has been called "the peculiar institution" might have been much shorter had Thomas Jefferson had his way. When Jefferson wrote the first draft of the declaration of Independence in Philadelphia during June of 1776, he included a paragraph denouncing the slave trade and slavery which was blamed on King George III (England was the primary slave trafficker at the time). If retained, this clause would have established the foundation for emancipating the slaves. Jefferson already had a plan for this called "the Jeffersonian solution." However, the Continental Congress deleted the paragraph from the final draft (Lincoln, 1968). The trafficking in African slaves, first sanctioned in the Virginia Colony in 1661, became an institutionalized practice in America that was to last over two hundred years before being brought to an end, largely as a result of the Civil War fought between North and South in which the issue of slavery was a major precipitating factor.

The Decades after the Civil War   In the aftermath of the Civil War (1861–1865), the Thirteenth, Fourteenth, and Fifteenth Amendments to the Constitution abolished slavery and gave males of African descent full citizenship and voting rights. Many of these freedoms were short-lived, however. The Ku Klux Klan, a white supremacist organization, brutalized black communities from the middle 1860s through the 1870s in an attempt to keep blacks from voting and engaging in other forms of participation in "white" society. During this period, assaults, murders, and nightly cross burnings were relatively common. In a backlash of institutional racism, several states began passing **"Jim Crow" laws** (named after a blackface minstrel dancer). Jim Crow laws were statutes passed by Southern states after the Civil War that denied blacks access to public facilities used by whites (e.g., restaurants, hotels, restrooms, rail cars, etc.).

The African American Experience: 1900 to 1954   The first half of the twentieth century did not bode well for the life chances of African Americans. The Jim Crow policy was upheld in 1896 by the U.S. Supreme Court in *Plessy v. Ferguson,* which stated that "separate but equal" facilities for blacks was reasonable accommodation for their needs (Woodward, 1974). This ruling ushered in a sixty year period of legally sanctioned racial segregation in which blacks sat at the back of the bus, prayed in separate churches, attended separate schools, and were set apart from white society in practically all aspects of social life. The Supreme Court finally set this policy aside in 1954 in *Brown v. the Board of Education,* which overturned the "separate but equal" doctrine as it applied to school facilities as unconstitutional. This, in part, helped set the stage for the Civil Rights movement of the 1960s.

Changing Life Chances: 1955 to the Present—Trends, Problems and Remaining Challenges   The period from 1955 to the present has been marked by social reforms and many institutional changes that have impacted significantly on African Americans as a consequence. In the wake of such events as the March on Selma and Dr. Martin Luther King, Jr.'s "I have a dream" speech in the 1960s, many changes came about for black Americans, some very positive and others not so positive.

Positive Trends   Groundbreaking federal legislation, including the Civil Rights Act of 1964, accompanied by vigorous enforcement of desegregation laws, reduced racial segregation in most communities. Federal programs in the areas of education, occupational training, housing, and urban renewal created unprecedented opportunities not only for African Americans but other minorities as well (Farley, 1977, 1984). Research conducted during this period indicated that attitudes in the white community also changed signifi-

© MONKEY BUSINESS IMAGES, 2009. USED UNDER LICENSE FROM SHUTTERSTOCK, INC.

Today, the black middle class is a growing phenomenon that accounts for over thirty-four percent of the black population (2000) and a projected forty to forty-five percent or more by 2015.

cantly and both prejudice and acts of discrimination declined (Farley, 1977, 1984). During the past half century, life chances for African Americans in general have improved considerably. The black middle class rose from less than ten percent of the total American population to thirty-four percent of black families with annual earnings of $50,000 or more by 2000 (U.S. Census Bureau, 2002). This was facilitated in large part by a percentage growth in African Americans.

And the number of elected black officials—including members of Congress and mayors of several major cities—increased to nearly 7,000 by the late 1980s as compared to less than 100 in 1955 (Gelman, et al., 1988). By the beginning of the 2000s, the number of black elected officials had increased over fivefold from under 1,800 in 1970 to over 9,000 in 2001 (Bositis, 2003).

Problems and Challenges   Despite the rise of the black middle class and an apparent decline of "race" as an important social concept to most Americans, there are still major problems and challenges facing the African American community. Racism in thought and deed still occurs and some forms of artificial segregation and denied opportunity still exist. However, the challenge today and in the future for both the black community and American society as a whole has more to do with class than race. (Wilson and Aponte, 1985). The poor are much more likely to be victimized by crime and to experience disorganized fractured families than are those occupying the more affluent classes. In addition, their children are only about half as likely to pursue postsecondary college degrees or technical education (Lareau, 2002).

Much of the challenge facing the African American community today is related to the family and demographic factors that impact on it. While affluent, college-educated African Americans usually move to the suburbs or gated urban areas, the underclass tend to be trapped in inner city neighborhoods which are in decay due to a lack of industry and jobs and a stagnating tax base which means poorly funded schools. Add to this the fact that only thirty-five percent of black children live in a two-parent home (compared to nearly seventy-six percent for white children) and just over fifty percent of black children live in a home maintained by a single mother, the consequences and implications for the life chances of black children are daunting (U.S. Bureau of the Census, 2006a). For example, twenty-eight percent of black, female-headed households live in poverty (Ibid.). Such dynamics contribute to high teenage pregnancy rates for girls and high rates of crime for adolescent males who (1) lack pro-social male success models in the inner city and (2) have little access to legitimate jobs, which are scarce and low paying.

Factors such as teenage pregnancy, coupled with lack of opportunity because of residual racism, low education, and the lack of job skills together create a vicious cycle that poor blacks find difficult to break. Consequently, African Americans as a whole have made tremendous strides since the 1950s, but several social conditions require change before they will be able to participate with realized life chances equal to those in the dominant group.

Asian Americans

Collectively, people of Asian descent represent the fastest growing minority group in America whose numbers more than tripled from three and one-half million in 1980 to nearly twelve million by 2004 (U.S. Bureau of the Census, 2004b; Kivisto and Ng, 2008). They represent several countries and regions of the world, most notably China, Japan, the Philippines, Korea, India, and Southeast Asia. Due largely to a greater participation in education than other Americans—eighty-five percent graduate from high school and fifty percent earn college degrees—Asian Americans are often referred to as the "model minority." While about twenty percent of white Americans are represented in managerial, professional, and executive occupations, the numbers for Americans of Asian descent—Asian Indians (forty-seven percent), Chinese (thirty percent), and Japanese (twenty-eight percent) for example—are significantly higher (Thompson and Hickey, 2008). If current immigration trends continue, Asian Americans are expected to triple in number to nearly thirty-three and one-half million by 2050 (U.S. Census Bureau, 2004).

The first immigrants from Asia came in the nineteenth century, predominantly from China and Japan. As late as 1970, three-quarters of all Asian Americans were from these two countries. However, with the dramatic influx of Filipinos, Koreans, East Indians, and Vietnamese in recent years, those of Japanese and Chinese descent now constitute only about one-third of all Asian Americans.

Chinese Americans   Of all Asian Americans, those of Chinese descent (nearly twenty-two and one-half percent) comprise the largest group (American Community Survey, 2005). As the first Asians to emigrate to the United States, the Chinese came mainly to California in the 1840s to escape economic problems and unrest in their own country (Kitano, 1985). At first, these new immigrants were accepted because they helped to alleviate an acute labor shortage in menial occupations. During the gold rush days of 1849 and 1850, there was a severe scarcity of women who traditionally did cooking, laundry, and other domestic chores. Although most Chinese immigrants were male, they were glad to do this work. They later worked as laborers in the mines and on the railroads.

As more and more Chinese came to the West Coast over the next several decades—at least three hundred thousand by 1880—their numbers, coupled with their very different racial and cultural characteristics, resulted in tremendous anti-Chinese sentiment. Many Californians, driven by fear that these strange, hardworking people would take their jobs, subjected the Chinese to scorn and racial slurs and beat and killed many of them. The Chinese, in reaction, found themselves forced to retreat to segregated communities called "Chinatowns." Californians, and later, leaders in Congress were so fearful of unchecked Chinese immigration—often called "the Yellow Peril"—that Congress passed the Chinese Exclusion Act in 1882, which banned further immigration for ten years. This exclusion was later made permanent and was not repealed until after World War II. Today, Chinese Americans are most likely of all Asian immigrants to complete college.

Japanese Americans   The immigration patterns of those who came to this country from Japan were somewhat different from the Chinese. When the Japanese government ended its two-hundred-year-old prohibition against foreign travel in 1865, some Japanese citizens began to emigrate to the United States. However, they did not arrive in significant numbers until about 1900 (Parrillo, 1980). Unlike the Chinese immigrants—who were almost exclusively single males—the Japanese came as married couples. Once in the United States, they established families and tried to assimilate into the American cultural mainstream. In addition, because jobs were difficult to obtain in the large cities and unions and

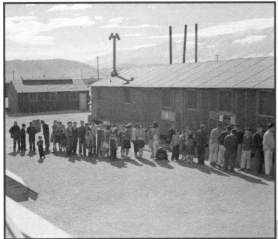

Because of a combination of war hysteria and racial bigotry, 110,000 persons of Japanese descent, most of whom were U.S. citizens, were forcibly relocated in 1942 to an American version of "concentration camps." Once relocated, they remained in these camps as prisoners of the U.S. military for the duration of World War II. Today, greater opportunities coupled with a strong work ethic have resulted in Japanese Americans and others of Asian descent becoming among the most upwardly mobile of minority groups.

their members considered Asians as a threat because they would work for lower wages, most Japanese Americans settled in rural outlying areas. There, they worked on farms, and some ultimately became successful tenant farmers and small farm and vineyard owners.

U.S. policy changed however, on December 7, 1941, when the Japanese bombed American naval installations at Pearl Harbor. The resulting war hysteria—many Americans feared a Japanese land invasion of California—resulted in the classification of Japanese Americans as a possible threat to national security. Consequently, 110,000 people of Japanese descent, 70,000 of whom were native-born, American citizens, were uprooted from their homes and businesses and schools and were relocated to detention camps in other states. There they remained for the duration of the war (Parrillo, 2009). They lost their homes and farms, and were not paid reparations after the war. In an ironic twist, the most highly decorated allied fighting unit in the European theater during World War II was the 442 Regimental Combat Team, a unit of Japanese American soldiers.

In August of 1988, forty-three years after the end of the war, President Ronald Reagan signed into law a bill designed to make reparations to the survivors of the forced imprisonment. Under this legislation, the U.S. government agreed to pay each of the estimated 62,000 Japanese American detainees still alive a reparation payment of $20,000 (Molotsky, 1988).

Asian Americans Today In recent years, Asian immigrants have come in large numbers from Indochina, a region in Southeast Asia. During the decade following the fall of South Vietnam in 1975, more than 840,000 immigrants, mainly refugees from countries including Vietnam, Laos, and Thailand (Rumbault, 1986). A large number have also immigrated from the Philippines.

Since the end of World War II, Asian Americans have become increasingly successful. Their families typically are tight-knit and stress self-discipline, hard work, and appreciation of education as the primary means of gaining upward mobility. Because of these values, Asian Americans, including more recent arrivals from the Philippines and Indochina, are among America's most successful minority groups. Japanese Americans, for example, have a higher per capita income than any other racial minority (Wilson and Hosokawa, 1980). Asian students are more likely to take college preparatory classes in math and science while in high school, devote more time to study, and are overrepresented in the freshman classes at the nation's leading universities in comparison with other Americans (Zigli, 1984; Butterfield, 1986; Parrillo, 2009).

ETHNICITY AND ETHNIC MINORITIES

The Nature of Ethnicity

Ethnicity refers to the specific cultural heritage that distinguishes one social category of people from others. In some societies, almost all inhabitants share essentially the same ethnicity. By comparison, the United States is a pluralistic society with citizens from dozens of different ethnic backgrounds. Nonetheless, those of European heritage, and particularly those of Anglo-Saxon descent, comprise the dominant or majority group today and have dominated both law and custom throughout American history. As a result, those with different ethnic backgrounds historically were seen as out-groups and often were denied equal life chances. Consequently, several groups became ethnic minorities that are regarded differently and treated unequally because of their cultural characteristics such as customs and country of origin.

It should be mentioned that racial minorities, as previously discussed, also have a distinctive ethnicity. However, the source of their unequal treatment has more to do with their visible physical characteristics than distinctive cultural attributes. The relocation of Japanese Americans into detention camps during World War II serves as a good example. The United States at that time was at war with the Axis Pact, which included Germany and Italy as well as Japan. While it is true that many German Americans were harassed during this time and some last names such as Mueller became Miller and DiBennedettos became Bennett, there was no serious attempt to systematically quarantine these groups of Caucasians. Only the Japanese Americans, because of their racial visibility, were perceived as potential enemies requiring involuntary relocation and detention.

Nonetheless, several ethnic minorities have been regarded and treated differently primarily because of their cultural backgrounds and characteristics. A brief discussion of some of these groups follows.

Hispanics

Today, the largest U. S. ethnic group is comprised of Hispanics who, by 2006, had grown in number to more than forty million, which is about double from their U.S. population in 1990. People of Hispanic background, most of whom are Spanish speaking, originally came to the United States from different countries with distinct cultural traditions. When racial background and ethnicity are considered, they represent the largest American minority, having surpassed African Americans in number as of 2001 as a result of both high fertility rates and rates of immigration (Parrillo, 2009).

Hispanics represent a diverse social category of people whose origins are such places as Mexico, Puerto Rico, Cuba, and various Central and South American and Caribbean countries. They share, however, certain characteristics in common including language, the Roman Catholic faith, and strong ethnic identification. Many Hispanics are found in large cities like Los Angeles, Houston, and Miami, and most are concentrated in two states, California and Texas. Other states including Arizona, New Mexico, New York, and Florida also have large Spanish-speaking populations.

Mexican Americans   The nearly thirty million Mexican Americans (by 2005) represents the largest Hispanic group in the United States, about sixty-six percent of all those of Latino origin (Thompson and Hickey, 2008). This estimate does not fully account for illegal immigrants from Mexico who number several million more (Kandel and Massey, 2002; Kivisto and Ng, 2005). Those of Spanish descent first migrated to what is now the American Southwest in the 1500s. Isolated Spanish missions designed to bring Christianity to various Indian groups grew to become settlements of significant size devoted to agriculture. When Mexico ceded one-third of its territory to the United States in 1848 following the Mexican-American War, many Mexican citizens suddenly found themselves living in the United States, which did not recognize their claims of land ownership that, in some cases, were granted much earlier by the King of Spain. Following political and economic unrest in Mexico during the late 1800s and early 1900s, many Mexicans came to America as agricultural workers or *braceros* who were in high demand because they accepted low wages.

During the late twentieth century and the first years of the new century, unstable political and poor economic conditions in Mexico have produced a flood of illegal immigrants desperate to earn a subsistence living. Both these people and U.S. citizens of Mexican descent have faced many problems, including the language barrier and economic and social discrimination. For example, until the 1960s, it was not uncommon for Mexican Americans to be denied service at restaurants and other businesses owned by white Anglo Americans.

Since the 1960s, however, the Chicano political movement has helped make Mexican Americans a more viable political force. Leaders have included Cesar Chavez, who organized Mexican migrant farm workers in the 1960s, and Henry Cisneros, former mayor of San Antonio who by the late 1980s had gained a national following. More recently, politicos such as Governor Bill Richardson, a Mexican American candidate for the Democratic presidential nomination in 2008, have been an influential force in addressing issues impacting on the life chances of Hispanics and other minorities. Political activism by Hispanics and others have allowed Mexican-American children who, until the late 1960s were not allowed to speak Spanish on school property, to have bilingual education to help them more readily acquire formal learning and, if designed properly, to become literate in English as well.

Nonetheless, Mexican Americans as a group remain significantly behind other Americans in terms of life chances. As of 2006, nearly twenty-four percent were living below the poverty line as compared to eighth and one-third percent for white non-Hispanics. Their plight is related to the fact that many first-generation Mexican Americans speak little or no English and just over thirty percent of twenty-two to twenty-four year olds (in 2005) had not finished high school (Parrillo, 2009).

Puerto Ricans   Governed by Spain for several hundred years, Puerto Rico was ceded to the United States by Spain in 1898 as a result of the Spanish-American War. At first there was little migration of these new Americans to the mainland even after they were granted citizenship in 1917. However, the collapse of the sugar industry after World War II coupled with such factors as low airline fares and the promise of jobs triggered one of the largest voluntary migrations in recent history. During the 1950s, one-half million Puerto Ricans—one of every six—left their native land and came to the mainland, most settling in New York City initially (Kitano, 1985). Because the majority were unskilled, poorly educated, and faced problems such as the language barrier and discrimination by labor unions, in housing, and in other areas, they were relegated to an underclass position.

Although increased opportunities in recent decades have made it possible for a larger number of Puerto Ricans to join the middle class, serious obstacles remain. In terms of positive life chance indicators, thirteen percent of Puerto Ricans were completing college in 2001 as compared to just over ten and one-half percent of all Hispanics and almost seven percent of Mexican Americans. However, Puerto Ricans, whom today live mainly in New York, New Jersey, Pennsylvania, and Florida, have obstacles to overcome that are similar to those of Mexican Americans and Hispanics as a whole. More than forty-three percent of their families are headed by a single parent as compared with thirty-two percent for Hispanics in general and thirty percent for Mexican Americans. Due to these and other factors, they have the highest unemployment rate (just over eight percent) of all Hispanics and represent the poorest of all Hispanic groups with nearly twenty-six percent (as of 2000) living below the poverty line (Therrien and Ramirez, 2001).

Cubans   Of all Hispanics, Cubans are closest to the American mainstream in annual family income and life chances. The majority—more than 910,000—have come to the United States since 1959 to escape communism under Fidel Castro. Once here, they have settled mainly in Miami, New York, and other major cities. Most of these people and their descendents are middle class, many with technical skills or college degrees (Parrillo, 2009). In terms of life chance indicators, twenty-three percent of Cuban Americans (as of 2000) complete college degrees, more than double that of Hispanics (just over ten and one-half percent) as a whole. In addition, just over seventeen percent live below the poverty line as compared to nearly twenty-three percent for Hispanics as a total group (Schaefer, 2008).

Although Cubans have faced both prejudice and discrimination, their class characteristics and education (as a group) have made it easier for them not only to survive but to prosper in a country with an urban business economy. Consequently, they have furnished positive role models for other Hispanics. According to sociologist Vincent B. Parrillo (2009),

> [T]he Cuban impact on Miami, now dubbed "Little Havana," has been significant. About 52 percent of all Cuban Americans live in Miami-Dade County, where Cuban influence has transformed Miami from a resort town to a year-round commercial center with linkages throughout Latin America and has turned it into a leading bilingual cultural center. Over 57percent of Miami-Dade County is now Hispanic with, including 657,000 Cubans, 80,000 Puerto Ricans, 38,000 Mexicans, and 522,000 others from Central and South America (p. 410).

White Ethnics

Those of largely non-Protestant European origin, termed "white ethnics," began emigrating to the United States in significant numbers a full half century before the following words included in a poem by Emma Lazarus were inscribed on the base of the Statue of Liberty in 1886:

> . . . Give me your tired, your poor,
> Your huddled masses yearning to breathe free,
> The wretched refuse of your teeming shore

They came primarily from Eastern and Western Europe for a variety of reasons, some out of desperation. Many Irish arrived during the 1840s in the wake of the potato famine in Ireland that ravaged the country causing economic devastation and, for some, starvation. Some Jews came to escape religious and political persecution in Europe. But mainly they came—the Italians and French, the Slavs, the Greeks, Poles, and others—to seek a better life in the emerging giant of a country called America.

Most white ethnics came to the United States in a great "second wave" between the 1870s and 1920s. The majority were poor and unskilled. Because of their meager resources, they settled mainly in eastern cities at or near their ports of entry. There, in places like New York and Chicago, they worked—men, women, and children—fourteen to sixteen hours a day, six or seven days a week, as laborers in industrial "sweat shops" and at other unskilled and semiskilled occupations. Many, because of low wages, were forced to live in vermin-infested tenements or "flophouses" in ethnic ghettos, where whole families of six or eight often lived in one or two rooms.

Although these people provided American industry at that time with a seemingly inexhaustible supply of cheap labor and were exploited before protective legislation began in the 1930s, they were not welcomed with open arms. Quite the contrary, they were subject to prejudice, discrimination, and racism for a variety of reasons. First, the sheer numbers of these "foreigners" struck at the ethnocentrism of Anglo-Saxons citizens who felt their culture threatened by the strange ways and customs of the newcomers. Many Protestants,

© TOMASZ PARYS, 2009. USED UNDER LICENSE FROM SHUTTERSTOCK, INC.

White ethnic families often occupied one or two rooms in "flop houses" when they came to America early in the twentieth century.

for example, rioted against Irish Catholics in the 1840s because of religious intolerance and later exhibited anti-Semitism toward the Jews. Others displayed racism against some newcomers because their swarthy Mediterranean complexions differed from those of lighter-skinned Caucasians from Northern Europe. In addition, these people were for the most part poor and unskilled and the more affluent considered them inferior. An editorial writer in 1886, for example, referred to them as "the very scum and offal of Europe" whom he described as "bad-smelling, . . . foreign wretches, who never did an honest hour's work in their lives" (quoted in Parrillo, 1985, p. 156).

Despite these obstacles, white ethnics as a whole have fared better than most minorities. Because they were Caucasian and understood the need to learn English, many of the first and second generations tried to assimilate into the American cultural mainstream with some success. In addition, many white ethnics changed their family names in order to "fit in" with the dominant Anglo-Saxon culture. As illustrated in Table 10-5, this pattern still exists to some degree.

Jewish Americans   Jewish Americans represent one example of a white ethnic group that came to this country. Although a few Jews from Spain and Portugal arrived as early as 1654, the most significant Jewish migration to America occurred around the turn of the twentieth century. Most early Jewish immigrants came voluntarily to seek a better life. However, some also came to escape religious persecution and political expulsion in Europe.

TABLE 10-5	Original Names of Selected White Ethnic Entertainers
Alan Alda: Alphonso D'Abruzzo	Ben Kingsley: Krisna Banji
Pat Benatar: Patricia Andrejewski	Cheryl Ladd: Cheryl Stoppelmoor
Tony Bennett: Tony Benedetto	Huey Lewis: Hugh Cregg
Joey Bishop: Joseph Gottleib	Jerry Lewis: Joseph LeVitch
Bono: Paul Hewson	Madonna: Madonna Louise Veronica Ciccone
David Bowie: David Robert Jones	Barry Manilow: Barry Allan Pincus
Nicolas Cage: Nicholas Coppala	Marilyn Manson: Brian Warner
Michael Caine: Maurice Mickelwhite	George Michael: Georgios Panayiotou
Tom Cruise: Thomas Mapother IV	Helen Mirren: Ilynea Lydia Mironoff
Danny Devito: Daniel Michaeli	Demi Moore: Demetria Guynes
Kathy Lee Gifford: Kathi Epstein	Bernadette Peters: Bernadette Lazzaro
Pee Wee Herman: Paul Reubenfeld	Joan Rivers: Joan Sandra Molinsky
Wynona Judd: Cristina Ciminella	Meg Ryan: Margaret Hyra
Elton John: Reginald Dwight	Winona Rider: Winono Horowitz
Carol King: Carole Klein	Jane Semour: Joyce Frankenburg
Larry King: Larry Ziegler	Randy Travis: Randy Trawick

As illustrated above, many white ethnic entertainers of North and East European and/or Jewish ancestry—for whatever reasons—have chosen to change their name, often to an anglicized version.

Source: *The World Almanac and Book of Facts.* 2008. New York: World Almanac Books, 227–228.

By the 1930s however, most Jews entering the United States were refugees fleeing from the tyranny of Germany's Third Reich.

Today, the United States is home to the largest concentration of Jews (forty-one percent) in the world. The largest concentration of America's nearly five and one-half million Jewish citizens reside in and around New York city, the center of Jewish culture in America (Schaefer, 2008). Contrary to myths and stereotypes held by some, Jewish identity is neither racial nor religious, but largely ethnic. Jews share a common cultural identity or "peoplehood," based at least partially on centuries of tradition and custom. Because most Jewish people who emigrated to America had been urban dwellers in Europe engaged in industrial occupations, they adapted readily to the American economic system and, as a group, have prospered.

One problem faced by Jewish people is **anti-Semitism**, prejudice and discrimination focused on people of Jewish culture or faith. The most extreme expression of Jewish persecution was the *Holocaust*, a systematic, state-sponsored attempt (1939–1945) by the Nazi German government to eliminate all Jewish people from the European continent. By the end of World War II, over six million European Jews had been exterminated in killing factories or concentration camps with their remains either buried in mass graves or cremated (Thio, 2008). This included two-thirds of Europe's entire Jewish population and ninety percent of all Jews from Austria, Germany, and Poland who were murdered (Schaefer, 2008). Although nothing this extreme has ever happened in America, numerous anti-Semitic incidents still occur in the United States each year. During 2006, for example, there were over fifteen hundred such episodes including eighty-one on college campuses, some perpetrated by anti-Semitic hate groups (Parrillo, 2009).

White Ethnics Today   In addition to the Jews, many other white ethnics had also been urban dwellers in Europe. Consequently, the transition to an industrial economy in the United States was relatively smooth for many of them, especially for those who have emigrated during the past several decades. Ethnic groups including the Irish, Italians, Germans, and Poles have made strong efforts to assimilate and today have family incomes competitive with most Americans (Greeley, 1976). Jewish Americans, for example, have higher median incomes than Americans in general, and almost twice as many, proportionally speaking, complete four years of college. Third generation white ethnics today are showing an ethnic pride that their parents and grandparents did not exhibit, because of the cultural climate in decades past. In 1960, John F. Kennedy, an Irish Catholic was narrowly elected president, although his Catholicism was an issue for more conservative Protestants. During 1988, Governor Michael Dukakis, the son of a Greek immigrant, was nominated by the Democratic Party to run for the same office. In 2004, a Jewish U.S. Senator named Joseph Lieberman was the Democratic Vice Presidential nominee (who ran with John Kerry) and an Austrian American named Arnold Schwartzenegar became Governor of California.

RACIAL AND ETHNIC RELATIONS IN PERSPECTIVE

The manner in which specific racial and ethnic minorities relate to the dominant group and culture is perhaps best illustrated by a polar typology as shown in Figure 10-2. On one side of the continuum are patterns of exclusion in varying degrees, which result in discrimination

Degrees of Exclusion ———————— ± ———————— Degrees of Participation

(genocide → / segregation → / accommodation → / assimilation → / pluralism)

Figure 10-2

Minority Exclusion and Participation: A Continuum

and denied or impaired life chances. On the other are differing degrees of participation and acceptance.

Patterns of Exclusion

As we have seen throughout this chapter, minority groups often have been excluded from social participation in varying degrees. The most extreme form of exclusion is **genocide**, an intentional and systematic attempt by one group to exterminate another. Throughout much of human history, there have been attempts at genocide at both micro (local) and macro (societal) levels. For example, the ancient Hebrews tried to eradicate the people of Canaan. During the colonial period in American history, both the colonists and Indians, on occasion, engaged in local massacres of one another. In addition to the *Holocaust* previously discussed, there have been others. Prominent examples include the murder of thirty million people by Soviet Union dictator Josef Stalin, Cambodia dictator Pol Pot's extermination of two million people—one-quarter of the country's population—from 1975–1980, and "the killing of hundreds of thousands of people in the Darfur region of the Sudan" in the 2000s (Macionis, 2007, pp. 313–314). A precondition for such barbarism is the dehumanization of the enemy (Duster, 1971).

Segregation involves the involuntary separation of a minority group from the dominant group in terms of general social contact and participation. There are two basic forms. *Defacto segregation* is separation "in fact" as established by social custom. *Dejure segregation* is separation mandated by law, such as that practiced in the United States during 1896–1954 and the apartheid system established in South Africa until abolished in 1994.

The least extreme form of exclusion is accommodation, a process in which members of a minority group attempt to coexist with the dominant group without making a significant effort to adopt the norms and values of the dominant society. Some, including Jewish and Cuban Americans have been able to gain relative prosperity while maintaining a strong ethnic identity, which includes a high value placed on economic independence and higher education. Others, including poor Mexican Americans and Puerto Ricans, have not fared so well, in part because they still cling to portions of orthodox Catholicism and the agricultural ethic that both encourage high rates of fertility. These factors combined with others—such as low levels of formal education—add up to a formula for continuing poverty.

Patterns of Participation

Minority groups may exhibit varying degrees of participation with or without the consent of the dominant group. Two of these patterns, diffusion and assimilation, were discussed earlier (Chapter 4) and will be mentioned only briefly here. *Diffusion* is cultural change brought about through direct contact of two cultures in which certain traits of one are borrowed from the other. In the context of minority relations, diffusion often is the first step toward full participation, in that members of a minority often will, for example, learn the language and acquire the skills valued in the larger society that are needed to improve their general life chances. *Assimilation* is a process whereby an immigrant or minority group changes its cultural patterns to conform and adapt to the ways of the dominant culture.

The key challenge for many minorities is not full assimilation but pluralism. **Pluralism** refers to equal social participation by diverse groups in society based on tolerance and mutual respect for each other's cultural distinctions in a climate of cooperation. In an atmosphere that is truly pluralistic, no one has to sacrifice their cultural heritage and identity but must learn to appreciate the richness that other cultural traditions can offer in enriching their own lives.

Usually the most complete level of participation is reached with some people who engage in **amalgamation**, the process through which members of the dominant group and a minority group combine to form a new group through intermarriage. State laws forbidding racial intermarriage were struck down as unconstitutional by the Supreme Court in 1967.

▶ CHAPTER SUMMARY

1. Minority relations in any society depend on the interaction between a dominant group and one or more minority groups. A dominant group is a social category comprised of those in society who are dominant in power, prestige, wealth, and culture. Historically, the United States has been dominated by those of white Anglo-Saxon heritage. A minority group is a social category of people distinguished by their physical or cultural characteristics whose members have experienced a historical pattern of prejudice and discrimination.

2. Sociologists generally distinguish between two overlapping types of minorities, racial minorities and ethnic minorities. A racial minority is a group whose members have suffered social disadvantages because of visible physical characteristics (such as skin color) seen as inferior by members of the dominant group. African Americans, American Indians, and Asian Americans are key examples. An ethnic minority is a group whose members have experienced social disadvantages primarily because of cultural characteristics, including traditional customs and nation of origin, which the dominant group has treated as inferior. Hispanics, Jewish Americans, and other white ethnics are typical of ethnic minorities in the United States today.

3. Prejudice and discrimination are two important factors that impact on minority relations. Prejudice is the judgment of individuals and groups based on preconceived ideas held about them. The three basic types of prejudice are exploitative prejudice, normative prejudice, and the authoritarian personality. Whereas prejudice is a judgmental attitude, discrimination involves differential treatment of people based on their membership in a particular social category. As such, discrimination may take both individual and institutional forms.

4. Another factor that influences minority relations is racism, which results from erroneous ways in which race is perceived. From a biological perspective, race involves certain visible physical characteristics of a group that are passed on to future generations. Scientists generally regard biological racial differences to be superficial at best and largely meaningless, because all humans belong to one species, *Homo sapiens sapiens*. From a sociological perspective, however, race involves a category of people (of both sexes and all age groups) perceived and treated differently because of certain visible physical characteristics. In some societies, racism may become prevalent as a doctrine that holds that one racial group is superior and all others are inferior. As a consequence, typically members of minorities are subject to victimization when one of the historically dominant forms of racism—individual or institutional—is used by the group in power to discriminate against and thus marginalize them. Although these forms of racism have declined tremendously since the 1960s, they still exist to a degree. In addition, new forms of racism have emerged (e.g., hate groups and reverse racism).

5. Racial minorities in the United States include African Americans (the largest), American Indians (the poorest) and Asian Americans (one of the fastest growing). All of these groups have experienced prejudice, discrimination, and racism throughout most of their histories in the United States. Blacks were enslaved for 200 years (1661–1865) and then forced to live under a system of legal and social segregation for the better part of another century. American Indians or Native Americans were alternately patronized and respected, vilified, slaughtered, and exploited for their lands. Asian Americans have endured economic exploitation, segregation, and in the case of the Japanese Americans, forcible detention as a group in camps during World War II. Nonetheless, conditions for racial minorities in general have improved significantly during the last several decades as a result of political activism, protective legislation, increased educational opportunities and levels of participation and educational attainment, and other factors.

6. Ethnic minorities include Hispanic Americans, Jews, and other white ethnics. These groups are distinguished primarily by their ethnicity or specific cultural heritage. In 2000, Hispanic Americans accounted for about twelve and one-half percent of the total U.S. population and included those of Mexican, Cuban, Puerto Rican, and Central and South American descent. Given such factors as fertility rates, religious beliefs, and traditional values borne out of a rural, agricultural heritage, Hispanics represent the largest and fastest growing minority group in America when racial background and ethnicity are considered. White ethnics are those of largely non-Protestant European origin who migrated to the United States during the nineteenth and early twentieth centuries. Jewish Americans, Irish Americans, and Italian Americans are only a few of over a hundred such groups.

7. Minority relations perhaps are best illustrated by a continuum, extreme exclusion on one end and almost if not complete acceptance and participation on the other. Patterns of exclusion range from genocide, the most extreme form, through segregation, to accommodation or tolerance in which the minority group coexists peaceably with the dominant and both groups more or less hold each other at arm's length. Patterns of participation begin generally with diffusion, then progress over two or three generations to assimilation, and then finally (or concurrently) for some members of both minority and dominant groups, pluralism and amalgamation occur.

TERMS TO KNOW

accommodation: a pattern of exclusion which members of a minority group attempt to coexist with the dominant group without making a significant effort to adopt the norms and values of the dominant society.

amalgamation: the intermarriage of minority group members with those belonging to the dominant group.

anti-Semitism: prejudice and discrimination focused on people of Jewish culture or faith.

authoritarian personality: a highly rigid and intolerant person who tends to exhibit a group of identifiable personality characteristics.

discrimination: differential treatment of people based on their membership in a particular social category.

dominant group: a social category comprised of those in society who are dominant in power, prestige, wealth, and culture.

ethnicity: a specific cultural heritage that distinguishes one social category of people from others.

ethnic minority: a social category whose members have experienced social disadvantages primarily because of cultural characteristics such as language or national origin.

exploitative prejudice: negative attitudes toward minority group members held by members of the majority group that are used as justification for keeping them in a subordinate position.

genocide: a pattern of exclusion that involves an intentional and systematic attempt by one group to exterminate another.

hate crimes: ordinary crimes in which victims are chosen because of some characteristic they possess such as racial background, religion, ethnicity, or sexual orientation.

individual discrimination: unequal treatment that occurs when individuals belonging to one group regard and treat individuals of another group differently because of their group membership.

individual racism: unequal treatment that occurs when ideas and actions based on a doctrine of racial supremacy are applied to members of one racial category by members of another. NOTE: This is a specific form of individual discrimination.

institutional discrimination: unequal treatment of certain categories of people as a result of inequities built into basic institutions.

institutional racism: unequal treatment of members of a racial category that occurs when ideas and actions based on a doctrine of racial inequality are embedded into the structure of basic institutions (e.g., government, education, and the economic system). NOTE: This is a specific form of institutional discrimination.

Jim Crow laws: statutes passed by Southern states after the Civil War that denied blacks access to public facilities used by whites (e.g., restaurants, hotels, restrooms, rail cars, etc.).

minority group: a social category of people distinguished by their physical or cultural characteristics whose members have experienced a historical pattern of prejudice and discrimination.

normative prejudice: negative attitudes toward members of a particular group that are accepted as "normal" through the process of socialization.

pan-Indianism: efforts by Indian groups to develop coalitions between several tribes to deal effectively with common problems.

pluralism: a process of equal social participation by diverse groups in society based on tolerance and mutual respect for each other's cultural distinctions in a climate of cooperation.

prejudice: the negative judgment of individuals and groups because of preconceived ideas held about them.

race: a social category of people (of both sexes and all age groups) perceived and treated in a distinct manner on the basis of certain visible physical characteristics.

racial minority: is a social category whose members have suffered social disadvantages because of visible physical characteristics (such as skin color).

racism: a doctrine—and acts stemming from it—that holds that one racial category is superior and all others, in varying degrees, are inferior.

reverse discrimination: unequal treatment of individuals based on their membership in the dominant group.

reverse racism: a resentment—and acts stemming from it—focused on the group in power by some minority members driven by deep-seated bitterness at the wrongs done to their ancestors by the ancestors of the dominant group.

segregation: a pattern of exclusion in which a minority group is involuntarily separated from the dominant group in terms of general social contact and participation.

stereotypes: fixed mental images about the characteristics of entire categories of people that are not tested against reality.

SUGGESTED READINGS

Brown, D. 2007. *Bury My Heart at Wounded Knee.* Reprinted ed. New York: Holt Paperbacks. An insightful portrayal of the experience of American Indians at the hands of the dominant group as told from a Native American perspective.

De Anda, R. M., ed. 2004. *Chicanas and Chicanos in Contemporary Society,* 2nd ed. Boston: Allyn & Bacon. A compilation of articles and essays about the roles of Mexican Americans and their family and community lives in present day American society.

Dent, D. J. 2001. *In Search of Black America: Discovering the African American Dream.* New York: Free Press. A thoughtful and detailed look into the lives of middle-class African Americans which shows them to be a very diverse group in terms of their opinions and world views on a variety of issues.

Min, P. G. 2005. *Asian Americans: Contemporary Trends and Issues.* Thousand Oaks, CA: Pine Oaks Press. A detailed and comprehensive examination of each of the major groups of Asian immigrants who have immigrated into the United States in terms of their histories and current issues that affect them.

Parrillo, V. N. 2008. *Diversity in America,* 3rd ed. Thousand Oaks, CA: Pine Forge Press. A brief general text that chronicles the historical development of the United States as a multicultural society from its colonial beginnings to the present.

Wise, T. J. 2005. *Affirmative Action: Racial Preference in Black and White.* New York: Routledge. A provocative, but engaging and well-researched book on the origins and development of affirmative action from its beginnings in 1961 to current applications.

PART FOUR

Issues, Institutions, and Change

Deviance and Social Control

▶ READING PREVIEW

Terms to Know

aberrant deviance
argot
astrology
atavistic theory
biological perspective
collective level deviance
compliant conformity
conflict approach to
    deviance
conformity
control theory
conventional conformity
crime
demonology
deviance

deviance by attributes
deviance resulting from an
    inability to conform
deviant
differential association
    theory
functionalist approach to
    deviance
group level deviance
index crimes
individual level deviance
innovation
interactionist approach to
    deviance
labeling theory

moral entrepreneurs
nonconforming deviance
primary deviance
rebellion
reductionism
retreatism
ritualism
secondary deviance
socially acceptable deviance
somotype theory
strain theory
XYY theory

His buddies call him Frog. At the age of thirteen, he was working the barrio areas of East Los Angeles and claims to have made several hundred a week as a crack dealer (Lamar, 1988). He also claims to have rented sports cars to drive on weekends, although he can barely see over the steering wheel. He takes pride in being a newly initiated member of the Crips, a notoriously violent juvenile gang. Not long ago, Frog was busted for possession of cocaine and placed in the Los Padrinos Juvenile Detention Center. There, the four-feet ten-inch, eighty-five pound juvenile was twice beaten severely by older and larger inmates and had two of his teeth knocked out.

Just recently Frog was placed in a foster home, where juvenile authorities will watch his activities closely. Like thousands of youngsters across the country from impoverished and disorganized family backgrounds, he was lured into crime by the excitement and easy money to be made from the booming drug trade. These young people are no different from American adolescents everywhere in that they are material girls and boys. They crave the glamorous clothes, cars, and jewelry they see advertised on TV, the beautiful things that only big money can buy. But many have grown up in fatherless homes, watching their mothers labor at low-paying jobs, struggling to stretch a welfare check. With the unemployment rate for black teenagers at thirty-seven percent, little work is available to unemployed, poorly educated youths. The handful of jobs that are open—flipping burgers, packing groceries—pay only minimum wages or "chump change," in the street vernacular.

So these youngsters turn to the most lucrative option they can find. In rapidly growing numbers, they are becoming the new criminal recruits of the inner city, the children who deal crack (Lamar, 1988, p. 20).

THE NATURE OF DEVIANCE

Deviance and Deviants

Frog represents only one of many Americans of different ages, backgrounds and present circumstances who engage in **deviance,** behavior that violates the dominant norms of a group or society. Such norms are established and enforced by those with the power to have their perceptions of appropriate behavior instituted as social policy and custom. Taken as a whole, these standards for behavior come to define for most of us what is legal, moral, appropriate, and even "normal." Through the socialization process, which begins in infancy, most people are conditioned to accept the dominant social standards they live under as right and normal not only for themselves but for others as well.

Deviance is a matter of degree. Each of us engages in minor acts of deviance from time to time. Being late for an appointment, receiving a ticket for speeding, or occasionally overdrawing a checking account are common examples. In this sense, deviance is a continuum ranging from minor infractions of folkways and social conventions to major violations of mores and laws relating to society's most cherished values. The analysis of deviance tells us how widely accepted a given set of norms is, along with the effectiveness of socialization and various social control mechanisms. Deviance sometimes results in serious social problems, like crime, while in other instances—the civil rights movement of the 1960s—it may help to bring about social reform and change. How deviance is defined, the forms it takes, why it arises, consequences that result from it, and related issues are of keen interest to sociologists and will be explored in this chapter.

Those who engage in ongoing, significant forms of deviance are called "deviants." A **deviant** is a person who violates the most highly regarded norms of a group or society. Crime and delinquency, prostitution, and drug abuse, for example, are recognized forms of deviance in the United States. The person defined as a deviant is often rejected as a person of value and is stigmatized and subjected to ostracism and, in many cases, severe punishment as well. (Clinard, 1974; Schur, 1971, 1984).

Deviance as a Social Definition

One commonly held misconception about deviance is the notion that the "don'ts" and "wrongs" specified by a given society are universal principles that apply everywhere. In actuality, *deviance is a social definition.* What is deemed unacceptable behavior varies according to several factors, most notably the particular society in which one lives. But who, in terms of the dominant group, makes the rules? An important question to ponder is this: Who in American society historically comprised the dominant group and, until recent decades, has largely determined most norms and policies? (See Chapter 10.)

Three of the most important factors relating to how deviance is defined—social context, position in society, and historical time frame—are briefly summarized as follows:

Deviance and One's Social Context

What is legal, moral, and acceptable varies from society to society. Emile Durkheim was one of the first sociologists to assert this principle: "It is no longer possible today to dispute the fact that law and morality vary from one social type to the next, nor that they change within the same type if the conditions of life are modified" (Durkheim, 1966, p. 70). In some societies, for example, it is not illegal to engage in public drunkenness, to marry multiple spouses, or to practice homosexuality. Countries such as Germany and Holland have legalized prostitution, whereas in the United States it is against the law except in certain portions of Nevada.

Deviance and One's Position in Society

What constitutes deviance in either law or custom also depends on one's position in society. Most Americans can legally purchase and own handguns, but convicted felons cannot. Children may not vote, persons under a certain age cannot draw social security retirement benefits, and employers are not allowed legally to employ undocumented aliens. Even in the 2000s, women who are assertive in the workplace are sometimes perceived as "argumentative" and "bitchy." Men engaged in the same behavior are seen positively as "take-charge" and "assertive" types.

Deviance and One's Historical Time Frame

As a third factor, what is seen as deviant depends on one's historical time frame as well. Interracial marriage, for instance, was illegal in parts of the United States prior to 1967. In similar fashion, various countries over the last few centuries have branded as deviant various behaviors not seen as deviant by modern American standards.

Deviance as a social definition: Prostitution. The practice of prostitution in the United States is a form of deviant behavior that is illegal everywhere except in portions of Nevada. In the photo on the left, this woman is in constant risk of being arrested. By contrast (right photo), the sale of sexual services is legal in some parts of Europe where sex workers are licensed.

A Prussian law of 1784 prohibited mothers and nurses from taking children under two years of age into their beds. The English villein [serf] of the fourteenth century was not allowed to send his son to school, and no one lower than a freeholder was permitted by law to keep a dog. The following have at different times been crimes: printing a book, professing the medical doctrine of the circulation of blood, driving with reins, [selling] coins to foreigners, having gold in the house, buying goods on the way to the market for the purpose of selling them at a higher price, [and] writing a check for less than one dollar (Sutherland and Cressey, 1970, pp. 15–16).

CONFORMITY AND HOW IT IS MAINTAINED

Social deviance occurs, in most cases, because of one or more of the following factors: (1) a decrease in the power and influence over people of certain norms in society, (2) a decrease in the relevance of these norms as a result of changing social conditions, or (3) a combination of these factors. In short, deviance occurs when certain members of society have neither the ability nor the motivation to conform to the dominant norms or social rules.

Consequently, a sociological analysis of deviant behavior perhaps should begin with the concept of **conformity**, behavior that is in basic agreement with the dominant norms of society. In addition to understanding the nature of conformity, it is also important to examine key factors relating to how it is maintained.

Sanctions and Social Controls

To the extent possible, the maintenance of conformity is ensured through established sanctions and other social controls. In Chapter 4: Culture, we discussed mechanisms of social control called *sanctions*, socially recognized and enforced rewards and punishments. Sanctions are applied to both conforming and deviant behavior and may be informal or formal. A smile from a loved one, for instance, is an informal positive sanction, while a frown is informal punishment. Similarly, a career promotion for exemplary job performance is a formal reward and a prison sentence for criminal conviction is a negative formal sanction.

In Chapter 6: Social Organization, we discussed how social order in society is maintained through sanctions in the form of both internal and external *social controls*. Through *internal social controls* developed primarily through family socialization, the child acquires a personal code of conduct or moral system that shapes future behavior. As a result, he or she becomes self-regulating in terms of behavior. To reinforce such conformity, society also makes use of various types of *external social controls*. They range from formally recognized rewards for socially valued acts of conformity to formally prescribed punishments for acts of deviance.

Mechanisms of Enforcement

Stated sanctions and social controls would mean little or nothing if not enforced. Therefore, to maintain conformity, several enforcement mechanisms are needed. First, most people learn to conform from childhood when confronted by various *authority figures*, beginning

Those who abide by established social norms obtain rewards by striving hard and following socially established paths to success. By contrast, criminals often attempt "shortcuts" to success that usually result in formal negative sanctions imposed by society.

with parents who teach their children norms (rules) and values. As these become accepted and internalized, they become the foundation for the child's personal social control system. Then, later, they are reinforced and expanded by other authority figures such as adult neighbors, teachers, employers, and police officers. A second source of social control is *peer group pressure.* Peer groups often shape behavior to a remarkable degree through the ongoing application of acceptance, praise and support for conformity and rejection, condemnation, and punishment for what is seen as deviance. Since we are social beings with a need for social approval and acceptance, we are very susceptible to the influence of both authority figures and peer groups. In addition, *physical coercion and punishment* is another mechanism of social control. When informal and formal sanctions and internal and external social controls prove ineffective, arrest, conviction, and incarceration by those in authority are sometimes necessary.

Language and the Use of Argots

Even language is used to distinguish conformity from deviance and to help maintain conformity. Symbolic interactionists argue that through the use of language, we structure a particular view of reality for ourselves. Our use of symbolic communication, along with certain words and phrases, helps us to conceptualize and communicate our views of conformity and deviance (Harroff, 1962). Further, the way people use language allows us to identify them as conformists or deviants, according to our perceptions within the context of our group and society. Likewise, the way we use language furnishes others with similar perceptions of us. If a person does not use "appropriate language," he or she does not "fit in" as far as the group is concerned and may be perceived as deviant.

What Is an Argot?   Sociologists have found that many groups possess an argot, a special form of language characteristic of subcultures. An argot involves the use of newly constructed words along with standard words and phrases with special meanings. These forms of communication are of particular value in studying conformity and deviance in highly stratified, pluralistic societies like the United States. Their use helps to establish boundaries between various groups. Since only group members tend to know the special meanings that go with certain words and phrases, a person's use or nonuse of a particular argot immediately identifies him or her to others as a "member" of their group and, thus, a conformist, or an "outsider." A person who wants to be accepted within the group learns the accepted form of language, or argot, in order to conform and be fully accepted.

Argots and Deviant Subcultures   Argots are characteristic of many groups and subcultures in America, conformist and deviant. Some permit identification based on such factors as age group, social class, or ethnic background. Adolescents have their own argot that changes from generation to generation. Black English or Ebonics is another example, as is the use of Yiddish terms and expressions by Jewish Americans. Even certain occupations and professions have argots, such as computer analysts, physicians, attorneys, and sociologists.

As illustrated in Table 11-1, deviant groups and subcultures also use certain idiomatic terms and expressions to establish a sense of exclusivity and to ensure internal conformity. Drug users, in their everyday speech, use such terms as "horse," "snow," "ludes," and "crank." Prostitutes have special meanings for terms like "date," "Greek," "French" and "half-and-half." While a few argot terms and expressions may find themselves into the general language of a culture, they have little to no meaning to most people in the general culture.

LEVELS AND TYPES OF DEVIANCE

Sociologists generally recognize three levels and four basic types of deviance that violate social standards. These behaviors range from the micro- to the macro levels of society.

Levels of Deviance

Deviance Carried Out by Individuals   First, there is **individual level deviance**, acts of antisocial behavior carried out by one person usually at the local community level. Examples include most suicides, behavior resulting from mental disorders, and many crimes of murder, rape, armed robbery, and burglary. Factors contributing to individual level deviance may include faulty socialization, poverty, and unequal opportunity, which can produce frustration and alienation.

Deviance Perpetrated by Groups   **Group level deviance** refers to socially unacceptable behavior by social groups, usually at the community level. Group deviance is often reinforced by a deviant subculture that furnishes its members with a set of socially unacceptable

TABLE 11-1 Argots: Examples from Two Deviant Subcultures

THE DRUG SUBCULTURE	LOS ANGELES STREET GANGS
Black Russian: black, potent hashish	Benzo: Mercedes Benz
Bag: a quantity of diluted heroin	Breakdown: shotgun (also gauge)
Blow: to inhale a drug (also sniff)	Bustin: to go out shooting (also Bust a cap)
Bluebirds; birds: amytal sodium capsules	Dead presidents: money
Change: a short jail or prison sentence	Duece-deuce: .22 caliber gun
Clean: not carrying or using narcotics	Do a ghost: leave (also Do a train)
Chinese white: potent white heroin	Fooled out: made a mistake
Connect: to find a source of drugs (also score)	Four-five: .45 caliber gun
Crystal palace: a place to take speed	Glass house: police headquarters
Flashing: glue sniffing	Hook: a phony person
Gorilla pills: barbiturates/other sedatives	Hoopy: car
Juice head: a person who drinks liquor	Jack: hijack
Luding out: using methaqualone	Kite: letter from prison
Mainline: to inject a drug	Mark: someone wanting to join a gang
Narc: any narcotics officer (any level)	Mud duck: ugly girl
Off: high on a drug (also to get rid of or kill)	Ride on: a drive by shooting
Peter: chloral hydrite (a sedative)	Squab: fight
Rifle range: withdrawal ward in hospital	Take out of the box: kill
Roach: a marijuana cigarette butt	Talking head: arguing
Rock: granulated heroin, cocaine, etc.	You got four feet?: Want to fight?

Sources: Adapted from Lingeman, R. R. 1974. *Drugs from A to Z: A Dictionary,* 2nd ed. New York: McGraw-Hill; The Los Angeles Times, 1988.

norms to follow. Individuals belonging to these groups—especially in urban America—often internalize deviant norms and values rather than those of the dominant society. Drug addicts and juvenile gangs, connected together in such groups, contribute significantly to the incidences of burglary and violent crime. Similarly, prostitutes have their own networks and support groups.

Deviance at the Macro Level of Society   Sometimes, however, the distinction between group deviance and collective level deviance becomes blurred. **Collective level deviance** is socially unacceptable behavior by large numbers of people at various levels of society. Such activities as those of organized crime, price fixing by some corporate executives, and various types of government corruption occur not only locally but also at the macro level of society. Take organized crime, for instance. In the United States, there are two or so dozen Mafia families—historically of Sicilian and Italian heritage—spread across

America with "a formal, oath-taking national membership of some 1700" (Magnuson, 1986). Of these, about one-half occupy five nationally powerful families headquartered in New York City. When drug trafficking, gambling, extortion, sex trafficking, and contract murder are the focus, organized crime is international in scope. Various ethnic crime networks in the United States have connections to other countries. They include Cubans (illegal gambling), Russians (extortion and contract killings, mainly in New York City), Columbians (cocaine smuggling), and various extortion organizations run by Chinese, Vietnamese, Japanese, and Korean groups (Thio, 2007). Collective level deviance also includes acts of civil disobedience carried out through social movements and occasional civil wars.

Sociological Types

Sociologists categorize deviance in a number of ways. However, five types, in particular, are perhaps most useful in illustrating the diversity of deviant behavior—aberrant deviance, nonconforming deviance, socially acceptable deviance, deviance resulting from an inability to conform, and deviance by attributes.

Aberrant Deviance   According to sociologist Robert Merton (1966), **aberrant deviance** is deviant behavior in which a person violates a norm for selfish reasons and attempts to escape detection and punishment. The criminal is one obvious example. The aberrant deviant acknowledges the validity of the norms being violated, but finds it advantageous to violate them for personal gain or satisfaction. Most criminals are aberrant deviants in that they commit illegal acts for selfish gain, attempting at the same time to avoid detection, capture, and punishment. Employees who feign illness to stay home from work and those who engage in extramarital sex—both typically covert in nature—offer additional examples.

Nonconforming Deviance   By contrast, Merton also identified **nonconforming deviance** as socially disapproved behavior in which the participant challenges the legitimacy of certain norms by violating them openly, regardless of the punishments that might be imposed. The nonconforming deviant acts out of conscience and often violates norms for unselfish reasons based on moral principles. In doing so, he or she often appeals to a higher moral good, an ultimate value that transcends particular norms of society. Although abortion is a legal right for women that most Americans tend to support, "pro-life" demonstrators in recent years have picketed abortion clinics and many have been arrested for civil disobedience and criminal offenses. Many colonial citizens during the American Revolution were nonconforming deviants committed to certain social ideals. Confederate soldiers during the Civil War and antiwar protesters and civil rights demonstrators during the 1960s–1970s provide additional examples.

Socially Acceptable Deviance   A third category is **socially acceptable deviance**, deviant behavior considered acceptable by significant portions of society (Sutherland, 1967). This can sometimes occur when laws or public policies result from pressure by interest groups instead of broad-based public support. Examples include the Eighteenth Amendment (prohibition of alcohol from 1919 until 1933) and laws (1950s through 1970s) that criminalized the possession of even small amounts of marijuana. Due to ongoing deviance by millions of Americans, prohibition was repealed and possession of small quantities of marijuana were largely decriminalized (Thio, 2007).

Sociologist Howard Becker (1963) coined the term **moral entrepreneurs** to refer to members of some groups who wish to impose their view of morality and policy on others. What such a person regards as a "problem" or "evil" is pursued as "an absolute ethic; what he sees is truly and totally evil with no qualification. Any means is justified to do away with it" (pp. 147–148). Other sociologists concur with Becker's view that socially acceptable deviance may occur in the wake of laws and policies instituted on ideological and moral grounds, rather than rational or even socially popular ones. In speaking to this, Eric Goode (1972, p. 186) has said that

> the moral entrepreneur is an ideological imperialist—it is his position that what he believes must also be right for everyone and that anyone doing what he disapproves of must be punished by the might of the law, by the state, by society as a whole. The existing rules do not satisfy him or her—some of the most influential moral entrepreneurs in history have been women, such as Carrie Nation, the alcohol prohibitionist.

> Naturally, all moral entrepreneurs believe that what they want to see passed into law *is good for others* and not merely a crystallization of their own personal views and prejudices. Thus, anti-marijuana crusaders do not see themselves as imposing their ideology and morality on the public. Rather, they see themselves as *doing good,* as helping others, as lifting up the drug user to see the error of his ways, protecting society from the damage that drug use can do to humanity. (But then, as Camus said, the welfare of humanity is always the alibi of tyrants.)

Deviance Resulting from an Inability to Conform   **Deviance resulting from an inability to conform** is a fourth type. This is a situational form of deviance in which a person either cannot control their behavior or is forced to commit a deviant act (Davis, 1964). For example:

- **Insanity: When a Person Cannot Control His or Her Behavior.** In criminal cases in which the accused allegedly suffers from a mental disorder, an insanity plea may be entered, although it is used only about four percent of the time in the American court system (Steadman and Cocozza, 1974). John Hinkley, for example, was the young man found not guilty by reason of insanity for shooting President Ronald Reagan and his Press Secretary James Brady in a 1981 assassination attempt. Today, Hinkley resides in a mental institution rather that a prison. Standards of accountability and punishment are applied differently to the mentally disturbed in criminal cases because, presumably, they were not in control of their mental faculties at the time the criminal act was committed (Bartol, 1980).

- **Duress: When a Person Is Forced to Commit a Deviant Act.** Likewise, a person forced to commit a deviant act against their will would not be held to the same accountability standards. Suppose a young bank officer receives a phone call one morning from a couple of criminals holding his wife and child for ransom. He is told that, unless he takes $50,000 from the bank's vault and leaves it at a designated drop point that afternoon, he will never see his wife and baby alive again. If he goes to the vault and obtains this money in order to get his family released safe and sound, most likely he will be met with only mild punishment, if any, from either his employer or the authorities. In addition, the bank officer most likely would not be indicted by a grand jury for criminal prosecution because of mitigating circumstances.

In a highly publicized Houston case, Andrea Yates was convicted of murdering her five children by drowning them one by one in a bathtub. At her retrial in 2006, she was judged insane. Testimony by psychiatrists convinced the jury that Ms. Yates was suffering from severe psychosis brought about by postpartum depression at the time she killed her children. She currently is confined in a mental institution.

~~ **The Legal Concept of Willful Intent.** In both subtypes illustrated above, the issue of willful intent is an important legal consideration. Suppose, however, a bank officer placed in the situation described above with his family being held for ransom goes to his employer's vault to get the ransom money to save his wife and child. But while there, he takes an extra $25,000 for himself, which he hides in the trunk of his car. In this case, there would be criminal intent on his part. If discovered, he would be prosecuted, most likely, for the theft of the additional money because of *willful intent.*

Deviance by Attributes   As a final and fifth category, there is deviance by attributes (Glaser, 1971). Deviance by attributes involves a process in which those with certain physical or social characteristics are perceived and/or treated as deviant (e.g., a physically handicapped person or the transgendered). The mentally challenged, dwarfs and midgets, those perceived by some as "freaks," the blind, the wheelchair bound, and other atypical people are sometimes treated in an obviously self-conscious way by those who may have more difficulty in dealing with the "special" characteristics of such people than with the people themselves. Consequently, they may choose to "deal" with such "different" people by simply avoiding them.

Crime: Trends and Issues

What Is a Crime?   A **crime** is a violation of criminal law enacted and enforced by government with formal penalties. Serious violations of criminal law involving severe penalties are *felony crimes.* Contrary to beliefs held by many, crime rates in recent decades (1990s and 2000s) for major felony index crimes have generally declined when compared to the 1980s.

Have Crime Rates Been Increasing or Declining?: The Eight Index Crimes   The most notable crimes are the **index crimes**, eight of the most serious violent and property crimes tracked each year by the U.S. Justice Department. Each year, data on four violent crimes—murder, rape, robbery, and aggravated assault—and four property crimes—burglary, larceny, motor vehicle theft, and arson—are compiled and tracked by the Federal Bureau of Investigation (FBI) based on arrest records by police departments across the nation. As can be found in the summary, changes in recent rates for these offenses, crime rates for major offenses have been declining overall in recent years (Table 11-2).

Do Perfect Crimes Exist?   In terms of perpetrators who are never apprehended, tried, convicted, and formally punished for a specific crime or crimes they committed, there are, indeed, perfect crimes, although habitual criminals who never get caught are very rare. Former labor leader, convicted felon (mail fraud), and alleged crime boss James "Jimmie" Hoffa (1913–1975?) disappeared and allegedly was murdered in 1975. Although various theories exist about his disappearance and "murder," this case today remains shrouded in mystery. In addition, most robberies are never solved and most rapes go unreported. Recent murder cases where no perpetrators to date have been convicted include the murders of Nicole Brown Simpson and Ron Goldman in 1994 and six-year-old JonBenet Ramsey in 1996. The disappearance of American teenager Natalie Holloway while on vacation in Aruba during May, 2005 also remains a mystery (CBS/AP, Feb. 1, 2008). Police authorities, ever hopeful, use the term "unsolved crimes" for these and other cases. However, some crimes, such as the "Jack the Ripper" serial murders in London, have remained unsolved for well over a century.

Three Preconditions Needed for the Perfect Crime (Never Getting Caught)
Three key prerequisites appear to be necessary in order for anyone to have a realistic expectation of committing a crime and never being caught and punished for it. Although each

TABLE 11-2	Eight Index Crimes: Percent Change 1994–2003
	Federal Bureau of Investigation Uniform Crime Reporting (UCR) Summary System

CRIME TYPE	PERCENT CHANGE: 1994–2003*
Murder and non-negligent manslaughter	−36.7%
Forcible rape	−18.2%
Robbery	−40.2%
Aggravated assault	−31.0%
Burglary	−28.9%
Larceny–theft	−20.2%
Motor vehicle theft	−26.7%
Arson	(Adequate data unavailable)

SOURCE: www.fbi.gov/ucr/ucrquest.htm (2004).

* Rate per 100,000 population.

will be identified and discussed, the author's purpose here is to discourage any potential criminal from engaging in crime. The reason is this: The odds are at least ten thousand to one against anyone being able to accomplish the following three things, as simple as they might seem.

Precondition 1 *The perpetrator must commit the crime him-/herself—alone, in person, and with no accomplices.* Very few criminals can do this. Acquiring assistance helps to bolster confidence and broadens criminal responsibility, particularly with complex crimes such as bank robbery, art and jewelry theft, and so on. However, acquiring the assistance of one or more "partners in crime" creates a critical weak link. When authorities bring in those suspected of the crime for questioning, suspects are placed in separate interrogation rooms and detectives often "play with their heads" by telling each that one or more of the others have confessed, plea bargained for a reduced sentence, and will testify for the prosecution at the trial. If the criminal had no partners, he or she would have much less vulnerability. In the celebrated case of Wanda Holloway, "the Cheerleader Mom" who hatched a murder plot in Channelview, Texas to hire a "hit man" to kill her neighbor Verna Heath, the mother of a her daughter's chief rival in cheerleader tryouts, she enlisted her brother to hire the professional killer. Holloway thought Amber, Verna's daughter, would be so distraught at her mother's death, she would lose in the cheerleading competition. Her brother lost his nerve and confessed to authorities. Holloway, who could not meet Precondition 1, was convicted of attempted murder for hire in 1991 (Rocky Mountain News, Denver CO; March 1, 1997).

Precondition 2 *The perpetrator must never ever tell anyone he/she committed the crime.* The overwhelming majority of criminals and other deviants just cannot "keep their mouths shut." For whatever reason—bragging rights, ego, the burden of guilt that requires that they confess to someone, and so on—criminals usually feel compelled to tell someone who then tells someone else. Within a relatively short span of time, either the word is out or authorities eventually are able to interrogate the right people to solve the crime. Examples are plentiful. President Richard Nixon, driven by ego, was compelled to tape record every conversation he had while in the White House. This ultimately was his undoing when, after a long court battle for custody of the tapes, Nixon had to surrender them. These tapes clearly showed his criminal complicity in the "Watergate Affair" and forced his resignation from office.

As an additional illustration, "unabomber" Ted Kaczynski killed and maimed people for seventeen years beginning in the late 1970s by sending them homemade, but carefully crafted bombs disguised as mailed packages. This resulted in both U.S. Postal Services Investigators and the FBI joining the manhunt. Kacynski, a brilliant scholar and former professor with a Ph.D. in math, alienated against modern technological society, made one critical error. He violated Precondition 2 by sending what amounted to "catch me if you can" notes to the authorities which gave investigators a large sample of his writing style. Then, in 1995, he sent a 35,000 word "Manifesto" to *The Washington Post* and *The New York Times*. In an accompanying note, he promised to halt his bombing if one or both papers published it. Both the *Post* and the *Times* did publish it. It was read by millions of Americans including Kaczynski's younger brother David and his wife Linda. They both recognized the writing style and themes as identical to that of David's older brother, Theodore. Concerned that he might be the unabomber, they contacted the FBI. On April 13, 1996, Theodore (Ted) Kaczynski was arrested and subsequently convicted of multiple counts of murder. He remains in prison today serving a life sentence (http://www.crimelibrary.com, 2004).

Precondition 3 *The perpetrator must never ever repeat the crime.* Most criminals (and practically all property criminals or thieves) are incapable of committing only one crime on one occasion. They get greedy, overconfident and "cocky." They may successfully rob a bank, steal a car, sell some drugs, embezzle from an employer, and so on, once or a few times. However, they usually cannot quit. The rewards are so easy, quick, and exciting that they repeat their offense over and over again. Eventually and inevitably, they get caught.

So-called "Perfect Crimes" in Perspective Even if a person manages to meet all three of the preconditions for a perfect crime just discussed, there are still dozens of ways to "get caught." Given the state of crime investigation forensics today, sometimes referred to as criminalistics, many criminals leave at the scene their DNA or that of their victims in violent offenses such as rape, assault, and murder. Assuming a crime scene can be secured and properly sealed within a relatively brief period of time after the crime, sound investigative techniques combined with persistence and good science usually result in the crime—sooner or later—being solved.

ℰARLY EXPLANATIONS OF DEVIANCE

The Basis for Early Explanation

Throughout history, humanity has sought to explain why certain individuals in society engage in deviant behavior. Early explanations centered on fear, myth, and superstition. Only during the past few decades have social scientists seen deviance from a perspective of cultural relativity. This comes from a realization that most forms of deviance do not involve moral or societal absolutes, but instead are determined by such factors as cultural context, people's perceptions of reality, and historical time frame. Nonetheless, people who are unfamiliar with the scientific method and sociological approaches continue to take an absolutist position on deviance.

Demonology

The earliest explanations of deviance took the form of **demonology**, a system of beliefs which holds that deviance is caused by evil spirits or demons that possess the body and made it act according to their will. In some early societies, the witch doctor or shaman was the "law giver" who interpreted the supernatural world. Anyone who violated the laws he established was seen as possessed by demons. He would then try to summon the good spirits to drive the demons away through such devices as the wearing of grotesque masks, dancing around the possessed victim to scare away evil spirits, using potions, or "grinding a hole in the person's skull with a sharp stone to let the demons out" (Fox, 1976, p. 10). The expression "scaring the hell out of a person" had its origins in the demonological traditions of early societies.

Explanations of deviance based on demonology were once prevalent in Europe and America. During the late 1600s, several young women in Massachusetts were convicted of practicing witchcraft and were executed by hanging.

Demonology has existed in numerous forms throughout the world and is still practiced (in Haiti, for example) where voodoo rituals are used to invoke or cast out demons. During the Middle Ages in Europe, rites of exorcism were used by the church to expel demons from the "possessed," and beliefs in the evil and deviant nature of witchcraft and sorcery were widely accepted. As a result of the witch trials held at Salem, Massachusetts, in 1692, nineteen women were put to death by hanging for practicing sorcery. Similar trials in America continued until about 1800, although no additional executions took place (Boyer and Nissenbaum, 1974).

Astrology

Astrology, which originated about five thousand years ago in Mesopotamia, has also been used in many cultures to explain deviance. **Astrology** refers to the notion that the movement of the planets and stars affects human behavior in general, and that the moon, in particular, influences deviant behavior. The concepts of "lunacy" and "lunatic," part of our popular vocabulary pertaining to the mentally disturbed, had their origins in this perspective during the eighteenth century (Fox, 1976). However, astrology had already been discredited as a serious science a century earlier. In the early 1600s, the astronomer Johannes Kepler (1571–1630), himself once an astrologer, discovered that the earth, a fairly insignificant speck in the grand scheme of things, was not the center of the universe. Today social scientists see astrology as having little or no value in explaining deviance or any other form of human behavior. Nonetheless, reading horoscopes remains a popular casual pastime for many who still take astrology seriously.

The Emergence of Science: Biological Explanations

By the late nineteenth century, explanations of deviance based on myth and superstition began to give way to those grounded in science. Since the behavioral sciences, including sociology, were then only in their infancy, the first attempts at scientific explanation of deviance emerged from the biological disciplines. The **biological perspective** argues that deviance is caused mainly by inborn physical traits or characteristics. Criminality and mental disorders thus began to be seen as being genetically inherited.

Lombroso's Atavistic Theory   The father of the biological school of deviance was Cesare Lombroso (1836–1909), an Italian psychiatrist. Lombroso developed what has been called **atavistic theory**, the argument that the violent criminal is an inherited type who represents a genetic throwback to primitive humans. In 1876, he published *L'Uomo Delinquente (Criminal Man)*, in which he argued that the criminal is a separate species from modern *Homo sapiens*, which he labeled *Homo delinquens*. Lombroso (1911) based his theory on data he gathered by comparing certain physical characteristics of Italian prison inmates with those of Italian soldiers. He also studied the skulls of several hundred criminals and compared them with those of prehistoric humans. He concluded that the criminal type could be identified by the presence of at least five of a large number of physical characteristics. They include a slanting forehead, prominent brow ridges, large ears, protruding lips, a heavy jaw, atypical eyes, a high tolerance for pain, and either excessive hairiness or a lack of body hair. The atavistic criminal lacked a sense of right or wrong (conscience), was egotistical and selfish, and cruel and impulsive. In his later writings, Lombroso did acknowledge the influence of environment in shaping the behavior of some criminals, but his basic explanation remained a genetic one (Wolfgang, 1972).

Both Lombroso's methods of analysis and his conclusions were strongly criticized by the scientific community, although his approach was fairly well received among popular audiences. In 1913, criminologist Charles Goring (1972) tested Lombroso's assertion that genetically inherited characteristics seriously affected crime. In comparing the characteristics of three thousand English prison inmates with those of a group of English college graduates, he found no significant difference between the two groups. The findings of this study were accepted by other criminologists, and Lombroso's theory of genetic causation was essentially laid to rest.

Sheldon's Somotype Theory   Another category of biological explanation is **somotype theory**, the argument that physique or body type is linked to both personality and deviance. Although scientific attempts to explain deviance in terms of body types have been prevalent since the 1850s, the most notable effort in recent times has been the work of anthropologist William H. Sheldon (1949). In his classification system, Sheldon divided body types into three broad categories: the *endomorph* (fat and flabby), the *ectomorph* (thin and frail), and the *mesomorph* (muscular and athletic). Furthermore, he asserted that the endomorph was outgoing and sociable in temperament, the ectomorph was shy and withdrawn, and the mesomorph had an aggressive and adventuresome personality. In studying delinquent males incarcerated in a rehabilitation home, Sheldon found that a disproportionate number were mesomorphic in body type. Subsequent studies on juvenile offenders have yielded similar results (Glueck and Glueck, 1950; Cortes and Gatti, 1972).

While it appears clear in some studies that mesomorphic body type is associated with delinquency, most sociologists reject the idea that there is a cause-and effect relationship between these two factors (Vold, 1958; Clinard and Meier, 1979). This would be like saying that because African Americans are disproportionately represented in the prison population, "race" could be a cause of crime. A large body of sociological research suggests otherwise. It is now clearly recognized that social and environment factors are the primary causes of delinquency, crime, and types and duration of incarceration. In addition, there are methodological problems associated with body type research. For example, delinquents in institutional settings are not representative of all delinquents any more than incarcerated criminals are representative of all criminals. It is just that they are the ones caught in the net of the justice system.

XYY Theory   A third type of biological explanation attempted to link chromosomes to crime. During the 1960s, the **XYY theory** experienced some popularity. This was the assertion that the presence of an extra Y chromosome in males was associated with criminal behavior. Typically, males have both X and Y chromosomes, or XY, and females have two X chromosomes, or XX. A few males have a chromosomal anomaly in which an extra Y chromosome is present. The result is XYY, which some researchers have claimed creates a "super male" of below average intelligence who is prone to violent criminal activity (Jacobs, et al., 1965). Although XYY males are indeed overrepresented in the prison population, their records indicate a lower incidence of violence against others than those of the more typical XY inmates (Price and Whatmore, 1967; Fox, 1971). In 1969, a conference of scientists sponsored by the National Institute of Mental Health concluded that evidence for the alleged relationship between the XYY chromosomal characteristic and crime was inconclusive (Public Health Reports, October 1969). More recent research has found little or no support for XYY theory as well (Ellis, 1982).

Biological Explanations in Perspective   Biological explanations for deviance in general and, more specifically, crime and delinquency have fallen short in explaining the complexities of deviance. Sociologists Edwin H. Sutherland and Donald Cressey (1970, p. 118)

© BETTMANN/CORBIS

Richard Speck, who murdered eight student nurses in a horrific dormitory killing spree in 1968, possessed the XYY chromosome and was the "poster boy" for XYY theory during this time. However, subsequent research has shown that evidentiary support for such biological explanations of deviance is very weak.

have commented that it is "impossible for criminality to be inherited as such, for crime is defined by acts of legislatures and these vary independently of the biological inheritance of the violators of the law." Most sociologists agree. Donald J. Mulvihill and Melvin Tumin (1969) assess the limitations of biological explanations of deviance as follows:

> [S]ome individuals are more likely than others to become criminals or violent as a result of biological makeup. But it is never "given" in the "nature" of any individual that he will be criminal or law abiding, pacific or violent, cooperative or competitive, selfish or altruistic. All these are complex forms of social behavior, which depend upon the social and cultural milieu of the developing individual (p. 424).

The Medicalization of Deviance

Similar attempts have been made to show a scientific basis for forms of so-called biologically derived deviance other than crime, including alcoholism, other forms of substance abuse, and mental disorders. While some of these behaviors, particularly some compulsive disorders, may indeed have a significant physiological component, the scientific evidence for biological causation, in most cases, is weak at best. With a few possible exceptions, physical or biological problems of deviance (e.g., physiological withdrawal in alcoholics) are little more than symptoms of larger and more fundamental social and environmental causes.

In recent decades, there have been ongoing attempts by some in the medical and psychiatric establishment to "medicalize" numerous forms of maladaptive behavior. This often represents a form of **reductionism**, a process in which the many complexities of a subject are reduced down to overly simplistic, single cause explanations. Consequently, what behavioral scientists see as problems of living, mental disorders, or compulsive behavioral disorders, many in the medical establishment label as diseases, addictions, or medical conditions.

Three prominent examples of such forms of biological reductionism—myths that are widely accepted by many in society—are discussed briefly below.

The Myth of Alcoholism as a "Disease"   Take alcoholism for example. Medical practitioners may be able to "dry out," "detoxify," and thus "cure" the physical dependence of a patient on alcohol. Such physical dependence occurs *after* a person has developed a habituated pattern of abusing alcohol as a maladaptive way of dealing with life stress. However, the medical and psychiatric community is ill equipped to deal with the root causes of alcoholism or "drug problems," in general, which lie deep within the fabric of society and the contextual dynamics of interpersonal relationships. Research suggests that there may be a biological predisposition toward "addictive" behavior in general. For example, the so-called A-1 gene present in some people has been found to blunt feelings of pleasure. The argument here is that abusers of alcohol use excessive drinking to achieve the pleasure that those who are genetically normal can experience without drinking (Noble, et al., 1991). However, assuming there might be something such as an "addictive gene" or trait, one might just as easily become "addicted" to fast food, sex, gambling, shopping, or any one of a hundred other things that, in the extreme, could be maladaptive. However, whether a predisposition toward such forms of behavior becomes suppressed or does, indeed, manifest itself in any one or combination of compulsive disorders is primarily a function of socialization. Consequently, medical treatment is a poor fit in dealing effectively with the direct root causes of alcoholism (Thio, 2007).

The Myth of Mental Illness   Likewise, the notion of "mental illness" and "psychiatric treatment" for most mental disorders sits on shaky scientific ground. Thomas Szasz (1974), himself a physician and psychiatrist, had this to say about "mental illness":

> [P]hysicians are trained to treat bodily ills—not economic, moral, racial, religious, or political "ills." And they themselves (except psychiatrists) expect, and in turn are expected by their patients, to treat bodily diseases, not envy and rage, fear and folly, poverty and stupidity, and all the other miseries that beset man. Strictly speaking, then, disease or illness can only affect the body. Hence, there can be no such thing as mental illness. The term "mental illness" is a metaphor.
>
> . . . In other words, I maintain that mental illness is a metaphorical disease: that bodily illness stands in the same relation to mental illness as a defective television set stands to a bad television program. Of course, the word "sick" is often used metaphorically. We call jokes "sick," sometimes even the whole world "sick"; but only when we call minds "sick" do we systematically mistake and strategically misinterpret metaphor for fact and send for the doctor to "cure" the "illness." It is as if a television viewer were to send for a television repairman because he dislikes the program he sees on the screen (pp. ix, x–xi).

The Myth of ADHD and the Use of Psychoactive Drugs Such as Ritalin in Its Treatment   Perhaps one of the most misunderstood and potentially damaging biological myths is the label of attention deficit hyperactivity disorder (ADHD) as a so-called "learning disorder." Many in the psychiatric community argue that ADHD is a neurologic disorder that prevents some children from being able to concentrate on specific tasks. The label ADHD is applied to millions of school-aged American children each year, particularly boys, who are then treated with various psychoactive drugs, most notably the stimulant Ritalin. Yet, criticism from prominent researchers and mental health practitioners

ILLUSTRATION BY EDWARD WINDSOR KEMBLE, COURTESY OF THE LIBRARY OF CONGRESS PRINTS AND PHOTOGRAPHS DIVISION

The mischievous, fictional exploits of Tom Sawyer and Huck Finn have been enjoyed by generations of young readers. Yet, were Tom and Huck to live in today's America, they might have the deviant label ADHD attached to them by school officials and medical doctors. Then, Tom's Aunt Polly and Huck's dad would be advised to put them on psychoactive drugs to make them easier to manage. In like manner, other ADHD candidates such as Leonardo DaVinci, Thomas Edison, and Albert Einstein might have been "diagnosed" the same.

against this label and treatment approach has grown in recent years and the charges levied against the psychiatric establishment have become blunt and withering. California neurologist Fred A. Baughman, M.D., for example, has stated that ADHD, as a disease, is "a total 100 percent fraud" (Baughman, 2006). In contrast to the profit-driven interests of the pharmaceutical industry and the self-serving, pseudo-science put forth by many in mainstream psychiatry, a more objective examination of this issue yields some interesting findings.

Psychologist Thomas Armstong (2004), for instance, has reported that there are no firmly established criteria from which to make a definitive and reliable diagnosis of ADD/ADHD. One child may act "hyper" in one situation yet remain very calm in another, while for his classmate or neighborhood friend the opposite will be true. Which child is hyperactive? It is probable, in many cases, that it is neither. When children do exhibit symptoms of hyperactivity, such behavior may stem from a variety or combination of origins. Causes may include—but are not limited to—anxiety, boredom, depression, environmentally-induced stress brought on by poverty or family abuse, an allergic reaction to dairy products, a high sugar or high fat content diet, or any one or a combination of other factors. Instead of treating each child as a unique individual with specific needs, public school officials and mental health professionals too often use a "one size fits all" approach and impose a deviant label on a child.

Once that diagnostic label is attached, such as "ADD child" or "ADHD," it then follows that many psychiatrists and other physicians often prescribe Ritalin or other similar drugs. Tragically, such forms of drug therapy often serve to mask symptoms rather than get at the real underlying causes of hyperactive behavior. Although this is often convenient for some teachers, counselors, and parents whose lives are made simpler by this "better behavior through chemistry" approach, the loser too often is the child whose real underlying needs are not addressed ("The Myth of Attention Deficit Disorder," www.thomasarmstrong.com 2004, p. 1).

Medicalization in Perspective   The dangers that accrue to various applications of biological reductionism go far beyond the three myths briefly discussed which represent but three of several prominent examples that could be cited. Since the American Psychiatric Association (APA) first published its Diagnostic and Statistical Manual of Mental Disorders (DSM) in 1952, the behavioral control movement masquerading as reliable hard science has proliferated. The number of identified psychiatric labels—many of which do appear valid—have proliferated from about one hundred to well over three hundred and counting. However, some of them, to the critical observer, clearly appear driven by political and/or economic agendas, not science, due to the fact that psychiatrists are often sought out by schools, human services organizations, courts, and other social and governmental entities as consultants and clinicians to assess, diagnose and "treat" troubled children (Thio, 2007, p 193). For example, behaviors such as hating school, being truant, exhibiting defiance or disrespect, and other forms of nonconformity—traits of "naughtiness" that endeared Tom Sawyer and Huckleberry Finn and their fictional exploits to generations of Americans—are now labeled as disorders in children that require "treatment" in the form of drug "therapy" (Diller, 1998, Thio, 2007). To this, sociologist Alex Thio says:

> Actually, many of these youngsters are victims of poverty, child abuse, or family misery, and their behaviors reflect a normal response to their abnormal environment. But instead of dealing with the abnormal environment that causes those troublesome behaviors, psychiatrists label those normal children "emotionally disturbed," then give them drug treatments

or isolate or incarcerate them. In short, kids who stand out as different are labeled mentally ill and controlled accordingly (2007, p. 193).

ODERN ANALYSIS: SOCIOLOGICAL EXPLANATIONS

The Functionalist Approach

As we discussed in Chapter 2, the *functionalist approach* to deviance maintains that society operates like an organism. That is, the various parts interact for the smooth functioning of the entire system. The resulting equilibrium forms the foundation for social order. Because deviance tends to disrupt that order, it is, in many cases, a negative and dysfunctional influence. Consequently, the **functionalist approach**, as applied to deviance, argues that deviant or antisocial behavior results from a strain on or breakdown of social order.

Functions (Social Benefits) and Dysfunctions (Social Problems) That Result from Deviance

Most people have a tendency to view acts of deviance—particularly those that violate laws and moral code—as "bad" or "detrimental" to society. Certainly many forms of deviance, including crime and family violence, do indeed undermine social order. However, deviance is a natural and inevitable product of social systems just as is conformity and, as such, has both positive and negative consequences for society. Deviants and conformists spring from the same social structure (Erikson, 1966). Indeed, some forms of deviance actually may be beneficial while others are disruptive and problematic.

Functions of Deviance

The following are some of the functions (benefits) that may be derived from antisocial behavior:

1. ***Deviance may increase group cohesion.*** Otherwise complacent and splintered groups sometimes unify when faced with an outside threat or "enemy." In this sense, deviance facilitates a sense of "community" as people close ranks and unite under a set of commonly held beliefs and purposes. At the micro level, a crime wave of burglary or drug pushing in a community may result in the formation of neighborhood associations and crime watch groups. This may help not only to neutralize the threat, but to bring neighbors together, as well. At the macro level, war with another country perceived as deviant may result in the development of the necessary unity and patriotism to repel the aggressor. The unity demonstrated by Americans in the wake of the September 11, 2001, terrorist attacks in New York and Washington, D.C. is a case in point.

2. ***Deviance may help to clarify social norms.*** Some norms are quite general, and deviance may serve to establish clear boundary lines of acceptable behavior. Rules of conduct are often ambiguous, relying on ill-defined standards of acceptability. Deviance confronts an issue and helps to set the outer limits concerning which behaviors will be tolerated and which will not. For example, two elementary school-teachers each tell their students that those who talk in class will be kept after school. Teacher A keeps any student after hours who so much as whispers to another student. Teacher B allows occasional whispering but, after giving a warning or two, will punish those offenders who persist. Students test the boundaries of norms with

each teacher to ascertain the limits of tolerance. Other similarly tested norms in society include unclear rules, policies, and laws perceived as out-of-date or unconstitutional. For example, reflecting societal changes in values, norms, and sensibilities that occurred during the 1950s and 1960s, the U.S. Supreme Court ruled in 1967 that state laws banning interracial marriage were unconstitutional.

3. ***The toleration of some deviance may help minimize more severe social problems and conflicts.*** Although some would see this as social hypocrisy, policymakers and enforcers often find it beneficial to tolerate or "close their eyes" to certain levels and forms of deviance. To combat major crime more effectively, law enforcement agencies and prosecutors often depend on informants (usually minor criminals) and a system of plea bargaining. These officials give minor offenders special consideration so that they can deal effectively with those perceived as the more dangerous threat to social order. The Roman Catholic Church, with its official policies against some birth control methods and prohibitions against noncelibacy and marriage for priests, also tolerates some deviance. Many American Catholics ignore the church's orthodox stand on birth control, and some priests keep a low profile while having sexual relationships or cohabiting with women. Given the church's traditional position and the ever-changing nature of American culture, these people feel it is unwise to be open about such practices. It might create a major schism in the Catholic Church. Toleration of limited deviance in these and other instances helps to preserve the social system and prevent the open rebellion that rigid enforcement would tend to produce.

4. ***Deviance may help to bring about changes in social policy.*** Deviance expressed as disagreement with policymakers and violation of their policies by significant numbers of people may indicate serious problems in the way a society is organized. If the needs of many, if not most, people are not being met by existing norms, a flaw in the social system may be evident and require some adjustment. The acts of civil disobedience by thousands of people during the civil rights movement of the 1960s is a case in point. Significant changes in law and social custom resulted from such "nonviolent protests."

Dysfunctions of Deviance   Just as deviance, in some cases, is functional or beneficial to society, it can also have very disruptive consequences. Serious social problems, including crime and delinquency, drug abuse, suicide, and family conflict, tend to be the images most people visualize when the term "deviance" is mentioned. Here are some of the most prevalent negative effects that stem from antisocial behavior:

1. ***Deviance disrupts social order.*** For any society to operate smoothly, its members must cooperate with each other by obeying social norms and respecting one another's rights. When there is a lack of cooperation and mutual respect, patterned social order and the resulting security and harmony become disrupted. High crime rates, for instance, cause people in many parts of the United States to feel insecure. To protect themselves and their property, many feel it necessary to have dead-bolt locks, burglar or window bars, electronic alarms, handguns in bedside tables, and large dogs in order to feel safe. The social and financial costs of maintaining police organizations, the courts, and the prisons also take their toll on the society at large.

2. ***Deviance destroys others' motivation to conform.*** For a child who observes that several of his or her friends have stolen toys from a department store and have not been caught, it might be tempting to engage in the same type of behavior. Similar situations occur when some students successfully cheat on an exam, delinquents vandalize a house, or criminals rob a bank. Those in the deviant's peer group and community may find it difficult to maintain their will to conform if they feel that others are not being caught and punished for their antisocial behavior. One consequence of the 1990s sex scandal involving President Bill Clinton and White House intern Monica Lewinsky was the message sent to young adolescents, twelve to sixteen years old, that oral sex is not real sex. A subsequent and immediately apparent increase in this type of behavior, even on school buses involving junior high schoolers, appears to have been one possible result.

3. ***Deviance undermines trust in organizations and institutions.*** How would you feel if your college instructors were chronically late or missed classes, returned exam scores a month late, and the college you attend did not send your grades as promised? What if department stores did not open and close according to posted hours, mail did not arrive at appropriate destinations much of the time, and car repairs you paid for were not done properly on several occasions? Like most people, at first you would probably feel anger, indignation, and, above all, surprise. However, you might soon feel helpless and lose all confidence in these areas of society. When deviance of this sort is perceived as pervasive and ongoing, people may lose faith in the proper functioning of organizations and institutions. The Watergate scandal of 1973–1974, for instance, resulted in a significant, though temporary, loss of confidence by many Americans in the existing political system. A sex scandal cost Senator Gary Hart his bid for the presidency in 1988. Likewise, revelations in 1988 concerning multiple liaisons between the television evangelist Jimmy Swaggart and a prostitute resulted in the dramatic loss of revenue for his ministry and a similar decline in enrollments at his Bible college. More recently, the "fallout" from the Clinton sex scandal most likely contributed in Albert Gore, Clinton's Vice President, losing the Presidential election to George Bush in 2000.

4. ***Deviance is expensive.*** The financial cost of combating and controlling deviance is high. Take crime, for example. In the United States, there are over two hundred million incidents of shoplifting a year that cost retail businesses up to $13.5 billion annually (Baumer and Rosenbaum, 1984; Schaeffer, 2006). Most of these costs are absorbed by the consumer, who must pay higher prices for goods and services. Consumer fraud—bank fraud, insurance fraud, deceptive advertising, antitrust violations, medicaid fraud, etc.—which may be the most prevalent of all crimes, costs an additional $25–30 billion each year (Barlow, 1987; Goode, 2001). This figure does not include the tens of billions in tax revenues it takes to maintain the criminal justice system comprised of law enforcement agencies and organizations, the courts, and penal institutions. Human costs are also high. During the 1980s in America, for example, the proportion of deaths by homicide was double that of the early 1960s (Currie and Skolnick, 1988). The amount of pain and suffering inflicted on the families of these victims is incalculable. However, American homicide rates have dropped significantly since that time. (See Table 11-3 for an overview of the functionalist perspective.)

TABLE 11-3	Deviance from a Functionalist Perspective: Possible Functions and Dysfunctions	
FUNCTIONS		**DYSFUNCTIONS**
1. May increase group cohesion		1. Disrupts social order
2. May help clarify social norms		2. Destroys motivation to conform
3. Toleration of less severe forms may minimize severe social problems		3. Undermines trust in organizations (if allowed to go unpunished)
4. May help bring about needed change		4. Is expensive to society

Durkheim and Merton: Deviance as a Response to Structural Strain   Perhaps the founding father of the functionalist approach, Emile Durkheim (1966), among his many contributions, coined the term "anomie." In his view, *anomie* represents a state of confused norms or normlessness brought on by rapid change and social complexity (see Chapter 2). As societies became industrialized, developed specialized institutions and divisions of labor, and thus became more complex, different sets of norms emerged to meet the needs of diverse groups and subcultures with differing attitudes, lifestyles, and preferences. Because the norms and values stressed by different segments of modern societies tend to conflict with one another, the "rights and wrongs" and "do's and don'ts" of society tend to become blurred and unclear, or no longer relevant in light of changing social conditions.

Building on Durkheim's work, Robert Merton (1968) extended the concept of anomie to the analysis of deviant behavior. In his **strain theory**, Merton asserted that deviance results from discrepancies that arise between culturally approved goals (culture) and access to the socially approved means (social structure) needed to achieve them.

Conformity: The Typical Adaptation   The typical individual, the **conformist**, is socialized to accept both culturally prescribed goals and means. Americans, in general, seek to achieve and sustain a middle-class lifestyle. They achieve this goal by first acquiring an education and then obtaining a job to support themselves and their families. Increasingly, a middle-class lifestyle and such material benefits as nice clothes, cars, and houses require a good education and a well-paying job. Historically, conformists, in Merton's view, have tended to be white, Anglo-Saxon protestants (WASPs). However, the poor, minorities, the young, and other groups often do not have equal access to either culturally approved goals or the social (structural) means to achieve them. The strain created by the discrepancy between a society's culture (which sets goals) and its social structure (which establishes means or opportunities to achieve them) can result in anomie or confusion. This, in turn, can cause a variety of deviant responses (see Table 11-4).

1. *Innovation.* **Innovation** is a deviant response in which a person accepts the culturally approved goals of society but rejects the socially approved means of achieving those goals. A teenager living in poverty may accept the goal of having an automobile and observes that many sixteen- and seventeen-year-olds have "wheels," which serve as an adolescent status symbol. However, because he or she has little access to

TABLE 11-4	Strain Theory: Merton's Four Types of Deviance	
METHOD OF ADAPTATION	**CULTURALLY APPROVED GOALS**	**SOCIALLY APPROVED MEANS**
CONFORMIST	Accepts	Accepts
DEVIANT		
Innovator	Accepts	Rejects
Ritualist	Rejects	Accepts
Retreatist	Rejects	Rejects
Rebel	Rejects	Rejects/Replaces

SOURCE: Adapted from Merton, R. K. (1957). *Social Theory and Social Structure*, 2nd ed., 140. New York: Free Press.

the socially approved means to obtain a car, pushing drugs to make money or stealing a car may serve as an illegitimate means to obtain the culturally approved goal.

2. ***Ritualism.*** An individual may also react to the cultural confusion resulting in anomie by engaging in **ritualism**. This is a deviant response in which a person rejects culturally approved goals but accepts the approved means. The ritualist responds to the confusion of anomie by grabbing onto any structured means or rules, just as a drowning person might grab for a life preserver. Culturally approved goals become secondary if not irrelevant as long as one has the security of a structured response to follow. Some bureaucrats are ritualists in that they become slaves to rules (means), while losing sight of organizational goals.

3. ***Retreatism.*** **Retreatism** is a deviant response in which a person rejects both culturally approved goals and socially acceptable means. In the wake of the stock market crash of 1929, millions of Americans during the Great Depression of the 1930s had their cultural rugs yanked out from under them in the form of economic disruption and collapse. Jobs, bank accounts, and homes were lost, and many had to struggle to survive. Thousands of men, formerly providers for their families, could not cope with this anomie and dropped out of society by hopping freight trains and living in "hobo jungles" at various train stops throughout the country. Today there are still a few hoboes, as well as other retreatists such as some of the street people, hard-core drug addicts, and teenage runaways. Participation in conventional society has become either meaningless or an extremely painful experience for such individuals. Other examples include some religious cults and other separatist groups who reject the conformity of the dominant society and seek to establish alternative lifestyles or communities.

4. ***Rebellion.*** A final form of deviance resulting from anomie is **rebellion**. Merton argues that rebels reject both culturally approved goals and means and seek to replace them with other goals and means. Political extremists (revolutionaries) bent on destroying a country's government and replacing it with another are representative of rebellion. The goals and tactics presently employed by Al Qaeda are a current example. Driven by adverse social conditions in their own countries, such as abject poverty, as well as a modern affluent world in Western societies they do not understand and

therefore reject, radical Islamists such as those affiliated with Al Qaeda seek to destroy Western Civilization. What they seek to replace it with is an extremely reactionary, anti-materialistic world ruled by men in which women will be treated as little more than chattel to serve men and bear and care for their children.

The Conflict Approach

As indicated by the previous discussion, functionalists see deviance as a disruption of the social order. Implicit in this approach is the assumption that, like physical organisms, "healthy" societies possess a certain balance or equilibrium. Deviance, like disease, can upset that balance and create harmful effects, known as social problems. Conflict theorists disagree.

The **conflict approach** to deviance argues that what is defined as "antisocial" or "deviant" arises out of a struggle for power between various groups. The segment of society with the most power and influence is then able to have its definitions of conformity and deviance legitimated as social policy. Those whose norms and values are not made into policy often become discontent, and out of such discontent arises antisocial behavior or deviance.

Deviance Resulting from Class Struggle   The conflict school in sociology, as first discussed in Chapter 2, originated with the work of Karl Marx, the nineteenth-century German philosopher and political economist. Marx saw history as a series of class struggles between two factions, the "haves" who made and benefited from social policy and the "have nots" who were forced to live under it.

Quinney: Corporate and White Collar Crime by Those in Privileged Classes   Following in this tradition, sociologist Richard Quinney (1974, 1980) argues that not only are policies and laws made by the ruling class but, when violated by members of the privileged group, penalties tend to be minimized. If we consider just five categories of crimes committed by U.S. corporations in recent years—bribery, fraud, illegal political contributions, tax evasion, and antitrust violations—the list of violators reads like a *Who's Who of American* companies. Those found guilty of one or more of these crimes include Bethlehem Steel, Gulf Oil, Firestone Tire & Rubber Co., DuPont Corporation, and International Paper (Ross, 1988).

Sociologist Amitai Etzioni (1985) reported that during the decade between 1975 and 1984, sixty-two percent of America's five hundred largest corporations had engaged in at least one form of illegal activity and 15 percent had participated in five or more types of crime. Yet, in many cases, charges brought by prosecutors were for minor criminal and misdemeanor offenses, and punishments tended to be suspended sentences and monetary fines. More recently, in the 2000s, the corporate fraud perpetrated by just three executives at Enron—Kenneth Lay, Andrew Fastow, and Jeffrey Skilling—ran into the hundreds of millions and brought down one of America's largest corporations. As another illustration, Dennis Kozlowski, Chief Executive of Tyco, an international corporate conglomerate, was charged in 2002 with stealing more than $600 million from his employer (Eisenburg, 2002).

Conflict theorists would argue that, compared to the costs—financial and human—and punishments involved with both violent and property crimes, corporate and white collar offenses perpetrated on society are perhaps much more serious. For example, those charged and convicted of criminal offenses, including assault, burglary, drug pushing, murder, and robbery, are generally punished much more severely by the criminal justice system. A burglar often is sentenced to several years in prison, while the "white-collar" criminal who embezzles $50,000 or more from an employer, as often as not, is never even prosecuted, much less spend any time in prison.

In terms of corporate crime in particular, the harm that perpetrators (both individuals and companies) do to society is well documented. According to U.S. Department of Justice figures compiled by the FBI, burglary and robbery account for $3.8 billion in losses each year. By contrast, estimates for health care fraud range from at least $100 billion, savings and loan fraud at least $300 billion, repair fraud $40 billion, and securities fraud $15 billion or more. In addition, there are deaths that increase the human costs of deviance. According to FBI statistics, there are 16,000 murders in the United States yearly, yet the death toll from occupational hazards such as black lung disease and asbestosis claim the lives of 56,000 Americans annually (Mokhiber, 2007).

The Poor and Minorities Receive the Harshest Punishments   In addition, the poor and minorities receive the most severe punishments from the criminal justice system. Nowhere is this better illustrated than with the death penalty, the harshest punishment of all. Almost 44 percent of all those on death row are black, and 5 percent are Hispanic (Bruck, 1988).

In a study published in 1980, criminologists William Bowers and Glen Pierce examined the sentencing process for homicide in three states: Florida, Georgia, and Texas. What they found was that in cases where white victims had been killed, black defendants in all three states were four to six times more likely to be sentenced to death than were white defendants. Both whites and blacks, moreover, faced a much greater danger of being executed where the murder victims were white than where the victims were black. A black defendant in Florida was thirty-seven times more likely to be sentenced to death if his victim was white than if his victim was black; in Georgia, black-on-white killings were punished by death thirty-three times more often than were black-on-black killings. And in Texas, the ratio climbed to an astounding eighty-four to one (reported in Bruck, 1988, p. 502).

The Drug Issue: An Application of Conflict Theory   One illustration of how conflict theorists approach the analysis of deviance is provided by the issue of drugs and how it was treated during the twentieth century in the United States. In the first two decades of the twentieth century, certain religious groups and their legislative counterparts in Congress waged a war against the "evils of drink." Primarily because of their lobbying efforts, they amassed enough support to secure passage of the Eighteenth Amendment to the Constitution. This prohibited the manufacture, sale, and distribution of beverages containing alcohol.

Although alcoholic beverages were banned, the prohibition amendment was an abysmal failure, in part because it focused on the use of alcohol rather than its abuse. Not only did the American public ignore prohibition, but alcohol consumption increased significantly. So did alcoholism and alcohol-related diseases and deaths (Wright and Weiss, 1980). Prohibition also enabled organized crime to establish a foothold in America by earning hundreds of millions of untaxed dollars from the sale of illegal alcohol. In 1933, after years

FROM THE NATIONAL PHOTO COMPANY COLLECTION, COURTESY OF THE LIBRARY OF CONGRESS PRINTS AND PHOTOGRAPHS DIVISION

The Eighteenth Amendment to the U.S. Constitution (called the Prohibition Amendment) was in effect during the 1920s. The "Roaring Twenties" was a time of bootleg whiskey and bathtub gin. Because of its failure to curb drinking, prohibition was later repealed in 1933 with the passage of the Twenty-First Amendment.

of public controversy and debate, prohibition was repealed by the passage of the Twenty-First Amendment.

In similar fashion, laws prohibiting the possession of such drugs as marijuana, cocaine, and opiate-narcotics have met with little success (Julian and Kornblum, 1986). Again, the focus has centered on the morality of using certain drugs rather than the problems stemming from their abuse. Like the prohibition issue of more than a century ago, critics argue that Congress has formulated a governmental drug policy in a climate of "bipartisan hysteria," rather than by an objective and rational appraisal of the real problems (Stark, 1988). By doing so, the more substantive issues of relative harm brought about by different drugs, drug abuse, and the need for effective drug treatment have been given scant attention.

It is, indeed, ironic that the most dangerous and harmful substances are more or less socially acceptable and "legal." Just two of these drugs—tobacco and alcohol—account for the deaths each year of 60 times more people in the united States than all so-called "harmful" illegal drugs (Caulkins, et al., 2005). Take cigarette smoking, for example. The tobacco and alcohol lobbies are powerful interest groups, which collectively spend billions of dollars annually on advertising and promotion that make their products seem relatively harmless. Yet, from the standpoint of deaths and health complications caused by harmful substances, cigarette smoking represents, by far, the number one drug problem in America. According to the Centers for Disease Control (CDC), the effects of cigarette smoking cause 430,000 premature deaths each year. Consequently, the toxicity in tobacco kills more people each year than all other drugs combined, legal or illegal. Abuse of alcohol—America's second most harmful drug and another legal substance—kills an estimated 100,000 to 150,000 annually (DiFranza and Lew, 1995; Goode, 2001). In comparison, fewer than 6,000 deaths each year have been attributable to illegal narcotics (reported in Stark, 1988).

The Interactionist Approach

The interactionist approach is quite distinct from those that view deviance as the product of social disruption (functionalism) or inter-group conflict (conflict theory). According to the **interactionist approach** to deviance, deviance results from certain types of interactions a person has with other people, as well as the acquisition of a deviant self-image. Two of the most prominent interactionist explanations are cultural transmission theory and labeling theory.

Sutherland: Differential Association Theory   Some sociologists subscribe to a general interactionist perspective called *cultural transmission theory,* the assertion that socialization experiences within certain groups and subcultures encourage the individual to engage in deviant behavior. One specific application of this approach, as applied to crime in particular, was developed by Edwin Sutherland in 1939. His perspective, called **differential association theory**, asserts that criminal behavior is learned in close-knit groups that encourage or condone antisocial behavior. When an individual has more contacts with these groups than with those who favor and encourage conformity, deviance is likely to occur.

Deviant Groups: Three Characteristics of Differential Association   Take, for example, deviant subcultures among some criminals—organized gangsters, prostitutes, narcotic drug users, and juvenile gangs. Such groups act as agents of socialization for their membership in transmitting a very different cultural orientation to its members than most people receive in the mainstream culture.

1. ***They have their own deviant norms.*** With these norms, deviant groups and subcultures define "right" and "wrong" very differently from the dominant society: wrong is often defined as right, bad as good, and the unacceptable as acceptable. For example, the fifteen year old who wants to join a juvenile gang might be given initiation tasks to perform to show his worthiness. His steps to earning gang entry might include stealing, vandalizing public or private property, and/or taking a violent beating from existing members to prove his "toughness." If he succeeds in completing these tasks successfully, he may have earned his "membership."

2. ***They provide education in the ways of the deviant life.*** In this sense, deviant groups teach their new or potential members in how to avoid negative sanctions imposed by society, such as arrest for a felony offense. In this regard, deviant group members serve as negative role models. Prostitutes, for example, need to learn "the ropes" from other prostitutes in how to "make" a "john" (customer) to ensure he is genuine rather than a police officer posing as a customer intent on "busting" her for solicitation. Likewise, car thieves and other property criminals have to learn how to "fence" their stolen merchandise to benefit from their criminal activity.

3. ***They provide emotional and social support.*** Deviant group participation may also provide participants or potential participants with emotional and social support that, in many cases, is not provided to them in other relationships. Consequently, those engaging in deviance, by having their basic emotional needs met through such relations, may find it easy to rationalize their behavior as acceptable. Pimps

often use techniques of emotional manipulation on young, socially isolated women by telling them they love them and will protect them. Some religious sects and cults also use such techniques. In other instances, the individual may feel some pangs of guilt or remorse over what he or she does in terms of violating law or custom, but receives enough peer pressure and/or emotional support from the deviant group to counter-balance and, thus, neutralize such dominant culture influences.

The learning of deviant responses, therefore, involves a socialization process very similar in some ways to that acquired by non-deviants. The values, motives, techniques, and rationalizations of deviance are, for the most part, learned in primary groups. These significant others provide the individual with more motivation and reinforcement for violating socially acceptable norms than for obeying them.

Reckless: Control Theory and Social Containment

In Chapter 5: Socialization, we discussed the importance of self-concept as a key factor in influencing our thoughts, feelings and behavior. In Chapter 6: Social Organization, one social need discussed that every society must provide is the maintenance of social order through the use of both internal and external social controls. What follows is an extension of these discussions.

One sociologist to establish a link between self-concept and deviance, particularly criminal behavior, was Walter Reckless (1973). In his **control theory**, he argues that conformity results when people resist pushes and pulls placed on them to violate social norms due to two sets of social controls, inner controls and outer controls. *Pushes* to deviate include environmental factors such as poverty, lack of opportunity, family problems, and peer pressure. *Pulls* include such internal factors as hostility, lack of impulse control, and antisocial wishes in opposition to dominant social standards. *Inner controls* are defined as those that lie within the individual that reflect the internalization of socially acceptable values and norms. Such inner regulators include a positive self-concept, self-discipline and ego-control, a strong set of ethical standards, and high resistance to socially unacceptable diversions. *Outer controls* include a range of structural reinforcers provided by the family and other groups, organizations and institutions that help to contain the individual (Barlow and Kauzlarich, 2002, p. 269). The combination of these inner and outer controls results in social containment or conformity.

Conformity and Its Two basic Forms

Building upon Reckless' assertion, an important aspect of understanding deviance is to discover what motivates people to conform to dominant social norms. We will now explore the issue of conformity (social containment) in some detail.

As previously defined, *conformity* is behavior that is in basic agreement with the dominant norms of society. Sociologists Mavis H. Beisanz and John Biesanz (1973) have made the distinction between two basic forms of conformity—conventional and compliant conformity.

Conventional Conformity

Conventional conformity is socially acceptable behavior that results from unconsciously following dominant norms. Conventional conformists, thus, act from habit. They have been successfully socialized (from the standpoint of society) with a set of socially dominant values that they have internalized as part of their identities. As a result, dominant norms are rarely questioned. If and when there are impulses or

In many neighborhoods across America, mowing one's lawn is one of many forms of conventional conformity practiced as social custom or habit.

temptations to deviate, conventional conformists are usually successful in suppressing them due to inner controls. Most of the folkways we subscribe to would fall into the category of conventional conformity. They include the foods we eat, the language patterns we use, and most of the folkways we follow. Our actions based on religious beliefs and basic moral principles are included as well.

Compliant Conformity   By comparison, **compliant conformity** is socially acceptable behavior that results from external social pressures. If such pressures—termed "outer controls" by Reckless—were suddenly removed, compliant conformists might feel they could "get away with" certain deviant acts and would not hesitate to engage in them. In other words, the primary reason for obeying norms in these instances is fear of the consequences, not any ingrained habit or moral conviction. Compliant conformists choose not to deviate because of their fear of discovery and punishment, fear of disapproval, and sometimes simply the lack of opportunity. Therefore, some people obey the laws, submit honest tax returns, and remain faithful to their spouses primarily because of these considerations.

In actuality, the socially acceptable behavior of most people includes both types of conformity. In some instances, people engage in conventional conformity, in other situations, compliant conformity prevails. It would appear, however, that in simple rural societies with low technology, little change, and homogeneous populations, conventional conformity often is the most prevalent. Children in such cultures tend to have a consistent and uniformly administered set of socialization experiences. What are viewed as both appropriate and deviant forms of behavior are clearly established and widely accepted by practically everyone. By contrast, compliant conformity is more likely to occur in modern, urban societies with high technology, rapid change, and heterogeneous populations. Children reared in these social systems grow up in an environment in which norms of appropriate conduct are much more vague and ill-defined.

Labeling Theory: Lemert's Primary and Secondary Deviance   Another interactionist explanation, labeling theory, is particularly useful in helping to explain why certain individuals, including prostitutes and criminals, become career deviants. Proponents of **labeling theory** assert that the way people perceive social reality determines (1) what behaviors are labeled as deviant and (2) how being labeled as deviant affects their behavior.

First of all, behavior viewed as deviant is not universally agreed upon but, instead, depends on such factors as the cultural context, the social situation, and "the eye of the beholder." As sociologist J. L. Simmons (1969) comments:

> [A]lmost every conceivable human . . . activity is pariah in somebody's eyes. This means that most people (you and I included) would be labeled deviant by some existing persons and groups. Anyone who moves around much from place to place or social world to social world has probably run into this. There is nothing inherently deviant in any human act; something is deviant only because some people have been successful in labeling it so. The labeling is a local matter that changes from place to place and even from time to time in the same place. To understand deviance we have to understand its environment[al] context. So we have to look at the people doing the labeling as much as the deviant himself (p. 4).

Those doing the labeling make the rules that define the limits of socially acceptable behavior. Individuals who violate these limits are labeled as deviant. In the United States, the development and enforcement of social norms historically have been dominated by affluent, white, Protestant, heterosexual males. Almost by definition, a person who did not fall into these categories was perceived as deviant. If a person was poor, non-white, non-Protestant, non-Christian, homosexual, or female, that individual was perceived as "non-typical," at best, and society applied different standards to his or her behavior. Such people have been perceived as outsiders and, in many instances, have often been labeled as deviant for engaging in the same behavior as the insiders (Becker, 1963). It was not too long ago that most Americans perceived any blacks as deviant for wanting to use the same public facilities as whites and saw a woman's place at the home rather than the workplace.

Edwin Lemert (1951), an early labeling theorist, identified two types of deviance—primary and secondary:

- **Primary deviance.** Primary deviance takes the form of impulsive episodes of socially unacceptable behavior that are temporary or experimental rather the habitual. Trying an illegal drug, shoplifting from a department store on a dare from one's friends, or cheating once on a college exam are examples. Individuals who engaged in these types of behavior would not perceive themselves as deviant nor would they be perceived as such by society in general. President George W. Bush, for example, admitted to having experimented with cocaine as a youth but quickly abandoned it.

- **Secondary deviance.** Secondary deviance, in comparison, is on-going and habitual behavior that violates social norms. Chronic drug users, thieves, prostitutes, and others who persistently violate standards of acceptability come to see themselves as deviant as a consequence of being labeled so by the dominant society. Once society attaches a label of deviance to a person—"pervert," "junkie," "whore," or "convict," to mention just a few—the deviant status becomes the imposed master status from the standpoint of society. Other aspects of the individual's personality and life, including social positions as a family member, citizen, and employee, are ignored (Semones, 1977). This, in turn, according to Lemert and other labeling theorists, encourages further deviance because the deviant image is internalized as part of the individual's self-concept. For instance, convicted felons who have "served time" are often labeled in this manner by the larger society after they are released from prison. Often they find it extremely difficult to obtain a job, partially because of the stigma attached to the label "ex-con." Especially for the many who have no stable family support system when they are released, it is common to take such a stigma and rejection to heart, become alienated from society, and develop a habituated pattern of criminal activity.

Sociological Explanations in Perspective

Despite their value, none of the three major sociological approaches to deviance discussed—functionalism, conflict theory, and interactionism—have escaped criticism. Functionalist explanations have been criticized on several grounds. Strain theory is useful in helping to explain various forms of deviance, ranging from several types of crime to retreatism. However, it does not adequately explain such other forms of deviance as mental disorders and rape. Not everyone in society agrees on what "socially acceptable goals" are or should be as discussed by Merton. Many of these criticisms have been leveled by conflict theorists, who argue that the natural state of society is competition and struggle between various groups rather than order and harmonious equilibrium.

Conflict explanations also have their critics. The value of conflict approaches in helping to explain some forms of deviance—including many forms of crime—is increasingly recognized. However, some forms of deviance, including crime, increased during most of the twentieth century in some modern societies, while exploitation and inequality declined (Davies, 1983). This suggests that other variables, in addition to conflict, may be of equal or greater importance.

Interactionist explanations, considered by themselves, also have their limitations. They are very useful in helping us understand how some career deviants, through differential socialization, come to perceive "appropriate behavior" very differently from most people. Labeling theory, for example, helps us understand how, through the vested interests of moral entrepreneurs and those in power, certain behaviors and individuals are "labeled" as inappropriate and deviant. The "deviant" individual may then come to feel stigmatized, as a result, and, thus, led to habitual deviance. However, some critics (Gove, 1980) argue that labeling theory fails to explain habitual deviants such as shoplifters and adulterers, who have not been caught (labeled) but nonetheless continue such behavior.

The limitations inherent in any single explanation of deviance only act to underscore the immense complexity of human behavior, in general, and deviance in particular. There are many varieties of deviance, each with several dimensions. Each of the sociological approaches briefly discussed focuses on a particular aspect of this very diverse and complex phenomenon. Other courses and texts in sociology—social problems, deviant behavior, criminology, drugs and drug abuse, human sexuality and so forth—address these issues specifically and in depth. In doing so, they use functionalist, conflict, interactionist, and other sociological approaches as diagnostic and explanatory tools of analysis to create a mosaic of understanding. Through the continued application of these and other sociological perspectives, those imbued with the sociological imagination will be able to build an increasingly integrated understanding of deviance and other forms of human behavior as we move through the twenty-first century.

► CHAPTER SUMMARY

1. In assessing the nature of deviant behavior, sociologists make a distinction between the concepts of deviance and deviant. Deviance is behavior that violates the dominate norms of a group or society. Most people engage in deviance from time to time. The deviant, however, is a person who violates the most highly regarded norms of a group or society. The criminal, for example, is stigmatized as such and is subject to ostracism, as well as severe punishment (incarceration) in many to most cases.

2. From the sociological perspective, deviance is a social definition. What constitutes socially unacceptable behavior varies from culture to culture, and often from situation to situation and even historical time frame. To have multiple spouses at the same time is viewed as deviance in American society, although it is permissible and even preferred in some cultures. Likewise, to kill an enemy in "combat" during a war is acceptable and, at times, seen as heroic, but to kill a neighbor in an argument is not. What is considered deviant also changes from one historical period to another. Behaviors such as interracial marriage and abortion, while legal today, were considered deviant and illegal until the late 1960s and early 1970s.

3. Any discussion of deviance should include some emphasis on conformity, behavior that is in basic agreement with the dominant norms of society. Conformity, in general, is maintained through sanctions (positive and negative, informal and formal). In addition to stated rewards for conformity and punishments for deviance, various enforcement mechanisms are necessary to reinforce conformity and deter or minimize deviance. They include authority figures, peer groups, and even physical coercion (in extreme cases). In addition, language and the use of argots by specific groups and subcultures allow us to perceive group boundaries involving insiders versus outsiders, accepted group members or deviants along with the reinforcement of acceptable versus unacceptable behavior.

4. The sociological analysis of deviance distinguishes between different levels and types of behavior seen as socially reprehensible. First, deviance occurs on three basic levels—individual, group, and collective levels. In addition, types of deviance include aberrant, nonconforming, and socially acceptable forms, as well as deviance resulting from the inability to conform and deviance defined by a person's characteristics or attributes. Crime, which may occur on any level of society and occupy any one of several types of deviance discussed, is tracked by the Federal Bureau of Investigation (FBI). According to the FBI's statistics compiled on eight index crimes over the past several decades, crime rates dropped overall during the 1990s and 2000s compared to earlier decades. Although one-time criminals—thieves and rapists, for example—often are never identified and caught, habitual criminals rarely ever go unpunished.

5. Early explanations of deviance centered on myth and superstition. Two illustrative examples are provided by demonology and astrology. Demonology is a system of beliefs which holds that deviant behavior is caused by evil spirits that possess the body and make it act according to their will. Astrology offers the notion that the movement of the planets and stars affects human behavior in general, and that the moon in particular influences deviant behavior.

6. By the last quarter of the nineteenth century, explanations of deviance based on science began to emerge. The first attempts at systematic explanation came from the biological approach and included atavistic theory, somotype theory, and XYY theory. Atavistic theory, developed by Cesare Lombroso, maintained that many criminals represented a genetic throwback to primitive humans. Somotype theory, proposed by William Sheldon, asserted that deviant behavior, such as delinquency, was related to physical body type. XYY theory argued that the presence of an extra Y chromosome in males was associated with criminal behavior. Atavistic theory has been discredited altogether, somotype and XYY theories are largely without substantiation, and few social scientists today place much stock in biological approaches as primary explanations of most forms of deviance.

7. Modern explanations of deviance are largely sociological. Functionalists stress the value of approaches such as Merton's strain theory, which argues that deviance results from anomie (structural strain). Such strain stems from discrepancies between culturally approved goals (socialized into people by their culture) and access to the socially approved means (opportunities provided by the social structure) needed to achieve them. Conflict theorists stress that what is "defined" as deviant arises out of a struggle for power between various groups. The segment of society with the most power is able to have its definition of conformity and deviance legitimated as social policy. Interactionists argue that deviance results from how we are taught to perceive reality from the interactions we have with others. Three of the more prominent interactionist explanations of deviances are (1) Sutherland's differential association theory (deviance as a different type of socialization from deviant groups), (2) Reckless's control theory with its emphasis on the mechanisms for self-containment (inner and outer controls), and (3) Lemert's application of labeling theory (primary vs. secondary deviance).

TERMS TO KNOW

aberrant deviance: deviant behavior in which a person violates a norm for selfish reasons and attempts to escape detection and punishment.

argot: a special type of language characteristic of subcultures.

astrology: the notion that the movement of the planets and stars affects human behavior, and that the moon in particular influences deviant behavior.

atavistic theory: a biological explanation of deviance which maintains that the violent criminal is an inherited type who represents a genetic throwback to primitive humans.

biological perspective: argues that deviance is caused primarily by inborn physical traits or characteristics.

collective level deviance: socially unacceptable behavior by large numbers of people at various levels of society.

compliant conformity: socially acceptable behavior that results from external social pressures.

conflict approach to deviance: the argument that what is defined as "antisocial" or "deviant" arises out of a struggle for power between various groups.

conformity: behavior that is in basic agreement with the dominant norms of society.

control theory: the assertion by Reckless that conformity results when people resist pushes and pulls placed on them to violate social norms due to two sets of social controls, inner controls and outer controls.

conventional conformity: socially acceptable behavior that results from unconsciously following dominant norms.

crime: a violation of criminal law enacted and enforced by government with formal penalties.

demonology: a system of beliefs which holds that deviance is caused by evil spirits that possess the body and make it act according to their will.

deviance: behavior that violates the dominant norms of a group or society.

deviance by attributes: a process in which those with certain physical or social characteristics are perceived and/or treated as deviant (e.g., a handicapped person or the transgendered).

deviance resulting from an inability to conform: a situational form of deviance in which a person either cannot control their behavior or is forced to commit a deviant act.

deviant: a person who violates the most highly regarded norms of a group or society.

differential association theory: the principle by Sutherland that criminal behavior is learned in close-knit groups that encourage or condone deviant behavior.

functionalist approach to deviance: argues that deviant or antisocial behavior results from a strain on or breakdown of social order.

group level deviance: socially unacceptable behavior carried out by social groups, usually at the community level.

index crimes: eight of the most serious violent and property crimes tracked each year by the U.S. Justice Department.

individual level deviance: acts of antisocial behavior carried out by one person, usually at the local community level.

innovation: a deviant response in which a person accepts culturally approved goals but rejects socially approved means of achieving them.

interactionist approach to deviance: the argument that deviance results from certain types of interactions a person has with other people, as well as the acquisition of a deviant self-image.

labeling theory: the assertion that the way people perceive social reality determines (1) what behaviors are labeled as deviant and (2) how being labeled as deviant affects their behavior.

moral entrepreneurs: Becker's term for members of some groups who try to impose their views of morality or policy on others.

nonconforming deviance: socially disapproved behavior in which the participant challenges the legitimacy of certain norms by violating them openly, regardless of the punishments that might be imposed.

primary deviance: impulsive episodes of socially unacceptable behavior that are temporary or experimental rather than habitual.

rebellion: a deviant response in which a person rejects both culturally approved goals and socially acceptable means and attempts to replace them with others goals and means.

reductionism: a process in which the many complexities of a subject are reduced down to overly simplistic, single cause explanations.

retreatism: a deviant response in which a person rejects both cultural goals and socially acceptable means.

ritualism: a deviant response in which a person rejects culturally approved goals but accepts the approved means.

secondary deviance: on-going and habitual behavior that violates social norms.

socially acceptable deviance: deviant behavior considered acceptable by significant portions of society.

somotype theory: a biological explanation of deviance by Shelton which asserted that physique or body type is linked to both personality and deviance.

strain theory: the perspective that deviance results from contradictions between culturally approved goals set by a culture and structural access to the socially approved means to achieve them.

XYY theory: a biological explanation of deviance which argues that the presence of an extra Y chromosome in males is associated with criminal behavior.

SUGGESTED READINGS

Barnett, O. W., C. L. Miller-Perrin, and R. D. Perrin. 2005. *Family Violence Across the Lifespan: An Introduction,* 2nd ed. Thousand Oaks, CA: Sage Publications. An excellent, research-based overview of family violence which covers issues and findings related to child abuse, spousal violence and abuse, and elder abuse. Causes, symptoms, perpetrators, consequences, and implications are all given useful treatment.

Chesler, P. 2005. *Women and Madness.* New York: Palgrave Macmillan. A penetrating look at the many sexist practices used in the psychiatric establishment in the therapeutic treatment of women. The authors combine a historical and contemporary approach.

Fox, J. A., J. Levin, and K. Quinet. 2005. *The Will to Kill: Making Sense of Senseless Murder.* Boston: Allyn & Bacon. A detailed analysis of several types of homicide. Topics, along with supporting research, focus on the nature of murder in its various forms. They include impulse murder, serial murder, school related homicide, mass murder, and cult murder.

Hawdon, J. E. 2005. *Drug and Alcohol Consumption as Functions of Social Structure: A Cross-Cultural Sociology.* Lewiston, NY: Edwin Mellon Press. A cross-cultural analysis of drug use and abuse in several societies around the world. The author explores the reasons why drug use is much more prevalent in some societies as compared with others.

Thio, A. 2007. *Deviant Behavior,* 9th ed. Boston, MA: Pearson Allyn & Bacon. A thorough, yet concise text on deviant behavior. Thio begins with deviance in general and then focuses on positivist and constructionist perspectives. The remainder examines a variety of topics using both of these major sociological perspectives.

Population and Human Ecology

▶ READING PREVIEW

Terms to Know

age specific fertility rate	greenhouse effect	mortality
age specific mortality rate	growth rate	mortality intervention
agricultural revolution	human ecology	population
census	immigration	population pyramid
crude birth rate	industrial revolution	postindustrial stage
crude death rate	infant mortality rate	posttransition stage
demographic transition	internal migration	pretransition stage
demography	international migration	pronatalism
dependency ratio	life expectancy	sex ratio
emigration	Mathusian theory	total fertility rate
fecundity	median age	transition stage
fertility	megacities	urban revolution
fertility rate	migration	vital statistics
global warming	momentum	

POPULATION: AN INTRODUCTION

People at present think that five sons are not too many and each son has five sons also, and before the death of the grandfather there are already 25 descendants. Therefore people are more and wealth is less; they work hard and receive little.

Han Fei-Tzu, ca. 500 BCE

To the size of states there is a limit, as there is to other things, plants, animals, implements; for none of these retain their natural power when they are too large or too small, but they either wholly lose their nature, or are spoiled.

Aristotle, 322 BCE

In the 25 seconds or so it takes you to read this paragraph, 51 new inhabitants will be born on the planet Earth. That equates to152 new people each minute and 9,122 each hour, every hour of every day. By the time you wake up tomorrow morning, there will be 219,000 new people worldwide who were not here yesterday. In fact, one of every ten people who have ever lived since humanity began are alive today. And the numbers and percentages continue to grow steadily ("World Vital Events Per Time Unit," U.S. Census Bureau, 2008).

For thousands of years in both Eastern and Western traditions, social thinkers warned that there were limits to growth. Few heeded these warnings because the problem seemed far off in the distant future, and somehow not relevant to "here and now" realities and concerns. Consequently, the world population grew and continued to grow.

Today, many Americans are as oblivious to the dangers of overpopulation as were the citizens of Ancient China and Ancient Greece during the times of Fei-Tzu and Aristotle. For those with a relatively high standard of living, a plentiful supply of food, and the technological benefits and conveniences of modern society, the problem of overpopulation seems distant and far away. Because of the low priority given this issue and related ecological concerns, this problem—until recently—has not been of major concern in presidential campaigns, has not constituted a major component of U.S. foreign or domestic policy, and has been given only passing attention in the national press. Mainly it has been only those in the scientific community and related organizations, particularly sociologists and biological scientists, who have seemed concerned. Meanwhile, the world population has continued to grow larger.

From a historical perspective, world population growth, until recently, has had more positive than negative consequences. It marked the transition from simple societies with low technology to complex ones with advanced industrial and postindustrial economies. These changes, in turn, made it possible for people in technologically advanced societies to enjoy a standard of living unprecedented in human history.

Consequently, it is indeed ironic that overpopulation is now among the most serious social problems facing humanity, one that along with nuclear war and international terrorism, could threaten not only modern civilization but the very survival of our species. From 1970 to 2004, the world's population grew from nearly three and one-half billion people to nearly six and one-half billion, enough new inhabitants (three billion) to occupy China, India, Japan, and the United States, four of the most populated nations on Earth. As of 2008, the total world population was increasing by eighty million people per year, or 219,000 each day. These are enough new people during each twenty-four-hour period to create a new Akron, Ohio. At this rate of increase, there could be six billion people in Asia, India, and Africa alone by the year 2040. According to Morris K. Udall, if world population growth continues to increase, "we could be fighting for food, space, and shelter with 15 billion people within the next century" (Udall, 1987, p. vii).

Obviously, this tremendous upsurge in population is a relatively new phenomenon that must be stopped and stopped soon. To accomplish this with a minimum of human suffering will require that people worldwide be informed about the scope of the problem as soon as possible. If birthrates worldwide are not reduced to replacement levels within the next few decades, the alternative will be increased death rates from malnutrition, disease, and, perhaps, wars, along with economic instability caused at least partially by the pressure of overpopulation. Currently, at least ten million people starve to death each year, six million of which are children under the age of five. Another 840 million people worldwide are chronically malnourished with about 799 million living in underdeveloped countries (World Hunger: Facts about Hunger, 2008). These figures can only rise in the future if nations throughout the world do not soon adopt comprehensive population control policies. Over twenty years ago, Werner Fornos (1987), president of the Population Institute, issued this warning:

> [I]f we permit the six-billion mark or the eight-billion mark to pass casually as we have the fifth, our children will pay the price. For the world they inherit from us will be one in which the nations of the developing world will have lost the struggle for economic

self-sufficiency. Staggering under the weight of huge and impoverished populations, . . . many of these nations would descend into a fierce cycle of economic deterioration and political and social instability.

Such conditions would have a direct and indisputable impact on the nations of the industrialized Northern Hemisphere as well. Americans, Canadians, Japanese, and Europeans would see their societies transformed by the pressures created by . . . the neighboring Third World, pressures that could well unhinge Western economies and undermine international security.

This bleak scenario does not arise from any defeatism or cynicism. Rather, it is founded on the most objective and realistic demographic data available and on science's best knowledge of the relationships between population and world environment. And it is offered in stark contrast to the striking opportunities and possibilities we have for a far brighter international future. For the fate of the world is not sealed; it is being determined by the choices and decisions we are now making (pp. 1– 2).

In the time since Dr. Wernos' statement, overpopulation pressures have increased in some parts of the world rather than being ameliorated and the planet—by 2013—will have seven billion or more inhabitants. Since the late 1980s, the consequences created at least in part by rapidly rising populations have contributed to a variety of problems experienced worldwide. These have included depletion of over one-fifth of the rain forests in the Amazon basin, the events of September 11, 2001, along with increasing threat of international terrorism, irrefutable scientific evidence of global warming, and gasoline prices that, by 2008, had tripled in two decades to more than $4 per gallon in parts of America and much higher in some European countries.

In this chapter, we will examine the nature of population in terms of characteristics, growth and change. When sociologists use the term **population**, they are speaking of the total number of persons who inhabit a country or other politically or geographically specified territory. Because of the worldwide importance of this topic as a social issue, much of the following discussion will focus on overpopulation as a social problem. To begin, we will examine how sociologists study this area of human behavior.

DEMOGRAPHY: THE STUDY OF POPULATION

The scientific study of population characteristics and change is **demography**. Although considered a subfield of sociology, demography is derived from such diverse disciplines as economics, statistics, medicine, and biology. It has been a part of sociology only during the last seventy-five years.

Specifically, demographers examine the size, composition, and distribution of human populations and how they change. They also examine the problems or potential problems associated with population growth, decline, and composition. Micro-, macro-, and international population characteristics and trends are analyzed. Some demographers, such as those employed by the U.S. Census Bureau, examine population factors primarily within the United States. They are interested in describing and explaining such things as rates of overall growth, trends regarding the size of the family, the ratio of rural to urban residence, which states and regions are gaining or losing population and why, and life expectancy. Others may be employed by international organizations, like the United Nations, and attempt to gather and analyze data on populations worldwide. Among other things, these scientists ascertain which countries have stable or declining populations, which have exploding populations and why, what political, social, and economic resources and solutions are needed to combat overpopulation and human suffering in certain countries, and which nations are hardest hit by the HIV epidemic and other health problems.

The Census

One way demographers gather data on populations is through census taking. A **census** is a relatively complete headcount of the people in a given society. The counting of populations can be traced back at least five thousand years to the ancient Sumerians and Egyptians. They most probably counted members of households along with their personal property for taxation purposes. In modern times, the taking of a formal census first emerged in democratic societies. The United States was the first modern country to make legal provision for a regular census.

The first U.S. census was taken in 1790. This initial effort showed a total U.S. population of 3.9 million people, fewer than the 4.1 million who currently live in the Houston, Texas metropolitan area. Since then, a census has been compiled every ten years and the American population has grown dramatically. Recent census research shows a total U.S. population of 179.3 million in 1960, 203.3 million in 1970, 226.5 million in 1980, 248.7 million in 1990, 281.4 million in 2000, and 295.7 million in 2004 (U.S. Census Bureau, 2004; Ibid, March 25, 2005). The margin of error in recent census studies has involved an underestimate of from one to two percent. By compiling population data, census takers also ascertain additional information, including each state's population by sex, race, rural or urban residence, and median age. To complete the 2010 census, it was estimated that 100,000 temporary, part-time employees or more would be needed by the U.S. Government (Table 12-1).

Census data are used by many individuals and organizations for several different purposes. Government officials use this information to assess needs for a variety of programs including social programs aimed at assisting the poor, the disabled, the young, and the elderly. Counseling professionals use these data to better assess family trends, pressures, and potential trouble spots. During the last fifty years, census figures have documented the rise of divorce and the proportion of children living in single-parent homes. Politicians running for national office use demographic statistics to better grasp the relative size and distribution of different voter constituencies at the state, regional, and national levels. And the corporate sector uses census information to assess and find markets for their products, develop advertising campaigns, and choose locations for production facilities, stores, and sales territories (Russell, 1984).

Vital Statistics

In addition to census data, demographers also make use of **vital statistics** to analyze population characteristics and change. These are records kept on the inhabitants of a nation or society, which include births, deaths, marriages, and incidences of disease. In early and medieval Europe, the church maintained many of these records, especially those documenting ceremonies related to births and baptisms, weddings, and burial services. However, these records documented only the ecclesiastical ceremonies that occurred after the fact,

TABLE 12-1	Total U.S. Population, Growth, and Density by Decade: 1790–2050 (Projected)		
CENSUS	POPULATION	POPULATION GROWTH (%)	PEOPLE PER SQUARE MILE OF LAND AREA
1790	3,929,214	—	4.5
1800	5,308,483	35.1	6.1
1810	7,239,881	36.4	4.3
1820	9,638,453	33.1	5.5
1830	12,866,020	33.5	7.4
1840	17,069,453	32.7	9.8
1850	23,191,876	35.9	7.9
1860	31,443,321	35.6	10.6
1870	39,818,449	26.6	11.2
1880	50,189,209	26.0	14.2
1890	62,979,766	25.5	17.8
1900	76,212,168	21.0	21.5
1910	92,228,496	21.0	26.0
1920	106,021,537	15.0	29.9
1930	123,202,624	16.2	34.7
1940	132,164,569	7.3	37.2
1950	151,325,798	14.5	42.6
1960	179,323,175	18.5	50.6
1970	203,302,031	13.4	57.5
1980	226,542,199	11.4	64.0
1990	248,718,302	9.8	70.3
2000	281,422,509	13.1	79.6
2010*	308,936,000	—	—
2020*	335,805,000	—	—
2030*	363,584,000	—	—
2040*	391,946,000	—	—
2050*	419,854,000	—	—

* 2010–2050 figures are projected estimates.
SOURCES: U.S. Bureau of the Census, 2004; Encyclopedia Britannica Almanac 2005, p. 763; Negative Population Growth. Accessed July 14, 2008 at *http://www.npg.org/popfacts.htm*

rather than the events themselves. Consequently, they were often incomplete. During the 1600s, Massachusetts became the first colony to mandate the recording of actual events rather than religious ceremonies related to them. As a result of placing record-keeping in the hands of civil authorities, records became much more reliable and accurate. Not until the twentieth century however, were comprehensive and accurate records being kept in all states. For instance, birth and death registrations in the United States were first reported and analyzed on a national basis in 1933 (Peterson, 1969).

Demographic Transition

One widely accepted explanation of population growth is the theory of **demographic transition**. This perspective maintains that population growth is a three-stage process in which developing nations move from a condition of high fertility and high mortality to one of low fertility and low mortality. Before the industrial revolution began in about 1750, the world's population was increasing but stable. High fertility rates in most societies were offset by high mortality rates. With industrialization, many societies began to experience demographic transition in which their mortality rates dropped. This created a period of rapid population growth. Then as these societies modernized, their fertility rates declined as well. Specifically, demographic transition involves the following three stages.

Stage 1: Pretransition Stage (Preindustrial Societies)

In what demographers call the first stage of demographic transition, the **pretransition stage**, there are *countries with high rates of both fertility and mortality*. Historically, this ratio between births and deaths has characterized preliterate societies before any modernization had taken place. High fertility rates were attributed to such factors as lack of understanding concerning birth control coupled with high mortality rates that made continued childbearing necessary. Having unlimited numbers of offspring was encouraged by both family and religious norms and cultural norms in general. High mortality was chiefly due to a lack of medical technology and modern health and sanitation practices. Few societies exist at this stage today except for possible isolated tribal and village cultures in parts of Africa, Asia, and South America.

Stage 2: Transition Stage (Industrializing [Developing] Societies)

The second stage of demographic transition, the **transition stage**, is characterized by *countries with high fertility rates and declining to low mortality rates*. As countries have modernized, mortality rates have dropped significantly because of access to modern medical technology and the adoption of better health practices. Historically, norms and values regarding births and family size, however, have lagged behind, sometimes for several decades. During the interim, population size often has risen dramatically. It takes time for people to realize the advantages of small families and leave old values behind. This imbalance between births and deaths characterized both Europe and the United States until the twentieth century. Today the pattern is most evident in parts of Africa, Asia, and Latin America, including such countries as Kenya, Nigeria, Zaire, India, Iran, the Philippines, Honduras, and Guatemala.

Stage 3: Posttransition Stage (Industrial Societies)

The third stage of demographic transition is the **posttransition stage**, which involves *countries with declining to low fertility and mortality rates*. This pattern characterizes countries near or at a state of full industrialization. In these societies, modern contraception coupled with cash economies have made low fertility rates not only possible but economically preferable to necessary. Because children do not participate significantly in modern economies and represent a drain on family resources, fertility rates have dropped accordingly. Likewise, advances in nutrition, public health and sanitation, and medical technology have resulted in lowered mortality rates. Taken together, lower rates of fertility and mortality have created a condition of population stability as the demographic transition has been completed. Countries that have completed this third stage include the United States, Canada, New Zealand, Great Britain, the Soviet Union, Japan, and Australia.

While demographic transition has characterized the history of industrial societies, demographers are divided as to whether it will accurately describe the future of today's developing nations. Unlike Europe and the United States, many of today's developing nations have higher initial rates of fertility and have experienced a much faster rate of decline in mortality (Teitelbaum, 1975). The result has been a literal "population explosion" that is unprecedented in history. The critical question is whether the complete cycle of demographic transition can be completed before many of these countries experience economic and ecological disaster. The future is beginning to look more encouraging for many of these nations, as we will see in the discussion to follow. However, successful transition is far from ensured, and the threat of severe dislocation and societal collapse from the pressures of overpopulation looms omnipresent on the horizon.

An Emerging Stage 4: Postindustrial Stage (Postindustrial Societies)   Demographers today increasingly are focused on an emerging fourth stage of demographic transition that represents a continuation of stage three—low fertility and mortality—with new forms of postindustrial economies. Postmodern societies—Western Europe, Japan, and the United States—are now moving into the *postindustrial stage* characterized by countries with information and service intensive economies and a continued lowering of fertility and mortality rates (Macionis, 2007).

Such recent changes are having a significant structural impact on several societies. Postindustrial countries, particularly the United States, have recently been outsourcing many manufacturing and lower-level service jobs to trained workers in less-developed countries where the wage scales are much lower. While this increases profits for American corporations and provides opportunities for workers abroad to improve their standards of living, it results in downward social mobility and hardships for many American workers and their families when they lose their jobs. But perhaps most problematic for the United States in particular and the developed world in general is international terrorism caused, in part, by demographic factors such as high fertility rates. This contributes to an increasing gap between the planet's "haves" and "have nots" as the world continues to change and develop technologically. However, some factions within some counties, particularly in parts of the Muslim world, refuse to join the modern world and react to their increasing poverty and frustration by seeking to destroy it.

Population Features of the United States as a Postindustrial Society   On Tuesday, October 17, 2006, at 7:46 A.M. Eastern Standard Time, the U.S. Bureau of the Census estimated that the population of the United States reached 300 million inhabitants (CNN, 2006. Wolf Blitzer's "Situation Room," October 17). When one examines the U.S. population growth rate from 1776 (an estimated 2.8 million), the rate of population growth has been accelerating just as it has been in other parts of the world (Table 12-2).

As the rate of U.S. population increase has accelerated, the composition of the population has been changing as well, with two notable trends involving both the aging and Latino populations. The first of the "baby boomer" generation (those born between 1946 and 1964) began turning 60 during 2006. Given the tremendous number of baby boomers, an estimated 77 million, there will be a definite "graying of America" in the next few decades as the median age of Americans continues to get higher. In 1900, the median age of Americans was a very young 22.9 years. As of 2006, it was 35.9 and it is projected that it will increase to 39 by 2030 with 19.6 percent of the population being 65 or older at that time. Latinos are also becoming more plentiful due to several factors including both high

TABLE 12-2 U.S. Population Growth by 100 Million Benchmarks		
BENCHMARK YEAR	U.S POPULATION	YEARS REQUIRED TO REACH NEW 100 MILLION BENCHMARK
1776	2,800,000	
1915	100,000,000	139
1967	200,000,000	52
2006	300,000,000	39
2043*	400,000,000	37

* Projected

SOURCE: Special Report: "A Nation in Full." *U.S. News and World Report,* October 2, 2006, Volume 141, No. 12, pp. 48–56.

immigration and fertility rates. As a consequence of these and other factors, the U.S. population is expected to top 400 million by 2043 (*U.S. News and World Report,* October 2, 2006, pp. 54–56).

POPULATION IN HISTORICAL PERSPECTIVE

Malthusian Theory

The idea that the Earth can become overpopulated is not new. In 1798, Thomas Malthus (1766–1834) wrote the first modern treatise on population entitled *An Essay on the Principle of Population.* In it, this English minister and economist presented a theory of population growth and, in later editions, proposed a set of solutions for the future overpopulation problem.

© BETTMANN/CORBIS

English economist Thomas Malthus (1766–1834) was one of the first modern scholars to predict a possible overpopulation crisis.

Malthus' Theory In setting forth what has come to be known as **Malthusian theory**, he argued that human societies increase their populations geometrically (1, 2, 4, 8, 16), while food supplies grow arithmetically (1, 2, 3, 4, 5). Malthus felt that this situation was deceptive in its initial stages because increases in food supply seemed to keep pace with the growth of human population. However, given the exponential growth of people, he predicted that biology would inevitably outdistance technology and the capacity to produce food would lag behind the numbers of people needing to be fed. This, in turn, would result in a world of misery overpopulated with malnourished people living in abject poverty.

Malthus' Checks on Population In subsequent editions of his essay, Malthus asserted that humanity had two essential choices in dealing with the problem. Although he seriously doubted this would occur, one choice was for individuals to implement the *preventive checks* of (1) postponed marriage and

(2) sexual abstinence. In lieu of such "moral restraint," the positive checks of (1) hunger, (2) disease, (3) war, and (4) "vice" would become the ultimate solution. He regarded artificial forms of birth control as a morally reprehensible "vice." Although "vice," as conceptualized by Malthus, would bring the population into balance, it would damn humans who practiced it to hell. Taken as a whole, positive checks would bring the population back into balance, but at a much higher cost in terms of human suffering and degradation than the inconveniences wrought by preventive checks. Although his ideas were accepted by some, Malthus was the subject of much ridicule and criticism.

His theory of population was severely criticized for its pessimism, and many scholars regarded Malthus as the "parson of doom." In some sectors, his ideas become identified with political conservatism. Some people used them to blame overpopulation on the poor who, it was charged, were least capable of practicing "moral restraint." One of his most vehement critics was Karl Marx (1906). Marx argued that starvation, where it occurred, was caused by social policies that allowed capitalists to hoard resources and accumulate wealth. Rather than blaming the poor for the lack of food, he felt that they were victims of the unequal distribution of wealth.

Mathusian Theory: An Assessment   First, it is clear that Malthus was short-sighted in several respects. He failed to anticipate the rapid decline in birthrates that accompanied demographic transition in industrialized countries. He did not foresee the technological revolution in agriculture during the nineteenth and twentieth centuries which, among, other things, made it possible to produce a much larger crop yield from an acre of ground. Neither did he anticipate the dramatic advances in communication and transportation that have made the distribution of vital resources, including food, less of a problem. And, of course, Malthus had no foresight regarding the advances of birth control during the twentieth century, which made it much easier to have small families. Consequently, his predictions of gross overpopulation have not come to pass in Europe and the United States.

A strong case can be made, however, for the argument that the less-developed nations have become caught in a Malthusian trap. This, in turn, could have a significant impact on the stability and quality of life not only for their populations, but for modern nations as well. Since the 1960s, Malthus' ideas have experienced a resurgence among those identified as the neo-Malthusian school (Morris, 1966; Ehrlich, 1970; Heilbroner, 1974; Ehrlich and Ehrlich, 1979). These scholars maintain that Malthus' basic thesis about runaway population growth accompanied by shortfalls in food and other vital resources was sound but premature.

Population Growth: Four Technological Revolutions

As briefly discussed in Chapter 6: Social Organization, *three technological revolutions—* agricultural, urban, and industrial—have played a key role in the evolutionary development of human societies. These critical historical periods have also sparked and accelerated population increase. In the section to follow, we will briefly discuss human social life in prehistory before the development of technology, three technological revolutions which set the stage for rapid population growth, and the emerging fourth technological revolution we are now experiencing (Table 12-3).

TABLE 12-3	Technological Revolutions: How They Sparked Population Growth

TECHNOLOGICAL REVOLUTION	TIME PERIOD	KEY CHARACTERISTICS	IMPACT ON HUMAN SOCIETIES
Pretechnology	Before 8000 BCE	Hunter-gatherer economies; Small roving bands of humans	Precarious existence; 25–35-year lifespan
Agricultural	8000–3500 BCE	Domestication of plants/animals; farm and pastoral economies	Stable/surplus food supply; social stability; growing population.
Urban	3500 BCE–1750 CE	City council government form; planned efficient economy; institutionalized leisure time.	rise of advanced civilizations; diversified division of labor that could support large populations.
Industrial	1750–1975	Mass production factory economy; Knowledge explosion in multiple fields (e.g., farming and medicine).	longer lifespans in advanced societies exponential population growth; short-fall of resources/poverty in Third World.
Information	1975–Present	Restructuring of institutions (e.g., economy, education); continuing knowledge explosion.	a world increasingly characterized by "haves" (the technological elite) who limit populations and "have nots" who do not.

Human Social Life in Prehistory: Hunter-Gatherer Societies At the dawn of pre-history, our ancestors lived in small, nomadic bands of twenty to thirty individuals and were hunters and food gathers. Because they had no means of storing food, they literally lived from meal to meal, from hand to mouth. Life was a constant struggle for food. In some cases, these early groups followed their primary source of food—caribou, reindeer, bison, and deer, for example—on the hoof. Such harsh conditions made a large population impossible, as the food supply tended to be unstable and often relatively small. The average life span during this period ranged from 25–35 years. As a result, the world's population remained small and grew very slowly.

The Agricultural Revolution About 10,000 years ago, a great change occurred with the **agricultural revolution**, the domestication of plants and animals. As the first technological revolution to spark population growth, it emerged about 8000 BCE with the development of simple slash-and-burn agriculture. It was marked by the cultivation of grains, including wheat and corn, and by the domestication of such animals as goats and poultry. Simple farming tools, including the hoe and a primitive, human-powered plow, were also invented during this time.

This was a monumental turning point because, for the first time in human history, a stable and surplus food supply became possible. With farming and animal husbandry, people could store grain and always have a supply of animal products available for sustenance. Groups could stay in one location permanently rather than have to forage for food. With such stability, the average life span began to increase, more children could be supported, and the size of the world's population began to rise steadily. As time passed, the agricultural revolution continued to gather momentum as farming methods slowly but steadily advanced.

The Urban Revolution   The next significant boost to population growth occurred about 5,500–6,000 years ago (4000–3500 BCE) with the rise of cities that created the **urban revolution**. With the technological base provided by slash-and-burn farming, first villages and later cities began to emerge in the Near East—Egypt, Greece, and Mesopotamia. Draft animals, such as oxen, were placed in front of a more advanced plow, and true agriculture began. Freed from depending on energy supplied by only their muscles, farmers could plant and harvest large fields rather than small plots (Peterson, 1969). Crop rotation, terraced fields, irrigation systems, and the development of metallurgy added to agricultural productivity.

To promote a more efficient form of agriculture and land use, soil and water resources were placed under the authority of a centralized city government. The economic and social growth of these cities was further facilitated by the establishment of trade relations with other cities. As time passed, the economic systems of these city-states became increasingly diversified and efficient, larger numbers of people could be sustained, and populations grew.

Modern civilization sprang from an urban social structure. The sheer efficiency of an urban society made it possible to institutionalize leisure time. Without having to spend every waking moment struggling for subsistence, some people were able to use their free time to ponder, think, imagine, invent, and inquire. Out of this environment came the cornerstones of modern civilization—art, music, architecture, literature, poetry, philosophy, and, ultimately, science. As these disciplines emerged and matured over a period of more than five thousand years, the stage was ultimately set for the emergence of the industrial Revolution.

The Industrial Revolution   The most dramatic increase in population began about 1750 with the beginning of the **industrial revolution**. Centralized facilities for mass production (factories) began to replace the home as the location for the production of goods and services. Bureaucratic forms of management were carried out by professionals who, in successfully coordinating complex and diverse work functions, heightened efficiency and greatly improved productivity.

With more and more goods and services being produced, a much larger population could be supported. As industrialization gathered momentum and developing nations went through demographic transition, mortality rates declined dramatically as a result of advances in medicine and health practices. Fertility rates remained high for a time and then declined to much lower levels. In the interim, population growth accelerated. Many of the less-developed nations today appear caught in this high fertility-low mortality ratio that is producing the current population explosion.

The Information Revolution: An Emerging Fourth Stage   The Industrial Revolution ended about 1975. With the development and increasing availability for home use of first desktop and then lap-top computers and, more recently, the internet and other communication technologies, we are now entering a new era of social organization that is transforming the ways in which societies are structured and the ways in which we live. Driven by the impact of this fourth technological revolution, the ways we work, organize education, shop for consumer goods, and even develop and maintain social relationships are changing and will continue to change and evolve as we experience the next century. Population characteristics—fertility rates, mortality rates, age and occupational distributions, and other demographic factors—will continue to impact how these technologies are used and in turn will continue to be impacted upon by such technologies. As a result, new world economic powers will emerge (e.g., China and India), the world increasingly will be characterized by "haves" in modern societies and "have nots" in the less-developed world, and hopefully, the world population will stabilize.

World Population Growth: Past, Present, and Future

Total Numbers: Past and Future At the beginning of the agricultural revolution, there were only about five million people inhabiting this planet. Over the next eight thousand years, the population grew slowly but steadily until there were approximately 250 million people by the year 1 CE This figure certainly would have been much greater without wars, epidemics, plagues, and famines that kept growth at a modest pace.

As shown in Table 12-4, the rate of population growth has increased dramatically since that time. By the year 1650, world population had doubled to 500 million (one-half billion). Then, between 1650 and 1850, something dramatic happened. That something was the *Industrial Revolution.* By 1850, the world's population was one billion people. As industrialization continued to gather momentum, doubling times became shorter and shorter. The world grew to two billion people by 1930 and four billion by 1975. In July 1986, we reached five billion people, and in October 1999, the world reached the six billion mark.

Demographers at the U.S. Bureau of the Census in 1985 estimated that the world population would exceed six billion by the year 2000 (*World Population Data Sheet*, 1985). This has been unprecedented because the world's population "tripled during a single human

TABLE 12-4 **World Population Growth: The Past 2000 Years**

YEAR	WORLD POPULATION	DOUBLING TIME (AND INCREASES PER BILLION)
1 CE	250 million ?	2,000–3,000 years
1650	500 million	1650 years
1850	1.0 billion	200 years
1930	2.0 billion	80 years
1975	4.0 billion	45 years
1986	5.0 billion	11 years
1999	6.0 billion	13 years
2009	6.8 billion	

SOURCES: *World Population Data Sheet*, 1985; U.S. Census Bureau, 1987, 1999, 2008.

lifetime from two billion to six billion during the 70 year period between 1930 and 2000. No one living at any previous time has witnessed such growth" (*Popline,* April 1986, p. 4). According to demographer Phillip Hauser writing in 1960, if the post-World War II rates of population growth were to continue for eight hundred years, the earth could indeed be a crowded place with "one person per square foot of the land surface." By 2008, these projections and predictions, as supported by the demographic data, were still fundamentally correct. Although the fertility rates around the world were declining overall and the rate of population increase was slowing down, the world population had reached 6.0 billion in 1999, and 6. 8 billion by 2009.

Accompanying Urbanization   World population growth has been accompanied by a corresponding increase in urbanization. At first, this occurred very slowly. Despite the urban revolution, ancient cities were relatively small by today's standards. Cities in early Mesopotamia and Egypt had between 5,000 and 20,000 people. Ancient Rome at its zenith had no more than 350,000. Urban areas during the Middle Ages rarely if ever contained more than 50,000 inhabitants. Even as late as 1800, less than five percent of the world's population were living in urban areas.

With the Industrial Revolution, urbanization began to accelerate. In the United States, for instance, the 1790 census showed only five percent of all American living in urban areas. By 1988, however, fully three-fourths of the population lived in areas defined as urban by the U.S. Bureau of the Census. Worldwide, the shift to cities has been much slower. Only twenty-nine percent of the global population lived in urban areas in 1950, forty percent in 1980, and the fifty and sixty percent marks were not expected to be reached until the years 2000 and 2025, respectively (*Popline,* October 1985, pp. 2–3).

The greatest impact of recent urbanization is being felt in less-developed nations. Traditionally rural, in 1980 these countries accounted for 54.8 percent of all urban dwellers worldwide and seventy-five percent of the earth's total human population. According to projections by the United Nations, seventy-seven percent of the world's urban population and eighty-three percent of all people will be living in less-developed nations by the year 2025 (United Nations, 1985).

The most striking trend in world population growth has been the recent and continuing development of **megacities**, those with ten million or more inhabitants (United Nations, 2003). In 1950, only two cities worldwide were in this category—New York and Shanghai. By the year 2000, the number of megacities had increased tenfold with a total of twenty such behemoths that together contained over 288 million people. Most of these cities are in less-developed nations and, without an industrial base to provide adequate jobs, most of their inhabitants live in abject squalor.

According to the Population Institute's predictions of two decades ago (*Popline,* April 1986), this trend would inevitably result in a situation in which:

> millions of rural inhabitants no longer able to earn a living in the farm economy move to cities in quest of a better life. Lacking money for housing, they construct makeshift structures in squatter cities, often on land unsuited for human habitation—such as next to a chemical plant in Bhopal, India, or next to a large petroleum storage facility in Mexico City.
>
> These squatter cities lack such basic amenities as sewage and water systems, electricity, police and fire protection, and, not infrequently, schools. Unremoved and untreated

human excrement is everywhere. In the warm sun, the excrement dries into a fine gray powder which the wind scatters over the entire city. A single squatter city can be home for hundreds of thousands and even millions of human beings.

The employment sought by rural to urban migrants is more often than not, illusory. With too many people chasing too few jobs, unemployment is high and wages are depressed. If they can find a job at all, these new urban dwellers may earn a dollar or less for 8 to 10 hours of heavy labor (p. 4).

This prediction indeed has indeed come true for many megacities and such rapid population growth has placed an almost impossible burden on their support services. To date, several of these cities, particularly those in the less-developed nations, have not been able to develop infrastructure at a pace needed to support an ever-growing population (Table 12-5).

$\mathcal{H}$OW POPULATIONS CHANGE

Human populations at all levels—community, society, and world—are not fixed and stable aggregates but are constantly changing in size, composition, and distribution because of a variety of factors. Chief among these are the variables of fertility, fertility, and migration. We next turn our attention to these factors and how they are measured by demographers.

TABLE 12-5 The World's Megacities (10 Million or More Inhabitants)

RANK	MEGACITY	COUNTRY	PROJECTION (2005)
1	Tokyo	Japan	35,327,000
2	Mexico City	Mexico	19,013,000
3	New York City–Newark	United States	18,498,000
4	Mumbai	India	18,336,000
5	Sao Paulo	Brazil	18,333,000
6	Delhi	India	15,334,000
7	Calcutto	India	14,299,000
8	Buenos Aires	Argentina	13,349,000
9	Jakarta	Indonesia	13,194,000
10	Shanghai	China	12,665,000
11	Dhaka	Bangladesh	12,560,000
12	Los Angeles–Long Beach	United States	12,146,000
13	Karachi	Pakistan	11,819,000
14	Rio de Janeiro	Brazil	11,469,000
15	Osaka–Kobe	Japan	11,286,000
16	Cairo	Egypt	11,146,000
17	Lagos	Nigeria	11,135,000
18	Beijing	China	10,849,000
19	Manila	Philippines	10,677,000
20	Moscow	Russia	10,672,000
21	Paris	France	9,854,000 *

SOURCE: United Nations, World Urbanization Prospects, 2003 Revision.
* Projected to reach ten million inhabitants by 2010.

In addition, we will also consider certain compositional characteristics of populations—such as median age and dependency ratios—that also bear directly on population change and the life chances of people in countries throughout the world.

Fertility

In demographic research, the term **fertility** refers to the number of births that occur in a population as measured by fertility rates. As applied to an individual woman, fertility is the number of children she gives birth to during her childbearing years.

For comparison purposes, demographers sometimes use the concept of **fecundity**, the biological potential for reproduction as applied either to an individual woman or to an entire population. The fecundity for the typical women is twenty to twenty-five offspring. However, because each woman would have to take motherhood seriously from puberty through menopause to have so many children, no society has reached or is anywhere near reaching its potential for reproduction.

However, a few women in some societies have exceeded the typical fecundity level in actual number of offspring. The world's record for documented fertility in an individual woman is sixty-nine. The wife of Feodor Vassilyev, a Russian peasant, in twenty-seven pregnancies between 1725 and 1765, "gave birth to 16 pairs of twins, 7 sets of triplets, and 4 sets of quadruplets" (McWhirter, 1982, p. 28).

Measures of Fertility Demographers measure fertility in several ways. The **crude birth rate (CBR)** (also known as *birth rate*) is the total number of births per one thousand people in a population during a given year. In 2001 the crude birth rate was twenty-eight for the world as a whole, compared to a high of forty-four in Africa and a low of thirteen for European nations on the average. In comparison, the United States had a CBR of 14.2 during the same year (*World Population Data Sheet, 2003*). This measure of fertility is valuable in that it gives demographers on over-all picture of birth characteristics. However, it does not inform them as to the specific characteristics of average families or of the women who are giving birth.

For more precise information demographers also compute fertility rates, total fertility rates, and age specific fertility rates. The **fertility rate (FR)** is the number of births per one thousand women of childbearing age (fifteen to forty-four years) in a country during a given year. This statistic aids demographers in (1) establishing average family size in specific countries and (2) making fertility comparisons between them. The United States in 2000, for example, had a fertility rate of 64.8 compared with FRs over twice as high in some less-developed countries (Current Population Reports, 2001; U.S. Census Bureau, 2001, 2004). The fertility rate affects the **total fertility rate (TFR)**, the total number of offspring a typical woman has during her lifetime in a given country. The United States has a TFR of about two while women in European nations and China average fewer than two children in a lifetime. By contrast, TFRs in African nations often approach or exceed six children per family (Table 12-7). The TFR in turn is affected by the **age specific fertility rate (ASFR)**, the number of births per one thousand women within specific age categories in a country during a given year. By amassing such information—what percentage of women in the age ranges 15–19, 20–24, 25–29, and so on, are giving birth—demographers determine at what ages women in a population are having their first child, their last child, and the largest number of children. In 2003, the average American woman was having her first child in the 25–29 year cohort. This is largely because the average age at first marriage for U.S. males and females was 26.9 and 25.3 years, respectively and most children were being born within marriage. By comparison, the average American woman in 1960 was having her first child in the 20–24 year age cohort, in part because the median age at marriage for U.S. women in that year was 20.3 (U.S. Census Bureau, 2005).

Mortality

Mortality is the number of deaths that occur in a population as measured by mortality rates. With fertility on top, mortality is the lower portion of a basic equation that shapes the characteristics of a population and how it changes.

The Measurement of Mortality Death rates are determined in several ways, the most fundamental of which is through computation of the crude death rate (also known as the *death rate*). The **crude death rate (CDR)** is the number of deaths per one thousand people in a population during a given year. The world's lowest CDRs are found in the countries of North America (eight) and Europe (seven), while the highest occur in African countries (fourteen). Even considering the tremendous suffering from hunger and malnutrition endured by the people of African nations and other less-developed countries, their death rates are still very low compared to their birth rates (*World Population Data Sheet*, 2005), due in large part to medical, health care, and other forms of assistance from the developed world.

As with fertility, demographers employ a variety of statistical techniques to more precisely assess mortality. Different segments of a population—such as those differentiated by age, sex, social class, race, and access to health care—have varying rates of mortality. The **age specific mortality rate (ASMR)**, for instance, measures the total number of deaths per one thousand people in a country within specific age categories during a given year. By computing this statistic, demographers are able to ascertain, among other things, the life expectancy of people in various age categories, such as those in the age groups of 20–24, 40–44, 60–64, and so on.

Infant mortality is also an important indicator. The **infant mortality rate (IMR)** is the total number of deaths per one thousand children under twelve months of age in a population within a given year. Because children are most vulnerable to disease during their first year of life, *infant mortality is the most sensitive indicator of death probabilities* in specific populations. In other words, infant mortality is a good predictor of **life expectancy**, the number of years a person in a specific country of a certain age can be expected to live.

This is clearly evident when one compares infant mortality rates between developed and less-developed nations. In countries like Japan and Sweden with infant mortality rates of 3.3 and 3.0, respectively, the life expectancy at birth is over 80 years. The United States, with an infant mortality rate of 6.6, has an average life expectancy of 77.6 years at birth (*World Population Data Sheet*, 2005). Contrast that with the relationship between infant mortality and life expectancy in less-developed countries. In Somalia, 118.5 children out of each 1,000 die before their first birthday, and the average life expectancy is 46.2 years. Afghanistan has an IMR of 165.9 (life expectancy 45.9 years), and Angola 182.3 (life expectancy 37.9 years) (Table 12-6).

Migration

Migration, a factor more difficult to explain and precisely measure than births and deaths, also affects population change. **Migration** refers to the movement of people from one geographical location to another for the purpose of establishing residence. In countries throughout the world, there is a constant shifting of populations internationally. Some people engage in *emigration* by leaving one country to seek settlement in another. Others at the end of their journey have participated in *immigration* by coming into a new country from another to establish residence.

TABLE 12-6	Countries with the Lowest and Highest Infant Mortality Rates (2004): A Comparison with Life Expectancies

THE TEN COUNTRIES WITH THE LOWEST INFANT MORTALITY RATES

	COUNTRY	INFANT MORTALITY RATE (DEATHS PER 1000 BORN)	LIFE EXPECTANCY (IN YEARS)
1	Singapore	2.28	81.5
2	Sweden	2.97	80.3
3	Japan	3.28	81.0
4	Iceland	3.31	80.2
5	Finland	3.59	77.4
6	Norway	3.73	79.3
7	Malta	3.94	77.9
8	Czech Republic	3.97	74.5
9	Andorra	4.05	83.5
10	Germany	4.20	77.1

THE TEN COUNTRIES WITH THE HIGHEST INFANT MORTALITY RATES

	COUNTRY	INFANT MORTALITY RATE (DEATHS PER 1000 BORN)	LIFE EXPECTANCY (IN YEARS)
1	Angola*	182.31	37.9
2	Afghanistan	165.96	38.3
3	Sierre Leon	145.24	45.3
4	Mozambique	137.08	37.5
5	Liberia	130.51	51.0
6	Niger	122.66	41.3
7	Somalia	118.52	46.2
8	Mali	117.99	46.7
9	Tijikistan	112.10	64.1
10	Guinea-Bissou	108.72	49.0

SOURCES: Geography.About.com; *CIA World Fact Book,* 2005; U.S Census Bureau, 2004.
* Information on Angola updated to 2008, *CIA World Fact Book,* 2008.

Types of Migration Demographers distinguish between two general forms of migration—international migration and internal migration. **International migration** involves movement of people from one country to another for the purpose of settlement. During a 150-year span between 1820 and 1970, forty-six million immigrants came to the United States mostly from Europe, but also from Asia and Latin America (Thomlinson, 1976). Some came to escape poverty and oppression, some to seek a better life in the spirit of adventure, and some for both reasons. More recently, significant rates of emigration have occurred in East Germany with the fall of the Berlin Wall and the reunification of Germany and in other areas of the world including Korea, Vietnam, Serbia, Rwanda, Bangladesh, Iran, and Mexico.

Internal migration involves movement of people from one place to another within a country. In the United States, for example, there have been significant internal migrations from East to West (1700–1900), South to North (1870–1940), and urban to suburban (1950 to the present). In addition, there has been some shift in U.S. population (and big business) since the 1970s away from the cold and heavily populated Northeast to the southwestern region of the county, commonly known as the Sunbelt.

Why Migration Occurs Shifts in population can be explained largely in terms of push and pull factors. *Push factors* are those which force people to leave their homes and communities because of conditions beyond their control. Thousands of Irish left their country during the 1840s because of the threat of starvation brought on by a potato blight that destroyed their crops. *Pull factors* are those which draw people to another geographical location because of the promise of a better life. In 1848, the discovery of gold by James Marshall near Sutter's Fort in California sparked a gold fever that drew eighty thousand "forty-niners" to that state the next year to seek their fortunes (Blum, et al., 1973).

William Peterson (1975) has identified several broad categories of migration that allow us to place push and pull factors in perspective. Push factors are chiefly responsible for what he terms primitive migration and impelled migration. *Primitive migration* occurs when people cannot control their natural environment. Those in hunting-gathering societies, for instance, are pushed to move on in search of food and water; those in horticultural societies may be forced to migrate in response to drought, famine, and other factors. Impelled migration typically results when people are forced to leave their homeland as a result of political pressure. The exodus of the Jews from Nazi Germany during the 1930s and 1940s provides one example. Pull factors are more prevalent with *free migration,* in which people freely decide to migrate to another location for their own personal reasons. Both push and pull factors may be involved with *group migration,* in which those who share common cultural bonds migrate together to retain their group or cultural identify. Several religious groups, including the Puritans (seventeenth century) and the Hutterites came to what is now the United States, both to escape religious persecution and to preserve their way of life.

Population Growth: The Bathtub Analogy

Taken together, the factors of fertility, mortality, and migration largely determine the size of human populations. To measure their relationship to each other, demographers compile and compare the annual growth rate of societies throughout the world. The **growth rate** is the annual percentage of growth or loss in a population. It is measured by adding the net difference between immigration and emigration per one thousand people in a particular population.

Positive Growth Rates   Most countries experience a positive growth rate. The rate of net annual growth, in turn, impacts on the amount of time it takes for a country to double its population. The developed countries of the world average annual growth rates of less than one percent per year. This translates into population doubling times of 70–100 years resulting in political, economic, and social stability. By comparison, several Asian and African counties have very high growth rates. Afghanistan, for instance, had an annual growth rate in 2006 of 4.5 percent which meant a doubling time of only 14.5 years (Rosenberg, 2006). If such a rate of growth is not reversed soon, Afghanistan, home to the Taliban and Al Qaeda, will become a failed state.

High growth rates have serious implications for other less-developed countries as well in which they are most prevalent. Many of these countries—Tanzania, Iran, Nigeria, Zaire, Pakistan, and the Philippines, for example—have exploding populations with doubling times that average twenty-five or fewer years. Population Biologist Paul Ehrlich has commented as follows:

> Think what it means for the population of a country to double in twenty-five years. In order to keep living standards at the present level, the food available to the people must be doubled. Every structure and road must be duplicated. The amounts of power must be duplicated. The capacity of the transport system must be doubled. The number of trained doctors, nurses, teachers, and administrators must be doubled. This would be a fantastically difficult job in the United States—a rich country with a fine agricultural system, immense industries, and rich natural resources. This of what this means to a country with none of these.
>
> Remember also that in all UDCs [underdeveloped countries], people have gotten the word about the better life it is possible to have. . . . They have what we like to call "rising expectations." If twice as many people are going to be happy, the miracle of doubling what they now have will not be enough. It will only maintain today's standard of living. There will have to be a tripling or better. Needless to say, they are not going to be happy (Ehrlich, 1970, pp. 22–23).

Negative Growth Rates   Some countries, however, have negative growth rates and a very different population problem, that of too few rather than too many people. These countries—including Hungary, Germany, Russia, and Romania—are beginning to experience shortages of both industrial and agricultural workers needed to maintain and expand their economies. Countries such as Germany and the Czech Republic, for example, have a zero percent growth rate, which means they must import workers to sustain economic viability (Rosenburg, 2006). Nonetheless, countries with under-population problems tend to be the exception today rather than the rule.

The Bathtub Analogy   To make sense of fertility, mortality, and migration in terms of their influence on population change, the bathtub analogy is useful. Imagine for a moment that a society is like a bathtub. They are both containers of a sort. One holds water and the other contains people. In addition, both have faucets and drains, or inputs and outputs. The bathtub has two faucets (or inputs), one each for the hot water and cold water. Society, like a bathtub, also has two faucets, one for fertility (the primary input) and one for immigration (the secondary input). Likewise, a bathtub and society both have drains, although the bathtub typically has only one, as compared to the two possessed by a society. A society's two drains are mortality (the primary output) and emigration (the secondary output).

From this brief analogy, it is relatively easy to understand the impact that fertility, mortality, and migration have on the changing size of a population. If more water goes into a bathtub than exits through the drain, the water level rises. If this condition persists long enough, the bathtub will overflow, and someone must deal with the excess water. A similar situation occurs within a society in terms of population. If more people enter a society through fertility and immigration (the two faucets) than exit through mortality and emigration (the two drains), the society as a container will overflow and will not be able to feed and care for the added people. If many societies have such an overflow and it persists—like so many overflowing bathtubs sitting in a giant swimming pool—the world itself, being a finite container like a swimming pool, is faced with a potential overflow as well.

The Composition of Populations: Age, Sex, and Population Pyramids

In addition to accounting for changes in population size, demographers also study the effects of various compositional factors on population change. In this sense, demographers are interested in how populations are composed and distributed according to such factors as age, sex, rural or urban residence, race and ethnicity, education, income, marital status, occupation, religion, national origin, and others. Of these, the composition of populations by age and sex are particularly important. This is because these two factors, taken together, largely determine the relative percentages of people who are economically productive in a given population.

Age Composition   The composition of a society in regard to the ages of most of its members plays an important role in terms of how it is structured as a social system. A population consisting mostly of children and/or the elderly has fewer options in social organization than one with smaller proportions of people in these age categories. Many less-developed countries have disproportionately large numbers of children and/or the elderly. Consequently, they cannot be as economically productive and flexible, in most cases, as developed nations. Indeed, such countries are placed under significant stress because of their age composition and, in many instances, may find it difficult to impossible to modernize as a result. Industrial and postindustrial economies require an adult labor force that is educated and technically trained. Yet many less-developed nations are so burdened with the costs of just maintaining their populations that comprehensive mass education is only a dream.

One method used to measure age composition is the calculation of the **dependency ratio**. This is the number of people in a population under 15 and over 65 years of age divided by the number of people between 15 and 65. For example, a country with a dependency ratio of 100 (100:100) has one dependent person for each productive person.

These ratios vary significantly between less-developed countries and modern nations. Dependency ratios for less-developed countries include Uganda (111), Yemen (103), Somalia (102) and Angola (100). These countries, therefore, have about one dependent person (or more) for every economically productive one. By comparison, developed nations like the United States (51), Italy (49), Japan (49), and China (43) have roughly one dependent person (or fewer) for every two economically productive ones (World Health Organization, 2003). The consequences in terms of both actual and potential economic productivity are obvious (Table 12-7).

TABLE 12-7	Dependency Ratios (per 100 Population) Selected Countries: 2003		
COUNTRIES WITH HIGH DEPENDENCY	**RATIO (PER 100)**	**COUNTRIES WITH LOW DEPENDENCY**	**RATIO (PER 100)**
Uganda	111	Denmark	51
Niger	109	United States	51
Mali	107	Cyprus	50
Burkina Faso	106	Finland	49
Yemen	103	Greece	49
Somalia	102	Italy	49
Guinea-Bissau	101	Japan	49
Angola	100	Germany	48
Malawi	100	Austria	47
Chad	100	Thailand	46
Zambia	99	Spain	45
Congo, Democratic Republic of the	98	China	43

SOURCES: World Health Organization, 2003. Accessed at Nationmaster.com on July 15, 2008. Health Statistics: Dependency Ratio per 100 Population. *http://www.nationmaster.com/graph/hea_dep_rat_per_100-health-dependency-ratio-per-100*

Median Age   The chief factor that affects the dependency ratio is **median age**, the mid-point or 50th percentile in the age distribution of a population. It is a type of average age at which one-half the population is older and one-half is younger. The median age has a profound impact on a variety of structural conditions in a society including per capita income and overall standard of living. Many less-developed countries cannot effectively industrialize because half or more of their people are under eighteen years. You must have most of the population in a given country as technically trained adults in the labor force in order to support a modern cash economy and generate the surpluses required in terms of tax revenues to build the schools, factories, and so on needed for a modern industrial or postindustrial state. Therefore, high fertility rates combined with low mortality rates result in low median ages and low per capita incomes (Table 12-8).

One additional age factor of particular concern to demographers is **momentum**, increases in a population that continue long after birth and death rates have been stabilized. The two-decade period after World War II (1946–1964) has been called the "baby boom" era in the United States. Fertility rates rose with social and economic prosperity. During this period, the average family had about 3.3 children. In the late 1960s, however, fertility rates began to drop, and from the middle 1970s until the present, the average American family included only 2 children. In fact, American families today have an average of about 2.0 children each, which is slightly below the replacement level of 2.1 (because some children die before adulthood).

TABLE 12-8	The Ten Richest Countries and Poorest Countries in Standard of Living: A Comparison using Selected Demographic Characteristics in 2002

THE TEN WEALTHIEST COUNTRIES IN PER CAPITA GROSS NATIONAL PRODUCT (GNP) (U.S.$)

RICHEST COUNTRIES IN RANK ORDER	PER CAPITA GNP	BIRTH RATE	DEATH RATE	% OF POPULATION UNDER 15	TOTAL FERTILITY RATE	LIFE EX-PECTANCY
1 Luxemburg	$55,100	12.3	8.9	18.9	1.6	78.0
2 Norway	$37,800	12.6	9.8	20.0	1.8	78.7
3 United States	$37,800	14.2	8.7	21.1	2.0	77.1
4 San Marino	$34,600	10.8	7.7	15.9	1.3	80.8
5 Switzerland	$32,700	10.1	8.8	17.0	1.4	80.2
6 Denmark	$31,100	12.0	10.9	18.6	1.7	77.1
7 Iceland	$30,900	14.6	6.9	23.2	1.3	80.0
8 Austria	$30,000	9.7	9.8	16.6	1.3	78.8
9 Canada	$29,800	11.2	7.5	19.0	1.6	78.8
10 Ireland	$29,600	14.6	8.1	21.6	2.0	76.6

THE TEN POOREST COUNTRIES IN TERMS OF PER CAPITA GNP (U.S.$)

POOREST COUNTRIES IN RANK ORDER	PER CAPITA GNP	BIRTH RATE	DEATH RATE	% OF POPULATION UNDER 15	TOTAL FERTILITY RATE	LIFE EX-PECTANCY
1 East Timor	$500	41.4	17.1	43.0	3.8	57.5
2 Somalia	$500	47.2	18.2	44.5	7.1	46.6
3 Sierra Leon	$500	45.1	19.2	44.7	6.1	45.7
4 Tanzania	$600	39.7	13.0	44.8	5.3	44.8
5 Burundi	$600	40.0	16.4	46.8	6.0	43.2
6 Congo, Republic	$700	46.0	15.2	48.2	6.8	48.7
7 Ethiopia	$700	44.7	17.8	47.2	5.7	42.5
8 Afghanistan	$700	41.4	17.7	42.2	5.7	46.6
9 Zambia	$800	41.5	22.0	47.4	5.4	35.3
10 Nigeria	$900	39.7	13.9	43.7	5.5	51.5

SOURCES: *CIA World Fact Book,* July 1, 2002; *Encyclopedia Britannica Almanac,* 2005.
NOTE: Statistics may vary slightly from table to table based on year, sources, and lag time in numbers quoted.

While this is encouraging, benefits in terms of a stabilized population have been delayed as a result of the lag effect produced by momentum. Although the typical American woman today is having fewer children, there are more women having children because of the larger pool of "mothers" created during the baby boom years. Thus, it takes several decades of sustained low fertility combined with other factors to produce a low- to no-growth population. When we consider the combined long-term effects of low age and high fertility in countries like Kenya, where the average women in 1988 was having eight children, we can understand why demographers are concerned.

Some Third World countries, however, have made significant progress toward attaining *a zero population growth rate* of 2.1 children per family (Rosenberg, 2006). Kenya, previously mentioned, offers one example. Although it has a long way to go, this country has reduced its TFR of 8.1 children per family in 1970 to 5.9 in 1990 and 5.0 in 2006. This has reduced Kenya's annual growth rate from 3.7 percent during 1970–1990 to 2.8 percent from 1990 through 2006. However, other countries in the Third World like Somalia (TFR of 7.1) and the Democratic Republic of the Congo (TFR of 6.8) remain problematic (UNICEF, 2008).

Sex Composition   The sex characteristics of a society are measured by the **sex ratio**, the number of males to every 100 females in a designated population. Males initially outnumber females by significant numbers. Because females are apparently more biologically hardy, however, higher mortality rates inevitably result in a shortage of males. At conception, there are 124 males to 100 females which, through higher rates of male fetal miscarriage, drops to 105 by birth. Until about the age of 15, there generally are more males than females. But, by that time, continuing male attrition begins to result in a surplus of females. This trend continues throughout the life cycle so that by the time people reach the 70–74 (years) age cohort, males are found in significantly fewer numbers than females. By the year 2100, when all age categories are considered, it is estimated that there will be 175 million more females in the world than males (*Popline*, July 1985).

Population Pyramids   Demographers often show the age and sex characteristics of populations as population pyramids. A **population pyramid** is a summary of age and sex compositions in a population portrayed in a graph or chart. As shown in Figure 12-1, those of less-developed countries like Kenya and Mexico look just like the name implies, an elongated pyramid. The broad base reflects high fertility rates and an overabundance of children and those under twenty years of age. The pointed top reflects the lower life expectancy in these countries and the very small number of both males and females over seventy years of age. Contrast this to population pyramids of more-developed nations like the United

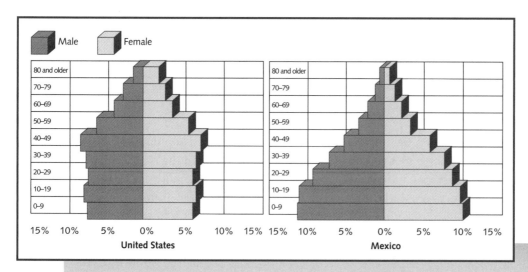

Figure 12-1

As shown in the examples above, the population pyramids in less-developed countries appear as a cone or pyramid that reflects high fertility rates and few people in older age categories. By contrast, population pyramids in advanced societies look more like a cylinder with a more evenly distributed population.

States and Sweden in which the graph, reflecting a more stable and evenly distributed population, appears more like a column.

THE POPULATION DILEMMA

As evidenced from the preceding discussion, the world has a problem and the problem is "us"—too many of us. The "whats" of the population dilemma are obvious to anyone who takes a rational and objective look at the major demographic and social indicators both past and present. They include exponential population growth, finite space and resources with which to support these growing numbers, and, ultimately, a dismal future for much if not all of humanity unless present trends are halted and reversed within the next few decades. The broad *"whys," implications,* and *solutions* to this problem are also relatively easy to understand. However, many of the specifics related to these concerns have themselves become controversial issues and "political footballs" that are fiercely debated by those in both the scientific community and several other segments of society. We now turn our attention to these and related topics.

The Whys of the Population Explosion

The recent and unprecedented explosion of population in the less-developed countries may be attributed to three general factors: mortality intervention, pronatalism, and inadequate contraception.

Mortality Intervention   Eric Breindel and Nick Eberstadt (1980, p. 42) in commenting on the population crisis emerging in less-developed nations during the 1980s, stated bluntly that the rapid growth in these countries has occurred "not because their people have suddenly started breeding like rabbits but because they have finally stopped dying like flies." Most of this growth has occurred since the end of World War II and is due primarily to **mortality intervention**, the provision of medical assistance and health technology and assistance to less-developed countries by developed nations. A small amount of this life-giving technology and aid have been acquired by the less-fortunate countries themselves through the natural process of diffusion. Increased technology and aid also have been furnished by religious and humanitarian organizations. However, the largest source of mortality intervention has come from the governments of modern, developed nations. The United States, for example, has furnished many billions of dollars in foreign aid to less-developed countries since 1945, much of it earmarked for medical and health services and supplies. The effect has been to contribute to the lowering of mortality rates and to the increasing of population growth rates in places like Latin America, Asia, Africa, and Oceania that today account for two-thirds of the world's inhabitants.

Pronatalism   Corresponding efforts and gains have not been made in terms of also reducing fertility rates in these countries to replacement or near replacement levels. It is one thing—and a noble thing at that—to save the life of a sick and starving baby through medical and caloric intervention. The child's relatives and neighbors often appreciate this "gift of life" for years to come. However, it is quite another thing to tell people that having too many children contributes to their economic woes. To suggest this is—from their perspective—to attack their most cherished values, religious beliefs, cultural traditions, and even their concepts of masculinity and femininity.

Many tradition-based societies still embrace **pronatalism**, a cultural orientation that strongly encourages childbearing. Historically, many of the world's religions have taught their followers that procreation is a near-sacred gift from the heavens and/or a moral duty. Having large numbers of offspring has been regarded as a sign of fertility (femininity) in women as well as an indicator of sexual potency (masculinity) in men. Children have been necessary to carry on the family name and gene pool and to inherit family property. In agricultural societies, children have participated directly in the economy and have contributed to their families' well-being. Given the prevalence of these norms and values throughout much of the world, many people in many societies today simply do not want to limit their offspring. Others want to have fewer children but lack the education and resources to know how.

Lack of Contraception   While mortality rates in less-developed countries sometimes approach the fertility rates of some advanced nations, their fertility rates are much higher which contributes to exploding populations. Crude birth rates (CBRs) in less-developed countries are three times higher on average than those in developed countries; the Democratic Republic of the Congo's CBR, at 48.2 per 1,000 (2003) is nearly four times as high (Table 12-8). These disparities are caused in large part by the difference between less-developed countries and technological nations in levels of contraception use. As a result of such factors as pronatalist norms and policies, the lack of education, and the low availability of contraceptives, birth control in less-developed countries historically has lagged behind modern nations.

Recent developments, however, have been somewhat encouraging for much of the less-developed world in that contraceptive use now approaches that of modern nations.

Due to such factors as mortality intervention, an ethic of pronatalism, and a lack of contraception, countries such as Somalia and the Republic of the Congo have exploding populations in which the average woman has about seven children.

About seventy percent of women in developed countries today use contraceptives ranging from sterilization, oral contraceptives, and intrauterine devices through a host of others including the use of condoms. Of the 700 million married women now in Asia, sixty six percent now use contraception. In Latin America and the Caribbean, sixty-nine percent of the eighty-four million women there are also using contraceptive technology. Among the poorest nations in the world in Africa, however, contraceptive usage among married women is only twenty-five percent (*UN Chronicle*, 2002).

The most serious contraceptive problem facing much of the less-developed world today has to do with distribution. According to projections by the United Nations, the number of women reaching childbearing age, using the year 2000 as a benchmark, will increase by 1.6 billion by 2015. The production capacity to meet this demand is more than adequate. The problem is in (1) distribution capability to reach the isolated villages of the much of the less-developed world along with (2) the necessary funds to purchase contraceptive supplies and (3) the infrastructure needed to deliver it to those who need it. In the year 2000, such supplies cost an estimated $810 million. By 2015, the costs will have increased to $1.8 billion. Yet donations needed to meet an anticipated shortfall in funds required have stagnated in recent years (Tarmann, 2001).

Implications for Human Ecology

There is a tendency for many of us to see our natural environment—the sunshine, forests, water, fossil fuels, and so forth—as part of the unlimited bounty of nature. For Americans, food must also be included in this equation. As a nation, Americans throw away and feed to their pets more food each year than some countries have to feed their people. However, we humans do not live in a vacuum. Our behavior not only impacts other people and societies but the fragile ecosystem called Earth as well.

What Is Human Ecology?   **Human ecology** is the scientific study of the relationship between human populations and their natural environment. Specifically, human ecologists are concerned with how social and cultural systems are organized within human populations to maintain harmony with the physical environment.

Population biologist Paul Ehrlich (1971) and other ecologists have warned that the accelerating growth of the world's population threatens to upset the ecological balance and pose serious potential problems related to long-term survival. As he has said:

> [M]an is not only running out of food, he is also destroying the life support systems of the Spaceship Earth. The situation was recently summarized very succinctly: "It is the top of the ninth inning. Man, always a threat at the plate, has been hitting nature hard. It is important to remember, however, that NATURE BATS LAST (p. 364).

Could it be that Ehrlich and others of like mind are alarmists who have greatly and pessimistically overstated a serious but nonthreatening problem? Many pronatalists think so. Their numbers include high-level clergy in the Catholic, Morman, and Islamic faiths, some on the pro-life side of the abortion issue, a few from the academic and scientific communities, some government officials, and many well-intentioned citizens. They feel that, like the boy in the folktale who cried "wolf" to play a joke on the woodcutter, ecologists are grossly exaggerating the so-called "overpopulation crisis" and "ecological imbalance."

While Ehrlich and those of like mind may have been a bit premature at times with some of their projected timetables, their basic findings are inescapable. Trained scientists who examine this issue comprehensively and objectively can hardly arrive at a different set of conclusions. If current trends of overpopulation and resource depletion—fresh water, oil and gas, and so on—are not stopped or dramatically reduced soon, an ecological crisis of grave proportion could face coming generations. Indeed, some scientists argue that the first stages—in such forms as food shortages, global warming, and international terrorism—are already well upon us.

Food   Despite the promise of a "green revolution" that would yield a much larger amount of grain from an acre of farmland, food production is not keeping pace with demand. During the 1980s and 1990s, this was partly due to temporary problems of internal political strife, poor crop yields due to drought, and distribution difficulties. However, many less-developed countries may be losing the struggle for adequate food resources. The United Nations has estimated that 2,300 calories of food per day are necessary to sustain the average person under normal conditions. However, almost two-thirds of the world's people—3.8 billion—live in 64 low-income, calorie deficit countries. United Nations projections show that, of these food insecure countries, 37 are in crisis requiring external food assistance. They include 21 countries in Africa (e.g., Chad, Somalia, Uganda), 10 in Asia (e.g., Afghanistan, China, Nepal), and 5 in Latin America (e.g., Bolivia, Ecuador, Nicaragua) (Food and Agriculture Organization, U.N., 2008).

Despite the shortfall in available food for the less-developed world, the largest and most developed countries—China, India, the EU, and the United States—are presently diverting large portions of their crop yield in grains toward the production of biofuels. While this may help to slow a potential world fuel crisis—driven mainly by population pressures and increasing industrialization—it, in effect, acts to take food out of the mouths of the world's poor to put into the gas tanks of the affluent, mainly those in developed countries. According to research by the World Bank, the global increase in corn (maize) production rose during 2004–2007 by about 51 million tons. During that same three-year period, consumption of biofuels (mostly ethanol) in just one developed country, the United States, increased by essentially the same amount (50 tons). The result: Almost the entire increase in cereal grains during 2004–2007 needed desperately to feed the poor in calorie deficit nations worldwide went to subsidize America's passion for fuel inefficient muscle cars, pickup trucks, and sports utility vehicles. In the next few years, the United States' consumption of corn-based ethanol is projected to require 114 tons of grain. This represents over double the amount of diverted grain resources needed to cover present food import needs of all low-income, food-deficit nations listed by the U.N.'s Food and Agriculture Organization (FAO). With global grain stockpiles now at the lowest levels in 25 years and the global population expected to reach 9 billion by 2050, the potential for future worldwide mass starvation is a growing possibility (Lynas, 2008).

Land Resources   One example of land resource depletion is the permanent destruction of the world's rain forests. These delicate ecosystems—located in tropical regions of Central and South America, Africa, and Asia—took 60 million years to develop. They play host to about one-half of all lower life forms on the planet with about 5 million species of insects, animals, and plants. Yet on a global level, these rainforests are being destroyed at the rate

© FRONTPAGE, 2009. USE UNDER LICENSE FROM SHUTTERSTOCK, INC.

This wasteland in Brazil was once a lush tropical forest a short time ago. Once the land has been "harvested" of mature hardwoods this way, there are no longer tree roots to hold the nutrients in the soil. The result is that tropical rains quickly wash the topsoil away. This leaves a permanent, irreversible tropical desert of mud where little will grow.

of about 50,000 acres per day. According to estimates by the World Wildlife Fund and the United Nations, that is 25–50 acres that are cut down or burned every minute and 50 million acres that are permanently lost each year. Harvard biologist E. O. Wilson has called this depletion of the world's rainforests as "the greatest extinction since the end of the age of dinosaurs" (Thinkquest, 2008). Worldwide, this amounts to the land resources of a country the size of Nepal disappearing each year (Peopleandplanet.net, May 8, 2008). Brazil perhaps offers the best example. Every year, Brazilian rainforests equal in size to the state of Connecticut are cut down. The Amazon Basin contains 1.5 million square miles of rain forests, an area the size of India that alone contains 40 percent of the world's supply. Tragically, about one-fifth of these forest lands have already been destroyed (Chang, 2007).

This alone results in a variety of unintended ecological consequences. Caused in large part by the press of the planet's growing population, much of the world's rain forest lands are being transformed into permanent tropical deserts and biodiversity is being reduced as hundreds of thousands of species become extinct. Depleting the forests of hardwoods, such as teak and mahogany for American and European markets, is one form of the destruction. Another is the razing of forests to provide pasture land for cattle, which are raised to provide the world's affluent populations with a cheap and plentiful supply of beef. The cattle completely denude the land within six to eight years and then are moved to other land to start the cycle over again. Soil nutrients, which lie near the surface, are soon washed away as tropical rains erode the soil because there are now no tree roots to hold the soil. The result is an irreversible tropical desert of mud where little will grow (*Popline*, September, 1987; Thinkquest, 2008.)

Energy As countries industrialize and populations worldwide become larger, the demand for energy rises rapidly. The most technologically developed areas—including the United States, Japan, and Western Europe—consume about 55 percent of the planet's energy yet comprise only 16 percent of the world's population. As populations worldwide continue to increase along with "rising expectations" concerning desired lifestyle and affluence, such levels of energy consumption will, of necessity, need to level off.

Yet developed countries in general and the United States especially continue to consume the planet's natural resources and energy at a relentless and growing pace. As a case in point, the United States contains only about 4.7 percent of the world's population. Yet Americans consume 25 percent of the globe's natural resources and produce at least an equal percentage of the planet's waste products. Compared to India, for example, Americans consume

> 50 times more steel, 56 times more energy, 170 times more synthetic rubber, 250 times more motor fuel, and 300 times more plastic. . . . Each American consumes as much grain as five Kenyans, and as much energy as 35 Indians, 150 Banglabeshis (a whole village) or five Ethiopians (Tufts Climate Initiative, 2005, p. 72).

Viewed from a global perspective, for the typical American to consume 250 times more fuel than the typical Indian and others in the developing world is dangerously reckless and irresponsible. Until 2008, when gasoline prices suddenly increased by one-third to $4 or more per gallon in six months, many to most Americans appeared blissfully ignorant of the fragility of the world's limited and rapidly depleting stores of petrochemicals

Pollution, the Greenhouse Effect, and Global Warming   The press of human numbers is also creating problems of land, water, and air degradation and pollution. For example, as the world's tropical rain forests are depleted in places like Asia and South America to infuse their countries with cash to feed their people and develop their countries, there are global ecological consequences. The rain forests are carbon reservoirs that worldwide contain about 830 billion tons of carbon. While trees are living, they take in and store carbon dioxide from the atmosphere. When they are cut down and processed, this carbon is released into the atmosphere. Carbon emissions from rainforest depletion account for about twenty-five percent of all carbon emissions generated by human activity that are released into the atmosphere each year (Peopleandplanet.com, May 8, 2008).

The primary sources for pollution, however, come from developed and developing nations. The United States alone, with less than five percent of the world's population, produces about twenty-five percent of CO_2 emissions, primarily from the burning of fossil fuels (*CIA World Fact Book*, 2008). China is second in CO_2 emissions and, by 2020, will most likely overtake the United States. Both China and India, with their huge coal reserves, have plans to burn enormous amounts of this carbon source for the energy they will need to run their growing industrial economies during the twenty-first century as they come to compete head to head with the United States (Lynas, 2005).

The dumping of five billion metric tons or more of carbon emissions and other pollutants—from the burning of fossil fuels and wood—into the atmosphere each year is producing adverse effects on the planet's ecosystem. One consequence is the **greenhouse effect**, increasing cloud cover caused by pollution that retains the warmth of the sun and produces higher ground temperatures. The ultimate result for the planet and its inhabitants is **global warming**, an unprecedented recent rise in greenhouse gas emissions and the Earth's temperatures caused largely by human intervention (Harvey, 2008). As the effects of global warming are felt, the impact on the planet includes melting of the polar ice including glaciers, rising sea levels that ultimately will displace millions of coastal residents worldwide, and changing precipitation patterns.

Far from being a myth, as some noisy and ill-informed critics have charged, global warming is very real. In 2007, the Intergovernmental Panel of Climate Change (IPCC)—the world's largest organization of climate scientists—announced that global warming was at least a ninety percent certainty and that human intervention was largely responsible (Harvey, 2008). The evidence is clear. Throughout the world, glaciers are melting at a disturbing rate. During the twentieth century, Mount Kilimanjaro in Africa lost over three-quarters of its ice cap. The Alps in Europe lost over fifty percent of its glacier ice during the same time frame. And in the United States, "the original 150 glaciers within Glacier National Park are now down to a mere fifty" (Lynas, 2005, p. 3)

TURNING THINGS AROUND: SOLUTIONS AND PROSPECTS

Despite the threats of overpopulation and ecological imbalance, many demographers and other scientists view the future with guarded optimism. The rate of the world population increase is beginning to decline. Government leaders of many countries have realized the gravity of the problem and have taken the first steps to address it directly. And some countries with historical problems of overpopulation, such as Japan and China, have already turned things around.

Because of a massive population control program established by the Chinese government during the 1980s, the average Chinese family today only has 1.5 children.

China: A Case Study in Population Control

China, currently the most populous country in the world with 1.3 billion people, has made tremendous strides in bringing its population growth under control. Traditionally a poor, agricultural society with a rapidly growing population, China experienced a sustained drought during the late 1950s. The resulting shortfall of food created the worst famine in history in which thirty million people died from starvation and malnutrition (*Population Today*, 1985). In response to this and related economic problems brought about by overpopulation, China instituted a two-child per family policy during the 1970s and passed laws mandating that couples could not marry until their late twenties (Whyte and Parrish, 1984).

Although birth rates declined significantly, government officials soon realized that, because of the momentum created by China's baby boom in the 1950s and 1960s, the population still would not stabilize for many decades. Therefore, in 1980 China adopted a constitution which, among other things, mandated a one-child-per-family rule.

Intent on limiting growth to 1.2 billion people by the year 2000, the government instituted a set of policies that might seem harsh by American standards. Couples who had only one child were rewarded with various incentives, including periodic cash bonuses, free contraceptives, jobs and job security, and priority schooling for their child. Those who had a second child were fined heavily, had their wages frozen, were denied grain allotments and pension benefits, and experienced tremendous ostracism from the community. After a couple had their first and only child, they were strongly encouraged to undergo sterilization. Women who again became pregnant were urged to have an abortion (Beck, et al., 1984; Jian, Tuan, and Jing-Yuan, 1985). In 1984, the government instituted a "1.5 child" policy. If the first child was a girl, a couple was allowed the birth of a second child. This more relaxed variation of the one child policy has remained up to the present. This has resulted in a total fertility rate in China of 1.47 offspring as of 2007 (Zeng, 2007). With an annual growth rate of under one percent and a continuing low fertility rate, China has stabilized its population.

Today, China is poised to experience the most dramatic transformation in economic fortunes the world has ever seen. Today, it has the world's largest human population at 1.3 billion, has experienced a tumultuous history, and remains under communist rule. Nonetheless, its economy has grown at the unprecedented rate of ten percent per year since the mid-1980s. To accomplish this, its economic output has had to double every seven and one-half years. Consequently, China's economy now ranks fourth in the world—behind the United States, Japan, and Germany—and it projected to attain the number two position by 2020 (Jin, 2007).

Needed Solutions for Population Stability

Turning the population crisis around is not only possible but probable, provided enough people with enough commitment engage in enough effort in enough time. To accomplish this, the following general solutions must be implemented.

A No-Growth Cultural Orientation

To reach a stable population, societies worldwide will have to adopt a "no-growth" cultural orientation toward fertility. This will necessitate an abandonment of the pronatalist traditions of the past in favor of a two-child per family value orientation. This cultural orientation, reinforced with legislation, was accomplished by Japan in the 1950s and China in the 1980s. The two-child cultural orientation remains dominant in most developed countries today as reflected in their fertility rates, which remain at or below replacement levels. The overpopulation issue aside, most people in these countries have learned that by maintaining small families of one or two children, they are better off not only economically, but in quality of life as well. Given current rates of world population growth plus the demographic factor of momentum, the less-developed world has perhaps only twenty years to learn the same lesson or we all will suffer the consequences.

Family Planning

To reach no-growth levels of fertility worldwide will require massive and comprehensive family planning programs. However, providing only the funds or the technology of birth control alone will not be sufficient. Much more effort will need to go into teaching people in less-developed countries about the need for a no-growth value orientation along with instruction at the grass-roots, village, and family level in how to use birth control devices effectively. Families with pronatalist views in several countries will not even think about using birth control until they already have four, five, or six children and desperate circumstances drive them to it. That mindset must change and change fairly soon before significant improvements can be made in their life chances.

Ethiopia, for example, provides a frustrating case in point. During the 1980s in that country, drought, famine, and an unstable political situation combined to cause many thousands of deaths from starvation, malnutrition, and disease. Massive humanitarian efforts were employed by governments, religious groups, and even entertainers who together raised millions of dollars for aid and tens of thousands were saved from starvation. However, if family planning program had been instituted there in 1970 with the modest goal of convincing thirty-five percent of the people to use contraception by the early 1980s, conditions by the time of the drought and famine would have been very different. Ethiopia's population would have been 1.7 million fewer, and much if not the large majority of the suffering and starvation could have been averted (*Popline*, 1985).

Unfortunately, not much has changed over the past quarter century there. In May of 2008, another drought placed up to six million Ethiopian children at risk of malnutrition and severe acute malnutrition threatened 126,000 children with death by starvation (Rice, 2008). Yet Ethiopia continues to have problems feeding its people today, in large part because only eight percent of the population practices birth control (USAID: Ethiopia, 2008). With a population that has more than doubled from 33.5 million in 1984 to 77 million in 2007, the future for this country currently looks bleak. Kevin Myers, a formerly idealistic British aid worker who was in Ethiopia trying to save lives in the early 1980s, had this to say about the present situation: "The wide-eyed boy child we saved 20 or so years ago is now a priapic, Kalashnikav-bearing hardy, siring children whenever the whim takes him" (Myers, 2008).

Leadership   Any societal or worldwide strategy for achieving population control and addressing and resolving related issues must include effective leadership at all levels. In February, 2005, the Kyoto Treaty aimed at curbing greenhouse emissions and global warming went into effect. The signatories to this treaty, which numbered 140 nations, committed themselves legally to meeting greenhouse gas emission goals by 2012. Sadly, the United States under President George W. Bush did not sign this treaty and this sent a very clear and negative signal to the rest of the world (Gifford, Sheets, and Poggioli, 2005). During the 2008 U.S. presidential campaign, both Republican candidate John McCain and Democrat candidate Barack Obama advocated the need for both population control and assistance, and the need to address the problems of greenhouse gas emissions and global warming both domestically and as a foreign policy issue. In addition, both McCain and Obama—along with the political parties they represent—pledged to develop and pass though congress a comprehensive energy policy to resolve the energy crisis. The next decade will be an important one which will determine whether and to what extent leaders in the United States and other countries address all these issues directly and decisively. To echo Mathus' warning over 200 years ago, "wars" loom ever-present as a positive check if modern preventive efforts to control the world's population and address related issues are not sufficient and effective. From a twenty-first century sociological perspective, a worst-case scenario from failed leadership could be global instability, economic breakdown, and/or a possible third world war.

Prospects for the Future

Despite some setbacks in a few areas, prospects for the future look more promising than in previous decades. Leaders and governments in the less-developed nations are, at an increasing rate, taking aggressive steps to protect the future of their people. Mexico's leadership helped to set the standard for such efforts over two decades ago. A success story in the Western hemisphere, Mexico won the 1986 United Nations Population Award for, among other things, reducing its growth rate by thirty-five percent from 1974 to 1985. As another example, India's government has instituted a series of economic incentives to encourage smaller families with the hope of seeing a two-child-per-family norm established in the near future. If current trends continue and expand, the combined efforts of the countries of the world should produce a stable global population within the next few decades. However, to achieve such goals, leaders throughout the world will need to remain steadfast and committed. The United States and other developed nations of the world will need to provide both moral leadership and financial support in both seeking less damaging forms of energy other than fossil fuels and in helping their less-developed neighbors do the same as well as reach replacement level fertility. Achieving these goals will remain a key challenge for the twenty-first century.

CHAPTER SUMMARY

1. A population is the total number of people who inhabit a country or other geographical territory. Sociologists who specialize in population engage in demography, the scientific study of population characteristics and change. Specifically, demographers study the size, composition, and distribution of human populations at micro-, macro-, and international levels. Primary sources of demographic information include taking a periodic census and amassing and evaluating ongoing records of vital statistics.

2. In examining population in historical perspective, important aspects include Malthusian theory, three technological revolutions that have sparked population growth, and estimates by demographers of actual population change. In 1798, Thomas Malthus proposed that populations increase geometrically (1, 2, 4, 8, 16), while food supplies increase arithmetically (I, 2, 3,4, 5). His doomsday predictions of a future population crisis, along with his proposed preventive solutions (postponed marriage and sexual abstinence), drew severe criticisms that have continued up to this day. Although his theory was naive and overly simplistic in some respects, modern scientists acknowledge that his basic premise of geometric population growth is approximately correct. Three technological revolutions to date over the past 10,000 years—agricultural, urban, and industrial—has produced a rate of population growth that, during the past 200 years, has been roughly geometrical. Whether Mathus' prediction of severe imbalance between people and food in the future comes true remains to be seen.

3. Populations change as a result of three basic factors: Fertility (births), mortality (deaths), and migration (movement of people from one place to another). Measures of fertility used by demographers include the computation of crude birth rates, fertility rates, total fertility rates, and age specific fertility rates within designated populations. Fertility in less-developed countries remains high compared with mortality rates. Mortality is measured by crude death rates, infant mortality rates, and age specific mortality rates. Migration, a third factor in assessing population change, is studied by demographers in terms of both international and internal (within a country) movements of people.

4. Demographers also study the composition of societies according to such factors as age and sex to ascertain how they impact on population change. The age composition of societies, as measured by such factors as the dependency ratio and median age, informs scientists as to the percentage of people in a population who are under fifteen and over sixty-five years of age. A country with a high dependency ratio and a low median age finds it structurally difficult if not impossible to modernize. This is due to the fact that most people must be in productive age categories in order for a country to build the infrastructure needed to support a modern economy and other institutions needed to support it. The sex composition of a society is measured by the sex ratio, the number of males to females. When age and sex compositions are combined into a population pyramid, demographers have a clear picture of a given society as compared with others regarding these characteristics.

5. The world currently is faced with the dilemma of overpopulation. The population explosion as it is sometimes called is a problem primarily in less-developed countries and stems from a variety of factors. The first is mortality intervention, the provision of medical and healthcare technology and assistance to less-developed nations by organizations and governments of modern developed nations. Such aid has significantly reduced mortality rates in these countries since 1945. However, corresponding progress has not been made in terms of reducing fertility rates with China representing a notable exception. Two other factors help account for overpopulation, namely pronatalism—a cultural orientation that strongly encourages lots of childbearing and the lack of available contraception education and technology.

6. Implications of overpopulation for human ecology are disturbing. There are significant food shortages in dozens of less-developed countries, as well as other problems including the depletion of land resources, pollution, potential energy crises, and the threat of the greenhouse effect and global warming. Nonetheless, the problem of overpopulation and its threat to the natural environment is beginning to turn around. Several countries, most notably China, Mexico, India and others have taken definitive steps to lower fertility rates and bring their populations under control. With the continued development of no-growth cultural orientations, family planning programs, and effective leadership, the countries of the world stand a good chance of stabilizing the global population within the next few decades.

TERMS TO KNOW

age specific fertility rate (ASFR): the number of births per 1,000 women in specific age categories during a given year.

age specific mortality rate (ASMR): the total number of deaths per 1,000 people in a population in specific age categories during a given year.

agricultural revolution: the first technological revolution to spark world population growth marked by the domestication of plants and animals which began about 10,000 years ago (8,000 BCE).

census: a relatively complete headcount of the people in a given society.

crude birth rate (CBR): the total number of births per 1,000 people in a population during a given year.

crude death rate (CDR): the number of deaths per 1,000 people in a population during a given year.

demographic transition: a three-stage process in which developing nations move from a condition of high fertility and high mortality to one of low fertility and low mortality.

demography: the scientific study of population characteristics and change.

dependency ratio: the number of people in a population under 15 and over 65 years of age divided by the number of people between 15 and 65.

emigration: leaving one country to seek settlement in another.

fecundity: the biological potential for reproduction as applied either to an individual woman or to an entire population.

fertility: the number of births that occur in a population as measured by fertility rates.

fertility rate (FR): the number of births per 1,000 women of childbearing age (15 to 44 years) in a population during a given year.

global warming: an unprecedented recent rise in greenhouse gas emissions and the earth's temperatures caused largely by human intervention.

greenhouse effect: increasing cloud cover caused by pollution which retains the warmth of the sun and produces higher ground temperatures.

growth rate: the annual percentage of growth or loss in a population.

human ecology: the scientific study of the relationship between human populations and their natural environment.

immigration: coming into a new country from another to establish residence.

industrial revolution: the third technological revolution to encourage world population growth marked by the rise of mass factory production which began about the year 1750.

infant mortality rate (IMR): the total number of deaths per 1,000 children under 12 months of age in a population within a given year.

internal migration: movement of people from one place to another within a country.

international migration: movement of people from one country to another for the purpose of settlement.

life expectancy: the number of years a person in a specific country of a certain age can be expected to live.

Malthusian theory: the argument proposed by Thomas Malthus that human societies increase their populations geometrically (1, 2, 4, 8, 16), while food supplies grow arithmetically (1, 2, 3, 4, 5).

median age: the mid-point or 50th percentile in the age distribution of a population.

megacities: cities with 10 million or more inhabitants.

migration: the movement of people from one geographical location to another for the purpose of establishing residence.

momentum: increases in a population that continue long after birth and death rates have been stabilized.

mortality: the number of deaths that occur in a population as measured by mortality rates.

mortality intervention: the provision of medical assistance and health technology and assistance to less-developed countries by developed nations.

population: the total number of persons who inhabit a country or other politically or geographically specified territory.

population pyramid: a summary of age and sex compositions in a population portrayed in a graph or chart.

postindustrial stage: an emerging fourth stage of demographic transition—countries with continuing low fertility and mortality—with new forms of postindustrial economies.

posttransition stage: the third stage of demographic transition which involves countries with declining to low fertility and mortality rates.

pretransition stage: the first stage of demographic transition which involves countries with high rates of both fertility and mortality.

pronatalism: a cultural orientation that strongly encourages childbearing.

sex ratio: the number of males to every 100 females in a designated population.

total fertility rate (TFR): the total number of offspring a typical woman has during her lifetime in a given country.

transition stage: the second stage of demographic transition characterized by countries with high fertility rates and declining to low mortality rates.

urban revolution: the second technological revolution to stimulate world population increase marked by the rise of cities which began about 3,500 BCE.

vital statistics: records kept on the inhabitants of a nation or society, which include births, deaths, marriages, and incidences of disease.

SUGGESTED READINGS

Anderson, Margo J., and S. E. Fienberg. 1999. *Who Counts? The Politics of Census-Taking in Contemporary America.* New York: Russel Sage Foundation. A tracing by the authors in the history of census-taking in the United States, current issues such as illegal immigration and undercounting, and projections as to how the U.S. population and the counting of it are likely to change.

Gore, A. 2006. *An Inconvenient Truth: The planetary Emergency of Global Warming and What We Can Do about It.* Rodale Press. The basis for the documentary film that won former Vice President Al Gore an Oscar for best documentary film, the author presents the scientific findings regarding global warming and the daunting challenges facing humans in stopping it and reversing it. For example, 20 of the hottest 22 years the planet has experienced in over 100 years are estimated to have occurred during the past 25 years.

Peterson, W. 2000. From *Birth to death: A Consumer's Guide to Population Studies.* New Brunswick, NJ: Transaction. A effective and well-written primer on population studies that presents the reader with a wide ranging discussion on a variety of population issues from fertility, mortality, and migration and population planning and control to the efficacy of Malthusian theory as applied to the modern world as we enter the twenty-first century.

Tobar, H. 2005. *Translation Nation.* New York: Riverhead. An examination of the growing trend in Hispanic immigrants to the United States during the past few decades, how Latinos are adjusting to America and how American culture is also changing as a result.

The Family: Most Basic of Institutions

Terms to Know

bride price	intimate partner abuse	polygyny
cenogamy	latchkey children	propinquity
child abuse	marriage	role discrepancy
cohabitation	marriage by exchange	romantic love
division of labor	marriage by mutual choice	rules of descent
dual earner	matriarchal authority	rules of residence
egalitarian authority	monogamy	same-sex marriage
endogamy	no fault divorce	serial monogamy
exogamy	nuclear family	single-parent family
extended family	patriarchal authority	stepfamily
family	pattern of authority	traditional monogamy
family universals	family polyandry	traditional nuclear family
incest taboo	polygamy	

There is an old joke among professors who teach marriage and family courses that they can use the same tests year after year because even though the questions remain the same, the answers keep changing.

—David Knox, 1988, p. 1

FAMILY: AN INTRODUCTION

As illustrated by Knox's tongue-in-cheek comment, the American family is indeed a changing institution. This is partially evident in the way it has been portrayed in the media during the last half century. Take television programming for instance. Beginning in the early 1950s, television audiences were entertained by the exploits of families including the Ricardos on *I Love Lucy* and the Nelsons on *Ozzie and Harriet*. These were followed in the 1960s by *Hazel* featuring the Baxter family and *Leave It to Beaver* with Ward and June Cleaver and their two sons. Almost without exception, these were middle- to upper-middle-class families in which the husband was the sole breadwinner and head of household, while the wife was a homemaker. For the most part, these shows painted an idyllic, stereotypical image of the model middle-class family as reflected in the dominant cultural values of this period.

Then, also in the 1960s, the structural characteristics of television families began to change, reflecting certain emerging trends and issues in the larger society. Shows including *The Partridge Family*, and *Family Affair* spotlighted the single-parent family, while *The Brady Bunch* reflected the growing number of stepfamilies. The next decade, the 1970s, gave us the generation gap which plagued the Bunkers on *All in the Family* and the second-marriage predicaments of middle-aged Maude and Walter Finley on *Maude.* During the 1980s and 1990s, many of us tuned in each week to observe these and other family types and arrangements, from the dysfunctional Bundy family in *Married with Children* to the dual-career family represented by the Huxtables on *The Cosby Show.* As we have entered the 2000s, a variety of family structures and situations have been portrayed including *Full House, Gilmore Girls,* and *Two and a Half Men,* an Emmy award-winning show about two unattached, heterosexual men occupying a household and raising a boy.

Several recent trends are apparent. About seventy percent of American families today have two breadwinners. The single-parent family has also become more prevalent as divorce rates overall have been higher than those experienced prior to the 1970s and rates of women giving birth to children outside of marriage have soared. The numbers of people opting for various lifestyle alternatives, including childlessness and unmarried cohabitation, have also risen. In contrast, the size of the American family is at an all-time low, reflecting lower fertility rates in recent decades. These and other developments both reflect and affect changes in the overall society as we move through the first decades of the twenty-first century.

Despite continuing change, the family remains the most basic of all social institutions. It represents the most important and durable source of primary group relations for most of us. In simple societies, it often represents the only institution with all basic social functions—socialization and emotional support, government, education, religion, and economic production—carried out within an extended family system. In modern societies, the family is but one of several specialized institutions, each designed to address a major area of needs.

Regardless of the type of society, the family, in the words of the late anthropologist Margaret Mead (1953), represents

the toughest institution we have. It is, in fact, the institution to which we owe our humanity. We know no other way of making human beings except by bringing them up in a family

© BILL REITZEL/CORBIS

Families portrayed on popular American television shows often reflect or model family trends in the larger society during a particular time frame.

. . . [W]e know no other way to bring up children to be human beings, able to act like men and women, and able to marry other men and women and bring up children, except through the family (p. 4).

THE FAMILY AS A SOCIAL INSTITUTION

In discussing what many sociologists consider the most fundamental and important of all institutions, we will begin with a definition of family that applies to almost all family types and specific variations worldwide. Then we will briefly examine several structural aspects of the family that are of particular value in assessing the similarities and differences between "families" in different parts of the world. These include family universals, basic family forms, and cross-cultural differences.

What Is a Family?

By **family**, sociologists mean two or more persons related by blood, marriage, or adoption who live together and cooperate economically. In societies worldwide, many people tend to have an ethnocentric bias concerning family that is based on their own socialization experiences in their culture of origin (Holtzman, 2005). Many Americans, for example, assume that monogamy, romantic love as a basis for marriage, and freedom of choice in selecting a mate are "normal" everywhere. They are not. Only about one-fourth of all societies insist on monogamy between a man and a woman as the only acceptable marriage form; romantic love as a basis for marriage is found mainly in Western societies; and, in several cultures, the parents of prospective spouses choose the person their child will marry. These and other issues related to family are explored in this chapter. First, we will examine the nature of the family institution from a global perspective. We will begin with the concept of family universals.

Family Universals

All known societies possess some form of family system. Within each system, **family universals**, characteristics common to families in all societies, may be found. Sociologist Kathleen Gough (1986) has identified four essential universals as the incest taboo, marriage, a division of labor pattern, and a pattern of authority.

The Incest Taboo   All societies possess the **incest taboo**, a norm that prohibits sexual relations and marriage between close family members. This prohibition, however, varies in strength from culture to culture. All societies "forbid mother–son mating, and most, father–daughter and brother–sister. Some societies allow relations but forbid marriage between certain degrees of kin" (Gough, 1986, p. 23). Nonetheless, the results of recent research indicate that incidents of incest may have taken place in up to eight percent of American families (Gordon and O' Keefe, 1984; Wilson, 2006). In this regard, the sexual abuse of children by close family members cuts across all social classes, racial and ethnic backgrounds, and occupational categories. According to available research on incested

American children and adolescents, the most likely perpetrator tends to be the father or step-father (Masters, Johnson, and Kolodny, 1992).

Marriage   All societies make some provision for **marriage**, a formally recognized, intimate relationship between two or more adults that is durable, relatively stable, and seen as desirable (Benokraitus, 2008). Marriage exists in various forms in different societies and, among other things, establishes the foundation for having and rearing children. Although motherhood is established biologically, fatherhood—as viewed from a global perspective—is based more on the social obligations of the husband to his wife and her child, particularly his ability to provide economic and protective support.

Monogamy   Acceptable forms of marriage vary significantly from society to society. The most widely accepted and practiced marriage form, both traditionally and presently, is **monogamy**, the marriage between two adults, usually a man and a woman. In many societies monogamy is the only acceptable marriage form, particularly modern societies like those of Europe and the United States with nuclear family systems.

There are two basic forms of monogamy, traditional and serial. **Traditional monogamy** is a form of marriage characterized by lifelong marriage to the same person. Given such factors as a rural, farm-based economy that required spouses to work together cooperatively, a short life span (forty-seven years in 1900), strong religious norms, and an expensive, *adversarial divorce* process that required both a plaintiff and defendant and demonstrated grounds such as adultery or desertion, lifelong monogamy was the dominant norm until well into the twentieth century. In the aftermath of World War II (1939–1945) and the structural changes that have occurred in American society since that time, an alternative to traditional monogamy has emerged as a viable and accepted alternative. This is **serial monogamy**, marriage to one partner at a time but two or more in a lifetime. Several social factors have influenced the development and acceptance of this form of monogamy. They include an increased lifespan, the increased participation of women in both the labor

© ANDREY STRATILATOV, 2009. USE UNDER LICENSE FROM SHUTTERSTOCK, INC.

Marriage is a family universal found in some form in all societies.

force and higher education (resulting in greater economic independence for women), the modern feminist movement, and the emergence of no-fault divorce as a replacement for fault grounds. Despite these changes, however, traditional monogamy remains the dominant American marriage pattern and divorce rates today are lower than those during the 1970s and 1980s.

Polygamy The other basic marriage form found in many parts of the world is **polygamy**, a marriage form that involves the taking of plural spouses. Sociologists and anthropologists distinguish between three types of polygamy: **polygyny** (one husband, two or more wives), **polyandry** (one wife, two or more husbands), and **cenogamy** (group marriage) that includes two or more husbands and wives involved together in a marital union.

Of these, *polygyny is, by far, the most common form of plural marriage.* It is found in most parts of the Muslim world, primarily in the Middle East countries such as Egypt, Saudi Arabia, and Iran. It is also common among tribal societies in Indonesia, New Guinea, and even isolated portions of the Amazon Basin in South America. Unofficial or informal forms of polygyny also occur in the United States and Canada. There are an estimated 300,000 polygynous families operating among orthodox, fundamentalist Mormans in portions of Utah, Texas, Arizona, and Canada (Divoky, 2002; Benokraitis, 2008). Polygyny has been quite popular and historically was the preferred form of marriage in three-quarters of the world's societies (Murdock, 1965). As patriarchy has given way to egalitarianism, plural marriage has declined as a social practice, has been outlawed in many formerly polygynous societies, and has been condemned by several international organizations, including the United Nations, as being exploitative of women.

By contrast, both polyandry and cenogamy (group marriages) are quite rare and are socially approved marriage forms in only a handful of the world's societies. Polyandry, for

© BETTMANN/CORBIS

In some Middle Eastern countries, a form of plural marriage (called polygyny) is practiced in which a man may have more than one wife. It appears to be on the decline, however, in some countries whose people are trying to modernize and adopt Western ways.

example, exists only in a handful of simple societies, such as the Todas of Southern India and a few mountain villages in Tibet (Benokraitis, 2008). It is perhaps best explained by a standard of living so low that one male cannot economically provide for a wife and off-spring by himself. Consequently, he may pool his meager assets with those of another two or three men, often his brothers, and share a wife.

A Division of Labor   A **division of labor** refers to the allocation of needed tasks to be performed in society to the necessary types and numbers of people. Historically, the assign-ment of these tasks was based largely on gender. Males essentially took care of govern-ment, hunting, fishing, farming, and war, while females handled child care, household duties, and related functions. This form of work allocation by gender still is prevalent in several parts of the world today including several countries in Africa and some Middle Eastern countries, especially those that embrace Islamic fundamentalism. Elements of a gender-based division of labor still may be found in modern, industrial and postindustrial societies like the United States, particularly among the less-educated sectors of society and also among first-generation immigrants who have migrated to the United States from tra-ditional, patriarchal societies. However, gender as a basis for allocating work, particularly economic functions, has become largely obsolete in the cultural mainstream of rapidly changing modern societies. As previously discussed in Chapter 6: Social Organization, occupational specialization, driven by credentials reflecting technical expertise, has become the modern world standard in the twenty-first century for allocating work.

A Pattern of Authority   Without exception, each of the world's societies has a **pattern of authority**, a group of norms that determine how status, authority, and decision making are to be distributed within the family and also within society as a whole. In this sense, there tend to be three patterns of authority.

Patriarchal Authority   Historically, male or **patriarchal authority**, a pattern of family decision making in which males are dominant in power, has been the dominant pattern. As previously discussed (Chapter 6), it is probable that early in human history, males, because of such factors as size, strength, and the lack of sex-related vulnerabilities (pregnancy, for instance), were able to assert and gain social and economic control. Therefore, family author-ity is very closely related to the economic division of labor. Many conditions in today's modern societies have changed fundamentally over the past several decades. Likewise, just as gender has become less of a factor in dividing work in modern economies, it has become equally irrel-evant in terms of defining authority in the family and other sectors of society as well.

Matriarchal Authority   **Matriarchal authority**, a pattern of family decision making in which females are dominant in power, requires special consideration. Some societies—including the Hopi Indians of America, the Ashanti of Ghana, and the Nayar of India—are characterized by *matrilineal descent,* in which property is passed from one generation to another within the woman's blood line. The husbands in these and other matrilineal cul-tures have little formal influence over their wives. However, the male members of a woman's kin group—her older brothers and maternal uncles, for example—typically exert authority over her in terms of "managing" her property. As Gough (1986) explains:

There is in fact no true "matriarchal," as distinct from "matrilineal," society in existence or known from literature, and the chances are there never has been. This does not mean that women and men have never had relations that were dignified and creative for both sexes, appropriate to the knowledge, skills and technology of their times. Nor does it mean that the sexes cannot be equal in the future or that the sexual division of labor cannot be abolished. I believe that it can and must be. But it is not necessary to believe myths of a feminist Golden Age in order to plan for parity in the future (p. 24).

Nonetheless, there no doubt exists in every society—including the most patriarchal cultures—individual families where the women are the dominant force and wield the most power. While the men may be the official heads of these families, they are heads in name only. This is due to the fact that, in many cases, their wives are the dominant personalities who, in effect, dominate or in some cases "rule" most of their husband's decisions. It is also fascinating to ponder the possible future results of an intriguing trend. If women—currently overrepresented in both college enrollments and recently earned baccalaureate degrees as compared with men—continue to dominate in these critical areas, they—rather than men—may come to occupy most of the dominate occupational positions in the future. Consequently, it is not only possible but feasible that changes during the next fifty years could result in the emergence of a truly matriarchal society in the United States dominated by women.

Egalitarian Authority   Finally, there is **egalitarian authority**, a pattern of family decision making in which males and females share power equally. This has become the dominant family authority pattern in the United States and is especially prevalent among college educated couples today. However, bastions of patriarchy still linger, especially in certain segments of the working class and among certain subcultural groups, including Christian fundamentalists and first-generation immigrants from predominantly Muslim countries, some Asian cultures, and portions of Latin America. However, with a growing proportion of women now participating in the work force and demonstrating increasing degrees of economic self-sufficiency, most of the traditional hold of men over women under the previous patriarchal system has evaporated in a rising tide of egalitarianism.

Basic Family Forms

As previously discussed in Chapter 6, kinship organization takes two basic forms, *affinal* (marriage as the primary family bond) and *consanguineal* (blood as the primary family bond). The structural forms of families that result are nuclear families and extended families, respectively. Nuclear families are found in hunter-gatherer, agricultural, and modern (industrial and postindustrial) societies. Extended families are found generally in agricultural societies.

The Nuclear Family   Specifically, a **nuclear family** consists of two or more related persons, usually including a married couple, who occupy a common household. Marriage is the primary bond, as most nuclear families consist of married couples who may or may not have children. A nuclear family, however, can also be made up of a single parent with one or more offspring, or even two or three adult brothers or sisters who reside together, with or without offspring.

Its Three Basic Characteristics   The American nuclear family has three major characteristics. First, *it has always been the dominant family form in America* from colonial times up to the present day. Although extended (three generation) families have always been part of the American experience, the majority of immigrants who migrated to the New World have come as single adults or married couples. Second, *marriage is the primary family bond* in the nuclear family. A person's primary obligation is to their spouse, not their blood kin. Finally, *the nuclear family is very short-lived.* It tends to disintegrate upon the marriage of the adult children or the death of the parents.

The Two Overlapping Nuclear Families   As shown in Figure 13-1, Most Americans belong to two overlapping nuclear families, the family of orientation and the family of procreation. The family we are born into and grow up in, which consists of our parents and siblings, is our *family of orientation.* This is the family of childhood socialization that "orients" us to our society as we progress toward adulthood. Then, after the onset of adulthood, the majority of people marry, and most married couples eventually have one or more children. This family we call the *family of procreation.* Making the transition from the first nuclear family to the second often involves two major adjustments. First, we must shift from the dependency of the adolescent role to the autonomy expected of a self-supporting adult. Then, often simultaneously, we must make the transition from a single person to a marriage partner, assuming the role obligations that go with this new position or status in society.

The Extended Family   Extended families are just what the names implies; that is, they are basic nuclear families that have been stretched, or extended, to include additional family members. Specifically, an **extended family** consists of two or more nuclear families, usually including married couples of different generations, and other relatives who all live together or near each other. Extended families are prevalent in agricultural societies and are sometimes found in the United States. The Waltons—a popular television series of the 1970s now seen on cable television—were portrayed in nostalgic fashion and experienced

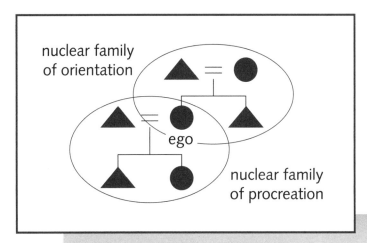

Figure 13-1

Nuclear Families: Orientation and Procreation
Source: Reprinted with permission from Leslie, G. R. 1979. *The Family in Social Context,* 4th ed., 15. New York: Oxford University Press.

the joys and struggles of a rural American family during the Great Depression. This was a time that spelled the "last hurrah" for the American extended family that, by the onset of World War II, was becoming somewhat rare. The Walton kids—John Boy, Mary Ellen, Joe Bob and several of the others as well—were lured off their mountain in rural Virginia by careers in writing, medicine, and other fields that promised a better way of life. As they and millions of real Americans moved to where their careers took them in urbanized areas occupying the cultural mainstream, their extended families were left "back home." Then, when they married, they formed what were usually much more isolated nuclear families.

Its Three Basic Characteristics   Like the nuclear family previously discussed, the extended family also has three major characteristics. First, despite the beliefs by some in the popular culture, the incidence of the American extended family has been greatly exaggerated. *This family form has never been dominant in America.* Most European immigrants were either single males or members of nuclear families. The American family, as it became established, was indeed patriarchal, and parents, particularly the father, influenced the marriages of their children by giving consent or approval. Most of their offspring, however, established their own relatively autonomous nuclear families. While it was common, if not expected, for elderly parents to be taken in by one of their married children—often the eldest son and his wife—most of their children had separate nuclear families.

On a cross-cultural basis, however, extended families are often quite different from the more familiar American family form. This brings us to the second characteristic. In the extended family, *the blood relationship is the primary family bond.* A person's primary obligation is to their blood relatives (particularly the parents), not the spouse. In some parts of the world even today, the blood bond is so dominant in many patriarchal societies that women are considered as little more that chattel (property). Upon marriage, they leave their homes at the behest of their parents, go to live with their husband and his extended family, and have little influence in affecting family decisions. Their influence is often diluted even further in several cultures by polygyny, a marriage practice that allows men to take multiple wives. Extreme forms of patriarchy, along with various forms of plural marriage, are still practiced today in such places as Africa, India, and the Middle East.

A third major characteristic of the extended family is that *it is very long-lived.* In fact, it may border on immortality. There are families in such places as India and China, for example, in which family landholdings and family name have both been passed down intact across dozens of generations for well over a thousand years.

The Family in Global Perspective

In addition to the four family universals previously discussed, both nuclear and extended family forms, societies throughout the world have also evolved other types of specialized norms with which to more fully organize family life. We will now discuss three of the most important of these—patterns of mate selection, rules of descent, and rules of residence—which represent three additional family universals.

Patterns of Mate Selection   Despite views by some that marriages "are made in heaven" and based mainly on romantic love, this notion represents a common ideal that is prevalent mainly in Western societies in Europe and the United States. The reality of mate selection tells quite a different story. Even in the United States, approximately one-fourth of all marriages take place primarily to solve a practical problem—pregnancy, escape from an abusive home environment, for companionship, and so on—and love has little to do with it. And in some parts of the Third World, the mate selection process takes what most Americans might think at first glance to be peculiar if not bizarre forms. However strange they may seem to American sensibilities, there are sociological explanations for all such practices that are rooted in traditional folklore and economic practicalities.

Take the practice of child marriage in India, for example, that can be traced back over a millennium. According to Hindu legend, the Muslims invaded portions of India about 800–900 CE. To protect their infant and young daughters from being raped or kidnapped as war booty, the Hindus evolved the custom of marrying off girls as young as one or two years of age. This practice of child marriage continues today. In addition, India remains one of the poorest countries in the world with family incomes for many rarely exceeding $600 to $800 per year. This provides families with a powerful economic incentive for marrying off their daughters as early as possible to ease their economic burden. Despite the Child Marriage Restraint Act first passed in 1929 and then revised in 1971, and the Hindu Marriage Act requiring a minimum age for women of eighteen at marriage and twenty-one for men, thousands of child marriages still take place in India each year.

Sociologists and anthropologists have noted and studied two basic patterns of mate selection that exist in various societies throughout the world. They are marriage by exchange and marriage by mutual choice which shall be briefly discussed as follows:

Marriage by Exchange   **Marriage by exchange** is a mate selection pattern involving a social and economic arrangement between the families of those to be married. This arrangement results in one or both parties to the marriage sacrificing their personal preferences to satisfy the needs and wishes of their blood kin. Historically, this system was rooted in extreme patriarchy in which women were treated as little more than commodities to be bought, sold, or traded. Valued for their labor and childbearing capacity, daughters and sisters were often exchanged to create alliances between families. Through the marriage of one family's son with another's daughter, the fields, livestock, and other property could be united and consolidated for inheritance by the next generation and the wealth and power acquired by these family alliances made each family stronger economically.

Marriages based on exchange still exist today, primarily in tradition-based, agricultural societies. Anthropologists Fred Plog and Daniel Bates (1980) have summarized the practice as follows:

> In some societies, interfamily alliances are created by exchanging daughters directly. Among the Tiv of Nigeria a man may exchange one of his sisters for the sister of another man, mutually binding the families together. But such direct exchange of women is relatively rare. More commonly, a man pays a family from which he takes a daughter in marriage (*bride price*) or works for it (*bride service*); the payment helps the family replace the daughter with a wife for one of his sons. This indirect exchange of women is found throughout the world (p. 267).

As indicated by the previous quote, there tend to be three basic forms of marriage by exchange, *bride price, bride service,* and *woman exchange.* **Bride price**—a mate selection practice in which a man pays a price to a family for the hand of their daughter in marriage—is by far the most common form of arranged marriage. The price for a bride may take several forms, ranging from cash or gold or heads of cattle, to bicycles or anything else of value. In most cultures using this system, the bride price is either stated or implied to be the price of a virgin. The woman must be a virgin at first marriage. To ensure virginity at marriage and a good bride price, *female circumcision* (removal of the clitoris and/or the vaginal lips) is still performed in about forty countries—mainly among practicing Muslims—on girls from eight to ten years old (Williams and Sobieszczyk, 1997).

Two far less common forms of marriage by exchange are bride service and woman exchange. *Bride service* is a mate selection practice in which a man works for a family for a period of time in exchange for their daughter's hand in marriage. Many Americans are familiar with the Old Testament story in the Christian tradition of Jacob who worked for seven years for Rachel's father in exchange for her hand in marriage. The rarest form of marriage by exchange is *woman exchange,* a mate selection practice in which two families exchange daughters or sisters directly. This method is practiced among a few tribal societies including the Tiv of Nigeria already mentioned.

Marriage by Mutual Choice

Marriage by mutual choice is a pattern of mate selection in which people freely choose their own spouse based on their mutual preferences rather than those of their extended blood kin. This marriage form is found primarily in modern, egalitarian societies and first emerged as an institutionalized form of mate selection primarily in response to the Industrial Revolution during the nineteenth century. As industrialization took hold, the extended family—once an all-encompassing institution—became less and less relevant and began to lose many traditional functions. The production of goods and services, for example, became the domain of a separate economic institution that furnished people with jobs and cash wages. Education likewise developed into a specialized institution needed to prepare children for a future in the emerging industrial economy. With these and other developments, young people in general and women in particular began to gain increasing independence from family elders. No longer rooted to the soil and a future on a farm, they could pursue their lives freely with few if any restrictions.

As the family evolved from an independent unit of production to a dependent unit of consumption, the emerging nuclear family became a specialized institution in its own right. The mass urban society of the twentieth century, with its emphasis on specialized role obligations and secondary group relations, became somewhat impersonal as compared to rural farm life. In this social environment, the family soon become the dominant to exclusive source of emotional support and interpersonal intimacy for all members. In terms of mate selection, romantic love and emotional compatibility—by the end of the nineteenth century—had largely replaced the practical considerations of the past as the basis for marriage.

Rules of Descent

Because of the biological potential for growth in numbers of kin, all societies have devised norms that act to reduce the number of such relatives to a manageable size (Peoples and Bailey, 1997). These norms, called **rules of descent**, socially define a person's relatives. This became necessary historically because of the fact that family obligations typically involved shared affection, economic cooperation, the provision of certain types of mutual aid when members were in need, and inheritance rights. Sociologist Gerald Leslie (1979) has stated that

> [t]here isn't enough affection to scatter indiscriminately over several hundred people, and to be entitled to aid from several hundred people is tantamount to receiving aid from no

one. The satisfactory performance of family duties requires a group of kin of manageable size with whom orderly relationships may be maintained (p. 45).

Rules of descent take several forms. The type found in the largest number of societies is *patrilineal descent,* a form of descent in which kinship and inheritance are traced through the father's bloodline (Leslie, 1979). Common in societies with an extended family system and patriarchal authority, its chief bond is one of blood ties between fathers, sons, and grandsons. Children are seen to have only one set of grandparents and other kin, those related to the father. Although in some cultures wives may continue relations with their blood kin, they and their children have primary obligations to the families of their husbands. The second most prevalent form is *bilateral descent,* in which kinship and inheritance are traced through both bloodlines equally. It is common in modern societies with nuclear family systems, like the United States, in which children have socially defined relatives on both paternal and maternal sides of the family equally. A relatively uncommon form is *matrilineal descent,* in which kinship and inheritance follow the mother's bloodline. Among societies that have been historically matrilineal are several American Indian groups (including the Navaho and Hopi), the Nayar of India, and the Bemba of Africa (Barnouw, 1978).

Rules of Residence   Societies also have **rules of residence**, norms that specify where a couple will live after marriage. Once the marriage takes place, at least one of the partners will have to change his or her residence. How this is determined is closely related to rules of descent. Societies defined by patrilineal descent tend toward *patrilocal residence,* in which, upon marriage, the couple goes to live with or near the husband's kin group (Ember and Ember, 1996). Likewise, societies of matrilineal descent tend toward matrilocal residence, in which the married couple resides with or near the wife's relatives. Modern societies like the United States with nuclear family structures tend toward *neolocal residence.* This norm stresses that couples, upon marriage, should establish a residence of their own apart from both families of blood kin (Clayton, 1979; Benokraitis, 2008) (Table 13-1).

STUDYING THE FAMILY: DIFFERENT SOCIOLOGICAL APPROACHES

Most people are experts when it comes to one family in particular, their own. It is indeed tempting sometimes to take the "facts" about our own family experience and generalize to the world of families everywhere. For some people, it is easy to assume that the way their families are structured and how their members interact with each other is typical or normal for all families. It is obvious from our discussions of global family variations that this usually is not the case.

From a scientific viewpoint, facts are relatively meaningless when they lie outside some means of systematic interpretation. Family sociologists examine thousands of representative families to determine patterns and trends, as well as to make comparisons. In doing so, they make use of a variety of different conceptual frameworks or perspectives. Some sociologists prefer the functionalist approach while others may use conflict, interactionist, or other perspectives. Still others may employ a combination of different approaches. Each sociological approach at examining the family reveals but one piece to a larger puzzle. Each

TABLE 13-1	Family Structure in Global Perspective	
STRUCTURAL CHARACTERISTICS (OF THE) →	NUCLEAR FAMILY (TYPICAL CHARACTERISTICS)	EXTENDED FAMILY (TYPICAL CHARACTERISTICS)
KINSHIP ORGANIZATION	Affinal (Marriage)	Consanguineal (Blood)
FORM OF MARRIAGE	Monogamy	Monogamy or Polygamy
PATTERN OF AUTHORITY	Patriarchal (Traditional) Egalitarian (Modern)	Patriarchal
PATTERN OF MATE SELECTION	Mutual Choice	Exchange (Arranged)
RULE OF DESCENT	Bilateral (Both Families Equally)	Patrilineal (from Male's) Matrilineal (from Female's)
RULE OF RESIDENCE	Neolocal (Independent)	Patrilocal or Matrilocal

is valuable because it focuses on different aspects of the family. Taken together, however, these basic approaches give us a composite view and help us to understand how and why the family operates as it does.

Functionalism

As discussed in Chapter 1 and throughout this book, structural functionalism emerged from the work of such nineteenth-century sociologists as Herbert Spencer and Emile Durkheim. Both of these early theorists used an *organic analogy* in which they compared a human society to a biological organism. Just as the physical body as a structural system has specialized organs that work in harmony with each other to maintain biological equilibrium or homeostasis, the human society as a social system likewise has specialized institutions that operate like organs of the body to maintain social equilibrium or stability.

During the twentieth century, functionalism was developed most notably by Talcott Parsons, and was later refined by others including Robert Merton. The chief proposition growing out of functionalism is that society as a social system operates (or functions) through its various structures (institutions) to maintain social order or equilibrium. Although the equilibrium developed is dynamic and thus constantly adjusting to account for change, order and harmony characterize the natural way a society should operate. Change and conflict, especially if they are dramatic and uncontrolled, are seen by functionalists as disruptive.

From a functionalist perspective, all major social structures or institutions in society provide functions (or benefits) that help to maintain social order and stability. Sociologists who use this approach argue that the overriding purpose of each of society's institutions—family, government, economy, religion, and education—is to promote such equilibrium and harmony. In this regard, the family is seen as the most fundamental and important of society's basic structural building blocks. In fact, some scholars today argue that "How goes the family goes society."

Functions of the Family   The first sociologist to identify and analyze how the family is organized to promote and maintain social order was William F. Ogburn (1964). He identified six key functions of the family discussed briefly in the following:

1. ***Reproduction.*** In order for the population in a society to be sustained, there must be some mechanism to ensure that those people who die or leave will be replaced. That mechanism—sexual reproduction—is supplied by the family, which is, practically speaking, the only institution equipped with the necessary characteristics needed to have and successfully raise children.

2. ***Physical Care and Protection.*** Being essentially devoid of the instincts possessed by the young of other species, human infants are virtually helpless at birth and incapable of sustaining themselves with the most basic of life's necessities such as food, shelter, and clothing. In addition, they are ill-equipped to protect themselves from potentially neglectful or harmful adults. Because humans are dependent on others of their kind for life essentials during a longer proportion of their lifespan than any of the other animals, the family provides this benefit or function in all societies. In the United States, for instance, the period of dependency for offspring—often well over two decades (twenty to twenty-five years)—is longer than for most societies. This is due mainly to increased demands for and costs of schooling needed for adults to participate meaningfully in today's postindustrial, high-tech economy.

3. ***Regulation of Sexual Expression.*** Because of the power and recurrent nature of the sex drive, all societies have found it necessary to regulate and limit its expression. Although other institutions also regulate sexual behavior—most notably religion and government—both the foundations and consequences of such regulation are rooted deeply in the family. As the primary agent of childhood socialization, the sexual norms of the larger culture are taught to children as part of their upbringing. These norms, either discussed openly or implied through silence, are taught to children as part of their socialization. As an example, the *incest taboo*—a cultural norm that forbids sex relations and marriage between close relatives—is forbidden in most forms in all societies.

   In most patriarchal societies historically and even today, *a double-standard* has stressed significant sexual freedom for single males but severe sexual restrictions to total abstinence for women. Yet most modern societies today are socializing their members with norms that stress the same sexual standards and freedoms for both males and females.

   However, young women today often face an unintended consequence for their recent sexual liberation. Sexually transmitted diseases (STDs) are often asymptomatic in women, in part because of the internal nature of their sexual anatomy. As a result of this and other factors, one-fourth of American teenage girls aged fifteen to nineteen currently are infected with a STD at any given point in time, according researchers at the Centers for Disease Control and Prevention. Such STDs, including human papillomavirus (HPV) and chlamydia, often result in no noticeable adverse health symptoms for several months or longer. By the time such young girls are diagnosed with a STD, many of them may have been rendered permanently sterile (Altman, 2008).

4. ***Socialization of Children.*** As discussed in Chapter 5: Socialization, children at birth essentially are *tabula raza*, or social blanks. The family represents the first, most intense, and most important social group in which they will hold membership until adulthood. Through the imposition of behavioral boundaries and sanctions for violating them, the family, most notably the parents, lead their children on a journey through the dependency and egocentrism of early childhood, the adjustments and lessons of late childhood, and finally the challenges and changes of adolescence as they make the journey to adulthood. Along the way, parents transmit the key elements of their culture—knowledge, beliefs, norms, values, symbols, ethics, language, and so on—to their children.

5. ***Emotional and Social Support.*** Behavioral research from several related disciplines has clearly demonstrated that human infants, children, adults, and senior adults all need intimacy and emotional and social support in addition to other life necessities. The family, as the center of our social and emotional world, is best equipped to satisfy these needs. As stated earlier, the family is our most enduring source of intense, personalized, and intimate relationships. An infant must learn to both receive and give love in an adaptive way in order to develop into a well-adjusted child. This, in turn, furnishes the foundation for developing a positive self-concept and sustaining strong friendships and an intimate pair-bond with a life partner later in adulthood. A child who is deficit in healthy and consistent emotional bonding and attachment while growing up often experiences attachment problems as an adult. In addition, adults who lose or get disconnected from meaningful interpersonal bonds are likely to experience chronic depression. If this is not relieved, maladaptive consequences can be the result including various addictions or suicide.

6. ***Social Placement.*** In order to achieve and maintain order and stability at both micro- and macrolevels of society, each individual must learn his or her status (position) or place in each group, organization, or institution he or she occupies. This process of learning one's social place is impacted significantly by one's social experiences with the world based on the interrelated categories of age, gender, racial or ethnic background, religious background, and class. These sources of interconnected identification are experienced as a totality within the family we grow up in. Parents—by their lessons and their actions—teach their children their place in the family, the community, and the society and world around them.

   For the sake of illustration, two examples should suffice to show the power of how social placement is taught to children by their family and its impact on them later in adulthood. If for example, parents are permissive and give their eight year old most of the choices and freedoms afforded an adult, the child likely will remain egocentric and may have serious interpersonal problems as an adult in relationships, school, and the workplace. Such children often grow up with a sense of personal entitlement that the larger world likely will not recognize and tolerate. Likewise, children who are taught by their family that their religion is the only true religion and everyone else in the world who worships differently must be converted to their faith or go to hell, will see and experience their place in the world very differently than children raised with religious tolerance and respect for other faiths.

Conflict Theory

While functionalism stresses the ways in which the family institution promotes order and stability in society as a whole, the conflict approach focuses on exploitation, opposition and change. Modern conflict theory, as previously discussed (Chapter 2), originated during the nineteenth century with the work of Karl Marx and his co-writer and colleague Friedrich Engels. Marx and Engels argued that the struggle and conflict between opposing forces were the most representative aspects of the human condition. Marx, who formulated the key ideas, argued that history was represented by a continuing series of struggles between the "haves" and the "have nots." In modern, industrial societies, the "haves" were comprised of the capitalist owners of industry—the bourgeoisie—who made profits from exploiting the labor of the "have nots"—the proletariat.

Conflict Theory and the Family: Macrolevel Applications   Both Marx and Engels saw the family as the basic social, economic, and political unit of society. They asserted that the family represented in microcosm the class struggle taking place in the larger society. This was manifested in the exploitation and oppression perpetrated by men against women. Engels (1902) stated that the family is a unit in which the husband "is the bourgeoisie and the wife represents the proletariat."

This view has become reflected in the writings of several more contemporary sociologists as well. Sociologist Arlene S. Skolnick (1987) states that

> the history of relations between the sexes is analogous to those between different races, classes, and castes. All such relationships have involved the domination of one group, defined by birth, by members of another group, also defined by birth. Thus patriarchy—the rule of men over women—must be placed alongside that of feudalism, despotism, slavery, aristocracy, and racism. In practice, however, such power arrangements appear natural and inevitable, and alternatives to them unthinkable. When religion is given as the major justification for behavior, subordination of one group by another is explained in religious terms. More recently, domination is usually justified in terms of biological necessity, irrevocable instincts, and inherent inferiority (pp. 185–186).

Conflict Theory and the Family: Microlevel Applications   In addition to macrolevel issues such as institutionalized gender inequality, the conflict approach also has some application at the microlevel regarding intrafamily conflict and family disorganization. What are the basic sources of family conflict among family members? How does conflict arise? What are its key forms? How can it be managed effectively? What are the major social problems arising out of family conflict and how can they be effectively addressed? These and other questions are explored and studied by conflict sociologists operating from a micro-perspective. Summarized below are a few of the many key issues raised by conflict theorists today that focus on the family:

1. ***The Nature of Family Conflict.*** Proponents of the conflict approach see conflict as a natural outgrowth of any relationship, particularly those within families. Conflict makes visible certain adjustments that we all have to make as we and our partners in relationships grow and change over time. In this sense, the absence of all conflict would perhaps indicate that family members no longer care enough to engage each

other and that true intimacy, as expressed in open communication and sharing, has been impaired or destroyed.

2. ***Sources of Conflict.*** Sources of conflict with family members may be internal or environmental (Rice, 1983). Internal sources include physical fatigue, illness, emotional upset, and mental disorders. Environmental sources of family conflict are much more varied. They include problems outside the home which spill over into the family—such as difficulties with a supervisor at work, interference by others—including well-meaning friends and in-laws, and situational pressures—including those caused by family finance, sexual performance issues, and children. All of these factors may create stress and tension that manifest themselves as family conflict.

3. ***Conflict Management and Resolution.*** Most conflict theorists agree that since some family discord is inevitable, normal, and not subject to complete resolution, it should be effectively and constructively managed. However, the best approach for accomplishing this is a subject of much debate, not just among sociologists, but among counselors and therapists from other disciplines as well. One method used by some therapists is *affective therapy,* an emotion-based form of marital therapy that focuses on the verbal release of conflict with or hostility toward the spouse or other family members in a controlled therapeutic environment. This approach—with a reported success rate of sixty to seventy-five percent—is based partially on the premise that such a form of couple therapy acts as a safety valve to release tensions and prevent a major explosion of hostility at a later time (Gurman and Fraenkel, 2002; Denton, 2007). Another approach is *constructive argument,* a technique used in family therapy in which family members work through a series of steps and techniques that place the focus on their problems rather than on their personalities. By avoiding the destructive consequences of quarreling, an immature form of conflict resolution, the parties involved can learn how to build a "win–win" rather than a "win–lose" solution.

4. ***Family Abuse and Violence.*** If family conflict is allowed to progress to the point of abuse and violence without some sort of effective intervention, the only recourse left for some may be escape and/or the reporting and filing of charges with appropriate authorities. Although many to most families are loving and supportive, others are characterized by neglect and abuse. When unequal power relationships and family discord are not managed effectively, they can become manifested as family abuse and violence. According to conflict theorists, these destructive family conditions result from unequal power arrangements in the family that, when coupled with identity and emotional problems experienced by some individuals and various forms of socially induced strain and stress, produce a variety of extreme family problems. These include intimate partner abuse, child abuse and neglect, and predatory and exploitative sexual behavior including incest. These offenses shall be discussed in greater detail later in this chapter.

Interactionism

Symbolic interactionism is a third approach. Developed and popularized early in the twentieth century by sociologists including Charles H. Cooley and George Herbert Mead, the interactionist perspective focuses on the personal meaning people assign to the social world around them (see Chapters 2 and 5) and their place in it. Also of importance are the ways in which people symbolically communicate their perceptions of reality to others. These unique perceptions are largely a product of our own particular socialization experiences.

Interactionism and the Family   When this approach is applied to the family, it is of particular value in helping to explain the complex interpersonal dynamics among members. As an illustration, we might examine the impact of significant others—such as the parents—on shaping the self-image of the developing child and his or her evolving perceptions of family relations. Small children, as first explained by George Herbert Mead, look to their parents as role models for their own future family behavior. As family sociologist Ira Reiss (1980) explains:

> [O]bserve them [children] playing house. The young female who plays the mother will usually indicate strong elements of her mother's role in her own play behavior. This indicates that she has learned her mother's role and, thus has role taken with her mother. The entire area of anticipatory socialization is involved here. We socialize our children ahead of time by our own behavior in the roles they will later perform. One can see this in everyday areas such as driving and drinking and smoking, but even more broadly in parental roles. The kind of parent-role conceptions children develop will be heavily influenced by their own parent's role behavior (p. 64).

Maturation and Role Expectations   As children come to maturity and look forward to establishing their own adult family roles, the perceptions they developed in childhood take the form of role expectations. They anticipate how they will act and should act in the roles of husband, wife, and then, later, as parent. They also develop role expectations about how their future spouse will and should act as well.

Consider the situation faced by an engaged couple as they near the date of their wedding. To increase the likelihood for marital success, they should openly communicate to each other, before marriage, their perceptions of married life, including the roles each person should play. To put it in blunt but metaphorical terms, they should "lay all their cards on the table," hold nothing back, and assume nothing on the part of their prospective partner concerning the key issues they will have to face together as a married couple. These include core values, life goals, money matters, sex, whether or not to have children and how many, parenting, and the roles their parents and in-laws will play in their marriage. The divorce courts are well-represented by those who did not do this before they married. Candidly discussing these issues, of course, is no panacea for all marital ills, nor is it a guarantee of long-term marital success. It simply means that, at the point of marriage, the two new partners have established a sound basis for compatibility and the lines of communication are open. The challenge after marriage is to keep them that way.

The Issue of Role Discrepancy   Those couples who enter marriage without openly and candidly communicating their perceptions and expectations about marriage and family to each other beforehand are likely candidates for role discrepancy, a possible source for marital discord. **Role discrepancy** is a condition produced in a marriage in which expectations about the nature and responsibilities of married life are inconsistent with its realities. Judson Landis and Mary Landis (1973) have commented as follows:

[I]n marriage, it is easy to be concerned with only one's own needs and expectations without seeing the other side of the question. . . . Couples contemplating marriage need to give thought to how well they understand each other and to what kinds of situations are tolerable or intolerable to each other. A competitive attitude toward each other during courtship may indicate conflicting role expectations. Each married couple must work out the husband-wife pattern according to the capacities and the adaptability of the partners and the circumstances of their lives. Whatever role patterns develop in any particular marriage, mutually supportive attitudes are essential to a good relationship (p. 28).

Changes in Role Relationships Over Time

Interactionism is also useful in examining the complexities of family role relationships over time (Stryker and Statham, 1985). A marriage is a process, not a "thing." To maintain a stable and growing relationship, each partner must guard against taking the other partner and the relationship for granted. Each person enters marriage with a definition of his or her role, that of their partner, and how they should interconnect. However, these definitions change and may become more complex as couples get older, have children, and add or rearrange goals and priorities. Children bring much added complexity to the dynamics of a marital relationship. Their arrival means that the marital role must be balanced with the parental role. Careers and financial priorities may add other complications. Certain events may occur—midlife crises, loss of job, children's growing up and leaving home, or loss of a family member through death or divorce—which call for other life adjustments.

Applications to Family Therapy

The interactionist perspective also provides family counselors and clinicians with a very useful therapeutic tool in helping individuals and families understand, achieve, maintain, and improve interpersonal relations with their loved ones. In fact, it is often recommended by behavioral scientists—your author included—that any couple contemplating marriage undergo premarital counseling with a professionally trained and certified marriage and family counselor or therapist. In addition, if problems and conflicts arise at any point in the marital or family relationship that family

TABLE 13-2	Studying the Family: Different Sociological Approaches	
SOCIOLOGICAL APPROACH	**BASIC FOCUS**	**SPECIFIC AREAS OF EXAMINATION AND ANALYSIS**
Functionalism	Social order, stability, and harmony	Functions Served: Reproduction; care and protection; regulation of sexuality; socialization of children; emotional and social support; and social placement
Conflict Theory	Opposition, exploitation, changing roles	The nature of family conflict; sources of conflict; family abuse and violence; and conflict management and resolution
Interactionism	Personal meaning; its impact on family; roles played and role expectations	Maturation and role expectations; the issue of role discrepancy; changes in role relationships over time; and applications to family therapy

members feel they cannot handle alone, a few sessions with a professional counselor or therapist can often facilitate a solution.

We live in a society in which many people do not hesitate to spend $22–$28 thousand dollars or more for a new car. They place a high value on transportation and see this as a "necessity." Is not the most fundamental and multidimensional relationship we have or perhaps will ever have with another human being also a necessity? If a marriage becomes characterized by conflict or some other impairment, is it not worth the few hundred dollars for counseling or therapy that could save or improve it? Only you can answer that question.

THE AMERICAN FAMILY TODAY

Today's American family is very different in its structure, in the issues facing it, and in its interpersonal dynamics than its counterpart in colonial America more than three hundred years ago. The industrial revolution is largely responsible for its transformation during the 1600s and 1700s from an independent unit of production (e.g., the farm family) to one characterized as a dependent unit of consumption today (e.g., multiple wage earners). Other factors during the last three-fourths of a century, including the Great Depression of the 1930s, World War II, the woman's movement, and post-war changes in the economy have resulted in diverse variations of the nuclear family as it exists today. We now turn our attention to an examination of these patterns as they have emerged.

Romantic Love

Its Origins *Romantic love* as a basis for marriage is a relatively new idea. Traditionally, societies saw marriage in very practical terms as necessary for procreation, inheritance rights for children, and cementing alliances between families. Romantic love in many societies was viewed as a type of emotional disorder. Among the ancient Greeks, it "was considered a form of madness that fortunately was 'cured' by marriage" (Coleman, 1988, p. 145). In modern times, it may be traced to the concept of courtly love in the eleventh and twelfth centuries. As a prevalent and institutionalized basis for marriage, romantic love first emerged in Europe among the middle and working classes during the sixteenth, seventeenth, and eighteenth centuries. It was brought to America by the Puritans and other European migrants as early as the 1600s. Today, partially as a result of the reinforcing factors of industrialization and a mass impersonal society, romantic love continues as the basis for marriage in the United States.

Romantic Love and Its Key Elements   Just what is this thing called love? **Romantic love** may be defined as the idealization of another person based on attachment, commitment, and intimacy. Three critical love elements have been identified by psychologist Zick Rubin (1970). According to Rubin, *attachment* involves the need to be physically near and emotionally supported by the other person. He uses the term "caring" for a second element, which involves concern for the well-being of the person loved along with a willingness to take some responsibility for maintaining and improving the relationship. The author actually prefers the term *commitment*, which involves demonstrated caring. Some people think they care and say they care ("I love you") but are unable for whatever reason to follow

The idealized relationship between feudal knights and ladies during the eleventh and twelfth centuries CE formed much of the basis for modern romantic love.

through. Commitment in an intimate pair-bond involves devoting significant amounts of time and energy as well as care and concern to the relationship. In the view of many scholars and clinicians, commitment is the glue that holds a relationship together. *Intimacy*, according to Rubin, involves a bonding process manifested in large part by open, extensive, and confidential communication.

Stages of Romantic Love

It is perhaps useful to distinguish between two types or stages of romantic love. *Initial romantic love* includes the elements of attachment, commitment, and intimacy along with passion and a sense of euphoria. In this context, *passion* refers to an intense physical and sexual attraction. *Euphoria* is a heightened sense of well-being. The second stage, *mature romantic love,* evolves out of initial romantic love. As such, it typically involves increased degrees of attachment, commitment, and intimacy, and diminished levels of both passion and euphoria. Mature love relationships typically involve a mellowing process in which the intensity and excitement of initial love evolves into a deep and enduring devotion (Rubin 1970).

Factors that Direct Cupid's Arrow: Propinquity, Endogamy, and Exogamy

We will now examine three key factors that tend to reduce the total pool of eligibles from which we might choose a mate down to a relatively small number of people. They are—in order of discussion—the propinquity principle and two mate selection norms, the rules of endogamy and exogamy.

Propinquity

One mate selection factor is **propinquity**, the principle that we choose a mate from among those who are near to us either in terms of geographical residence or our spheres of social relations. Until World War II (the 1940s), there was a tendency for many to most Americans to marry their high school sweetheart or the boy or girl "next door" or from a nearby neighborhood. However, after the Great Depression of the 1930s and the war, the post-war boom period that followed (created by the growing, ever-technical, urban, industrial economy) caused many Americans to become more geographically mobile.

With the demands of school and career taking many far from their neighborhoods, towns, and states of origin, a key result was a shift from residential propinquity to geographical propinquity as a factor in mate selection. People began to choose mates from among the pool of eligibles near to them in their spheres of social relations at the point in their life cycle at which they were most vulnerable to mate selection. This pattern continues even today. For example, you go off to school in another city or state to attend college and there he or she is, in your biology lab or sociology course. This person, whom you fall in love with and marry, is from another state, fifteen hundred miles from your home town. Had you both not gone to that college at that time, you most likely would never have met.

Endogamy and Exogamy   Cultural norms also strongly influence mate selection. Whether one lives in a society that stresses marriage by exchange or marriage by mutual choice, all societies have norms that attempt to regulate the pool of potential partners from which a mate is chosen.

Two of the more powerful mate selection norms in most societies involve the rules of endogamy and exogamy. **Endogamy** is a norm that encourages or requires people to marry within certain culturally defined groups. In many cultures such as the United States, people typically are put under some pressure by family and peers to marry a person similar to themselves according to such factors as age, racial or ethnic background, religion, and class. **Exogamy** is a norm that encourages or requires people to marry outside of certain culturally defined groups. The most universal application of exogamy is the incest taboo that prohibits sexual relations or marriage between certain close relatives. In all fifty states in the United States one may not marry a parent or grandparent, child or grandchild, sibling, or a blood-related aunt, uncle, niece, or nephew and, in most states, first cousins and half-siblings as well (Cox, 1987). In addition, the large majority of states prohibit marriage between people of the same gender.

Dick and Jane: The Traditional Nuclear Family

During the 1940s, 1950s, and most of the 1960s, elementary school children in the United States learned to read in the first few grades by following the exploits of Dick and Jane in their reading books. Dick and Jane were white, middle-class children who lived in the suburbs with their parents, a little sister named Sally, and a couple of pets, Spot the dog and Puff the cat. Dad wore a suit each weekday and carried a briefcase to work in the city, while Mom stayed home and engaged in domestic chores. This was a portrayal of the **traditional nuclear family**, one consisting of a full-time working husband, a homemaker wife, and one or more school-age children. The implicit message conveyed in elementary readers during the 1940s to the 1960s was that Dick and Jane would grow up, each find and marry a spouse, and live in the suburbs where they would follow their parents' pattern in the next generation.

In most cases, the family lives of young people growing up in America from the 1940s on have not turned out that way. Instead, the traditional nuclear family today in the twenty-first century has become somewhat of an endangered species. According to the U.S. Census Bureau (1985, November), seventy percent of all U.S. households consisted of traditional nuclear families in 1950, up from sixty-six percent in 1940 (Clay, 2005). However, despite this brief post World War II upward spike, the statistics since that period have gone in the opposite direction. By the year 2000, the percentage of traditional "Dick and Jane" families had declined to just under twenty-four percent of all households (Schmitt, 2001; CensusScope, 2001). Projections by the U.S. Bureau of Labor Statistics indicate that by the year 2030, only seventeen percent of households will consist of traditional nuclear families (Clay, 2005).

The primary reasons for this change in structural characteristics of the American family include rising affluence during the post-war period (from 1945 onward), a focus on personal needs and fulfillment, and the emergence of less-restrictive laws—reinforced by supreme court decisions—pertaining to marriage and divorce. A key consequence of these and other social trends has been the emergence of increasingly diverse family variations and alternative life style choices. We will next examine some of the recently prevalent family patterns that are commonly found today.

The Dual-Earner Family

The family form that has largely replaced the traditional nuclear family is the **dual-earner family**, a family form in which both married partners generate income and share in home and child-rearing responsibilities. This is the dominant American family form today, with approximately two-thirds of U.S. married couple households consisting of couples who both work (Roehling and Moen, 2003). Even so, married life for two-income couples appears to be more complex than for traditional couples in several respects.

Authority and Careers   In a traditional marriage, if the husband's career necessitated a move to another city or state, the wife and children moved with him. However, in today's two-income marriage, there are two-careers to consider. Whose career is more important?

© ZSOLT NYULASZI, 2009. USE UNDER LICENSE FROM SHUTTERSTOCK, INC.

Two-thirds of today's married couples in the United States are dual-earner families in which both spouses work outside the home.

Should one or the other make a sacrifice? What if the other spouse cannot find a job in their chosen occupation or profession in the new location? Of course, there are no ready-made solutions. Each couple has to resolve this type of problem based on their own values and priorities.

Certainly, two-income families have become more egalitarian, as women in the workforce today have many more options than did their mothers and grandmothers. Even so, the career of the husband today often is still regarded as the more important, the wife agreeing to make the move even if it may jeopardize her career (Cooper, et al., 1986). This situation is caused, at least in part, by the lag that still exists between women's pay versus men's pay for comparable jobs. A second factor in some marriages is the effect of traditional male socialization on men who may feel their masculinity compromised if their careers are lost or inhibited. The effects of traditional childhood socialization on women who were taught the importance of a man's career may also play a part. However, about one-third of all working married women in the United States now have higher incomes than their husbands. Among these marriages, husbands are more likely to make sacrifices in their careers (Frieswick, 2007).

Commuter Marriages   Sometimes, circumstances necessitate a *commuter marriage*, a marriage in which a couple, due to career priorities, live apart for a period of time in separate cities or states and visit each other when they can. As a significant life style element among modern couples, this is a relatively new phenomenon. Consequently, serious research on commuter marriages did not begin until the 1970s. The United States is a highly mobile society with about fifteen million families that move each year, a pattern that appears likely to continue. With an estimated one-fourth of all American workers changing or planning to change their occupations each year, coupled with the rise in two-income families, a significant growth in the number of commuter marriages appears inevitable (Porter, 1986).

These marriages, which increased thirty percent from 2000 to 2005 to 3.6 million, are increasingly characteristic of college-educated professionals (Cullen, 2007). The fact that partners live in different cities and/or states means that they may see each other only on weekends at best. Disadvantages include loneliness, the costs of maintaining two households, and impaired marital and sexual adjustment if the situation lasts for an extended period of time. To combat these effects, recent technological innovations such as cell phones and email have made daily interaction more practical and cost effective than in the past, a luxury that commuter couples prior to the 2000s usually did not have. Nonetheless, this arrangement is seen by most couples as temporary until both can find occupational positions in the same location.

Prenuptial Agreements and Personal Marriage Contracts   When a couple marries, the partners enter into a civil contract with legal rights and responsibilities specified for each person according to the laws of the state. These rights and obligations include living together as husband and wife in a common residence, property and inheritance rights, and reasonable sexual obligations (Broderick, 1988). Therefore, marriage is not simply a personal commitment but a legal contract entered into with the state as the third party. To dissolve this contract permanently, all three parties—the husband, wife, and state—become involved in a legal process called divorce.

Given the complexities of modern marital and family life, a small but growing number of couples are electing to enter into a prenuptial agreement, a marriage contract, or both. A *prenuptial agreement* is a signed, notarized contract between two people about to marry that specifies how financial assets will be divided in case of divorce (Stritof and Stritof, 2008). "Prenups," as they are often called, are valid in all fifty states and the District of Columbia. They perhaps are most useful to couples in which one (or both) has significant financial assets and/or income-generating potential. One or both parties in pursuit of an advanced degree or with an existing business may wish to have the income generating potential of that degree or business excluded from the marital assets. Although critics argue that prenups benefit the person with the most assets, in actuality both parties can benefit and be protected by knowing specifically what they will receive financially should the marriage fail (Larson, 2003).

A much broader and inclusive form of premarital agreement is represented by a *personal marriage contract*. This is a written agreement between two about-to-be-married people that specifies the expectations, rights, and obligations of each party to the marriage, along with the conditions of the relationship. Critics argue that such contracts interfere with marital spontaneity and "natural growth" because they are calculated and based on distrust. Proponents argue just the opposite. They claim that the process of two people coming together and agreeing to the basic structure and direction of their relationship brings all-important issues into the open and facilitates the building of a relationship based on trust and open communication.

Sociologists Mary Ann Lamanna and Agnes Reidman (1985, p. 267) state that "writing a personal agreement can allow partners to understand each other's role expectations." Other family sociologists and therapists argue that a personal marriage contract facilitates a more egalitarian marriage in which the man and woman are equal participants. Sociologist F. Phillip Rice (1983) has commented as follows:

> When a couple supports and signs such an agreement, husbands are more likely to share in household chores, to look upon their wives as equal partners, and to be relieved of the entire responsibility of earning family income. Advocates also point out that issues are clarified and conflicts are minimized. . . . There are even marriage counselors who use the contract principle of negotiation and reciprocity to assist couples in working out their problems (pp. 369–370).
>
> . . . Proponents of a personal contract emphasize that this is one way to that difficulties can be avoided; the couple learn to talk about everything with each other, they enhance their decision-making capability, and they develop negotiating skills and their own personal and social identities. They derive real security from knowing what to expect in the future (p. 371).

Third Party Childcare

A familiar early morning sight today is that of one or more parents driving to work with their preschool child strapped into a protective car seat. Before the parent or parents arrive at work, the child is dropped off at a childcare facility.

Third-party daycare for children under six years old is a growing phenomenon resulting from the increasing numbers of both dual-income and single-parent families. Yet, day care is increasingly expensive. For instance, Texas in 2006 ranked thirty-seven of fifty states in the average annual cost for third party child care at $85 per week, or $380 per month and $4,427 per year. Single parents had a much higher financial burden at 21.7 percent of

TABLE 13-3	Annual Median Costs of Third-Party Childcare: 2006 (State-by-State: Highest and Lowest)		
COST RANKING BY STATE*	AVERAGE ANNUAL COST FOR PRESCHOOLER CARE**	% OF MEDIAN SINGLE-PARENT INCOME SPENT***	% OF MEDIAN TWO-PARENT INCOME SPENT***
Five Highest Cost States			
1. New York	$8,530	40.4%	11.5%
2. Minnesota	$8,832	31.1.%	11.4%
3. California	$7,576	31.1%	10.9%
4. Massachusetts	$9,628	40.7%	10.6%
5. Virginia	$7,852	34.6%	10.3%
Five Lowest Cost States			
46. South Carolina	$4,180	22.8%	6.2%
47. Missouri	$3,967	18.7%	6.1%
48. Arkansas	$3,384	22.3%	6.1%
49. Nevada	$3,200	14.3%	5.3%
50. Alabama	$3,010	18.3%	4.8%

*Ranking based on average cost per state for a four-year-old child.

**Average annual costs figures are for each state (infant care through age five, which varies by state)

***Percentage of income spent for single-parent households and two-parent households vary based on average incomes for each state, which also are different for each state.

Sources: National Association of Childcare Referral Agencies, 2006; Armour, S. 2006. High cost of childcare can lead to lifestyle changes and adjustments. *USA Today.* April 18, 2006.

their median annual income as compared to two-income households at 7.2 percent (Armour, 2006). However, research has found that children in the better child-care centers with low child-to-caregiver ratios and well-trained staff receive adequate care in a warm and nurturing environment (Cochran and Gunnarsson, 1985; Meredith, 1986). Parents need to be selective, nonetheless, to ensure that their child is receiving adequate care. See Table 13-3 for U.S. state-by-state comparisons.

Latchkey Children   By some estimates, more than 7.5 million U.S. children today—or ten percent of all children between six and nine years of age—spend one to several hours each day during most weekdays caring for themselves without the presence of responsible adults. For ten to twelve year olds, the figures add up to thirty-five percent (Capizzano and Adams, 2000; Vandivere, et al., 2003). These are **latchkey children**, children who spend significant amounts of time alone each day with no adult supervision. These are older school-aged children who spend an average of two and one-half hours daily after school without the presence of responsible adults (Turkington, 1983). This situation may pose little or no danger to some children, who may learn to be more self-reliant and responsible (Wattenberg, 1985; Collins, 1988). No doubt in other cases, latchkey children are more likely to have accidents and get into trouble because they are left alone too often and for too long without supervision. According to some cognitive development researchers, children under ten years old do not possess the intellectual skills and judgment to adequately care for themselves without adult supervision Therefore, they see the latchkey phenomenon to be a growing social problem (Belle, 1999; Vandivere, et al., 2003).

The Single-Parent Family

Over the past several decades, the percentage of households headed by unmarried adults with children has tripled. According to the U.S. Census Bureau (1982), the proportion of one-parent families increased from eleven percent of all families in 1971 to twenty-one percent by 1981. By 1985, the figure was twenty-six percent (U.S. Census Bureau, 1986 C). This trend has continued. There are nearly thirteen million such families today which constitute approximately one out of every three (30.6 percent) families (U.S. Census Bureau, 2005b). Most projections estimate that more than one-half of all American children in the foreseeable future will spend at least some time in a single-parent family.

As defined by sociologists, a **single-parent family** consists of a single, separated, divorced, or widowed adult with one or more offspring. Of all such families in the United States, eighty-three percent are headed by women (Welch, 2008). Most single parents are separated or divorced, although about twenty-five percent are women who have never been married (Hanson and Sporakowski, 1986).

Single parents face many problems and challenges. Because of the gap in earnings between men and women, single parents who are women face many more financial problems

© ENNA VAN DUINEN, 2009. USE UNDER LICENSE FROM SHUTTERSTOCK, INC.

Nearly one-third of all families today are headed by a single parent. Parenting without a partner involves special challenges and sacrifices. However, many single parents today appear able to successfully handle such responsibilities.

and are increasingly likely to be poor (Glick, 1981). The effect of the absence of a father or mother figure for the child presents a special challenge for the single parent in trying to find surrogate role models for the absent gender parent. As an illustration, both young boys and girls whose fathers are absent may become too dependent on their mothers and experience problems in peer relationships, as compared with fewer of these problems among children in father-present families (Santrock, 1970; Biller, 1971). Other problems include emotional overload by the single parent because there is no partner to "take up the slack," and responsibility overload because there is no one with whom to share decisions in disciplining and advising the children (Coleman, 1988). Despite these and other difficulties, many single parents appear successful in raising their children and report satisfaction even though their personal sacrifices are often great.

The Stepfamily

A **stepfamily** is a family formed when two people marry and stepparent and stepsibling relationships are established. During much of the twentieth century, divorce rates increased significantly. Because most divorced people at that time remarried and the majority of them were also parents, stepfamily relationships were formed in increasing numbers. Today, stepfamilies account for slightly more than one-sixth (sixteen percent) of all families, and about thirty-five to fifty percent of all children born today will spend some time in a stepfamily before their eighteenth birthday (Johnson, 1986; Skolnick and Skolnick, 2007). Many of these children will grow up with stepsiblings in addition to their own brothers and sisters.

The chief characteristic of stepfamilies is complexity. A person who marries a divorced person with one or more children enters a complex web of relationships. This often includes an ex-spouse who at minimum must be tolerated for the sake of the children. Stepchildren must be won over in terms of love and respect, which often takes some time and much patience. When two divorced people marry, each with children from a previous relationship, it is sometimes a case of "my children, your children, and our children" if they decide to also have children together. Providing equal amounts of love and consistent emotional support to all these children becomes a challenge few people would envy. Remarkably, marriage partners who form stepfamilies seem to be as happy in the beginning as couples in first marriages. However, their relationships tend to be more unstable over time. According to projections, more than forty percent of those in first marriages will divorce compared to sixty percent in second marriages, many of which involve stepfamilies (Glick, 1984). This suggests that the majority of people contemplating the formation of a stepfamily or those already in one could benefit from premarital and marital counseling to assess their relationship and keep it on stable footing.

FAMILY CRISIS AND CONFLICT

The complexities and pressures of life in modern society often contribute to family conflict and crisis. Two of the most fundamental types of family problems today are marital breakdown and family violence.

Marital Breakdown

The Period of Rising Divorce Rates: 1860–1985
In terms of the **crude divorce rate** (i.e., the number of divorces each year per 1,000 people), the general trend during the last half of the nineteenth century and most of the twentieth century was upward. In 1860, the crude divorce rate was about .3 per 1,000 people, compared to an increase to 1.0 in 1900 and 2.0 in 1940 (U.S. National Center for Health Statistics, March, 1979). During the next forty-five years, the divorce rate more than doubled, reaching a high of 5.1 per 1,000 people in 1980 and remaining nearly as high at 5.0 in 1985 (*Newsweek*, August 24, 1987). These figures—as projected into the future—indicated that by the mid-1980s, nearly one of two marriages would eventually end in divorce as compared to the projected divorce rate of one of seven for those marriages that took place in 1920 (Kenkel, 1973; U.S. Census Bureau, 1988, Welch, 2007).

Contributing Factors for Rising Divorce Rates: 1860–1985
Why did American divorce rates rise so dramatically over this period? First and perhaps most important were changes in rights for women that expanded their political rights and gave them greater economic freedom. By the post-World War II period from the 1940s to the 1980s, women whose mothers and grandmothers may have been locked into miserable marriages because of economic dependence on their husbands, found themselves with increased options. They found themselves empowered to support themselves and their children if necessary. In addition, the social stigma once attached to divorce by the church, the workplace, and society in general began to subside by 1950 and was practically nonexistent by the 1980s. A third factor was represented by significant changes in the divorce process itself. The old adversarial system of divorce, in which one party had to be found "guilty" under the fault grounds established by each state, began to be challenged by the late 1960s, and by the 1970s was dismantled state by state. By the 1980s, **no fault divorce** had became the norm nationally. No fault divorce is a form of divorce in which dissolution of marriage is little more than a formality in which needed papers are filed with the court without fault grounds required. Assuming there is no conflict over child custody and/or division of property,an attorney can file the necessary papers with the court, often for a fee of less than $300 dollars. In community property states like California and Texas, noncontested divorces have become commonplace and individuals can file all needed paperwork themselves by purchasing a book—with all needed forms and steps included—with titles like *How to Do Your Own Divorce in Texas*.

The Recent Period of Declining Divorce Rates: 1986–Present
From the mid-1980s until now, U.S. divorce rates have dropped significantly. In 1986, for instance, the rate was 4.8 per 1,000 people, down .2 from 5.0 per 1,000 in 1985 (*Newsweek*, Aug. 24, 1987). Since that time, marital dissolution rates for the U.S. population in general have continued to trend downward—4.7 in 1990, 4.2 in 2000, and by 2005, the divorce rate had dropped to 3.6 per 1,000, the lowest rate since 1970 (Centers for Disease Control, 2006; Welch, 2007, p. 436) (Table 13-4).

Crude divorce rates, however, do not tell the whole story regarding the prevalence or likelihood of divorce. While divorce rates are down significantly for most Americans—who occupy the middle class—they are not down for everyone. For those who use nonmarital

TABLE 13-4	The Rise and Fall of U.S. Crude Divorce Rates: 1900–2005

YEAR	SELECTED CRUDE DIVORCE RATE (PER 1,000 MARRIAGES PER YEAR)
1900	0.7
1920	1.6
1940	2.0
1960	2.2
1970	3.5
1980	5.2
1985	5.0
1990	4.7
1995	4.4
2000	4.1
2005	3.6

Source: Centers for Disease Control. 2006. "Births, Marriages, Divorces, and Deaths: Provisional Data for 2005." *National Vital Statistics Reports*. Vol. 54, No. 20, July 21.; Welch, Kelly J. 2007. *Family Life Now*. Boston, MA: Pearson Education, Inc., p. 436.

cohabitation as a stage of courtship—and their numbers have grown exponentially in recent years—there is a higher likelihood of eventual divorce (Heaton, 2002). In addition, for those with a high school diploma or less, divorce rates are much higher than are rates of marital dissolution among the college educated (Martin, 2006). Other predictors of a higher likelihood of divorce include premarital pregnancy or childbearing (Teachman, 2002), parents who were divorced (Armato and DeBoer, 2001), and lack of marital preparation as indicated by those who marry before age twenty (Bramlett and Mosher, 2001; Amato and Previti, 2004). Racial and ethnic background also represents an important factor that intersects with other predictors. For example, African Americans are less likely to marry than whites and Hispanics and among blacks who do, their marriages are twice as likely to end in divorce (Sweeney and Phillips, 2004).

Family Abuse and Violence

When family conflict remains unresolved, it can evolve into violence. About 5.3 million violent acts occur within intimate relationships and families each year in the United States. Cumulatively, they result in injuries to two million men, women, and children and 1,300 deaths annually (Durose, et al., 2005). Of these, the two most prevalent forms of family violence are intimate partner abuse and child abuse.

Intimate Partner Abuse By far, the most common form of family abuse is **intimate partner abuse**, the use of overt aggression by one spouse or intimate partner against another which can produce emotional problems, physical injury or both. According to available research, twenty percent of women and three percent of men report having been physically abused by a spouse or intimate partner at some point in their lifetime (Rennison, 2003). In this sense, partner abuse can take many forms, including—but not limited to—verbal abuse, repeated blows with either a closed fist or open palm, kicking, repeated pushing, restraining, hitting with objects, burning and other forms of mutilation, and even rape or attempted rape. Of these variations, the two most commonly used criteria in assessing what factors constitute physical abuse tend to be *physical injury* and repeated acts. Available national research indicates that intimate partner abuse is the most common form of family violence.

Partner abuse may be initiated by either person. However, the victims are most often women. According to estimates by the FBI, and others, 84.3 percent of domestic violence victims involving spouses are wives and 85.9 percent involving unmarried intimate partners are girlfriends (Durose, et al., 2005). Immediate causes that trigger violence include jealousy, alcohol and drugs, and arguments over money or children (Roscoe and Benaske, 1985). Underlying causes are varied. *Socioeconomic status* is one factor, since family violence in general is more prevalent among the poor and disadvantaged. *Childhood socialization* also plays a role, as many spouse and child abusers were themselves exposed to violence or abused in their families as children. *Chronic stress* stemming from poverty, unemployment or job-related problems, and pregnancy are also associated with family violence. Although spouse abuse remains a serious social problem, it appears to be gradually declining as a result of efforts in education and treatment. The increasing availability of shelters, "safe houses," and "hotlines" for abused women is also furnishing them with resources and opportunities (Gelles, 1980; Coleman, 1988).

Child Abuse   **Child abuse** refers to neglect or overt acts of aggression by a parent or other adult against a child that produces physical injury, emotional problems, or both. Such treatment takes several forms, including excessive verbal cruelty and intimidation, physical beatings, and sexual contact. It is difficult to estimate the incidence of child abuse, because it usually takes place behind closed doors. From reported cases, however, it is clear that over three million children suffer abuse or neglect at the hands of their caregivers each year and over two thousand infants and children are killed annually by their parents or other caregivers (U.S. Department of Health and Human Services, 2005, 2007). Although reported cases of child abuse declined from 1994 to 2004 (from 15.2 to 11.9 per 1,000 children), "almost thirty percent of U.S. children live in partner-violent families" (Benokraitus, 2008, p. 421)

Parents and other caretakers who abuse children usually fit a general profile. Many are very *authoritarian* and make use of few positive reinforcements in dealing with children. Abusers also tend to be *emotionally immature,* prone to emotional outbursts of hostility when faced with frustration, and therefore have little self-control. They also tend toward low self-esteem, depression, and dependence on alcohol and other drugs (Gelles, 1973; Enfer and Scheewind, 1982). Like spouse abusers, those who mistreat children *often were themselves abused as children* (Coleman and Cressy, 1984). Because violence in the home was often part of their own socialization, it often becomes internalized in their minds as an appropriate response to stress and frustration in adulthood. Unless this destructive cycle is broken, family violence becomes contagious and may perpetuate itself across generations.

Given the vulnerability of children caught up in this web of violence, the general public is encouraged to report all instances of child abuse. Early intervention, in some cases, has saved children who otherwise might have become maimed or killed at the hands of their parents. Types of treatment include the psychological-psychiatric approach, which stresses individual and group therapy, and the sociological approach, which emphasizes education in marriage and family life, family planning, and marital and family counseling (Rice, 1983).

ALTERNATIVE LIFESTYLES AND FAMILY FORMS

Despite its problems, the family is an amazingly diverse and adaptable institution and in little danger of disappearing. In fact, the reverse seems to be true. As we move fully into the twenty-first century, several additional lifestyle alternatives and family subtypes are emerging. To put this in perspective, the words of sociologist Suzanne Keller (1985) seem appropriate:

> [I]f we wish to understand what is happening to the family—to our own family—in our own day, we must examine and observe it in the here and now. In doing so, it would be well to keep in mind that the family is an abstraction at best serving as guide and image of what a particular society considers desirable and appropriate in family relations, not what takes place in actual fact. In reality, there are always a number of empirical family types at variance with this (p. 521).

Being Single

One interesting trend in recent years has been the increasing percentages of men and women who elect to postpone or forego marriage. In 1970, less than 28 percent of American adults were single. By 2005, that percentage had increased significantly to forty-four percent of U.S. households being headed by single men or women. A portion of this phenomenon is reflected in the steady rise of age at first marriage among Americans. In 1973, the median age at first marriage was 23.2 for men and 21.0 for women. However, by 2004, it had risen to 27.4 and 25.8, respectively (U.S. Bureau of the Census, 2005c). Contributing factors include the impact of the woman's movement on lifestyle choices among women including the increasing pursuit of higher education, the evaporation of social stigma associated with both premarital sex and nonmarital cohabitation among most sectors of society, and a growing emphasis on personal fulfillment (Campbell, 2002; Waite and Joyner, 2001). As a result, there is less pressure for most people to feel they must marry in their early to mid-twenties or, for that matter, to marry at all. Consequently, the largest category of single people today consists of the never married. Given the evolution of a supportive singles subculture in recent years—singles clubs, housing, resorts, publications, and so forth—pressure to marry may decline even further in the future.

Nonmarital Cohabitation

The U.S. Census Bureau defines it as POSSLQ, an acronym which means Persons of the Opposite Sex Sharing Living Quarters. Prior to the 1960s, "living together" without benefit of marriage was seen as a violation of Christian religious norms by many to most Americans and carried the stigmatizing label of "living in sin" or "shacking up." Today, it is termed **cohabitation** by sociologists, a relationship between two unrelated, unmarried adults who share a common residence and an assumed sexual relationship (Hyde and Delamater, 2008).

Since the 1970s, cohabitation has grown almost exponentially. Between 1970 and 1985, the numbers of heterosexual cohabiting couples quadrupled from 523,000 to 2,000,000 (U.S. Census Bureau, 1985, November). Since that time, research has shown consistently that one-half or more of the couples who apply for marriage licenses already are living together (Gwartney-Gibbs, 1986). This shows that cohabitation has become normative in recent years as an institutionalized form of trial marriage or as a stage of courtship for an increasing number of couples. As evidence of this, the U.S. Census Bureau reported that the number of American cohabiting couples reached 6.4 million in 2007 (Jayson, 2008). An additional one million households are occupied by same-sex couples (Kreider and Fields, 2005).

Marriage without Children

Childless or child-free couples are also on the increase. A certain percentage of married couples (about ten to twelve percent) have always remained childless involuntarily because of medical reasons. However, since the 1960s, there has been a growing number of couples who have made an active choice either to postpone parenting or to not have children at all (*Newsweek*, 1986). From 1970 to 2003, the percentage of all intact married couples of all ages with children under 18 living at home dropped from forty percent to twenty-three percent (Benokraitis, 2008, p. 21).

Consequently, the "three's a crowd" sentiment, particularly among college-educated married couples, has become a growing trend. Some couples appear to drift into a state of permanent childlessness due to a series of postponements which often entail education, career, changing values and priorities, and increasing financial costs. Take costs, for example. According to the U.S. Department of labor projections, a middle-income couple

© ROB MARMION, 2009. USE UNDER LICENSE FROM SHUTTERSTOCK, INC.

An increasing number of couples today are electing to remain childless by choice. Called DINKS by some (double income, no kids), these couples claim advantages that include a simpler and less stressful home environment, increased affluence, and more leisure time. Nonetheless, the majority of Americans still wish to experience both the joys and challenges of parenthood.

($40,000-$70,000 in annual income) can expect to pay over $200,000 to raise a child from birth through high school graduation, excluding the costs for college (Vorozkko, 2008). Couples with combined annual incomes of less than $40,000 can expect to pay over $134,000 and affluent couples with annual incomes over $70,000 will spend an average of about $270, 000 (MSN Money, 2008).

In today's society, this is often possible for young college-educated couples or DINKS (double income, no kids) but unattainable for many middle-aged couples with children. Other factors include a decline in pronatalism due to overpopulation, changes in sex roles for women that offer alternatives to motherhood, uncertainty about the future due to recent national trends in the national economy, and support groups, including the National Organization for Nonparents, which use slogans like "None Is Fun." Consequently, many couples seem quite fulfilled by choosing not to have children. However, most married couples today still want to have and rear children and experience both the joys and challenges of parenthood.

Same-Sex Marriage

In a benchmark decision handed down by the U.S. Supreme Court in *Lawrence v. Texas* during 2003, the court ruled that sodomy laws both in Texas and nationally were unconstitutional. In essence, this meant that the private sex lives of consenting adults were protected by the Fourteenth Amendment and, therefore, not subject to regulation by the state. Although this ruling did not address the issue of gay marriage directly, it nullified—in the opinion of some legal scholars—a constitutional basis for forbidding such marriages (Von Drehle, 2003). This opened up a fervent debate on both state and national levels regarding the efficacy of such marriages that continues to this day.

The trend worldwide in recent years has been to begin legalizing **same-sex marriage**, a marital union between two gay males or lesbian females. The gay marriage movement actually began in Northern Europe and can be traced to 1989 when Denmark became the first nation to recognize same-sex civil unions, although it fell short in allowing full marital rights and church weddings. This was followed by 1996 in Iceland, Norway, and Sweden, neighboring Germany in 2001, and Finland during 2002. The first country to legalize full civil marriage rights for gay couples was the Netherlands in 2001, followed by Belgium in 2003 and Spain during 2005. Some variation of "registered partnership" or full marital status for same-sex couples has now been formally approved by countries throughout the world. They include France, Luxemburg, and Britain in Europe, South Africa on that continent, New Zealand, and, in the Western hemisphere, Canada, Argentina, and in a handful of states, the United States as well (BBC News, 2005). In the United States, Connecticut, Iowa, Massachusetts, and Vermont (as of this writing) have legalized same-sex marriages, which are also recognized by New York. In 2008, ten additional states were nearing passage of either civil unions or legal marriage for gay or lesbian couples (Head, 2008). However, there has been a backlash in some states. In November of 2008, California voters, for example, passed a measure that, in effect, banned same-sex marriage, which was legal there for a brief period. Nonetheless, the incidence of same-sex unions globally is gradually trending toward increased acceptance. Reasons for these trends include changing sexual mores around the world, in part driven by the findings and conclusions of most researchers and clinicians. In summarizing the current positions of a variety of scientific and professional organizations—including the American Psychiatric Association—"the evidence does not support the notion that homosexuals are 'sick' or poorly adjusted" (Hyde and DeLamater, 2008). In addition, religious arguments against homosexuality and same-sex marriages increasingly are being challenged (*Newsweek*, December 15, 2008).

The Family of the Future: Current Projections

As with modern society in general and its major institutions, the family in its various forms represents a series of dynamic structures and relationships that are constantly evolving and changing. What modern families might look like in fifty years is anybody's guess. However, sociologists who make it a subject for scientific study can predict likely family aspects and patterns based on recent changes and current trends. Patriarchy is unlikely to return, as egalitarian values and norms have become firmly established in modern societies. With this shift to gender equality, dual-earner families and single-parent families likely will remain equally if not more prevalent. In addition, more and more people likely will remain single longer and engage a variety of single life styles that most likely will include one or more nonmarital cohabitation relationships before marriage. Also, as the general public learns more about findings in science concerning sexual behavior and functioning, same-sex marriage likely will gradually gain more acceptance and legitimacy as an alternative marriage form in the United States as international trends also indicate.

Finally, the author—who has a marriage and family counseling background—has two key recommendations regarding the stability of the family now and in the future. First, couples contemplating marriage should benefit immensely from premarital counseling from a qualified, credentialed counselor or therapist. And second, children should benefit if their parents would (1) take a course or two in lifespan psychology, psychology of child development, and/or sociology of marriage and the family before having children and (2) plan and space their children carefully to increase the probability that they will experience marital and childrearing success.

TERMS TO KNOW

bride price: a mate selection practice in which a man pays a price to a family for the hand of their daughter in marriage; the most common form of arranged marriage.

cenogamy: the marriage of two or more men and two or more women; also known as group marriage.

child abuse: neglect or overt acts of aggression by a parent or other adult against a child that produces physical injury, emotional problems, or both.

cohabitation: a relationship between two unrelated, unmarried adults who share a common residence and an assumed sexual relationship.

division of labor: the allocation of needed tasks to be performed in society to the necessary types and numbers of people.

dual-earner family: a family form in which both married partners generate income and share in home and child-rearing responsibilities.

egalitarian authority: a pattern of family decision making in which males and females share power equally.

endogamy: a norm that encourages or requires people to marry within certain culturally defined groups.

exogamy: a norm that encourages or requires people to marry outside of certain culturally defined groups.

extended family: two or more nuclear families, usually including married couples of different generations, and other relatives who all live together or near each other.

family: two or more persons related by blood, marriage, or adoption who live together and cooperate economically.

family universals: characteristics common to families in all societies.

incest taboo: a norm that prohibits sex relations and marriage between close family members.

intimate partner abuse: the use of overt aggression by one spouse or intimate partner against another which can produce emotional problems, physical injury, or both.

latchkey children: children who spend significant amounts of time alone each day with no adult supervision.

marriage: a formally recognized, intimate relationship between two or more adults that is durable, relatively stable, and seen as desirable.

marriage by exchange: a pattern of mate selection involving a social and economic arrangement between the families of those to be married.

marriage by mutual choice: a pattern of mate selection in which the people to be married freely choose their own spouse based on their mutual preferences rather than those of their extended blood kin.

matriarchal authority: a pattern of family decision making in which females are dominant in power.

monogamy: the marriage of one man to one woman or, in a few countries and jurisdictions, the marriage of two persons of the same gender, which is also accepted.

no fault divorce: a form of divorce in which dissolution of marriage is little more than a formality and needed papers are filed with the court without fault grounds required.

nuclear family: two or more related persons, usually including a married couple, who occupy a common household.

patriarchal authority: a pattern of family decision making in which males are dominant in power.

pattern of authority: a group of norms that determine how status, authority, and decision making are to be distributed within the family and also within society as a whole.

polyandry: the marriage of one woman to two or more men.

polygamy: a marriage form that involves the taking of plural spouses.

polygyny: the marriage of one man to two or more women.

propinquity: the principle that we chose a mate from among those who are near to us either in terms of geographical residence or our spheres of social relations.

role discrepancy: a condition produced in a marriage in which expectations about the nature and responsibilities of married life are inconsistent with its realities.

romantic love: the idealization of another person based on attachment, commitment, and intimacy.

rules of descent: norms in society that socially define a person's relatives.

rules of residence: norms in society that specify where a couple will go to live after marriage.

same-sex marriage: a marital union between two gay males or lesbian females.

serial monogamy: marriage to one partner at a time but two or more in a lifetime.

single-parent family: a single, separated, divorced, or widowed adult with one or more offspring.

stepfamily: a family formed when two people marry and stepparent and stepsibling relationships are established.

traditional monogamy: a form of marriage characterized by lifelong marriage to the same person.

traditional nuclear family: a family consisting of a full-time working husband, a homemaker wife, and one or more school-age children.

SUGGESTED READINGS

Benokraitis, N. V. 2008. *Marriages & Families: Changes, Choices, and Constraints.* Upper Saddle River, NJ: Pearson-Prentice Hall. An excellent text that focuses primarily on the American family, past, present, and future. A few of the topics covered by the author include the changing family, studying marriage and the family, the family in historical perspective, love and loving relationships, dating and mate selection, raising children, and conflicts and crises.

Coontz, S. 2006. *Marriage: A History: From Obedience to Intimacy, or How Love Conquered Marriage.* New York: Penguin Books. An engaging account of how marriage in America evolved from the practical and economic arrangements of the colonial period to the modern emphasis today on romantic love and individual fulfillment.

Sternberg, R. 1998. *Love Is a Story: A New Theory of Relationships.* New York: Oxford University Press. The author discusses his triangular theory of love—passion, intimacy, and commitment—and describes 27 stories of love along with a scale for determining which story or stories (e.g., the knitting story, pornography story, cookbook story, etc.) each person identifies as a close fit to their style of loving.

Welch, K. J. 2007. *Family Life Now: A Conversation About Marriages, Families, and Relationships.* Boston: Pearson Education. A text with an excellent coverage of the contemporary American family, issues confronting it, and the challenges it faces now and in the future.

Collective Behavior and Social Change

Terms to Know

acting crowd	expressive crowd	public opinion
anonymity	fads	reactionary movements
bystander apathy	fashions	reform movements
casual crowd	game perspective	revolutionary movements
censorship	generalized belief	rumor
circular reaction	mass behavior	separatist movements
collective behavior	mass hysteria	social contagion theory
conservative movements	media	social control
conventional crowd	mob	social movement
convergence theory	mobilization of participants	social strain
crazes	precipitating factors	structural conduciveness
crowd (also physical aggregate)	propaganda	urban legend
emergent norm theory	public	value added theory

It was after dark when Sally, tired from a long day at work, finally shut down her computer and left the office to go home. As she walked across the dimly-lit parking lot and slowly climbed into her car, she thought of how nice it was going to be to soak in a nice warm tub. Five minutes later, still preoccupied with her thoughts, she was unaware that she was being followed by a large man in pickup truck. As she reached a desolate stretch of road, she was jarred into reality by the bright lights of the pickup in her rearview mirror. Seconds later, she found herself being forced off the road by a menacing-looking stranger.

In a desperate move, Sally floored the accelerator and lurched ahead of the truck and back onto the road. As she sped on through the night and passed her house, she was unable to shake the truck, which alternately held back from and clung to her bumper, the driver periodically turning on and off his high beams.

Finally, she noticed a busy truck stop ahead, quickly turned in at high speed, and braked suddenly to a sliding halt with the pickup right behind her. As she ran in tears to three burly truckers for help, she suddenly became puzzled when she heard the stranger asking for help as well. For, you see, in the back seat of her car, there was an escaped mental patient with a butcher knife who had been incarcerated for slashing to death his entire family, including a daughter who looked very similar to Sally. The "menacing" stranger, it turned out, had spotted the man in the back of Sally's car and, by following the young woman, had probably saved her life.

While this makes an interesting story, it is only one of several variations of "the killer in the backseat" legend that has little, if any, basis in truth (Brunvand, 1986). Stories such as this, called urban legends, start as rumors in local communities and, in a mobile society of corporate travelers and the proliferating use of the internet, are soon spread nationwide with many variations. No doubt you have heard some of them. They include such standbys as "the escaped one-armed killer with a hook," and more recent legends such as "the choking Doberman" and "the dog in the microwave." Generated spontaneously and spread in an unplanned and unstructured way, urban legends are a product of but one aspect of collective behavior, which is the focus of this chapter.

THE NATURE AND SCOPE OF COLLECTIVE BEHAVIOR

Most social behavior involves somewhat patterned responses to established norms. In our coverage of culture (Chapter 4), we discussed how its cognitive, normative, material, and language elements give our lives order and predictability. These patterns for thinking, feeling, and acting are then imparted to us through socialization (Chapter 5). In addition, the ways in which we react to and act on them form the basis for social organization (Chapter 6) at all levels of society. Together, these processes—culture, socialization, and social organization—operate in a dynamic interplay which, in large part, give our lives structure and routine. The majority of us, thus, operate in most spheres of life such as family, school, and work in a fairly patterned way. However, just as there are order and structure in society and social life, so are there changes and, at times, some unpredictability. Sociologists address the issue of change in a variety of ways, including the study of collective behavior, a very broad area of social investigation.

Briefly defined, **collective behavior** consists of people's relatively spontaneous and unstructured actions in response to ambiguous or changing social conditions (Zygmunt, 1986). Especially in situations of rapid social change, conventional social norms may become blurred or not applicable, and habitual patterns of response may not seem appropriate. Individuals and groups in some situations are left to improvise and cope as best they can. This is typical with some crowds. A crowd is a group of people that often forms very quickly, seeks to move forward with a life of its own, may involve highly charged emotions, and may disperse as quickly as it formed. In other circumstances, large groups of people form and elect to participate in what sociologists call a social movement. Such movements—through the combined effort of their members—impose their will on a social condition and develop norms, organization, and goals for others to follow. Those who become involved in social movements make a concerted effort to influence public opinion and sometimes are able to affect significant changes in public policy.

Given its unstructured, unpredictable, temporary, and often emotional nature, collective behavior represents a complex and diverse area of investigation. At one end of the continuum are the most temporary and least organized forms, such as crowds and crowd behavior. By comparison, public opinion at times can be fairly stable. Social movements, the most organized form of collective behavior, can be durable and have been known to last for long periods of time. The civil rights movement in the United States, now in its mature phase, continues after more than fifty years, although its goals and tactics have changed considerably, particularly as gains have been made.

In general, sociologists divide collective behavior into four broad categories: crowds and crowd behavior, mass behavior, public opinion, and social movements. The thrust of this chapter will be to discuss each of these topics in some detail. Let us begin by first examining some of the preconditions that lead to spontaneous or other relatively fluid and unstructured forms of social behavior.

 PRECONDITIONS FOR COLLECTIVE BEHAVIOR

Sociologist Neil Smelser (1963) developed *value-added theory,* one of the first and most widely used approaches to understanding collective behavior. In doing so, he has attempted to combine elements of various perspectives—functionalist, conflict, and interactionist—in explaining many of the social conditions that underlie collective behavior. In essence, **value-added theory** argues that six conditions in society, when added together in sequential order, create a cumulative effect that increases the likelihood of relatively spontaneous group behavior. While collective behavior does not automatically follow from these conditions, each one that is added tends to decrease conventional options and increase pressure placed on people to act out in spontaneous and unstructured ways. These six factors are briefly discussed as follows:

Structural Conduciveness

The first of Smelser's preconditions, **structural conduciveness**, refers to elements built into a society's social structure that encourage collective behavior. Simple nonindustrial societies are low in structural conduciveness because they tend to be slow-changing, tradition-based, and homogeneous regarding their people's lifestyle. Life in these village-focused societies tends to be highly structured, affording little opportunity for innovation or other forms of change. Since everyone tends to have the same or similar occupations, values, beliefs, and worldview, there is little basis for conflict.

Modern industrial and postindustrial societies, however, have a high degree of structural conduciveness. These are fast-changing, urban social systems that are not bound by tradition and have very diverse populations. When this ever-changing mix of occupations, value orientations, and world perspectives among people is combined with burgeoning technology and increasingly sophisticated communications and information processing capabilities, conditions are ripe for collective behavior of several varieties. Consequently, the openness and flexibility these societies possess, along with some confusion and probable conflict, make it much easier for crowds, fads, rumors, and even social movements to emerge.

Social Strain

Societies with high structural conduciveness are more likely to experience **social strain**, a social condition in which (1) intergroup conflicts develop between certain segments of the population and/or (2) dramatic social changes occur. Intergroup conflicts serve as one source of strain. In August of 1988, Universal Studios released the movie *The Last Temptation of Christ,* creating a furor among Christian fundamentalists. Incensed by a fictionalized "human" portrayal of Christ, which included a dream sequence of Jesus having sex with Mary Magdalene, thousands of protesters, mainly fundamentalists, signed petitions, picketed movie theaters, and tried unsuccessfully to have the movie banned. Other

© ROBERT A. MANSKER, 2009. USE UNDER LICENSE FROM SHUTTERSTOCK, INC.

Dramatic social changes such as the stranding of thousands of people in New Orleans in the wake of Hurricane Katrina during 2005 can heighten social strain.

conflicts have arisen among diverse groups in recent years on issues ranging from the Iraq War to abortion, gun control, and illegal immigration.

Dramatic social changes can also produce social strain. Our behavior is governed to a significant degree by the routines or habits we acquire from our culture. If these routines are suddenly interrupted, circumstances force us to innovate or adapt to the situation. Dramatic changes might be brought on at various levels of society by such dramatic events as economic downturns, industrial accidents that cause the leak of poisonous chemicals, political assassinations, violent acts of war such as the September 11 attack on the United States in 2001, and natural disasters such as what occurred in 2005 with Hurricane Katrina that devastated New Orleans and Hurricane Ike that seriously impacted Galveston and the Houston metropolitan area in 2008. Sometimes people are able to react and adapt to such things in an orderly fashion, while at other times, they panic or rebel. Collective behavior resulting from such conditions might include rumors, crowd behavior, mobs and riots, looting, shifts in public opinion, and social movements.

Generalized Belief

For collective behavior to actually occur, however, other conditions in addition to ideal structural conditions also are needed. One of these is what Smelser calls **generalized belief**, a situation in which (1) intergroup conflicts develop between certain segments of the population and/or (2) dramatic social changes occur. Social strain is unsettling to many people who require an "explanation" to a perceived condition that disturbs them. When the stock market crashed in late October, 1929, this dramatic event led to the generalized belief that the entire economy was going to collapse. This shared perception of reality by millions of people set the stage for a run on the banks, which, due to the lack of safeguards, did, indeed, collapse in the wake of an enormous mass panic.

© MELISSA BRANDES, 2009. USE UNDER LICENSE FROM SHUTTERSTOCK, INC.

Sometimes demonstrations, such as those portrayed above by these "prolifers" and their signs, end peacefully. At other times, they act as precipitating events that lead to social breakdown and possibly violence.

Precipitating Factors

Even with the three preceding conditions firmly in place, collective behavior does not always result. What may be needed to spark people into action are **precipitating factors**, events or actions that sharpen the focus of structural conduciveness and social strain and create or reinforce generalized belief that can lead to collective behavior. The bombing of Pearl Harbor on December 7, 1941, triggered American involvement in World War II. During the racial unrest of the 1960s, alleged incidents involving both "police brutality" and "inner city snipers" helped to spark riots in several American cities.

Another precipitating event in January, 1989, created the critical mass for touching off intergroup conflict resulting in explosive violence between native-born blacks in Miami, Florida, and Hispanic immigrants. A Colombian-born police officer, in an attempt to stop a speeding motor cycle, shot and killed its operator in Overtown, an inner-city Miami ghetto. The rear passenger of the motorcycle, also black, died from injuries received in the resulting crash. This event sparked two nights of rioting in which one participant was killed, 22 wounded, and 385 arrested for looting, arson, and random shooting. The property damage amounted to approximately $1 million (*Time,* January 30, 1989).

Similar precipitating events continue to act as catalysts for collective action. What occurred in the immediate wake of Hurricane Ike, which pounded the Texas coast on September 12, 2008, serves as a case in point. The negative consequences were minimized due to local and state officials' planning and prudent actions who had learned much from Hurricanes Katrina and Rita that pounded the Gulf Coast in 2005.

Mobilization of Participants for Action

Once conduciveness and strain are in place and people feel through generalized belief and participating events that 'the evidence is in," all that remains is to engage in collective action. To accomplish this, the leadership and activism of a few individuals will result in the **mobilization of participants**. This is a process in which, through the directions and actions of a few leaders, enough people with sufficient motivation can be brought together and given the focus to act either positively or negatively. The resulting "critical mass" makes collective behavior inevitable (Oliver, Marwell, and Teixeira, 1985). At one extreme are leaders and activists in crowds, who seize the moment and urge the group to act. At the opposite end of the continuum are leaders of social movements who often develop carefully articulated goals and the strategies designed to meet them.

A case in point from the middle range of the above-cited continuum occurred during the first 48 hours following the devastating arrival of Hurricane Ike on September 12–13, 2008, to the Texas Gulf Coast. Despite FEMA's promises to provide immediate and substantive on-the-ground assistance to deal effectively with the aftermath of this devastating storm, essentials such as bottled water, food and ice needed for first-responders charged with rescue efforts and evacuation assistance were not adequately available from federal officials. Much-needed assets were ineffectively planned by FEMA, not in place when the storm hit, and not immediately forthcoming. Several hundred police officers, firefighters, and other emergency personnel in Houston were without necessary supplies for up to eighteen hours.

In response to calls for citizen assistance from proactive community leaders broadcast on local television and radio stations, hundreds of local citizens rose to the challenge by assisting in numerous ways. Many brought critical supplies, such as nonperishable food and bottled water, to staging areas for first responders. In addition, looting was minimized by strict curfews put in place and enforced by several Gulf Coast communities as police and other emergency personnel carried out their duties, for the most part, efficiently and effectively. And local citizens, armed with chain saws and other tools, helped clear away debris, such as fallen trees and heavy limbs, from their own neighborhoods and streets (Feibel and Olson, 2008).

Although FEMA performed significantly better overall than it did in its woefully inadequate performance during the 2005 Hurricane Katrina fiasco and aftermath, the Katrina effect (Chapter 2) was still observable in its first real test of "lessons learned" after three years.

Social Control

The direction collective behavior takes once it is initiated depends in part on how agents of *social control* use their power to minimize or interrupt its potentially negative effects. **Social control**, in a collective behavior context, refers to how authorities' actions can facilitate a smooth process of spontaneous group expression or promote conflict and cause a tense situation to become more volatile.

A now-classic example of the latter situation is the tragic incident that occurred on the campus of Kent State University in May of 1970, during a period marked by much discord and unrest over America's involvement in Vietnam. In the wake of antiwar demonstrations on campus and rowdiness by an estimated three hundred students, which included the firebombing of the campus ROTC building, the mayor of Kent, Ohio requested that then-Governor James Rhodes send in the National Guard. Rhodes complied, declared martial

© BETTMANN/CORBIS

According to sociologist Jerry M. Lewis (1972), all six of Neil Smelser's six preconditions for collective behavior were present in the tragic events that took place at Kent State University during May of 1970. In the wake of student antiwar demonstrations, members of the Ohio National Guard fired on some students, killing four of them and wounding several others.

law, and, to set the tone, even showed up himself on the KSU campus. There, in a public address, he attributed the situations to students "worse than the 'brown shirt' and the communist element and also the night riders in the vigilantes . . . the worst type of people we harbor in America." He also said. "We are going to eradicate the problem. . . . It's over with in Ohio" (*Newsweek*, May 18, 1970).

The members of the Guard, mobilized under the general belief that they would be dealing with a dangerous mob of unified demonstrators, arrived on campus in force with loaded M-16 rifles and gas masks. There, during a confrontation with some of the demonstrators who hurled insults and rocks at the Guard, a continent of about sixteen soldiers fired thirty-five rounds directly into the crowd, which consisted mainly of spectators and students going to and from classes. Four students were killed and ten were wounded, including one paralyzed from the waist down. None of the soldiers hit by rocks required hospitalization.

Sociologist Jerry M. Lewis (1972), in his analysis of this incident, found that all six of Smelser's preconditions had been present. He also found that the motivations of the crowd participants were diverse; that some were demonstrators and others were not involved at all.

Newsweek magazine, reporting on the story a week after it happened, had this to say in their cover story:

Not one of the four dead had been closer than 75 feet to the troops who had killed them— and there was not the slightest suggestion that they had been singled out as targets because of anything they had done. Indeed, all available evidence indicated that the four dead students . . . were probably innocent bystanders.

. . . Kent State faculty members rendered a verdict of their own. Prevented from meeting on campus, they crowded into a nearby Akron Unitarian Church and passed this resolution:

"We hold the guardsmen acting directly under orders and under severe psychological pressures, less responsible than are Governor Rhodes and Adjutant General [Sylvester] Del Corso, whose inflammatory statements produced these pressures (May 18, 1970, pp. 32, 33 f)."

CROWDS AND CROWD BEHAVIOR

Some of the most spontaneous, unstructured, and short-lived forms of collective behavior occur within crowds. A **crowd** is a type of group that sociologists also call a *physical aggregate*—a temporary and relatively unstructured group, distinguished primarily by the physical proximity of its members. This concept was first introduced in Chapter 7 as one of the five basic types of groups in society. Now we will discuss in some detail the nature of crowds, their different forms, and how they operate.

The Nature of Crowds

Crowds are emergent groups that tend to develop in response to a variety of social situations, including planned events, sudden changes, and perceived injustices. They are often formed spontaneously, and, when the stimulus that attracted people ceases to be of interest, they can disperse just as quickly. Unlike other types of groups, such as social groups and formal organizations, crowds are "now" oriented and have no history and no future. Their members have no social positions with attendant role responsibilities to perform, no division of labor, and no commonly agreed-upon goals in most cases. Members, drawn by their individual motivations based on curiosity, interest, or motivation, find themselves in crowds as spectators, active participants, or just "floaters" passing through.

One of the most pervasive characteristics of crowds is **anonymity**, a condition in which a person's identity becomes lost in a crowd. When people feel anonymous because of their insulation by others in a large mass of people, they may also feel free to engage in behavior they would not have considered had they been acting alone. From the perspective of participants, it is almost as if the rules or laws are suspended and they feel immune from conventional norms because "no one will ever know it was I." In several civil disturbances throughout the twentieth and into the twenty-first century, crowds involved in various antisocial activities, including lynching, looting, and the destruction of property, have been influenced by anonymity. The sheer numbers of people involved have protected the identities of most members and furnished them with feelings of security. Some members of the Ku Klux Klan, for instance, have been prominent citizens in their local communities. They often felt immune from public scrutiny and possible sanctions because they operated in secrecy and hid their identities under white robes and hoods.

According to several social scientists' results, anonymity may also result in *bystander apathy* (Darley and Latane, 1968; Schwartz and Gottlieb, 1980). **Bystander apathy** is a condition in which, during emergency situations requiring responsible action, onlookers at the scene fail to act. Most people, when alone and aware that others are aware of their presence, will feel some pressure to render aid, in part because they do not want others to think poorly of them if they do not. However, they may be much less likely to act in a large crowd where their identity is unknown.

A dramatic illustration is represented by the brutal murder in 1962 of a young woman named Kitty Genovese. Returning home one night from her job, she was attacked in the parking lot adjacent to her apartment building by a single assailant with a knife. Stabbed repeatedly in an attack that took thirty-five minutes in three separate episodes of violence, the young woman screamed loudly for her life: "Oh God, he stabbed me! Please help me! Please help me! . . . I'm dying! I'm dying!" In all, thirty-eight people raised their windows and watched portions of these multiple attacks in which the assailant slowly took the life of his victim. One person shouted once for the attacker to stop, but no one tried otherwise to interfere with the slow butchering of this woman. No one tried to rescue her. Some went back to bed. And no one called the police. When questioned later by investigating authorities, one of Genovese's neighbors reported that he did not want to get involved (Rosenthal, 1964).

Types of Crowds

Crowds exhibit different characteristics and engage in a wide variety of activities. Some are relatively calm and somewhat formal. Others are quite volatile and have little, if any, focus or structure. There are murderous crowds and peaceful crowds, joyous crowds and sad crowds. Sociologist Herbert Blumer (1957) developed a most useful and comprehensive system for categorizing such groups. He divided crowds into four general categories—casual, conventional, expressive, and acting—which are briefly explained as follows:

1. *Casual Crowds.* A **casual crowd** is a temporary crowd formed spontaneously with members that tend to come and go. Spectators gathered to watch a building burn or to view the effects of a car accident are representative examples. So are shoppers at a mall that gather to watch a group of street dancers. Casual crowds are the most unstructured of all crowds, their members having little, if any, focus or emotional involvement. Members will often pass through the crowd on their way to some other activity and be a member for only a few moments. There is very little, if any, interaction between members because, in this type of crowd, there is a high degree of anonymity. It is fairly common for casual crowds to last for only a few minutes.

2. *Conventional Crowds.* A **conventional crowd** is a fairly structured crowd that conforms to established norms. Unlike a casual crowd, this group typically has a common goal among members and acts according to an agreed to set of norms. Religious assemblies on Sunday morning, movie audiences, and groups in attendance at symphony concerts fall into this category.

3. *Expressive Crowds.* An **expressive crowd** is one that has as its primary purpose the free expression of emotions by participants. In these groups, some allowances are made for those who want to "let go" emotionally in their own individual ways. Among fundamentalists, some funerals as well as religious revivals involve crowds that are particularly expressive of their emotions. As an additional illustration, parties may involve a free release of emotions as people "unwind" and have a good time. Victory celebrations for successful professional sports teams or political candidates serve as an added example.

4. *Acting Crowds.* An **acting crowd** is a highly aroused crowd focused on a specific situation or problem that members are willing to act on impulse to resolve. Unlike

expressive crowds, which have no concentrated focus, acting crowds are usually charged with negative emotions that are concentrated on some source of agitation. They tend to be very volatile and, thus, potentially dangerous to those who might get in their way. A **mob** is the most extreme form of acting crowd whose members are out of control and willing to engage in violence if it suits their ends.

Explanations of Crowd Behavior

In addition to Smelser's value-added theory, there are other, more specific, approaches that seem more suitable in helping us to understand the wide diversity of crowd behaviors and motivations. Of these, two of the most prominent explanations have been social contagion theory and emergent norm theory.

Social Contagion Theory   In 1895, French social psychologist Gustave Le Bon (1968) argued that people in crowds are so greatly influenced by the behavior of others that their own rational, decision-making capabilities are stifled. They fall under the influence of the powerful, almost hypnotic, "collective mind" of the crowd. So strong is the pull of some crowds, Le Bon asserted, that people who are typically peaceful and civilized when alone can be turned into violent barbarians under the influence of the crowd. Today, Le Bon is credited with being the originator of **social contagion theory**, the assertion that the mood and behavior of crowds become dominant in shaping the emotions and behavior of individual participants.

As initially formulated, contagion theory essentially was a psychological approach. It was based on the reductionist argument that the "collective mind" of the crowd influenced the minds of individuals who got caught up in a type of crowd mentality. There are, indeed, instances in which individuals seem to do little more than react mindlessly to a crowd. When this occurs with certain crowds, two contagion principles sometimes can be observed.

First, people will often engage in *imitation,* doing what they see others doing. In a shopping mall, for example, if one hears a strange sound, such as music, and observes others going to see what it is, it is very tempting for many to follow them and thus contribute to the formation of a crowd. Second, it is also very easy to react because of suggestibility, the tendency for people to be influenced in their behavior by the suggestions, directions, and actions of others once a crowd is formed. Crowds are often unstructured in that conventional norms are either absent or do not seem to apply. In such a situation, people tend to look to others for clues as to how to act. Consequently, they are susceptible to following the directions of those who possess decisive leadership qualities.

Some sociologists from the interactionist school, such as Herbert Blumer, have rejected the concept of the "collective mind" as being too simplistic. Nonetheless, some social scientists still subscribe to the contagion thesis that ordinary people in everyday situations can and do become "caught up" in crowds that alter their behavior. Blumer argues that this process is as interactive as it is reactive. Through his principle of **circular reaction**, he asserts that members of crowds, particularly in conditions of unrest and heightened tension, reinforce one another's feelings and behavior in a back-and-forth or circular fashion. A crowd's emotions and behavior in a tense situation are spread to others who not only model the behavior of the original group but reinforce their actions as well. This circular process of mutual reinforcement then acts to intensify many crowd situations, producing panics, angry mobs, or looting crowds.

Emergent Norm Theory   In contrast to the contagion approach is the **emergent norm theory**, the perspective that individuals become members of crowds for numerous reasons and, through interaction with others, adopt the group norms that develop from the particular situation. The original proponents of this theory, Ralph Turner and Lewis Killian (1957, 1987), offer an approach that differs from the social contagion theory in two key respects. First, rather than having unanimity of motive for their behavior, they argue that people may have a multitude of reasons for joining a crowd (Turner, 1980, McPhail and Wohlstein, 1983). In a mob, for example, some people may be incensed about something and want retribution, while others may simply want to use the situation as a cover to loot and steal for personal gain. Still others may be spectators who do not actively participate or those just passing through the crowd to reach another destination.

Second, Turner and Killian argue that, in most cases, people in crowds do not simply react to or even reinforce the emotions of the moment. Instead, they conform to norms that emerge from a crowd in much the same way they would in most conventional situations. Group norms govern appropriate behavior in almost all social encounters. Emergent norm theorists maintain that the same processes occur in crowds. A few visible leaders may define norms by expression or by example. Those who disagree often will not voice dissent because of the size of the group, which may be intimidating, or their fear of negative sanctions that may range from ridicule and embarrassment to the threat of physical punishment (Shibutani, 1986). Emergent norms in crowds, thus, say whether it is appropriate to applaud or jeer, laugh or cry, become "involved" or uninvolved, or, in some cases, whether to stand up (as in a movie ticket line) or sit down (as a member of the audience in a theatre).

Other Explanations   Although a popular theory for much of the twentieth century, the contagion approach, in particular, has drawn some criticism from some critics. Sociologist Richard Berk (1974) has used a **game perspective**, which argues that crowds are not irrational entities that catch people up in something "bigger than themselves." Instead, he asserts, crowds are often very rational and individuals are usually in complete control. In this sense, "selling off" one's stocks in a stock market crash may seem to be a logical thing to do to minimize losses. The riots that took place in the Watts section of Los Angeles during the summer of 1965 provide another example. In this violent upheaval in the impoverished black community, destruction was selective. Black-owned businesses were spared while white-owned businesses were looted and burned (Task Force Report, 1967). In addition, some looters driving cars were observed stopping for traffic lights and stop signs.

Other social scientists subscribe to **convergence theory**. They maintain that crowds tend to draw particular types of people with definite interests and values rather than a representative cross section of people from the community. Consequently, one would not see many Episcopalians at religious revivals, country-western fans as jazz music festivals, or well-educated, professional people at lynch mobs. In essence, proponents of this approach argue that people tend to participate in many crowd situations because of their wish to do with others what they enjoy doing by themselves. What attracts them is not mere curiosity but a set of interests and values.

Placing these varied explanations of crowds in perspective—Smelser's six preconditions, social contagion theory, emergent norm theory, and others—one realizes that all have some value in explaining the extremely diverse phenomenon of crowd behavior, but none is adequate in explaining all such behavior. Some crowds exhibit all six of Smelser's stages in sequence while others do not (Milgram, 1977). Social contagion occurs in certain instances in which a crowd seems to react with unanimity, while in others, critics assert, people have a variety of motives and react in a variety of ways (Turner, 1964). In addition, these approaches are not mutually exclusive. In specific crowds, specific elements of two or more of these perspectives may apply.

*M*ASS BEHAVIOR

Whereas crowd behavior typically occurs at the microlevel of society, mass behavior involves essentially the same process extended to the macrolevel. Briefly defined, **mass behavior** is unstructured social behavior characteristic of large collectivities of people who operate outside of one another's presence. The perspectives that are useful in explaining what happens in crowds also have some application to mass behavior. In fact, some sociologists consider "masses" as little more than diffuse crowds. Masses are, however, quite distinct from crowds. Unlike crowds, they are much larger and consist of persons "spatially dispersed and anonymous, reacting to one or more of the same stimuli but acting individually without regard to one another." (Hoult, 1969, p. 194).

Fads, Crazes, and Fashions

Fads, crazes, and fashions were first introduced in Chapter 4 as variations of folkways, broad-based norms in the form of customs and social conventions. However, they also represent forms of collective behavior in that they are temporary, relatively unstructured, and often have tremendous mass appeal. **Fads** are folkways popular for a brief period of time among a limited segment of the population. They take a variety of slang language forms

© MALIBUBOOKS, 2009. USED UNDER LICENSE FROM SHUTTERSTOCK, INC.

With the run up of gasoline to prices that nudged $4.00 per gallon during 2008, large "gas guzzler" vehicles went out of fashion and contributed to the needed government "bailout" of the big three U.S. automakers during 2008–2009. They overbuilt fuel-inefficient vehicles that, by early 2009, had plummeted in sales.

including "groovy" in the 1960s, "bad" in the 1980s, and "arm candy" (desirable for a date) in 2008–2009. Fads are also evident in musical preferences, modes of dress, and even diets. **Crazes** are fads which, among a limited segment of society, become obsessive. They vary from the hero worship of cult personalities like athletes, motion picture stars, and musical entertainers to certain consumer preferences such as "pet rocks" in the 1970s to the "Pokeman" and "Nintendo" game crazes during the early 2000s. **Fashions** are folkways more durable than fads that gain widespread acceptance among a large portion of society for a substantial period of time. Informal and varied clothing styles, driving smaller, more fuel-efficient cars, eating "heart-healthy," two-career families, and not smoking are fashionable forms of behavior and life style preferences today that are almost mirror opposites to what was fashionable a half a century ago during the 1950s and 1960s.

As forms of collective behavior, fads, crazes, and fashions, are important for their dynamic, rather than normative, aspects. Although often trivial—fads and crazes—and even frivolous in some instances, they sometimes act as indicators of significant social change. In a rapidly changing society like the United States, what begins as a fad or fashion can sometimes become an institutionalized part of a society's culture. Fast foods like ice cream cones, hot dogs, hamburgers, and coffee shops—which have now become a permanent part of Americana—began as fads and "caught on." The same thing could be said of sports like golf and tennis, bras for women, radios in automobiles, and even automobiles themselves. As another illustration, today, you can go to practically any airport, mall, or Starbucks coffee shop in America and see dozens of people with their laptops plugged into practically every available electrical outlet on evenings and weekends. This phenomenon was practically nonexistent until laptops, Google, and other related technologies became available, cost-effective, and "caught on" beginning just a few years ago with the dawn of the twenty-first century.

Likewise, crazes may come and go to provide stimulation and variety for a mass culture but sometimes become institutionalized as well. During the 1630s, the Dutch developed a passion for tulips. Individuals at all levels of society wanted tulip bulbs for their gardens, and soon the demand greatly outstripped the supply. Tulip mania reached such an extreme that people were paying more for a single tulip bulb than for a cow or a sheep, and soon bulbs were worth their weight in gold. This fever caused people to sell their farms and liquidate other property to invest in tulip bulbs, and a few people became rich overnight. A rumor was started, however, that the price of tulip bulbs was about to collapse. A selling panic resulted as thousands tried to sell their tulip bulbs and flowers all at once. The tulip market collapsed and many people were financially ruined. Nonetheless, what began at first as a prosperous and then disastrous craze gained a permanent place in the culture of Dutch society. Today, when one thinks of Holland, its world-renowned tulips, which are still grown with pride in that country, often come to mind.

Rumors

Just as one unverified story set in motion a panic and the subsequent collapse of the tulip market in Holland several centuries ago, rumors today can and do help to initiate and reinforce a variety of collective behavior forms. A **rumor** is an unconfirmed story that is spread rather quickly from person to person. Such unsubstantiated stories often emerge from conditions of social strain and confusion. When authoritative information is unavailable or formal channels of communication are blocked or not functioning effectively, conditions are ripe for the spread of rumors. Given such circumstances, few people in society—even the most educated and sophisticated—are immune from the temptation, at times, to listen to and perhaps spread rumors. These stories tend to originate and spread most easily among people of low prestige who crave attention, those who are socially isolated, and those with little education who lack the critical thinking skills to seek verification (Buckner, 1969). Regardless of who spreads unverified stories, the central reason for rumors, sociologist Tamotso Shibutani (1966) argues, is clear:

> Rumor is a substitute for news; in fact, it is news that does not develop in institutionalized channels. Unsatisfied demand for news—the discrepancy between information needed to come to terms with a changing environment and what is provided by formal news channels—constitutes the crucial condition of rumor construction (p. 62).

Rumors can be very destructive; for example, they touched off and fueled several riots during the 1960s. The Watts riot of 1965 in Los Angeles was precipitated by an incident of alleged "police brutality" in which a police officer jabbed a young black youth in the stomach with his baton (Governor's Commission, 1965; Cohen, 1969). However, by the time the story was told a few times, rumor had it that the police had beaten a pregnant woman. During the Newark, New Jersey riot of 1967, a young National Guardsman fired a warning shot to scare an inner-city resident away from a window. A rumor spread among police and guardsmen, alike, that the shot was fired by a sniper. Shortly thereafter, some fireworks going off were mistaken for snipers and police and two columns of guardsmen riddled a housing project with intense fire (*Report of the National Advisory Commission on Civil Disorders,* 1968, pp. 3-4).

The National Advisory Commission on Civil Disorders, charged with investigating both underlying and immediate causes of the urban riots of the 1960s, reported as follows:

> Rumors significantly aggravated tension and disorder in more than 65 percent of the disorders studied by the commission. Sometimes, as in Tampa and New Haven, rumor served as the spark that turned an incident into a civil disorder. Elsewhere, notably Detroit and Newark, even where they were not precipitating or motivating factors, inflaming rumors made the police and community leaders' jobs far more difficult (1968, p. 326).

Rumors have also affected reputations and careers and created problems for individuals and organizations. In 1985, Proctor and Gamble, a major producer of household products, abandoned their logo of 103 years depicting the man in the moon surrounded by thirteen stars (Salmans, 1985). For several years, fundamentalists had spread the rumor that the logo was a Satanic symbol. Although this was not true, this controversy created more problems for the company than it thought the logo was worth and it was discontinued. What makes rumors so insidious is that from time to time some of them turn out to be partially true. During the late summer of 2008, certain sources among the tabloid press news media "leaked" a story that former Democrat Senator John Edwards who had run for the Presidential nomination during the primary season earlier in the year, had been having an extramarital affair with a campaign staffer and had fathered a "love child" with this woman. Although Edwards emphatically denied these rumors, this story would not go away and finally was picked up and investigated by the mainstream media. Although the "love child" may or may not have been fathered by Edwards, he did finally admit to having had the affair, which effectively ended his further political aspirations for at least the foreseeable future (Schwartz, Ross, and Francecani, 2008).

© NEAL PRESTON/CORBIS

Despite widespread rumors that Paul McCartney had died (during the 1960s) and Dolly Parton had succumbed suddenly due to heart failure in 2008, both of these very popular entertainers were alive and well in 2010.

Two popular forms of rumor that become widespread from time to time focus on the "death" of a popular personality or media star or fantastic feats that defy death. During the 1960s, many fans of the pop music group The Beatles temporarily reached a state of near hysteria when it became widespread that lead singer and songwriter Paul McCartney had died. Of course today, nearly a half century later, McCartney is still very much alive. In the days following the September 11, 2001, attack on the World Trade Center, a rumor spread like wildfire that—as one of the towers fell—an elderly man surfed the falling debris down eighty floors to safety (Tyrangiel, 2001). More recently, the rumor was circulated that Dolly Parton, country-western singer, song-writer, and icon had died of congestive heart failure at age 62, despite the fact that she was very much alive and well (Fox News, August 25, 2008).

How do rumors spread? What interpersonal dynamics take place among those who initiate and pass them along? Social scientists Gordon Allport and Leo Postman (1965) studied rumors for several years. They found that, among several factors, leveling and sharpening seem to be of particular value. *Leveling* is a process by which, as a rumor is told and retold, it becomes more concise and retains only a few key details. This makes the story easier to grasp and spread to others. The distortion is then heightened in some cases by *sharpening,* a process in which the details that are retained as the story is passed on then increase in importance and, in essence, become the main story.

Two other processes—correcting and exaggeration—add to the development of rumors in some cases. When a story is reduced and distorted by leveling and sharpening, the details that remain and are passed on may not logically fit together anymore. The result is often correcting, a process in which people—either knowingly or unknowingly—make changes in an already distorted rumor so that its details seem to fit together more "logically." The addition of new details—never included in the original account—through *exaggeration* can then make an interesting story even more exciting.

Urban Legends

A phenomenon similar to rumors is what Jan Harold Brunvand (1980, 1981, 1986) has called the **urban legend**. An urban legend is an unsubstantiated story, much more durable than a rumor, that is spread over an entire society or country, usually with several local variations. These stories usually contain themes consistent with issues, problems, fears, and mysteries of modern life. How such tales are spread nationwide is not known for certain, although it appears that business people who travel by plane often spread them fairly quickly from coast to coast. Brunvand (1981, p. 10) says that a rumor tends to become an urban legend when it meets three criteria: (1) it makes for a good story, (2) it is plausible in the mind of the public, and (3) it serves as a moral object lesson. One popular theme in urban legends is the "suppressed truth" story. "The Martians have landed" has been a very popular story in recent decades, reaching urban legend status:

Supposedly, a UFO from the planet Mars with a number of humanoid creatures aboard crashed in the Midwest many years ago, and U.S. Air Force personnel recovered part of the craft and its occupants, one or two of them still alive before the rest of the spacecraft was destroyed in the resulting fire and explosion. The remaining UFO parts and the creatures were moved to an isolated hanger in the desert of Arizona (Texas, New Mexico, etc.), and the men involved in the action were sworn to secrecy or lied to about the nature of their mission. . . . The occupants were described as "three-foot tall, humanlike creatures wrapped in fine metallic cloth" (Brunvand, 1986, p. 198).

Other prevalent themes include "unusual uses of technology" (microwaves, cars, freezers, and so on), "restroom legends," "unfortunate pets legends," "sex scandal legends," and "unusual forms of revenge." The following example (Brunvand, 1986) combines two of the more common urban legend themes:

A woman went home on her lunch hour to pick up some items she needed for work, though she normally ate lunch at work. Upon her arrival home, she noticed her husband's car in the driveway. When she entered the house, she heard voices coming from the bedroom and she realized what she had walked in on. She immediately left the house, returned to work, and plotted her revenge. When she went home that evening, she cooked her husband's favorite dinner, changed into a sexy negligee, lit the candles, chilled the wine, and enjoyed a romantic evening with her husband. After dinner she enticed him into the bedroom, undressed him, and sexually aroused him, and when he was fully erect, she superglued his penis to his abdomen. He required surgery for its removal (p. 146).

Mass Hysteria

Sometimes mass behavior occurs so quickly that it becomes what sociologists call **mass hysteria**, a spontaneous excited reaction by large numbers of people to a mysterious social condition or event perceived as a threat. During May of 1981, for example, a large group of elementary school students in Massachusetts were practicing in a school auditorium for their spring concert. Suddenly, in a matter of minutes, nine children fainted. Forty children became ill with symptoms of nausea and dizziness, and six were taken to a local hospital.

When thirty children became ill at the concert later that evening, public health officials began an investigation. They concluded that the children suffered from no organic illness even though they did experience physical symptoms (Matchan, 1983). These children were probably anxious about performing before their parents and the community. Their anxiety, combined with close supervision by teachers creating a "captive audience" effect, peer pressure, and the pressure from all concerned to "get ready" for the big event, most likely produced an unbearable level of stress. Consequently, it is probable that a single child got dizzy and fainted in reaction to the pressure, which in turn provided an "escape mechanism" for others, who quickly developed similar physiological symptoms and responded accordingly.

The phenomenon of group panic, although localized at the micro level in the preceding illustration, also takes place at the macro level and has occurred throughout much of history. During the Middle Ages, the bubonic plague, or "Black Death," killed millions of Europeans and produced a mass panic. In the late 1600s, a "witch scare" swept across Massachusetts. Several young women and men were put on trial and later convicted and executed by hanging for practicing witchcraft (Boyer and Nissenbaum, 1974). A witch hunt

© BETTMANN/CORBIS

During the early 1950s, Senator Joseph McCarthy led a movement to find, expose, and discredit American communists. The actions of McCarthy and his followers created a form of mass hysteria that had many Americans worried over the "communist threat." Before he was finally discredited as an inflammatory demagogue who greatly exaggerated the communist presence and influence, hundreds of innocent Americans had had their reputations and careers destroyed.

of a quite different type occurred in the United States during the early 1950s. Senator Joseph McCarthy led a crusade to root out American communists, whom he and others felt were plotting to undermine the American way of life (Belfrage, 1963). Although McCarthy was finally discredited as an inflammatory demagogue, the inquisition he led produced a "red scare" that caused the blacklisting of many people in the entertainment industry—actors, screenwriters, playwrights, and so on—and ruined the reputations and careers of hundreds of innocent Americans.

The War of the Worlds Martian Invasion Case   One of the most fascinating incidences of mass hysteria during the twentieth century took place in 1938. On October 30, Orson Welles broadcast a dramatic and modernized version of H. G. Wells's *War of the Worlds* from the Mercury Theatre in New York City. Although Wells issued a disclaimer at the beginning of the radio program informing listeners that the story was fictional, many people tuned in during the middle of the program and thought the United States was being invaded by hostile Martians. In the story, the Martians first landed at a farm in Grover's Mill, New Jersey. After fighting a battle with U.S. troops, they moved on to New York City, where they proceeded to kill its inhabitants with poison gas. All this took place before the first thirty-minute station break. Of an estimated six million listeners, one million went into panic.

They called relatives to say farewell, fled from the area by car, and many gathered in bars and other public places to await "the end." It was obvious to a careful listener that there were too many events crammed into the short time of the radio broadcast to have taken place in real life. However, radio technology was relatively new, and many people, lacking media sophistication, were convinced that a Martian invasion from outer space was really happening (Houseman, 1948; Cantril, 1982).

The Melbourne Airport "Gassing" Phenomenon   Incidences of mass hysteria continue to occur, and several recent examples are cited in the literature. One of the more curious incidences occurred at the domestic terminal at Melbourne Airport on February 21, 2005. At just after 7:00 A.M., a woman working at a magazine stand collapsed near an escalator fifteen yards from her work station. Shortly thereafter, another airport employee fairly nearby became dizzy and started vomiting. Before the day was over, fifty-seven people had succumbed to this mysterious illness—with symptoms including dizziness, headaches, nausea, and vomiting—and forty-seven were taken to a nearby hospital. The generalized belief that spread fairly quickly throughout the airport was that a "gas leak" had caused the sudden illness. After thorough testing of air quality, emergency officials found no evidence of accidental or intentional release of chemical agents. The conclusion reached by a three-month Australian government investigation called it simply a "mystery." Sociogenic causes were never considered in the report of the incident, which cost one airline alone about $3 million. This episode, which disrupted one-third of domestic flights coming into and out of Melbourne Airport for two days, was most likely caused by mass hysteria (Bartholomew, 2005).

PUBLICS AND PUBLIC OPINION

Mass societies like the United States are characterized by, among other things, constantly changing policies, issues, and trends. The inhabitants of such societies often form publics which assess and react to these changing conditions in the form of public opinion. Some very visible issues occupying the minds of publics in recent decades included the civil rights and women's movements and the Vietnam conflict during the 1960s and 1970s, the HIV epidemic and "AIDS scare" in the 1980s, and "nuclear proliferation" during the 1990s. Major issues of public concern during the first decade of the 2000s included U.S. military involvement in Iraq and Afghanistan, the issue of homosexual marriage, and whether or not—in the view of the American public—global warming exists and, if so, whether or not human actions have been a significant factor. These and other concerns cause specific publics to emerge from the larger society which, in turn, may have an impact on social policies and trends.

Publics and Their Characteristics

A **public** is a large, widely dispersed group of people who share an interest in or concern about an issue or group of issues. Modern society contains many such publics. There is a voting public, a baseball public, and an investment public, as well as those focused on dozens of other concerns including abortion, gun control, pornography, women's rights, and other issues too numerous to mention. Therefore, every issue seen as significant in society tends to have its own public that is interested in how it is handled.

It is generally true that the more complex, urban, and technologically advanced a society is, the larger is its number of different publics. This is due mainly to rapid technological change and the diversity of occupations and lifestyles of a society's inhabitants. These changes and varied characteristics and interests of the people create conditions ripe for the emergence of different types of publics.

Characteristics of Publics   Although there are several ways to describe publics, they tend to have the following three basic characteristics:

1. ***The Membership of a Public Constantly Changes.*** People may freely enter or leave a public at any time. Consequently, some individuals become newly intrigued or disturbed by a particular issue while others become bored, tired, or disenchanted with it and shift interest to other issues or activities.

2. ***A Public is Usually Temporary.*** Publics tend to emerge and grow with an event or issue and, likewise, lose their focus or disintegrate when the event is over or the issue dies and fades away. A viewing public for a popular television show, for instance, will form and disband during a one-hour period each week, as analyzed by polls designed to measure the audience share each show receives. Likewise, a motion picture, which may take over a year to produce, film, edit, and promote, may become a commercial success or failure based on box office receipts paid by a public that formed around seeing it over a three- to four-week period. At best, voting publics, particularly in U.S. national elections, have a lifespan of only a few months as interest builds. Then, after the election, politics suddenly is a nonissue in the minds of most people. As a case in point, Hillary Clinton, during the her 2008 run for the Presidency, had a huge public of eighteen million supporters who voted her to victory in over two dozen state primaries during the Democratic primary. Narrowly defeated for the Democratic nomination, most of her public—with her encouragement—then shifted their allegiance to Senator Barack Obama from Illinois.

3. ***A Public Critically Assesses the Topic or Issue at Hand.*** Members take sides on an issue and seek information about it. Moviegoers read the critics' reviews, voters listen to the candidates and media pundits, and investors and business people follow the stock market and read financial columns. Publics communicate through and seek information primarily from media sources. For example, the magazines people subscribe to often identify the publics to which they belong. What publics would you guess are represented by most subscribers to *The Wall Street Journal, Ms. Magazine, Golf Digest,* and *Guns and Ammo?*

Public Opinion and Factors Affecting It

Public opinion refers to the dominant attitude held by a specific public or a society's population at large. As such, it is influenced by a variety of factors. First of all, the particular stand taken by a public on an issue is affected by the organizational affiliations held by its members, as well as the reference groups with which they identify (Blumer, 1948). It would be unlikely, therefore, for Republicans to favor strict gun control or for members of the National Organization for Women (NOW) to take a stand against abortion. In addition, community and national leaders exert a significant degree of influence in shaping the opinions held by members of certain publics who look to them for guidance and direction (Katz and Lazarsfeld, 1955). For example, in recent years, leaders like Hillary Clinton, Al Sharpton, Mich Romney, and Rudy Giuliani have each had their own constituencies. However, three factors impacting public opinion seem most worthy of expanded discussion: media, censorship, and propaganda.

Media   Media plays a dominant role in affecting public opinion. This is amply demonstrated by the billions of dollars spent annually on advertising by the producers of various consumer goods. Then, too, there is the emphasis and money spent on creating the proper "image" and gaining adequate media exposure for politicians who run for national, state, and even local office.

Media refer to the systematic ways used to transmit information to specific publics or the population at large. In the United States, television, newspapers, and internet blogs furnish most adults with their primary sources of information about what is happening in the world, nation, and local community. The impact of media on public opinion is substantial. From the Vietnam conflict ending in the 1970s to the operations of today's U.S. military personnel placed in harm's way in places like Afghanistan, war actions displayed in vivid color live as it happens or within hours of its occurrence have brought home in vivid clarity the horrors of war and the human toll it takes on combatants as well as citizens in the countries where the violence occurs. Since the Vietnam era of the 1970s, American families have seen sons, husbands, and fathers, as well as women family members, carried away on stretchers to waiting helicopters for evacuation. Until this modern era, war had been distant and much easier to defend and even romanticize. The stark realism of media imagery today no doubt has influenced American public opinion concerning U.S. involvement in Iraq and other places.

Sociologist Gary Marx (1986) has argued that media are used in the United States in a calculated manner as social control mechanisms, a trend that has been on the increase in recent decades. A long list of examples include the following: computerized databanks containing various kinds of personal information about most citizens; video surveillance cameras in public and work locations; increasingly sophisticated "eavesdropping" technology, including wiretapping; satellite surveillance capability; electronic ankle devices worn by those on house arrest, probation, or parole that allow authorities to track their locations; and crime hotlines for reporting anonymous tips.

Marx warns that while these new uses of media technology may be attractive in combating crime, they can also be used to discourage free speech, creativity, and most forms of nonconformity. If such a trend were to lead gradually to an insidious form of totalitarianism—in which people's lives and actions are increasingly micromanaged and controlled by bureaucrats whose use of such burgeoning technology is used to justify their positions—it would have a chilling effect on free speech and creativity and, with it, a dramatic impact on public opinion as well. If this occurs, which Marx fears is likely, public opinion and public discourse could be controlled, because people would become afraid to speak their true feelings anywhere.

Censorship   Limitations placed on the information made available to the public are called **censorship**. One form of such restriction—the form usually thought of—is governmental censorship of sensitive information for national security reasons. During World War II, for instance, thousands of scientists and government employees worked on the $2 billion Manhattan Project aimed at developing the atomic bomb. Yet only a very few knew the entire story, scope, and goals, which later turned out to be the best-kept secret of the twentieth century (Blum, et al., 1973).

Limitations on information take a variety of forms. In the space allowed in a newspaper story or the time available for a news broadcast, those who control the media decide which information to leave in and which to exclude. Parents, likewise, censor the information their small children receive, especially in regard to violence and sexual content; motion pictures do the same within the guidelines established for the motion picture industry, and manufacturers, particularly in "high tech" industries, maintain tight security in guarding corporate secrets.

Propaganda   While censorship acts to delete all or a part of a certain message, propaganda also distorts the information needed for the public to assess an issue freely. This is accomplished by only presenting one side of an argument or otherwise engaging in a calculated attempt to persuade in a biased and often misleading manner.

Propaganda refers to the use of calculated and biased methods of persuasion based on emotional appeal. The propagandist may be a government or one of its agencies, a politician, a manufacturer or advertising executive, a church minister, or even a teacher or friend. Unlike the aims of *brainwashing*, which are to "reprogram" an individual or group with a different value orientation, those of propaganda are temporary and superficial, in most cases. The goals of propagandists focus on influencing people just enough to persuade them to vote for a particular candidate, support a specific cause or position, sign a petition, or buy a product.

Methods of persuasion are usually aimed at a specific target population and are planned accordingly. The tobacco industry, for example, markets dozens of brands of cigarettes. With the exception of low tar and nicotine content cigarettes, there is little difference between the various "blends" of tobacco except in the way they are packaged and marketed to specific publics. What type of targeted group is Marlboro aimed at? What about Virginia Slims or Eve? Likewise, how would you compare what is advertised on the Sunday evening news program 60 Minutes with the products advertised on Saturday morning cartoon shows. What type of audience watches each program? Advertisers find out through what is called psychographic research and then carefully craft propaganda to appeal to each targeted group.

Some of the more common propaganda approaches, as identified by Sociologists Leonard Broom and Phillip Selznick (1968), are gaining attention, associating, concealing identity and aims, raising anxieties, and showing strength:

1. ***Gaining Attention.*** *Attention getting* involves the use of a variety of catch phrases, eye-catching devices, and other gimmicks to influence public opinion. Politicians make use of such attention getters as grand entrances, brass bands, and media exposure. Those determined to discredit a politician or other public figure use a variation of the "big lie," in which some half-truth about the person is exaggerated and taken out of context. The media often blows such things out of proportion because it is sensational and "sells copy," or may increase "audience share" to maximize profits. When apologies are sometimes made and the negative item is put in its proper perspective, it is not "real news" and tends to get buried in a brief statement on a back page. In the mind of the public, however, the sensational headline or lead story is the one remembered, even though the credibility of the public figure might be damaged or destroyed.

   Likewise, advertisers selling a product in both print and the electronic media use a variety of attention-getting devices. Words like "free" and "sale" are very effective, as are musical jingles and catch phrases. Memorable phrases from the 1970s through the 2000s have included "You deserve a break today," "Where's the beef?," "Be all that you can be," and, recently, the Lexus ad which says, "The relentless pursuit of perfection" and for Nike running shoes, "Just do it." Politicians also use attention getting devices. During the 2008 U.S. Presidential Campaign, for example, the Democrats promoting Obama used the catch phrases "We can do it" and "Change we can believe in" while the McCain-led Republicans countered with "the straight talk express." Those with a profit-making motive, like advertisers, also use attention getters, which include sex and sexual imagery, delicious-looking food, and adorable children and animals.

2. ***Associating a Cause or Product with Values, Beliefs, or Symbols Held or Used by the Public.*** Politicians, for example, may talk in *glittering generalities* about such things as home, family values, God, and country as a diversionary tactic to keep away from the substantive issues. Some voters, impressed with this "image" that seems to be in line with cherished values, may succumb to the orchestrated allure of such a candidate. Another associating technique used by politicians and others is to appear as *plain folks.* Advertisers and other propagandists may also use *testimonials* by famous actors, professional athletes, and other personalities to grace a product or cause. This, again, is a diversionary tactic used to avoid a direct and substantive discussion of the issue or issues at hand. Finally, propagandists sometimes use the *band wagon* technique in an attempt to convince the audience that everyone is "doing it," "buying it," "accepting it," or otherwise "jumping on the bandwagon" (Lee and Lee, 1971).

3. ***Concealing Real Identity and Goals.*** Sometimes, because of prevailing attitudes in a community or society, propagandists feel they must hide their true identities and aims. Extremist groups and organized crime families, for example, may hide behind legitimate, socially acceptable, "front organizations" or causes. They convince many in the public that they are acceptable when, in reality, they are engaged in covert, destructive activities (Broom and Selznick, 1968). In similar fashion, governments of countries like the United States and Russia try to convince their citizens that they are giving aid to less developed countries primarily for humanitarian reasons when other motivations, such as the geopolitical importance of these countries and/or access to their natural resources, are equally compelling.

4. ***Raising Fears and Anxieties.*** On occasion, politicians will attempt to raise fears by emphasizing *hidden enemies.* Advertisers will often attempt to raise people's anxieties concerning a whole host of issues including their health, sex life, weight, or social standing. In television commercials, there is a standard formula. During the first few seconds, a person in the story is portrayed with a life complication. Next comes the introduction of the product, often with a demonstration of its effectiveness. This is followed immediately by an "instant miracle" in which the person's life is changed for the better because he or she used the product.

5. ***Showing Strength.*** Propagandists use this persuasive technique in an attempt to show the merits of a particular point of view, cause, or product. Organized groups and social movements with few resources can impact public opinion by staging dramatic, visible events, and then using authoritative sources, such as the press, to gain

maximum public exposure (Kielbowiez and Scherer, 1986). Marches, demonstrations, sit-ins, and other devices used by various groups in recent years serve as representative examples. Advertisers also show products' strength through the use of statistical claims, product comparisons, demonstrations, and independent tests.

Propaganda in Perspective   Two additional points concerning propaganda should be mentioned. First, the categories of techniques listed above are not mutually exclusive. Instead, propagandists often incorporate several approaches in attempting persuasion. For example, in 1985, the late actor Yul Brynner, who was a five-pack-per-day smoker, made an antismoking television commercial for the American Cancer Society a few weeks before he died of cancer. In this poignant attempt to persuade viewers to quit smoking, elements of associating, raising fears and anxieties, and showing strength were used.

Second, propaganda is often limited in its total effectiveness by several factors. These include competing propagandas, the level of education and sophistication of the audience, and existing norms and cultural trends. Well-informed people are much more resistant to propaganda than the naive and poorly educated. Likewise, propaganda that goes against existing cultural norms is usually ineffective.

SOCIAL MOVEMENTS

A **social movement** is a dedicated effort by a fairly large group to promote or resist change in the existing social system (Tilly, 2004). Social movements represent the most highly organized form of collective behavior and are often the longest lasting. Historically, they have taken place primarily in societies characterized by complexity, growth, and change. In 1517, for example, Martin Luther set in motion one of the most significant movements of the last five hundred years when he nailed his *Ninety-Five Theses* to the church door in Wittenburg. The Protestant Reformation that followed helped to reshape social, political, and economic thought in Europe and affected the worldview of those who first emigrated from their countries of origin to come to America in order to escape religious persecution (Bronowski and Mazlish, 1962).

Since that time, social movements have taken various forms. All have distinct goals. Some try to affect social values as did the recent civil rights and women's movements. Other movements attempt to gain power, such as that of the Nazis in Germany during the 1930s and 1940s, and more recently during the 2000s, the communist movement in Venezuela led by Hugo Chavez who, like his hero Fidel Castro, has seized private property and corporate infrastructure, nationalized the economy, and curtailed human rights. There are also movements focused on achieving personal benefits and psychological rewards for participants, including back-to-nature movements, and religious movements like those of the Mormons during the nineteenth century and the fundamentalist evangelicals today (Turner and Killian, 1987).

Characteristics

Although social movements vary significantly in terms of goals, they usually have similar characteristics (Broom and Selznick, 1968; DeFleur, D'Antonio, and D'Fleur, 1976). First, they tend to have a *different perspective* from the status quo, or existing social policy. The women's movement, as a case in point, has succeeded in helping to redefine the role and status of women in contemporary society. Second, social movements exhibit *idealism among members.* Such idealism is particularly important as a morale booster since members of many social movements must face hardships and resistance. During the civil rights movement of the 1960s, many participants in demonstrations—often the objects of taunts, assaults, and arrest—linked arms and sang "We shall overcome," which became the theme song of the movement. In addition, members of social movements have an *action orientation.* They are dedicated to engaging in the action necessary to change some aspect of society through petitions, debates, speeches, demonstrations, and other approaches. Finally, most movements consist of multiple organizations. Even though each may have its specific objectives, a coalition is often established to enable numerous organizations to work for a common cause.

Stages

According to Herbert Blumer (1939), social movements typically progress through a life cycle of four distinct stages. The first of these, the *social unrest stage,* emerges as a response to conflicts between various segments of society, unresolved social problems that sometimes appear to be getting worse, and a general state of dissatisfaction and restlessness concerning one or more issues. In such conditions of social unrest and confusion, leaders initially tend to be malcontents who do little more than heighten feelings of discontent.

Such leadership, however, tends to result in greater focus as the movement enters the *popular stage,* in which dissatisfied individuals see the need to close ranks and work together for a commonly held goal. During this period in the lifespan of a movement, two types of leaders may emerge—prophets and reformers. Prophets tend to be charismatic individuals with a vision, who have the ability to inspire followers to pursue a commonly held goal. Reformers are much more pragmatic and may have an agenda for addressing specific problems and overcoming them a step at a time.

The third and fourth periods in the life of a social movement are the formalization and institutional stages. During the *formalization stage,* goals and strategies become clearly defined and standardized. The movement develops calculated formation with clearly established levels and areas of leadership and authority. Policies and plans of action emerge which may resemble those of bureaucracies and formal organizations. Negotiators and master strategists take over the reins of leadership from the prophets and reformers. Finally, during the *institutional stage,* the movement is fully accepted and becomes part of the institutional fabric of mainstream society. Leaders become power brokers and administrators, concerned chiefly with consolidating and managing the gains that have been achieved.

Malcolm Spector and John Kitsuse (1977) have suggested an additional stage—reemergence or *renewal,* in some social movements. A portion of the original membership may come to feel that the movement has become too "status quo" in orientation and has lost its original sense of mission or purpose. Perceiving stagnation and discontent, these people may feel a need to renew efforts or perhaps begin a new movement based on the gains already achieved. The women's movements of the twentieth century furnish us with a good illustration. During the first decade of this century, the goal for reform-oriented women was suffrage, the right to vote. By the late 1960s, a process of renewal was clearly evident as women focused their efforts on a much broader range of issues—abortion rights, pay equity, the equal rights amendment, breaking the glass ceiling for women wishing to reach the highest possible levels in their careers, and so on—aimed at much broader participation in society. With some of these goals accomplished and others—such as shattering the glass ceilings—making definite progress, it is not unrealistic to expect perhaps a second feminist renewal sometime during the first half of the twenty-first century (Marx and McAdam, 1994).

Types

Perhaps the most useful way to distinguish between different types of social movements is to examine their goals and the means or tactics used to achieve them. Accordingly, most social movements may be placed in one of the following categories:

1. ***Reactionary Movements.*** **Reactionary movements** are those that reject existing social policy and attempt to restore earlier values, norms, and policies, through violent means, if necessary. The Ku Klux Klan historically has supported the doctrine of white supremacy and complete segregation of the races. In attempting to reach this goal, members of the Klan and other segregationist groups have periodically engaged in acts of terrorism and violence.

2. ***Conservative Movements.*** **Conservative movements** work within the system to preserve aspects of the status quo and thus resist certain forms of social change. The National Rifle Association, for instance, continues to work diligently in an attempt to preserve what it believes to be American citizens' constitutional right—under the Second amendment—to keep and bear arms with as few restrictions on law-abiding citizens as possible.

3. ***Reform Movements.*** **Reform movements** are those that work within the social system for changes in specific values, norms, and policies. Both the civil rights and women's movements during the twentieth century have been reform movements, in that they have attempted to change customs and laws to provide minorities and women with improved opportunities and greater participation in society. In regard to both goals, these movements have both achieved significant, if not dramatic, success over the past several decades.

4. ***Revolutionary Movements.*** **Revolutionary movements** seek to replace a portion or all of an existing social system with something different, through violent means if necessary. Examples include the American Revolution of 1776–1789 and the Russian Revolution of 1917. How those involved in a revolutionary struggle are perceived and characterized depends on one's vantage point and vested interests. During the American Revolution, the "Sons of Liberty" were seen as heroes by many colonists but were vilified by those still loyal to the British Crown.

5. ***Separatist movements.*** **Separatist movements** are those that find the existing social system unacceptable and seek to set up alternative organizations, communities, or societies. Some social scientists prefer the term "utopian" in referring to

these movements (Alexander and Gill, 1984). Their members attempt to operate outside the mainstream of the host society. Their goal is the achievement of a form of personal expression and a lifestyle directed inward toward themselves and their group or community, rather than outward toward the larger world of contemporary society. Some of the most notable of these isolationist movements are religious in orientation. In the United States, they include the Shakers, the Amish, and more recently, fundamentalist Morman polygamous groups, such as the Yearning for Zion Ranch group previously discussed in Chapter 8.

CHAPTER SUMMARY

1. Collective behavior consists of people's relatively spontaneous and unstructured actions in response to ambiguous or changing social conditions. In general, sociologists divide investigation of this type of behavior into four broad categories: crowds and crowd behavior, mass behavior, public opinion, and social movements. This chapter is devoted primarily to a discussion of these topics.

2. We must first, however, discuss the preconditions that set the stage for collective behavior. In this regard, sociologist Neil Smelser has developed the value-added theory, the assertion that six conditions in society, when added together in sequential order, create a cumulative effect that increases the likelihood of collective behavior. These six factors are structural conduciveness, social strain, generalized belief, precipitating factors, mobilization of participants and social control.

3. Crowds are emergent groups that tend to develop in response to a variety of social situations, including planned events, sudden changes, and perceived injustices. One of the most pervasive characteristics of crowds is anonymity, a condition in which a person's identity becomes lost in a crowd. This, combined with bystander apathy, can significantly influence the forms of behavior within such groupings. Crowds are generally divided into four basic types: casual, conventional, expressive, and acting.

4. Two of the most dominant explanations of crowd behavior are provided by social contagion theory and emergent norm theory. Contagion theorists hold that the mood and behavior of crowds becomes dominant in shaping the emotions and behavior of the individuals who participate in them. Through such processes as imitation, suggestibility, and circular reaction, the behavior patterns of a crowd spread to include additional members. An alternative to the social contagion approach is the emergent norm theory, the perspective that individuals become members of crowds for numerous reasons and, through interaction with others, adopt the group norms that develop from the situation.

5. Mass behavior is unstructured social behavior characteristic of large collectivities of people who operate outside of each other's presence. This form of collective behavior includes fads, crazes, and fashions (discussed in Chapter 4), as well as rumors, urban legends, and mass hysteria. A rumor is an unconfirmed story that is spread rather quickly from person to person. Such unverified stories tend to emerge from conditions of social strain and confusion and take form through processes of what sociologists have named leveling, sharpening, correcting, and exaggeration. An urban legend is an unsubstantiated story much more durable than a rumor, that is spread over an entire society or country. This kind of story usually involves themes consistent with the issues, problems, fears, and mysteries of modern life. A third form of mass behavior is mass hysteria, a spontaneous excited reaction by large numbers of people to a mysterious social condition or event perceived as a threat.

6. Publics and public opinion represent an additional form of collective behavior. A public is a large, widely dispersed group of people who share an interest in or concern about a particular issue or group of issues. Every major issue in a given society has a

public devoted to it. Public opinion refers to the dominant attitude held by a specific public or a society's population at large. It is influenced by several factors including media, censorship, and propaganda.

7. The most highly organized form of collective behavior is represented by the social movement, a dedicated effort by a fairly large group to promote or resist change in the existing social system. In terms of characteristics, most social movements tend to have a different perspective from the status quo, exhibit idealism among members, maintain an action orientation, and consist of multiple organizations. Specific types of social movements include the reactionary, conservative, reform, revolutionary, and separatist forms.

TERMS TO KNOW

acting crowd: a highly aroused crowd focused on a specific situation or problem that members are willing to act on impulse to resolve.

anonymity: a condition in which a person's identity becomes lost in a crowd.

bystander apathy: a condition in which, during emergency situations requiring responsible action, onlookers at the scene fail to act.

casual crowd: a temporary crowd formed spontaneously with members that tend to come and go.

censorship: limitations placed on the information that is made available to the public.

circular reaction: the principle that members of crowds, particularly in conditions of unrest and heightened tension, reinforce one another's feelings and behavior in a back-and-forth or circular fashion.

collective behavior: a pattern of social behavior that consists of people's relatively spontaneous and unstructured actions in response to ambiguous or changing social conditions.

conservative movements: those that work within the system to preserve aspects of the status quo and thus resist certain forms of social change.

conventional crowd: a fairly structured crowd that conforms to established norms.

convergence theory: the perspective that crowds tend to draw particular types of people with definite interests and values rather than a representative cross-section from the community.

crazes: fads which, among a limited segment of society, become obsessive.

crowd (also physical aggregate): a temporary and relatively unstructured group distinguished primarily by the physical proximity of its members.

emergent norm theory: the perspective that individuals become members of crowds for numerous reasons and, through interaction with others, adopt the group norms that develop from the particular situation.

expressive crowd: a crowd that has as its primary purpose the free expression of emotions by participants.

fads: folkways popular for a brief period of time among a limited segment of the population

fashions: folkways more durable than fads that gain widespread acceptance among a large portion of society for a substantial period of time.

game perspective: the argument that crowds are often very rational with participants who act logically under their own control in ways that benefit them.

generalized belief: a situation in which (1) intergroup conflicts develop between certain segments of the population and/or (2) dramatic social changes occur which can precipitate incidents of collective behavior.

mass behavior: unstructured social behavior characteristic of large collectivities of people who operate outside of one another's presence.

mass hysteria: a spontaneous excited reaction by large numbers of people to a mysterious social condition or event perceived as a threat.

media: the systematic ways used to transmit information to specific publics or the population at large.

mob: the most extreme form of acting crowd, whose members are out of control and willing to engage in violence if it suits their ends.

mobilization of participants: a process in which, through the directions and actions of a few leaders, enough people with sufficient motivation can be brought together and given the focus to act either positively or negatively.

precipitating factors: events or actions that sharpen the focus of structural conduciveness and social strain and create or reinforce generalized belief that can lead to collective behavior.

propaganda: calculated and biased methods of persuasion based on emotional appeal.

public: a large, widely dispersed group of people who share an interest in or concern about an issue or group of issues.

public opinion: the dominant attitude held by a specific public or a society's population at large.

reactionary movements: those that reject existing social policy and attempt to restore earlier values, norms, and policies, through violent means, if necessary.

reform movements: those that work within the social system for changes in specific values, norms, and policies.

revolutionary movements: those that seek to replace a portion or all of an existing social system with something different, through violent means, if necessary.

rumor: an unconfirmed story that is spread rather quickly from person to person.

separatist movements: those that find the existing social system unacceptable and seek to set up alternative organizations, communities, or societies.

social contagion theory: the assertion that the mood and behavior of crowds become dominant in shaping the emotions and behavior of individual participants.

social control: the process of how, in a collective behavior context, the actions of authorities can facilitate a smooth process of spontaneous group expression or promote conflict and cause a tense situation to become more volatile.

social movement: a dedicated effort by a fairly large group to promote or resist change in the existing social system.

social strain: a social condition in which (1) intergroup conflicts develop between certain segments of the population and/or (2) dramatic social changes occur.

structural conduciveness: a condition in which certain elements built into a society's social structure act to encourage collective behavior.

urban legend: an unsubstantiated story, much more durable than a rumor, that is spread over an entire society or country, usually with several local variations.

value-added theory: the argument that certain conditions in society, when added together in sequential order, create a cumulative effect that increases the likelihood of relatively spontaneous group behavior.

SUGGESTED READINGS

Best, J. 2006. *Flavor of the Month: Why Smart People Fall for Fads.* Berkeley, CA: University of California Press. A tracking of fad phenomena throughout American pop culture using examples from the 1950s to the present. A very entertaining and penetrating look at how "fickle" popular tastes are and how quickly they can change.

Marx, G. T., and D. McAdam. 1994. *Collective Behavior and Social Movements: Structure and Process.* Englewood Cliffs, NJ: Prentice-Hall. A well-written, brief overview of the major topics and techniques used in the sociological analysis of collective behavior.

Rubin, B. A. 1996. *Shifts in the Social Contract: Understanding Change in American Society.* Thousand Oaks, CA: Pine Forge Press. An analysis of how fundamental shifts are occurring in several sectors of postmodern society as we move away from stable, long-term relationships to dynamic, short-term ones that tend to be temporary.

Tilly, C. 2004. *Social Movements. 1768–2004.* Boulder, CO: Paradigm Publishers. A fascinating look at the history of social movements in the United States, from the late colonial period to contemporary times, that is punctuated with fascinating examples from each period of American society as it has evolved.

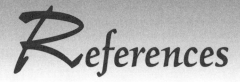

References

Abegglen, J. C. 1958. *The Japanese factory.* New York: Free Press.

Adams, N. 1974. Heredity and environment. *Encyclopedia of sociology,* 126. Guilford: CT: The Duskin Publishing Group.

Adorno, T. W., E. Frenkel-Brunswick, D. J. Levinson, and R. N. Sanford. 1950. *The authoritarian personality.* New York: Wiley.

Aguilar, A., and R. Baillargeon. 1999. 2.5-month-old infant's reasoning about when objects should and should not be occluded. *Cognitive Psychology* 39: 116–157.

Aldous, J. 1986. Cuts in selected welfare programs: The effects on U. S. families. *Journal of Family Issues* (June).

Alexander, P., and R. Gill, eds. 1984. *Utopias.* London: Duckworth.

Allport, G. 1954. *The nature of prejudice.* Reading, MA: Addison-Wesley.

Allport, G., and L. Postman. 1965. *The psychology of rumor.* New York: Holt, Rinehart and Winston. Originally published in 1947.

Altman, L. 2008. Sex infections found in quarter of teenaged girls. *The New York Times.* March 12. Accessed on September 24, 2008 at http://www.nytimes.com/2008/03/12/science/12std.html

American Academy of Pediatrics, Committee on Public Education. 2001. Policy statement: Children, adolescents, and television. *Pediatrics* 107 (February): 423–426.

American Sociological Association, Committee on Professional Ethics. 1968. Toward a code of ethics for sociologists. *American Sociologist* 3 (November): 316–318.

American Sociological Association 1980. Revised A. S. A. code of ethics. *A. S. A. Footnotes* 8 (August): 12–13; 52.

American Sociological Association. 1999. Employed social scientists with bachelors degrees by Sector, 1999. Updated October 23, 2008.

Amidei, N. 1981. Testimony, U.S. Congress, House Committee on Energy and Commerce, Subcommittee on Health and the Environment (October): 459.

Anderson, J. 2008. Wall Street winners get billion dollar paydays. *International Herald Tribune.* April 16.

Anderson, M. J, and S. E. Fienberg, 1999. *Who counts: The politics of census-taking in contemporary America.* New York: Russell Sage Foundation.

Anderson, N. 1923. *The hobo.* Chicago: The University of Chicago Press.

APP News. 1998. *American Journal of Pediatrics* (May).

Archer, D., and R. Gartner. 1984. *Violence and crime in cross-national perspective.* New Haven, CT: Yale University Press.

Armato, P., and DeBoer, D. B. 2001. The transmission of marital instability across generations: Relationship skills or commitment to marriage? *Journal of Marriage and Family* 63: 1038–1051.

Armato, P., and Previti, D. 2004. People's reasons for divorcing: Gender, social class, the life course, and adjustment. *Journal of Family Issues* 24: 602–606.

Armour, S. 2006. High cost of child care can lead to lifestyle changes, adjustments. *USA Today,* April 18. Accessed on September 24, 2008 at http://usatoday.com/money/perfi/general/2006-4-18-child-costs-usat_x.htm

Armstrong, T. 2004. *The myth of the attention deficit child.* 1. Accessed on November 22, 2008 at www.thomasarmstrong.com

Asch, S. E. 1955. Opinions and social pressure. *Scientific American* 193: 4–8.

Asch, S. 1965. Effects of group pressure upon the modification and distortion of judgments. In H. Proshansky and B. Seldenberg, eds. *Basic studies in psychology.* New York: Holt, Rinehart and Winston, 393–401.

Babbie, E. 1983. *The practice of social research.* 3rd ed. Belmont, CA: Wadsworth.

Babbie, E. 1994. *The sociological spirit.* Belmont, CA: Wadsworth.

Bachman, J. P., P. M. O'Malley, and J. Johnston. 1978. *Adolescence to adulthood: Change and stability in the lives of young men.* Vol. 4, *Youth in transition.* Ann Arbor: MI: Institute for Social Research.

Bailey, W. T. 1998. Deterrence, brutalization, and the death penalty: Another examination of Oklahoma's return to capital punishment. *Criminology* 36: 711–733.

Bailey, T. 1966. *The American pageant: A history of the republic,* 3rd ed. Boston: D. C. Heath.

Bales, R. F. 1950. *Interaction process analysis.* Reading: MA: Addison-Wesley.

Bales, R. F. 1953. The equilibrium problem in small groups. In T. Parsons et al., eds. *Working papers in the theory of action.* Glencoe, IL: Free Press.

Bales, R. F. 1970. *Personality and interpersonal behavior.* New York: Holt, Rinehart and Winston.

Bales, R. F., and P. E. Slater. 1955. Role differentiation in small decision-making groups. In T. Parsons and R. F. Bales, eds. *Family, socialization, and interaction process.* New York: Free Press.

Bales, R. F.,and F. L. Strodtbeck. 1951. Phases in group problem-solving. *Journal of Abnormal and Social Psychology* 46 (October): 485–495.

Ball-Rokeach, S. J. M. Rokeach, and J. W. Grube. 1984. *The great American values test: Influencing behavior and belief through television.* New York: Free Press.

Barbujani, G., A. Magagni, E. Minch, and L. L. Cavelli-Sforza. 1997. An apportionment of human DNA diversity. *Proceedings of the National Academy of Sciences* 94(9): 4516–4519.

Barlow, H. 1987. *Introduction to criminology,* 4th ed. Boston: Little, Brown.

Barlow, H. D., and D. Kauzlarich. 2002. *Introduction to criminology,* 8th ed. Upper Saddle River, NJ: Prentice-Hall/Pearson Education.

Barnett, O. W., C. L. Miller-Perrin, and R. D. Perrin. 2005. *Family violence across the lifespan: An introduction,* 2nd ed. Thousand Oaks, CA: Sage Publications.

Barnouw, V. 1978. *Ethnology: An introduction to anthropology,* 3rd ed. Homewood, IL: Dorsey Press.

Bart, P., and L. Frankel. 1986. *The student sociologist's handbook,* 4th ed. New York: Random House.

Bartholomew, R. E. 2005. "Mystery Illness at Melbourne airport: Toxic poisoning or mass hysteria." *The Medical Journal of Australia* 183 (11/12): 564–566.

Bartol, C. R. 1980. *Criminal behavior: A psychosocial approach.* Englewood Cliffs, NJ: Prentice-Hall.

Baughman, F. A. Jr. 2006. *The ADHD fraud: How psychiatrists make "patients" of normal children.* USA: Trafford Publishing.

Baumer, T. L., and D. P. Rosenbaum. 1984. *Combating retail theft: Programs and strategies.* Boston: Butterworth.

Baumrind, D. 1968. Authoritarian versus authoritative parental control. *Adolescence* 3: 255–72.

Baumrind, D. 1989. Rearing competent children. In *Child development today and tomorrow,* ed. W. Damon, 349–378. San Francisco: Jossey-Bass.

Bavelas, A. 1962. Communication patterns in task-oriented groups In *Group dynamics,* 2nd ed., eds. D. Cartright and A. F. Zander, 669–682. New York: Harper & Row.

BBC News, 2005. Gay marriage around the globe. *BBC News,* July 22, 2005. Accessed September 29, 2008 at http://news.bbc.co.uk/1/hi/world/americas/4081999.stm

BBC Homepage, 2005. Religion and ethics—Hinduism. 11-14-05. Accessed November 22, 2008 at http://www.bbc.co.uk/religion/religions/Hinduism/living/caste.shtml

BBC News, 2005. Child slavery worldwide. *BBC News,* May 11, 2005.

Beach, L. R. 1973. *Psychology: Core concepts and special topics.* New York: Holt, Rinehart and Winston.

Becker, H. S. 1963. *The outsiders: Studies in the sociology of deviance.* New York: Free Press.

Becker, H. 1967. Whose side are we on? *Social Problems* 14: 239–247.

Becker, H. 1998. *Tricks of the trade: How to think about your research while you're doing it.* Chicago: University of Chicago Press.

Becker, H., and H. E. Barnes. 1961. *Social thought from lore to science,* Vol. 1, 3rd ed. New York: Free Press.

Beeghley, L. 2008. *The structure of social stratification in the United States,* 5th ed. Boston: Allyn and Bacon

Beeghley, L., and E. W. Butler. 1974. The consequences of intelligence testing in the public schools before and after desegregation. *Social Problems* 21:740–754.

Belfrage, C. 1963. *The American inquisition, 1945–1960.* New York: Bobbs-Merrill.

Bell, D. 1973. *The coming of the post-industrial society.* New York: Basic Books.

Bell, R. R. 1979. *Marriage and family interaction,* 5th ed. Homewood, Illinois: Dorsey Press.

Belle, D. 1999. *The afterschool lives of children alone with others while parents work.* Mahwah, NJ: Erlbaum.

Bendix, R. ed. 1960. *Max Weber: An intellectual portrait.* Garden City, NY: Doubleday.

Benokraitis, N. V. 2008. *Marriages and families: Changes, choices, and constraints,* 6th ed. Upper Saddle River, NJ: Pearson-Prentice Hall.

Berger, P. L. 1963. *Invitation to sociology: A humanistic perspective.* Garden City, NY: Doubleday.

Berger, P. L., and S. P. Huntington, eds. 2002. *Many globalizations: Cultural diversity in the contemporary world.* New York: Oxford University Press.

Berk, R. 1974. A gaming approach to crowd behavior. *American Journal of Sociology* 79:355–373.

Bernard, L. L. 1924. *Instinct.* New York: Holt, Rinehart, and Winston.

Best, Joel. 2006. *Flavor of the month: Why smart people fall for fads.* Berkeley, CA: University of California Press.

Biesanz, L. L., and J. Biesanz. 1973. *Introduction to sociology,* 2nd ed. Englewood Cliffs, NJ: Prentice-Hall.

Biller, H. B. 1971. *Father, child, and sex role: Paternal determinants of personality development.* Lexington, MA: D. C. Heath.

Billson, J. M., and B. J. Huber. 1993. *Embarking on a career with an undergraduate degree in Sociology,* 2nd ed. Washington, DC: American Sociological Association.

Black, J. A., and D. J. Champion, 1976. *Methods and issues in social research.* New York: Wiley.

Blau, P. 1964. *Exchange and power in social life.* New York: Wiley.

Blau, P. M., and M. W. Meyer. 1971. *Bureaucracy in modern society,* 2nd ed. New York: Random House.

Blau, P. M., and W. R. Scott. 1962. *Formal organizations.* San Francisco: Chandler.

Bloomfield, M. 1970. Dixon's The leopard's spots: A study in popular fascism. In *White racism: It's history, pathology, and practice,* eds. B. N. Schwartz and R. Disch. New York: Dell.

Blum, J. W., et al. 1973. *The national experience: A history of the United States,* 3rd. ed. New York: Harcourt Brace Jovanovich.

Blumer, H. 1948. Public opinion and public opinion polling. *American Sociological Review* 13: 542–549.

Blumer, H. 1957. Collective Behavior. In *Principles of sociology,* ed. A. M. Lee. New York: Barnes and Noble.

Boas, F. 1911. *The mind of primitive man.* New York: Macmillan.

Bogardus, E. S. 1959. *Social distance.* Yellow Springs, Ohio: Antioch Press.

Borg, W. R., and M. D. Gall. 1979. *Educational research: An introduction.* New York: Longman.

Borgatta, E. F. ed. 1992. *Encyclopedia of sociology.* New York: Macmillan.

Borofsky, R., and B. Albert. 2006. *Yanomani: The fierce controversity and what we can learn from it.* Berkley, CA: University of California Press.

Bositis, D. A. 2003. Black elected officials reach historic highs. *Focus* (November/December) 31: 3–4.

Bottomore, T. B. 1966. *Classes in modern society.* New York: Pantheon Books.

Boyer, S., and S. Nissenbaum. 1974. *Salem possessed: The social origins of witchcraft.* Cambridge, MA: Harvard University Press.

Brake, M. 1985. *Comparative youth culture: The sociology of youth cultures and youth subcultures in America, Britain, and Canada.* Boston/London: Rutledge and Kegan Paul.

Bramlett, M. D., and Mosher, W. D. 2001. First marriage dissolution, divorce, and remarriage: United States. *Vital and Health Statistics,* 323. Hyattville, MD: National Center for Health Statistics.

Breindel, E. M., and N. Eberstadt. 1980. Paradoxes of population. *Commentary* 70 (August 8): 42.

Brian, J. A. 1965. Apprenticeships in prostitution. *Social problems* 12 (Winter): 287–297.

Broderick, C. B. 1988. *Marriage and the family,* 3rd ed. Englewood Cliffs, NJ: Prentice-Hall.

Bronowski, J., and B. Mazlish. 1962. *The Western intellectual tradition: From Leonardo to Hegel,* 76–85. New York: Harper Torchbooks.

Broom, L., and P. Selznick. 1968. *Sociology: A text with adapted readings,* 4th ed. New York: Harper & Row.

Brown, D. 2007. *Bury my heart at wounded knee.* Reprinted ed. New York: Holt Paperbacks

Brown, L., ed. 1946. *The world's great scriptures.* New York: Macmillan.

Bruck, D. 1988. Decisions of death. In *Crisis in American institutions,* 7th ed. ed. J. H. Skolnick and E. Currie. Glenview, IL: Scott, Foresman.

Brunvand, J. H. 1980. Urban legends: Folklore for today. *Psychology Today* 14 (June): 50.

Brunvand. J. H. 1981. *The vanishing hiker: American urban legends and their meanings.* New York: Norton.

Brunvand, J. H. 1986. *The choking Doberman and other new urban legends.* New York: Norton.

Buckner, H. T. 1969. A theory of rumor transmission. In *Readings on collective behavior,* ed. R. R. Evans. Chicago: Rand McNally.

Burke, P. J. 1967. The development of tasks and socioemotional role differentiation. *Sociometry* 30 (December): 379–392.

Burke, P. J. 1968. Role differentiation and the legitimization of task activity. *Sociometry* 31 (December): 404–411.

Butterfield, F. 1986. Why Asians are going to the head of the class. *The New York Times* (August 3): Section 12, 18–23.

Butterfield, H. 1957. *The origins of modern science,* Rev. ed. New York: Free Press.

Campbell, A., P. E. Converse, and W. L. Rogers. 1976. *The quality of life in America: Perceptions, evaluations, and satisfactions.* New York: Russell Sage Foundation.

Campbell, K. 2002. Today's courtship. White teeth, root beer, and email? *Christian Science Monitor,* pp. 1–4.

Canli, T. 2004. Functional brainmapping of extraversion and neuroticism: Learning from individual differences in emotion processing. *Journal of Personality* 72: 1105–1132.

Canli, T.; Amin, Z.; Haas, B.; Omura. K., & Constable, R. T. 2004. A double dissociation between mood states and personality in the anterior cingulate. *Behavioral Neuroscience,* 118, 897–904.

Canli, T., Sivers, H., Whitfield, L., Gotlib, I. H., and Gabrieli, J. D. E. 2002. Amygdala response to happy faces as a function of extraversion. *Science* 296: 2191.

Cantril, H., with H. Gaudet and H. Herzog. 1982. *The invasion from Mars.* Princeton, NJ: Princeton University Press.

Cappizano, J., and G. Adams. 2000. The number of childcare arrangements used by children under five: Variation across states. The Urban Institute. www.newfederalism.urban.org

Capizzano, J., G. Adams, and J. Ost. 2006. The childcare patterns of white, black and hispanic children. The Urban Institute. www.urban.org

Caplow, T. 1969. *Two against one: Coalitions in triads.* EnglewoodCliffs: NJ: Prentice-Hall.

Caulkins, J. P., et al. 2005. *How Goes the "War on Drugs?"* Santa Monica, CA: Rand.

CensusScope. 2001. Household and family structure, 1990–2000. Social Science Data Analysis Network. Accessed on September 26, 2008 at http://censusscope.org/us/chart_house.html

Centers for Disease Control. 2006. "Births, marriages, divorces, and deaths: Provisional data for 2005." *National Vital Statistics Reports,* Vol. 54, No. 20, July 21.

Central Intelligence Agency. 2002. *CIA: The World Fact Book.* United States (July, 1).

Central Intelligence Agency. 2008. *CIA: The World Fact Book.* United States. Accessed on July 27, 2008 at https://www.cia.gov/library/publications/the-world-factbook/geos/us.html

Chagnon, N. A. 1983. *Yanomamo: A fierce people,* 3th ed. New York: Holt, Rinehart and Winston.

Chagnon, N. A. 1997. *Yanomamo: A fierce people,* 5th ed. New York: Harcourt Brace Jovanovich.

Chang, J. 2008. New satellite photos show Amazon rainforest shrinking. *Atlanta Journal Constitution* (June 3).

Charon, J. M. 2007. *Symbolic interactionism: An Introduction, an interpretation,* 9th ed. Upper Saddle River, NJ: Prentice-Hall.

Clayton, R. R. 1979. *Cross cultural variations of the family. The family, marriage, and social change,* 2nd ed. Lexington, MA: D. C. Heath.

Chesler, P. 2005. *Women and madness.* New York: Palgrave Macmillan.

Clay, R. 2005. Dual-earner families: Making working families work. *APA Monitor* Vol. 36, No. 11, Dec.

Clinard, M. B. 1974. *Sociology of deviant behavior.* New York: Holt, Rinehart and Winston.

Clinard, M. B., and R. F. Meier. 1979. *Sociology of deviant behavior,* 31. New York: Holt, Rinehart and Winston.

CNN. 2006. Wolf Blitzer's "Situation Room" Television News Broadcast, October 17.

CNNMoney.com. 2008. Fortune magazines' best companies. Accessed on November 22, 2008 at http://money.cnn.com/magazines/fortune/bestcompanies/2008/

Cochran, J. K., M. B. Chamlin, and M. Seth. 1994. Deterrence or brutalization: An impact assessment of Oklahoma's return to capital punishment. *Criminology* 32: 107–134.

Cochran, M. M., and I. Gunnarsson, 1985. A follow-up study of group day-care and family-based childbearing patterns. *Journal of Marriage and Family* 47 (May): 297–309.

Cohen, N., ed. 1969. *The Los Angeles riots: A socio-psychological study.* New York: Macmillan.

Coleman, J. 1988. *Intimate relationships, marriage and family,* 2nd ed. New York: Macmillan.

Collins, R. 1988. *Sociology of marriage and the family: Gender, love, and property,* 2nd ed. New York: Harper & Row.

Cooley, C. H. 1902. *Human nature and social order.* New York: Scribner's.

Cooley, C. H. 1909. *Social organization.* New York: Scribner's.

Cooley, C. H. 1956. *Social organization: Human nature and the social order.* New York: Free Press. Originally published in 1909).

Cooley, C. H. 1964. *Human nature and the social order.* New York: Schocken Books. (First published in 1902 by Scribner's).

Coontz, S. 2006. Marriage: *A history: From obedience to intimacy, or how love conquered marriage.* New York: Penguin Books.

Cooper, K., L. Chassin, S. Braver, K. Zeiss, and K. A. Khavari. 1986. Correlates in mood and marital satisfaction. Among dual-workers and single-worker couples. *Social psychology quarterly* 49: 322–329.

Corsaro, W. A. 2004. *The sociology of childhood, 2nd ed.* Thousand Oaks, CA: Sage.

Cortez, J. B., and F. M. Gatti. 1972. *Delinquency and crime: A biopsychological approach.* New York: Seminar Press.

Coser, L. A. 1956. *The functions of social conflict.* New York: Free Press (Later edition in 1964).

Coser, L. A. 1971. *Masters of sociological thought.* New York: Harcourt, Brace, and Jovanovich. First published in 1956.

Cox, F. D. 1987. *Human intimacy: Marriage, the family and its meanings,* 4th ed. New York: West.

Crime library.com 2004. Ted Kaczynski, unabomber. Accessed at http://www.crimelibrary.com

Croteau, D., and W. Hoynes. 2000. *Media/society: Industries, images, and audiences.* Thousand Oaks, CA: Pine Forge Press.

Cullen, J. B., and S. M. Novick. 1979. The Davis-Moore theory of stratification: A further examination and extension. *American Journal of Sociology* 84 (May): 1424–1427.

Cullen, L. T. 2007. Till work us do part. *Time* (Thursday, Sept. 27). Accessed September 25, 2008 at http://www.time/magazine/article/0,9171,1666269,00.html

Currie, E., and J. H. Skolnick. 1988. *America's problems: Social issues and public policy,* 2nd ed. Glenview, IL: Scott Foresman.

Curtiss, S. 1977. *Genie: A psycholinguistic study of a modern-day "wild child."* New York: Academic Press.

Dahl, R. 1961. *Who governs?* New Haven, CT: Yale University Press.

Dahrendorf, R. 1959. *Class and class conflict in industrial society.* Stanford, CA: Stanford University Press.

Darley, J., and B. Latane. 1968. Bystander intervention in emergencies: Diffusion of responsibility. *Journal of Personality and Social Psychology* 8: 377–383.

Darwin, C. 1859. *On the origin of species.* New York: Macmillan, 1927.

Davies, C. 1983. Crime, bureaucracy, and equality. *Policy Review* 23: 89–105.

Davis, A. , B. B. Gardner, and M. R. Gardner. 1965. *Deep South: A social anthropological study of caste and class.* Chicago: University of Chicago Press.

Davis, F. 1964. Deviance disavowal: The management of strained interaction by the visually handicapped. In *The other side,* ed. H. Becker, 119–137. New York: Free Press.

Davis, K. 1940. Extreme social isolation of a child. *American Journal of Sociology* 45: 554–564.

Davis, K. 1947. Final note on a case of extreme isolation. *American Journal of Sociology* 50: 432–437.

Davis, K. 1948. *Human society.* New York: Macmillan.

Davis, K., and W. Moore. 1945. Some principles of stratification. *American Sociological Review* 10 (April): 242–249.

DeAnda, R. M. 2004. Ed. *Chicanas and chicanos in contemporary society,* 2nd. ed. Boston: Allyn & Bacon.

Deegan, M. J. 1987. *Jane Addams and the men of the Chicago school, 1892–1918.* New Brunswick, NJ: Transaction.

Defleur, M. L., W. V. D'Antonio, and L. B. Defleur. 1981. *Sociology: Human society,* 3rd ed. Glenview, IL: Scott, Foresman. (also 1976 2nd ed.)

Dent, D. J. 2001. *In search of Black America: Discovering the African American dream.* New York: Free Press.

Denton, W. H. 2007. The role of affect in marital therapy. *Journal of Marital and Family Therapy* 17 (June): 257–261.

Deloria, V. 1970. *Custer died for your sins. An Indian manifesto.* New York: Avon.

DeParle, J. 2004. *American dream: Three women, ten kids, and a nation's drive to end welfare.* New York: Penguin Books.

Dewalt, K. M., and B. R. Dewalt. 2002. *Participant observation.* Altamira Press ISBN-13 9780759100459.

Diamond, J. 2005. *Collapse: How societies choose to fail or succeed.* New York: Viking Press.

DiFranza, J. R., and R. A. Lew. 1995. Effects of maternal cigarette smoking on pregnancy complications and sudden deaths syndrome. *Journal of Family Practice* 40 (April): 385–394.

Dilanian, K. 2008. Clintons' income, $109M since 2000. *USA Today.* April 4

Diller, L. 1998. *Running on ritalin.* New York: Bantam Books.

Divoky, D. 2002. Utah women to highlight hazards of polygamy. Women's E-News. Accessed on September 24, 2008 at http://www.womensenews.org

Domhoff, G. W. 1967. *Who rules America?* Englewood Cliffs, NJ: Prentice-Hall.

Dorius, C. J., S. J. Bahr, J.P. Hoffman, and E. L. Harmon. 2004. Parenting practices as moderators of the relationship between peers and adolescent marijuana use. *Journal of Mmarriage and Family* 66 (February): 163–178.

Du Bois, W. E. B.. 1899. *The Philadephia negro: A social study.* Philadephia: University of Pennsylvania Press.

Du Bois, W. E. B. 1903. *The souls of black folks.* New York: Dover.

Duncan, G. 1984. *Times of poverty, times of plenty.* Ann Arbor, MI: University of Michigan Press.

Dunn, J., and C. Kendrick. 1983. *Siblings: Love, envy, and understanding.* Cambridge, MA: Harvard University Press.

Durkheim, E. 1933. *The division of labor in society,* 2nd ed. New York: Free Press (Originally published in 1899, 1893).

Durkheim, E. 1966. *Suicide.* Trans. J. A. Spaulding and G. Simpson. New York: Free Press (First published in 1897).

Durkheim, E. 1966. *The rules of sociological method.* Trans. S. A. Solovay and J. H. Mueller Ed. E. G. Catlin. New York: Free Press. (First published in French in 1893; in English, 1938).

Durose, M. R., C. W. Harlow, P. A. Langan, M. Motivans, R. R. Rantala, and E. L. Smith. 2005. Family violence statistics: Including statistics on strangers and acquaintances. Washington, DC: United States Department of Justice Statistics. Available at www.ojp.usdoj.gov/bjs (April 4, 2006)

Duster, T. 1971. Conditions for a guilt-free massacre. In *Sanctions for evil: Sources of social Destructiveness,* eds. N. Sanford, C. Comsbock, et al. Boston: Beacon Press.

Dye, T. R. 1986. *Who's running America: The conservative years,* 4th ed. Englewood Cliffs, NJ: Prentice-Hall.

Eastman, C. M. 1975. *Aspects of language and culture.* San Francisco: Chandler and Sharp.

Edwards, T.. 2000. Flying solo. *Time,* August 28, pp. 47–53.

Ehrenreich, B. 2001. *Nickel and dimed: On (not) getting by in America.* New York: Metropolitan.

Ehrlich, P. R. 1970. *The population bomb.* New York: Ballantine Books.

Ehrlich, P. R., and A. H. Ehrlich, 1979. What happened to the population bomb? *Human Nature* (January): 88–92.

Eight Index Crimes: Percent Change (1994–2003). 2004. Federal Bureau of Investigation. Accessed on November 19, 2008 at www.fbi.gov/ucr/ucrquest.htm

Eisenburg, D. 2002. Dennis the menace. *Time.* June 17, pp. 46-49.

Eisenburg, N., et al. 2005. Relations between positive parenting, children's effortful control, and externalizing problems: A three wave longitudinal study. *Child Development* 76 (Sept./Oct.): 1055–1071.

Elkin, A. P. 1954. *The Australian aborigines,* 3rd ed. Sydney and London, Also 1964. New York: Doubleday.

Elkin, F., and G. Handel. 1984. *The child and society.* New York: Random House.

Ellis, L. 1982. Genetics and criminal behavior. *Criminology* 20 (May): 42–46.

Ember, C. R., and M. Ember. 1996. *Cultural Anthropology,* 8th ed. Upper Saddle River, NJ: Prentice-Hall, 1996.

Encyclopedia Britannica Almanac. 2005. 763. U.S. population growth.

Engfer, A., and K. A. Scheewind. 1982. Causes and consequences of harsh parental punishment. *Child abuse and neglect, The Interactionist Journal* 6: 129–140.

Engels, F. 1902. *The origins of the family, private property and the state.* Chicago: Charles H. Kerr. (First published in 1884).

Erikson, K. T. 1966. *Wayward puritans: A study in the sociology of deviance.* New York: Wiley.

Erikson, K. T. 1967. A comment on disguised observation in sociology. *Social Problems* 14 (Spring): 366–373.

Etter, L. 2006. Welfare reform: Ten years later. *Wall Street Journal,* August 26, p. A9.

Etzioni, A. 1964. *Modern organizations.* Englewood Cliffs, NJ: Prentice-Hall.

Etzioni, A. 1975. *A comparative analysis of complex organizations.* New York: Free Press. First published in 1961.

Etzioni, A. 1985. Shady corporate practices. *New York Times* (November 15): 204.

Etzioni, A. 2001. *Next: The road to a good society.* New York: Basic Books.

Farley, R. 1977. Trends in racial inequalities: Have the gains of the 1960s disappeared in the 1970s? *American Sociological Review* 42 (April): 189–207.

Farley, R. 1984. *Blacks and whites.* Cambridge, MA: Harvard University Press.

Fass, S., and N. K. Cauthen. 2006. *Who are America's poor children? The official story.* National Center for Children in Poverty. Columbia University, Mailman school of Public Health. December. Accessed 7/1/08 at http://www.nccp.org/publications/pub_684.html

Feibel, C., and B. Olson. 2008. Politicians, FEMA blame each other for relief mishaps. *Houston Chronicle,* September 15.

Fiedler, F. E. 1981. Leadership effectiveness. *American Behavioral Scientist* 24: 619–632.

Firestone, I. J., C. M. Lichtman, and J. Calamosa. 1975. Leader effectiveness and leader conferral as determinents of helping in a medical emergency. *Journal of Personality and Social Psychology* 31 (February): 345–348.

Fishman, J. 1985. *The rise and fall of the ethnic revival: Perspectives on language and ethnicity.* Berlin: Mouton.

Fletcher, L. 2008. Hedge fund manager Paulson earns 3.7 billion. *Yahoo News.* Wednesday April 16.

Forbes, 2006. Special Issue. *Forbes 400: The richest people in America* (October 9).

Food and Agriculture Organization (FAO). 2008. *Crop prospects and food situation—No. 2,* April. FAO corporate document repository. United Nations.

Forer, L. K. 1976. *The birth order factor.* New York: David McKay.

Fox, G. R. 1971. The XYY offender: A modern myth? *The Journal of Criminal Law, Criminology and Police Science* 62 (March): 59–73.

Fox, J. A., J. Levin, and K. Quinet. 2005. *The will to kill: Making sense of senseless murder.* Boston: Allyn & Bacon.

Fox News. 2008. Dolly Parton 'alive and well' despite death Rumor. August 25. Accessed on September 22, 2008 at http://foxnews.com/story/0,2933,410042,00.html

Fox, V. 1976. *Introduction to criminology.* Englewood Cliffs: NJ: Prentice-Hall.

Freeman, H. E., R. E. Dynes, P. H. Rossi, and W. F. Whyte, eds. 1983. *Applied sociology.* San Francisco: Jossey-Bass.

French, J. R. P., Jr., and B. Raven. 1968. The bases of social power. In *Group dynamics,* 3rd ed., eds. D. Cartright and A. Zander, 259–269. New York: Harper & Row.

Freud, S. 1930. *Civilization and its discontents.* Trans. J. Strachey. New York: Norton.

Friedrich, L. K., and A. H. Stein. 1975. Prosocial television and young people. *Child Development* 46: 27–38.

Friedsam, H. J. 1965. Competition. In *A dictionary of the social sciences,* ed. J. Gould and W. L. Kolb, 118–119. New York: Free Press.

Frieswick, K. 2007. A job without benefits. *The Boston Globe.* March 11. Accessed on September 26, 2008 at http:/www.boston.com/news/globe/magazine/articles/2007/03/11/the_job_without_benefits/

Fussel, P. 1983. *Class.* New York: Ballantine Books.

Gallo, A. E., J. A. Zellner, and D. M. Smallwood. 1980. The rich, the poor, and the money they spent for food. (Consumer research) *National Food Review* (Summer): 16–18.

Gans, H. J. 1972. The positive functions of poverty. *American Journal of Sociology* 78 (September): 275–289.

Gans, H. J. 1973. *More equality.* New York: Pantheon.

Gelles, R. J. 1973. Child abuse as psychopathology: A sociological critique and reformation. American *Journal of Orthopsychiatry* 43: 611–621.

Gelles, R. J. 1980. Violence in the family: A review of the research of the 1970s. *Journal of Marriage and the Family* 42: 873–875.

Gelman, D., M. Springen, K. Brailsford, and M. Miller. 1988. Black and white in America. *Newsweek* (March 7): 18–23.

Gerbner, G., L. Gross, M. Morgan, and N. Signorielli. 1994. In J. Bryant and D. Zillmann, eds. *Media effects: Advances in theory and research,* 17–41. Hillsdale, NJ: Erlbaum.

Gergen, K. J., and M. M. Gergen. 1981. *Social psychology.* New York: Harcourt Brace Jovanovich.

Gerth, H. H., and C. W. Mills, eds. And trans. 1946. *From Max Weber: Essays in sociology.* New York: Oxford University Press.

Giallombardo, R. 1970. Social roles in a prison for women. In *The sociology of organizations: Basic studies,* eds. O. Grusky and F. A. Miller, 393–408. New York: Basic Books.

Glick, P. C. 1981. Children from one-parent families: Recent data and projections. Paper presented at the Special Institutes on Critical Issues in Education sponsored by the Charles F. Kettering Foundation and held at the American University, Washington, DC, June 20, 1981.

Glick, P. C. 1984. Marriage, divorce, and living arrangements. *Journal of Family Issues* 5: 7–26.

Glueck, S., and E. Glueck, 1950. *Unraveling juvenile delinquency.* New York: Harper & Row.

Gibbs, N. R., et al. 1988. Grays on the go. *Time* (February 22): 66–75.

Gifford, R., L. Sheets, and S. Poggoili. 2005. Kyoto accords take effect. Feb. 16, 2005. NPR. Accessed on July 27, 2008 at Http://www.npr.org/template/story/story.php?storyId=4501237

Ginsburg, H., and S. Opper. 1969. *Piaget's theory of intellectual development.* Englewood Cliffs, NJ: Prentice-Hall.

Goffman, E. 1961. *Asylums.* Garden City, NY: Doubleday.

Goffman, E. 1963. *Behavior in public places.* New York: Free Press.

Goffman, E. 1959. *The presentation of self in everyday life.* New York: Doubleday

Goffman, E. 1967. *Interaction ritual: Essays on face-to-face behavior,* 5, Garden City, NY: Doubleday. (Anchor Books, 1992)

Goffman, E. 1972. Territories of the self. In *Relations in public,* ed. E. Goffman. New York: Harper, Colophon.

Goode, E. 1972. *Drugs in American society.* New York: Knopf.

Goode, E. 2001. *Legal drugs: The use of alcohol and tobacco. Deviant behavior,* 6th ed. Upper Saddle River,NJ: Prentice-Hall.

Goode, W. J. 1960. A theory of role strain. *American Sociological Review* 25: 483–496.

Goode, W. J., and P. K. Hatt. 1952. *Methods in social research.* New York, McGraw-Hill

Gordon, L., and P. O'Keefe. 1984. Incest as a form of family violence. *Journal of Marriage and the Family* 46: 27–34.

Gore, A. 2006. *An inconvenient truth: The planetary emergency of global warming and what we can do about it.* Rodale Press.

Goring, C. 1972. *The English convict: A statistical study.* Montclair, NJ: Patterson Smith.

Gortmaker, S. 1979. Poverty and infant mortality in the United States. *American Sociological Review* 44 (April): 280–297.

Gough, K. 1986. The origin of the family. In *Family in transition: Rethinking marriage, sexuality, childbearing, and family organization,* eds. A. S. Skolnick and H. H. Skolnick, 22–39. Boston, MA: Little, Brown.

Gouldner, A. W. 1954. *Patterns of industrial bureaucracy.* Glencoe, IL: Free Press.

Gouldner, A. W. 1960. The norm of reciprocity. *American Sociological Review* 25. (February): 161–178.

Gove, W. R., ed. 1980. *The labeling of deviance: Evaluation of a perspective.* Beverly Hills, CA: Sage.

Governor's Commission on the Los Angeles Riots. 1965. *Violence in the city: An end or a beginning.* Los Angeles.

Greeley, A. M. 1976. Political attitudes among American white ethnics. In *Sociological essays and research,* ed. C. H. Anderson. Homewood, IL: Dorsey.

Green, A. W. 1968. *Sociology: An analysis of life in modern society.* New York: McGraw-Hill.

Greenhouse, L. 2008. Justices rule for individual gun rights. *New York Times.* June 27. Accessed on September 3, 2008 at http://www.nytimes.com/2008/06/27/washington/27scotuscnd.html

Gregory, D. 1967. *Nigger.* New York: Simon & Schuster, Pocket Books edition.

Griffin, J. H. 1961. *Black like me.* New York: Norton.

Gupta, M. 1983. The basis for friendly dyadic interpersonal relationships. *Small Group Behavior* 14 (February): 15–33.

Gurman, A. S. and P. Fraenkel. 2002. The history of couple therapy: A millennial view. *Family Process* (July), Vol. 41, No. 2, pp. 199–260.

Guterman, S. S., 1969. In defense of Wirth's "Urbanism as a way of life." *American Journal of Sociology* 74 (March): 492–493.

Gwartney-Gibbs, P. A. 1986. The institutionalization of premarital cohabitation: Estimates from marriage licence applications 1970 and 1980. *Journal of Marriage and Family* 48 (May): 423–424.

Haas, J. E., and T. E. Drabek 1973. *Complex organizations: A sociological perspective.* New York: Macmillan.

Haber, A., and R. P. Runyon. 1974. *Fundamentals of psychology.* Reading, MA: Addison-Wesley.

Halloran, L. 2008. Reverend Wright's Re-emergence Could Spell Trouble for Obama Campaign. Tuesday, April 29. www.usnews.com

Halsell, G. 1969. *Soul sister.* New York: Fawcett.

Hare, P. A. P. 1962. *Handbook of small group research.* Glencoe, IL: Free Press. 229.

Harlow, H. F., and M. K. Harlow. 1966. Learning to love. *Scientific American* 215: 244–272.

Harlow, H. F., and R. Z. Zimmerman. 1959. Affectional responses in the infant monkey. *Science* 130: 421–432.

Harmatz, M. G., and M. A. Novak, 1983. *Human sexuality.* New York: Harper & Row.

Harrington, M. 1984. *The new American poverty.* New York: Holt, Rinehart and Winston.

Harris, M. 1977. *Cannibals and kings. The origins of culture.* New York: Random House.

Harris, M. 1980. *Cultural materialism.* New York: Random House, Vintage edition.

Harris, M. 1987. India's sacred cow. In *Conformity and conflict: Readings in cultural anthropology,* 6th ed., eds. J. P. Spradley and D. W. McCurdy. Boston: MA: Little, Brown.

Harroff, P. B. 1962. On language. In *Readings in sociology,* eds. J. F. Cuber and P. Harroff, 61–88. New York: Appleton-Century-Crofts.

Harvey, L. D. Danny. 2000. *Global warning: The hard science.* London: Pearson Education.

Hausbeck, K., and B. Brent. 2006. *McDonaldization of the Sex Industries: The Business of Sex,* ed. G. Ritzer, McDonaldization: The reader. Thousand Oaks, CA: Pineridge Press.

Havighurst, R. J., and B. L. Neugarten. 1967. *Society and education*, 3rd ed., 78–79. Boston: Allyn and Bacon.

Hawdon, J. E. 2005. *Drug and alcohol consumption as functions of social structure: A cross-cultural sociology.* Lewiston, NY: Edwin Mellon Press.

Head, T. 2008. States that may soon allow legal gay marriages or new civil unions. About.com Civil liberties. Accessed on September 29, 2008 at http://civilliberty.about.com/od/gendersexuality/tp/newgaystates.htm

Heaton, T. B. 2002. Factors contributing to increased marital stability in the United States. *Journal of Family Issues* 23: 392–409.

Hedley, R. A., and Adams, S. M. 1982. The job market for bachelor degree holders: A cumulation. *The American Sociologist* 17: 155–163.

Heilbroner, R. L. 1974. *An inquiry into the human prospect.* New York: Norton

Helmreich, W. B. 1982. *The things they say behind your back.* New York: Doubleday.

Hobbes, T. 1881. *Leviathan.* Oxford: James Thornton. First published in 1651.

Hochenbury, D. H., and S. E. Hockenbury. 2006. *Psychology,* 4th ed. New York: Worth Publishers.

Hodge, R., and D. Treiman. 1968. Class identification in the United States. *American Journal of Sociology* 73: 312.

Hollander, G. P. 1964. *Leaders, groups, and influence*, 11–26. New York: Oxford University Press.

Holtzman, M. 2005. The family definitions continuum. *National Council of Family Relations Report* 50 (June): F1, F3.

Holusha, J., and K. Johnson. 2008. Polygamist sect's children ordered released by judge. *New York Times* (June 2).

Homans, G. C. 2001. *The human group.* New Brunswick, NJ: Transaction Publishers. First published in 1950 by Harcourt Brace.

Hoover, R. K. 1988. *The elements of social scientific thinking*, 4th ed. New York: St. Martin's Press.

Horowitz, I. L. ed. 1967. *The rise and fall of project Camelot.* Cambridge, MA: M.I.T. Press.

Hoult, T. F. 1969. *Dictionary of modern sociology*, 5. Totowa, NJ: Littlefield, Adams, and Company.

Houseman, J. 1948. The men from Mars. *Harper's* 197 (December): 74–82.

Hunt, S. J. 2006. *The life course: A sociological introduction.* New York: Palgrave Macmillan.

Hyde, J. S., and J. D. Delamater. 2008. *Understanding human sexuality*, 10th ed. Boston, MA: McGraw-Hill Higher Education.

Hyman, H. H. 1942. The psychology of status. *The Archives of Psychology* 37: 15.

Jackman, M. R., and R. W. Jackman. 1983. *Class awareness in the United States.* Berkeley, CA: University of California Press.

Jacobs, P. A., M. Brunton, H. M. Melville, R. P. Brittain, and W. F. McClemont. 1965. Aggressive Behavior, mental subnormality and the XYY male. *Nature* 208: 1351–1352.

Janis, I. L., and L. Mann. 1977. *Decision making.* New York: Free Press.

Janis, I. L. 1982 A. *Victims of groupthink: A psychological study of foreign policy decisions and fiascos.* Boston: Houghton Mifflin.

Janis. I. L. 1982 B. Counteracting the adverse effects of concurrence-seeking in policy-planning Groups: Theory and research perspectives, eds., I. H. Brandstatter, J. Davis, and G. Stocker-Kreichgauer. 477-501. *Group decisionmaking:* New York.: Academic Press.

Jacoby, S. M. 2004. *The embedded corporation: Corporate governance and employee relations in Japan and the United States.* Princeton University Press.

James, J. 1951. A preliminary study of the size determinant in small group interaction. *American Sociological Review* 16: 474–477.

James, W. 1890. *The principles of psychology.* New York: Dover.

Janis, I. L., and L. Mann. 1977. *Decision making.* New York: Free Press.

Jayson, S. 2008. Census reports more unmarried couples living together. *USA Today.* 7/28/08. Accessed September 27, 2008 at http://www.usatoday.com/news/nation/census/2008-07-28-cohabitation-census_N.htm

Jencks, C. 1972. *Inequality.* New York: Basic Books.

Jian, S., C. H. Tuan, and Y. Jing-Yuan. 1985. *Population control in China.* New York: Praeger.

Jin, L. 2007. China. Time. Wednesday, Aug. 1, 2007. Accessed on July 21, 2008 at http://www.time.com/time/topics/article/0,8599,1648769,00.html

Johnson, J. 1986. The 90's home: Make room for stepfamilies. *USA Today* (March 6): 1-A.

Johnston, D. 2002. Traces of terror: News analysis; A plea suited to both sides. *New York Times.* July 16, 2002.

Julian, J., and W. Kornblum. 1986. *Social problems,* 5th ed. Englewood, Cliffs, NJ: Prentice-Hall.

Kandel, W., and D. Massey. 2002. The culture of Mexican migration: A theoretical and empirical analysis. *Social Forces* 80 (3): 981–1004.

Kang, S. 2003. Hot item or old hat? *Wall Street Journal,* October 24, pp. B1, B4.

Kannan, S. 2005. McDonalds in India: Capitalism and cow worship. *The Daily Reckoning.* London, England. Wednesday, December 7.

Karpov, Y., and H. C. Harwood. 1998. Two ways to elaborate Vygotsky's concept of mediation: Implications for instruction. *American Psychologist* 53: 27–36.

Kattak, C. P., and K. A. Kozaitus. 2008. *On being different: Diversity and multiculturalism in the North American mainstream,* 3rd ed. Boston: McGraw Hill.

Katz, E., and P. F. Lazarsfeld. 1955. *Personal influence.* New York: Free Press.

Keilbowiez, R. B., and R. Scherer, 1986. The role of the press in the dynamics of social movements. *Research in Social Movements, Conflict and Change* 9: 71–96.

Keister, L. A. 2005. *Getting rich: America's new rich and how they got that way.* New York: Cambridge University Press.

Keller, S. 1985. Does the family have a future? In *Rethinking marriage, sexuality, childbearing, and family organization,* 5th ed., eds., A. S. Skolnick and J. H. Skolnick. Boston, MA: Little, Brown.

Kempe, R. and H. Kempe. 1978. *Child abuse.* Cambridge, MA: Harvard University Press.

Kenkel, W. F. 1973. *The family in perspective.* Englewood Cliffs, NJ: Prentice-Hall.

Kennell, J. H. , D. K. Voos, and M. H. Klaus. 1979. Parent-infant bonding. In *Handbook of infant Development,* ed. J. D. Osofsky, 786–798. New York: Wiley.

Kephart, W. M., and W. W. Zellner. 2000. *Extraordinary groups: The sociology of unconventional life-styles,* 7th ed. New York: Worth.

Kessen, W. 1996. American psychology just before Piaget. *Psychological Science* 7: 196–199.

Khaldun, Ibn. 1950. *An Arab philosophy of history; Selection of the prolegomena of Ibn Khaldun.* Trans. C. Issawi. London: John Murray.

Kikkawa, T. 2005. "Recent research trends on Japan's economy and corporate systems." *Social Science Japan Journal* 8 (2): 273–279.

Kimmel, M., and A. Aronson. 2009. *Sociology now.* Boston: Pearson-Allyn & Bacon.

King, D. C., and M. R. Koller. 1975. *Foundations of sociology,* 27–30. San Francisco, CA: Rinehart Press/Holt, Rinehart and Winston.

Kinsey, A. C., W. B. Pomeroy, and C. E. Martin. 1948. *Sexual behavior in the human male.* Philadephia, PA: Saunders.

Kitano, H. 1985. *Race relations,* 3rd. ed. Englewood Cliffs, NJ: Prentice-Hall.

Kivisto, P., and W. Ng. 2005. *Americans all: Racial and ethnic relations in historical, structural, and comparative perspectives,* 2nd ed. Los Angeles, CA: Roxbury Publishing Company.

Klaus, M. H., et al. 1972. Maternal bonding: Importance of the first postpartum days. *New England Journal of Medicine* 286: 460–463.

Klaus, M. H., and J. H. Kennell. 1982. *Parent-infant bonding,* 2nd ed. St. Louis: Mosby.

Knox, D. 1988. *Choices in relationships: An introduction to marriage and the family*, 2nd ed. St. Paul, MN West.

Koepp, S. 1987. Pul-eeze! Will somebody help me? Frustrated Americans wonder where the service went. *Time* 129 (February 28): 48–55.

Kohn, M. L. 1963. Social class and parent-child relationships: An interpretation. *American Journal of Sociology* 68: 471–480.

Kohn, M. L. 1977. *Class and conformity*, 2nd ed. Homewood, IL: Dorsey.

Kosova, W. 2007. The power that was. *Newsweek*, April 23, pp. 24–31.

Kottak, C. P., and K. A. Kozaitus. 2008. *On being different: Diversity and multiculturalism in the North American mainstream*, 3rd ed. Boston: McGraw Hill.

Krantz, D. S., N. E. Grunberg, and A. Baum. 1985. Health psychology. *Annual Review of Psychology* 36: 349–384.

Kreider, R. M., and Fields, J. M. 2005. Living arrangements of children: 2001. United States Census Bureau. Current population reports, July, P70-104. Washington, DC: U.S. Government Printing Office.

Kroeber, A. L. 1948. *Anthropology.* New York: Harcourt Brace and World.

Lamanna, M. A., and A. Reidman. 1985. *Marriages and families: Making choices throughout the life cycle,* 2nd ed. Belmont, CA: Wadsworth.

Lamar, J. V. 1899. Kids who sell crack. *Time* (May 9): 20–23.

Lambert, S. E. 1997. *Great jobs for sociology majors: A career guide.* Stephen E. Lambert: VGM Career Publications.

Landis, J. T., and M. G. Landis. 1973. *Building a successful marriage,* 6th ed. Englewood Cliffs, NJ: Prentice Hall.

Langford, T., and L. Sandberg. 2008. Sect Children to Remain in State Custody. *Houston Chronicle,* Vol. 107, No. 189 (Saturday, April 19), pp. A1, A12.

Lareau, A. 2002. Juvenile inequality: Social class and childrearing in black families and white families. *American Sociological Review* (October) 67: 747–776.

Larson, A. 2003. The prenuptial agreement. Expert law library, family law. August. Accessed September 23, 2008 at http://www.expertlaw.com/library/family_law/ prenuptial_agreements.html

Larson, C. J. 1995. Theory and applied sociology. *Journal of Applied Sociology* 12(9): 13–29.

Lauer, R. H., and W. H. Handel. 1983. *Social psychology: The theory and application of symbolic Interactionism,* 2nd ed. Englewood Cliffs, NJ: Prentice-Hall.

Le Bon, G. 1985. *The crowd: The study of the popular mind.* London: Ernest Bonn. Originally published in 1896.

Lee, A. M., and E. B. Lee. 1971. *The fine art of propaganda.* New York: Octagon.

Lee, R. M. 1995. *Dangerous fieldwork.* London: Sage.

Lee, R. R., and I. DeVore, eds. 1976. *Kalihari hunter-gatherers: Studies of the !Kung San and their neighbors.* Cambridge, MA: Harvard University Press.

Leinhard, J. 2008. "Engines of our ingenuity" Episode 1531. KTUH Radio: Houston.

Lemert, E. M. 1951. *Social pathology.* New York: McGraw-Hill.

Lenski, G. 1966. *Power and privilege: A theory of social stratification.* New York: McGraw-Hill.

Leslie, G. R. 1979. 1979. *The family in social context,* 4th ed. New York: Oxford University Press.

Lewin, K. 1954. Experiments of K. Lewin, R. Lippitt, and R. K. White reported by H. H. Kelly and J. W. Thibault. In *Handbook of social psychology,* Vol. 2, ed. G. Lindsey, 776–777. Reading, MA: Addison-Wesley.

Lewis, J. W. 1972. A study of the Kent State incident using Smelser's theory of collective behavior. *Sociological Inquiry* 42: 87–96.

Lewis, O. 1961. *The children of Sanchez: Autobiography of a Mexican family.* New York: Vintage Books.

Lewis, O. 1966. The culture of poverty. *Scientific American* 215 (October): 19–25.

Lewis, O. 1968. *A study of slum culture.* New York: Random House.

Light, D., and S. Keller. 1982. *Sociology,* 3rd ed. New York: Knopf.

Lincoln, C. E. 1968. *Chronicles of black protest.* New York: New American Library, Mentor edition.

Lingeman, R. R. 1984. *Drugs from A to Z: A dictionary,* 2nd ed. New York: McGraw-Hill.

Linsey, L. L. and S. Beach. 2000. *Sociology: Social life and social issues.* Upper Saddle River, New Jersey: Prentice Hall.

Lipset, S. M. (Ed.) 1962. *Harriet Martineau: Society in America.* New York: Doubleday

Lipset, S. M. 1962. *The third century: America as a postindustrial society.* Chicago: University of Chicago Press.

Lipset, S. M. 1979. *The third century: America as a postindustrial society.* Chicago: University of Chicago Press.

Lipset, S. M. 1994. The state of American sociology. *Sociological Forum* 9: 199–220.

Little, R. W. 1970. Buddy relations and combat performance. In *The sociology of organizations: Basic studies,* ed. O. Grusky and G. A. Miller, 361–375. New York: Free Pres.

Locke, J. 1690. *Two treatises of government.*

Lombroso, C. 1911. *Crime, its causes and remedies.* Boston: Little, Brown.

Los Angeles Times. 1973. Syphilis study of 600 blacks called racist. Los Angeles: UPI Dispatch (May 13): 1A, 6.

Luo, J., and R. Baillargeon, L. Brueckner, and Y. Munakata. 2003. Reasoning about a hidden object after a delay: Evidence for robust representations in 5-month-old infants. *Cognition,* B23–B32.

Lynas, M. 2005. Stormy path to a warmer world. Peopleandplanet.net. Accessed on July, 21, 2008 at http://www.peopleandplanet.net/doc.php?id=754&section=8

Lynas, M. 2008. How the rich starved the world. *New Statesman.* April 17. Accessed on July 15, 2008 at http://www.newstatesman.com/world-affairs/2008/04/food-prices-lynas-Biofuels

Lyson, T. A., and G. D. Squires. 1993. The lost generation of sociologists. *ASA Footnotes* 21: 4–5.

Macionis, J. J. 2007. *Society: The basics,* 9th ed. Upper Saddle River: NJ Pearson-Prentice Hall.

MacIver, R. M. 1948. *The more perfect union.* New York: Macmillan.

Malson, L. 1972. *Wolf children and the problem of human nature.* New York: Monthly Review Press.

Magnuson, E. 1986. Hitting the mafia: A wave of trials is putting the nation's crime bosses behind bars. *Time* 128 (September 29): 16–22.

Marable, M. 1986. *W. E. B. Du Bois: Black radical democrat.* Boston: Twayne Publishers.

Mare, R. D. 1982. Socioeconomic effects on child mortality in the United States. *American Journal of Public Health* (June): 541–543.

Marsden, P. V. 1987. Core discussion networks of Americans. *American Sociological Review* 52 (February): 122–131.

Martin, R. 1977. *The sociology of power.* London: Routledge and Kegan Paul.

Martin, S. 2006a. *Growing evidence for a 'divorce divide'?: Education, race, and marital dissolution rates in the U.S. since the 1970s.* New York: Russell Sage Foundation.

Martin, S. P. 2006b. Trends in marital dissolution by women's education in the United States. *Demographic Research,* December 13, 2006. Vol. 15, No. 20, pp. 537–560.

Marx, G. T. 1986. The iron fist and the velvet glove: Totalitarian potentials within democratic structures. In *The social fabric: Dimensions and issues,* ed. J. F. Short, Jr. Newbury Park: CA: Sage.

Marx, G. T., and D. McAdam. 1994. *Collective behavior and social movements: structure and process.* Englewood Cliffs, NJ: Prentice-Hall.

Marx, K. 1906/1894. *Capital,* Vol. 1. New York: Modern Library. First published in 1867 as Das Kapital.

Marx, K., and F. Engels. 1939/1846. *The German ideology.* New York: International Publishers Edition. First published in 1846.

Marx, K., and F. Engels. 1969/1848. *The communist manifesto.* New York: Penguin.

Massey, G. 1975. Studying social class: The case of embourgeoisement and the culture of Poverty. *Social Problems* 22 (June): 595–608.

Masters, W. E., V. E. Johnson, and R. C. Kolodny. 1992. *Human sexuality,* 4th ed. New York: HarperCollins.

Matchan, L. 1983. *Boston Globe* (October 17): 41–43.

McCall, R. B. 1975. *Intelligence and heredity.* Homewood, IL: Learning Systems Company.

McCullough, D. W., ed. 1984. *Great detectives: A century of the best mysteries from England and America.* New York: Pantheon.

McGuire, M. 2002. Conducting field research. In *Religion: The social context,* 327–334. Belmont, CA: Wadsworth.

McPhail, C., and R. T. Wolstein. 1983. Individuals and collective behaviors within gatherings, demonstrations, and riots. *Annual Review of Sociology,* 9. Palo Alto, CA.

McWhirter, N. 1982. *Guinness book of world records,* 28. New York: Bantam Books.

Mead, G. H. 1934. *Mind, self, and other.* Chicago: University of Chicago Press.

Mead, G. H. (1934/1967). *Mind, self, and society: From the standpoint of a social behaviorist.* Chicago: University of Chicago Press.

Mead, M. 1953. *The impact of cultural changes on the family. The family in the urban community.* Detroit: The Merrill-Palmer School.

Mead, M. 1971. Comment. In *Discussions on child development,* ed., J. Tanner and B. Inbelder. New York: International Universities Press.

Meese, R. L. 2005. A few new children: Postinstitutionalized children of intercountry adoption. *Journal of Special Education* 39: 157–167.

Meredith, D. 1986. Day-care: The nine to five dilemma. *Psychology Today* 20 (February): 36–44.

Merton, R. K. 1957. *Social theory and social structure,* 2nd ed. New York: Free Press.

Merton, R. K. 1968. *Social theory and social structure.* Engl. ed. New York: Free Press.

Merton, R. K. 1959. Notes on problem-finding in sociology. In *Sociology today: Problems and prospects,* ed. R. K. Merton, L. Broom, and L. S. Cottrell, Jr., ix–xxxiv. New York: Basic Books.

Merton, R. K. 1976. *Sociological ambivalence and other essays.* New York: Morrow.

Merton, R. K. 1976. Discrimination and the American creed. In *Sociological ambivalence and other essays,* 190–199. New York: Morrow.

Merton, R. K., and A. S. Rossi. 1968. Contributions to the theory of reference group behavior. In *Social theory and social structure.* Engl. ed., 319–322. New York: Free Press.

Michelmore, P. N. 1986. A knife in the heart. *Reader's Digest* (April): 109–114.

Michels, R. 1966. Political parties: *A sociological study of the oligarchic tendencies of modern democracy.* New York: Free Press Paperback. (Originally published in 1911.).

Miles, D. 2008. Surge strategy working in Iraq, but challenges remain; Patraeus says. American Services Press Service News Articles. U.S. Department of Defense Jan. 8, 2008. Washington, DC: Accessed June 17, 2008 at http://www.defencelink.mil/news/newsarticle

Milgram, S. 1965. Some conditions of obedience and disobedience to authority. *Human Relations* 18: 57–75.

Milgram, S. 1974. *Obediance to authority.* New York: Harper & Row.

Milgram, S. 1977. *The individual in a social world.* Reading, MA: Addison-Wesley.

Miller, E. L. 1987. *Questions that matter: An invitation to philosophy.* New York: McGraw-Hill.

Mills, C. W. 1956. *The power elite.* New York: The Oxford University Press.

Mills, C. W. 1959. *The sociological imagination.* New York: Oxford University Press.

Mills, C. W. 2000. *The sociological imagination.* New York: Oxford University Press. First published in 1959.

Min, P. G. 2005. *Asian Americans: Contemporary trends and issues.* Thousand Oaks, CA: Pine Oaks Press.

Molotsky, I. 1988. Senate votes to compensate Japanese-American internees. *New York Times,* April 21, pp. 1, 9.

Montague, A. 1972. *Statement on race.* New York: Oxford University Press.

Mooney, C. 2008. *Storm world: Hurricanes, politics, and the battle over global warming.* New York: Harcourt Trade.

Morris, J. K. 1966. Professor Mathus and his essay. *The Population Bulletin* 22 (February): 7–27.

Mortimer, J. T., and R. G. Simmons. 1978. Adult socialization. *Annual Review of Sociology* 4: 421–454.

Moses, A. M. 2008. *Impacts of television viewing on young children's literacy development in the United States.*

Moskos, C. Jr. 1975. The American combat soldier in Vietnam. *Journal of Social Issues* (Fall): 25–37.

MSN Money, 2008. Raising your quarter million dollar baby. Reuters. Accessed September 30, 2008 at http://moneycentral.msn.com/content/collegeandfamily/raisekids/p37245.asp

Muller, B. 1974. *Brainwashing. Encyclopedia of sociology.* Guilford, CT: The Duskin Publishing Group.

Mulvihill, D. J., and M. Tumin (with L. Curtis). 1969. *Crimes of violence: Staff report to the national commission on the causes and prevention of violence.* Washington, DC: U.S. Government Printing Office.

Murdock, P. M. 1945. The common denominator of cultures. In *The science of man and the world crisis,* ed. R. Linton. New York: Columbia University Press.

Murdock, P. M. 1945. 1965. *Social structure.* New York: Free Press. Originally published in 1949.

Myers, K. 2008. Africa is giving nothing to anyone—apart from AIDs. July 10. Accessed on July 27, 2008 at http://www.independent.ie/opinion/columns/kevin-myers/africa-is-gining-nothing away-to-anyone-apart-from-aids-1430428.html/

Myrdal, G. 1962. *Challenge to affluence.* New York: Random House.

Nachmias, D., and C. Nachmias. 1987. *Research methods in the social sciences,* 3rd. ed. New York: St. Martins Press.

Naisbitt, J. 1984. *Megatrends: Ten new directions transforming our lives.* New York: Warner Books.

National Advisory Commission on Civil Disorders. 1968. *Report.* New York: Bantam.

National Institute of Mental Health. 1982. *Television and behavior: Ten years of scientific progress and implication for the eighties.* Washington, DC: U.S. Government Printing Office.

National Opinion Research Center. 2001. *General social surveys 1972–2000: Cumulative Codebook.* Storrs, CT: Roper center for public opinion research.

Nationmaster.com 2008. Health Statistics>Dependency ratio per 100 (most recent by country). http://www.nationmaster.com/graph/hea_dep_rat_per_100-health-dependency-ratio-per-100

Neuman, W. L. 2005. Social research methods: *Qualitative and quantitative approaches,* 6th ed. Boston: Allyn & Bacon.

Negative population growth. 2008. Accessed on July 14 at http://www.npg.org/popfacts.htm

Newsweek, 1970. My god, they're killing us. (May 18): 31–33, 33F.

Newsweek, 1986, (September, 1): 3.

Newsweek, 1987. How to stay married (August 24): 53.

Nisbet, R. A. 1965. *Emile Durkheim.* Englewood Cliffs, NJ: Prentice Hall.

Nisbet. R. A. 1966. *The sociological tradition.* New York: Basic Books.

Nisbet, R. A. 1970. *The social bond,* 66–69. New York: Knopf.

NLADA Update. 2008. High court orders Texas to reunite polygamist sect's children with their Parents. National Legal and Defender Association. June 10, 2008; Volume 10, No. 9. Accessed June 22, 2008 at http://www.lada.org/Publications/Update08_0610

Noble, E. P., et al. 1991. Allelic association of the D2 dopamine receptor gene with receptor-binding characteristics in alcoholism. *Archives of General Psychiatry* 48: 648–654.

Noda, K. 1975. Big business organization. *In Modern Japanese organization and decision making,* ed. E. F. Vogel. Berkeley, CA: University of California Press.

Nottingham, E. K. 1971. *Religion: A sociological view.* New York: Random House.

Novak, M. A. 1979. Social recovery of monkeys isolated for the first year of life: II. Long term assessment. *Developmental Psychology* 11: 453–461.

Nye, J. L., and A. M. Brower (Eds.). 1996. *What's social about social cognition?* Thousand Oaks, CA: Sage.

Olmsted, M. S., and A. P. Hare. 1978. *The small group,* 2nd ed. New York: Free Press.

Ogburn. W. F. 1922. *Social change: With respect to culture and original nature.* New York: Huebsch.

Ogburn, W. F. 1930. The folk-ways of scientific sociology. *Scientific Monthly* 30 (April): 300–306.

Ogburn, W. F. 1959. The wolf boy of Agra. *American Journal of Sociology* 46 (March): 499–554.

Ogburn, W. F. 1964. *On Cultural and social change: Selected papers.* Chicago: University of Chicago Press.

Oliver, P., G. Marwell, and R. Teixeira. 1985. A theory of the critical mass: Interdependence, group heterogeneity, and the production of collective action. *American Journal of Ssociology* 91: 522–556.

Orshansky, M. Who's who among the poor: A demographic view of poverty. *Social Security Bulletin* 28 (July): 3–32.

Ouchi, W. G. 1981. *Theory Z: How American business can meet the Japanese challenge.* Reading, MA: Addison-Wesley.

Parrillo, V. N. 1985. *Strangers to these shores,* 2nd ed. New York: Wiley.

Parrillo, V. N. 2009. *Strangers to these shores,* 9th ed. Boston: Allyn & Bacon/Pearson Education.

Parkinson, C. N. 1957. *Parkinson's law and other studies in administration.* Boston: Houghton Mifflin.

Parsons, T. 1937. *The structure of social action.* New York: McGraw-Hill.

Parsons, T., ed. 1947. *Max Weber: The theory of social and economic organization.* New York: Oxford University Press.

Parsons, T. 1947. Introduction, ed. M. Weber, *The theory of social and economic organization.* New York: Oxford University Press.

Parsons, T. 1951. *The social system.* Glencoe, IL: Free Press.

Parsons, T. 1956. Suggestions for a sociological approach to theory of organizations. *Administrative Science Quarterly* 1 (June): 63–85.

Pear, R. 1986. Poverty rate shows slight drop for '85 census, bureau says. *New York Times* (August 27): 1, 9.

Peoples, J., and G. Bailey. 1997. *Humanity: An introduction to cultural anthropology,* 4th ed. Belmont, CA: West/Wadsworth.

Perrow, C. 1967. A framework for the comparative analysis of organizations. *American Sociological Review* 32 (April): 194–208.

Peter, L. J., and R. Hull. 1969. *The Peter principle: Why things always go wrong.* New York: Morrow.

Peters, T. J., and R. J. Waterman, Jr. 1982. *In search of excellence: Lessons from America's best run companies.* New York: Macmillan.

Peterson, R. D., and W. C. Bailey. 1991. Felony murder and capital punishment: An examination of the deterrence question. *Criminology* 29: 367–395.

Peterson, W. 1969. *Population.* 115. New York: Macmillan.

Peterson, W. 1975. *Population,* 3rd ed. New York: Macmillan.

Peternson, W. 2000. *From birth to death: A consumer's guide to population studies.* New Brunswick, NJ: Transaction.

Pettigrew, T. F. 1980. *Prejudice. Harvard encyclopedia of American ethnic groups.* Cambridge, MA: Belnap Press.

Piaget, J. 1929. *The child's conception of the world.* New York: Harcourt, Brace, and World.

Piaget, J., and B. Inhelder. 1969. *The psychology of the child.* New York: Basic Books.

Plog, F., and D. G. Bates. 1980. *Cultural anthropology,* 2nd. ed. New York: Knopf.

Polansky, N. A., M. A. Chalmers, E. Buttenseiser, and D. P. Williams. 1981. *Damaged parents, an anatomy of child neglect.* Chicago: University of Chicago Press.

Popline. 1985. A bitter struggle with millions of lives at stake. (April): 1. Washington, DC: The Population Institute.

Popline. 1985. 20 million more men. (July). Washington, DC: The Population Institute.

Popline. 1985. 100 new mega-cities expected. (September): 3. Washington, DC: The Population Institute.

Popline. 1986. Mega-cities: New 3rd world phenomenon. (April): 4–8. Washington, DC: Population Reference Bureau.

Popline. 1987. Population growth is contributing to rainforest decline. (September): 3. Washington, DC: Population Reference Bureau.

Population Reports. 2000. Feeding a future world. Volume XXVIII, Number 3, Fall. United Nations.

Population Today. 1985 (March). China's demographic disaster of 1958–1962. 13: 2

Porter, A. 1986. *Work in the new information age. The futurist.* 20 (September-October): 9–14.

Porteus, L. 2004. Group Think led to Iraq WMD weapons assessment. FoxNews, Sunday July 11, 2004. Accessed on June 18, 2008 at http://www.foxnews.com/story/0,2933,125123,00.html

Price, W. H., and P. B. Whatmore. 1967. Behavior disorders and patterns of crime among XYY males identified at a maximum security hospital. *British Medical Journal* 1: 533–536.

Public Health Reports. 1969. Link between XYY syndrome and criminality not clear. 89 (October): 914.

Putnam, R. 2000. *Bowling alone: The collapse and revival of American community.* New York: Simon & Schuster: New York.

Putnam, R. 2003. *Better together: Restoring the American community.* New York: Simon & Schuster.

Quarles, B. 1969. *The Negro in the making of America.* New York: Macmillan.

Quinney, R. 1974. *Critique of legal order: Crime control in capitalist society.* Boston: Little, Brown.

Quinney, R. 1980. *Class, state and crime,* 2nd ed. New York: Longman.

Reckless, W. 1973. *The crime problem,* 5th ed. Englewood Cliffs, NJ: Prentice-Hall.

Reisman, D. 1961. *The lonely crowd.* New Haven, CT: Yale University Press.

Reiss, I. 1980. *Family systems in America,* 3rd ed. New York: Holt, Rinehart and Winston.

Reitermann, T. 1982. *Raven: The untold story of the Rev. Jim Jones and his temple.* New York: Dutton.

Rennison, C. M. 2003. *Intimate partner violence, 1993–2001.* Washington, DC: U.S. Department of Justice.

Renzetti, C. M., and D. J. Curran. 1998. *Living sociology.* Boston: Allyn and Bacon.

Report of the national advisory committee on civil disorders, 1968, 3–4. New York: Bantam Books.

Rice, F. P. 1983. *Contemporary marriage.* Boston: Allyn and Bacon.

Rice, X. 2008. Six million Ethiopian children at risk of malnutrition as crops fail. Wednesday May 21. Guardian News and Media Limited. Accessed on July 27, 2008 at http://www.guardian.co.uk/world/2008/may/20/ethiopia

Richardson, B. 2006. Kenneth Lay: A fallen hero. BBC News, International Version, July 5, 2006. Accessed on June 18, 2008 at http://news.bbc.co.uk/2/hi/business/3875941.stm

Ridley, F. F., ed. 1979. *Government and administration in Western Europe.* New York: St. Martin's Press.

Ritzer, G. 1983. *Sociological theory.* New York: Knopf.

Ritzer, G. 1996. *The McDonaldization of society,* revised ed. Thousand Oaks, CA: Pine Forge Press.

Ritzer, G. 2008. *Classic sociological theory,* 5th ed. New York: McGraw-Hill.

Rivlin, G. 2005. Hate messages on Google site draws concerns. *New York Times,* February 7, C1, C7.

Robertson, I. 1974. Counterculture. In the *Encyclopedia of sociology,* 60–61. Guilford, CT: Duskin Publishing Group.

Robertson, I. 1974. Indian caste system. In the *Encyclopedia of sociology.* Guilford, CT: Duskin Publishing Group.

Robertson, I. 1980. *Social problems,* 2nd. ed. New York: Random House.

Roediger, H. L., J. P. Rushton, E. D. Capaldi, and S. G. Paris. 1984. *Psychology.* Boston: Little, Brown.

Roehling, P. V., and P. Moen. 2003. Dual earner couples (2003). Sloan work and family research network. Encyclopedia. 3/05/03. Accessed on September 23, 2008 at http://wfnetwork.bc.edu/ encyclopedia_entry.php?id=229&area=All

Roethlisberger, F. J., and W. J. Dickson. 1939. *Management and the worker.* Cambridge, MA: Harvard University Press.

Rogoff, B. 1990. *Apprenticeship in thinking: Cognitive development in social context.* New York: Oxford University Press.

Rosenberg, M. 2006. Population growth rates and doubling times. About.com: Geography January 1, 2006. Accessed on July 29, 2008 at http://geography.about.com/od/populationgeography/ a/ populationgrow.htm

Rosenthal, A. M. 1964. *Thirty-eight witnesses.* New York: McGraw-Hill.

Rosenthal, E., and A. C. Revkin. 2007. Science panel called global warming 'unequivocal." *New York Times* (February 3).

Ross, J. B., and M. M. McLaughlin, eds. 1949. *The portable medieval reader.* New York: Viking Press.

Ross, J. B. 1988. How lawless are big companies? In *Crisis in American institutions,* 7th ed. ed. J. H. Skolnick and E. Currie. Glenview, IL: Scott, Foresman.

Roscoe, B., and N. Benaske. 1985. Courtship violence experienced by abused wives: Similarities in patterns of abuse. *Family Relations* 34: 419–424.

Rossides, D. W. 1998. *Social stratification: The interplay of class, race, and gender,* 2nd ed. Upper Saddle River, NJ: Prentice-Hall.

Rothschild, J. 1986. Alternatives to Bureaucracy: Democratic participation in the economy. *Annual Review of Sociology* 12: 307–328.

Rothschild-Whitt, J. 1979. The collectivist organization: An alternative to rational bureaucratic Models. *American Sociological Review* 44: 509–527.

Rousseau, J. J. 1762. *A treatise on the social compact.*

RP News Wires, 2008. New fortune 500 list unveiled; Big oil dominates top five. Reliable plant magazine, May, June. Accessed at www.reliableplant.com on May 28, 2008, p. 2.

Ruben, Z. 1970. Measurement of romantic love. *Journal of Personality and Social Psychology* 16: 265–273.

Rubin, B. A. 1996. *Shifts in the social contract: Understanding change in American society.* Thousand Oaks, CA: Pine Forge Press.

Rumbaut, G. R. 1986. Southeast Asian refugees in the United States: A portrait of a case of migration and resettlement, 1975–1985. Paper presented at the annual meeting of the American Sociological Association.

Russell, C. 1984. The business of demographics. *Population Bulletin* 39 (June): 1–40.

Rymer, R. 1994. *Genie: A scientific tragedy.* New York: Harper Perennial Library.

Sahadi, J. 2006. TNS financial services. Top 10 millionaire counties. CNNMoney.com March 29. http://money.cnn.com/2006/03/28/news/economy/millionaires/

Salmans, S. 1985. Man in the moon loses job at P&G. *New York Times* 25 (April).

Santrock, J. W. 1970. Influence of onset and type of parental absence on the first four Eriksonian developmental crises. *Developmental Psychology* 3: 273–274.

Sapir, E. 1929. The status of linguistics as a science. *Language* 5: 207–214.

Saxton, L. 1972. *The individual, marriage and the family,* 2nd ed. Belmont, CA: Wadsworth.

Scarr, S., and R. A. Weinberg. 1976. IQ test performance in black children adopted by white families. *American Ppsychologist* 31 (April): 726–739.

Schaefer, R. T. 1985. *Racial and ethnic groups,* 2nd ed. Boston: Little Brown.

Schaefer, R. T. 2006. *Sociology: A brief introduction,* 6th ed. Boston: McGraw-Hill

Schaefer, R. T. 2008. *Racial and ethnic groups,* 11th ed. Upper Saddle River, NJ: Pearson Prentice-Hall.

Schelling, T. C. 1978. *Micromotives and macrobehavior.* New York: Norton.

Schmitt, E. 2001. For the first time, nuclear families drop below 25% of households. *The New York Times,* May 15, A1, A18.

Schor, J. 1999. *The overspent American. Why we want what we don't need.* New York: Harper-Collins.

Schultz, E. A., and R. H. LaVenda. 1987. *Cultural anthropology: A perspective on the human condition.* New York: West.

Schur, E. M. 1971. *Labeling deviant behavior: Its sociological implications.* New York: Harper & Row.

Schur, E. M. 1984. *Labeling women as deviant: Gender, stigma, and social control.* New York: Random House.

Schwartz, S., and A. Gottlieb. 1980. Bystander anonymity and reaction to emergencies. *Journal of Personality and Social Psychology* 39: 418–440.

Schwartz, R., B. Ross, and C. Francescani. 2008. Edwards admits sexual affair: Lied as presidential candidate. ABC News. The Blotter from Brian Ross & the Investigative Team. Accessed September 22, 2008 at http://abcnews.go.com/Blotter/story?id=5441195&page=1

ScienceDaily. 2006. American's circle of friends is Shrinking, new study shows. *Science News.* June 23, 2006. Accessed on June 17, 2008 at http://www.sciencedaily.com/releases/2006/06/060623093533

Semones, J. K. 1977. *Sociology: A core text.* Dubuque, IA: Kendall/Hunt.

Semones, J. K. 1990. *Sociology: A core text.* Forth Worth, TX: Holt, Rinehart, and Winston, Inc.

Semones, J. K. 1991. *Effective study skills: A step-by step system for achieving student success.* Forth Worth: Holt, Rinehart and Winston, Inc.

Semones, J. K. 1992. *The experiential guide to effective study skills.* New York: Harcourt Brace Jovanovich College Publishers.

Semones, J. K. 2005. *Survival readings in sociology.* Houston, TX: ESS Enterprises.

Semones, J. K., and L. M. Romero, 2007. Reisman's 'the lonely crowd' revisited: The loss of meaningful personal connection and intimacy in a cyber-directed world. A paper presented at Persons and sexuality: Probing the boundaries, 4th Global Conference (November 19–22), Salzburg, Austria. Section 5: Intimacy, November 21.

Service, Elman. R. 1971. *Profiles in ethnology.* Revised Edition. New York: Harper & Row.

Sharif, I., and J. D. Sargent. 2006. Association between television, movie, and video game exposure and school performance. *Pediatrics,* Vol. 118, No. 4 (October), e1061–e1070.

Sheldon. W. H. 1949. *Varieties of delinquent youth: An introduction to constitutional psychiatry.* New York: Harper & Row.

Shibutani, T. 1966. *Improvised news: A sociological study of rumor,* 62. Indianapolis: Bobbs-Merrill.

Shibutani, T. 1986. *Social processes: An introduction to sociology.* Berkeley, CA: University of California Press.

Shils, E. O. 1950. Primary groups in the American army. In *Continuities in social research,* eds. R. K. Merton and P. F. Lazarsfeld. New York: Free Press.

Shils, E. A., and M. Janowitz. 1948. Cohesion and disintegration in the Wehrmacht in World War II. *Public Opinion Quarterly* (Summer): 280–315.

Shipler, D. K. 2005. *The working poor: Invisible in America.* New York: Vintage.

Shirk, M., N. G. Bennett, and J. L. Aber. 1999. *Lives on the line: American families and the struggle to make ends meet.* Boulder, CO: Westview Press.

Sikh, Pakistani shot in USA. 2001. *The Tribune.* Online edition. September 17. Accessed June 10, 2008 at http://www.tribuneindia.com/2001/20010917/main.4.htm

Simon, J. L., and P. Burstein. 1985. *Basic research methods in social science,* 3rd. ed. New York: Random House.

Simmel, G. 1950 A. The metropolis and mental life. In *The sociology of Georg Simmel,* ed. and trans. K. Wolff. New York: Free Press. (This article was first published in 1918.)

Simmel, G. 1950 B. Quantitative aspects of the group. In *The sociology of Georg Simmel,* ed. and trans. K. Wolff. New York: Free Press. (This article was first published in 1905.)

Simmel, G. 1955. *Conflict and the web of group affiliations.* New York: Free Press.

Simmons, J. L. 1969. *Deviants.* Berkeley, CA: The Glendessary Press.

Sjoberg, G. 1967. Project Camelot: Selected readings and personal reflections. In *Ethics, politics, and social research,* ed. G. Sjoberg. Cambridge, MA: Schenkman.

Skolnick, A. S. 1987. *The intimate environment: Exploring marriage and the family,* 4th ed. Boston: Little, Brown.

Skolnick, A. S., and J. H. 2007. *Family in transition,* 14th ed. Boston: Allyn and Bacon.

Slater, P. E. 1955. Role differentiation in small groups. In *Small groups: Studies in social interaction,* ed. A. P. Hare, et al. New York: Knopf.

Smelser, N. 1963. *Theory of collective behavior.* Glencoe, IL: Free Press.

Solomon, Z., M. Mikulincer, and S. E. Hobfoll. 1986. Effects of social support and battle intensity on lonliness and breakdown during combat. *Journal of Personality and Social Psychology* 51: 1269–1276.

Sorenson, A. B. 1975. The structure of intragenerational mobility. *American Sociological Review* 40: 456–471.

Southern Poverty Law Center. 2008. *Hate groups in America.* Headquarters, Atlanta, GA.

Spencer, H. 1860. *The social organism.* London: Greenwood.

Spencer, H. 1874. *The study of sociology.* New York: Appleton.

Spector, M., and J. I. Kitsuse, 1977. *Constructing social problems.* Menlo Park, CA: Cummings.

Spiegelman, A. 2004. *In the shadow of no towers.* New York: Pantheon.

Spitz, R. 1945. Hospitalization: An inquiry into the genesis of psychiatric conditions in early childhood. In *The Psychoanalytic study of the child,* ed. A. Freud. New York: International Universities Press.

Stark, P. 1988. A drug test for members of congress. *Playboy* (November): 49, 54.

Stark, R. 1989. *Sociology,* 3rd ed. Belmont, CA: Wadsworth.

Steadman, H. J. and J. J. Cocozza. 1974. *Careers of the criminally insane.* Lexington, MA: Lexington Books.

Steele, S. 1990. *The content of our character.* New York: HarperCollins.

Steinbeck, J. 1939. *The grapes of wrath.* New York: The Viking Press.

Stephens. W. R. 2004. *Careers in sociology,* 4th ed. Boston, MA: Pearson Education.

Sternberg, R. 1998. *Love is a story: A new theory of relationships.* New York: The Oxford University Press.

Stevens, W. A. 1970. A cross-cultural study of modesty and obscenity. In *Technical reports of the commission on Obscenity and Pornography.* Washington, DC: IX.

Strasburger, V. C. 1993. Adolescents and the media: Five crucial issues. *Adolescent Medicine* 4: 479–493.

Stritof, S., and B. Stritof. 2008. Prenuptial marriage agreements: For love or money. Accessed September 23, 2008 at http://marriage.about.com/cs/agreements/a/loveormoney/.html

Stout, D. 2003. Supreme Court splits on diversity efforts at University of Michigan. (On-line). Obtained June 23, 2003 at http://news.yahoo.com

Stryker, S., and A. Statham. 1985. Symbolic interactionism and role theory. In *Handbook of social psychology: Vol. 1*, 3rd ed., ed. G. Lindsey and E. Aronson. New York: Random House.

Stuckert, R. P. 1976. "Race" mixture: The black ancestry of white Americans. In *Physical anthropology and archeology*, ed. P. B. Hammond. New York: Macmillan.

Suchman, E. A. 1968. The "hang-loose" ethic and the spirit of drug use. *Journal of Health and Social Behavior* (June): 146–155.

Sumner, W. G. 1960. *Folkways*. New York: The New American Library. (Originally published in 1906.)

Sutherland, E. H. 1939. *Principles of criminology*. Philadelphia: Lippincott.

Sutherland, E. H. 1967. *White collar crime*. New York: Holt, Rinehart and Winston.

Sutherland, E. H., and D. R. Cressey. 1970. *Criminology*, 8th ed. Philadelphia: Lippincott.

Sweeney, M. M., and Phillips, J. A. 2004. Understanding racial differences in marital disruptions: Recent trends and explanations. *Journal of Marriage and Family* 66: 239–250.

Szasz, T. S. 1974. *The myth of mental illness*. New York: Harper & Row.

Taft, D. R., and R. W. England. 1966. *Criminology*, 4th ed. New York: Macmillan.

Taneja, V. S., R. S. Beri., V. Sreenhivas, R. Aggarwal, R. Kaur, and J. M. Puliyel. 2002. "Not by bread alone": Impact of a structured 90 minute play session on development of children in an orphanage. *Child Care, Health & Development* 28: 95–100.

Tanikawa, M. 1995. Earning it; In Japan, some shun lifetime jobs to chase dreams. *New York Times:* June 25.

Tarmann, A. 2001. Contraceptive shortages loom in less developed countries. *Population Today* August/September: 1–2.

Task force report: Crime and its impact. 1967. President's Commission on Law Enforcement and Administration of Justice. Washington, DC: U.S. Government Printing Office.

Teachman, J. D. 2002. Childhood living arrangements and the intergenerational transmission of divorce. *Journal of Marriage and Family* 64: 717–729.

Teitelbaum, M. S. 1975. Relevance of demographic transition theory for developing countries. *Science* 188 (May): 420–425.

Television, computers, and brain development. 2004. Speechgoals.org.

Therrien, M., and R. R. Ramirez. 2001. The Hispanic population in the United States, March 2000. Current Population Reports. Ser. P20, No. 535. Washington, DC: U. S. Government Printing Office. (10) Accessed on July 16 at http://library.thinkquest.org/26026/Environmental_Problems/rain_forest_destruction.html

Thio, A. 2007. *Deviant behavior*, 9th ed. Boston: Allyn & Bacon/Pearson Education.

Tilly, C. 2004. *Social Movements. 1768–2004*. Boulder, CO: Paradigm Publishers.

Timasheff, N. S. 1967. *Sociological theory: Its nature and growth*, 3rd ed. New York: Random House.

The Associated Press. 2008a. Obama denounces former pastor. MSNBC.com. Tues. April 29, pp. 1–2.

The World Almanac and Book of Facts. 2005. New York: World Almanac Books.

The World Almanac and Book of Facts. 2008. New York: World Almanac Books.

Thomas, W. I., and M. Thomas. 1928. *The child in America: Behavior problems and programs*. New York: Knopf.

Thomson, W. E., and J. V. Hickey. 2008. *Society in focus*, 6th ed. Boston: Pearson-Allyn & Bacon.

Thrasher, F. M. 1927. *The gang*. Chicaco: University of Chicago Press.

Thurstone, L. L. 1938. Primary mental abilities. *Psychometric Monographs,* No. 1. Chicago: University of Chicago Press.

Time. 1989. A brightly colored tinderbox. (January 30): 28–29.

Toffler, A. 1980. *The third wave.* New York: Morrow.

Tönnies, F. 1957. *Community and society: Gemeinschaft and Gesellschaft.* Ed. and trans. C. A. Loomis. East Lansing, MI: Michigan State University Press. Originally published in 1887.

Tönnies, F. 2003. *Community and Society.* New York: Dover Publications. Originally published in 1887 in German as *Gemeinschaft und Gellschaft.*

Toufexis, A., et al. 1988. Older—but coming on strong. *Time* (February 22): 76–79.

Tovar, H. 2005. *Translation nation.* New York: Riverhead.

Truzzi, M. 1974. *Sociology for pleasure.* Englewood Cliffs, NJ: Prentice-Hall.

Tumin, M. 1953. Some principles of stratification: A critical analysis. *American Sociological Review* 18: 387–394.

Turkington, C. 1983. Lifetime of fear may be the legacy of latchkey children. Monitor. Washington, DC: *American Psychological Association* (November): 19.

Turner, R. H. 1964. Collective behavior. In *Handbook of modern sociology,* ed. R. E. L. Fatis. Chicago: Rand McNally.

Turner, R. H. 1980. New theoretical frameworks. In *Collective behavior: A source book,* ed. M. D. Pugh, 31–41.

Turner, R. H., and L. M. Killian, eds. 1957. *Collective behavior.* Englewood Cliffs, NJ: Prentice Hall. (Third edition 1987.)

Turner, V. 1967. *The forest of symbols,* 3. Ithaca, NY: Cornell University Press.

Tyrangiel, Josh, 2001. Did you hear about . . . . *Time,* October 8, p. 77.

Udall, M. K. 1987. *Introduction. Gaining people, losing ground,* vii, ed. W. Fornos,Washington, DC: The Population Institute.

UNICEF. 2008. Kenya statistics. Accessed on July 29, 2008 at http://www.unicef.org/infobycountry/kenya_statistics.html

United Nations. 1985. *Estimates and projections of urban, rural, and city population. 1950–2025.*

United Nations. 2003. *World urbanization prospects,* Megacities.

USAID: Ethiopia: 2008. United nations tells Ethiopia to decriminalize abortion; publically fund contraception. *Program Data Sheet.* LifeSiteNews.com Jan 4, 2004.

UN Chronicle. 2002. Substantial increase in 1990s—world contraceptive use—2001. Sept–Nov. United Nations Publications.

USA Today. 2008. NAACP to hold funeral for 'N' word. April 30. Accessed on May 25, 2008 at http://www.usatoday.com/news/nation/2007-04-30-n-word-funeral_N.htm

U.S. Census Bureau. 1985. November. Marital Status and living arrangements, March 1985. *Current population reports,* Series P-120, No. 410. Washington, DC: U.S. Printing Office.

U.S. Census Bureau. 1986a. Money income and poverty status of families and persons in the United States, 1985. *Current population reports,* Series P-60. No. 154:13. Washington, DC: U.S. Government Printing Office.

U.S. Census Bureau. 1986b. Money income and poverty status of families and persons in the United States, 1985. *Current population reports,* Series P-60, No. 154:13. Washington, DC: U.S. Printing Office.

U.S. Census Bureau. 1986c. November. Households, families, marital status, and living arrangements. March, 1986. Advance report. *Current population reports,* Series P-20, No. 410. Washington, DC: U.S. Government Printing Office.

U.S. Census. 1987. Money income and poverty status of families in the United States, 1986. *Current population reports,* Series P-60, No. 157. Washington, DC: U. S. Government Printing Office.

U.S. Census Bureau. 1988. Money income and poverty status of families in the United States, 1987. *Current population reports.* Washington, DC: U.S. Government Printing Office.

U.S. Census Bureau. 2000a. Percentage of the U.S. population over 65 years of age.

U.S. Census Bureau. 2002. Household and family characteristics, March 1981. *Current population reports,* Series P-20, No. 372. Washington, DC: U.S. Government Printing Office.

U.S. Census Bureau. 2002a. *Black population in the United States: 2002,* pp. 5–6.

U.S. Census Bureau. 2001. *Current population reports.*

U.S. Census Bureau. 2004. *Current population reports.*

U.S. Census Bureau. 2004a. The Black Population in the United States: March, 2004. *Current population survey,* PPL -186, Table 17.

U.S. Census Bureau. 2004b. The Asian Alone Population in the United States: March 2004, Table 1.1

U.S. Census Bureau. 2004c. More diversity, slower growth: Census Bureau projects tripling of Hispanic and Asian populations in fifty years; nonhispanic whites may drop to half of total Population. Washington, DC: U.S. Department of Commerce. March 18.

U.S. U.S. Census Bureau. 2001. *Current population reports.*

U. S. Census Bureau. 2005. *Current population reports.* Age specific fertility in women.

U.S. Census Bureau. 2005a. *College degree nearly doubles annual earnings.* Census Bureau Reports CB05-58, Table 10.

U.S. Census Bureau. 2005b. "Table H-3. Mean household income received by each fifth and top 5 percent, all races, 1967 to 2004." Accessed on September 27, 2008 at http://www.census.gov/hhes/www/income

U.S. Census Bureau, 2005c. Estimated median age at first marriage. *Current population survey:* March and annual social and economic supplements, 2005 and earlier.

U.S. Census Bureau. 2006a. 2005 March *Current population reports.* Detailed tables, Table 3C.

U.S. Census Bureau. 2006b. *Current population survey* 2006 Annual social and economic supplement.

U.S. Census Bureau. 2008. *World vital events per time unit: 2008.* Accessed on July 15, 2008 at http://www.census.gov/cgi-bin/ipc/pcwe

U.S. Department of Health and Human Services, 2005. Health Resources Services Administration. *Domestic violence.* Rockville, Maryland.

U.S. Department of Health and Human Services. 2007. Health Resources Services Administration, *Women's health USA 2007.* Rockville, Maryland.

U.S. Department of Health and Human Services. 2008. Annual Update, poverty guidelines: Posted January 23.

U.S. Department of Justice. 2006. Federal Bureau of Investigation. *Hate crime statistics,* Table 3.

U.S. National Center for Health Statistics. 1979. March. Department of Health, Education, and Welfare, Publication No. (PHS) 78-1120. Washington, DC: U.S. Government Printing Office.

U.S. News and World Report. 2006. A Nation in Full. October 2, 2006, Volume 141, No. 12, pp. 48–56.

Van Creveld, M. 1982. *Fighting power: U.S. and German army performance, 1939–1945.* Westport, CT: Greenwood Press.

Money income and poverty status of families in the United States: 1987. Current Population Reports. Washington, DC: U. S. Government Printing Office.

Van den Berghe, P. *Race and racism: A comparative perspective,* 2nd ed. New York: Wiley.

Vander Zanden, J. W. 1972. *American minority relations: The sociology of race and ethnic groups,* 3rd ed., 46–47. New York: Ronald Press.

Vander Zanden, J. W. 1983. *American minority relations,* 4th ed. New York: Knopf.

Vander Zanden, J. W. 1985. *Human development,* 3rd ed. New York: Knopf.

Vandivere, S., K. Tout, J. Capizzano, and M. Zaslow. 2003. Left unsupervised: A look at the most vulnerable children. Washington, DC: The Urban Institute. Accessed January 28, 2009 at www.childtrends.org/files/UnsupervisedRB.pdf

Vogel, E. 1979. *Japan as number one: Lessons for America.* Cambridge, MA: Harvard University Press.

Vold, G. 1958. *Theoretical criminology,* 74. New York: Harvard University Press.

Von Drehle, D. 2003. Debate on Marriage and More Looms. WashingtonPost.com. June 27, 2003, pp. 1–5.

Vorozkko, T. 2008. U.S. parents face the high costs of raising children. Voice of America, September 18. Accessed on 9/29/08 at http://www.voanews.com/english/2008-09-18-voa30.cfm

Vygotsky, L. 1978. *Mind in society.* Cambridge, MA: Harvard University Press.

Wagley, C., and M. Harris. 1964. *Minorities in the new world.* New York: Columbia University Press.

Waite L., and Joyner, K. 2001. Emotional satisfaction, and physical pleasure in sexual unions: Time horizon, sexual behavior, and sexual exclusivity. *Journal of Marriage and Family* 63: 247–264.

Wallace, W. 1972. *The logic of science in sociology,* 18. Chicago: Aldine-Atherton,

Wallerstein, I. 2005. *Katrina: The politics of incompetence and decline.* Fernand Baudel Center, Binghampton University: England. Commentary no. 169, September 15.

Warner, W. L. 1949. *Democracy in Jonesville.* New York: Harper & Row.

Warner, W. L., and P. S. Lunt. 1941. *The social life of a modern community.* New Haven, CT: Yale University Press.

Warner, W. L., M. Meeker, and K. Ells. 1949. *Social class in America.* Chicago: Science Research Associates.

Waters, H. P. 1977. What TV does to kids. *Newsweek,* 21. February: 107–112

Watkins, L. M. 1986. Liberal arts graduates in the job market grow brighter. *Wall Street Journal,* (May 6): 29.

Watson, J. B. 1924. *Behavior.* New York: Norton.

Wattenburg, B. J. 1985. *The good news is the bad news is wrong.* New York: Simon and Shuster.

Welch, Kelly J. 2007. *Family life now: A conversation about marriages, families, and relationship,* 436s. Boston, MA: Pearson Education, Inc.

Westhoff, B. 2008. Not your father's N-Word. *Houston Press.* April 3. Accessed May 25, 2008 at http://www.houstonpress.com/2008-04-03/music/not-your-father-s-n-word/

Weber, M. 1905/1977. *The protestant ethnic and the spirit of capitalism,* trans. T. Parsons. New York: Scribner's.

Weber, M. 1922/1968. *Economy and society.* New York: Bedminster Press.

Weber, M. 1946. Class, status, and party. From *Max Weber: Essays in sociology,* ed. and trans. H. Gerth and C. W. Mills, 180–195. New York: Oxford University Press.

Weber, M. 1946. The sociology of charismatic authority, From *Max Weber: Essays in sociology,* ed. and trans. H. Gerth and C. W. Mills, 245–252. New York: Oxford University Press.

Weiss, R. S. 2004. In their own words: Making the most of qualitative interviews. *Contexts.* Fall: 44–51.

White, J. E. 1997. "I'm Just Who I Am." *Time* May 5, 149: 32–34, 36.

White, R. K., and R. O. Lippitt. 1960. *Autocracy and democracy.* New York: Harper & Row.

Whitman, M. N. 1999. *New world, new rules: The changing role of the American corporation.* Boston: Harvard University Press.

Whyte, M. K., and W. L. Parrish. 1984. *Urban life in contemporary China.* Chicago: University of Chicago Press.

Wilensky, H. L., and C. N. Lebeaux. 1958. *Industrial society and social welfare.* New York: Russell Sage Foundation.

Wilkinson, D. 1980. Applied sociology: Is it pure? *A.S.A. Footnotes* 8 (May 3). Quoted from Ward, L. F. 1906. *Applied Sociology,* 3. Boston, MA: Ginn.

Williams, R. M. Jr. 1970. *American society: A sociological interpretation,* 3rd ed. New York: Knopf.

Williams, L. and Sobieszczyk. 1997. Attitudes surrounding the continuation of female circumcision in the Sudan: Passing tradition on to the next generation. *Journal of Marriage and the Family,* 59, 966–981 (13).

Wilson, E. O. 1975. *Sociobiology: The new synthesis.* Cambridge, MA: Harvard University Press.

Wilson, E. O. 1978. What is sociobiology? *Society* 15 (September-October): 6.

Wilson, J. Q. 2000. *Bureaucracy: What government agencies do and why they do it.* New York: Basic Books.

Wilson, R. A., and B. Hosokawa. 1980. *East to America: A history of the Japanese in the United States.* New York: Morrow.

Wilson, R. F. 2006. Sexually predatory parents and the children in their care: Remove the threat, not the child. In *Handbook on children, violence, and culture,* eds. N. E. Dowd, D. G. Singer, and R. F. Wilson, 39–58. Thousand Oaks, CA: Sage.

Wilson, W., et al. 1976. Authoritarianism left and right. *Bulletin of the Psychonomic Society* 7 (March): 271–274.

Wilson, W. J., and R. Aponte. 1985. Urban poverty. *Annual Review of Sociology* 11: 231–258.

Winn, P. 2008. Female airmen deadly in Iraq, Afganistan. AirforceTimes. Sunday, Jan. 13, 2008. Accessed June 23, 2008 at http://www.airforce.com/news/2007/12/airforce_deadly_ women_ 071229w/

Wirth, L. 1938. Urbanism as a way of life. *American Journal of Sociology* 44 (July): 1–2.

Wirth, L. 1945. The problem of minority groups. In *The science of man in the world crisis,* ed. R. Linton, 347v372. New York: Columbia University Press.

Wise, T. 2005. *Affirmative action: Racial preference in black and white.* New York: Routledge.

Witherspoon, G. 1975. *Navajo kinship and marriage.* Chicago: University of Chicago Press.

Witherspoon, D. J., S. Wooding, A. R. Rogers, E. E. Marchani, W. S. Watkins, M. A. Batzer, and L. B. Jorde. 2007. Genetic similarities within and between human populations. *Genetics* May 1; 176(1): 351–359.

Wolfgang, M. E. 1972. Cesare Lombroso (1835–1909). In *Pioneers in criminology,* ed. H. Mannheim. Montclair, NJ: Patterson Smith.

Woodward, C. V. 1974. *The strange career of Jim Crow,* 3rd ed. New York: Oxford University Press.

World Health Organization. 2003. Accessed at Nationmaster.com on July 15, 2008. Health Statistics, dependency ratio per 100 population.

World Hunger: Facts about Hunger. 2008. CARE. Accessed on July 19, 2008 at http://www.care.org/ campaigns/world-hunger/facts.asp

World Population Data Sheet. 1985. Washington, DC: Population Reference Bureau.

World Population Data Sheet. 1987. Washington, DC: Population Reference Bureau.

World Population Data Sheet. 2003. Washington, DC: Population Reference Bureau.

*World Population Data Sheet.*2005. Washington, DC: Population Reference Bureau.

Wright, B., and J. B. Weiss. 1980. *Social problems.* Boston: Little, Brown.

Wrong, D. H. 1959. The functional theory of stratification: Some neglected considerations. *American Sociological Review* 24: 772–782.

Wysocki, D. K., ed. 2008. *Readings in social research methods,* 3rd ed. Belmont, CA: Wadsworth.

Yinger, J. M. 1982. *Countercultures.* New York: Free Press.

Zeng, Y. 2007. Options for fertility policy in China. Population and policy review. The population council. June 1, 2007. Accessed on July 21 at http://www.accessmy library.com/coms2/summary_ 0286-31855448_ITM (12)

Zigli, B. 1984. Asian-Americans beat others in academic drive. *USA Today* 25 April, 1D.

Zimbardo, P. G. 1972. Pathology of imprisonment. *Society* 9 (April): 4–8.

Zygmunt, J. E. 1986. Collective behavior as a phase of societal life. Blumer's emergent views and Their implications. *Research in Social Movements, Conflicts and Change* 9: 25–46.

Glossary

aberrant deviance: deviant behavior in which a person violates a norm for selfish reasons and attempts to escape detection and punishment.

absolute poverty: a condition that exists when people lack essential resources, such as food and shelter, for survival.

accommodation (general definition): a pattern of social interaction that fosters the reduction or resolution of conflict so that opposing parties can function together successfully.

accommodation (in minority relations): a pattern of exclusion which members of a minority group attempt to coexist with the dominant group without making a significant effort to adopt the norms and values of the dominant society.

achieved status: a social position earned through individual effort.

acting crowd: a highly aroused crowd focused on a specific situation or problem that members are willing to act on impulse to resolve.

affective therapy: emotion-based marital therapy that focuses on the verbal release of conflict with or hostility toward the spouse or other family members in a controlled therapeutic environment.

affinal kinship: a type of family organization based primarily on marital ties.

age specific fertility rate (ASFR): the number of births per 1,000 women in specific age categories during a given year.

age specific mortality rate (ASMR): the total number of deaths per 1,000 people in a population in specific age categories during a given year.

agricultural revolution: the first technological revolution to spark world population growth marked by the domestication of plants and animals which began about 10,000 years ago (8,000 BCE).

agrarian societies: social systems organized around advanced agricultural methods for subsistence and centralized governmental authority.

amalgamation: the intermarriage of minority group members with those belonging to the dominant group.

anomie: Durkheim's term for a state of confused norms or normlessness (the absence of norms) brought on by rapid change or social complexity.

anonymity: a condition in which a person's identity becomes lost in a crowd.

anticipatory socialization: the informal preparation for future life stages and life responsibilities.

anti-Semitism: prejudice and discrimination focused on people of Jewish culture or faith.

applied research: the study of how sociological principles and knowledge might be applied to social issues, programs, and problems.

apprenticeship in thinking: a process in which an unskilled person (novice learner) develops mastery of a cognitive competency through active involvement with one or more skilled mentors (Vygotsky).

argot: a special type of language characteristic of subcultures.

artifacts: physical objects that represent a specific culture.

ascribed status: a social position assigned to a person at birth or otherwise imposed by society.

assimilation: a process whereby an immigrant or minority group changes its cultural patterns to conform and adapt to the ways of a dominant culture.

astrology: the notion that the movement of the planets and stars affects human behavior, and that the moon in particular influences deviant behavior.

atavistic theory: a biological explanation of deviance which maintains that the violent criminal is an inherited type who represents a genetic throwback to primitive humans.

authoritarian personality: a highly rigid and intolerant person who tends to exhibit a group of identifiable personality characteristics.

authority: legitimated power generally recognized and supported by those over whom it is exercised.

"bad blood" theory: the early view that deviant behavior (such as crime and drug addiction) was caused by the biological makeup of a person who had "bad blood" or who was a "bad seed."

beliefs: propositions about reality that either are not based on scientific evidence or cannot be demonstrated through scientific means.

biased sample: an unscientific sample that lacks random selection and, in some cases, involves self-selection by participants (e.g., straw polls, letters to the editor).

biological perspective (on deviance): argues that deviance is caused primarily by inborn physical traits or characteristics.

bonding: the process of forming close personal relationships with other people, such as the relationship between a parent and child.

bottom-up decision making: a characteristic of Japanese corporations in which information and decisions based on group consensus travel from bottom to top, rather than from top to bottom in the organization.

bourgeoisie: Marx's term for the capitalist owners of industry, the "haves" who made profits from exploiting the labor of the workers.

brainwashing: a process of almost complete thought control in which the victim's existing values and beliefs are made useless and replaced with those desired by the agent of influence.

bride price: a mate selection practice in which a man pays a price to a family for the hand of their daughter in marriage; the most common form of arranged marriage.

bureaucracy: a form of social organization in which the work of participants in large-scale organizations is rationally coordinated by professionally trained managers.

bystander apathy: a condition in which, during emergency situations requiring responsible action, onlookers at the scene fail to act.

calculated formation: the action taken by group members to organize together in pursuit of one or more specific, practical goals.

careers: positions held by managerial and professional officials through which, in exchange for loyal and adequate performance, extended employment and opportunities for advancement are provided.

caste system: a rigid and closed system of social ranking in which most statuses are ascribed and tend to remain so.

casual crowd: a temporary crowd formed spontaneously with members that tend to come and go.

cenogamy: the marriage of two or more men and two or more women; also known as group marriage.

censorship: limitations placed on the information that is made available to the public.

census: a relatively complete headcount of the people in a given society.

charismatic authority: Weber's term for authority based on the commonly accepted belief by followers that a leader possesses special qualities or unique characteristics (e.g., military heroism or divine grace).

"Chicago school": A unified school of thought primarily established by sociologists at the University of Chicago in the 1920s and 1930s that stressed urban problems and a reform perspective.

child abuse: neglect or overt acts of aggression by a parent or other adult against a child that produces physical injury, emotional problems, or both.

circular reaction: the principle that members of crowds, particularly in conditions of unrest and heightened tension, reinforce one another's feelings and behavior in a back-and-forth or circular fashion.

collective behavior: a pattern of social behavior that consists of people's relatively spontaneous and unstructured actions in response to ambiguous or changing social conditions.

class system: a relatively open and flexible system of social ranking in which most statuses are achieved.

clinical sociology: an applied profession within sociology dedicated to helping people better cope with their social identities and social relations through the use of sociological principles.

coalition: in the context of group dynamics, it is a relationship formed when some group members align themselves against others.

coercive organization: Etzioni's term for an organization in which people participate due to force or the threat of force.

cognitive culture: the ways in which a culture defines what is real or what exists (e.g., knowledge, beliefs, and ideologies).

cognitive development theory: Piaget's perspective that examined changes in thought processes and intellectual abilities that occur in four stages as children mature.

cohabitation: a relationship between two unrelated, unmarried adults who share a common residence and an assumed sexual relationship.

collective conscience: in Durkheim's view, a state of mental and moral agreement among members of a society concerning basic norms and values.

collective level deviance: socially unacceptable behavior by large numbers of people at various levels of society.

collectives: alternative organizations consisting mainly of small businesses and nonprofit volunteer groups that function on nonbureaucratic principles.

common attributes: the characteristics members of a group share in common with one another.

competition: a pattern of social interaction that occurs when two or more parties attempt to reach a mutually prized goal that is limited in quantity.

compliant conformity: socially acceptable behavior that results from external social pressures.

Comteian synthesis: Auguste Comte's integration of three themes in Western civilization—Socratic skepticism, Platonic idealism, and the scientific method—that formed the basis for the emergence of sociology as a science.

concrete operations: the third stage in cognitive development (Piaget) in which cause-and-effect relationships in the real world become understood and concrete reasoning ability is developed.

conflict: a pattern of social interaction in which two or more parties seek to reach a goal by neutralizing, dominating, or destroying all adversaries against their will.

conflict approach to deviance: the argument that what is defined as "antisocial" or "deviant" arises out of a struggle for power between various groups.

conflict perspective (on stratification): an approach that sees stratification as harmful to society because it allows those with the most power, prestige, and wealth to dominate and exploit the less advantaged and maintain a condition of inequity.

conflict theory: a modern sociological perspective that analyses conflict and power as they relate to social policy and change in society.

conformity: behavior that is in basic agreement with the dominant norms of society.

consanguineal kinship: a type of family organization based primarily on blood ties.

consciousness of kind: the tendency of people to recognize others like themselves and, in many cases, to feel a common sense of identification or connection as a result.

conservative movements: those that work within the system to preserve aspects of the status quo and thus resist certain forms of social change.

constructive argument: a family therapy method in which family members work through steps and techniques that place the focus on their problem rather than on their personalities.

content analysis: a research design in which the content of communication (media) is studied to assess its impact on social attitudes and behavior.

contract: a social bond between two or more parties that involves the exchange of one promise for another.

control group: the group in an experiment not exposed to the independent variable.

control theory: the assertion by Reckless that conformity results when people resist pushes and pulls placed on them to violate social norms due to two sets of social controls, inner controls and outer controls.

conventional conformity: socially acceptable behavior that results from unconsciously following dominant norms.

conventional crowd: a fairly structured crowd that conforms to established norms.

convergence theory: the perspective that crowds tend to draw particular types of people with definite interests and values rather than a representative cross-section from the community.

cooperation: a pattern of social interaction that involves the sharing of responsibility by people who work together to reach a shared goal.

correlation: the simultaneous occurrence of two variables together in a particular type of relationship.

counterculture: a type of subculture that is in basic disagreement or conflict with the ways of the dominant culture of a society.

crazes: fads which among a limited segment of society, become obsessive.

crime: a violation of criminal law enacted and enforced by government with formal penalties.

cross-sectional study: a broad-based study that takes place over a brief period of time (one to two days to a few weeks).

crowd (also physical aggregate): a temporary and relatively unstructured group distinguished primarily by the physical proximity of its members.

crude birth rate (CBR): the total number of births per 1,000 people in a population during a given year.

crude death rate (CDR): the number of deaths per 1,000 people in a population during a given year.

cultural lag: a condition in which material culture (technology) changes more rapidly than nonmaterial or adaptive culture, causing a period of strain (lag) between the two.

cultural mediation: the process by which children learn or internalize the ways of their culture and how to use them as tools to succeed both as a society member and as an individual.

cultural relativity: the principle that each culture should be seen and understood in its own context apart from a biased comparison with others.

cultural universals: patterns and practices common to all cultures.

culture: the socially established patterns of perceiving and acting that one acquires as a member of society. NORMS, Values, —

culture of poverty hypothesis: Oscar Lewis's argument that poverty involves a subculture that socializes its children with attitudes of despair and acceptance of being poor as natural and normal for them.

culture shock: a disorientation that occurs when one is placed in a cultural setting significantly different from one's own.

cumulative knowledge: a characteristic of science in which what is known (the state of knowledge) is constantly being added to, modified, and refined.

demographic transition: a three-stage process in which developing nations move from a condition of high fertility and high mortality to one of low fertility and low mortality.

demography: the scientific study of population characteristics and change.

demonology: a system of beliefs which holds that deviance is caused by evil spirits that possess the body and make it act according to their will.

dependency ratio: the number of people in a population under fifteen and over sixty-five years of age divided by the number of people between fifteen and sixty-five.

dependent variable: in science, the effect (or result) that the research attempts to account for or explain.

deviance: behavior that violates the dominant norms of a group or society.

deviance by attributes: a process in which those with certain physical or social characteristics are perceived and/or treated as deviant (e.g., a handicapped person or the transgendered).

deviance resulting from an inability to conform: a situational form of deviance in which a person either cannot control their behavior or is forced to commit a deviant act.

deviant: a person who violates the most highly regarded norms of a group or society.

didactic teaching: the actual hands-on instruction of a child by a parent in some skill or activity.

differential association theory: the principle by Sutherland that criminal behavior is learned in close-knit groups that encourage or condone deviant behavior.

diffusion: cultural change brought about through the direct contact of two cultures (or more) in which certain traits of one are borrowed by the other.

discovery: the realization and sharing of newfound knowledge about something not previously known about or understood.

discrimination: differential treatment of people based on their membership in a particular social category.

division of labor: a system in society through which essential tasks are assigned to and carried out by the necessary numbers of people.

dominant group: a social category comprised of those in society who are dominant in power, prestige, wealth, and culture.

dramaturgical analysis: Goffman's approach to socialization which studies how and why people intentionally interact with each others like actors in a play titled "society."

drive: a physiological state in the form of internal tension that signals an individual that a particular need demands satisfaction.

dual-earner family: a family form in which both married partners generate income and share in home and child-rearing responsibilities.

dyad: a two person group.

dynamics: the study of how the various parts of society evolve and change.

dysfunctions: negative or disruptive consequences (problems) that that result from certain structural parts of society (e.g., child abuse in the family; deficit spending by government).

egalitarian authority: a pattern of family decision making in which males and females share power equally.

ego: Freud's term for the rational part of the self which acts as the governor or manager of the personality.

emergent norm theory: the perspective that individuals become members of crowds for numerous reasons and, through interaction with others, adopt the group norms that develop from the particular situation.

emigration: leaving one country to seek settlement in another.

empiricism: a characteristic of science in which evidence in science is gathered through the organized use of the senses.

endogamy: a norm that encourages or requires people to marry within certain culturally defined groups.

epistemology: an area in the philosophy of science devoted to the study of knowledge and how it is validated.

ethnicity: a specific cultural heritage that distinguishes one social category of people from others.

ethnic minority: ia social category whose members have experienced social disadvantages primarily because of cultural characteristics such as language or national origin.

ethnocentrism: the tendency to regard one's own culture as superior and other cultures as inferior.

evaluation research: examines the consequences of various public policies by evaluating their degree of effectiveness or ineffectiveness.

evolutionary perspective: the first theoretical approach used in the emerging science of sociology that early sociologists borrowed largely from Charles Darwin's biological model of natural selection.

evolutionary perspective (on stratification): an approach that attempts to integrate both functionalist and conflict explanations of stratification.

exchange: a pattern of social interaction in which allo parties expect to benefit by receiving a reward.

exogamy: a norm that encourages or requires people to marry outside of certain culturally defined groups.

experiment: a research design in which two matched groups of people are compared in terms of how they act in a specially designed social situation.

experimental group: the group in an experiment that is exposed to the independent variable.

exploitative prejudice: negative attitudes toward minority group members held by members of the majority group that are used as justification for keeping them in a subordinate position.

expressive crowd: a crowd that has as its primary purpose the free expression of emotions by participants.

expressive group purpose: the focus of relations in primary groups in which the main goal is the emotional benefit derived from participation as an end in itself.

extended family: two or more nuclear families, usually including married couples of different generations, and other relatives who all who all live together or near each other.

fads are folkways popular for a brief period of time among a limited segment of the population.

family: two or more persons related by blood, marriage, or adoption who live together and cooperate economically.

family universals: characteristics common to families in all societies.

fashions are folkways more durable than fads that gain widespread acceptance among a large portion of society for a substantial period of time.

fealty: a form of social organization involving the personal loyalty of a follower toward a leader.

fecundity: the biological potential for reproduction as applied either to an individual woman or to an entire population.

felt poverty: a condition of hardship experienced by families that fall slightly above the poverty line and/or those whose members experience emotional deprivation because their standard of living has been reduced.

fertility: the number of births that occur in a population as measured by fertility rates.

fertility rate (FR): the number of births per 1,000 women of childbearing age (15 to 44 years) in a population during a given year.

field research: the study of certain forms of social behavior within their natural settings.

folkways: broad-based norms such as general customs and social conventions that, when violated, result in only mild punishment, if any.

formal operations: the last and most advanced stage of cognitive development (Piaget) characterized by the development of higher order or abstract thinking abilities.

formal organization: a group deliberately formed to pursue one or more specific practical goals.

formal structure: the official set of goals, policies, and procedures of an organization that specify the behavior of its members.

functionalism: a modern sociological perspective that analyses the various parts or structures in society (e.g., institutions such as the family, government, and education) in terms of how they function to promote social order and stability.

functionalist approach to deviance: the argument that deviant or antisocial behavior results from a strain on or breakdown of social order.

functionalist perspective (on stratification): an approach that sees stratification as necessary and beneficial to society because it uses a system of rewards to motivate people to acquire the skills needed to obtain the most valued positions.

functions: benefits that result from a particular social structure or activity that help to promote social order and harmony.

game perspective: the argument that crowds are often very rational with participants who act logically under their own control in ways that benefit them.

game stage: Mead's term for middle to late childhood and early adolescence, during which the individual learns to play the game of society according to the rules, in terms of role obligations.

gemeinschaft: Tönnies's term for a community-oriented society in which most social relations are personal, informal, and tend to be based on tradition.

generalized belief: an emergent popular explanation that includes both the causes and "solutions" to a perceived social problem (structural strain).

generalized other: Mead's term for the standards of community behavior expected of anyone placed in a given social position.

genocide: a pattern of exclusion that involves an intentional and systematic attempt by one group to exterminate another.

gesellschaft: Tönnies's term for an urban, industrial society with impersonal and somewhat informal relations that tend to be based on contract.

global sociology: the use of the content, methods, and tools of sociology to examine the comparative and interdependent nature of social behavior among people throughout the world.

global warming: an unprecedented recent rise in greenhouse gas emissions and the earth's temperatures caused largely by human intervention.

goal displacement: a problem in which the means (rules) of an organization become substituted for the goals and many to most participants lose sight of their original objectives.

greenhouse effect: increasing cloud cover caused by pollution which retains the warmth of the sun and produces higher ground temperatures.

group: two or more people with one or more characteristics in common.

group dynamics: the systematic study of small group processes.

group level deviance: socially unacceptable behavior carried out by social groups, usually at the community level.

groupthink: a form of over-conformity in which, for the sake of cohesion and "good relations," group decisions are make uncritically with little if any conflict.

growth rate: the annual percentage of growth or loss in a population.

guided participation: a process by which a skilled member of society serving as mentor—a parent or teacher, for example,—actively assists an unskilled learner in mastering a particular cognitive competency (Vygotsky).

hate crimes: ordinary crimes in which victims are chosen because of some characteristic they possess such as racial background, religion, ethnicity, or sexual orientation.

Hawthorne effect: a temporary change in the behavior of people in a group because of the presence and influence of outsiders.

hierarchical authority: a process in which "offices" or positions in an organization are arranged vertically in terms of authority and responsibility.

horizontal mobility: change in social position, usually occupation, without any significant impact on social class level.

horticultural societies: village focused social systems that rely on simple slash-and-burn agriculture and the use of domesticated animals for subsistence.

human ecology: the scientific study of the relationship between human populations and their natural environment.

hunting-gathering societies: small bands of nomadic hunters and food gatherers who, because they lack the technology to produce or preserve food, literally take life a meal at a time.

hypothesis: a formal statement in science of an expected relationship between two variables which can be tested (Step 3 in conducting a study).

id: Freud's term for a person's natural urges and "instincts," such as sex and aggression.

ideal type: a conceptual model or pure type of something (e.g., urban as a pure type) that is used as a basis for comparing things as they actually exist.

ideology: a set of ideas aimed at promoting the interests of a particular segment of society.

imitative stage: Mead's term for infancy and early childhood (0–3 years), during which children learn to imitate the behavior of parents and others in their immediate environment.

immigration: coming into a new country from another to establish residence.

incest taboo: a norm that prohibits sex relations and marriage between close family members.

independent variable: in science, the causal or influencing variable that affects to some extent the occurrence of another variable.

index crimes: eight of the most serious violent and property crimes tracked each year by the U.S. Justice Department.

individual discrimination: unequal treatment that occurs when individuals belonging to one group regard and treat individuals of another group differently because of their group membership.

individual level deviance: acts of antisocial behavior carried out by one person, usually at the local community level.

individual racism: unequal treatment that occurs when ideas and actions based on a doctrine of racial supremacy are applied to members of one racial category by members of another. Note: a specific form of individual discrimination.

industrial revolution: the third technological revolution to encourage world population growth marked by the rise of mass factory production which began about the year 1750.

industrial societies: complex and technologically advanced social systems with a cash economy, mass production, specialized occupations, and bureaucratic management.

infant mortality rate (IMR): the total number of deaths per 1,000 children under twelve months of age in a population within a given year.

informal structure: the nonofficial norms and interaction patterns of an organization that emerge from the interaction patterns of its participants.

in-group: a group a person belongs to or identifies with.

inner-directed: adults with a positive self-concept and an internal moral compass formed mainly during childhood which guides them during their life course.

innovation: a deviant response in which a person accepts cultural approved goals but rejects socially approved means of achieving them.

instinct: a genetically determined imperative for complex behavior.

instinct theory: the argument that human behavior was shaped largely by genetically inherited predispositions that were called instincts.

institution: a major structural part of a society that addresses a special area of human needs.

institutional discrimination: unequal treatment of certain categories of people as a result of inequities built into basic institutions.

institutional racism: unequal treatment of members of a racial category that occurs when ideas and actions based on a doctrine of racial inequality are embedded into the structure of basic institutions (e.g., government, education, and the economic system). Note: a specific form of institutional discrimination.

instrumental group purpose: the focus of relations in secondary groups in which the group is used as a means to an end to achieve a practical goal.

interactionism: a modern sociological perspective that studies the personal meaning people assign to the social world around them and how they communicate these perceptions to others through the use of language.

interactionist approach to deviance: the argument that deviance results from certain types of interactions a person has with other people, as well as the acquisition of a deviant self-image.

intergenerational mobility: change in social class level that occurs across generations between parents and their children.

internal migration: movement of people from one place to another within a country.

international migration: movement of people from one country to another for the purpose of settlement.

interview: the direct questioning of research subjects by an investigator that is sometimes used in survey research.

intimate partner abuse: the use of overt aggression by one spouse or intimate partner against another which can produce emotional problems, physical injury, or both.

instrumental group purpose: the focus of relations in secondary groups in which the group is used as a means to an end to achieve a practical goal.

intragenerational mobility: changes people experience in social rank within their own lifetimes or careers.

invention: the development and application of existing objects and knowledge in ways not used before.

iron law of oligarchy: Michels' principle that power in organizations invariably becomes concentrated in the hands of a few people who use it to further their self-interests.

Jim Crow laws: statutes passed by Southern states after the Civil War that denied blacks access to public facilities used by whites (e.g., restaurants, hotels, restrooms, rail cars, etc.).

Katrina effect: an unnecessary expansion of social breakdown (anomie) caused when authorities fail to act decisively to a known, sudden change while it is immediately imminent and/or after a disaster occurs.

kinship: a form of social organization involving the manner in which family relations are organized.

knowledge: propositions about reality that have been scientifically verified.

labeling theory: the assertion that the way people perceive social reality determines (1) what behaviors are labeled as deviant and (2) how being labeled as deviant affects their behavior.

language: a learned system of symbolic communication that furnishes the framework for the sharing of meaning and culture.

latchkey children: children who spend significant amounts of time alone each day with no adult supervision.

latent functions: unintended and unrecognized benefits that result from certain structural parts of society that promote order and stability.

laws: officially recorded norms formulated and enforced by government.

life chances: opportunities for survival and prosperity in society (Max Weber).

life expectancy: the number of years a person in a specific country of a certain age can be expected to live.

lifestyle: the general value orientation, tastes and preferences, and pattern of living characteristic of those belonging to a particular group or social class.

longitudinal study: a study focused on a single group of people over an extended period of time (sometimes several years).

looking-glass self: Cooley's term for how people see themselves based on their assessment of how others see them.

macrolevel organization: the manner in which large-scale organizations, basic institutions, and societies are organized and interact with one another.

macrosociology: the study of major institutions and entire societies or civilizations.

Malthusian theory: the argument proposed by Thomas Malthus that human societies increase their populations geometrically (1, 2, 4, 8, 16), while food supplies grow arithmetically (1, 2, 3, 4, 5).

manifest functions: intended and recognized benefits that result from certain structural parts of society that promote social order and stability.

marriage: a formally recognized, intimate relationship between two or more adults that is durable, relatively stable, and seen as desirable.

marriage by exchange: a pattern of mate selection involving a social and economic arrangement between the families of those to be married.

marriage by mutual choice: ia pattern of mate selection in which the people to be married freely choose their own spouse based on their mutual preferences rather than those of their extended blood kin.

mass behavior: unstructured social behavior characteristic of large collectivities of people who operate outside of one another's presence.

mass hysteria: a spontaneous excited reaction by large numbers of people to a mysterious social condition or event perceived as a threat.

mass media: the various methods used to transmit information to large numbers of people in an organized manner.

master status: the social position held by a person that becomes the primary source of his or her identity.

material culture: cultural aspects, including technologies, that for the most part are physical and tangible in form such as artifacts and symbols.

matriarchal authority: a pattern of family decision making in which females are dominant in power.

means of subsistence: the specific process used by a society to provide food and other resources needed by its people for survival and prosperity.

mechanical solidarity: Durkheim's term for the solidarity (cohesion) of resemblance characteristic of traditional nonindustrial societies.

media: the systematic ways used to transmit information to specific publics or the population at large.

median age: the mid-point or fiftieth percentile in the age distribution of a population.

megacities: cities with ten million or more inhabitants.

microlevel organization: the patterned ways people act at the local community level in social encounters, relationships, and groups.

microsociology: the study of social behavior primarily at the interpersonal, local, and community levels of society.

migration: the movement of people from one geographical location to another for the purpose of establishing residence

minority group: a social category of people distinguished by their physical or cultural characteristics whose members have experienced a historical pattern of prejudice and discrimination.

mob: the most extreme form of acting crowd, whose members are out of control and willing to engage in violence if it suits their ends.

mobilization of participants: a process in which, through the directions and actions of a few leaders, enough people with sufficient motivation can be brought together and given the focus to act either positively or negatively.

momentum: increases in a population that continue long after birth and death rates have been stabilized.

monogamy: the marriage of one man to one woman or, in a few countries and jurisdictions, the marriage of two persons of the same gender which is also accepted.

moral entrepreneurs: Becker's term for members of some groups who try to impose their views of morality or policy on others.

mores: norms with a compelling moral connotation whose violation is met with general condemnation and sometimes severe punishment.

mortality: the number of deaths that occur in a population as measured by mortality rates.

mortality intervention: the provision of medical assistance and health technology and assistance to less-developed countries by developed nations.

mortification: a process in which a person's old identity is stripped away through a systematic program of degradation and humiliation, and replaced with a new self more suitable to the organization.

networking: the conscious and planned cultivation of social networks to achieve personal or practical goals.

no fault divorce: a form of divorce in which dissolution of marriage is little more than a formality and needed papers are filed with the court without fault grounds required.

nonconforming deviance: social disapproved behavior in which the participant challenges the legitimacy of certain norms by violating them openly, regardless of the punishments that might be imposed.

normative culture: socially agreed-upon standards for thinking, feeling, and acting in society (e.g., norms, values, laws and technicways).

normative prejudice: negative attitudes towards members of a particular group which are accepted as "normal" through the process of socialization.

norms: cultural rules that specify appropriate and inappropriate behavior.

nuclear family: two or more related persons, usually including a married couple, who occupy a common household.

objective approach (in stratification analysis): a method of stratification analysis that makes use of standardized criteria—such as occupation, education, and income—for objectively measuring social rank.

objective poverty: a state of official deprivation as determined by an agreed-upon standard of measurement (e.g., the poverty line for a family of four).

objectivity: a characteristic of science that involves an unbiased and unprejudiced approach aimed at determining truth.

organic analogy: a construct discussed by Spencer and Durkheim that compares a society or social organism made up of institutions, with an individual's body with internal organs that work in harmony with one another to promote a healthy biological organism.

organic solidarity: Durkheim's term for the solidarity (cohesion) of differences found in modern complex societies.

other-directed: adults with a negative self-concept who, largely as a result, allow others to guide their basic life decisions and shape their actions.

out-group: a group a person does not belong to or identify with.

pan-Indianism: efforts by Indian groups to develop coalitions between several tribes to deal effectively with common problems.

Parkinson's law: a problem in organizations in which "work expands to fill the time available for its completion."

participant observation: a form of field research in which the investigator actually joins the group being studied in order to obtain an inside view of social behavior.

patriarchal authority: a pattern of family decision making in which males are dominant in power.

pattern of authority: a group of norms that determine how status, authority, and decision-making are to be distributed within the family and also within society as a whole.

patterned social relations: a process by which group members influence the feelings, attitudes, and behavior of one another through personal social interaction.

peer groups: groups of people of about the same age and social position whose members have significant influence on one another.

personality: the sum total of a person's unique yet consistent patterns of thoughts, feelings, and actions.

Peter principle: the assertion that officials within an organization tend to keep rising until they eventually reach their level of incompetence.

philosophy: a systematic and rational method for organizing the thought processes that is used to address critical questions.

physical aggregate: a type of group distinguished primarily by the physical proximity of its members (e.g., a crowd).

physical sciences: the sciences that study the physical and biological world.

Platonic idealism: a key element in the emergence of sociology because of its emphasis on social planning and reform for the improvement of society; a key element of the Comteian synthesis.

play stage: Mead's term for middle childhood, during which the child begins to seriously act out the roles of adults.

pluralism: a process of equal social participation by diverse groups in society based on tolerance and mutual respect for each other's cultural distinctions in a climate of cooperation.

pluralistic theory (of power): the assertion that power in America is distributed among a wide variety of interest groups which tend to cancel each other out, thus preventing any one group from dominating public policy.

polar typology: a tool of analysis in which two dissimilar ideal types are placed at either end of a continuum for the purposes of comparison.

policy research: studies related to social issues and problems whose results may be used as a basis for the formation of public policy, international policy, and social reform.

polyandry: the marriage of one woman to two or more men.

polygamy: a marriage form that involves the taking of plural spouses.

polygyny: the marriage of one man to two or more women.

population (in demography): the total number of persons who inhabit a country or other politically or geographically specified territory.

population (in social research): the total group of people with specific characteristics being studied (in most sociological studies).

population pyramid: a summary of age and sex compositions in a population portrayed in a graph or chart.

postindustrial societies: emerging social systems—countries with continuing low fertility and mortality—which increasingly are becoming dominated by service and information economies.

postindustrial stage: an emerging fourth stage of demographic transition—low fertility and mortality—with new forms of postindustrial economies.

posttransition stage: the third stage of demographic transition which involves countries with declining to low fertility and mortality rates.

poverty: a condition experienced by those who possess the lowest levels of life chances in a given society.

power: the ability to influence or control the behavior of others with or without their consent.

power elite theory (of power): the assertion by Mills that American society is shaped largely by an informal unified group of elites from the highest levels of government, the military, and the corporate sector.

precipitating factors: events or actions that sharpen the focus of structural conduciveness and social strain and create or reinforce generalized belief that can lead to collective behavior.

prejudice: the negative judgment of individuals and groups because of preconceived ideas held about them.

preoperations: the second stage of cognitive development (Piaget) in which children develop the ability to think in symbolic terms and use language to communicate with others.

presociologists: early thinkers who, although they lacked the tools of science to apply to their questions, learned how to ask important sociological questions about their societies and how they functioned.

prestige: the relative degree of honor and respect a person receives from others.

pretransition stage: the first stage of demographic transition which involves countries with high rates of both fertility and mortality.

PR-HD-OAR: an acronym useful in learning the seven steps of the scientific research cycle which are Problem, Review, Hypotheses, Design, Observations, Analysis, and Reporting.

primary group: a small group characterized by personalized, ongoing relationships.

primary deviance: impulsive episodes of socially unacceptable behavior that are temporary or experimental rather than habitual (Lemert).

principle of synergy: a principle borrowed from the physical sciences (the whole is greater than the sum of its parts) and reformulated by Durkheim as follows: Society as a whole is greater than the sum of its parts, the individuals that interact within it.

proletariat: Marx's term for the industrial workers, the "have nots," who were paid only enough to barely survive.

pronatalism: a cultural orientation that strongly encourages childbearing.

propaganda: calculated and biased methods of persuasion based on emotional appeal.

propinquity: the principle that we chose a mate from among those who are near to us either in terms of geographical residence or our spheres of social relations.

protection of incompetence: a problem that occurs when an organization fails to first identify and then to promptly develop, reassign, or remove inadequate performers.

public: a large, widely dispersed group of people who share an interest in or concern about an issue or group of issues.

public opinion: the dominant attitude held by a specific public or a society's population at large.

pure research: scientific investigation aimed at expanding the base of knowledge.

race: a social category of people (of both sexes and all age groups) perceived and treated in a distinct manner on the basis of certain visible physical characteristics

racial minority: a social category whose members have suffered social disadvantages because of visible physical characteristics (such as skin color).

racism: a doctrine—and acts stemming from it—which holds that one racial category is superior and all others, in varying degrees, are inferior.

random sample: a sample chosen in such a way that every member of the larger population being studied has an equal chance of being included.

rational-legal authority: Weber's term for a type of authority based on the legitimacy of a formal set of laws or rules that define the scope of a leader's rights and responsibilities.

reactionary movements: those that reject existing social policy and attempt to restore earlier values, norms, and policies, through violent means if necessary.

rebellion: a deviant response in which a person rejects both culturally approved goals and socially acceptable means and attempts to replace them with others goals and means.

reductionism: a process in which the many complexities of a subject are reduced down to overly simplistic, single cause explanations.

reference group: a group to which a person may or may not belong, which is used as a standard of comparison to evaluate his or her values, behavior, and goals.

reflex: an automatic physical response to an external stimulus by the nervous system.

reform movements: those that work within the social system for changes in specific values, norms, and policies

relative poverty: a standard of living that is substandard in relation to that of the majority of society members.

religion: a method of explaining human life and the universe usually through the concepts of the sacred and divine as acknowledged through ritual and worship.

reputational approach (in stratification analysis): a method of stratification analysis that asks people to identify the social class of others in their community.

research design: the use of a particular method in making scientific observations.

research problem: the statement of a specific research problem (topic) related to a general scientific theory.

resocialization: an abrupt and often basic change in life style and life priorities.

retreatism: a deviant response in which a person rejects both culturally approach goals and socially acceptable means.

reverse discrimination: unequal treatment of individuals based on their membership in the dominant group.

reverse racism: a resentment—and acts stemming from it—focused on the group in power by some minority members driven by deep-seated bitterness at the wrongs done to their ancestors by the ancestors of the dominant group.

review of the literature: a thorough examination of previous research concerning the scientific theory that is to be tested.

revolutionary movements: those that seek to replace a portion or all of an existing social system with something different, through violent means if necessary.

rites of passage: formal events that signal the end of one position or stage in life and the beginning of another.

ritualism (in a bureaucracy): a problem involving over-conformity to the rules of the organization by an individual participant.

ritualism (as a form of deviance): a deviant response in which a person rejects culturally approved goals but accepts the approved means.

role: the expected forms of behavior, obligation, and privilege that go with a social status.

role ambiguity: a situation that occurs when the obligations attached to a social status are unclear.

role conflict: stress caused when conflicting role demands are built into separate statuses or positions, each of which an individual is expected to carry out successfully.

role discrepancy: a condition produced in a marriage in which expectations about the nature and responsibilities of married life are inconsistent with its realities.

role set: two or more distinct roles that relate to a single status or social position.

role strain: stress that occurs when (1) conflicting role demands are built into a single status, (2) a person cannot fulfill the role demands of a given position, or both

role taking: the ability to imagine ourselves in the social roles of other people and act them out in order to learn the social standards that will be applied to our behavior.

romantic love: the idealization of another person based on attachment, commitment, and intimacy.

rules of descent: norms in society that socially define a person's relatives.

rules of residence: norms in society that specify where a couple will go to live after marriage.

rumor: an unconfirmed story that is spread rather quickly from person to person.

same-sex marriage: a marital union between two gay males or lesbian females.

sample: a smaller number of people taken from the larger population being studied.

sampling error: the degree to which characteristics of a sample do not represent those of the population from which it was drawn.

sanctions: socially recognized and enforced rewards and punishments that are applied to conforming and nonconforming behavior.

Sapir-Whorf hypothesis: the perspective that language structures the way people in different cultures think about and perceive reality.

science: an objective and systematic method of observing and explaining reality in a verifiable manner.

scientific research cycle: the process by which the seven steps in scientific research are completed in a circular or cyclical manner (just as the minute hand moves around the face of a watch in the course of an hour).

scientific theory: clearly stated propositions (statements) about reality that have been verified to some degree (a characteristic of science).

secondary deviance: on-going and habitual behavior that violates social norms.

secondary group: a relatively large collection of people with whom one has superficial and somewhat impersonal relations.

segregation: a pattern of exclusion in which a minority group is involuntarily separated from the dominant group in terms of general social contact and participation.

self-concept: the personal assessment people have of their own identity and self- worth and how they fit into the larger community and society.

self-fulfilling prophesy: a prediction by a person that something will occur which is then caused to happen by his or her actions.

sensorimotor stage: the first stage of cognitive development (Piaget) in which children develop motor intelligence and learn to distinguish different objects.

separatist movements: those that find the existing social system unacceptable and seek to set up alternative organizations, communities, or societies.

serial monogamy: marriage to one partner at a time but two or more in a lifetime.

single parent family: a single, separated, divorced, or widowed adult with one or more offspring.

stepfamily: a family formed when two people marry and stepparent and stepsibling relationships are established.

sex ratio: the number of males to every one hundred females in a designated population.

significant others: Mead's term for people with whom the individual has close personal ties.

slavery: an involuntary system of bondage in which human beings are bought, sold, or exchanged for money or other resources.

social action: the meaning people assign to their own behavior and their relations with others and society, and how this personal assessment of reality affects their own behavior and that of others.

social category: a type of group distinguished by its members having one or more visible or otherwise identifiable special features or characteristics in common.

social class: a grouping of people on the socioeconomic continuum who share similar levels and types of power, prestige, and wealth.

social contagion theory: the assertion that the mood and behavior of crowds become dominant in shaping the emotions and behavior of individual participants.

social control: a process designed to maintain conformity to dominant norms.

social control (as applied to collective behavior): the process of how, in a collective behavior context, the actions of authorities can facilitate a smooth process of spontaneous group expression or promote conflict and cause a tense situation to become more volatile.

social Darwinism: the nineteenth century view, espoused by Herbert Spencer, that governments should not interfere in the lives of individuals or the operation of organizations so that the fittest can survive.

social distance: the degree of acceptance an individual feels toward those who belong to various groups to which he or she does not belong.

social facts: Durkheim's term for things or events external to the individual, such as customs, that have the power to shape behavior.

social group: a type of group consisting of people bound together by common interests and values in a definite pattern of social relations.

social integration: a social condition in which most people in a community or society basically agree on social rules (norms) and values which causes them to feel socially connected and secure as a result.

social interaction: the process through which two or more individuals mutually influence each other's thoughts, feelings, and actions.

social isolates: children deprived of adequate social contact and stimulation in their early years who do not develop into functional adults as a result.

socialization: the process through which culture is transmitted to the individual and the personality and self-concept are developed.

socially acceptable deviance: deviant behavior considered acceptable by significant portions of society.

social mobility: the ability to move from one social location or level in society to another.

social movement: a dedicated effort by a fairly large group to promote or resist change in the existing social system.

social networks: linkages maintained with specific types of people for the satisfaction of personal and practical needs.

social organization: the process by which society is structured as a system of social interaction to meet the needs of its members.

social sciences: the sciences that examine human behavior.

social solidarity: Durkheim's term for social order and its fundamental causes.

social strain: a social condition in which (1) intergroup conflicts develop between certain segments of the population and/or (2) dramatic social changes occur.

social stratification: a system in each society that defines how social rank is determined and social rewards are distributed.

social structure: a set of organized norms that govern how people are to interact with each other in various social situations.

society: the largest possible grouping of individuals with specific characteristics in a particular system of social interaction.

sociobiology: the study of the biological aspects of social behavior in all species including humans .

sociocultural theory: a socialization perspective that focuses on the dynamic interplay between developing children and their guided participation in society by competent adults (Vygotsky).

socioemotional leaders: those who concentrate their energies on expressive group purposes aimed at promoting morale and harmony among members.

sociological fluency: the ability to accurately read about, comprehend, and apply the language, perspectives, and methods of sociology to analyze and better understand human social behavior.

sociological imagination: the ability of individuals to see how interrelated their private lives are with the nature of their society.

sociology: the science of human social behavior at all levels of society.

Socratic method: the asking of logical, penetrating questions about anything and everything, including the nature of one's society.

Socratic skepticism: a method that focuses on the persistent asking of critical, penetrating questions which is a critical component of both science and sociology today; a key element of the Comteian synthesis.

somotype theory: a biological explanation of deviance by Shelton which asserted that physique or bodytype is linked to both personality and deviance.

specialized division of labor: a process in which participants in large-scale organizations are assigned positions that center on specific, specialized tasks.

spurious correlation: the simultaneous occurrence of two variables caused by a third or intervening variable.

statics: the study of how the various parts (institutions)of society are structured to promote social order and stability.

statistical category: a type of group not formed by the members themselves but by researchers for the purposes of social analysis

statistics: mathematical procedures that describe the characteristics of variables and explain or measure the relationships between them.

status: a socially defined place or position a person occupies in society, along with a set of expected behavior patterns that act to regulate their behavior.

status inconsistency: a contradiction or mismatch between statuses in which a person ranks high in one and low in another.

status set: the sum total of statuses (social positions) a person occupies in his or her life situation.

stereotypes: fixed mental images about the characteristics of entire categories of people that are not tested against reality.

strain theory: the perspective that deviance results from contradictions between culturally approved goals set by a culture and structural access to the socially approved means to achieve them.

stratified random sample: a random sample chosen in such a way that certain characteristics of the population being studied are represented in accurate proportions.

structural conduciveness: a condition in which certain elements built into a society's social structure act to encourage collective behavior.

structural unemployment: the loss of employment as a result of changes in the economy that render certain occupations obsolete.

subculture: the heritage and lifestyle of a particular group that, although in basic harmony with the dominant culture, has some distinctive cultural features of its own.

subjective approach (in stratification analysis): a method of stratification analysis in which people are asked to identify their own social class category.

superego: Freud's term for the idealized part of the self or conscience that makes us feel proud when we act properly and guilty when we do wrong.

Survey approach: a research design that involves the use of questionnaires to gather information about people's attitudes and their social behavior.

symbols: objects or acts that have a special meaning within a specific culture.

task leaders: those who focus their attention on instrumental group purposes aimed at reaching practical goals.

technical competence: in Weber's model, the basis for rewards (placement and promotion) in a bureaucracy as measured by formal education, training, experience, and job performance.

technicways: rules for carrying out skills or habits associated with the use of technology.

test for statistical significance: a measure designed to determine the likelihood that the correlation found between two variables was due to chance.

Thomas theorem: the assertion by W. I. Thomas that when individuals "define situations as real, they are real in their consequences."

total fertility rate (TFR): the total number of offspring a typical woman has during her lifetime in a given country.

total institution: an extreme form of coercive organization that exerts 24 hour a day control over participants

traditional authority: a type of authority based on followers' acceptance of the legitimacy contained in long-standing traditions and customs (e.g., authority possessed by a king or queen).

traditional monogamy: a form of marriage characterized by lifelong marriage to the same person.

traditional nuclear family: a family consisting of a full-time working husband, a homemaker wife, and one or more school-age children.

transition stage: the second stage of demographic transition characterized by countries with high fertility rates and declining to low mortality rates.

triad: a three-person group.

urban revolution: the second technological revolution to stimulate world population increase marked by the rise of cities which began about 3,500 BCE.

urban legend: an unsubstantiated story, much more durable than a rumor, that is spread over an entire society or country, usually with several local variations.

utilitarian organization: Etzioni's term for an organization in which people participate for practical gain or profit.

value-added theory: the argument that certain conditions in society, when added together in sequential order, create a cumulative effect that increases the likelihood of relatively spontaneous group behavior.

value neutrality: view put forth by Weber that the sociologist as a scientist must remain value-free or ethically neutral in matters of research methods and social policy and reform.

values: the standards used by people to evaluate the relative desirability and worth of practically everything in their lives and in the social world around them.

variable: in sociology, any social characteristic or form of social behavior that may differ in some regard or change.

verified propositions: the *hallmark* that distinguishes science from other forms of explanation such as religion or philosophy.

verstehen: a German term used by Weber that means an empathetic understanding of how individuals and groups perceive the social world and their place in it.

vertical mobility: any upward or downward change that occurs in a person's social class level.

visual sociology: the application of sociological concepts, perspectives, and techniques to better understand human behavior by using visual media such as photographs, movies, television, etc.

vital statistics: records kept on the inhabitants of a nation or society, which include births, deaths, marriages, and incidences of disease.

voluntary organization: Etzioni's term for an organization people join freely as a part-time activity because they agree with its values, norms, and goals.

wealth: the net worth of an individual or group in terms of property and income.

xenocentrism: a preference for the ways of a foreign culture or cultures and a rejection of part or all of one's native way of life.

xenophobia: an irrational fear of foreigners or of cultures significantly different from one's own.

XYY theory: a biological explanation of deviance which argues that the presence of an extra Y chromosome in males is associated with criminal behavior.

youth subculture: life-style characteristics and preferences among children and adolescents very distinct from those of their parents.

zone of proximal development (ZPD): the potential for learning that a child possesses which can be developed with help from skilled mentors as compared to what the child already knows or can learn on his or her own.